The Muslim Brotherhood

The Muslim Brotherhood

Evolution of an Islamist Movement

Carrie Rosefsky Wickham

PRINCETON UNIVERSITY PRESS

PRINCETON AND OXFORD

Jacket photograph: Supporters of Muslim Brotherhood's Muhammad Mursi celebrate his victory in Cairo, Egypt, on June 24, 2012. © Amru Salahuddien/Xinhua Press/Corbis

Library of Congress Cataloging-in-Publication Data

Wickham, Carrie Rosefsky, 1962–
The Muslim Brotherhood : evolution of an Islamist movement / Carrie Rosefsky Wickham.
pages cm
Includes bibliographical references and index.
ISBN 978-0-691-14940-0 (hardcover)
Ikhwan al-Muslimun—History.   2. Islamic fundamentalism—History.   I. Title.
BP10.I385W53 2013
322.4′20956—dc23   2013003231

British Library Cataloging-in-Publication Data is available

This book has been composed in Minion family with Helvetica Neue for display

Printed on acid-free paper. ∞

Printed in the United States of America

10 9 8 7 6 5 4 3 2 1

To my beloved daughters,
Anna and Iris,
for their understanding

Contents

Preface	ix
Acknowledgments	xiii
Note on Transliteration	xvii

CHAPTER ONE
Conceptualizing Islamist Movement Change — 1

CHAPTER TWO
The Brotherhood's Early Years — 20

CHAPTER THREE
The Brotherhood's Foray into Electoral Politics — 46

CHAPTER FOUR
The Wasat Party Initiative and the Brotherhood's Response — 76

CHAPTER FIVE
The Brotherhood's Seesaw between Self-Assertion
and Self-Restraint — 96

CHAPTER SIX
Repression and Retrenchment — 120

CHAPTER SEVEN
The Brotherhood and the Egyptian Uprising — 154

CHAPTER EIGHT
Egypt's Islamist Movement in Comparative Perspective — 196

CHAPTER NINE
The Muslim Brotherhood in (Egypt's) Transition — 247

Notes	289
List of Interviews	327
Selected Bibliography	331
Index	347

Preface

THE IDEA FOR THIS BOOK EMERGED during the course of my research for *Mobilizing Islam: Religion, Activism and Political Change in Egypt* (2002), which was an updated and theoretically revised version of my dissertation. Based on data gathered during eighteen months of fieldwork from 1990 to 1991, as well as during three additional research trips to Egypt from 1993 to 2000, *Mobilizing Islam* sought to explain how the Muslim Brotherhood managed to attract a wide following among urban, educated youth under the shadow of an authoritarian state.

During the research for my first book, I was struck by the fact that many of the Islamist leaders I interviewed emphasized how dramatically their worldviews and priorities had changed over time. This trend was particularly pronounced among younger-generation Islamists, then in their thirties and forties, who had begun to openly question the positions and practices of their elders. My first attempt to chart the rise of the "reformist trend" within the Brotherhood was an article I wrote in 2004 on the Wasat party, formed by a group that broke from the Brotherhood in 1996.[1] In 2004 I received a major research grant from the Carnegie Corporation of New York to undertake a deeper and more systematic investigation of emerging patterns of internal debate and contestation over movement goals, strategies, and practices within the Muslim Brotherhood, as well as within the leading organizations of the Sunni Islamist revivalist movement in Jordan, Kuwait, and Morocco. From the outset, I sensed that characterizing Islamist movement change strictly as a process of strategic adaptation failed to capture important shifts in the ideological commitments of certain leaders and factions. Yet how and why such shifts had occurred remained undertheorized and underexplored.

With support from the Carnegie Scholars program, as well as supplemental grants from the United States Institute of Peace and the Woodruff Research Fund of Emory University, I gathered information for this project over the course of five research trips from 2004 to 2008, including three trips to Egypt (2004, 2005, 2008), a trip to Jordan and Kuwait (2004), and a trip to Morocco (2006). In April and July 2011 I made two additional trips to Egypt, the first as a member of a Carter Center delegation and the second on my own. As part of the Carter Center delegation in April, I helped conduct interviews with senior political and civic leaders in order to gain a clearer sense of the general features of Egypt's political transition. In July, supported by an Emory research grant, I returned to Egypt to investigate the role of the Brotherhood in Egypt's popular uprising and the transition that ensued in its wake. From 2004 to 2011, I conducted 124 interviews with Islamist and secular civic and political activists, academics, and journalists in Egypt, Jordan, Morocco, and Kuwait, including a few Islamist leaders in Egypt whom I interviewed multiple times over a period of several years. Whether the interviews were conducted in Arabic or English depended on the relative proficiency of my Arabic to their English; with the exception of a few Arab journalists, academics, and secular democracy activists, the large majority of my respondents chose to converse with me in Arabic. Lasting from thirty minutes to several hours, the interviews were loosely structured around a predetermined set of questions, but I also allowed the direction they took to be shaped by the issues deemed especially relevant and important by the respondents themselves. In addition to such interview material, the book draws on scores of Arabic-language primary source documents, books, research reports, and media articles, many of which remain largely unaccessed by other Western researchers. Further, it incorporates relevant information and insights from English- and French-language studies of the Islamist groups included in my study.

Given that my interest in the question of Islamist movement change was sparked by observations made during my dissertation fieldwork on the Muslim Brotherhood from 1990 to 1991, and much of my research has remained focused on the Brotherhood ever since, it is not an exaggeration to characterize this book as the product of twenty-two years spent in the examination of a single case. What, one might reasonably ask, is the value of studying any one thing for so long?

With the rise of large-n quantitative research to a dominant position in the field of comparative politics, the analytic payoff of case study research has been judged with growing skepticism. Yet the close study of one or a small number of cases entails several advantages that its critics often fail to appreciate. First, when dealing with an organization like the Muslim Brotherhood, which has remained technically illegal for most of its history and for good reasons has sought to shield itself from public scrutiny, the information available to us about its internal workings is sketchy and incomplete. For example, for all of the attention the Brotherhood has attracted since the 2011 uprising catapulted it to the center stage of Egyptian public life, we still know very little about the balance of power among its internal factions, the distribution of authority among its administrative subunits, its patterns of internal decision making, its strategies of recruitment and socialization, and its methods of enforcing internal conformity and discipline, all of which are exceedingly difficult to determine from easily accessed statements or position papers alone. As a result, when one Brotherhood leader makes a reassuring statement while another leader makes an inflammatory one, it is difficult to determine whether they are expressing a personal opinion, the view of a particular faction, or a position on which there is a consensus within the group as a whole. In such instances, deriving valid causal inferences from observed data hinges on the contextual knowledge of the researcher, that is, on his/her capacity to interpret discrete bits of evidence in light of a deeper and more holistic understanding of the group's internal dynamics. Further, the intensive study of a large and internally differentiated organization like the Muslim Brotherhood reveals how nonsensical and absurd it is to describe the group in simple terms like "radical" or "moderate" that do violence to its complexity, albeit in different ways. We likewise come to appreciate the inadequacy of accounts that focus solely on elements of continuity with the group's anti-system past and those that focus only on progressive shifts. Finally, we become aware of the overgeneralization inherent in blanket claims about, say, the impact of regime accommodation or repression on Islamist groups, as if external conditions invariably produce one type of outcome when in fact they can, and often do, produce contradictory effects.

In addition, by interacting with certain Brotherhood leaders over many years, I have watched them mature, both in a chronological and evolutionary sense, with my own eyes. Like all of us, in some respects they are the same as they were twenty years ago, and in other ways they are not. More broadly, such interactions have enabled me to see these leaders not as two-dimensional stand-ins for the organization they represent but as complex individuals with conflicting motivations whose values and priorities have been shaped, and at times radically altered, by life experience. Through sustained discussions with Islamist leaders, I came to appreciate the importance of religious commitment as a motive for people to set aside daily concerns and pursue a higher cause but also to appreciate the fluidity and elasticity of the particular objectives and purposes they saw themselves as religiously obligated to fulfill.

In sum, the value of an intensive, long-term study of the individuals and institutions of a single movement is that it enables one to develop a more complete and persuasive account of their evolution than can be derived from a thumbnail sketch that glosses over inconsistencies, ambiguities, and contradictions that are a vital part of the story itself. At the same time, it forces us to confront the limits of our knowledge by exposing the dimensions of internal group dynamics we do not fully understand. It hence impels us to be more humble in the claims we make and more skeptical of sweeping generalizations that derive more from a researcher's pre-judgments than from a robust empirical investigation of the subject itself.

Acknowledgments

I AM GRATEFUL TO MANY INDIVIDUALS AND INSTITUTIONS for their support of this project. First, I would like to thank the Carnegie Corporation of New York for awarding me a major grant that funded research and course relief from 2004 to 2006. Special thanks are due to Patricia Rosenfield, Chair of the Carnegie Scholars Program, for her mentorship and support of this project from its conception. I would also like to thank the United State Institute of Peace for providing me with a supplemental grant in support of my research, and for the opportunity to present my preliminary findings at a USIP-sponsored round-table discussion on April 21, 2005. In particular, I would like to thank Steve Riskin and Judy Barsalou for their enthusiastic interest in and support of my work.

I also owe a deep debt of gratitude to Emory University. In particular, I am grateful to the Woodruff Research Fund, which supported summer research in Egypt in 2008 and 2011, and to the Bill and Carol Fox Center for Humanistic Inquiry, which awarded me a senior fellowship in 2009–10, freeing me from teaching responsibilities to write the first half of the book. My thanks to Martina Brownley, Keith Anthony, Colette Barlow, and Amy Erbil for making my term as a Fox Center fellow a high point of my academic career—as well as to other fellows at the Center whose lively intellectual discussions enriched my work. I am also very grateful to Emory College for awarding me an Associate Completion Leave in 2011–12, which enabled me to finish writing the book and extend its scope to include developments since the Arab Spring. Special thanks to the Department of Political Science, and in particular to its consecutive chairs, Thomas Remington and Dan Reiter, for supporting my research project and approving the course relief that allowed me to bring it to completion. Finally, my thanks to David Carroll and the Democracy Program at the Carter Center, for inviting me to participate in a fact-finding mission in April 2011 and to serve as an international election witness during Egypt's presidential run-off in June 2012.

I am also grateful to Princeton University Press for its support of my project. Thanks to my anonymous reviewers for their constructive feedback on the first draft of the manuscript, and to Chuck Myers, then Senior Editor for Political Science and Law, for his astute advice and support at various stages of the book's development. I would also like to thank Jennifer Backer, my outstanding copyeditor, for her thoughtful and judicious edits, and to Debbie Tegarden, my indefatigable production editor. Thanks also to Eric Crahan, who succeeded Chuck Myers as Princeton's new Senior Editor for Political Science and American History, and to Eric Henney, Robert Tempio, and other members of the Press's editorial, production, marketing, and publicity staff for their efforts on the book's behalf.

David Marcus's assistance during copyediting was invaluable, first by establishing a rubric for the transliteration of Arabic terms into English and later by reviewing the entire manuscript for maximum consistency in this regard.

Let me also thank the political and civil society activists, scholars, and journalists in Egypt, Jordan, Kuwait, and Morocco who shared their experiences and insights about the dynamics of Islamist movement change. Our candid open-ended conversations, which often continued for several hours, enabled me to gain a far deeper understanding of emerging trends in Arab politics and society than was available from published sources alone. My particular thanks go to leaders in the Muslim Brotherhood and other Islamist groups for setting aside their initial reservations about sharing sensitive information with a female American researcher. It is my hope that they will see their views faithfully represented, in all their nuance and complexity, in the pages of this book.

Thanks also to the two Egyptian families who welcomed me into their lives and their hearts nearly thirty years ago and to whom I remain close to this day. To Maha, Amina, Youseria, and their growing families—which now span three generations—thank you for your home-cooked meals, your ongoing interest in my work and concern for my well-being, and the consummate kindness and generosity with which you have treated me since we first met. Your grace under adversity encourages me to believe in, and rely on, my own inner strength. It is because of you that Egypt feels like a second home.

Let me also acknowledge a special debt of gratitude to three dear Egyptian colleagues and friends, Hisham Mubarak, Ahmad Abdallah Roza, and Hisham Tammam, each of whom enlightened us all with a profound understanding of Egyptian politics and culture and who have all left this world all too soon. It is a tribute to their wisdom and humanity that they will long be remembered and deeply missed.

In Jordan, Kuwait, and Morocco, several of my interview subjects also helped me establish contacts and provided sage advice that was critical to the success of my research. In particular, I thank Hani Hourani in Jordan, Ghanim al-Najjar and Shafiq Ghabra in Kuwait, Mustafa Khalfi (whom I met in Washington, D.C.), and Jamal Benrahman in Morocco.

The research and writing of this book has spanned the course of many years. Throughout this period I have benefitted greatly from an ongoing intellectual exchange with many scholars who engaged with the ideas in this book and contributed to their refinement. Let me thank the following individuals: Khalil al-Anani, Eva Bellin, Nathan Brown, Jason Brownlee, Daniel Brumberg, Janine Clark, Kathleen Collins, Richard Doner, Israel Elad-Altman, John Entelis, John Esposito, James Gelvin, Jeroen Gunning, Amr Hamzawy, Michael Herb, Charles Kurzman, Stephane La Croix, Ellen Lust, Marc Lynch, Abdeslam Maghraoui, Peter Mandeville, Tarek Masoud, Quinn Mecham, Roel Meijer, Emile Nakhleh, Vali Nasr, David Patel, Diya Rishwan, Curtis Ryan, Jillian Schwedler, Samer Shehata, Joshua Stacher, Bjorn Utvik, Michael Willis, Stacey Philbrick Yadav, Malika Zghlal, and Barbara Zollner. If I have inadvertently missed someone who merits inclusion on this list, please forgive me. While I have benefitted tremendously from my conversations with these scholars, the responsibility for any errors or omissions in this book is my own.

During the research and writing of the book, I also benefited from the help of several Emory PhD candidates who worked as my research assistants at various times. Special thanks to Nicole Baerg, Karolyn Benger, Nadya Hajj, Jakub Kakietek, Andrew Kirkpatrick, Amanda Murdie, Grace Park, Christina Parowczenko, and Sara Jackson Wade for the research they conducted on my behalf.

Thanks also to my uncle, Arthur Greenbaum, a retired intellectual property lawyer, for his ongoing support and for coming up with the title of the book.

During the long years it took me to bring this project to fruition, those who have borne the greatest burden are the members of my family. I am indebted to Joe, my husband, for supporting me in all my endeavors, for "holding the fort" during my numerous absences from home, both during field trips to the Middle East and on the many week nights and weekends when I was sequestered away with my computer, for helping me navigate through moments of self-doubt, and for assuring me countless times that all the time and energy I had invested in this project would pay off in the end. To my parents, my gratitude for filling in with child care, cooking and other household chores, and for their ongoing encouragement and support. Finally, and most of all, to Anna and Iris, my two daughters and shining stars, who have coped with the heavy demands made by my career with generosity and forbearance. I hope that they are compensated, at least in part, for the time I spent away from them by the knowledge of how much they are loved.

Note on Transliteration

ARABIC-TO-ENGLISH TRANSLITERATION methods have been simplified in this text, following the conventions employed in social science texts that deal with the Arab world. Common terms and names of individuals that appear widely in Western media, such as Quran, Abdel Nasser, Mahmoud, Khaled, Omar Suleiman, Osama, Kefaya, Baradei, jihad, and ulema, appear as they normally do in English. To transliterate all other terms, an abbreviated phonetic system is employed, including the symbol ʿ for *ayn*, and the symbol ʾ for medial and final hamza. Initial hamza is omitted (*Abu, al-Ahram*). Initial *ayn* is indicated, except in the case of names beginning with *Abd al-*. We omit all other Arabic diacriticals, including the underdot for emphatic consonants and the overbar for long vowels. For clarity's sake, here is a list of certain Arabic consonants and their transliterations in this book:

ء	hamza
ث	th
ح	h
خ	kh
ذ	dh
ص	s
ض	d
ط	t
ظ	dh
ع	ayn
غ	gh
ق	q
ك	k
ه	h

Doubled consonants are indicated with two English consonants (*Muhammad, Gazzar, tayyar, mutahammisin*), except where this leads to awkward spellings (*muwadhaf*, not *muwadhdhaf*). The short vowels *a*, *i*, and *u* are preferred over *e* and *o*, and *i* is used for final *yaa'* (*Fahmi, Misri*). The long vowel *ou* is used (*Mahmoud, dustour, hudoud*) but not the long *aa* and *ii* (*tayyar,* not *tayyaar*).The definite article is spelled *al-* regardless of its pronunciation (*al-turath,* not *at-turath*), with the exception of the religious phrase *al-munkar 'an in-nahy*. In addition, the *a* in *al-* is elided after certain short prepositions, as in *fi'l-yawm* or *li'l-Islam*. When there is a discrepancy, the consonants and vowels of formal Arabic are preferred to those of spoken Arabic (*nidham* rather than *nizam, yawm* rather than *youm*).

The greatest transliteration challenge in this book, however, is the spelling of the personal names of public figures, especially of those Middle Easterners who are already widely discussed in the Western media. English versions of their names are often erratic and phonetically incorrect. For example, nine different spellings of *Aboul 'Ela Madi* appear in respected journalistic sources, and none of them follows the rubric noted above. Following a name's correct Arabic phonemes and word division, on the other hand, can tax the reader's eye: *Abu 'l'Ila Madi.*

The following compromise is adopted in this book. First, the Arabic names of authors who publish in English appear as they have chosen to transliterate them in English (*Mamoun Hudeibi* and *Kassem,* not *Ma'moun al-Hudaybi* or *Qaasim*). For most other names, the traditional Arabic short vowels (*a, i,* and *u*) are used as much as possible (*Muhammad Mursi,* not *Muhamed Morsi*), and we present most "*Idafa* names" as they would be in Arabic (*Abd al-Fattah* rather than *Abdel Fattah*). However, we bend these rules either to preserve the spoken pronunciation (*Hudeibi, 'Usman, 'Abdalla,* and *Muhyiddin*) or to follow other English usage preferences (such as *e* over *i* in *'Esam* and *'Ezzat*).

Except where indicated, all translations in this book are by the author.

The Muslim Brotherhood

CHAPTER ONE

Conceptualizing Islamist Movement Change

ON JUNE 30, 2012, Muhammad Mursi, a leader in the Muslim Brotherhood, was sworn in as Egypt's new president. To longtime observers of politics in the region, the event felt surreal. An Islamist organization that had spent most of its existence denied legal status and subject to the depredations of a hostile authoritarian state was now in charge of the very apparatus once used to repress it. And it had reached those heights not by way of coup or revolution but through the ballot box.

Just eighteen months earlier, the idea of a Brotherhood president of Egypt was so far-fetched as to be laughable. The Mubarak regime appeared too deeply entrenched and the Egyptian people too afraid of the security police and too exhausted by daily struggles to survive to imagine a breakthrough occurring any time soon. Yet on January 25, 2011, a massive uprising broke out in cities and towns across the country, and eighteen days later, after thirty years in power, President Mubarak was forced to step down.

The Egyptian uprising was part of a seismic wave of protest that began in Tunisia and rapidly spread to other Arab states. Millions of men, women, and children poured into the streets to demand their freedom, and Middle East experts, as surprised by the protests as everyone else, struggled to explain why what were considered some of the region's most durable regimes had proven more fragile than anyone had thought.

The "Arab Spring" has set a new dynamic in motion in a region long afflicted by political stagnation. Though the contours of the region's new landscape are still taking shape, one trend is clear: the power of mainstream Islamist groups is on the rise. As the largest, most popular, and best-organized sector of the opposition in most Arab states before the protests erupted, Islamist groups were uniquely positioned to ride the openings that occurred in their wake. In Tunisia and Egypt, Islamist parties emerged as the resounding victors in parliamentary elections, and in Egypt, a Brotherhood career politician was elected president. Even in countries where longstanding rulers retained power, Islamists gained ground. For example, in Morocco constitutional reforms enacted after the Arab Spring prompted King Muhammad VI to appoint the head of the Islamist-oriented Justice and Development Party, the largest group in parliament, as prime minister.

The emergence of Islamist actors as a leading force in Arab politics has triggered competing reactions in the region and around the globe. While some have witnessed this development with equanimity, others have reacted with consternation and dismay. Such different reactions reflect the fact that the motives of such actors are hard to fathom. The information we have about Islamist groups is sketchy and incomplete, and the observations we have to go on are subject to conflicting interpretations. As a result, the broader implications of the Islamist surge, including its impact on the future of democratic governance, economic development, peace, and stability in the region, are open to dispute.

Perhaps the central issue is whether and to what extent contemporary Islamist groups have moved away from the illiberal features that characterized them in the past, including their support of violence, their rejection of democracy as an "alien" system imported from the West, and their calls for the application of Shari'a, or Islamic law, based on a conservative reading of Islam's sacred texts and juristic precedents. While Islamist leaders have welcomed and, indeed, actively supported recent democratic reforms, skeptics contend that they do not support democracy as an end in itself but as the first step toward establishing a system governed by the laws of God as they define them. From this perspective, the greater the influence of Islamist groups in the Arab world, the dimmer the region's prospects for democracy and freedom. Others, by contrast, claim that mainstream Islamist groups that once rejected democracy have become some of its greatest proponents and that the region's nascent transitions to democracy will hinge on their support.

The main objective of this book is to challenge these and other sweeping generalizations. Taking aim at much of what has been written about the Egyptian Muslim Brotherhood and other Arab Islamist groups in recent years, I argue that they cannot be described as "for" or "against" democracy, any more than they can be characterized as "moderate" or "extremist." First, by "breaking into the black box" of Islamist movement organizations and exposing the factional divisions and debates within them, I show that they are not monolithic entities whose members think and act in lockstep. Second, while demonstrating that Islamist groups have undergone an important evolution, I show that it has not been a linear, unidimensional progression toward greater "moderation." Rather, such groups have traced a path marked by profound inconsistencies and contradictions, yielding agendas in which newly embraced themes of freedom and democracy coexist uneasily with illiberal religious concepts carried over from the past. Third, I highlight the complex motivations of Islamist actors and demonstrate that recent shifts in their rhetoric and behavior cannot be attributed to a single chain of cause and effect. I argue that such shifts bear the imprint of strategic and ideational processes of change occurring simultaneously.

To gain leverage on the scope and limits of Islamist movement change, as well as its underlying causes and dynamics, I examine the trajectories of mainstream Sunni revivalist movement organizations in four Arab states. The main contribution of the book is a finely grained analysis of the evolution of the Muslim Brotherhood in Egypt from its founding in 1928 to the inauguration of Muhammad Mursi as president in 2012. My analysis draws on insights and observations from twenty-two years of research on the Brotherhood, beginning with the fieldwork I conducted in 1990 and 1991 for my first book, *Mobilizing Islam* (2002), and including research conducted specifically for this project during multiple trips to the region between 2004 and 2012. Rather than treat the Brotherhood as a unitary actor, this book highlights ongoing disagreements within the organization over ideology and strategy as well as the shifting power balance among its competing factions. In so doing, it endeavors to explain why the Brotherhood opted for one path over another at various points in the past and to illuminate how such developments have shaped its priorities today.

Toward the end of the book, I compare the trajectory of the Egyptian Brotherhood to those of its counterparts in Jordan, Kuwait, and Morocco, highlighting the features they share as well as those that set them apart. In Jordan and Kuwait, I focus on regional offshoots of the Brotherhood, as well as their political affiliates, the Islamic Action Front (IAF) in Jordan and the Islamic Constitutional Movement (ICM) in Kuwait. In Morocco, I focus on the Movement of Unity and Reform (MUR) and its political arm, the Justice and Development Party (Parti de Justice et Developpement, or PJD). While formally independent of the Brotherhood's network, the MUR and the PJD were historically influenced by the Brotherhood's ideas and institutional arrangements and retain a close "family resemblance" to their Brotherhood counterparts.

To be clear, the four cases chosen for inclusion in this book cannot be said to represent the wider universe of Islamist movement groups and organizations around the globe, or even within the Arab states of the Middle East and North Africa. All of the groups covered in this study are situated within the movement of Sunni revivalist Islam. They also have focused primarily on issues of domestic social and political reform, committed themselves to a path of nonviolence in pursuit of their objectives, and accrued long records of participating in electoral politics. Such characteristics distinguish them from Shi'ite Islamist groups and parties, "national resistance" movements like Hamas (Sunni) and Hizbollah (Shi'ite), and militant Islamist groups engaged in a holy war or jihad against incumbent rulers and their foreign patrons, such as al-Qa'ida and its regional affiliates. They also distinguish them from Islamist movement organizations such as al-'Adl wa al-Ihsan (Justice and Charity) in Morocco that have chosen to boycott the formal political system. Likewise, such characteristics set them apart from Salafi Islamist groups that engage in grassroots religious outreach but, except in Kuwait, have not until recently participated in electoral contests for political power.

The four Islamist groups included in this study hence constitute a distinctive subset within the broader matrix of groups and movements that define their identities and objectives in Islamic terms. My objective is not to articulate a general set of propositions that apply to all Islamist groups. Rather, it is to capture the impact of political participation on four groups that started out with similar agendas and sought to pursue them under roughly similar conditions: as nonviolent opposition groups situated within systems of authoritarian rule.

In all four of the countries under study, Islamist groups took advantage of regime experiments with political liberalization in the 1980s and 1990s by expanding their participation in electoral politics. Participating in the political systems of "un-Islamic" regimes was intended to advance such groups' partisan objectives, but it triggered fundamental changes in the Islamic movement itself. The aim of this book is to specify the changes that have occurred, the causal processes that produced them, and the impact they will have on Arab politics and society. My hope is that by offering new leverage on such issues the book will make a significant contribution to the fields of Middle East studies and comparative politics, as well as to the study of social movements and contentious politics more generally.

Yet as those who have worked the longest and thought the hardest about such matters are often the first to admit, the effects of participation on the goals and strategies of Islamist opposition groups are extraordinarily difficult to pin down. In recent years, a number of Middle East scholars have begun to explore the impact of political participation on Islamist movement organizations, goals, and strategies. A pathbreaking work in this regard is Jillian Schwedler's *Faith in Moderation* (2006), which traced the divergent effects of participation on Islamist groups in Jordan and Yemen. Other scholars who have made noteworthy contributions to the analysis of Islamist participation within and across countries in the Middle East and North Africa (including the non-Arab states of Turkey and Iran) include Asef Bayat, Michelle Browers, Nathan Brown, Janine Clark, Mona El-Ghobashy, 'Amr Hamzawy, Quinn Mecham, Curtis Ryan, Samer Shehata, Joshua Stacher, Gunes Murat Tezcur, Eva Wegner, and Michael Willis. In order to gain traction on such issues, some Middle East scholars, myself included, have turned to the work of Przeworski and Sprague (1988) and Kalyvas (1996) on the democratic integration of socialist and Catholic parties in late nineteenth- and early twentieth-century western Europe and of Share (1985), Huntington (1991), Mainwaring (1992), and others on the deradicalization of leftist parties and movements during "third wave" democratic transitions in southern Europe and Latin America. Although they differ in their particulars, such studies generally frame the ideological and behavioral moderation of former radicals as a response to incentives generated by the democratic (or democratizing) environments in which they are embedded. For example, socialist parties renounced violence and diluted their calls for revolutionary change in order to gain the acceptance of erstwhile rivals, achieve legal status, and appeal to wider sectors of the electorate. Hence the prime movers in such accounts are considerations of strategic advantage, which prompted "rational" movement actors to adapt their goals and methods to changing political opportunities and constraints.

Yet the application of causal models derived from Western scenarios to the analysis of contemporary Islamist groups is hardly a straightforward endeavor. First, it is unclear whether groups that seek to establish a political system based on God's instructions for humankind are analogous to leftist parties, or even to Catholic parties that have a religious foundation but whose platforms contain nothing akin to the call for the application of a comprehensive system of divine law. Second, the participation of Islamist groups during the time frame in question occurred within the context of stable "semi-authoritarian" regimes, not within established democracies or during turbulent and open-ended periods of regime change. Finally, the resonance of Islam, the weakness of rival secular ideologies, and the limited—and largely disappointing—record of previous experiments in democracy in the Arab world have arguably lessened the pressures facing Islamist groups to dilute their agendas in order to appeal to wider sectors of the electorate. Indeed, the leaders of mainstream Islamist groups routinely contend that their agendas are already supported by a majority of the public at large.

Equally if not more vexing for those seeking to capture the effects of participation on Islamist groups in the Arab world is the fact that key terms in the "participation-moderation" thesis remain woefully underspecified. Indeed, a review of the literature on the subject reveals a striking lack of consensus on the definition of the outcome(s) to be explained, the conditions under which they occur, and the causal processes presumed to be at play. Let me describe each of these areas of contention and briefly explain how I will approach them in this book.

CHARACTERIZING ISLAMIST MOVEMENT CHANGE

Much of the literature on contemporary Islamist groups seeks to identify whether and how their participation in the domain of formal politics has contributed to the "moderation" of their goals and strategies. Yet the concept of "moderation" suffers from a high degree of imprecision. First and most obvious, it can refer to both an end state and a process. Second, as a relative rather than an absolute concept, it begs the question, "Moderate in comparison to what?" Third, it may refer to changes in behavior, such as a renunciation of violence, and/or to changes in broader worldviews, goals, and values, such as a growing commitment to freedom of expression or women's rights. Fourth, the term can be applied to changes both at the level of individual actors and at the level of the complex organizations of which they are a part. Yet when used as a descriptor of an Islamist organization as a whole (the Muslim Brotherhood is or is not "moderate") or to capture change over time in an organization's rhetoric and behavior (the Muslim Brotherhood is or is not "moderating"), it may gloss over some important vectors of internal differentiation. First, the term implies an overarching, internally consistent, and linear process of behavioral or ideological change when in fact an Islamist group may "moderate" its official rhetoric and practice in some areas while retaining, or even radicalizing, them in others.[1] Second, treating Islamist organizations as unitary actors entails the risk of exaggerating the extent of the ideological and behavior uniformity within them—that is, of failing to discern instances in which the beliefs and practices of some individuals or factions of a group have changed while those of others have not.

Rather than aiming to determine whether the Egyptian Muslim Brotherhood and similar groups are "moderating," I take a more open-ended approach to the study of Islamist movement change. That is, I seek to capture the effects of participation on Islamist groups without assuming a priori that such change is likely to assume a particular form or direction. Like many other Middle East scholars, I am particularly interested in the type of changes implied by the concept of "moderation." But rather than employ "moderation" as a shorthand, I disaggregate the concept and attempt to specify the multiple dimensions of change it encompasses while leaving open the question of whether such changes have in fact occurred. Below I summarize the dimensions of primary interest.

To begin, I consider whether Islamist groups have renounced violence and come to support the democratic alternation of power, a system in which leaders are chosen through free and fair elections. Further, I seek to determine whether and to what extent Islamist groups as a whole—or some individuals and factions within them—have adjusted their broader worldviews, values, and beliefs along four dimensions. First is whether they have moved toward a more relativistic approach to religion—that is, they have begun to frame their interpretation of Islam as one among many—as opposed to equating that interpretation with Islam itself. Second is whether they have moved toward greater toleration of the expression of values and perspectives that conflict with their own, not only in the domain of politics but also in the spheres of art, literature, film, and scholarship. Third is whether they have deepened their commitment to the legal guarantee of individual rights and freedoms, including the right to make life choices (with respect to styles of dress, forms of recreation, social interactions, and sexual conduct) that violate Islamic mandates as they define them. Fourth is the extent to which they have embraced the principle of equal citizenship rights, both for Muslims and non-Muslims and for men and women, with the latter extending to support for gender equality in the "private" domains of marriage, divorce, and inheritance. What should be amply clear is that such ideological changes go far beyond support for the procedural aspects of democracy and the principle of majority rule. What may be less obvious is that they do not necessarily entail or require a shift from a religious frame of reference to a secular one, though they do require a fundamental break with the letter and spirit of Shari'a rulings inherited from the past.

In addition to the ideational dimensions of Islamist movement change, the book investigates changes in the relationships of Islamist groups with other social and political forces, as well as the types of issues and activities to which they devote their time, energy, and resources. Further, to the extent that available information permits, it examines changes in their institutional norms and decision-making processes. At issue here is whether and to what extent Islamist groups are becoming more transparent, rule based, and internally democratic, as well as more accommodating of members with different views and opinions, including those advocating the reform of group norms and practices.

One might argue that a focus on the "progressive" dimensions of movement change reflects a preference for the kinds of values and institutions associated with liberal democratic systems in the West. That is, whether we define the outcome as "moderation" or as a series of discrete changes, as I propose instead, the questions animating my research exhibit a normative slant. I fully concede that the types of changes described above are consistent with my own culturally specific values and preferences. Yet I would argue that no social science research is in fact "value free" and that our normative preferences do not preempt a sober-minded analysis of real-world trends, as long as we consciously guard against the temptation to exaggerate features that conform with our preferences and to ignore, discount, or attempt to explain away those that do not.

As noted earlier, whether or not progressive changes are occurring in Islamist worldviews, values and practices can be analyzed at the level of individuals, at the level of organizations, or both. With this in mind, I attempt to distinguish between individual and collective processes of change and address the crucial problem of aggregation—of whether, when, and how ideological innovation spreads from the level of individuals or subsets of individuals to the broader organizations in which they are embedded. One of the central contentions of this book is that the Muslim Brotherhood in Egypt and its analogues in Jordan, Kuwait, and Morocco are large umbrella organizations encompassing individuals and factions with different and at times conflicting worldviews, values, and opinions. Moreover, such variation cannot be neatly captured by a single ideological spectrum, with "hard-liners" on one end and "moderates" on the other, because the composition of internal alignments hinges on the issue at hand. Hence it is important to examine when and why certain issues have emerged as a focus of internal contention and debate. In particular, we need to assess whether those who advocate progressive changes in the historic agendas and practices of Islamist groups have managed to acquire the influence and authority to shape group policy over the objections of their detractors. This in turn requires greater attention to the balance of power among competing factions within Islamist groups and the conditions under which it may shift over time.

DISAGGREGATING PARTICIPATION

Another central problem in the literature on the "participation-moderation linkage" is that the concept of "participation" is underspecified and hence is ill equipped to provide a conceptual anchor for the analysis of Islamist movement change. In general terms, "participation" refers to the involvement of movement organizations and parties in competitive elections for parliament and, in some cases, for positions in local government councils, student unions, faculty clubs, and professional syndicates. *Yet which dimension(s) of participation act as triggers of movement change—and how—remain unclear.* First, there is the question of whether participation under authoritarian constraints differs in its overall effects from participation in established or emerging democracies. Second, regardless of the institutional context, "participation" arguably encompasses several discrete processes at once. For example, it entails a party or movement organization running candidates in elections and, if they secure enough votes, the ascent of their members to positions of public office, necessitating decisions about how they will respond to the needs and concerns of their constituents, including those who did not vote for them and, in some cases, actively oppose their agendas. In addition, participation often propels movement actors into sustained interaction with regime officials, security personnel, and the leaders of other political parties, movement organizations, and civil society groups, as well as domestic and international media outlets. Since these different dimensions of participation may be presumed to have different effects, lumping them all together under a single rubric is problematic. Hence we need to disaggregate the concept of "participation" and investigate how the different processes it encompasses have shaped the trajectories of Islamist opposition groups in the Arab world.

THE CAUSAL MECHANISMS OF ISLAMIST MOVEMENT CHANGE

If the key terms in the "participation-moderation" thesis require greater theoretic specification, so too does the presumed causal relationship between them. One of the central propositions advanced by Prezeworksi and Sprague, Mainwaring, Huntington, Kalyvas, and others is that even ideologically motivated individuals and organizations are apt to adjust their rhetoric and behavior to advance their partisan interests. That is, the leaders of socialist and Catholic parties can be portrayed as "rational actors" responsive to the incentives for "moderation" generated by their surrounding democratic (or democratizing) environments. Hence, for example, socialist party leaders renounced violence and postponed or abandoned their call for a radical restructuring of the foundations of economic and political power in "bourgeois" democracies in order to avoid repression, gain legal recognition, and appeal to wider sectors of the electorate. The deradicalization of party goals and strategies thus occurred in the service of maximizing the party's influence and power. A key feature of this causal model is that adjustments in ideology are characterized as guided by, and ultimately subordinate to, considerations of strategic advantage. Conspicuously missing is any serious effort to identify a set of factors that might prompt deeper changes in radical actors' underlying worldviews, orientations, and beliefs, other than to frame such changes as a natural outcome of "democratic habituation," that is, a gradual adaptation to the norms and values of the political systems in which they are embedded.

The question of whether rational actor models offer a persuasive account of movement deradicalization in the West exceeds the scope of this study. But such models strike me as too simplistic and deterministic to fully capture the dynamics of Islamist movement change. First, the contention that Islamist actors adjust their rhetoric and behavior to maximize group interests hinges on the assumption that such interests are ranked within a well-defined and stable hierarchy accessible to the external observer, enabling him or her to predict their response to environmental cues with a high degree of certainty. This becomes problematic if, as I suggest is the case, Islamist actors and organizations can (and often do) pursue diverse objectives simultaneously and the priority they attach to any one of them is open to internal debate and subject to change over time. Hence, even if the goals and interests of Islamist actors are shaped by the institutional parameters within which they operate, it is difficult to determine a priori how they will respond to a given set of institutional cues. This is particularly the case when Islamist actors and organizations are simultaneously attempting to advance their long-term objectives, maintain the support of their mass base, and effectively manage their relationships with regime authorities and rival social and political forces. In such instances, the costs and benefits associated with any given course of action are susceptible to diverse interpretations—not just by external observers but by Islamist actors themselves.

Beyond Strategic Adaptation

Characterizing Islamist movement change as a process of strategic adaptation is useful but incomplete because it does not address the potentially transformative effects of participation on the ideological commitments of Islamist actors and, in particular, on how the broader purposes of the Islamist movement should be defined. One reason the ideational dimensions of Islamist movement change remain underexplored is that it is extraordinarily difficult to confirm them empirically. For example, what explains the dramatic shift in the discourse of Islamist groups on democracy from its depiction as an alien system imported from the West to a type of political system mandated by Islam itself? The problem is that this shift is susceptible to conflicting interpretations, each of which implies a different set of causal triggers and dynamics. Here I highlight the distinctive features of these different causal models and explain why I find some of them more persuasive than others.

From one perspective, the rhetoric and behavior of Islamist groups are open to change, but the fundamental character of the movement is not. As characterized by those with this outlook, Islamists are rational, even Machiavellian actors who routinely and systematically adjust their tactics in whatever way they deem necessary to achieve a fixed set of higher goals—namely, to impose a system based on the traditional rulings of Shari'a, or Islamic law. Hence their statements in favor of democracy, pluralism, and equal citizenship rights can be dismissed as a form of strategic posturing, designed to mask their radical intentions behind a moderate veneer. Likewise, Islamist groups' support for democratic procedures can be discounted as purely self-serving, since such procedures offer them a means to convert their mass support into political power. Indeed, widespread doubts and suspicions about the ulterior motives of Islamist leaders have caused them to be routinely accused of practicing *taqiyya* (dissimulation, a term borrowed into mainstream Arab discourse from Shi'ite Islam)— that is, of engaging in a prolonged, deliberate, and self-conscious effort to deceive the wider public. Though this perspective offers a simple and coherent explanation of Islamist movement change, it is nearly impossible to falsify, since any pro-democratic statements and actions by Islamist actors can be dismissed out of hand as strategically motivated, no matter how consistently they express such views or how intense the approbation they incur as a result. Further, the idea that recent shifts in Islamist movement rhetoric, strategy, and organization, involving thousands of individuals over more than twenty years, are the result of some elaborate ruse strikes me as highly implausible given the enormous coordination problems that such a conspiracy would inevitably entail. Indeed, as I will demonstrate in the chapters to come, the portrayal of mainstream Islamist actors as single-mindedly bent on seizing power to achieve a set of fixed goals is a gross oversimplification—indeed a caricature—that cannot survive close empirical scrutiny.

That said, it is nevertheless plausible that shifts in the rhetoric and behavior of Islamist actors and organizations are driven by considerations of group advantage. Hence a second and to my mind more persuasive strategic explanation of Islamist movement change posits that Islamist groups have come to place a greater emphasis on democracy and the expansion of public freedoms *not for the purpose of deception but out of a realization that such reforms align with their group interests.* As opposition groups in authoritarian settings, Islamist groups would benefit directly from a lifting of restrictions on freedom of expression and assembly and the establishment of stricter constitutional limits on state power. Further, in countries where the mobilizing power of Islamist groups vastly exceeds that of their secular counterparts, they are likely to perform well in free and fair elections. Hence they have a powerful vested interest in the process of democratic reform.

As I will demonstrate in the chapters to come, the dynamics of Islamist movement change in Egypt, Jordan, Kuwait, and Morocco do in fact conform to a strategic logic, at least in part. In particular, considerations of short-term political advantage—the desire to gain (and preserve) a legal foothold in the political system, avoid repression, and gain social acceptance—have encouraged Islamist groups to exercise pragmatic self-restraint in the domains of both rhetoric and practice. For example, such considerations have led Islamist groups to soft-pedal their calls for Shari'a rule by postponing it far into the future and/ or by redefining it as the application of a general set of principles rather than equating it with the imposition of traditional rulings inherited from the past. In addition, Islamist groups have limited their participation in competitive elections to avoid too large a margin of victory. Further, they have allied with secular parties and organizations to amplify pressure for democratic reform.

Yet a strategic account of Islamist movement change takes us only so far. This is because it fails to acknowledge and explore the conditions under which the ideological commitments—as well as the strategic interests—of Islamist actors are open to change over time.

The dominance of rational actor models of behavior in the field of political science has diverted attention away from the role of values and ideas—as opposed to interests—as a basis for political action. Yet in recent years a promising field of study has emerged as part of the "constructivist" turn in international relations theory, which focuses on how the preferences of political actors are formed and how and why they change over time. These questions are typically bracketed by rational choice theorists, who tend to treat such preferences as given.[2] Constructivist scholars emphasize that the preferences of individual actors are socially constructed through their interactions with others within specific institutional and cultural environments.[3] Further, unlike strict rational choice theory, which presumes that actors seek, always and everywhere, to maximize their interests, constructivists emphasize the role of identities, values, and beliefs as key drivers of political action. In so doing, they highlight the possibility that changes in the rhetoric and behavior of, say, a state official or an opposition activist may stem from unconscious or conscious change in his/her values and beliefs.[4]

Constructivist scholars identify two distinct causal processes that can produce such change. First, the sustained participation of political actors in new institutional settings can trigger a reflexive and unconscious process of socialization variously described in the literature as "role playing," "mimicking," "copying," and "emulating" prescribed norms of behavior.[5] When political actors enter a new institutional environment, they are under pressure to conform with its established rules of speech and conduct. And once they adapt to such expectations, they must justify this adaptation to themselves and others. As a result, "they may later adapt their preferences to these justifications, in this way reducing cognitive dissonance."[6] *Changes in the behavior of political actors, iterated over time, may thus produce change in their beliefs.* As Zürn and Checkel have argued, "Acting in accordance with role expectations may lead to the internalization of these expectations,"[7] a situation in which, to borrow an elegant turn of phrase from Suzanne Hoeber Rudolph, "the mask becomes the face."[8] As Islamist actors have assumed new roles and responsibilities, it can be theorized that they have developed new competencies and skills and adapted their behavior to the norms and expectations of the institutions of which they are a part. As a result, the type of issues they focus on, and the ways they seek to address them, may diverge considerably from their original goals and strategies.

Political Engagement and Value-Change

Islamist movement change can be conceptualized as entailing another set of causal processes that go beyond strategic adaptation. As constructivist scholars observe, new forms of political engagement can also produce self-conscious shifts in the commitments of political actors as a result of new experiences and/ or exposure to new information and ideas.[9] Checkel and his colleagues focused on changes in the preferences of national politicians resulting from processes of deliberation and persuasion within the institutions of the European Union, but this process of value-change can be discerned among other types of actors in other settings as well. For example, studies by Bermeo, Roberts, and McCoy on the evolution of the radical left during "third wave" democratic transitions in southern Europe and Latin America suggest that the views of socialist leaders were fundamentally transformed by their close interactions with leaders of other groups in exile or in prison. Such interactions triggered a process of soul-searching and a critical reexamination of the rigid ideological certainties that had fueled their calls for revolution in the past.[10] Given that the leaders of Islamist groups are more numerous, the institutional environments within which they operate are more diffuse, and the interactions that might exert an influence on their preferences have taken place over a longer period of time, the chains of cause and effect are less tightly connected and therefore more difficult to verify. Nevertheless, it is worth investigating how the experiences gained by Islamist actors as participants in the formal political system—including their involvement in intensive forms of dialogue, deliberation, and cooperation with figures outside the Islamist movement—have affected their values and beliefs. As I will argue in the chapters to come, the participation of Islamist groups in the political process not only generated new strategic interests but also prompted internal debates about their ultimate goals and purposes. In recent decades, Islamist actors have begun to break out of the insular networks of movement politics and interact on a regular basis with government officials and leaders of other civil and political groups. In addition, they have been sought out by international media outlets, as well as by foreign researchers, party and NGO activists, and even, in some instances, officials of foreign governments. Through such contacts, Islamist leaders have been more intensively exposed to the global discourse on democracy and human rights as well as to local arguments in favor of comprehensive democratic reform. Among some Islamist leaders, such exposure increased the resonance of new and more progressive readings of Islam. The availability of alternative interpretive frameworks, articulated by independent Islamist thinkers with considerable religious authority, facilitated the "hybridization" of democratic values or their re-articulation in a local idiom.[11] For the Islamist actors in question, the internalization of new and more progressive interpretations of Islam was not the result of a single discrete event but the cumulative effect of hundreds, if not thousands, of conversations, debates, and arguments in the public domain over many years. Islamist leaders often describe the impact of these experiences on their outlook as a holistic, profound, and emotional-affective journey through which "a whole new world opened up" and their outlook changed "180 degrees." Moreover, such individual trajectories eventually set a wider evolution in motion, as Islamist leaders who were gradually transformed by their experience became proponents of change in the Islamist movement itself.

Indeed, one of the central objectives of this book is to highlight the emergence of a new "reformist" (*islahi*) trend within Arab Islamist opposition groups, which refers here not to the reform of society and state but the reform of the self (*al-islah al-dhati*) or what we might translate into English as "auto-reform." In recent years leaders affiliated with this trend have called for the progressive revision of Islamist groups' traditional positions on such key issues as the scope for political and intellectual pluralism, the rights of women and non-Muslims, and relations with the West. In addition, they have criticized their "culture of obedience," their lack of routinized procedures for selecting leaders and setting policy, and their historic isolation from other forces in society. Finally, though still committed to the ultimate goal of establishing a political system based on Shari'a, Islamists affiliated with the "reformist" trend have begun to articulate a different vision of what this would mean in practice. In particular, they have developed a new Islamist agenda, which—in sharp contrast to the totalizing ambitions of Islamist groups in the past—endorses strict limits on the exercise of state power and the legal protection of a broad range of civil and political rights.

In sum, the emergence of the "reformist" trend has triggered new debates within Islamist circles. Such debates, which have typically occurred behind closed doors in settings removed from public scrutiny, have taken the form of puzzling, arguing, and deliberating about the modern coordinates of Shari'a rule. And they show that not just the *means* but also the *ends* of the Sunni revivalist movement are open to change over time.

The process of value-change described above occurred first and foremost at the level of individual actors. This seemingly straightforward point has several important implications. First, owing to differences in the life histories, motivations, reasoning patterns, and emotions of Islamist actors, as well as in the positions they occupy within Islamist groups and the character and intensity of their engagement in the broader political system, we cannot expect them to have the same set of experiences or to react to them in the same way. As a result, it is virtually impossible to identify a general matrix of ideological and behavioral shifts that applies to the cadres of the Islamist movement as a whole. On the contrary, Islamist leaders within the same country, and even within the same group, have come to assume very different positions on such "meta-issues" as the definition of Shari'a rule, as well as on various policy matters of the day, such as whether a controversial film should be banned. Such incoherence exposes Islamist groups to the charge that they "speak in a double language," when in fact it reflects differences in their members' personalities, orientations, and beliefs.

Second, value-change proceeds from a particular ideological starting point shaped by the social and cultural milieu of revivalist Islam. It does not entail "wiping the slate clean" so much as a grafting of new ideas and sensibilities into preexisting ideological frameworks by recasting them in movement-valid terms. It should come as no surprise that this process of ideological "hybridization" is fraught with contradictions and ambiguities rather than yielding a seamless integration of the old and new. Third, the pace and scope of ideological revision under way within mainstream Islamist groups is uneven. The support of some Islamist leaders for suicide-bombing operations against civilians in Palestine and Iraq at the same time that they have begun to incorporate the concept of human rights into their agendas at home highlights the selective and contingent nature of value-change and the difficulty of framing it as a monolithic and unilinear process. Fourth, even the most ardent supporters of Islamist movement reform have not suddenly morphed into liberal democrats, nor should we expect them to do so any time soon. Such leaders remain committed to a vision of Islam as *din wa dawla*, both religion and state, and aspire to the eventual establishment of Islamic rule. But *what Islamic rule would mean in practice and how it should be pursued have become moving targets*, with new and more progressive interpretations of Islam being deployed by some members of the movement to challenge the profoundly illiberal conceptions of Islamic rule supported by others.

Finally, understanding value-change as a process of individual—rather than collective—transformation forces us to confront the crucial problem of aggregation. That is, we need to investigate whether, how, and under what conditions ideological innovation spreads from the level of individual actors to the organizations and movements of which they are a part. More specifically, we need to identify whether and how the advocates of Islamist auto-reform are able to mobilize internal support for their agendas and acquire the capacity to influence the official programs and policies of Islamist groups. It is to these issues that we now turn.

THE SCOPE AND LIMITS OF ISLAMIST SELF-REFORM

The rise of an Islamist reformist trend in Egypt, Jordan, Morocco, and Kuwait is an important phenomenon in its own right, but we cannot determine its significance without assessing its impact on the official policies and practices of mainstream Islamist groups. Do the advocates of movement reform remain "voices in the wilderness," blocked from positions of decision-making power within such organizations and lacking an institutional platform from which to reach their base? Or have they begun to coalesce into a coherent bloc with sufficient resources, networks, and moral authority to challenge the status and power of movement hard-liners? As I will demonstrate in the chapters to come, the influence of the "reformist" trend varies considerably from one Islamist group to another, having achieved the greatest influence, among the cases here, in the Justice and Development Party (JDP) in Morocco. Such variation reflects differences in the power of reformist leaders within the leadership of such groups, as well as in the receptivity of group members to their ideas.

The impact of the reformist trend on mainstream Arab Islamist political organizations is also shaped by domestic, regional, and global developments. In countries like Egypt and Jordan, the chronic vulnerability of Islamist groups to harassment and repression by authoritarian state establishments, as well as unresolved conflicts over territory and power in Palestine and Iraq, long bolstered appeals for Islamic movement unity and solidarity at the expense of calls for internal critique and reform. In addition, the departure of some of the most outspoken and charismatic proponents of reform from these groups diluted the influence of the reformist current within the "mother organizations" they left behind. Hence the impact of the reformist trend was more muted than it might have been under different circumstances.

THE VALUE OF COMPARATIVE HISTORICAL ANALYSIS

The purpose of this book is to identify the scope and limits of Islamist movement change, as well as its underlying causes and dynamics, through a focus on the historical evolution of the Muslim Brotherhood in Egypt and similar Islamist groups in Jordan, Kuwait, and Morocco. My approach proceeds from the premise that significant real-world trends and events are rarely, if ever, caused by a small set of factors or "variables" operating in regular and consistent ways across space and time. On the contrary, they are typically the result of the complex interaction of multiple causal factors, the effects of which are shaped by the context in which they are embedded, what Charles Ragin has described as "multiple conjunctural causation."[12] Rooting my work within the broader tradition of comparative historical analysis in the social sciences, I trace the causal processes that have produced changes in Islamist rhetoric and behavior through a close, in-depth empirical investigation of a small number of cases. As Peter Hall observed, an argument about causes must specify the process by which they generate an outcome, and "the explanatory power of a theory rests, in large measure, on the specification of such a process." Through "systematic process analysis," Hall notes, "the causal theories to be tested are interrogated for the predictions they contain about how events will unfold. . . . The point is to see if the multiple actions and statements of the actors at each stage of the causal process are consistent with the image of the world implied by each theory." According to Hall, the ultimate purpose of such analysis is to establish the superiority of one theory over others, based on the "congruence between predictions and observations."[13] Yet there are times when the observations we gather in the field are susceptible to a "double interpretation"; that is, they are consistent with conflicting causal explanations.[14] In such cases, I would argue, we need to assess how closely a given sequence of events conforms to the logic of a particular causal process while remaining open to the possibility that a single outcome or set of outcomes might be generated by multiple causal processes operating at the same time.

Another distinctive feature of this book is that it traces the evolution of Islamist rhetoric, behavior, and practices over a long time frame. In Chapters 2 through 7 and in Chapter 9, I trace the development of the Muslim Brotherhood in Egypt from its formation in 1928 to the election of Muhammad Mursi as president in 2012, an arc of more than eighty years. In Chapter 8, I examine the trajectories of mainstream Islamist opposition groups in Jordan, Kuwait, and Morocco beginning with the formation of their movement associations in the 1940s, 1960s, and 1970s, respectively. By starting at the beginning, so to speak, I am able to identify the core characteristics of Islamist organizations *before* they entered the fray of competitive electoral politics, establishing a clear baseline against which subsequent developments can be judged. Further, as Hall and other advocates and practitioners of comparative historical analysis have observed, tracking the development of groups and institutions over a long period enables us to investigate how decisions made in the distant past impact later outcomes. This is true whether we conceive of "path dependence" as a series of "critical junctures" at which a group or institution undergoes an abrupt and dramatic shift in course and/or as the cumulative impact of more incremental and continuous processes of change. Further, the close examination of a single case or a limited number of cases over time enables us to establish tighter and better empirically supported relationships of cause and effect than is possible in large-n studies, which of necessity characterize patterns of causation in more schematic terms. Of particular importance for my purposes, the close examination of discrete trends and events over time *permits an investigation of both the strategic and nonstrategic dimensions of Islamist movement change within a unified analytic framework.*

In sum, by "telling the story" of the evolution of mainstream Islamist groups in Egypt, Jordan, Kuwait, and Morocco through parallel historical narratives, the book aims to specify the causal processes at work in each case, as well as to identify the broader pattern of Islamist movement change suggested by the elements they have in common. My central argument is that observable changes in Islamist group rhetoric and behavior cannot be explained as an outcome of *either* strategic adaptation *or* ideational change but rather exhibit features of both. It is hence an argument for complexity over parsimony both in the analysis of the motivations of Islamist actors and in the analysis of the wider developments in the movements and organizations of which they are a part.

THE ORGANIZATION OF THE BOOK

In Chapter 2, I trace the early history of the Brotherhood from its founding in 1928 through the end of the Sadat era. In so doing, I seek to provide a more nuanced and complex picture of the "starting point" for the changes in Brotherhood ideology, strategy, and organization that occurred from the mid-1980s forward. In Chapter 3, I trace the Brotherhood's entry into parliament, professional associations, and faculty clubs from the mid-1980s to the mid-1990s and demonstrate how its leaders justified the group's participation in electoral politics in an "unIslamic" regime. Further, I show that the professional associations in particular became important sites of contact between Islamist and secular public figures and that the cross-partisan interactions within them helped nurture the formation of a new "reformist trend" within the Brotherhood's ranks. I show that leaders affiliated with this trend launched a critical reassessment of the movement's anti-system past and called for a redefinition of its historic mission based on new and more progressive interpretations of Islam. Yet I also demonstrate that calls for movement reform encountered stiff resistance from "old-guard" leaders who retained a monopoly of seats on the Brotherhood's executive board.

Chapter 4 explains how and why growing internal tensions led to a rift in the Brotherhood's ranks in the mid-1990s with the formation of the Wasat (Center) party by a breakaway group of reformist leaders. I demonstrate that this rift occurred in the context of—and in reaction to—a new wave of repression directed at violent and nonviolent Islamist groups alike. I show that rather than augment and embolden the reformist current within the Brotherhood, the Wasat initiative actually worked to undermine it by splitting the reformist camp in two and diluting its influence within the Brotherhood itself.

In Chapters 5 and 6, I analyze the path taken by the Brotherhood during the final decade of the Mubarak era. I demonstrate that the Brotherhood's efforts to navigate an unforgiving political environment yielded a zigzag course, with periods of bold self-assertion followed by periods of retreat. These chapters highlight the waning influence of the reformist trend within the Brotherhood in the context of a closing political environment, the conservative *da'wa* faction's success in achieving a near total monopoly of power in the Guidance Bureau, and the growing influence of the Salafi trend among the members of its base.

In Chapter 7, I analyze the role of the Brotherhood in the 2011 Egyptian uprising and the course it pursued after the Supreme Council of the Armed Forces (SCAF) assumed power and launched a transition to a new political order. I show that although the Brotherhood did not lead the uprising, it ended up as one of its greatest beneficiaries. While moving quickly to form a party and gear up for parliamentary elections in the fall, the Brotherhood took pains to emphasize that it sought to "participate, not dominate" the new political institutions that would be seated by popular vote.

Chapter 8 compares the evolution of the Egyptian Muslim Brotherhood with those of its counterparts in Jordan, Kuwait, and Morocco. In so doing, it enables us to discern a general pattern of Islamist movement change that transcends the particulars of any single country case. Yet Chapter 8 also shows that the trajectory of each Islamist group was shaped by the institutional environment in which it was embedded, the social profile of its base, and the balance of power among its internal factions. More broadly, each group's evolution bears the imprint of the distinctive features of its host country's society and culture, producing a set of outcomes best described as "variations on a theme."

In Chapter 9, I return to the case of Egypt, highlighting the Brotherhood's striking gains in recent parliamentary and presidential elections, as well as the series of constitutional and political crises that attended its rise to new heights of political power. Though the Brotherhood has emerged as the clear victor in recent elections, it has confronted significant pushback from the institutions of the "deep state" carried over from the Mubarak era. The Brotherhood has thus been forced to walk a fine line, attempting to defend its mandate to govern without provoking a backlash that could place the transition—and its own gains—at risk.

At the same time, Brotherhood leaders have come to realize that the consolidation of Egypt's fragile democratic institutions and the revival of economic growth will require the support of domestic and foreign actors external to—and in some cases deeply suspicious of—the Islamist movement. Against this backdrop, the Brotherhood faces a second challenge: winning the trust and cooperation of other groups while assuring supporters of its fidelity to the Islamic cause.

Chapter 9 concludes with a summary of the book's main analytic findings, a key one of which is that some dimensions of Islamist movement change conform to a strategic logic and others do not. By highlighting the ideational dimension of Islamist movement change, I reveal the speciousness of the premise that the ideological commitments of Islamist actors and organizations are fixed, as well as the inability of strict rational actor models to explain when, why, and how they change over time. Hence I show that findings derived from contextually grounded, finely grained small-n research can help problematize reigning paradigms in the discipline of political science and provide a more nuanced and persuasive account of real-world social and political change.

CHAPTER TWO

The Brotherhood's Early Years

FOUNDED BY HASAN AL-BANNA in Egypt in 1928, the Muslim Brotherhood is the flagship organization of Sunni revivalist Islam and has been in existence longer than any other contemporary Islamist group in the Arab world. Today it is the most powerful nonstate actor in Egypt, with over eighty million people, the largest Arab country. It is also the "mother organization" of Brotherhood affiliates in Jordan, Palestine, Kuwait, Syria, Iraq, Sudan, and Bahrain and has served as a model and source of inspiration for Sunni revivalist groups in Arab North Africa as well.

Aside from the Brotherhood's obvious real-world importance, its path over the past eighty years raises some broader questions. How did the Brotherhood evolve from a small religious and charitable society into the largest and most effective sector of the opposition during Egypt's long years under authoritarian rule? Further, what prompted it to enter the fray of electoral politics, and how did that decision and the series of institutional adjustments that succeeded it affect its leaders' interests, values, and beliefs, including their conception of the desired end state of Shari'a rule? To answer these questions, we need to establish a clear baseline against which subsequent developments can be compared. How did the founders of the Brotherhood originally define its mission, and how was it shaped by the social and political conditions of their time?

THE ORIGINS OF THE MUSLIM BROTHERHOOD

No one but God knows how many nights we spent reviewing the state of the nation . . . analyzing the sickness, and thinking of the possible remedies. So disturbed were we that we reached the point of tears.

Hasan al-Banna, 1939

The Society of the Muslim Brothers (Jam'iyyat al-Ikhwan al-Muslimin) was founded by Hasan al-Banna in 1928.[1] As detailed in Richard Mitchell's seminal

1969 book on the group's formative years in Egypt before 1952, al-Banna was born in 1906 in the small town of Mahmudiyya, located about ninety miles northwest of Cairo in the fertile agricultural region of the Delta. The son of a local sheikh who had been educated at Al-Azhar, al-Banna was raised in a home shaped by his father's "classical and traditional religious learning and piety."[2] As a boy, al-Banna became involved in the Order of the Hasafiyya, a Sufi mystic circle, and at the age of thirteen was appointed secretary of a new group affiliated with the Hasafiyya order that aimed to "fight for the preservation of Islamic morality and to resist the work of Christian missionaries in the town."[3] After graduating from the Primary Teacher Training School in Damanhour, al-Banna moved to Cairo at the age of sixteen and enrolled in Dar al-ʿUlum, founded in 1873 as Egypt's first "modern" institute of higher education. As a student in Cairo, al-Banna was dismayed by the petty rivalries and factionalism that divided Egypt's political elite in the wake of the national revolution of 1919, as well as by the secular orientations of the new Egyptian university and the literary and social salons, newspapers, and magazines, which seemed intent on "weakening the influence of religion."[4] And like many of his contemporaries, al-Banna reacted bitterly to the continued presence of British troops on Egyptian soil as well as ongoing British interference in the country's political life, which continued even after the country achieved nominal independence in 1923. In his last year at Dar al-ʿUlum, al-Banna decided that he would make it his own personal mission to return educated youth to the Islamic way of life by preaching, teaching, and providing guidance to them and their parents.

In 1927, al-Banna received his first teaching position at a government primary school in the Suez Canal Zone town of Ismailiyya, the site of a large British military installation as well as the headquarters of the European-owned Suez Canal Company. When not occupied with lessons at school, al-Banna spread his call for a return to Islam in local mosques and coffeehouses, developing a reputation as a skilled and magnetic speaker. In 1928, at the age of twenty-two, al-Banna was approached by six laborers from a British military camp on the outskirts of Ismailiyya, who, inspired by his commitment to Islam and the welfare of Muslims, asked him to lead them. Mitchell describes his response:

> Banna, duly moved, accepted the burden imposed on him, and together they took an oath to God to be "troops [*jund*] for the message of Islam." The name was selected by Banna: "We are brothers in the service of Islam; hence we are the ʿMuslim Brothers.ʾ"[5]

In its first few years of existence, the Muslim Brotherhood developed a following in Ismailiyya through direct outreach in mosques, coffeehouses, and private homes; in addition, it built a mosque, a school for boys, a boys' club, and a school for girls, a pattern of establishing local community service projects that it would later replicate in other Egyptian cities and towns.[6] At the time of its formation, the Brotherhood was just one of several religious societies seeking to reinforce popular adherence to Islam and combat the threat posed by the spread of Western cultural values and lifestyles in a context of rapid social and political change. Yet in the two decades that followed, under al-Banna's charismatic leadership, the Brotherhood rapidly expanded into a broad national organization with a large membership base and a network of social and welfare institutions that eclipsed those of any other civic association, religious or otherwise, in the country. As observed by Mitchell, the number of its branches rose from four in 1929 to two thousand in 1949; by the mid-1940s, the Brotherhood had grown to encompass an estimated three hundred to six hundred thousand members.[7]

The Muslim Brotherhood in its early years was a classic case of an "anti-system" group situated outside—and against—the established political order. Al-Banna condemned the factional infighting and petty strife that pitted the country's political parties and leading politicians against each other during the interwar years, arguing that such partisan conflict (*hizbiyya*, or partyism) undermined the nation's unity and thereby made it more vulnerable to foreign domination. Continued British intervention throughout the 1930s and 1940s served to underscore the failure of established politicians to assert effective control over the country's sovereign affairs. Further, al-Banna highlighted the incapacity or unwillingness of the elected parliament, dominated at the time by large landowning and commercial elites, to address the country's highly skewed distribution of wealth and alleviate the suffering of the Egyptian masses, whose living conditions were further eroded by rampant inflation and basic food shortages.[8]

Such seeming proof of the bankruptcy of the constitutional order established in 1923 was also emphasized by other anti-system groups and movements at the time, including the militant nationalist Misr al-Fatah and various leftist and communist groups. What distinguished the Brotherhood was its religious interpretation of the causes of the country's malaise and the proper framework for its solution. To al-Banna and other religious conservatives, the problems of foreign economic, political, and military domination were compounded by the spread of Western secular values and practices. The secular models of law and education borrowed from Europe were out of touch with the religious beliefs and sentiments of Egyptian society; likewise, the "cheap," "lewd," and "suggestive" content of popular media, films, and music undermined traditional values and created moral and sexual problems for youth. Finally, the seeming eagerness of the country's political elite to "ape" Western ways—as indicated, among other things, by the free mixing of their women with unrelated men at private parties and official functions and the spread of alcohol, gambling, and prostitution—signaled their betrayal of the country's Islamic heritage.[9]

In the view of the Muslim Brotherhood, the key to the country's moral and social renewal—as well as the only effective means to wrest it free from foreign control—was a return to Islam. In what would become the hallmark of Sunni revivalist groups across the region in subsequent decades, the Brotherhood propagated a vision of Islam as *din wa dawla* (religion and state), that is, not only a guide to private belief and ritual but a comprehensive system of values and governance intrinsically different from—and superior to—the secular political systems of the West.[10] Though framed as a return to the "pure" and "true" Islam of the Prophet Muhammad and his Companions, the Brotherhood's understanding of Islam was itself a product of modern times, influenced directly by the ideas of Rashid Rida and Muhibb al-Din al-Khatib, disciples of the early twentieth-century modernist Islamist thinker Muhammad Abduh. In their hands, Abduh's conception of a national renaissance based on a return to the Islam of the first Muslims (the Aslaf, or pious ancestors) lost its emphasis on the "rational" spirit of Islam and its openness to learning from the West and assumed a more strident tone.[11] For example, they asserted that an Islamic order (*al-nidham al-islami*) based on Shari'a embodied all of the virtues of democratic and socialist systems in the West while avoiding all their defects. As the newspaper of the Brotherhood boldly proclaimed:

> If the French Revolution decreed the rights of man and declared for freedom, equality and brotherhood, and if the Russian revolution brought closer the classes and social justice for people, the great Islamic revolution decreed all that 1,300 years before.[12]

Further, against a backdrop of global economic depression and world war, it was clear that despite its past scientific and material achievements, Western civilization was now "bankrupt and in decline." As al-Banna observed:

> Its foundations are crumbling, and its institutions and guiding principles are falling apart. Its political foundations are being destroyed by dictatorships, and its economic foundations are being swept away by crises. The millions of its wretched unemployed and hungry offer their testimony against it. . . . Their congresses are failures, their treaties are broken and their covenants torn to pieces: their League of Nations is a phantasm, possessing neither spirit nor influence, while their strong men, along with other things, are overthrowing its covenant of peace and security.[13]

The Brotherhood sought to raise the level of religious commitment in Egyptian society by providing its own members with a rigorous Islamic "upbringing" (*tarbiya*) and subsequently enlisting them in religious outreach (*da'wa*) to the wider public. Communicating their ideas through face-to-face contact with friends, neighbors, relatives, schoolmates, and fellow office workers, the Brotherhood sought to enlarge the circle of "committed" Muslims until it eventually encompassed society as a whole. At the same time, Brotherhood-sponsored local social service and community projects, including schools, health clinics, and charitable foundations, demonstrated the Brotherhood's concern with the public welfare and created new avenues for recruitment. The ambitiousness of the Brotherhood's agenda—which amounted to no less than a systematic effort to capture the hearts and minds of the educated youth of Egypt's cities and provincial towns—as well as its claims to act in the broad interests of society, rather than those of a partisan group or faction within it, made al-Banna reluctant to pigeonhole the organization into any conventional political category. As al-Banna exhorted its members in his first *risala*, or public message, written just before the outbreak of World War II:

> Brethren, you are not a benevolent organization, nor a political party, nor a local association with strictly limited aims. Rather you are a new spirit making its way into the heart of this nation and revivifying it through the Quran; a new light dawning and scattering the darkness of materialism through the knowledge of God; a resounding voice rising and echoing the message of the Prophet.[14]

The Brotherhood never offered a detailed and coherent vision of the Islamic order it sought to create. In part, this stemmed from the group's emphasis on "action" (*'amal*) and "organization" (*tandhiim*) over "ideology" (*fikra*), as well as perhaps a sense that any efforts to work out the details at such a preliminary stage were premature.[15] As a result, the character of the Brothers' political thought is susceptible to conflicting interpretations. Some observers see the group's rejection of partisan conflict and its calls for the establishment of a "comprehensive" Islamic order as evidence of a coercive project to gain state power and impose its agenda by force.[16] Yet this characterization of the early Brotherhood misses some important nuances. First, according to sources cited by Mitchell, al-Banna took pains to emphasize that the Brotherhood did not seek to acquire power for itself but aimed to facilitate a wider process of social reform. Second, while Brotherhood leaders believed that the establishment of a legal system consistent with Shari'a would require the backing of a government authority, they envisioned this as the end point of a long period of preparatory outreach when the people would demand an Islamic government for themselves.[17] Third, several of the leading religious scholars associated with the Brotherhood expressed support for the institution of parliament, the choice of rulers via popular elections, the establishment of an independent judiciary, and the protection of the rights of citizens by law.[18] Finally, rather than insist on the literal application of traditional Shari'a rulings inherited from the past, Brotherhood leaders emphasized the need for *ijtihad*, the exercise of human reason, to construct laws derived from the sacred texts of Islam that were relevant to the needs of the Muslim community in modern times.

Despite the progressive positions taken by some Brotherhood-affiliated religious scholars, it is nevertheless the case that its political discourse exhibited a number of unresolved contradictions and ambiguities. First and most important was the tension between the ultimate authority of God as expressed by the Shari'a and the authority of the nation's elected representatives in parliament or local councils to enact laws in accordance with the popular will. How—and by whom—should the conformity of human-made legislation with the principles of Shari'a be ensured? A second aspect of the Brotherhood's thought that lacked clarity was its position on the rights of those—whether Christians or fellow Muslims—who did not subscribe to its agenda. At issue was not just whether the Brotherhood supported pluralism in the political arena but also whether it supported intellectual and artistic freedom and respected the right of private citizens to choose their own values and lifestyles. In claiming to represent all Muslims and portraying its message as the only "true" and "correct" understanding of Islam, the Brotherhood exhibited, in Mitchell's words, "a self-righteousness born of sanctimonious claims to omniscience" as well as a "basic intolerance of dissent."[19] Even if the Brotherhood did not intend to seize power and impose its agenda by force, its arrogation to itself of the exclusive authority to interpret God's will—and rejection of the legitimacy of opposing viewpoints—gave its ideology a rigid and coercive tone.

A third feature of the Brotherhood was its ambivalence toward formal political institutions like parliament and political parties. On the one hand, the Brotherhood condemned the corruption and elitism of the political system, as well as its continued vulnerability to British interference. Yet at the group's sixth general conference in 1941, it decided "at the appropriate time" to field candidates for parliament. Seventeen Brotherhood candidates were slated to participate in the 1942 parliamentary elections, with al-Banna himself as a candidate for the district of Ismailiyya; al-Banna was subsequently summoned by the Wafdist government and pressured to withdraw from the race. In 1945, al-Banna and five other Brothers ran for parliament, but amid widespread allegations of electoral fraud, all of them were defeated.[20] Such disappointing results, which, as Mitchell recounts, precipitated "charges of forgery, cast in the form of denunciations of parties, partyism, and anything related," likely deepened the Brotherhood's alienation from the formal political order and reinforced its "anti-system" orientation.

While most of the Brotherhood's activities in its formative years were devoted to the incremental reform of society from the bottom up, Hasan al-Banna and other leaders also embraced the Islamist concept of jihad. The Brotherhood's understanding of jihad drew on the Quran and the Hadith (the narrative records of the Sunna, the speech and practices of the Prophet and his Companions), as well as the legal rulings of classical Muslim jurists. Beyond the general meaning of jihad as "struggle," the Brotherhood viewed it as the legitimate use of force, both as a method to enlarge the territory under Islamic rule and as a means to defend the Muslim community when it was subjected to the rule of unbelievers and was vulnerable to external threats. In the latter circumstances, which according to al-Banna accurately described the situation of the Muslim world in his day, jihad became the religious obligation of every Muslim:

Today the Muslims, as you know, are compelled to humble themselves before non-Muslims, and are ruled by unbelievers. Their lands have been trampled over, and their honor besmirched. Their adversaries are in charge of their affairs, and the rites of their religion have fallen into abeyance within their own domains. . . . Hence it has become an individual obligation, which there is no evading, on every Muslim to prepare his equipment, to make up his mind to engage in *jihad*, and to get ready for it until the opportunity is ripe and God decrees a matter which is sure to be accomplished.[21]

The primary targets of jihad were the Western imperialists and Zionists who had colonized Muslim lands and asserted control over their sovereign affairs. Yet the principle of jihad was also invoked in the Brotherhood's confrontations with rival opposition groups and the Egyptian government. In the 1930s the Brotherhood established paramilitary formations known as the Rovers (*jawwala*) and Battalions (*kata'ib*), which provided committed youth with rigorous spiritual and physical training. Drawing inspiration from the fascist youth organizations of interwar Europe, the Brotherhood's militias and the parallel militias set up by rival groups (including the Green Shirts of the ultranationalist Young Egypt movement and the Blue Shirts of the Wafd party) engaged in pitched street battles with each other. Such armed groups were both a symptom of and a factor contributing to the general breakdown of law and order and the legitimation of violence as a method of political struggle.[22] In addition, late in 1942 or early 1943, the Brotherhood established a separate unit within the organization that came to be known inside the group as the "special section" (*al-nidham al-khass*) and outside it as the "secret apparatus" (*al-jihaz al-sirri*), which was implicated in a series of attacks on British military installations as well as Egyptian police and government targets. After the United Nations approved the establishment of a Jewish state in Palestine in November 1947, al-Banna activated the group's military units and in April 1948 sent three battalions to fight in the Palestine War.[23] The war triggered rioting and attacks on Egyptian Jewish residences and business establishments in which scores of people were killed or injured and property destroyed; the "secret apparatus" was apparently involved in at least some of these incidents.[24]

The assassination of a prominent judge by members of the secret apparatus in March 1948, together with other charges of violence and weapons training, led to the dissolution of the Brotherhood in December 1948. A few weeks later, a member of the Brotherhood shot and killed Prime Minister Nuqrashi Pasha, and on February 12, 1949, al-Banna himself was gunned down by government agents.[25] At the conclusion of the court case, the order dissolving the Brotherhood was lifted, and in October 1951 Hasan al-Hudeibi, a respected judge with twenty-five years on the bench, was appointed the organization's new Supreme Guide.

The Muslim Brotherhood under the Nasser Regime

The Free Officers' coup of 1952, which overthrew Egypt's constitutional monarchy and brought the country's troubled experiment with liberal politics to a close, was initially welcomed by the Muslim Brotherhood. Indeed, Brotherhood leaders saw themselves as having provided the "inspiration" for the rebellion and saw the establishment of the new regime as a fulfillment of the aspirations of the Brotherhood itself.[26] Yet as the main organizational rival to the new regime, the Brotherhood soon became a target of brutal repression, as Mitchell notes:

> On July 23, 1952 the Muslim Brothers joined with the rest of Egypt in celebrating the dawn of a new era; twenty-nine months later, six of the Society's members died on the gallows, and the organization was destroyed almost beyond repair.[27]

By 1954, Gamal Abdel Nasser had consolidated his position as the undisputed head of the new "revolutionary" government. The Brotherhood's repeated calls for the application of Shari'a and its public support for General Muhammad Naguib, Nasser's rival in the power struggle that followed the Free Officers' takeover, had already provoked Nasser's antipathy, but by 1954 the Brotherhood's continued existence as an independent movement with the capacity to flex its muscles whenever it saw fit had become intolerable. Following a clash between Brotherhood university students and the police, Nasser dissolved the Brotherhood on January 13, 1954.[28] The dissolution decree spurred the "secret apparatus" to reorganize and prepare for what it saw as an inevitable confrontation with the regime.

On October 19 Nasser signed an evacuation treaty with Britain, which, in its concessions to British security interests, was condemned by some in the Brotherhood for "giving away the rights of the nation."[29] The same day, Mahmud Abd al-Latif, a member of the Brotherhood's secret apparatus, accepted the mission to assassinate Nasser, and one week later, on October 26, he fired eight shots at Nasser at an open-air rally, none of which reached its target. Although the Brotherhood's leadership condemned the attack and denied any prior knowledge of it,[30] the assassination attempt gave Nasser the pretext he needed to crush the organization once and for all. Alleging that the Brotherhood aimed to overthrow the government and seize power for itself, the regime destroyed its headquarters and tried a thousand Brotherhood leaders in court. In December, six of its members were hanged.[31]

From 1954 to 1970, the Brotherhood remained a prime target of the Nasserist state. Thousands of Brotherhood members languished in desert prison camps,[32] where many were deprived of basic necessities and repeatedly subjected to brutal acts of torture, while those not caught up in the regime's security net fled into exile or were forced underground. Islamist books and pamphlets published after Nasser's death capture the Brotherhood's *mihna* (ordeal) with titles and images depicting gallows, blood, and death. The regime's harsh crackdown on the Brotherhood provoked the rise of new schisms within the organization's ranks by encouraging the ideological radicalization of some of its members, who reached the conclusion that any regime that could inflict such enormous suffering was irredeemably corrupt and could only be combated through force of arms. Such ideas received their fullest expression in the works of Brotherhood ideologue Sayyid Qutb, which he wrote from his prison cell while serving a sentence of twenty-five years with hard labor.[33] In his most influential tract, *Ma'alim fii al-Tariq* (Signposts Along the Path), Qutb developed the concepts of *jahiliyya* and *hakimiyya* initially proposed by the Pakistani revivalist Islamist thinkers Ala' al-Mawdudi and Abu Hasan al-Nadwi and, by applying them directly to an analysis of the Brotherhood's persecution under Nasser, gave them new clarity and force. *Jahiliyya* (from *jahl*, ignorance) originally referred to society in Arabia prior to the advent of Islam. In its modern formulation, as elaborated upon and popularized by Qutb, it referred to a state of willful blindness to God's sovereign power. All systems based on man-made laws, whatever their orientation, fell within the category of *jahiliyya*, including the democratic systems of the West. Against *jahiliyya* stood one alternative, *hakimiyyat Allah* (the absolute sovereignty of God), meaning the imposition of a system of Islamic law derived from the texts of the Quran and the Sunna. The Nasser regime, "as seen from the vantage point of a man who knew only its concentration camps,"[34] epitomized the intrinsic flaws and excesses of all *jahili* systems, exposing the depths of human suffering that resulted when some of God's subjects arrogated the right to rule over others. In Signposts, Qutb exhorted Muslim youth to form a vanguard (*tali'a*) ready to launch a holy war (jihad) against the modern *jahili* system and all who supported it, with the ultimate objective of establishing a system based on the laws of God.

In 1957 and 1958 a group of Brotherhood activists, some of whom had just been released from prison, organized a secret network and asked Sayyid Qutb to serve as their spiritual guide. In fact, it has been suggested that Qutb wrote Signposts as a text to be used in the group's instruction.[35] Uncovered by the security police in 1965, members of the network (dubbed in court as "Organization 1965") were accused of plotting to overthrow the regime. Named as the group's primary source of inspiration (with the police claiming that "copies of Signposts had been found in each and every search"), Qutb, who had been released from prison at the behest of Iraqi president 'Abd al-Salam 'Arif in late 1964, was re-arrested, tried in court, and hanged on August 29, 1966, thereafter to be honored as a martyr (*shahid*) for the Islamic cause.[36]

The harsh trials and sentences that followed the exposure of Organization 1965 triggered a heated debate among Brotherhood members in prison on the religious validity of Qutb's radical thought. As Barbara Zollner notes, the

"Qutbists adopted the idea of an irreconcilable division between Islam and *jahiliyya*, Muslim and *kafir* (non-believer), and fully embraced the concept of revolutionary Islamic activism as the true expression of Islamic duty."[37] This viewpoint entailed an explicit rejection of the rightful authority of Hasan al-Hudeibi, the Brotherhood's *murshid* (Supreme Guide): "Not only did they consider the *murshid*'s political maneuverings, as practiced in the years before the *mihna*, to be indecisive, weak, and therefore the main cause of the persecution, but they also accused him of cooperating with a '*jahili* state system.'"[38]

Hudeibi, apparently with extensive input from other senior Brotherhood leaders and established Islamic jurists, wrote *Du'ah La Qudah* (Preachers, Not Judges) to refute the ideas embraced by Qutb's followers and provide a theological justification for a continuation of the Brotherhood's gradualist approach to Islamic reform. Although the text never mentioned Sayyid Qutb by name, *Du'ah La Qudah* sought to correct the mistaken ideas of those who claimed to represent his legacy after his death.[39] By emphasizing the flexible nature of the Shari'a and the historical role of human interpretation in its development, the text argued against "the idea of reducing Islamic government to the implementation of an essentialist view of law under the pretext of God's sovereignty."[40] Likewise, in direct challenge to the rigid distinction Qutb had drawn between *jahiliyya* and Islamic rule, it stressed that it was both possible and desirable for committed Muslims to live their lives in conformity with the "laws of God" even in the absence of an Islamic state.[41]

Du'ah La Qudah appeared in February 1969 and was circulated among Brothers in prison. Yet its broader impact on the views of the Brothers' mass base is unclear; in fact, it was not published and available for wider distribution until 1977. The importance of the tract derived rather from the fact that it offered a systematic exposition of the views of al-Hudeibi and his close associates in the Brotherhood's Guidance Bureau, several of whom would eventually be appointed to the position of *murshid* in later years. It was through a consolidation of the influence of members of al-Hudeibi's inner circle within the organization's highest leadership ranks that *Du'ah La Qudah* worked to inform the main lines of the Brotherhood's ideology and strategy when it was permitted to resume a role in public life after Nasser's death.[42]

The Muslim Brotherhood in the Sadat Era

In 1970 Gamal Abdel Nasser died and was succeeded in his post by Vice President Anwar Sadat. In an effort to break out of the shadow of his larger-than-life predecessor and reflecting his own discomfort with the radical social and economic policies Nasser had enacted in the name of "Arab socialism" in the late 1960s, Sadat called for a "correction of the revolution" shortly after assuming power. Among other things, this involved a purge of diehard Nasserists and socialists, who were removed from their posts in the upper echelons of the regime and the Arab Socialist Union, the country's sole legal political body.[43] Sadat also attempted to boost his authority by invoking religious themes and values, presenting himself as the "Believer-President" and appearing on numerous television broadcasts entering and exiting public mosques on Fridays and Islamic holidays.[44]

As part of this broader reorientation, Sadat granted a general amnesty to the Muslim Brotherhood and released its members from prison in stages, beginning in 1971 and continuing through March 1975. In addition, Sadat encouraged Brotherhood members living in exile in Saudi Arabia and other Gulf states to return home.[45] Sadat's overture to the Brothers reflected his hope that the group would pose a counterweight to the Nasserist left, which he viewed as the greatest challenge to his authority at that time. When al-Hudeibi died in 1973, no official successor was appointed, but 'Umar al-Tilmisani emerged as the group's main spokesman, and as a veteran who had spent seventeen years in prison and the group's oldest member, he was eventually selected as the new Supreme Guide, a position he held until his death in 1986.[46] When the Brotherhood resumed publication of its journal al-Da'wa, he was appointed editor in chief.[47] Until it was banned in 1981, al-Da'wa served as the Brotherhood's primary mouthpiece, providing its senior leaders with the opportunity to explain their outlook and objectives to members and the wider public. As Abdel Azim Ramadan noted, with the revival of al-Da'wa, "the Muslim Brotherhood reclaimed a public voice for the first time since 1954."[48] Its circulation was reported to have reached eighty to a hundred thousand per month at its height.[49]

As the chief spokesman for the Brotherhood and its third Supreme Guide, al-Tilmisani consolidated Hasan al-Hudeibi's gradualist approach to the Islamic reform of society and state. The brutal repression the Brotherhood suffered during the Nasser era convinced senior leaders of the catastrophic results of a direct confrontation with the regime. In public speeches and in the pages of al-Da'wa, al-Tilmisani made the Brotherhood's rejection of violent action against the state patently clear: "If what is meant by *haraka* (movement) is to confront the regime by force and violence, then we believe that this is a futile use of the people's strength which benefits no one but the enemies of this country."[50] In addition, he stressed, what concerned the Brotherhood was not the person of the ruler but the type of government, particularly the harmony of its laws with the principles of the Shari'a.[51]

In 1976 Sadat launched a controlled experiment in political liberalization, beginning with the establishment of three platforms (*manaber*) within the Arab Socialist Union, purportedly to represent the right, left, and center of the ideological spectrum. Following parliamentary elections in 1976, in which the regime-backed center platform won an overwhelming majority of seats, Sadat authorized the conversion of the *manaber* into legal political parties.[52] In the pages of *al-Daʿwa*, several Brotherhood leaders confidently predicted that they would eventually be permitted to form a party of their own,[53] but these expectations were dashed by the passage of the Political Parties Law of 1977, which expressly prohibited the formation of parties on the basis of religion. In a private meeting with Sadat around 1979, al-Tilmisani broached the idea of forming a Brotherhood party, which Sadat rejected, perhaps concerned that the government would be placed in the awkward position of having to defend its record on the implementation of Shariʿa against the interrogations of an official party.[54] Sadat offered instead to register the Brotherhood as an association under the authority of the Ministry of Social Affairs. According to various reports, al-Tilmisani rejected Sadat's proposal because it would both limit the scope of the Brotherhood's activities to the narrow domain of social and charitable work and compromise its independence.[55] Thus the Brotherhood remained "both inside and outside the system," permitted to publish its own journal and lobby parliament but lacking formal recognition as either a *jamʿiyya* (association) or a political party.

Despite its tenuous legal status, the Brotherhood was in a propitious environment to advance the cause of Shariʿa rule as a result of Sadat's own efforts to consolidate the status of Islam as a primary foundation of the political order. Article 2 of the new Egyptian Constitution promulgated by Sadat in 1971 declared the principles of the Islamic Shariʿa to be a "chief source of legislation," and through the 1970s several parliamentary committees were formed to study its implementation, in consultation with members of the judiciary and senior faculty at Al-Azhar University, the crown of the state religious establishment.[56] In 1976 six members of the Brotherhood won seats in parliament, including Sheikh Salah Abu Ismaʿil, who played a leading role in promoting Shariʿa-based initiatives within the assembly. In addition, the Brotherhood lobbied other members of parliament to support their cause.[57] As Hala Mustafa observed, the Brotherhood's efforts to promote Shariʿa rule took two forms: first, pressing for an upgrade of the status of Shariʿa in Article 2 from "a primary source" (implying parity with other sources) to "the primary source" of legislation; and second, repeatedly petitioning parliament for the immediate repeal of laws that allegedly contradicted Shariʿa principles and, as such, violated the constitution itself.[58] Examples of the latter included appeals to prohibit the sale, production, and distribution of alcohol; applying the *hudoud* (Quranic punishments for serious crimes like murder and adultery); establishing penalties for breaking the fast during the holy month of Ramadan; and reconciling the laws governing marriage and divorce with Shariʿa mandates.[59] A rise in the number of deputies in parliament from the countryside, many of whom shared the Brotherhood's conservative religious views, helped the Brotherhood gain support for these proposals and ensure their inclusion on the assembly's schedule.[60]

Brotherhood leaders elected to parliament took pains to stress that their participation did not imply their support for a democratic system in which the

personal opinions of legislators trumped the laws of God. As Sheikh Abu Is-
maʻil explained:

> One cannot say that we are part of a democratic system, as there is a huge difference
> between democracy which grants absolute authority to the majority, and *shura* [con-
> sultation] in Islam, which does not intervene in the domain over which God rules,
> but rather exerts their efforts with an Islamic spirit in those areas which the text [of
> the revealed sources] has left to opinion. . . . If democracy grants sovereignty to the
> people, then we must mobilize the believing majority so that they are the decision-
> makers, and at that time, personal opinion will not butt horns with the text of the
> Shariʻa but rather will prostrate itself before it.[61]

The Brotherhood's participation in parliament hence evinced a distinct instrumental logic: it would work within the framework of existing laws and institutions in order to transform them.

Yet Sadat was unwilling to permit either the Muslim Brotherhood or the
country's senior religious authorities to define the terms of the state's engagement with Islam, a prerogative he jealously guarded for himself. Hence the response of the regime and its allies to the Shariʻa-based proposals raised in parliament took the form of welcoming them in principle but postponing their
implementation by allowing them to become tied up in parliamentary subcom-
mittees, then proceeding to substitute similar initiatives of their own.[62] Further,
in November 1979, when parliament was not in session, Sadat used his executive privilege to issue a new personal status law expanding the rights of women
in marriage and divorce, reportedly at the urging of his Western-educated wife,
Jehan (as a result of which it was informally known as "Jehan's law"), a move
that provoked bitter opposition from the Brotherhood and other religious conservatives.[63] Yet shortly thereafter, Sadat reversed track and took an historic step
toward the Islamization of Egyptian law. On April 30, 1980, the government-
dominated parliament overwhelmingly approved the amendment of Article 2
of the constitution to define "the principles of Islamic Shariʻa as *the* chief source
of legislation"; on May 22 the bill was ratified and made into law.[64] From that
point forward, the Brotherhood could argue that the revision of existing laws to
conform with Shariʻa mandates was in fact demanded by the constitution
itself.

By the late 1970s, the Brotherhood's tactical alliance with the Sadat regime
had begun to wear thin, as indicated by the group's increasingly strident criticism of its policies. The Brotherhood condemned the growing social and economic inequality stemming from the *Infitah* (opening) of the Egyptian economy to market forces, as well as the president's more frequent resort to
dictatorial and heavy-handed methods of dealing with dissent, particularly
after the food riots of January 1977. But what provoked the Brotherhood's greatest ire was Sadat's visit to Jerusalem in November 1977 and his signing of a
peace treaty with Israel in 1979. The Brotherhood's jaundiced view of the peace
negotiations reflected not only its support of the Palestinian cause but the deep

vein of anti-Semitism that pervaded its thinking, according to which the Jews were inherently corrupt and duplicitous, cursed by God, and described in the Quran as an existential enemy of Islam and the Muslim people.[65] Brotherhood leaders denounced the modern state of Israel as based on the illegal and illegitimate usurpation of Muslim territory and advocated jihad in order to liberate the Muslim holy site of Jerusalem. As Gilles Kepel observed, the Brothers' vehement opposition to the peace negotiations led them to openly challenge the religious legitimacy of the regime for the first time. As al-Tilmisani stated in al-Da'wa in 1978:

> If the Muslims renounce the effort to recover any part of their alienated land when it is possible for them to do so, they are all in a state of sin. History will judge the present generation harshly, rulers and ruled alike, for having preferred material well-being to honor and religion.[66]

Forced onto the defensive, Sadat's rhetoric became increasingly combative. He publicly castigated the Brotherhood for abusing its newfound freedoms and warned that he would not "tolerate those who try to tamper with the high interests of the state under the guise of religion."[67] Further, in multiple speeches at the time, Sadat insisted on the "total separation of religion and politics." In fact, he wanted to remain free to manipulate religion to legitimate his own policy decisions while blocking its use by his opponents. Such hypocrisy was not lost on observers at the time. As Muhammad Abd al-Qudus, an independent Islamist thinker, wrote in al-Da'wa: "When the Sheikh of Al-Azhar issued a statement glorifying the peace treaty, it was published on the front page of Al-Ahram [the government-controlled daily]. No one dares charge that religion was involved in politics."[68]

By 1981, Sadat's tolerance for dissent emanating from any quarter had reached its limit. In September the regime arrested more than 1,500 civic and political leaders from across the ideological spectrum, including al-Tilmisani and other senior Brotherhood leaders, and banned several opposition journals, including al-Da'wa.[69] Among those caught up in the security net was Muhammad al-Islambuli, an Islamist student activist from Asyut, whose brother Khaled, acting on orders from the militant Islamic group al-Jihad, gunned down the president less than a month later on October 6, 1981.

The Muslim Brotherhood and Jihadist Groups

The expansion of the Islamic movement in Egypt in the 1970s included the rise of new groups outside the Brotherhood's fold. First, several militant Islamic cells emerged that drew inspiration from the radical thought of Sayyid Qutb and embraced the practice of takfir (the act of designating a nominally Muslim individual, group, or government insufficiently committed to Islam as a kafir or non-believer). The leaders of these cells condemned the gradualist approach advocated by the Brothers' senior leadership and established independent networks committed to jihad. Among the most prominent of these groups was the Military Academy Group led by Salih Sirriyya, a Palestinian, which attempted to incite a rebellion at a military institute in a suburb of Cairo in 1974, and Shukri Mustafa's Society of Muslims, which kidnapped and killed Sheikh Muhammad al-Dhahabi, a former minister of religious endowments, in 1977.[70] According to one senior Brotherhood leader, the brutal mistreatment that Brotherhood members had suffered in Nasser's prisons and concentrations camps had convinced some of them that the regime and the society that supported it could not be Muslim, hence paving the way to their characterization as "infidels" and, as such, legitimate targets of jihad.[71] Both cells were ultimately uncovered by the security police, their members imprisoned, and their top leaders executed. In 1975 a new group calling itself al-Jihad was established, originally drawing members from Salih Sirriyya's organization. The group was uncovered in 1977 and its leaders arrested on charges of aiming to "forcefully overthrow and change the constitution of the state . . . on the pretext that the system is in conflict with the regulations of the Islamic Shari'a."[72] The primary successor to this group, which also called itself al-Jihad, was formed by Muhammad Abd al-Salam Faraj in 1979. In his tract *Al-Farida al-Gha'iba* (The Hidden Imperative), Faraj drew on the rulings of Ibn Taymiyya, a thirteenth-century Islamic jurist, to argue that a ruler who did not govern according to the Shari'a must be combatted through jihad and that doing so was a religious obligation incumbent upon every Muslim.[73] It was Faraj's group, which merged in 1980 with militant Islamist student leaders from the Sa'id (Upper Egypt), that assassinated President Anwar Sadat on October 6, 1981.

The views of Islamist militants on social and moral issues did not differ all that much from those of the Brotherhood in the 1970s. As Raymond Hinnebusch noted, they both "adhered to the standard positions on the status and segregation of women; accepted the traditional view of the ideal political system as a pious ruler implementing the Shari'a, and wanted a non-aligned self-sufficient Egypt."[74] What distinguished the militants was their radical rejection of the existing order and their efforts to overthrow it by force. While the jihadists denounced the Brotherhood's conciliatory methods, the Brotherhood condemned the jihadists' depiction of ordinary Muslims as infidels and portrayed their resort to violence against the state as a futile exercise that would only end up damaging the movement itself.[75]

The Islamic Student Associations in the Sadat Era

The period of the 1970s also witnessed the rise of independent Islamist student associations, which quickly grew from a modest base to become the dominant force in Egyptian student politics. In the early 1970s, small religious societies (*usar*, clubs or families) began to appear on Egyptian university campuses, typically anchored by the activities of one or two students known for their strict religious observance.[76] Rather than participate in the political demonstrations and conferences organized by Nasserist and leftist students at the time—such as the massive student protests of 1972 demanding that Sadat launch a new war with Israel to avenge the Arab defeat of June 1967—such Islamic religious societies confined themselves to holding religious lessons, promoting the memorization of the Quran, and calling for the segregation of male and female students in college lecture halls.[77]

Prompted by the same logic that pushed him into a tactical alliance with the Brotherhood, Sadat extended state support to the religious societies in the hope that they would develop into an effective counterweight to student groups on the left.[78] A key figure in the regime's outreach to such groups was Muhammad 'Uthman Isma'il, first as organization secretary of the Arab Socialist Union and later as the governor of the province of Asyut, a post he held from 1973 to 1982. By encouraging the religious societies to expand their activities, Isma'il helped spur their transformation into a nationwide network of Islamic student associations (*jama'at*), which within a few years eclipsed the left as the leading force in the Egyptian student movement.[79] In addition, as we will see, some Islamist student leaders went on to join the Brotherhood, infusing it with new blood.

In 1973 Islamist student leaders began to hold annual summer camps financed in part by government subsidies, which provided an intensive and holistic experience of Islamic indoctrination and solidarity and hence served as an important training ground for a new generation of committed Islamist youth. As Kepel observed:

> The participants did not spend all their time contemplating the Koran . . . but also trained in various group sports and self-defense, prayed collectively, and, at dusk, listened to preachers expound Islamicist solutions to the bitter disappointments of contemporary Egyptian society. The camps were micro-cosmic experiments in Islamicist utopia, past and future.[80]

By the mid-1970s, Islamist student organizations representing the Islamic Group (*al-jama'a al-islamiyya*) had become active within each of Egypt's national universities, gaining particular strength in the natural sciences (the Faculties of Engineering, Medicine, Pharmacy, and Agriculture). Shura Councils headed by *amirs* were formed at the faculty and university levels, and a national Shura Council made up of the leading *amirs* at each university was established to coordinate the Islamist student movement's activities across the country as a whole. This national council was in turn headed by the *amir al-umara'* (the "amir of amirs" or "leader of leaders"), a position held by Hilmi Gazzar, a medical student at Cairo University, in the mid-1970s.[81]

The Islamist student associations gained support by addressing the real-life needs of economically marginalized and socially conservative students who were struggling to cope in the university environment. They published cheap study guides, offered tutoring sessions in the mosques, and, to prevent female students from being harassed en route to campus, established microbus routes reserved for women and arranged for the segregation of lecture halls, with men and women in different rows.[82] They sponsored conferences and seminars around various national and religious themes that featured leading Islamic preachers and scholars, organized Islamic book fairs, and published small booklets and pamphlets to introduce their ideas to a broad cross-section of Egyptian youth. In addition, they sponsored huge open-air collective prayer sessions in the public squares of Cairo and other cities during Islamic holidays. The impressive crowds of veiled women and bearded young men in white *jalabiyyas* (ankle-length robes) served as both a powerful visual display of the movement's mobilizing power and a means to usher a new Islamic public sphere into being within society at large.

Beginning in 1975, Islamist student groups entered the General Egyptian Students' Union and quickly gained control of several of its committees. As Kepel noted, through its control of the union's national information and publishing committee, the *jama'at*

> were able to use both government money and student contributions to pursue a vigorous policy of producing low cost Islamicist pamphlets: the collection called *Sawt al-Haqq* (Voice of the Truth) . . . made available to every student not only the densest passages of [Qutb's] *Signposts*, copies of which were still difficult to find in Egypt at the time, but also selections from leading twentieth-century authors of the Islamicist movement.[83]

As the popularity of leftist student groups and the resonance of Arab nationalist slogans steadily declined after the 1973 war, the *jama'at* consolidated their position as the leading force in the General Egyptian Students' Union. Landslide victories in university-wide student elections in the academic years of 1976–77 and 1977–78, and in elections for the union's national board in 1978–79, confirmed the *jama'at*'s success in wooing university youth away from the Nasserist and communist groups that had dominated student politics in the past.[84]

Yet the growing autonomy of the *jama'at* and their increasingly outspoken criticism of regime policy, particularly after Sadat opened negotiations with Israel, soon pushed the Islamic student movement into a direct confrontation with the regime. In 1979 the lenient Egyptian Student Union Charter was replaced with a more restrictive version, which limited union activities to the faculty level and placed them under the supervision of university administrators. The Islamic summer camps were discontinued, security guards were returned to university campuses, and six hundred Islamist students were arrested in a massive security roundup in September 1981.[85] Clearly, by the end of the Sadat era, the regime's alliance with the Islamist student movement had come to an end.

THE WORLDVIEW OF ISLAMIST STUDENT LEADERS

Members of the Islamist student associations saw themselves—and were either heroized or vilified by others—as exceptionally *mutahammasin* (zealous) in applying the principles of Islam as they understood them to their own lives and their relations with other members of society. Their outlook was influenced more by Sayyid Qutb and Salafi thinkers than by Hasan al-Banna and Hasan al-Hudeibi, and they aspired to create a pure Islamic society modeled on the first Islamic community that existed at the time of the Prophet.[86] Detaching themselves from mainstream culture, they established their own social norms (for example, exiting class in the middle of a lecture in order to pray) and developed their own distinctive greetings and modes of dress (the *lihya*, or untrimmed beard, and *jalabiyya*, or robe, for men; full-length dresses and veils for women).[87] From their perspective, the more freewheeling behavior of less observant students, from smoking to drinking alcohol to attendance at mixed-sex parties, were signs of moral laxity and deviation. In some instances, the Islamist students' dedication to fulfilling the Quranic injunction to "promote good and prohibit evil" (*al-'amr bi'l-ma'arouf wa'n-nahy 'an il-munkar*) led to instances of physical violence and psychological intimidation. As Kepel noted:

> Couples were physically attacked for violations of upright Islamic morals; films could not be shown; concerts and evening dances could not be held. . . . All artistic and cinematic exhibitions were considered provocations against the *jama'at* and as such were forbidden.[88]

It is difficult to gauge how frequently and extensively Islamist student groups resorted to coercion in an attempt to impose their norms on students outside their own circle. Nevertheless, there is sufficient evidence to suggest that instances of intimidation and harassment occurred, at least sporadically, at every university and were especially pronounced in the Sa'id (Upper Egypt), such as in Minya and Asyut.[89]

In assuming new roles and responsibilities in the management of campus affairs, some Islamist youth leaders began to interact on a regular basis with a wider mix of university staff and students. Those who rose to high-profile leadership positions included Abd al-Mun'im Abu al-Futouh, president of Cairo University's student union; 'Esam al-'Aryan, *amir* of the *jama'a* in the Medical Faculty at Cairo University; Ibrahim al-Za'farani, *amir* of the *jama'a* at Alexandria University; Hilmi Gazzar, a medical student at Cairo University who was elected *amir al-umara'* (the top leader of the *jama'at* in the nation as a whole); Muhyiddin al-Zayyat, *amir* of the *jama'a* at 'Ayn Shams University; and Aboul 'Ela Madi, *amir* of the *jama'a* in the Engineering Faculty at Al-Minya University and subsequently president of the student union at Al-Minya University.[90] Such figures were pulled into meetings with university and government authorities, as well as with members of other student groups. Though initially suspicious of each other, Islamist and secular youth leaders discovered some common ground. As Diya' Rishwan, now a researcher at the Al-Ahram Center for Political and Strategic Studies, recalled:

> ['Esam al-'Aryan] and I were at university at the same time, when I was active in the Nasserist Club. There were some confrontations [between our groups] in the beginning, but after Camp David, there were many instances of discussion and cooperation. Both the Nasserists and the Islamists came from non-elite [*sha'bi*] backgrounds; we were sons of the lower-middle class, but with a university education. This shared background encouraged us to listen and speak to each other.[91]

Seeking to attract a wider base, the *jama'at* leaders initiated programs to address the needs of the broader student population and began to prioritize issues, such as the expansion of democracy, that were also becoming increasingly important to students outside the Islamist camp. As Hilmi Gazzar observed, in the 1970s Islamist student groups focused on such issues as the importance of Islamic dress (for example, the veil and a long-sleeved, loose-fitting dress for females). But over time,

> Our discourse changed and began to emphasize freedom and democracy and serving the needs of students and providing them with cheap references and revision manuals. This was the more logical discourse through which to attract students and win elections. I see this as a positive development, not a negative one. For any social sector, the one who claims to represent it is the one who serves it.[92]

In sum, the interaction between students of different ideological backgrounds on Egyptian campuses in the mid-1970s helped nurture the formation of a new cadre of self-confident and politically savvy Islamist youth leaders, some of whom managed to attract a broad following within the student community at large.

Arguably the most charismatic and widely respected figure in the Islamic student movement at the time was Abd al-Mun'im Abu al-Futouh. Elected president of the Cairo University student union in 1976–77, Abu al-Futouh worked closely with student leaders across the ideological spectrum. As Ahmed Abdalla observed, Abu al-Futouh would later defend the record of the Islamist student movement by highlighting instances "in which he had shown solidarity with his opponents (sponsoring lawyers to defend them, for example) and democratic attitudes in dealing with them (such as allowing them to issue wall posters and to address meetings)."[93] Abu al-Futouh gained national prominence following a direct confrontation with President Sadat during a highly publicized meeting with student leaders in the town of Qantara in February 1977. In the presence of a distinguished array of senior government officials, Sadat denounced the massive food riots of the previous month, defended his record as one of "democracy" and "freedoms" and "opening the economy to save the country from bankruptcy," and, after warning student leaders that political activity and expression should not be conducted through "rudeness," exhorted them to help instill proper values and principles among the country's youth.[94] After Sadat concluded his remarks, Abu al-Futouh, reportedly the only representative of the Islamic student movement at the meeting, requested permission to speak. He then launched into a passionate rebuttal, challenging Sadat "to define the freedoms and values he was referring to, at a time that freedoms were being destroyed and citizens were being arrested and Islamic scholars were being prevented from calling youth to Islam and educating them in its principles," citing the case of Sheikh Muhammad al-Ghazzali, who had been prohibited from delivering sermons at the 'Amr Ibn al-'As mosque in Cairo, and ending by advising Sadat to "take the pulse of the people and get to know the problems of the masses far away from your entourage."[95] The effect of his speech was electrifying. As Badr Muhammad Badr, a former Islamist student leader, recalled:

> When Sadat saw this young man with a black untrimmed beard, speaking with such unexpected courage and clarity and force, he erupted into anger, pointing his finger at the young man in front of him—"Stop where you are! (*Qif Makanak!*) I will not allow any one to contradict me!"[96]

Abu al-Futouh's public act of defiance, recounted with pride by Islamist activists across the country both at the time and for years thereafter, underscored the willingness of Islamist student leaders to "speak truth to power" at the highest levels.

THE MUSLIM BROTHERHOOD'S OUTREACH TO THE ISLAMIST STUDENT ASSOCIATIONS

The Muslim Brotherhood openly encouraged the growth of Islamist student groups, providing them with publicity and moral support. For example, the Brotherhood journal *al-Da'wa* featured a regular column with news of their activities and successes in student union elections, and published articles by Islamist student leaders themselves.[97] Yet the Brotherhood also worked closely with regime authorities to rein in more extremist elements in the student movement taken with the ideas of *takfir* and jihad. In an interview published in *al-Musawwar* on January 22, 1982, and cited by Raymond Baker, al-Tilmisani "frankly acknowledged assisting Nabawy Isma'il, then Minister of the Interior":

> Whenever anything happened, he used to call and take my advice. . . . The Minister used to send me to some university faculties. When I spoke to the students, they responded to me . . . they accepted my arguments against violence, demonstrations, strikes and sabotage.[98]

Nevertheless, when Sadat began to crack down on the *jama'at*, the Brotherhood rose to their defense and condemned the regime's intervention in student affairs.[99]

The Brotherhood looked to the Islamist student associations with the hope that they could help replenish its base, which had atrophied considerably during the organization's dark years under Nasser. As Baker observed, "from the Brotherhood perspective, the Islamic groups' strong appeal to youth was potentially a great resource."[100] During the second half of the 1970s, the Brotherhood made a concerted effort to reach out to student leaders and persuade them to join its ranks. For example, 'Umar al-Tilmisani and Mustafa Mashhour, both senior members of the Guidance Bureau, attended seminars and conferences sponsored by the *jama'at* and made presentations on the Brotherhood's goals and methods, which they portrayed as based on a "proper" and "correct" understanding of Islam, as opposed to the "mistaken" views of the jihadist groups with whom they were competing for the students' support. To enhance the Brotherhood's attractiveness vis-à-vis such militant upstarts, al-Tilmisani, Mashhour, and other leaders emphasized the group's long history of "resistance" and "martyrdom" on behalf of the Islamic call and appealed for "unity"—meaning the unity of the Islamic movement under the Brotherhood's command.[101]

As reported in several Arabic-language sources and confirmed by my own interviews, many Islamist student leaders were initially reluctant to join the Brotherhood's fold. First, they harbored doubts about the Brotherhood's *minhaj* (general method or approach), which struck them as too conciliatory, both toward the regime and toward acts of moral deviation in society at large. As Tal'at Fu'ad Qasim, an Islamist activist at Al-Minya University, recalled, in 1978

> [t]he Brotherhood organized an Islamic camp at 'Ayn Shams University for *jama'at* leaders from universities across the country. Senior leaders of the Brotherhood, including Mustafa Mashhour and Salah Abu Isma'il and others, spoke frankly with us and told us that we must join the Brotherhood, considering that it was the mother organization [of the Islamic movement], and we refused, based on the differences in our approach from theirs, and this was the position taken by the majority of Islamist student leaders in the Sa'id.[102]

In addition, Islamist youth leaders questioned the depth of some Brotherhood leaders' religious commitments. As Aboul 'Ela Madi explained:

> The Brotherhood tried several times to get us to join them but at first we weren't convinced. The Brotherhood at that time was very weak, with a limited popular presence . . . it was stronger in some areas of the Delta, like Mansoura, but was virtually absent from the Sa'id. Beginning in 1977, Mustafa Mashhour, in his capacity as head of the Brotherhood's committee Youth and Universities, came to Minya to meet with student leaders. We slept overnight at the mosque and had long discussions, but we were not persuaded by him at all. For one thing, we weren't con-

vinced of his religious commitment; we said, "How can we accept him as a leader when he isn't even *multahi* [does not have a *lihya*]?" We considered this a religious deficiency. Hearing of our doubts, Mashhour grew a *lihya*, but still we were not convinced.[103]

The first cadre of Islamist student leaders to join the Muslim Brotherhood was a small group based at the country's main urban universities: Cairo, 'Ayn Shams, and Alexandria. Given the visibility and prestige of such leaders within the Islamic student movement as a whole, their choice encouraged others to follow suit. As Aboul 'Ela Madi recalled: "Their decision to join had a big effect on us. We respected them because they were bold and courageous. After they joined, they tried to persuade other *jama'at* leaders to join as well."[104]

Within a short time, student leaders affiliated with the Brotherhood had become the dominant force in the *jama'at* at Cairo and Alexandria universities. In the universities of Upper Egypt, by contrast, opinion on the Brotherhood remained divided. Two of the first Islamist student leaders in the region to join the Brotherhood were Aboul 'Ela Madi and Muhyiddin Ahmad 'Isa, both based at Al-Minya University, who joined the group after their release from prison in 1979. Madi clarified the reasoning that led to their decision:

> As we saw it, there were two paths ahead. One was to create a new independent mass Islamist association, but we lacked the strong popular leadership that would be needed to accomplish this. The second was to join an already existing organization, namely the Brotherhood. We knew the Brotherhood was weak and that it had virtually no following in Minya or anywhere else in the Said. But our idea was that we would breathe new life into the organization. So we decided to join and I gave my *bay'a* [oath of allegiance] to Mustafa Mashhour.[105]

As Madi noted in a published interview, he and 'Isa were warmly welcomed by 'Umar al-Tilmisani, and their decision prompted hundreds of other *jama'at* activists in the region to join as well.[106]

By contrast, other *jama'at* leaders in Upper Egypt rebuffed the Brotherhood's overtures and insisted on preserving their organizational autonomy.[107] This schism initially created some confusion, as both Brotherhood-affiliated and anti-Brotherhood groups continued to act in the name of the *jama'a* (Islamic Group) in Minya and Asyut.[108] The rejectionists included Karam Zuhdi, a charismatic, ultrazealous student leader at Al-Minya University, as well as most *jama'at* leaders in Asyut. As Hisham Mubarak observed, the rigid mentality of such leaders, which entailed a commitment to "promote virtue and prohibit vice" by force if necessary, was fundamentally out of sync with the Brotherhood's gradualist approach to change.[109] After the defection of some Sai'di student leaders to the Brotherhood, such hard-liners coalesced into more militant Islamist cells, and eventually Karam Zuhdi's group merged with the Jihad organization of Muhammad Salim al-Faraj in Cairo.[110]

In sum, by the end of the Sadat era, the Muslim Brotherhood had managed to harness some of the energy and mass appeal of the Islamic student movement by incorporating many of its most talented and dynamic leaders into its ranks. And it was this cadre of *shabab* (youth), who would subsequently become known as the "middle generation" within the Brotherhood, that would spearhead its entry into broader spheres of public life in the years to come.

CONCLUSION

The objective of this chapter was to trace the development of the Muslim Brotherhood in Egypt since its founding in 1928 to the end of the Sadat era and, in doing so, to establish a baseline for its entry into wider areas of public life in the 1980s and the transformations that followed. Yet as is obvious from this brief review of the Brotherhood's evolution over the course of more than fifty years, this "starting point" is a long and complicated one, encompassing conflicting trends, which is why it is so difficult to summarize and why it is susceptible to different interpretations. In concluding this chapter, I highlight five key aspects of the Brotherhood's early development that, taken together, represent the historic legacy that would become a focus of critical review and debate in the Mubarak era.

As noted at the outset, the Brotherhood began as an organization outside and against the political order. Its goal was not to seize power for itself but to launch a broad process of social reform that would lead eventually and inevitably to the establishment of an Islamic state. Owing in part to the Brotherhood's emphasis on action over ideology, its conception of Islamic rule remained vague and ill defined, framed less as a particular form of government than as a utopian end state offering a panacea to all of the problems confronting the Muslim community in modern times. In addition, the rhetoric and practice of the Brotherhood under the leadership of Hasan al-Banna provided historic precedent and ideological legitimation for both the gradualist and revolutionary strategies of change pursued by those reared in the Brotherhood's *minhaj* (program) after al-Banna's death. For example, al-Banna's stress on *tarbiya*, the bottom-up spiritual and moral formation of society needed to pave the way for Islamic rule, gave credence to the gradualist approach articulated by Hasan al-Hudeibi and perpetuated by 'Umar al-Tilmisani after the group's rehabilitation by Sadat. At the same time, al-Banna's categorical rejection of *hizbiyya* (partyism), his glorification of jihad and martyrdom in the path of God, and the violent acts perpetrated by the group's "secret apparatus" in the final chaotic years of the constitutional monarchy set the stage for the rise of a militant Islamic trend dedicated to the forcible overthrow of the political order after 1952.

A second point is that Nasser's brutal repression of the Brotherhood paradoxically served to reinforce both the gradualist and revolutionary wings of the movement, as members derived different lessons from the Brotherhood's *mihna* (ordeal). While al-Hudeibi and his associates in the Guidance Bureau reached the conclusion that direct confrontation with a deeply entrenched police state could only lead to disaster, Sayyid Qutb and those who sought to carry on his legacy arrived at the opposing view that such a regime could only be combated by force.

A third point is that the partial and uneven political liberalization of the Sadat era, characterized by halting progress and subsequent reversals in the broadening of public freedoms of expression and assembly, had contradictory effects on the Brotherhood's development as well. On the one hand, Sadat's initial accommodation of the Brotherhood created new incentives for the group to enter the domain of formal politics, primarily in the form of lobbying members of parliament to revise Egyptian laws in accordance with the provisions of Shari'a. Further, by distancing itself from jihadist groups—and indeed, by assisting the government in trying to dissuade such groups from resorting to violence—the Brotherhood demonstrated its usefulness to regime authorities, a point not lost on Sadat's successor. As Baker observed, "The strategic decision of the Brothers' leadership in the seventies for limited cooperation with the regime laid the intellectual and practical foundations for the legal expansion in the eighties into nearly all aspects of political life."[111]

At the same time, however, the Sadat regime quashed any hopes that the Brotherhood might be allowed to form its own party and became increasingly intolerant of its criticism of regime policy, a trend that culminated in the arrest and imprisonment of al-Tilmisani and other Brotherhood leaders in a general sweep of the opposition in 1981. Sadat thus impeded the professionalization and routinization of the Brotherhood and its conversion into a "normal" political actor and reinforced the inclination of its senior leaders to remain outside the formal legal system where they could operate beyond the reach of direct state control. That the Brotherhood's continued existence as an organization active in public life but "denied legal status" (*mahjoub 'an al-shar'iyya*) was not just an outcome of political constraints but also a strategic choice is suggested by al-Tilmisani's rejection of Sadat's offer to register the Brotherhood as a legal association under the jurisdiction of the Ministry of Social Affairs, as well as by the Guidance Bureau's reluctance to launch a serious initiative to form a Brotherhood party. Apart from the perceived futility of submitting an application to form a party, which was virtually guaranteed to go nowhere, the Brotherhood's veteran leaders did not want to be forced to submit to the rules governing the country's legal political parties, which might require them to limit or even abandon the *da'wa* and social service activities that had enabled them to develop a strong base of support. In sum, though the Brotherhood's senior leaders might have been open, when the time was ripe, to establish a Brotherhood party *alongside* its religious outreach association, they did not want a party to *replace* it.[112]

A fourth and particularly important point is that although the senior leaders of the Brotherhood in the 1970s favored a gradualist, nonviolent approach to Islamic change, their ultimate objectives remained profoundly illiberal in tone and content, as indicated by the priority they attached to the application of traditional Shariʿa rulings, such as the *hudoud* punishments, inherited from the past. Moreover, the Brotherhood continued to depict itself as representing the "believing majority" of Egyptians, implying that those who disagreed with its agenda stood against the public will. In response to Sadat's increasingly dictatorial approach to the Islamic movement and the political opposition in general, Brotherhood leaders began to frame their criticism of regime policy as a call for public freedom and democracy. Yet when one looks at their discourse at the time, it becomes apparent that such leaders advocated greater freedom *for themselves* but not for those with opposing views and goals. For example, Sheikh Salah Abu Ismaʿil, who entered parliament in 1976, warned of the dangers to the nation when legislation and oversight rest with "the secularists and the Masons and the atheists and the Communists and those who have sold themselves to the devil, who block the application of the Shariʿa with their personal opinions, and who permit what is forbidden and prohibit what is permitted."[113] In sum, at least some Brotherhood leaders persisted in characterizing those who did not share their commitment to Shariʿa rule as morally unfit to participate in the formation of state policy.

The Brotherhood also retained a conservative outlook on social and cultural issues, seeking to preserve the special privileges historically accorded to Muslim males in the public sphere and the domain of the family. Finally, for the first fifty or so years of its existence, the Brotherhood's top leaders remained aloof from secular civil and political groups, whose agendas they regarded with hostility and suspicion. In particular, liberal and leftist groups were seen as promoting ideas imported from the West that threatened the country's Islamic values and way of life. The Brotherhood's self-isolation and ideological rigidity were thus mutually reinforcing. As ʿAmr al-Chobaki observed:

> The isolation of the Brotherhood from political life [in the 1970s] led it to retreat into a cocoon of closed ideological concepts, cordoning off the religious and ideological views of the group from any interactions with society.[114]

The Brotherhood's commitment to a conception of Shariʿa rule based on a highly conservative reading of Islam's sacred texts and juristic precedents clearly conflicted with the norms of liberal democracy, as its critics were quick to point out. At the same time, the Brotherhood was criticized by hard-liners in the Egyptian Islamic movement for its commitment to gradualism and its willingness to participate in a political system not based on the laws of Islam. Here it is worth recalling that many Islamist student leaders were initially reluctant to join the Brotherhood, in part because of the gulf between the Brotherhood's gradualist approach to social change and the inclination of some Islamist youth to directly and immediately combat instances of "moral deviation" (the use of alcohol, intermixing of the sexes, etc.) in their midst. Due in part to the ideological influence of Sayyid Qutb and other Salafi thinkers, many Islamist student leaders had an ultrapuritanical mind-set and were inclined to view the Brotherhood as deficient in religious zeal and rigor. Yet paradoxically, some of these very student leaders were about to undergo a dramatic ideological transformation. Spearheading the Brotherhood's entry into various spheres of public life in the 1980s and 1990s, such leaders would be pulled into sustained engagement with wider forces in Egyptian society, the region, and around the globe, and in many cases, their worldviews and sensibilities would change as a result. Indeed, some former student leaders would eventually articulate a profound and far-reaching critique of the Brotherhood's historic mission, based on new interpretations of Islam that privileged ideas of democracy, pluralism, and equal citizenship rights. It is to these personal transformations, and the environmental conditions that shaped their wider impact, that we now turn.

CHAPTER THREE

The Brotherhood's Foray into Electoral Politics

Hosni Mubarak's inauguration as Egypt's president in 1981 set the stage for a new phase in the Brotherhood's development. Beginning in the mid-1980s, the Brotherhood expanded its presence in various spheres of public life and quickly established itself as the leading edge of the opposition. From this point forward, we see a marked increase in the Brotherhood's references to global norms of democracy and human rights. The Brotherhood invoked the language of democracy in part to challenge the conditions of its own exclusion. Yet this new emphasis also reflected the sensibilities of a cadre of Brotherhood activists who came to refer to themselves as *al-tayyar al-islahi*, the reformist trend. As I will demonstrate in this chapter, the life experience of such figures as elected public officials in parliament, faculty clubs, and professional associations triggered a gradual process of psychological and ideological transformation that ultimately set them apart from—and drove them into confrontation with—the Brotherhood's old guard.

Political Participation as an Extension of the Brotherhood's Da'wa Mission

The first three years of the Mubarak era were relatively calm, with both the regime and the opposition seeking to avoid a resumption of the cycle of protest and repression that had culminated in Sadat's assassination. In the fall of 1981, Mubarak signaled his commitment to a gradual increase in public freedoms with the release in stages of opposition activists Sadat had imprisoned. Under the leadership of 'Umar al-Tilmisani, the Brotherhood took some time to evaluate its options and assess how it might take advantage of the country's more open political climate. In what can be seen in retrospect as a time of preparation for the major initiatives to come, during the first three years of the Mubarak presidency, "Islamist activists and issues were conspicuous in their absence."[1]

Among the Brotherhood's senior leaders, it was 'Umar al-Tilmisani who emerged as the most forceful advocate of expanding the group's role in public life. At his initiative, in May 1984 the Brotherhood entered parliamentary elections as an organized force for the first time since its unsuccessful run in the 1940s.[2] Under Law 114 of 1983, a party-list system had replaced competition for individual seats. Independent candidates were prohibited, and a relatively high threshold (8%) was established for parties to qualify for representation. Votes for all parties that did not meet this minimum were automatically transferred to the largest party, which in practice padded the number of seats allocated to the government's National Democratic Party. Parties that crossed the minimum percentage of votes obtained seats on a proportional basis.[3]

In the May 1984 elections, the Brotherhood entered into a tactical alliance with the secular nationalist Wafd party. According to a deal worked out between al-Tilmisani and Wafd chairman Fu'ad Siraj al-Din in February, the Brothers would run their own slate of candidates on the Wafd party list. As Mona El-Ghobashy observed, "The eminently reasonable logic was that the Wafd provided a legal channel while the Ikhwan [Brotherhood] offered a popular base," thereby enabling "both to reclaim their place on the national stage after long years of state-enforced absence."[4]

Perhaps as a condition of gaining the cover of a legal party, the Brothers acquiesced to a role as the Wafd's "junior partner." Of the fifty-eight seats won by the Wafd-Brotherhood alliance, only eight went to Muslim Brotherhood candidates (though an additional two went to independent Islamist candidates on the Wafd list).[5]

Three years later, in the parliamentary elections of April 1987, the Brotherhood joined with the Socialist Labor Party and Liberal Party (neither of which had managed to cross the minimum vote threshold in 1984) to form the Islamic Alliance (al-Tahaluf al-Islami) under the banner "Islam Is the Solution" (al-Islam Huwa al-Hal).[6] The Brotherhood was clearly the dominant force in the Alliance, both the chief architect of its electoral program and its prime magnet of support.[7] During the campaign period, which "witnessed the greatest public displays of pro-Islamicist sentiment in the history of Egyptian parliamentary elections," the Brotherhood "blanketed the country with posters carrying messages such as "Give your vote to Allah, Give it to the Muslim Brotherhood."[8] The Alliance won fifty-six seats, of which thirty-six went to the Muslim Brotherhood, compared with thirty-five for the Wafd, making the Brotherhood the single largest opposition bloc in parliament for the first time.[9]

Al-Tilmisani's decision to enter the fray of electoral politics in the mid-1980s reflected his view that it would be irresponsible for the Brotherhood to squander the opportunities for participation that had opened up. As he later recalled:

When we were released from the 1981 detention, we were in a state of near-recession. We set to looking for a lawful means to carry out our activities without troubling security or challenging the laws. Allah saw fit to find us a lawful way in the views of officials. The parliamentary session had just ended and thinking began on the new parliamentary elections. It was the opportunity of a lifetime; had the *Ikhwan* [Brotherhood] let it slip from their hands they would surely have counted among the ranks of the neglectful.[10]

Yet by choosing to run candidates for parliament, the Brotherhood leadership exposed themselves to the charge that they were allowing themselves to be co-opted into a system that did not uphold Shari'a precepts. That the decision to entangle the Brotherhood in the political game was a controversial one is suggested by the strenuous efforts that were taken to justify it. As Mamoun Hudeibi opined in the Islamist journal *Liwa' al-Islam*, "I've said many times, we entered elections under the slogan 'Islam is the Solution.' How can it be said that we participate in the existing system when we are trying to change it in the preferred manner—by changing institutions with institutions?"[11] Above all, proponents of the Brotherhood's new strategy emphasized, electoral participation was not a substitute for the group's *da'wa* mission, but a means to extend it into a new domain.

In the months leading up to the May 1984 elections, al-Tilmisani explained how the Brotherhood's entry into politics served its broader goals. First, unlike other groups, the Brotherhood did not enter the political fray seeking power for itself but to spread the word of God. As he noted in an interview with *Ahrar* on November 7, 1983:

When the Brotherhood talks of politics, they don't speak as political men but as Islamic *du'ah* [messengers of the *da'wa*, or call to God]. . . . Some think that when we speak on political matters that this has nothing to do with religion and that this is the talk of parties, but this is not true, because the parties seek to achieve power and that is not our approach. . . . We don't work for ourselves, we work for God.[12]

Likewise, in an interview with *al-Majalla* on April 28, 1984, when asked why the Brotherhood had entered into an electoral alliance with the Wafd, al-Tilmisani replied:

Our goal is not what you would call a political victory but rather what concerns us is achieving a victory for God and the application of his Law, hence if we entered parliament, we don't consider this a victory according to the criteria of other people; rather we consider it a *minbar* (pulpit) which is capable of spreading the *da'wa* of God. . . . Our entry into parliament is not a goal in and of itself but rather a means, and if one strategy does not succeed, we will abandon it and seek out another strategy [that is more effective].[13]

Given the National Democratic Party's ability to secure a large majority of votes in every parliamentary election, as well as the sparse number of Brotherhood candidates on the Wafd party list, the number of seats the Brotherhood could reasonably hope to win was small. Yet al-Tilmisani rejected electoral gains and losses as a metric of the Brotherhood's success. Instead, he stressed that regardless of their numbers, the Brotherhood's deputies could use parliament as a *minbar* (pulpit; the same word used to describe the dais from which imams preached in the mosques) from which to disseminate their ideas to the public at large.

Al-Tilmisani was confident that the group's message would elicit a positive response once the Egyptian people had a chance to hear it. As he explained in an interview in March 1984, "the only thing the Brotherhood cares about is the spread of its ideas," and the proof of its success could be gleaned from "recent surveys" indicating that the base of the movement had grown to encompass two million members. Despite all of the legal constraints and obstacles it had faced in recent times, "it is clear to what extent the Brotherhood has managed to spread its ideas and entrench them within the souls of the country's youth."[14]

Mustafa Mashhour echoed such themes in the pages of the Brotherhood-affiliated journal *Liwa' al-Islam*. In an article published in 1987,[15] Mashhour offered a detailed exposition of the Brotherhood's rationale for participating in elections and, in so doing, sought to allay any doubts and reservations harbored by the journal's readership.

First, Mashhour observed, "as to the question of whether [the Brotherhood's] entry into parliamentary elections represents a new path," the answer was clearly no, given that Hasan al-Banna himself stood as a candidate for parliament in the 1940s, and individuals affiliated with the Brotherhood served in parliament during the Sadat era. Second, the Brotherhood could take advantage of the campaign period preceding elections, as well as the political immunity of Brotherhood representatives in parliament, to "educate the people" and "combat the mistaken ideas which the evangelists and Orientalists and secularists have carried to our country and our educational institutions which have distorted the image of Islam." Through its representation in parliament, the Brotherhood could achieve a "complete transformation in the thinking of all toward God and the Shari'a," paving the way to Islamic rule. To those who argued that participation would jeopardize the Brotherhood's core mission of *tarbiya* (the spiritual and religious formation of society), Mashhour replied that it would in fact enhance the mission by providing Brotherhood members with new skills and experience.

Further, Mashhour noted, Brotherhood deputies in parliament could hold the government accountable for its actions and provide it with guidance based on the public interest and the principles of the Shari'a. Mashhour frankly conceded that "as long as the majority in the assembly belongs to the ruling party, the response is likely to be limited." Nevertheless, the very act of offering such advice served the Brotherhood's goals. If the assembly responded favorably, that was all to the good, but if it did not, then it would redound to the Brotherhood's benefit by casting its representatives in a positive light. More broadly, echoing al-Tilmisani, Mashhour expressed his confidence in the religious devotion of the Egyptian people and their support for the Islamic cause.

If Brotherhood leaders took pains to justify their decision to enter the fray of competitive politics in general, two initiatives proved especially controversial. First, al-Tilmisani needed to persuade members of the legitimacy of the Brotherhood's alliance with the Wafd party in 1984, a problem given the latter's secular orientation. In a salvo to mollify the Brotherhood and boost its mass appeal, Wafd party leaders revised the group's platform shortly before the May 1984 elections to include a passage affirming the party's belief "in what the Constitution stipulates, that Islam is the religion of the state and the principles of Islamic Shari'a are the primary source of legislation," prompting some party members to resign in protest.[16] In this the Wafd was not alone, as several other parties—including the government-backed National Democratic Party (NDP)—introduced similar language into their platforms around the same time.[17] Yet the contradiction between the Wafd's ostensible commitment to the Shari'a and its historic call for the separation of religion and state was particularly jarring, making the actions of both the Wafd and the Brotherhood appear to be driven by political expediency. The ideological divide between the two partners resurfaced after the elections when, despite officially endorsing the call for Shari'a rule, the Wafd "did as little as possible to pressure the government to that end."[18]

Another point of contention within the Brotherhood was whether its drive for participation should include a bid to establish a party of its own. The thought of a Brotherhood party was not new; indeed, al-Tilmisani had floated the idea in a conversation with Sadat years earlier, only to be rebuffed. Further, shortly after his release from prison in November 1981, al-Tilmisani had drafted an open letter to the minister of the interior demanding full legal status for the Brotherhood akin to that of other parties. Once again, there was no response.

It soon became clear that President Mubarak was just as opposed to the formation of a Brotherhood party as his successor had been.[19] Brotherhood leaders were reluctant to push too hard on the issue lest they trigger a broader conflict with the regime. Yet their ambivalence also ran deeper, reflecting the conspicuous absence of parties in traditional Islamic political thought and practice, as well as al-Banna's negative view of *hizbiyya* (partyism) as undermining the unity of the nation and increasing its vulnerability to foreign domination.[20] Further, as Mustapha Kamal al-Sayyid observed:

> The Brotherhood also rejected party status because they believed this would imply that the Brotherhood was just one of several legitimate parties. They believed that their sacred call for an Islamic society put them above all other parties and that their goal deserved the support of all Muslims.[21]

Al-Tilmisani expressed his own reservations about the legitimacy of parties in an interview with *al-Ahrar* on November 7, 1983:

The Parties Law has blocked the Brotherhood from every outlet it might have pursued, but as another matter, the Brotherhood has never thought of forming its own party, because Islam does not recognize the word parties; if you read the Quran from start to finish you will not find the word parties. Hence we don't accept the idea of parties.[22]

Yet once the Brotherhood decided to participate in an electoral system that favored parties, al-Tilmisani's views changed, and in mid-1984 he formed a special committee charged with drafting a Brotherhood party platform. According to Hisham al-Awadi, two separate party manifestos were prepared, one for a party to be known as the Egyptian Reform Party (Hizb al-Islah al-Misri) and the other for the Consultation Party (Hizb al-Shura), with members of the Brotherhood consulting Islamist party leaders in Jordan, Turkey, and Yemen to learn from their experience.[23] In various public statements at the time, al-Tilmisani stressed that any party established by the Brotherhood would not substitute for the *jama'a* (the movement association) but would function as a subsidiary under its control.[24] In addition, he framed the party initiative as a matter of strategic necessity. For example, in an interview in November 1984 he noted that "if all other outlets through which to carry on our activities as Muslims and as citizens have been closed before us, then we are forced to establish a party," citing the traditional proverb: "If the only way for those on water to reach the shore is to walk across their swords, then they must do so."[25] Further, al-Tilmisani stressed, not only the Brotherhood but also the communists and the Nasserists (who, like the Brotherhood, were denied legal status) should have the right to form parties of their own:

> On the day that I prohibit any party from being established, I condemn myself to execution . . . because he can say—"You deprived me of my freedom, so now you are denied your freedom also."[26]

Al-Tilmisani floated the idea of a Brotherhood party several times during the mid-1980s. Nevertheless, as Joshua Stacher notes, "no attempt to apply for a party license was ever taken through formal channels."[27] When al-Tilmisani died on May 22, 1986, the party initiative was shelved, suggesting that other Brotherhood leaders continued to harbor serious reservations about the party project.[28] In addition to arguing that the time was not ripe, they expressed the fear that a bid for party status would divert time and energy away from the group's *da'wa* activities and, if successful, would place the Brotherhood's activities under tighter government surveillance and control. Some leaders also expressed concern that the concessions the Brotherhood would have to make to secure party status would trigger internal protest and hence weaken the group's ideological and organizational cohesion.[29] Finally, as noted earlier, some leaders opposed the conversion of the Brotherhood into "just one party among many," thereby undermining its claim to represent all Muslims.[30] As Hossam Tammam succinctly observed, many Brothers, including several influential figures in the Guidance Bureau, concluded that "the costs of legality exceeded its benefits."[31]

Al-Tilmisani's willingness to embrace the costs and risks of a deeper engagement with the state and other opposition groups within the framework of existing political constraints set him apart from other members of the Brotherhood's senior leadership, whose support for his initiatives remained tepid at best. Yet veteran leaders also realized that al-Tilmisani, with his courteous and professional demeanor, could play a useful role as the "public face" of the Brotherhood. As Aboul 'Ela Madi recalled, "The old guard were against him, but they also realized that they needed him. Al-Tilmisani was very polite and sensitive to the views of others; he also had a certain charisma [which they lacked]."[32]

Al-Tilmisani's strategy of participation received its strongest endorsement from younger members, including many former Islamists student leaders who joined the Brotherhood in the late 1970s and early 1980s; indeed, Aboul 'Ela Madi described him as the "spiritual father" (*ab ruhi*) of this age cohort. While still in their twenties and early thirties, this cohort, which later came to be known as the "middle generation," helped engineer the Brotherhood's electoral alliances in 1984 and 1987 and figured as some of the Brotherhood's most dynamic representatives in parliament. As El-Ghobashy noted,

> Muhammad Abd al-Qudus, currently a member of the press syndicate board and a leading Muslim Brothers figure, participated in the 1984 meeting that produced the Wafd-Brotherhood alliance. Abd al-Moneim [Abd al-Mun'im] Abu al-Futuh, now a member of the Society's Guidance Bureau, was a member of the meeting that clinched the Muslim Brothers-Labor Alliance in 1987. [And] the physician 'Esam Al-Eryan and the lawyer Mokhtar Nouh were two of the most active Brotherhood MPs in the 1987 parliament.[33]

Further, with al-Tilmisani's blessing, it was members of this generation who spearheaded the Brotherhood's entry into Egypt's professional syndicates and university faculty clubs, as will be discussed in greater detail later in this chapter.

First, however, let us examine the priorities of Brotherhood deputies in parliament in the early years of the Mubarak era.

THE BROTHERHOOD UNDER THE DOME OF PARLIAMENT, 1984–90

During the 1980s, the Brotherhood continued to push for the application of Shari'a and succeeded in making it a major focus of discussion in the People's Assembly. For example, in 1984 and 1985 parliament held several sessions on the issue, to which various political and religious figures, including al-Tilmisani, were invited to offer their advice. As the 1985 Arab Strategic Report observed, "a general consensus was reached in these sessions on the necessity of applying the Shari'a in a gradual manner, beginning with the cleansing of existing laws, that is, the removal of elements in conflict with Shari'a rulings."[34] Further, Brotherhood deputies in parliament, together with senior figures in the state religious establishment, lobbied hard for the repeal of "Jehan's law," the progressive reform of Egypt's Personal Status Code that Sadat had issued by decree a few years earlier. In a partial concession to Islamist demands, the NDP majority in parliament amended the law to restore some of the privileged rights of men in marriage and divorce that Sadat's reform had weakened or abolished completely.[35]

As the Brotherhood's Supreme Guide, al-Tilmisani was careful to avoid pushing for the application of Shari'a in a manner that would antagonize the Mubarak regime and alienate secular parties. In the years before his death in 1986, al-Tilmisani repeatedly stressed that the Brotherhood favored the *gradual* application of Shari'a, to be preceded by a careful and thorough review of existing laws, rather than a mindless rush to impose Shari'a dictates that could produce adverse results.[36] Not all Brotherhood leaders were equally circumspect, however. For example, in an interview with the Kuwaiti Islamist journal *al-Mujtama'* published in July 1985, Salah Shadi, a veteran hard-liner, argued that the full application of Shari'a in Egypt should be "concluded as quickly as possible," noting that this was an issue "on which no Muslim can possibly disagree" and, indeed, that it represented the demands of the Egyptian people as well as those in all other Muslim states.[37] In his insistence that the Egyptian people were ready—indeed, eager—for the immediate application of Shari'a, Shadi was not alone. In fact, the same argument was made repeatedly by Brotherhood deputies in parliament from 1987 to 1990. Let us look more closely at the Brotherhood's push for Shari'a "under the dome of parliament."

As noted earlier, in 1987 the Brotherhood joined with the Labor and Liberal parties to form the Islamic Alliance under the banner al-Islam Huwa al-Hal (Islam Is the Solution). The Alliance was facilitated by the prior evolution of the Labor Party (which, as the successor to the "Young Egypt" [Misr al-Fatah] movement, had historically encompassed a vague mix of nationalist, socialist, and religious elements) toward a greater emphasis on Islam.[38] Indeed, both Ibrahim Shukri, the party chairman, and 'Adil Hussein, editor of al-Sha'b, the party's newspaper, were former leftists turned Islamists. The Labor Party's alliance with the Brotherhood, which led some of its last remaining secular leaders to resign in protest, consolidated the party's Islamic orientation, and al-Sha'b welcomed a growing number of Brotherhood editorialists and journalists.[39] The tiny Ahrar (Liberal) party followed a similar path, and its party newspaper became another outlet for Islamist opinion.

In 1987 the Brotherhood emerged as the single largest opposition bloc in parliament for the first time. Shortly after that year's elections, Hamid Abu Nasr, the Brotherhood's newly appointed Supreme Guide, sought to reassure the movement's critics by emphasizing, as al-Tilmisani had done before him, that the Brotherhood supported a gradualist approach to the implementation of Shari'a, "just as the Shari'a itself had appeared gradually in the history of Islam."[40] Yet the Brotherhood's strong showing in the 1987 elections boosted the confidence of its deputies in parliament, prompting their demands for Shari'a to assume a more strident tone. As can be seen in the Brotherhood position statements collected in Muhammad 'Abdalla al-Khatib's 1990 book *Al-Ikhwan al-Muslimin Taht Qubbat al-Barlaman* (The Muslim Brotherhood under the Dome of Parliament), Brotherhood deputies repeatedly expressed their exasperation at the slow pace of the government's progress toward the application of Shari'a and challenged the NDP majority to justify the ongoing delays.[41] In addition, they stressed that the partial adjustment of existing laws was not enough. As Mamoun Hudeibi, head of the Brotherhood's parliamentary bloc, put it in a speech before parliament on January 8, 1988, "Either you have God's law or you don't; there is no middle ground between them."[42] Although the NDP's large majority in the assembly sharply limited the Brotherhood's ability to initiate legislation, the latter could still exploit its presence in parliament to enhance its reputation as a proponent of Islamic rule. As Hudeibi noted in a June 1988 interview with *al-Anba'*:

> No one imagines that, with our small numbers, we can impose our opinions, beliefs, programs and broad strategy; we know that the path we have embarked upon is fraught with difficulties, and this period is best summed up in the words of God the Most Blessed and Most High: "Speak out, and as long as you are outspoken you are not required to achieve a dominant position", meaning that our presence in parliament is in order to speak out and to utter the word of Truth at all times.[43]

With no practical responsibility for lawmaking, Brotherhood deputies indulged a penchant for grandstanding before their assembled peers. Mamoun Hudeibi in particular frequently gave long and rambling speeches that strayed off topic and exceeded his time limits, prompting the Speaker to interrupt him mid-sentence and beseech him to bring his remarks to a speedy conclusion.[44] Not only did Brotherhood representatives offer "guidance" to the NDP majority in parliament, but on at least one memorable occasion they also directly addressed the president of the republic himself. As Muhammad Habib stated before parliament on June 25, 1987:

> Another issue of the greatest importance is the government's lack of seriousness, and I do not think that I am overstepping my bounds in saying that this responsibility ultimately lies with the President of the state, Muhammad Hosni Mubarak. With all due respect, it is he who forms the government, and thus he who is accountable for any deficiency or gap in what it does, hence I blame the President of the Republic because he knows that the sympathy of the people is with Islam, and despite this, he does not take the necessary step, and it is my greatest hope and I ask God Most Blessed and High to open his heart to the acceptance of this step, since

we find Ministers who justify what they do as "based on the instructions of the President of the Republic", so where are the instructions of the President with respect to the application of the Laws of God? The government is not serious about purifying the Islamic society of moral abominations and depravities and that could be done by one stroke of the pen from the President; so I ask of him from atop this *minbar* to do this and shut down the liquor factories and forbidden entertainment places, and direct the media and especially the television to the protection of our sons and daughters and our wives.[45]

The Brotherhood's deputies in parliament did not spend all their time pontificating in support of Shariʿa rule. They also began to address a broader range of national and regional issues, both in their day-to-day committee work and through their involvement in assembly-wide deliberation and debate, occasions when their relationship with the NDP majority vacillated depending on the issues and circumstances at hand. As El-Ghobashy observed,

> The *Ikhwan* [Brotherhood] deputies' behavior under the rotunda veered between dramatic performances in plenary sessions, in intricate coordination with Parliamentary Speaker Rifʿat al-Mahgoub, and routine committee work away from the limelight. Parliamentary leaders from the NDP and the *Ikhwan* MPs incessantly negotiated and renegotiated their terms of interaction, alternately escalating and containing criticisms in response to each other's cues and events transpiring outside Parliament.[46]

Brotherhood members in parliament thus began to develop new competencies and skills, including the ability to maneuver around the agenda of the NDP majority. In addition, they began to articulate positions on issues related only indirectly to the advance of Shariʿa rule. For example, the speeches and interpellations of Brotherhood deputies during this period included calls to raise educational standards, address housing shortages, expand the country's sewage and electricity grids, increase domestic wheat production, raise the wages of government employees, and stimulate Egyptian private investment in local industry, as well as demanding attention to such regional issues as the increase in Soviet Jewish immigration to Israel and, in 1990, the Iraqi invasion of Kuwait and the amassing of U.S. troops in the Gulf.[47]

During the same period, Brotherhood deputies vigorously condemned the extension of the country's Emergency Laws and protested the restrictive nature of the laws governing the formation of political parties and the licensing of newspapers and journals, which, they claimed, failed to guarantee all Egyptian citizens a voice in the country's affairs. The Brotherhood's new emphasis on public freedoms and citizenship rights exhibited a clear instrumental logic, given that, at least by its own reckoning, the primary victim of existing restrictions was the Brotherhood itself. As Salah Shadi bluntly asserted, to begin the process of applying the Shariʿa, "the government must first commit itself to freedom, as this is the foundation upon which and through which the Shariʿa is built."[48] Further, the Brotherhood used the regime's own references to democracy against it by highlighting the gap between its rhetoric and practice. As Mamoun Hudeibi stated before parliament on January 9, 1988:

> The President of the Cabinet claimed in a recent speech that the government has opted for democracy with the utmost faith and conviction, and it is the primary foundation for social and economic development . . . but we are forced to wonder about the real extent to which these words are applied in practice. The Emergency Law which invalidates all the provisions of the Constitution and defies all of the protections guaranteed within it—does this achieve democracy?[49]

In addition, Brotherhood deputies argued that if the government were truly faithful to the principles of democracy, it would proceed without further delay to apply Shariʿa laws in accession to the people's will. As Hudeibi argued, "If democracy is rule of the people by the people and in the interest of the people, as we know, well then, the people of Egypt believe in their religion and their Shariʿa and have repeated time and again that they want to be ruled according to laws which conform with their beliefs and opinions and feelings."[50] Finally, Brotherhood MPs stressed that the application of Shariʿa was mandated by the Egyptian Constitution itself. As Ahmad Sayf al-Islam al-Banna declared before parliament:

> We ask the government to implement the provisions of Article 2 of the Constitution in promoting Islamic Shariʿa, as it is the decisive criterion and the predominant demand of this nation as the religion of Islam is deeply entrenched in their hearts and feelings, so I ask clearly and frankly when and how will the government fulfill this task?[51]

In sum, Brotherhood deputies began to justify their efforts to secure a larger role in the political system, as well as to expedite the application of Shariʿa, by referring to the principles of democracy, citizenship, and the rule of law. As part of this trend, its discourse evinced a growing emphasis on procedural issues, such as the rules governing the conduct of elections, the formation of parties, and the conduct of regime officials. When the regime revised the country's electoral laws, after the High Constitutional Court ruled that the party-list system in force during the 1987 elections was unconstitutional, the Brotherhood joined several secular opposition parties in boycotting the 1990 elections on the grounds that the revisions had not gone far enough to ensure that the elections would be fully free and fair.[52] As Hudeibi put it,

> We wanted a free and fair election. . . . Our demands were refused. We asked for judicial supervision; this was refused. We asked that voters prove their identity; this was refused. The Minister of Interior is controlling everything. Everyone is under his orders. There are no guarantees.[53]

Hence the boycott did not signal a rejection of participation by the Brotherhood but a push for changes in the system that would enable them to expand it. As Abed-Kotob observed, "the boycott of 1990 was not a withdrawal from the entire electoral process; it was a protest against the government's attempts to decrease the Brotherhood's presence in the People's Assembly."[54]

The Muslim Brotherhood and the "Dual Games" of Electoral Authoritarian Regimes

Drawing on the work of Scott Mainwaring, Mona El-Ghobashy has argued that the Brotherhood's rhetoric and behavior in parliament during the 1980s demonstrated the challenges facing opposition groups in "authoritarian-democracy hybrids where the contest for votes is stunted by state repression." In these settings, opposition parties play "dual games" simultaneously: the objective of the "electoral game" is to win votes and seats, while that of the "regime game" is to push for a transition to democracy and/or to undermine the legitimacy of authoritarian incumbents.[55] According to this logic, the Brotherhood can be said to have prioritized the "electoral game" in 1984 and 1987 and shifted to an emphasis on the "regime game" when it decided to boycott the parliamentary elections in 1990.

The concept of opposition groups playing "dual games" in authoritarian settings is useful, but two important qualifications must be made, at least with respect to the options available to the Muslim Brotherhood at the time. First, the Brotherhood's engagement in the "electoral game" risked diminishing its leverage in the "regime game," and vice versa. The Brotherhood's participation in parliamentary elections hinged on the regime's blessing, or at least forbearance, thus requiring some measure of organizational self-restraint, while its efforts to challenge the legitimacy of the regime's authoritarian laws and practices necessitated a shift to a more confrontational type of rhetoric and behavior. Yet the more openly and aggressively the Brotherhood challenged regime policy, the more it exposed itself to repression, thereby narrowing the margin for any future electoral gains. The Brotherhood thus had to walk a fine line: accommodating enough to retain some access to the system under existing political constraints on the one hand while bold enough to mobilize effective pressure to lift those constraints on the other. In the face of such conflicting pressures, it was difficult for Brotherhood leaders—not to mention for an "objective" observer—to determine what course of action would best serve the group's interests, which helps explain why the Brotherhood's approach vacillated between enthusiastic participation and deliberate withdrawal as a form of political protest.

A second and perhaps even more important qualification is that the objective of the Brotherhood in playing the "regime game" was not to effect a transition to democracy but to prepare the way for Shari'a rule. Throughout the period in question, senior Brotherhood leaders deliberately refrained from calling for "democracy," due to both its secular and Western connotations and its designation of the people—rather than God—as the highest source of lawmaking authority. Instead, the Brotherhood framed its support for the peaceful alternation of power through elections as deriving from the Islamic principle of *shura* (consultation), according to which the selection of the ruler and the authority he exercised should hinge on popular consent. The crucial difference between democracy and a political system based on *shura* was that the latter presumed the existence of a state that governed in accordance with Shari'a law.[56] Despite the Brotherhood's repeated claims that the Egyptian people wanted to be governed by Shari'a, it is clear that the wishes of the people were not all-determining. As Brotherhood MP Muhammad Tawfiq Qasim argued before parliament, "Only the Creator knows what is best for his creations. Hence submission to the Shari'a is not voluntary, it is not a choice; rather it is an obligation [of the Muslim faith]."[57]

Hence even as Brotherhood deputies adjusted to a changing landscape of political opportunities and constraints, they retained their core ideological commitment to the establishment of a system based on the laws of God. While Brotherhood deputies gained skill and experience in the exercise of democratic rules and procedures, their mission remained fundamentally at odds with the principle that human beings should be free to establish laws of their own choosing. Yet the Brotherhood's traditional conception of its mission, as well as its position on democracy, were soon to become matters of vigorous internal scrutiny and debate. Next I explore the sequence of events that led to the emergence of a "reformist bloc" within the Muslim Brotherhood and that triggered its eventual collision with the movement's old guard.

The Muslim Brotherhood in the Professional Associations and the Rise of the "Reformist Trend"

In addition to running for seats in parliament, the Brotherhood decided to field candidates for seats on the boards of Egypt's professional associations. With roots dating back in some instances to the pre-1952 liberal era, such associations were transformed during the Nasser era into state-chartered "syndicates" (*niqabat*) representing the members of each profession. Despite their continued reliance on state funding and support, by the 1970s certain syndicates—most notably those in journalism and law—had managed to reassert some measure of independence, as indicated by their public opposition to Sadat's peace treaty with Israel and their condemnation of the dictatorial practices to which he resorted with mounting frequency toward the end of his reign. But up to the mid-1980s, most of the country's professional syndicates functioned largely as extensions of the state apparatus. Indeed, both the position of syndicate president (*naqib*) and a majority of seats on their executive boards were monopolized by pro-government figures, ensuring their docility and acquiescence to the main lines of state policy.[58] At a time when the most noteworthy feature of the professional syndicates was their perceived political irrelevance, the Brotherhood decided to field candidates for leadership positions within them. Within less than a decade, the Brotherhood had gained controlling majorities on the boards of several of the largest and most influential associations in the country and converted them into what was arguably the most active and dynamic sector of Egyptian civil society.

The Brotherhood's growing influence in the professional syndicates can be largely credited to the age cohort of Brotherhood activists known since the 1990s as the "middle generation," sandwiched between the old guard and more recent recruits. As noted earlier, many middle-generation activists had gained valuable skill and experience as Islamist student leaders in the 1970s, and after graduating and joining the Brotherhood in the late 1970s and early 1980s they injected a new element of dynamism into its ranks. In their first step up the chain of command, middle-generation activists were given responsibility for the Brotherhood's outreach to university students in the early 1980s. As Aboul 'Ela Madi recalled, "I was in charge of the Sa'id region, while Hilmi Gazzar was responsible for Greater Cairo. We organized a lot of activities, including Islamist camps in which thousands of students took part."[59] With the active encouragement of 'Umar al-Tilmisani, they subsequently channeled their energies into professional syndicate elections and later, as board members, into the development of a wide range of programmatic initiatives that, in scope and ambition, far exceeded anything that the syndicates had attempted previously. To effectively manage these programs, such middle-generation leaders worked to cultivate the trust and cooperation of a wide range of professionals, government officials, political parties, and civil society groups that were not affiliated with the Islamic trend. Over time, their involvement in sustained dialogue and cooperation with figures outside the Islamic movement, including Coptic Christians, assertive, unveiled Muslim women, and, eventually, representatives of various charitable, relief, and human rights organizations around the globe transformed their worldviews, values, and beliefs, creating new tensions within the Brotherhood and ultimately triggering an open rift with the veteran leaders at its helm.

The Brotherhood's involvement in elections for the boards of the professional syndicates began in 1984, the same year it fielded candidates for parliament under the Wafd party list. Given that many of the group's most active leaders were based in the natural sciences, it is not coincidental that their first forays –and largest victories—occurred in these fields. In 1984 a group of Brotherhood activists, headed by Abd al-Mun'im Abu al-Futouh and calling their list the Islamic Voice (*as-sawt al-islami*), entered the doctors' syndicate elections and by 1986 had won a majority of seats on its executive board. By 1990 the Brotherhood controlled twenty of the twenty-five seats, "after deliberately choosing not to contest the remaining seats in order to accommodate representatives of other groups," and retained a controlling majority from that time forward. In 1985 the Brotherhood fielded candidates in the engineers' syndicate elections under the banner of the Islamic Trend (*al-tayyar al-islami*), achieving its first major victory when it won fifty-four of the sixty-one seats on its executive board in 1987. The Islamic Trend retained a majority on the executive board until 1995, when the syndicate was placed under government supervision. The Brotherhood also achieved noteworthy gains in the pharmacists' and scientists' syndicates, but its most stunning victory occurred on September 11, 1992, when it won eighteen of twenty-four seats on the executive board of the lawyers' syndicate, thereby gaining control of one of the country's last bastions of secular liberal and Arab nationalist opinion.[60]

On a parallel track, Brotherhood activists gained a dominant position in the faculty clubs at many Egyptian universities. For example, they won a majority of seats on the governing board of the Faculty Club of Asyut University in 1985 and on the board of the Cairo University Faculty Club in 1986, proceeding to win all twelve seats on the latter in 1990. Likewise, in the Delta region, they won a majority of seats on the board of Zagazig University's Faculty Club in 1993.[61]

The Brotherhood's landslide victories in the syndicates and faculty clubs reveal little about the preferences of Egypt's professionals, since only a minority of them actually turned out to vote. Rather, they demonstrated the Brotherhood's superior organization, financing, and electoral tactics, which enabled it to mobilize supporters in electoral contests from which other organized trends were conspicuously absent.[62]

The Brotherhood activists who contested for seats on the syndicates' executive boards did not formally acknowledge their affiliation with the Brotherhood, choosing instead to refer to themselves as the Islamic Voice or the Islamic Trend. In part, this reflected the risk of identifying with what remained a technically illegal organization, but it can also be viewed as an effort on their part to assert a certain measure of independence from the Brotherhood's old guard. In contrast to the meetings of the Brotherhood's senior leadership, which took place in secret, Brotherhood activists in the professional associations held their meetings at syndicate headquarters, in full view of members allied with the government and with other opposition groups. As Salah Abd al-Karim, an Islamic Trend leader in the engineers' syndicate, recalled:

> Even members who were not necessarily sympathetic to the Islamic cause supported us. We never identified ourselves with the Muslim Brothers. We held all of our meetings in public in the syndicate headquarters, as opposed to the Muslim Brother veterans who were accustomed to conducting business underground.[63]

In a clear sign of pragmatism, the Islamic Trend did not contest the position of *naqib*, or syndicate president, a position traditionally held by a government minister or other high-ranking official, so as not to undermine the syndicates' relations with the state, upon which they continued to depend for financial and operational support. Yet within these parameters, the professional associations provided a new generation of Brotherhood leaders with a space relatively insulated from both the regime and the Brotherhood's old guard in which to develop their own ideas and programs.

As elected public officials at the helm of large national organizations, Islamic Trend leaders became accountable to all syndicate members, not just those who shared their partisan sympathies. In the doctors' and engineers' syndicates, where Islamic Trend board members were particularly entrepreneurial and energetic, they leveraged their new authority to address the practical needs of syndicate members and bring their concerns to the attention of the wider public. For example, the engineers' syndicate held a conference focused on the more than twenty thousand predominantly young engineers without work, and the doctors' syndicate conducted a survey of nearly twenty-five thousand doctors in twelve governorates, in which 84% of those interviewed claimed that their salaries were not sufficient to cover their living costs. Further, within existing budgetary constraints, the Islamist-led boards reinvigorated existing programs or established new ones to help struggling members. For example, "they organized advanced training courses, offered health and 'emergency' insurance, extended low-interest loans to help young members get married and/or establish their own small business, and facilitated the purchase of consumer durables and furniture on long-term installment plans."[64] Such initiatives, duly reported in the Islamic Trend's electoral propaganda, boosted the impression that its leaders were genuinely concerned about the welfare of the syndicates' younger and more economically vulnerable members, and thereby helped win their support.

Islamic Trend leaders eventually addressed a wider array of domestic and regional issues as well. Beginning in the late 1980s, the doctors' and engineers' syndicates organized a series of workshops and conferences on matters far exceeding the conventional bounds of interest-group politics, in which scores of professionals and civil and political leaders, researchers, journalists, and businessmen participated.[65] For example, the engineers' syndicate sponsored a conference titled "Unemployment in Egyptian Society" in January 1989; the "Freedom and Development" conference in February 1990; and a conference called "Terrorism" in June 1992. In a bold move, the engineers' syndicate planned a conference titled "On Behalf of an Egypt United against Torture" but was forced to cancel it after security forces established a cordon around the syndicate's headquarters on the day the event was scheduled and threatened to arrest anyone who dared cross it.[66] In a sign of the growing scope of its activities, the engineers' syndicate eventually came to include over forty committees focused on issues ranging from development in China to the crisis in Bosnia.

The engagement of the syndicates with broader topics of national debate accelerated with the formation of the Professional Syndicates' Coordinating Committee, the first time the syndicates had formed an independent body to coordinate their actions since 1952. The committee held its inaugural conference at the headquarters of the doctors' syndicate on February 18, 1990. With representatives from seventeen syndicates in attendance, the conference addressed a wide variety of topics from housing to unemployment to political freedoms. The committee held subsequent annual conferences from 1991 to 1994. Involving civil and political activists from across the ideological spectrum, they provided an important forum for cross-partisan dialogue and debate. In what can be seen as the culmination of this trend, the fifth annual conference, held on February 9, 1994, and titled "The Conference of the National Dialogue," focused directly on issues of constitutional and political reform. On October 15 and 16, 1994, a second conference was convened to discuss the concept of "freedoms" (*hurriyyaat*) in greater depth.[67] With panel discussions organized around four themes—"Public Freedoms," "Syndicate Freedoms," "Personal Freedoms," and "Freedoms and the Principles of Islam"—the conference was attended by more than five hundred individuals, including syndicate, party, and nongovernmental (NGO) activists; academics; journalists; publishers; businessmen; and government officials. It concluded with the formation of a cross-partisan committee to draft a new national charter as the basis for future political reform.[68]

As elected officials of large public institutions, Islamic Trend leaders negotiated with government officials and worked with fellow professionals to administer programs and organize events on matters of national concern. In addition, they met with syndicate branch leaders from the provinces, consulted with activists from NGOs, and gave frequent interviews to reporters. They also made a self-conscious effort to develop their management skills. As Aboul 'Ela Madi recalled, in 1985 he and fourteen other Islamist leaders took part in a three-day seminar on political negotiations taught by professors from the American University in Cairo, despite the controversy associated with taking instruction from faculty affiliated with a "foreign" institution.[69] More generally, in the day-to-day fulfillment of their duties as syndicate officials, Islamic Trend leaders arguably underwent a largely unconscious process of professional socialization, becoming habituated to—and adept in the exercise of—routine administrative procedures and moving toward greater pragmatism in their relations with individuals and institutions outside the movement's ranks. For example, in his capacity as the assistant secretary-general of the engineers' syndicate, Aboul 'Ela Madi lobbied hard (and successfully) to convince a staunchly secular engineering professor to lead a series of advanced training workshops for young engineers. Further, as head of the committee in charge of supervising the syndicate's internal elections, Madi was a stickler for the rules, emphasizing that, unlike elections for parliament, the syndicate's elections would conform with correct procedures. Indeed, the fairness and integrity of syndicate elections carried out under Islamist supervision were acknowledged by their rivals, even when they resulted in overwhelming Islamist victories.[70] At the same time, the Brotherhood was willing to concede defeat when its own candidates lost seats. As Abd al-Mun'im Abu al-Futouh noted, the Islamic Trend lost its majority on the executive board of the veterinary syndicate in 1990, in elections supervised by the Islamic Trend itself. The Islamic Trend's board members' willingness to step down, Abu al-Futouh stressed, offered a concrete example of their respect for the peaceful alternation of power.[71]

Over time, the participation of middle-generation leaders in the syndicates and other fields of public life produced some striking changes in their demeanor and behavior. As I noted in *Mobilizing Islam*, drawing on research I conducted in the syndicates in the early 1990s:

> In shifting from *emirs* to association officials, the middle-generation Islamists moved closer, in appearance and in practice, to the norms of the status quo. Gone in most cases were the untrimmed beards of their defiant student days; instead, most were clean shaven or had neatly trimmed beards and wore standard Western or civil service style suits. From modest dormitory rooms, they had moved into the air-conditioned offices of the associations headquarters, where they supervised a large staff, received visitors from the provinces, were interviewed by journalists, and met with other associations or party leaders to coordinate strategy on issues of shared concern.[72]

As syndicate officials, Islamic Trend leaders broke out of the Brotherhood's insular networks and engaged in closer and more sustained dialogue and cooperation with other individuals and groups. This was a clear departure from the pattern of self-isolation that had distinguished their behavior in the past. As Muhammad Siman, former secretary-general of the Cairo branch of the engineers' syndicate, recalled,

> When those of us affiliated with the Brotherhood first became involved in the syndicate, we kept to ourselves. But by the early 1990s, there was a widening in our viewpoint (*infitah ru'iyya*) involving a greater openness to others in society, and a greater willingness to cooperate with them. . . . You see, initially we clung to a mistaken understanding of Islam; we thought that those of us in the movement should only interact with each other. But then we looked at the early period of Islam and discovered that the Prophet was open to everyone. We realized that isolation doesn't give you strength, but that being open to others does. We came to this realization through experience. Because, you see, the syndicate is a civil institution, not a religious one, and to run its affairs properly, you need the most qualified people to assist you, whether or not they are from the *Ikhwan*.[73]

In part, Islamic Trend leaders' desire to become more effective administrators motivated them to seek advice from figures outside their ranks. As Sayyid
Abd al-Sattar, former general secretary of the scientists' syndicate, observed,

> We wanted to benefit from Western thought, to improve the means of administra-
> tion. So we needed to learn effective technical procedures for elections and consul-
> tation in decision-making. This helped trigger our opening to others in society, and
> to the West.[74]

Close interaction (*ihtikak*) between Islamic Trend leaders and individuals outside the movement, including intensive deliberation and debate on sensitive
matters, had a transformative effect on the worldviews of Islamist actors, a point
stressed by virtually every middle-generation leader I interviewed during my
research.[75] As 'Esam Sultan, a prominent Islamist in the lawyers' syndicate,
observed,

> When we were leaders in the student unions, we had a utopian and idealistic mind-
> set, content to act on the basis of such slogans as "Islam Is the Solution" without
> concerning ourselves with the details. There was also a rejection of the Other and a
> lack of acceptance of him. We thought we were the only ones qualified to manage
> the affairs of the country; other opinions and viewpoints were always mistaken. For
> us, Muslim women who did not wear a veil were a problem. I'm talking in general
> here, not just about myself. But through our participation in public life, in the stu-
> dent unions, and then in the professional associations and the faculty clubs, our
> interaction (*ihtikak*) with others groups changed our convictions.[76]

Or as Sayyid Abd al-Sattar explained:

> Through our interaction and dialogue, cooperating with others and listening to
> other points of view, we took a new look at our positions, to evaluate if they were
> right or wrong. This came from our practical experience. . . . And we realized that
> Hasan al-Banna advocated good relations with everyone in society; he did not cut
> off relations with people of other religions or people from other parties.[77]

Islamic Trend leaders justified their interaction with other groups by citing
the behavior of the Prophet Muhammad and Brotherhood founder, Hasan al-
Banna, thereby framing their openness as consistent with the spirit of Islam and
the Brotherhood's own *minhaj* (program). Yet some leaders frankly admitted
that their new thinking represented a fundamental break with the past. As
Aboul 'Ela Madi put it,

> Since the 1970s, continuing through the 1980s, 1990s, up to today, you see an evo-
> lution in thinking. The senior leaders of the Brotherhood don't want to admit that
> a change has occurred, but I admit it. Changing one's thinking is a sign of strength,
> not a sign of weakness. The weak one is the one who insists on maintaining his old
> ideas in the face of new realities.

When I asked if this was a matter of self-confidence, Madi agreed: "Yes, that's it. If you are self-confident you can be open to the influence of others but also in a position to influence them."[78]

As Ibrahim Bayoumi Ghanim, another middle-generation activist, described it, the shift in the thinking of Islamic Trend leaders involved a dawning recognition of the absolute value of human rights and freedoms:

> Those of us in the new generation, we studied and read widely and we interacted with those outside the circles of the Islamic movement. This had a huge effect on our thinking. We talked about human rights, respect for human life, democracy, and freedom. We saw that totalitarian regimes are based on a lack of respect for human life, and hence the solution is democracy and freedom. Through our readings, through our travels, and through our participation in public life, we asked questions, we investigated, and we realized that the problem of the system was that it was not democratic. And when we reviewed the legacy of Muslim political thought, we found no contradiction between democracy and Islam.[79]

Other Islamic Trend leaders acknowledged that a change had occurred but stressed that it was a gradual and incremental process, as well as a natural outcome of increasing experience and maturity. As Abd al-Mun'im Abu al-Futouh explained,

> There was a change in our views, but it was not a change all at once, and it wasn't drastic. The most important impetus for this change was our engagement with the broader society through parliament, elections, etcetera. Through such engagement we gained a clearer understanding of the problems in our society and of the people's interests. And we came to the realization that the scope for agreement and cooperation [with other social and political trends] was in fact quite broad. This was a sign of our greater political awareness and maturity.[80]

The rise of middle-generation Brotherhood activists as the leading force in the professional syndicates was a point of pride for the group's veteran leaders, but it was also a source of trepidation, as the latter saw the Islamist-led syndicates turning into rival centers of power. As Aboul 'Ela Madi recalled,

> In the Brotherhood they were the authorities, but in the syndicates we were the authorities. We had tens of millions of dollars in our budgets; we interacted with the national banks, with government ministers, and with the leaders of political parties. [Unlike them,] we had a real presence in public life, in the media, and in civil society.[81]

The contrast between the syndicate offices in Cairo, which buzzed with activity, and the relative quiet and obscurity of the Brotherhood's headquarters, which received little traffic apart from the small cadre of senior leaders who maintained offices there, was vividly captured in 1995 by a reporter from the leftist journal *al-Yasar*:

If you had an opportunity to sit in the Brotherhood's office in Tawfiqiyya [the head-quarters of the Brotherhood before it was shut down], and then to visit the reception hall of the Engineers' Syndicate, which was recently refurbished with gleaming ceramic tiles, you can't help but be struck by the impression that all of the dynamism and blessing inheres in the latter. And one might expect under these circumstances that the current Supreme Guide, who will remain in that position until his death, will become nothing more than an honorary office; and those who describe the Engineers' Syndicate as under the aegis of the Brotherhood, directed by the Supreme Guide, will be compelled to change their minds, for the Brotherhood group in the syndicate functions not just as a political party which issues its own publications and hosts its own seminars on Bosnia-Herzegovina and Chechnya, but has developed into a complete entity with its own initiatives and procedures and resources.[82]

As middle-generation leaders' involvement in public life increased, so too did their self-confidence and the sense that they were entitled to a greater share of decision-making power within the Brotherhood itself. Over time, they became increasingly frustrated by what they saw as the self-perpetuating rule of the old guard, manifested in their intense personal loyalty to one another, their routine flouting of formal rules and procedures, and their continued monopoly of seats in the Guidance Bureau. Indeed, for many years only one middle-generation leader, Abd al-Mun'im Abu al-Futouh, occupied a seat on the Guidance Bureau, a position he assumed in 1985.

The return of several veteran leaders to Egypt in the early 1980s following long years of exile in the Gulf and in Europe set the stage for the flare of open tensions between the middle-generation leaders and the old guard a decade later. The returnees included Mustafa Mashhour (who had lived in Kuwait and Germany), Mahmoud 'Ezzat (who returned from exile in Yemen and London), Khayrat al-Shatir (who also returned from exile in Yemen and London), Mamoun Hudeibi (who served for many years as an advisor to the Ministry of the Interior in Saudi Arabia), and Muhammad Mahdi 'Aqif (who returned from exile in Saudi Arabia and Germany).[83] They joined with other leaders of the same age cohort to form a tight-knit group that sought to assert its control over the Islamist movement's "mother organization" in Egypt. As seen by such veterans, who had devoted their lives to the *jama'a* and made tremendous personal sacrifices on its behalf, the young upstarts who had joined the Brotherhood more recently and risen to prominence in the professional syndicates had no right to question their authority. A journalist for *al-Hayat* described the outlook of the old guard as follows:

During the years of their imprisonment they didn't read and didn't keep apprised [of what was going on outside the prison walls], which increased their pride in their own experience of suffering and torture and their tendency to use it as a standard against which to judge others. Hence they would say to the youth leaders with a bitterness which was difficult for them to conceal: "You are *khawajat* [foreigners] to the Brotherhood, who were studying and enjoying a comfortable and easy life while we were in the prison camps!"

Meanwhile, the journalist observed with a trace of irony, "these '*khawajat*' were running the affairs of many syndicates, including the Engineers' Syndicate with 115 regional branches and an annual budget of 150 million Egyptian pounds."[84]

Tensions between the old guard and middle-generation leaders in the Brotherhood mounted over time. The entrenchment of the former in the Guidance Bureau effectively blocked the latter from advancing into senior positions of decision-making power. Further, middle-generation leaders became increasingly critical of the old guard's mind-set, which they saw as warped by the long years they had spent in prison or in exile, cut off from broader changes in Egyptian society. In particular, they criticized veteran leaders' insistence that Brotherhood members exhibit absolute loyalty and obedience to their elders, their tendency to conduct their affairs in secret, and the "victim complex" that distorted their relations with the state.[85] Such attitudes, they noted, bore the imprint of the "secret apparatus," from whose ranks several leaders in the Guidance Bureau had sprung, including Mustafa Mashhour and Mohammad Mahdi 'Aqif, both of whom eventually went on to occupy the position of Supreme Guide.[86] Finally, they argued, the persecution that veteran leaders had suffered made any psychological opening to the broader society extremely difficult. As Ibrahim Bayoumi Ghanim put it,

> The brutal repression the veteran leaders of the Brotherhood endured subjected them to a crisis. They spent a good part of their life in prison, sometimes as long as twenty or twenty-five years, and many of them were subjected to torture. They developed a mind-set that the whole world is against us. You can't expect them to forget all this and say *yallah nidardish* [Come on, let's talk].[87]

Further, some middle-generation leaders complained, the old guard persisted in defining a member's qualifications for leadership in terms of the number of years he had spent in prison or the onerousness of the hardships he had endured on the movement's behalf, rather than considering his skill and effectiveness in representing the Brotherhood in public life.

As their ideas coalesced and gained clarity and force, this emerging cadre of internal critics began to refer to themselves as the "reformist group" (*al-majmu' al-islahi*) or the "reformist trend" (*al-tayyar al-islami*). Though dominated by middle-generation leaders active in the professional syndicates and other spheres of public life, the reformist trend gained the support of some older and younger members as well. As Aboul 'Ela Madi noted, "The conflict was not one between generations but between two visions [of the Brotherhood's mission and the path it should take in the future]."[88] Many leaders affiliated with the reformist trend occupied seats in the Brotherhood's legislative assembly (Majlis al-Shura).[89] During assembly sessions, and in informal conversations, they began to lobby for change in the Brotherhood's traditional positions on such issues as the legitimate scope of political and ideological pluralism and the rights of women and Coptic Christians.[90]

According to several middle-generation leaders I interviewed, such calls for change provoked a series of intense and at times deeply acrimonious debates within Brotherhood circles. A central pivot of contention was how the broad objectives (al-maqasid al-'amma) of the Shari'a should be defined. Proponents of reform emphasized that the values of freedom, pluralism, and human rights could be found in the Quran and in the example set by the Prophet Muhammad. In addition, they revisited the famous tracts (rasa'il) of Hasan al-Banna and highlighted those in which he described the Western constitutional parliamentary system as closest to the Islamic ideal. Further, they criticized the Brotherhood's traditional views on women, including the idea that women's participation in society should be limited to their roles as wives and mothers and that they should be confined to the home. To the reformists, such "backward" attitudes violated the egalitarian spirit of Islam and contravened the example set by the Prophet Muhammad, who had treated women with respect. In a rare move, Ibrahim Bayoumi Ghanim went so far as to directly criticize Hasan al-Banna for his narrow views on women's rights, provoking an outcry from those in the movement who continued to insist that "all his ideas were right."[91]

Brotherhood leaders affiliated with the reformist trend were professionals and political activists, not Islamic scholars. They lacked the religious training and credentials to issue authoritative statements on matters of the faith. As it turns out, much of the substantive content and authority associated with their ideas was supplied by independent Islamist scholars and intellectuals who, during the 1980s and 1990s, began to articulate more progressive interpretations of Islam in a broad assortment of books, articles, and speeches known simply as the New Islamic Discourse (al-khitab al-islami al-jadid). Contributors to this new school of Islamic thought included two prolific and globally recognized Egyptian religious scholars, Yusuf al-Qaradawi and Muhammad al-Ghazzali, as well as such prominent independent Egyptian Islamist thinkers as Muhammad Salim al-'Awa, Tariq Bishri, Muhammad 'Imara, Abd al-Wahhab al-Messiri, 'Adil Hussein, and Fahmi Huweidi. These Islamist thinkers—some of whom, incidentally, had switched to the Islamic movement from the left[92]—articulated powerful arguments in favor of pluralism, democracy, and the citizenship rights of women and non-Muslims in terms of Islam's sacred texts and historical precedents and gave these arguments an air of gravitas and authority they would otherwise have lacked.[93] The "new Islamist intellectuals" found a receptive audience among the Brotherhood's middle-generation activists, who read their work, invited them to conferences and workshops, and sought them out for guidance and advice. Such activists embraced the new interpretations of

Islam advanced by al-Qaradawi, al-'Awa, al-Bishri, and others because they resonated with their own experience, and it was through their efforts that the ideas of such thinkers were translated into concrete programs and initiatives.

Efforts to reform the Brotherhood's traditional discourse and practice—which took the form of reasoned deliberation in some instances and bitter rhetorical outbursts in others—produced some tangible results. For example, the influence of the reformist trend can be clearly discerned in two official position papers (*bayanat*) issued by the Muslim Brotherhood in the mid-1990s. The first statement, "The Muslim Woman in Muslim Society and *Shura* and Party Pluralism," issued in March 1994, stipulated that the *umma* (Muslim nation) is the source of all political authority (*masdar al-sulutat*) and affirmed the Brotherhood's support for party pluralism as a natural expression of God-given differences, a position, El-Ghobashy observes, "in blatant contradiction to Hasan al-Banna's famously hostile attitude toward parties."[94] Yet a close reading of the text indicates that the domain for party pluralism was in fact narrower than in the secular democratic systems of the West, insofar as it presupposed a social consensus on the primacy of Shari'a law. As the text reads:

> We believe in political pluralism in *an Islamic society* in which there is no need for the authorities to impose any constraints on the formation and activity of political groups and parties, and to leave each group free to disseminate its ideas and clarify its programs *as long as the Islamic Shari'a is the highest Constitution* [*al-dustour al-asma*], and is the law which an independent judiciary upholds free of political intervention . . . and this should be sufficient . . . to take the appropriate legal measures toward *those matters which violate the basic principles upon which there is no disagreement among Muslim scholars and jurists and which are considered the fundamental elements* [*al-maqumat al-asasiyya*] *of society* [emphasis added].[95]

It is difficult to gauge whether this statement—in which support for political pluralism is predicated on society's recognition of the supreme authority of Shari'a—reflected the actual views of Brotherhood reformers or their failure to gain support for a more expansive definition of pluralism in the face of internal opposition. Regardless, the statement can be seen as an attempt by the Brotherhood to strike a balance between party pluralism and preserving the Islamic character of Egyptian society.

The 1994 statement also exhibited a striking evolution in the Brotherhood's discourse on women. The text asserted that Quranic verse 4:34 establishing the authority of men over women applied only to the domain of the family and should be understood as a component of the reciprocal obligations of husband and wife. Further, while emphasizing the crucial roles women play in raising children and managing the home, it endorsed their right to work and participate in public affairs. The statement said women had the right to vote and to run as candidates in legislative elections, "finding nothing in the Shari'a texts which prohibits them from doing so" and observing that in other Islamic countries, denying women the right to vote tended to limit the gains of Islamist candidates. Several middle-generation leaders I interviewed said that the Brotherhood's official endorsement of the political rights of women was preceded by heated internal debate. Further, painstaking efforts were made in the *bayan* itself to rebut traditional objections to granting women the right to vote and run for office, from doubts regarding their mental fitness to fears that their participation in politics would compromise the fulfillment of their duties at home. For example, the *bayan* observed that candidates in most elected councils must fulfill a minimum age requirement, which is typically around forty, at which time most women have already completed the task of raising children. And to ensure that the involvement of women in public affairs did not compromise their modesty and dignity, the *bayan* advised women to wear Islamic dress when they went out to vote and when they sat in assembly sessions, and advocated establishing separate polling stations for men and women to avoid any improper mixing of the sexes. Finally, the *bayan* stipulated that women were entitled to serve in all elected positions *except* the head of state, noting that on the question of whether a woman can serve as a judge, "the opinions of Muslim jurists are divided" and should be open to review in light of Shari'a sources and the interests of society. As in its discussion of political pluralism, the *bayan's* discourse on women sought to walk a fine line—in this case, supporting the expansion of women's roles on the one hand and emphasizing the obligations of women as wives and mothers and seeking to preserve their chastity and modesty on the other.

The second statement, known as the "Statement to the People" (Bayan lil-Naas) or, less formally, the "Statement on Democracy," was issued in April 1995. In what was "the closest the group had come to a public announcement of its revamped ideology," the statement defined the Brotherhood's position on non-Muslims, the relationship between religion and politics, violence, and human rights. In addition to including a strong restatement of the Brotherhood's support for political pluralism, the statement endorsed the principle of popular sovereignty: "The legitimacy of government in a Muslim society should be derived from the consent and choice of the people," who have the right "to invent different systems, formulas and techniques that suit their conditions." The statement also emphasized the Brotherhood's support of full citizenship rights for Egypt's Coptic Christians, noting that they "have the same rights and duties as we do."[96] However, a speech given by Mustafa Mashhour two years later revealed that not all Brotherhood members accepted this formula. As Mashhour declared, "Coptic citizens should be barred from top positions in the army to ensure complete loyalty in confronting hostile Christian states" and should be expected to pay the *jizya*, the tax historically paid by minority religious communities in return for their protection.[97]

CALLS FOR THE DEMOCRATIC REFORM OF
THE BROTHERHOOD'S INTERNAL PRACTICES

In addition to advocating a revision of the Brotherhood's positions on sensitive political and social matters, reformist trend leaders advocated changes in the Brotherhood's internal practices in favor of a broader distribution of power and a strengthening of democratic norms and procedures. As Aboul 'Ela Madi explained, "Unlike the old guard, we believed in democracy and pluralism of ideas, and starting in the mid-1980s, we began to exert pressure to make the organization conform more directly with our views."[98]

Reliable information on the internal workings of the Brotherhood is notoriously difficult to come by. As the Al-Ahram Center's 1995 *Taqrir 'an al-Hala al-Diniyya fii Misr* (Report on Religious Conditions in Egypt) observed, since its return to public life in the early 1980s, the Brotherhood had not released any documents on its membership, administrative structure, or mode of operations, forcing researchers to rely on media reports and evidence derived from state security investigations. Indeed, the best source of data on plans to restructure the Brotherhood at the time was a cache of documents captured by government security agents in 1992 in what came to be known as the "Salsabil Affair." Named for the computer company run by Khayrat al-Shatir, a businessman and Brotherhood activist, from whose office the documents were seized, the Salsabil Affair documents were cited by the government as proof that the Brotherhood was attempting to "rebuild its organization." According to the terms of the Brotherhood's revised charter, both the Guidance Bureau (expanded from 13 to 16 members) and the legislative assembly or Majlis al-Shura (comprising 75 members, down from 100–150 members in the past) were to be elected by secret ballot. Further, several new standing divisions (*aqsam*) were added to the older structure, including the Political Apparatus, the Planning Apparatus, the Committee on Elections and Parliamentary Affairs, the Committee on State Security, and the Committee on Human Rights. In addition, several standing committees were established under the aegis of the Administrative Office (Hay'at al-Maktab) responsible for the group's day-to-day operations, including committees on membership, politics, economics, publishing, and statistics and research.

The creation of such new committees suggests an increasing specialization of roles and a reduction in the scope of the activities directly controlled by the Guidance Bureau and the Supreme Guide. Further, in a clear departure from the past, the revised charter made no reference to the historic norm by which the Supreme Guide remained in his position for life. According to various sources, this reflected internal calls for term limits, in particular for restricting the position of Supreme Guide to a renewable six-year term.[99] Indeed, when

Mustafa Mashhour acceded to the position after the death of Hamid Abu Nasr in 1996, it was reportedly decided that he would serve for only six years.

Middle- and younger-generation leaders provided much of the impetus for the administrative restructuring of the Brotherhood and the revision of its internal rules and procedures.[100] The push for a greater specialization of roles and functions in the jama'a, the demand that positions in its executive bodies be filled by elections with a secret ballot, and calls for term limits for the post of Supreme Guide reflected in part such leaders' growing internalization of democratic norms. At the same time, these demands reflected the aspirations of middle-generation leaders for a greater share of power in the setting of Brotherhood policy and the administration of its affairs. Despite their prominent role in parliament and the professional syndicates, younger leaders found that their access to senior positions in the Brotherhood remained blocked because the old guard was in a position to appoint whomever they wished to strategic posts, as well as to marshal support for their chosen candidates in internal elections. According to the Salsabil documents, of the eighty-three candidates who ran for seats on the Guidance Bureau in 1992, twenty-seven were under the age of sixty, including several individuals in their forties. But the number of candidates under the age of sixty who won positions was "limited to the extreme";[101] indeed, following the 1992 elections, the only individual in the Guidance Bureau from the ranks of the middle generation was Abd al-Mun'im Abu al-Futouh.

Another point of conflict between the reformist trend and the old guard was the issue of the Brotherhood's unresolved legal standing. In the reformists' view, the Brotherhood's status as a technically illegal organization placed it in a state of chronic vulnerability to repression and impeded its full integration into the political system. In an effort to resolve this predicament, some Islamic Trend leaders revived al-Tilmisani's earlier proposals to establish a Brotherhood party. A draft program for the Islah (Reform) party was floated in the early 1990s, and again in 1995, under the sponsorship of Abd al-Mun'im Abu al-Futouh.[102] But in a repetition of what happened in the mid-1980s, neither of these proposals was ever formally submitted to the government's Political Parties Committee, and they were shelved once again. Senior Brotherhood leaders justified the jama'a's reluctance to pursue the issue as a function of existing political constraints: there was no use expending political capital on an initiative sure to be rejected by the authorities. Yet as some middle-generation leaders saw it, the old guard's unwillingness to pursue a bid for party status with any seriousness also reflected their fear that the establishment of a Brotherhood party might force the jama'a to scale back or give up its da'wa and social service networks, thereby eroding some of their most important bases of control. As Aboul 'Ela Madi put it:

> The old guard preferred the option of illegalism to maintain their control over the organization. If they joined the system they would have to give up many of their

activities. We [in the reformist trend] said the Brotherhood has to choose: either it is a movement association or a party; it can't be both. We debated this issue inside the Brotherhood for ten years before it broke out into the open.[103]

From 1985 to 1995, tensions between the old guard and the reformist bloc remained largely hidden from public view. Middle-generation leaders associated with the latter channeled their energies into changing the jama'a from within, while the old guard worked to manage the group's internal conflicts and prevent defections from its ranks.[104] But when the Brotherhood was targeted by a new wave of repression in the mid-1990s, such tensions broke into the open, and a prominent group of reformist figures announced their decision to form a new party of their own.

INTERPRETING THE RISE OF THE REFORMIST TREND: THEORETICAL AND METHODOLOGICAL ISSUES

Before analyzing the sequence of events that led to this watershed moment in the next chapter, let us step back for a moment and address some of the broader theoretical and methodological questions raised by the trajectory of the "reformist trend." First, it behooves us to revisit the argument that change in the discourse of middle-generation leaders toward greater support of tolerance, pluralism, democracy, and greater rights for women and non-Muslims was nothing but a strategic ploy, intended to mask the Brotherhood's radical intentions behind a moderate veneer. To put it another way, how can we know if some form of value-change did in fact occur? The simple answer to this question is that any claims about the motives driving an actor's observable rhetoric and behavior will always fail to meet the standard of scientific "proof," as those motives are by definition inaccessible to an outside observer. Even when a middle-generation leader insists that his values—or, in the language of rational choice theory, "preferences"—have changed, his speech and action will remain susceptible to a strategic explanation based on the interests they are alleged to serve. Yet the cumulative record of reformist leaders' rhetoric and behavior, including their increasingly emphatic calls for change in the Brotherhood's agenda and practices during intragroup discussions removed from the public eye, places enormous strain on the plausibility of the claim that their push for reform was nothing more than a form of subterfuge designed for external consumption. Further, to make their case, those who characterize the reformist impulse as a strategic maneuver would have to demonstrate convincingly that the processes of socialization and cross-partisan interaction described earlier had no meaningful effect on Islamist leaders' values and beliefs. That said, the argument developed here concedes, and indeed emphasizes, that internal calls for reform were inextricably linked with middle-generation leaders' efforts to break the old guard's monopoly on power. Hence it highlights the complex matrix of ideas and interests shaping the behavior of reformist leaders at the time.

So if, in fact, a value shift occurred, what caused it? A first point worth stressing is that *changes in the beliefs and orientations of reformist trend leaders were not a function of "participation" per se.* The involvement of Brotherhood leaders in elections for seats in various representative bodies was not enough to produce such change. Indeed, when we review the Brotherhood's activity in parliament from 1984 to 1990, what is most striking is the continuity in its deputies' calls for the application of Shariʿa rule. So what was it about the experience of middle-generation leaders in the professional syndicates that catalyzed their ideological transformation? In my view, it was their sustained interaction with individuals and groups outside the Islamist movement, in the form of intensive deliberation and debate on contentious issues and cooperation in pursuit of common goals. As noted earlier, it was the professional syndicates, which were once deemed marginal enough by regime authorities to function with a minimum of interference, that served as the primary site for such new types of cross-partisan engagement. Further, it can be argued that the middle-generation Islamists who assumed a leading role in the syndicates were more disposed to such interactions—or, more accurately, less resistant to them—because their socialization into the Brotherhood's insular culture was less absolute and all-encompassing. In contrast to veteran leaders who had been raised on the Brotherhood *minhaj* (program) and operated within its ranks for decades, middle-generation activists joined the Brotherhood in the late 1970s and early 1980s, and their internalization of its norms—including the principle of absolute loyalty to the Supreme Guide and the expectation that all of one's dealings and relationships should be restricted to other Brotherhood members—was arguably less complete. Moreover, they were shaped by their prior experience as independent student leaders when they had interacted with other political and ideological groups on a regular basis. Further, as elected public officials in the syndicates, they began reaching out to individuals outside the Brotherhood's networks in an effort to meet the needs of syndicate members.

To clarify my argument through counterfactual conjecture, had middle-generation leaders previously undergone a longer and deeper process of socialization into Brotherhood culture and/or encountered weaker strategic incentives for sustained engagement with members of other groups, the transformative effects of participation on their values and beliefs would have been less pronounced.

Another question raised by the preceding narrative is whether and to what extent the reformist trend was the main force driving change in the Brotherhood's official agenda in the 1990s, as well as the parallel move to reorganize its internal administrative structure. This question reflects a broader problem: we often know more about the *outcomes* of the Brotherhood's decisions than the *processes* that led up to them. Ideally, evidence of reformist leaders' impact would include direct observations of the formal sessions and informal meetings in which such reforms were discussed. But such deliberations typically occurred behind closed doors. My evidence is thus limited to the retrospective accounts of individuals involved in these sessions, as well as the judgments of Egyptian researchers and journalists familiar with Brotherhood affairs. Yet here, too, the preponderance of the available evidence suggests that middle-generation reformist leaders provided much of the impetus for change, even if the scope of their influence, and the methods by which they exerted it, cannot be fully ascertained here.

In the next chapter we will look at the sequence of events that led to an open rift between the old guard and the reformists and some members of the reformist bloc and how it ended up diluting the reformist impulse within the Brotherhood in the years that followed.

CHAPTER FOUR

The Wasat Party Initiative and the Brotherhood's Response

IN RETROSPECT, THE FIRST decade of Mubarak's rule can be seen as the high point of the Brotherhood's participation within a system of authoritarian rule. During that time, the *jama'a* enjoyed a greater margin of freedom than at any time since 1952,[1] only to see it erode considerably in the years to come. The regime's hands-off approach to the Brotherhood at the time did not signal its acceptance of the group as a legitimate political actor so much as its desire to avoid conflict and maintain the social peace. As Egyptian scholar Ahmed Abdalla observed:

> Deferring confrontation was an instinctual trade-off, not a carefully thought out state policy. The government turned a blind eye to Islamist grassroots power. In return, the Islamists did not confront state corruption and inefficiency.[2]

Yet by the late 1980s, the Brotherhood's growing influence began to provoke concern within regime circles, prompting a revival of the charge that the Brotherhood and jihadist groups were in fact two sides of the same coin. As Zaki Badr, then minister of the interior, stated in 1989: "There is no conflict between the two tendencies, as some want to believe, and they are in fact a single association."[3] In 1990, the Brotherhood's boycott of the parliamentary elections was seen as a move to embarrass the government, as was its outspoken criticism of regime policy. For example, after parliament renewed the country's Emergency Laws, Brotherhood spokesman Mamoun Hudeibi declared, "The government system is based on oppression and dictatorship, which is why it hides behind emergency laws."[4] A few months later, on January 20, 1991, the Brotherhood-led syndicates issued a joint statement denouncing the involvement of Egyptian troops in the Gulf War.[5] As 'Esam al-'Aryan recalled,

> I see it as the straw that broke the camel's back. When we met in the medical syndicate to write the statement, we did so in a very provocative manner. Only then do I

assume that the regime said to itself, "That is enough. The syndicates have over-stepped the line," where the lines comprised the state's foreign policy and the army.[6]

Tensions mounted in October when the Brotherhood issued a public statement condemning Egypt's participation in the Madrid peace talks and the Islamist-controlled doctors' syndicate organized a rally, attended by twenty thousand demonstrators, in protest. The rally culminated in the arrest of fifteen Brotherhood members who were described by the state as "extremists, terrorists, fanatics and infiltrators."[7] In the wake of the arrests, the Ministry of the Interior redoubled its efforts to gather information on the Brotherhood's leadership and operations. In February 1992, security agents raided the offices of the Salsabil firm and seized a large cache of documents that were later cited by the government as proof of the group's efforts to "revive an illegal organization opposed to the state and the public order."[8]

The regime's dawning perception that the Brotherhood posed a threat to its vital interests was reinforced after a major earthquake struck Cairo and surrounding areas on October 12, 1992. The Brotherhood-led doctors' and engineers' syndicates were first on the scene providing tents, blankets, food, and clothes to the victims, which they dispensed from first aid clinics and emergency shelters plastered with banners and posters declaring "Islam Is the Solution."[9] The Brotherhood's quick response to the earthquake and its efficient mobilization of relief funds and supplies in the days that followed through such groups as the doctors' syndicate–affiliated Humanitarian Relief Committee was in stark contrast to the government's slow-footed response, exacerbated by the fact that President Mubarak was in China at the time and the earthquake occurred on a Thursday after most state offices had closed for the weekend. As Sa'd al-Din Ibrahim noted, "By the time the government got its act together, 36 hours had passed."[10] The holdup was widely reported in the Arab and Western media, tarnishing the government's image at home and abroad.

The Brotherhood's high-profile relief drive following the 1992 earthquake convinced some government officials that the unchecked expansion of its activity in the public domain could no longer be tolerated. As Abdel Halim Musa, the minister of the interior, complained: "What is going on here? Do we have a state within the state?"[11] Together with the Brotherhood's electoral victory in the lawyers' syndicate the previous month, the doctors' and engineers' syndicates' upstaging of the government after the earthquake prompted the government to solicit a confidential report on the Brotherhood's activities in the syndicates from Amani Qandil, an Egyptian expert on civil society groups. As Qandil recalled:

Obviously the regime still did not have a clue about what was going on in the syndicates, but was troubled and puzzled by the ability of the Islamists to secure a majority in their elections. In my report to the regime, I tried to identify the mechanisms of the Brothers' influence and to explain why they had become a legitimate force in the syndicates.[12]

Regime efforts to wrest the syndicates from Brotherhood control began the following year. On February 16, 1993, the National Democratic Party hastily passed a new bill through parliament. Titled the "Law to Guarantee Democracy in the Professional Associations," the bill established a minimum voter turnout rate for syndicate elections (50% in the first round and 33% in the second); if not met, the results would be voided and the association would be placed under the supervision of a panel of appointed judges.[13] According to its backers, the new law would prevent an "organized minority" from dominating the syndicates for its own political ends.[14] The law triggered a chorus of protest from the Brotherhood and other opposition groups. At one demonstration in front of the Cairo headquarters of the engineers' syndicate, an estimated fifteen thousand professionals listened to impassioned speeches against the law, the ruling party, and the Mubarak regime amid posters denouncing the "earthquake of February 16" and the "assassination of the professional associations in parliament."[15] In May, after accusing the Islamist-controlled board of financial mismanagement, the government placed the engineers' syndicate under judicial sequestration. Further, in a move to limit the power of the Brotherhood-dominated faculty clubs, the Egyptian Universities Act was amended in June 1994 to repeal the election of faculty deans and limit representation in university councils, formerly constituted mostly of elected members, to government appointees.[16]

The regime's efforts to rein in the Brotherhood occurred against the backdrop of a sharp increase in violent attacks by militant Islamist groups. As Sa'd al-Din Ibrahim observed, Islamist violence produced 33 casualties (the total number of deaths and injuries) in the period from 1982 to 1985, but that number rose to 1,164 from 1990 to 1993, marking that period as "by far the bloodiest, not only during the Mubarak presidency but also in this century."[17] Islamic militants assassinated Rif'at al-Mahgoub, a former Speaker of Parliament, as well as four police generals, and made attempts on the lives of the minister of information, the minister of the interior, and the prime minister. In June 1992 they assassinated Egypt's most prominent secular critic of the Islamist movement, Farag Fouda, and eventually broadened their attacks to include a wider range of civilian targets, such as Coptic Christians and secular Muslim intellectuals, as well as cinemas, nightclubs, cafés, and video shops.[18]

The tactics of Islamist militants during this period exhibited a marked increase in skill and sophistication, due in part to the return of combat-hardened veterans from the jihad against the Soviets in Afghanistan. As Sa'd al-Din Ibrahim noted, "Not only did they demonstrate skillful use of arms, explosives, and remote control devices, but also manufactured some [of them] themselves. They [also] displayed remarkable abilities in their system of intelligence."[19] The escalation in violence provided regime officials with an opportunity to paint the

Brotherhood as guilty by association with the movement's more radical elements. Around this time, the regime launched a campaign against the Brotherhood in the semiofficial media, characterizing it as an illegal organization opposed to the existing order and accusing it of providing material, logistical, and moral support to jihadist groups.[20] Such accusations escalated after a march by several hundred lawyers on May 17, 1994, to protest the death in state custody of Abd al-Harith Madani, a defense lawyer for some of the militants caught up in the latest wave of arrests. As the dominant force in the lawyers' syndicate, the Brotherhood was held responsible for the march and the public uproar that followed.[21]

The regime's new zero-tolerance approach to the Brotherhood was starkly revealed in several interviews President Mubarak gave to members of the foreign press. For example, in an interview with the American journalist Mary Ann Weaver in late 1994, published in the *New Yorker* in January 1995, Mubarak ominously warned,

> I must tell you, this whole problem of terrorism throughout the Middle East is a by-product of our own illegal Muslim Brotherhood—whether it is al-Jihad, Hizbollah in Lebanon or Hamas, they all spring from underneath the umbrella of the Muslim Brotherhood. They say that they have renounced violence, but in reality they are responsible for all the violence, and the time will come when they will be uncovered.[22]

Following a series of small-scale arrests in the early 1990s, the regime's offensive against the Brotherhood intensified in 1995. During that year, hundreds of Brotherhood members were arrested, and the cases of eighty-one prominent leaders were transferred to military courts for the first time since 1965.[23] Those charged in the military trials of 1995 included several key figures with direct responsibility for the Brotherhood's activities in the professional associations, as well as the faculty clubs and student groups on university campuses. Rather than targeting the organization's old guard, the trials aimed to disrupt the work of the middle-generation activists who had spearheaded the dramatic expansion of the group's involvement in public life.[24]

Following trials in military court, fifty-four of the Brotherhood defendants received sentences of up to five years with hard labor. In conjunction with these sentences, the court shut down the Brotherhood's headquarters in the Tawfiqiyya district of downtown Cairo and confiscated its funds.[25]

The timing of the sentences, which were handed down just a week before parliamentary elections commenced on November 29, suggests that they were intended by the regime to undermine the Brotherhood's ability to run an effective electoral campaign. As al-Awadi observed, the stakes of that year's elections were especially high because the 1995 assembly was set to nominate Mubarak for a fourth term as president. If the Brotherhood won more than a third of the

seats, it would be in a position to obstruct his nomination.[26] Senior regime officials feared that "Egypt could become another Algeria," a reference to the fact
that in January 1992, Islamists there had been poised to win control of parliament before the military stepped in and canceled the results. Makram Mohammad Ahmad, editor of the semiofficial journal *al-Musawwar*, explained the regime's anxiety:

> The *Ikhwan* are very organized and extremely popular, and if they contested the
> elections, they could easily win against the NDP. A trend within the regime thinks
> that the *Ikhwan* constitute the greatest political threat to Mubarak, and fears that
> what happened in Algeria could happen in Egypt.[27]

It is thus not surprising that the parliamentary elections of 1995 exhibited an
unprecedented level of government intervention, including widespread harassment and intimidation of voters by state security officers and police. By the end
of the two-day voting period, over eight hundred people had been injured and
fifty-one had died.[28] According to the Egyptian Organization for Human Rights,
security forces arrested over a thousand Islamist campaign workers and sympathizers and "systematically targeted Islamist candidates country-wide, using
techniques such as intimidation, illegal search and seizure of campaign offices,
and arbitrary arrests."[29] Under the new electoral system introduced in 1990,
candidates in the elections ran as independents rather than on party lists. Although the Brotherhood put forward an estimated 150 candidates, it won only
one seat, which was subsequently contested in court.[30]

The regime's campaign against the Brotherhood, though justified in terms of
its alleged ties with jihadist groups, arguably sought to contain a highly visible
and dynamic organization operating within legal channels, a point not lost on
members of the Brotherhood itself. As Mustafa Mashhour, then first deputy to
the Supreme Guide, observed,

> The Brotherhood has shown that it has been successful in the professional associa-
> tions because those elections were generally free and without irregularities, and this
> indicates that the opinion of the educated class is with the Brotherhood. And per-
> haps the government is afraid that if the Brotherhood forms a political party or is
> allowed to participate in political life more generally, then it will be able to turn
> public opinion to its side. . . . If free elections were held for the People's Assembly
> the Brotherhood would win, and this would de-stabilize the position of those who
> occupy the senior most positions in the state. . . . They want to remain in power and
> hence they place restrictions on us and try to freeze our activities and falsify election
> results so our candidates don't win, and that is the reason for all of the harassment
> which the Brotherhood has endured.[31]

The repression of the mid-1990s dealt a serious blow to the Brotherhood.
The sentences handed down in the military trials of 1995 placed some of its
most capable and experienced leaders behind bars and, according to Egyptian

law, blocked them from contesting seats in parliament and serving on the boards of public organizations for a period of time equal to double their sentences (ten years for defendants who received the maximum sentence) after their release.[32] In addition, the crackdown exacerbated ideological and generational tensions within the Brotherhood's own ranks, culminating in the eruption of an open rift in 1996. We now turn to the sequence of events leading up to this rift and its impact on the evolution of the Brotherhood in the years that followed.

THE WASAT PARTY INITIATIVE

On January 10, 1996, a group of leaders associated with the Brotherhood's "reformist" current, led by thirty-seven-year-old engineer Aboul 'Ela Madi, announced their plans to form a new party and submitted their proposal to the government's Political Parties Committee. Defined by Madi as "a civic platform based on the Islamic faith, which believes in pluralism and the alternation of power," the Wasat (Center) party built directly on the earlier party programs that had been raised—and shelved—by the Brotherhood. Sixty-two of the party's seventy-four founders were members of the Brotherhood; the other twelve included several women and Christians.[33] At first the regime viewed the initiative as a Brotherhood ploy, and Madi and two other cofounders were among thirteen Brotherhood members arrested on April 2 and accused by the State Security Prosecution Office of "belonging to an illegal organization," "preparing anti-regime publications," "carrying out political activities without permission," and "attempting to form the Wasat party as a front from the banned Muslim Brotherhood."[34] Yet it soon became clear that the party founders were acting on their own, a point underscored by the hostile response of the Brotherhood's senior leadership. In August, Madi and his colleagues were released without ever standing trial or being formally charged.[35]

In interviews with the press, Mamoun Hudeibi, a prominent figure in the Brotherhood's Guidance Bureau and an official spokesman for the group, explained that although the idea of forming a party was nothing new and was accepted in principle, the Wasat party founders had erred by rushing to pursue it before the time was right. Given that regime authorities remained adamantly opposed to a party based on religion, any effort to force the issue was not just foolhardy but dangerous, as it could set the Brotherhood on a collision course with the government.[36] In stark contrast with such reasoned public discourse, the Brotherhood's old guard reacted furiously behind the scenes to what they regarded as an intolerable affront to their authority. According to various news reports, Hudeibi ordered the Brothers on the Wasat party list to withdraw their names or risk expulsion, a directive to which many of them acquiesced. This decreased the number of registrants to below the minimum number of fifty, leading the Political Parties Committee to reject the proposal on procedural grounds on May 13.[37] On May 27, in his capacity as the Wasat founders' lawyer, Muhammad Salim al-'Awa filed an appeal in High Administrative Court against the government's ruling, which was signed by several prominent secular lawyers as well.[38] As 'Esam Sultan recalled, after al-'Awa read the appeal at the court hearing, lawyers for the Brotherhood took the floor and spoke against it.[39] Later that year, as pressure from the Brotherhood leadership mounted, Madi and fifteen other Wasat founders submitted their resignations from the Brotherhood to the Supreme Guide.[40]

Over the next year, with its legal appeal pending, the Wasat party received vocal encouragement and support from leaders in the secular opposition, as well as from independent Islamist figures such as Yusuf al-Qaradawi.[41] By contrast, the Brotherhood's old guard denounced the initiative, placing them in the awkward position of siding with the regime and the die-hard anti-Islamist left. As Salah 'Isa, a leftist intellectual supportive of the Wasat trend, observed with unconcealed derision,

> Hence this laughable front has been formed, full of contradictions, which includes the government, and the Tagammu' Party, together with the Brotherhood's old guard and the *jihadists*, all working together on behalf of one goal: to bring down the project to establish the *Wasat* Party.[42]

On May 9, 1998, the High Administrative Court announced that it had rejected the party's appeal on the grounds that the party "did not contribute anything new to the existing political parties" and hence failed to meet the requirements of the Political Parties Law of 1977.[43] Undeterred, Madi submitted a revised and expanded party platform, called Hizb al-Wasat al-Misri (Egyptian Center Party), to the Political Parties Committee two days later. Of the expanded list of ninety-three founding members, only twenty-four were ex-Brothers; the group also included nineteen women and three Christians. The Political Parties Committee rejected the second Wasat party bid for legal status on September 21, 1998. In an unprecedented move, Madi demanded a meeting with committee members to discuss the grounds for their decision, a right which, though stipulated by the Political Parties Law of 1977, had never been invoked. In the ensuing meeting, Madi recalled that he sat across an oval table from several high-ranking government officials, including the minister of the interior and the minister of parliamentary affairs, but they refused to engage in any serious discussion of the party's ideas.[44] The Wasat party once again appealed the committee's decision in the High Administrative Court, which ruled against their appeal on June 5, 1999.[45] Madi would eventually submit a third proposal to the Political Parties Committee for Hizb al-Wasat al-Jadid (New Wasat Party), with an expanded membership and more detailed platform, in 2004.

The platform of the Egyptian Wasat party, drafted by Islamist engineer Salah Abd al-Karim in consultation with other party members, was a forty-nine-page document that elaborated on the party's vision and objectives in substantial depth.[46] As I have analyzed the platform in detail elsewhere,[47] it will suffice here to highlight a few of its most salient themes. First, the party sought to establish a "center" or "middle" position between the rigid defense of Islamic tradition and the wholesale adoption of values and institutions imported from the West. Second, in contrast to the traditional Islamist conception of the *umma* as the Muslim community of believers, the platform defined the *umma* as encompassing all Egyptians, Muslims, and Christians who shared a common cultural reference and identity shaped by the history and values of Arab-Islamic civilization. Third, the platform asserted that the "most important civilizational principle of our *umma*, and hence of the public order of the *umma*, is pluralism," elaborating that "we mean pluralism in its many dimensions, not just political pluralism, because the *umma* has been based throughout history on religious, cultural and social pluralism, as well as other types," and observing that "pluralism within a single civilizational framework" was in reality not a weakness but a source of the *umma*'s strength.[48] Fourth, the platform defined the *umma* as the "first" and "only" source of all political authority; emphasized its right to select its representatives in "a genuine choice free of coercion or material or psychological pressure"; and affirmed the equal rights and obligations of all citizens irrespective of religious affiliation or gender.[49]

If in these respects the Wasat platform conformed with the norms and values of secular democracy, it departed from them in others. First, the platform did not advocate the separation of religion and state but affirmed the primacy of Shari'a, or Islamic law, as the basis of the constitutional order. Second, it stipulated that the "clear rulings" contained in the sacred texts of Islam must be applied to all Muslims. At the same time, the platform emphasized that given the limited number of such explicit rulings, the scope for human legislation was in fact quite broad and affirmed the right of all citizens, Muslims and non-Muslims alike, to engage in *ijtihad* (human reasoning) to adapt Shari'a principles to the circumstances of modern times. The platform remained vague on the critical question of which individuals or institutions possessed the legal authority to interpret the Shari'a and to veto legislation deemed to violate its content and spirit. Rather, it simply stated that all legislation must be grounded within an Islamic frame of reference (*marja'iyya islamiyya*) or, as phrased elsewhere in the platform, must be consistent with the "enduring values of the nation" (*thawabet al-umma*). The platform did not provide a detailed and comprehensive definition of these values but emphasized two constitutive elements of the Arab-Islamic heritage: the identity of the family, rather than the individual, as its primary social unit, and the religious character of society. By defining these elements as essential features of Arab-Islamic culture and identity, it removed them from the domain of public debate, in effect granting them the same transcendent status accorded to the "clear rulings" in Islam's sacred texts.[50] The party platform can thus be said to exhibit a tension between two competing impulses: to enlarge the sphere for free political, intellectual, and cultural expression on the one hand, and to defend the conservative religious values and institutions of the *umma* against the depredations of Western secularism and individualism on the other.

More than a decade after its release, the Wasat party platform of 1998 can be seen as a work in progress, reflecting the consensus of its founders at a particular point in time, which would undergo further revision in the years to come. The main themes of the platform bore the imprint of the New Islamic Discourse, and especially the ideas of Muhammad Salim al-'Awa and Tariq Bishri, with whom its founders consulted on a regular basis and upon whom they relied for authoritative (re-)interpretations of Islam's historical precedents and sacred texts.[51] At the same time, the platform reflected changes in the interests, values, and priorities of middle-generation activists that stemmed from their close engagement with leaders from other political and ideological trends over the preceding decade.

Given the group's strong endorsement of pluralism and equal citizenship rights for women and non-Muslims, the novelty of which was accentuated by its founders' historic ties with the Muslim Brotherhood, the Wasat party initiative generated enormous attention in the Egyptian and Arab press. Dozens of articles about the party, including lengthy interviews with Aboul 'Ela Madi, its affable and charismatic founder, appeared in numerous regional newspapers and journals, frequently adorned by large photos or artist sketches of his face.[52] In addition, Madi and other Wasat party Islamists made the rounds on Arabic satellite television programs and sat for lengthy interviews with journalists from Europe, the United States, and Japan. They also elaborated on the party's agenda, which they pointedly described as a "human interpretation of Islam open to discussion" in various seminars and workshops sponsored by secular civil society groups.[53] The Wasat initiative received support from several influential secular commentators, such as leftist Salah 'Isa, editor in chief of *al-Qahira*, a weekly journal. As 'Isa remarked:

> We must open a democratic space for engagement with the Islamists in order to encourage their moderation. We welcomed the Wasat party, seeing it as the most important trend toward moderation in the Islamic trend, because its platform is based on citizenship and not on religion. I can accept the idea of a shared identity rooted in Arab-Islamic civilization, but if you say that we have to apply Islamic juridical rulings, that is a problem.[54]

Although generally receptive to the Wasat initiative, 'Isa and other secular Egyptian figures objected to certain elements of the party's agenda, especially its seeming elevation of the Shari'a and *thawabet al-umma* beyond the reach of public scrutiny and debate.[55] For example, the concept of *thawabet al-umma* came under harsh criticism at a seminar titled "Political Forces and Their Positions on Freedom of Opinion and Thought and Belief," organized by the Egyptian Organization for Human Rights on October, 14, 1996, in which Madi participated. Shaken by the verbal attacks directed by some of the speakers "on everything Islamic," Madi wrote a response, published in *al-Sha'b* on October 25, in which he strongly defended the idea that freedom of expression must be bound by respect for the community's shared values and beliefs. As he asked with no small amount of exasperation,

> Is it all right to abuse and insult sacred principles (*al-muqaddasat*) in the name of freedom? From the viewpoint of belief, and from the perspective of morals, is the call for, say, sexual licentiousness included in the freedoms which some people call for or not? Are there limits to these freedoms or not? This question must be answered: Are there religious and moral values of this society or not? And what are they; we need to define them so that no one oversteps them or adds anything to them.[56]

In contrast to the secular commentators who endorsed the Wasat party initiative but remained ill at ease with certain aspects of its platform, other secularists rejected the Wasat party experiment altogether, characterizing it as a front for the Brotherhood and/or openly deriding its alleged moderation. As Muhammad al-Shibh opined in a December 1996 article, "its founders, as Islamist student leaders in the 1970s, never once showed a concern for democracy or pluralism, so why should we believe they support them now?"[57]

The Back Story of the Wasat Founders' Split from the Brotherhood

The Wasat party initiative did not emerge out of thin air but was the culmination of growing tensions between the Brotherhood's old guard and their internal critics. Why did such conflict reach a peak in the mid-1990s and ultimately trigger an open rift?

Middle-generation leaders' frustrations with the perceived ideological rigidity of the Brotherhood's old guard reached a new height before the break. Several factors contributed to this development. At the conclusion of the joint professional syndicates' conference titled "Freedoms and Civil Society" in October 1994, which extended the discussion of issues first raised during a conference called "The National Dialogue" the preceding February, a committee was formed to draft a National Charter (Mithaq al-Wifaq al-Watani) representing a national consensus on a framework for constitutional and political reform. Mamoun Hudeibi, Abd al-Mun'im Abu al-Futouh, and Aboul 'Ela Madi, served on the committee—Hudeibi and Abu al-Futouh as Brotherhood delegates and

Madi as a representative of the professional syndicates. During the committee's sessions, which took place over a period of ten months from October 1994 to August 1995, heated debates broke out between Hudeibi and secular civic and political leaders on the status of the Shari'a in the constitution of the state. Sayyid al-Naggar, the founder of the liberal New Civic Forum, was particularly adamant that the charter make no reference to the Shari'a or religion over the bitter objections of Mamoun Hudeibi. As al-Naggar recalled:

> I said this charter is not going to have one word about religion, for the reason that 10% of the population are non-Muslims. You can't speak about Shari'a if 10% of the people are Copts. This is discrimination. Hudeibi said, "Are you against Article 2 of the Constitution?" and I said, "Yes, this was a mistake. It was imposed as a matter of political expediency." Hudeibi and I had many heated discussions on this issue. I said, "You want to cut off the hand of the thief and throw stones at adulterers?" and he answered, "This is in the Quran," and I replied, "This was for seventh-century Muslims, not for Muslims of the twentieth century," and he said, "That is *kufr* [unbelief]."[58]

Interestingly, al-Naggar's acquaintance with Hudeibi went back fifty years. As al-Naggar noted:

> I graduated from the faculty of law in 1942, and some of the members of my generation fell under the influence of the Brotherhood. Hudeibi was in the same class as I was. I was the number one student and he was number nine or ten. We studied together but eventually we had a falling out. . . . I am a thorough secularist, so I absolutely refuse to cite religion when I am dealing with a secular question. I reject the line of reasoning that "'Umar [the second caliph] said this, or such-and-such a verse of the Quran says that." Our foundation is an enlightened faith in the human mind, in the ability of the human mind to deal with problems in a manner derived from the surrounding culture of our society. So I wanted to see no reference in the charter to religion at all. This was accepted by all of the other members of the committee except Hudeibi. At our last meeting, he declared "this is an atheist National Charter" and refused to sign it because it made no reference to the Shari'a and Islam.[59]

In the end, the initiative collapsed in August 1995 when only six of the original twelve members of the committee signed the National Charter. As Madi and other middle-generation leaders saw it, Hudeibi's intransigence not only triggered the breakdown of an important civil initiative but also reinforced public perceptions of the Brotherhood as an obstacle to democratic reform and contributed to the overwhelming defeat of Brotherhood candidates in the November parliamentary elections.[60]

More generally, Mamoun Hudeibi, with his strong personality and combative rhetoric, served as a flashpoint for the grievances of younger leaders, who complained about his arrogance and high-handedness in meetings and discussions with other Brotherhood members.[61] Hudeibi, a longtime member of the Guidance Bureau and an official spokesman for the group, was also criticized for arrogating dictatorial powers to himself and making policy decisions without consulting others. Especially galling to reformist trend leaders was his refusal to move forward with plans to establish a party to represent the Brotherhood in public life. As Madi noted in a 2003 article in *Sawt al-Umma*:

> If you spoke with him for two minutes, his answer would take ten minutes, [and he'd become] very agitated . . . he would try to impose his point of view; the *Majlis al-Shura* (the Brotherhood's legislative assembly) issued several decisions to form a party for the Brotherhood, but he always blocked them, despite the fact that 90% of the members of the Assembly supported them, and after all that Hudeibi would say that we must respect the decisions of the *jama'a*, so why didn't he do so himself?[62]

Just as vexing was the old guard's continued monopoly of power in the Guidance Bureau and control over appointments in the Brotherhood's branch offices, which deprived the reformists of an institutional platform from which to connect with members of the group's base.

In what Madi described as the "Great Theft" (*al-satw al-kubra*):

> Those of us in the reformist group worked in public relations, while the old guard worked to control the organization [*tandhim*]. They controlled the backbone of the organization and this enabled them to steal the younger generation from us. The old guard leaders would say, "Loyalty should be to the *jama'a*, not to individuals," but in reality this meant loyalty to them. Hence the views of the new generations, those who entered the *jama'a* in the 1980s and 1990s, were based on what the old guard said.[63]

REVISITING THE REPRESSION-RADICALIZATION THESIS

If the split of the Wasat party founders from the Brotherhood reflected the culmination of a long history of internal conflict, its proximate trigger was a spike in repression that peaked with the military trials of 1995 and the government's campaign against Brotherhood candidates and their supporters in the parliamentary elections that same year. The sentencing of some of the Brotherhood's most prominent middle-generation figures to prison, including Abd al-Mun'im Abu al-Futouh, 'Esam al-'Aryan, Sayyid Abd al-Sattar, and Ibrahim al-Za'farani, triggered a bitter outcry from other middle-generation leaders, who accused the old guard of trapping the *jama'a* in an ongoing confrontation with the state, of which they were the greatest victims.[64] They were also angered when, after four members of the Guidance Bureau were sent to prison, Hudeibi and other members of the Executive Council handpicked their replacements, violating group rules requiring that they be chosen through internal elections.[65]

Further, the Brotherhood's abysmal showing in the parliamentary elections of November and December 1995 reinforced middle-generation leaders' conviction that as long as the Brotherhood remained deprived of legal status, its opportunity for meaningful participation in the political system would be blocked. As a candidate for the district of Helwan (an industrial area of Cairo), Madi witnessed the government's interference in the race firsthand, as did twelve other founding members of the Wasat party who stood as candidates.[66] As a result, they became even more determined to the shed the handicap of illegalism and secure the status of a "normal" political actor. As Madi explained in *al-Anba'* in March 1996, the formation of the Wasat party "reflects our commitment to peaceful work (*al-'amal al-silmi*) as the only alternative in light of the circumstances which the *umma* faces today." He went on:

> We declared our commitment to peaceful work in the aftermath of the great waves of anger which welled up from Egyptian society after the announcement of the last parliamentary elections, and the party saw at that time that there was a broad reaction that violence is the solution, but we said to them that peaceful work is the solution, and our positions were astonishing to everyone given that the Islamic Trend suffered the greatest harm and endured the greatest losses in those elections.[67]

The response of the Wasat party founders to the regime crackdown flies in the face of conventional arguments that the exclusion and repression of opposition groups encourages their radicalization. For example, in "Fulfilling Prophecies: State Policy and Islamist Radicalism," Lisa Anderson cited Giovanni Sartori on the effects of political exclusion on the development of opposition groups in Europe:

> An opposition which knows that it may be called to "respond," i.e.[,] which is oriented towards governing and has a reasonable chance to govern, or to have access to governmental responsibility, is likely to behave responsibly, in a restrained and responsible way. On the other hand, a "permanent opposition" which is far removed from government turnover and thereby knows that it will *not* be called to "respond," is likely to take the path of "irresponsible opposition," that is, the path of promising wildly and outbidding.[68]

Extending the same logic to the behavior of Islamist opposition groups in the Arab world, Anderson argued:

> By the very fact that they are illegal, unrecognized Islamist movements had no motivation to accommodate their opponents and embrace democracy and ample incentives to adopt a "rejectionist" posture.... Arbitrary and unpredictable government behavior engenders its own opposition.... The goals of opposition in these circumstances cannot be but the overthrow of the system and the establishment of another regime in which the disenfranchised will benefit.[69]

Yet the exclusionary policies of authoritarian regimes do not always produce the radical and irresponsible type of opposition they so richly deserve. There is no doubt that in some cases, state repression triggered the radicalization and militarization of elements within the Islamist movement. This occurred after the military aborted the democratic process and banned the Islamic Salvation Front in Algeria in 1992, a case highlighted by Anderson in support of her broader claims. But as the Wasat party founders' response to the sequence of events described above indicates, the reaction of opposition actors to exclusion and repression can assume different forms. To this group of Islamists, the repressive turn of the mid-1990s *did not demonstrate the necessity of militancy but rather underscored its futility.* Just as the Brotherhood's ordeal in the Nasser era generated divergent responses, pushing some members toward radicalization while persuading others, including the Supreme Guide and his closest associates, of the risks of direct confrontation with a police state, the Mubarak regime's crackdown on the Brotherhood in the mid-1990s was open to conflicting interpretations. In this instance, it increased the determination of Brotherhood reformers to obtain a legal foothold in the system as a means to operate effectively under existing political constraints.

The escalation of regime pressure on the Brotherhood in the mid-1990s increased the perceived costs of the *jama'a's* continued existence outside the formal political order, while the old guard's continued monopoly on power within it diminished the perceived prospects for meaningful change. As Aboul 'Ela Madi noted, "When we realized that a transition toward legal status was not in the interest of the most influential leaders in the Brotherhood, I personally felt a loss of hope . . . especially after elections in January 1995 for vacant posts in the Guidance Bureau produced 0% change."[70] Hence a group of middle-generation leaders decided to seize the initiative and establish a party of their own. As Salah Abd al-Karim explained,

> The crisis manifested itself over a period of about ten years. We always felt we had something to give to society and the state, but the [Brotherhood] leadership always denied us. So we decided to give the *Wasat* a trial run.[71]

BROTHER AGAINST BROTHER: THE REFORMIST CRITIQUE OF THE OLD GUARD BECOMES PUBLIC

The intensive media coverage of the Wasat party initiative, prolonged by the fits and starts of its successive bids for legal status, placed the Brotherhood in an awkward position. Discussions in the press, including lengthy interviews with party founders, highlighted the Wasat party's "progressive" and "liberal" interpretation of Islam and invariably cast the Brotherhood, either implicitly or through direct comparison, in a negative light. But even more damaging was the public criticism directed by Brotherhood "insiders" against the group's leaders and institutional culture. Freed from disciplinary pressures, the Wasat party founders no longer felt obligated to censor their opinions. As Madi bluntly asserted,

> We sought to make a difference inside the organization itself by pushing for more internal democracy and accountability. We also worked hard to push the organization to take more progressive positions on a wide array of issues including democracy, and equal rights for all citizens regardless of gender or religion. After almost twenty years of repeated frustrations, we realized that such changes were vehemently resisted by the powers that be inside the organization. At that point we decided to quit and establish our own more progressive and tolerant project: the Wasat party.[72]

The Wasat leaders' critique was particularly devastating because it was mounted by figures with a long history of involvement in the Brotherhood itself. Such insider status gave them privileged access to intimate details about how the organization was run and what transpired during its meetings and discussions, lending their claims added force. Particularly embarrassing was the Wasat founders' claim that while their ideas had evolved and matured as a result of their extensive interaction with other social and political forces at home and abroad, the mentality of the Brothers' senior leaders had remained trapped in the past. As Madi stated in numerous interviews with the press, his countless meetings and discussions with secular activists and intellectuals, as well as his various missions to other Arab countries and to Europe and the United States— for example, to raise funds for Bosnian refugees—had a profound effect on his thinking, a trend that extended to other leaders of the Wasat cohort as well. The most important development, he emphasized, was "our realization that we don't have a monopoly on the Truth." Hence, Madi and other Wasat founders explained, they offered their party program as a "human interpretation of Islam" open to discussion and debate.[73] By contrast, they argued, the Brotherhood's veteran leaders, who had insulated themselves from other forces in society, clung to the traditional conception of the Brotherhood's mission as an expression of Islam itself.

New information on the history of internal conflict within the Brotherhood came to light with the publication in early 1997 of Tal'at Ramih's book, Al-Wasat wa al-Ikhwan (The Wasat and the Brotherhood).[74] Tracing the events leading to the formation of the Wasat party from a highly sympathetic point of view, the book describes Aboul 'Ela Madi and other middle-generation leaders in glowing, almost reverential terms as a dynamic and progressive force that had struggled to assert itself within the Brotherhood for over a decade. Among the most revealing sections of the book are previously unpublished documents highlighting the middle generation's critique of the old guard as the conflict between them was unfolding. Among them was a lecture titled "[Toward a]

Broad Psychological and Practical Opening" (al-Infitah al-Nafsi wa al-ʿAmali al-ʿAm), which was presented by a Wasat party leader to a Brotherhood audience, though its date and location are not identified. Given the highly evocative tone and content of the lecture, it is worth excerpting here:

> The reality of Muslims in the modern era at both the local and global levels is one of backwardness and defeat, and tension in the relations between Muslims and those who have defeated them, and culture wars and a global rejection of everything Islamic. And such conditions have led to reactions to the situation of Muslims ranging from buried feelings of defeatism and retreat, and a lack of self-confidence and an inability to confront the Other and embarrassment and hiding behind religion, to the opposite psychological state of excessive arrogance and feelings of superiority, and accusations against the Other (all Others). . . .
>
> And conditions in the world have shifted from rejection and wars to mutual acceptance and truce and co-existence and understanding and admiration, but this global change in views on Islam and Muslims has not been accompanied by a change in our repertoires of activity and our movement which would enable Muslims to benefit from this development. And thus a golden opportunity has been squandered, and tensions have resumed.

The lecture goes on to identify a wide repertoire of damaging behaviors, including the "tribal" (clannish) practice of limiting one's interactions to others in the movement; painting a harsh and rigid picture of what a Muslim should be; a pattern of self-concealment and isolation from advocates of reform; and an unwillingness to adapt the Brotherhood's methods to changing circumstances.

Likewise, the lecture criticizes the atavistic character of current Islamist rhetoric, as indicated by:

1. "The use of historic terms which frighten others and are not accepted in modern times in our interactions with non-Muslims, like *Dar al-Harb* [the domain of war] and *Dar al-Islam* [the domain of Islam] and the *jizya* [the poll tax paid by non-Muslims under Islamic rule]";
2. "The use of frightening and absolutist expressions in our relations with Muslims which emphasize our differences and cloak us with an aura of superiority—like 'penetration' and 'inundation' and 'challenge' as a means to describe our mission and our guidance and service to the people"; and
3. "Demanding the impossible from people and the lack of [a commitment to] gradualism."

Finally, the lecture warns against

> [t]aking positions which the Shariʿa does not require of us, and indeed which flow from the personal views of individuals, and may even lead to consequences which contradict what the Shariʿa demands.[75]

Perhaps more than any articles in the press, this lecture—not intended for public consumption but directed to the Brotherhood's own ranks—illuminates the sea change in the worldview of its reformist cadres and reveals that their calls for change in the Brotherhood's goals and strategies were bound up with a profound and far-reaching critique of the defensive psychological complexes created and reproduced by the group's institutional culture.

With the departure of the Wasat party founders billed in the press as an "explosion" and as the "greatest conflict in the Brotherhood's history," Hudeibi and other senior leaders sought to downplay the threat it posed to the *jama'a's* ideological and organizational unity. In an interview with *al-Hayat* on February 20, 1996, Hudeibi protested the characterization of the incident as a "schism," asking "how many people have actually left the *jama'a*?" In addition, he stressed, the Brotherhood's objection to the initiative stemmed from its overriding concern with "the preservation of the *jama'a* itself, and the principles and rules and foundations upon which it is based, which have always come before anything else, and have preserved the *jama'a* since its establishment in 1928."[76]

The Wasat party initiative placed middle-generation reformers who chose to stay with the Brotherhood in an especially difficult position. Such figures subscribed to the same ideas as the Wasat party founders but remained subject to the group's disciplinary pressures and were hence obliged, at least in public, to back those at its helm. Several reformist figures were reportedly upset by the old guard's harsh response to the Wasat party initiative, and one sent a letter to the Supreme Guide from prison to register his objections.[77] At the same time, however, they contributed to the group's collective efforts at damage control by framing the Brotherhood's dispute with the Wasat party as simply a matter of strategy and timing. In particular, they argued that the ideas expressed by the Wasat party leaders had also become part of the overarching vision of the Brotherhood itself.

The Wasat party experiment highlighted an influential trend of self-critique and self-reform within the Brotherhood. Yet it also revealed the limits of the reformist impulse in two crucial respects.

First, while scores of media reports waxed rhapsodic about the "liberal," "tolerant," "moderate," and "democratic" aspects of the Wasat party platform, a closer reading indicates that it remained firmly committed to the revivalist Islamist understanding of Islam as *din wa dawla*, that is, both a matter of private belief and practice and the guiding principle for the organization of society and state. While the platform exhibited a significant set of ideological developments, particularly with respect to its definition of Islam as a civilizational reference, its emphasis on pluralism, and its support for the full citizenship rights of women and non-Muslims, it also exhibited a clear continuity with the past in its efforts to defend conservative religious values. *By defining such values as intrinsic features of Arab-Islamic culture and identity, the Wasat platform placed them beyond the reach of public scrutiny and debate.* In sum, the Wasat platforms of 1996 and 1998 did not constitute a sharp break from the central priorities of the Islamist movement. Rather, they represented an effort to articulate an Islamist ideological framework more consistent with reformist sensibilities and better adapted to existing political constraints. Further, they sought to translate the vague and abstract slogans of the Islamist movement into concrete policy positions and programs and, in doing so, to differentiate the Wasat party from the Brotherhood on the one hand, and the secular opposition on the other.

The Wasat party initiative, and the old guard's response to it, exposed the limits of the reformist impulse in a second way as well. On the question of whether the initiative could be characterized as a schism within the Brotherhood's ranks, Hudeibi was right. It did *not* represent a schism because it had no significant impact on the Brotherhood's core structures and bases of power. The overwhelming majority of the *jama'a's* members remained loyal to its senior leadership, due in part to the fact that Hudeibi and other members of the Guidance Bureau had managed to fill strategic administrative posts in the group's regional and local branches with individuals beholden to them and vested in their conception of the group's mission. Against this backdrop, the Wasat party initiative can more accurately be described as a *split in the cadre of middle-generation leaders who had pushed for internal reform of the movement over the preceding decade.* Further, the departure of the Wasat party founders diluted the influence of the reformist trend within the Brotherhood itself. While reformists who remained, like Abd al-Mun'im Abu al-Futouh, continued to lobby for progressive changes in the Brotherhood's policy positions and internal practices and in favor of deeper engagement with other groups in society, they became increasingly marginalized in the face of heightened security pressures on the Brotherhood on the one hand and a strengthening of the conservative faction at the apex of the group on the other.

During the second half of the 1990s, the old guard reasserted its control over the Brotherhood and reaffirmed the relevance and wisdom of its historic mission. In the wake of the public uproar sparked by the Wasat party split, the Brotherhood's senior leaders issued a statement, "Fawa'id Min al-Shada'id" (The Virtues of Hardship), directed at the members of its base. At certain times, the statement observed, it is necessary to review one's course in order to ascertain whether it is still on the right path and ensure that, in the sweep of events, it has not lost its sense of purpose or become detached from its foundations. With numerous references to the Quran, the Hadith, and the example set by the Prophet and his Companions, the statement affirmed that the higher purpose of the Brotherhood remained the same as it was in the past. At the core of our belief, it claimed, is that "Our *da'wa* [call or mission] is the call to God, and that God is its protector and defender." It went on to explain that "trials and hardships are one of the obligations of the *da'wa* mission" and hence that Brothers must take this burden upon themselves whether they are under the protection of a legal cover or not. The statement asked rhetorically whether anyone seriously believed that gaining legal status would protect those engaged in the *da'wa*, noting that the Brotherhood's adversaries would never grant the *jama'a* legal status, "since when have they ever respected the law or the constitution or justice or reason or honor?"

The statement went on to explain why the formation of a party under present circumstances contravened the Brotherhood's higher mission. Islam, it noted, is a comprehensive religion that covers all aspects of life. Therefore, "the *da'wa* cannot be restricted to the framework of a political party governed by laws which prohibit the establishment of parties on a religious basis and determine the scope of its activities and restrict its operations to the field of politics only without embracing the other dimensions of life." In short, political work subject to governmental control could not substitute for ongoing religious outreach in society at large.

The statement then addressed how differences in opinion among Brotherhood members should be adjudicated to ensure that they did not undermine the *jama'a*'s unity or higher purpose. It affirmed that *shura* (consultation) is an Islamic principle, not just in politics but in all fields of human endeavor, but insisted that it conform with certain rules and protocols. In particular, one should not insist on the rightness of his opinion if it goes against the preferences of the majority, for this is the height of tyranny and arrogance. Once a decision is made and confirmed by the *jama'a*'s established leadership, it is necessary for its members to listen and obey and to express their confidence in the *da'wa* and the leaders who work on its behalf. Further, internal disputes must be resolved through proper channels, not outside them; if not, they will lead to conflict (*fitna*) and chaos (*fawda*).

In conclusion, the statement noted that "respect for one's elders is a duty of the faith," particularly given that the steadfastness of the *jama'a*'s veteran leaders was among the main reasons the *da'wa* and its principles had survived. Hence members must give them respect, affirm their full confidence in them, and offer them their thanks. The statement warned members of the *jama'a* not to allow internal disputes to form the basis of "reports" and "stories" that would distract them from the group's higher purpose and lead to a dissipation of its time and effort. Instead they should align their loyalties with the *jama'a*, noting that "the obligation of allegiance is grounded in the morals of our faith."[78]

Around the same time, the Brotherhood sought to explain its mission to a Western audience with the publication in 1997 of a booklet by Mamoun Hudeibi titled *Politics in Islam*.[79] The booklet, which offers a detailed exposition of the Brotherhood's *da'wa* mission and positions on key issues in English, has an interesting provenance, as it was written in response to a query from the student-run *Harvard International Review*. Like the Brotherhood position papers released in 1994 and 1995, *Politics in Islam* exhibits an incoherent mix of religious and democratic themes. For example, it asserts that the "*umma* is the source of authority" but immediately undercuts this statement by emphasizing that members of the *umma* are obligated to submit to the provisions of Islamic law. As it declares,

> The Muslim Nation is obligated to submit to Allah alone and to sanctify the laws of the Glorious Quran and the blessed Sunna [Traditions of the Prophet], and believes that man does not have the right to rule except with that which was revealed by Allah in the form of Shari'a. In that sense, it cannot nominate anyone to act on its behalf except if he is willing to rule in accordance with the Law of Allah.[80]

Elsewhere the text affirms that the specific rulings contained in the sacred texts of Islam must be enforced:

> The Shari'a includes texts relating to systems which nowadays are considered to be an integral part of politics. We, the Muslim Brotherhood, demand that these particular Islamic injunctions be adhered to and acted upon. They cannot be disregarded, neglected, or their application and enforcement ignored.[81]

Hence even in a statement directed to a Western audience, Hudeibi continued to frame the program of the Brotherhood as aiming toward the ultimate establishment of Shari'a rule.

In sum, the Brotherhood's veteran leaders responded to growing external and internal criticism by affirming their commitment to the Brotherhood's historic *da'wa* mission and emphasizing the duty of absolute loyalty and obedience to those at its helm. Indeed, if anything, the embarrassing public rift with the Wasat party founders accentuated their determination to manage the group's internal conflicts and prevent such an incident from happening again. At the same time, the repressive turn of the mid-1990s and the additional waves of arrests that followed underscored the Brotherhood's vulnerability to state repression and prompted its senior leaders to exercise greater self-restraint in their public rhetoric and behavior. Seeking to cultivate new allies and avoid another direct confrontation with the state, the Brotherhood began to soft-pedal its calls for the immediate application of Shari'a rule and attempt to recast itself as an agent of democratic reform. These trends are discussed in the next chapter.

CHAPTER FIVE

The Brotherhood's Seesaw between Self-Assertion and Self-Restraint

THE PARADOXICAL STATUS of the Muslim Brotherhood on the eve of the Egyptian uprising is striking. It was the largest and best-organized sector of the political opposition—and an illegal group accused of seeking to undermine the public order and the state. During the last decade of the Mubarak era, the Brotherhood walked a fine line, seeking to avoid a collision with the regime while asserting its right to a leading role in public life. The arc of the Brotherhood's strategy during this period can be likened to the swing of a pendulum, seesawing between moments of self-assertion and moments of self-restraint. Moreover, the Brotherhood's trajectory did not trace a linear path toward greater integration into the political system. Instead it took the form of a sequence of fits and starts, its leaders continually recalibrating the terms of their engagement in an effort to expand their influence without jeopardizing the group's survival. More specifically, the Brotherhood's trajectory in the decade before the uprising arguably encompassed three distinct phases: (1) an initial period of guardedness in which the group attempted to recover from the repressive measures taken against it in the mid- to late 1990s (2000–2003); (2) a period of bolder self-assertion against the backdrop of a short-lived political opening (2004–5); and (3) a reversion to self-restraint following the onset of a new wave of repression (2005–10).

Yet we can also discern a wider pattern in which a combination of external pressure and internal group dynamics worked to limit the pace and scope of "auto-reform." As we will see in this chapter and the next, the Brotherhood adjusted itself to the rules and procedures of electoral politics without undertaking the type of deeper ideological and institutional changes that would have effected a more decisive break with its anti-system past.

The Egyptian Muslim Brotherhood as a Self-Limiting Actor, 2000–2003

The Brotherhood entered the new millennium seeking to avoid another round of confrontation with the state. The last of the Brotherhood leaders jailed after the military trials of 1995, including 'Esam al-'Aryan and Abd al-Mun'im Abu al-Futouh (who had suffered a heart attack in prison), were released in 2000. Acclaimed as "martyrs" for the cause, they resumed an active role in the group and helped orchestrate its campaign for the parliamentary elections scheduled in the fall. Yet chastened by—and still reeling from—the regime's latest assault, the Brotherhood sought to limit their electoral gains to "acceptable" levels. In the 2000 parliamentary elections, the Brotherhood decided to run for only 75 of the 444 seats open to contestation, or roughly half the number of seats it had contested in 1995.[1]

In addition to limiting its participation to certain districts, the Brotherhood's list of candidates (all of whom were technically running as independents) generally avoided high-profile figures and was weighted in favor of local—and in many cases younger and less experienced—candidates not well-known outside their own districts.[2] Hence the Brotherhood chose candidates in a better position to campaign under the radar of state security. In another sign of the Brotherhood's lower-key approach, many of its candidates focused on issues specific to the circumstances of their districts rather than engaging in ideological grandstanding.[3] Further, Brotherhood campaign posters and banners avoided the controversial slogan "Islam Is the Solution" ("Al-Islam huwa al-Hal") it had used in the past. Instead, their banners declared that "The Constitution Is the Solution" ("Al-Dustour Huwa al-Hal") or demanded "Apply the Constitution!"[4] signaling the Brotherhood's commitment to the rule of law while implicitly calling for the application of Shari'a, since Article 2 of the constitution defined the principles of the Shari'a as the country's primary source of legislation.

Following a July 2000 Supreme Constitutional Court ruling deeming the results of the previous two elections invalid because they were not subject to judicial control, President Mubarak consented to full judicial supervision of the elections and, with great fanfare, heralded the move as a significant step toward democracy.[5] To ensure that judges could supervise the balloting at all of the country's ten thousand polling sessions, the elections were spread out across three phases from October 18 to November 15. Yet the regime still intervened to limit the Brotherhood's gains. As local observers noted, the elections were "clean on the inside but dirty on the outside." The presence of judges inside the polling stations reduced the incidence of outright fraud, but the regime was still unwilling to create a level playing field for opposition candidates. A few days before the elections, twenty would-be Brotherhood candidates were rounded up and tried before a military tribunal.[6] In addition, the voting process was marred by the government's harassment of opposition candidates and supporters, including the eruption of open clashes between security police and voters being blocked from entering the polling stations in hotly contested districts, which occurred with greater frequency in the second and third rounds of the balloting. Predictably, the Brotherhood bore the brunt of this meddling. According to one report, of the 1,400 individuals arrested during the second round of elections, more than 1,000 were supporters of the Muslim Brotherhood who were arrested to prevent them from reaching the polling stations.[7] The security cordon was particularly tight in the Dokki district of Cairo, where Mamoun Hudeibi was running against Amal 'Usman, a high-ranking NDP member and government official, and in the Raml district in Alexandria, where, for the first time, the Brotherhood ran a female candidate, Jihan al-Halafawi, the wife of Brotherhood leader Ibrahim al-Za'farani. When al-Halafawi outperformed the NDP's candidate in the first round, the Ministry of the Interior promptly stepped in and canceled the results, leaving the district without representation for two years until a by-election in 2002 held under tight security produced victories for two NDP candidates.[8]

Whether the government's interference in the elections would have been even more pronounced had the Brotherhood chosen to run more candidates, included more prominent leaders on its list, challenged more high-ranking NDP party officials, and/or resorted to its old brow-raising slogans remains open to speculation, but it appears that the group's restrained electoral strategy paid off. After gaining only one seat in 1995, the Brotherhood managed to win seventeen seats in the 2000 elections, equal to the number of seats won by all other opposition candidates combined.[9] While this was nowhere near enough to challenge the NDP's stronghold in parliament (particularly after the overwhelming majority of independent candidates who had defected from the NDP before the elections rejoined it),[10] the Brotherhood emerged as the single largest opposition group in parliament.

After the elections, Brotherhood leaders sought to soften the impact of their strong showing. For example, while noting that, in principle, the Brotherhood should be allowed to form a party given the support it enjoyed among members of the Egyptian public, group leaders stressed that they would not push the issue at the present time. As Abd al-Mun'im Abu al-Futouh explained: "We are not going to submit an application unless we are certain that the government will accept it. Our goal is not to put the government in an embarrassing situation." Further, Abu al-Futouh stressed, the Brotherhood would limit its participation to the channels available to it under the law:

What the Muslim Brotherhood suffered in the past years and our stand in the recent elections provide clear evidence that we prefer the public interest to self-interest. As much as we are interested in participating in political action, we care for the country's security and peace.[11]

Abu al-Futouh also emphasized that the Brotherhood "wants to participate in the system, not to overthrow it" and, along the same lines, stressed that "we don't want to change the Constitution," since Article 2 already defined the Shariʿa as the primary source of legislation. Further, the Brotherhood supported the right of all groups, including the communists, to establish legal parties, with Abu al-Futouh noting that "what we ask for ourselves we must extend to others" and that "it is up to the people to decide which group they want to support." Finally, in what would become a hallmark of Brotherhood rhetoric in the coming years, Abu al-Futouh soft-pedaled the group's call for the application of Shariʿa, leading instead with the demand for democratic reform. As Abu al-Futouh noted: "The first priority for us is the same as it is for all other groups—freedom [al-hurriyya]; real democracy and real freedom for everyone."[12]

The Brotherhood also exhibited notable self-restraint in the lawyers' syndicate elections of 2001 when the Brotherhood joined a "national slate" for all twenty-four seats open to contestation that encompassed figures from various opposition groups as well as members of the ruling party and independents. According to the agreement worked out between the parties in advance, only eight of the twenty-four seats on the syndicate board would be allocated to the Brotherhood. Further, according to observers, the mix of "Islamist" and "professional/syndicate" content in the Brotherhood's electoral propaganda clearly tilted toward the latter, in marked contrast to the partisan slant of its earlier campaigns.[13] In what can be seen as an implicit trade-off between power and social acceptance, the Brotherhood clearly opted for the latter. As Abd al-Munʿim Abu al-Futouh told a reporter from the *Christian Science Monitor*:

> We changed from wanting to dominate the syndicates to allowing more plural boards because even though we know we could win control easily with total Brotherhood slates we'd be excluding a lot of people. What we want out of our involvement in the syndicates is to give an Islamic democratic model, to show that it works in practice.[14]

Finally, the Brotherhood exercised restraint in its response to regional developments that provoked widespread anger in the Arab world. The outbreak of the second Palestinian intifada in the fall of 2000 triggered a new round of conflict involving harsh Israeli military reprisals and incursions into Palestinian towns. Like Egypt's Arab nationalist and leftist groups, the Brotherhood was quick to denounce Israel's actions and to express solidarity with the Palestinian people. Yet it was small, grassroots networks on the left, such as the Egyptian People's Committee for Support of the Palestinian Intifada (EPCSPI)—and not the Brotherhood—that "broke the sacred red lines" and called protestors into the streets.[15] The EPCSPI included a wide mix of human rights groups, Nasserists, communists, and independent socialists, as well as some Islamists, mainly from the (now suspended) Labor Party.[16] Though the anti-Israel protests of the time were largely spontaneous, the EPCSPI played an important role behind the scenes. Protestors demanded that the Israeli Embassy in Cairo be closed and called for a boycott of Israeli and American goods. In addition, they denounced the complacency of Arab regimes in the face of Israeli aggression and, in a momentous shift, extended their outrage to conditions in Egypt itself.[17] As protestors shouted at a pro-Palestinian rally at Cairo University on April 8, 2002, "We want a new government because we've hit rock bottom."[18]

Despite its firm stand against "Zionist and American aggression" and the inflammatory comments of some individual leaders urging jihad against Israel and the United States, the Muslim Brotherhood was largely conspicuous by its absence from the pro-Palestinian protests, sit-ins, and hunger strikes that swept the country from 2000 to 2002.[19] Moreover, unlike its leftist counterparts, the Brotherhood assiduously avoided expanding its list of targets to include the Mubarak regime, arguing that the country must be unified in the face of external threats. As Mamoun Hudeibi stressed:

We shouldn't fight over secondary issues and leave the major causes. We shouldn't break our ranks. Instead, we have to unite the front against the external aggression. We are careful that the popular support for the *intifada* would never be directed towards confronting the regime. No one benefits from that but the enemy.[20]

Likewise, in January and February 2003, it was activists on the left who organized the first street rallies against the impending U.S.-led invasion of Iraq. Once again, the slogans shouted by the crowds quickly assumed an anti-regime tone, such as "Baghdad Is Cairo! Jerusalem Is Cairo!" and "We Want Egypt to Be Free, Life Has Become Bitter!"[21] As reporters observed, the Brotherhood was largely absent from the protests of February 18 and 22.[22] When it later joined the fray, it did so with the regime's blessing. On February 27, the Brotherhood obtained a permit to hold an antiwar demonstration in Cairo Stadium. The event, which reportedly drew more than a hundred thousand people, was much larger than any protest organized by the left, but it was peaceful and refrained from chanting anti-regime slogans.[23] By contrast, demonstrations in Tahrir Square staged by leftist groups on March 20 and 21, a few hours after the first air strikes on Iraq, quickly morphed into anti-regime protests, as did the demonstrations they organized to mark the first-year anniversary of the war in March the following year.[24]

Paradoxically, the Brotherhood's superior mobilizing power raised the price of "crossing the red lines," since Brotherhood leaders knew that any demonstration they headed would be seen as more threatening to the regime than those led by marginal groups on the left and would hence be more likely to provoke a violent crackdown. This helps explain why it was the left—and not the Brotherhood—that took the lead in the antiwar protests. Likewise, it was leftist activists who took the bold step of directing popular outrage against the regime, chanting slogans protesting the wide gulf between rich and poor, the corruption of government leaders, and the president's rumored choice of his son Gamal as his successor.[25]

Incentives for self-restraint were augmented by the attacks of September 11, 2001, which prompted the Brotherhood to attempt to distance itself from al-Qaʻida and other militant Islamist groups. The Brotherhood's condemnation of al-Qaʻida's attacks on civilian targets in the United States as unethical and un-Islamic stood in awkward contradiction, to say the least, with its support for martyrdom operations against civilian targets in Palestine and Iraq. While the Brotherhood positioned itself in moral solidarity with Palestinians and Iraqis under occupation, it was unwilling to justify direct attacks on the United States and, by extension, the Arab regimes allied with it. More generally, the sharp rise in global and domestic scrutiny of Islamist groups as purveyors of terrorism and extremism placed the Brotherhood on the defensive and increased its reluctance to launch any move that could trigger another round of conflict with the state.

The self-restraint exhibited by the Brotherhood during the period from 2000 to 2004 did not reflect a consensus among the Brotherhood's rank and file. For example, during the pro-Palestinian protests in the spring of 2002, the branch office of the Brotherhood in Alexandria called for a "million-man march" to mark the fifty-fourth anniversary of the *nakba* (disaster), the creation of Israel and the dispossession of the Palestinians in 1948. Tens of thousands reportedly showed up for the march even after its organizers were arrested.[26] Yet such initiatives were rare, given the cautious stance of the group's senior leadership, who were convinced that the Brotherhood was "too big to react" without bringing disaster upon itself. Asked in early 2003 whether the Brotherhood, as the country's largest opposition group, was ready to "shatter the red line" and take to the streets, Abd al-Munʻim Abu al-Futouh responded:

> We are not prepared to bear the consequences! You ask me: "Can you mobilize a 10,000 strong demonstration?" I'll tell you: We can mobilize 50,000. But if it's only us, then the government would try us in the military courts and not the leftists. We don't want blood, and we don't want a civil war in the streets![27]

The Brotherhood's self-restraint from 2000 to 2004 was also a function of the death of two aging Supreme Guides in rapid succession, which diverted the group's energy and attention toward the selection of their replacements. How the Brotherhood's tenuous legal status, as well as the tensions between rival factions within it, shaped the turnover of its leadership is examined next.

THE BROTHERHOOD'S LEADERSHIP SUCCESSION STRUGGLES, 2002–4

The death of Mustafa Mashhour, the fifth Supreme Guide, on November 13, 2002, and of Mamoun Hudeibi, the sixth Supreme Guide, on January 8, 2004, posed a set of acute technical challenges for the Brotherhood. Over the previous decade, reformist leaders had begun to insist that the Supreme Guide be elected by the group's legislative assembly (*majlis al-shura*) rather than chosen by seniority as had been the norm. Yet others pointed out that a meeting of the assembly to elect a new Supreme Guide would likely trigger a new round of repression, as it did in 1995, when a similar effort led to the arrest of several prominent Brotherhood leaders on charges of "trying to revive an illegal organization." The state of siege in which the Brotherhood found itself hence put a brake on internal reform. As Abd al Mun'im Abu al-Futouh explained in an interview in October 2002, "the climate of repression and exclusion has aborted the conduct of internal elections within the Brotherhood and strengthened the hand of those who reject the growth of democracy within the group to the point that it has stopped completely."[28]

In late October 2002, shortly before Mashhour's death, the Guidance Bureau appointed a committee to vet the preferences of Shura Council members regarding his replacement, meeting in small groups and as individuals "to avoid being entrapped by the security forces, the mistake they made in 1995." Such members apparently supported Mamoun Hudeibi as the new Supreme Guide, a post he assumed on November 27, 2002.[29] Yet Hudeibi's death in January 2004 left the group's highest post vacant once again. As Diya' Rishwan observed, Hudeibi was "the last great figure of his generation"[30] and left behind no obvious successor. Just days after Hudeibi's death, Mohammed Mahdi 'Akef was selected as the new Supreme Guide. According to Hossam Tammam, the quick endorsement of 'Akef by the Guidance Bureau and Shura Council members reflected the perception that he was more capable than other candidates of bridging the group's internal divides.[31] Like Mashhour, 'Akef had been an active member of the "secret apparatus" during the interwar period, and during the Nasser era he had served twenty years in prison (1954–74). Though clearly affiliated by age and life experience with the Brotherhood's old guard, 'Akef was seen as having a more flexible personality than other senior Guidance Bureau members. Further, while many of the latter had spent their entire careers administering group affairs "from the inside," 'Akef had broader experience in public life. For example, he served in parliament from 1987 to 1990 as a member of the Islamic Alliance and ran again as an independent in 1995 and 2000.[32] Such experience enhanced his credibility among the Brotherhood's middle-generation activists. As Tammam observed, "it was widely known that he was the closest of the members of the Guidance Bureau to this generation, and the best equipped to absorb them and reach an understanding with their leaders."[33] In another nod toward inclusiveness, Muhammad Habib, a former science professor, was chosen as the Supreme Guide's first deputy, and Khayrat al-Shatir, a businessman, as his second deputy; both were younger than the members of the Brotherhood's old guard and maintained good relations with middle- and younger-generation reformists within its ranks.[34]

FOREIGN "DEMOCRACY PROMOTION" AS A NEW FACTOR IN EGYPTIAN PUBLIC LIFE

'Akef's selection as the Brotherhood's new Supreme Guide coincided with a marked shift in the policy agendas of the Bush administration and European governments toward a new focus on the "democracy deficit" in the Arab world. To a large extent, this policy shift can be traced back to the attacks of September 11, 2001, which, as Joseph S, Nye put it, exposed the fact that "dreadful conditions in poor weak countries halfway around the world can have terrible consequences for the United States."[35] Conditions of poverty and dictatorship in the Arab world came to be seen as a breeding ground for terrorism and hence a direct threat to U.S. national security. The promotion of democracy, human rights, the rule of law, and economic development—objectives long overshadowed by concerns with regional stability, Arab-Israeli peace, and ensuring a steady supply of cheap oil to global markets—hence surged to the top of the U.S. foreign policy agenda. In a speech at the National Endowment for Democracy on November 6, 2003, President George W. Bush justified this new focus:

> Sixty years of Western nations excusing and accommodating the lack of freedom in the Middle East did nothing to make us safer—because in the long run, stability cannot be preserved at the expense of liberty. As long as the Middle East remains a place where freedom does not flourish, it will remain a place of stagnation, resentment and violence ready for export. . . . Therefore the United States has adopted a new policy, a forward strategy of freedom in the Middle East.[36]

In February 2004 a draft proposal for a "Greater Middle East Initiative," prepared by U.S. policymakers for discussion at an upcoming summit of G-8 nations, was leaked to the press. In response to criticisms of the draft from European and Arab quarters, the proposal was revised, and the final version, renamed the "Broader Middle East and North Africa Initiative" (BMENA), was approved at the G-8 summit in June.[37] The BMENA initiative envisioned a multilateral approach to political and economic liberalization in the region. At the prompting of European officials, as well as in concession to Arab sensitivities, the new version stressed that reform cannot be imposed from the outside; framed Arab political, business, and NGO leaders as "full partners" in the reform process; acknowledged that the pace and scope of reform would vary according to the individual circumstances of each country; and emphasized the urgent need for progress toward a resolution of the Israeli-Palestinian conflict and the restoration of full national sovereignty in Iraq.[38]

Despite the lofty rhetoric and the flurry of new programmatic initiatives, what is most striking in retrospect about this new "freedom first" strategy was the limited nature of its impact, as indicated by the modest revenues allocated to it (particularly in comparison with the enormous cost of the military occupation of Iraq) and the unwillingness of U.S. and European policymakers to give such initiatives any teeth by setting clear time lines and benchmarks for reform and establishing mechanisms for their enforcement.[39] Further, the new emphasis on democracy did nothing to lessen the reliance of Western governments on "friendly" authoritarian regimes in the region. As Martina Ottaway and Thomas Carothers observed,

> It seems clear that the administration is unwilling to push the envelope and adopt a much more assertive policy toward non-democratic and largely non-reforming but friendly Middle Eastern states. Despite all the talk about a new paradigm for U.S. policy in the region, U.S. policy makers are still effectively paralyzed by an old problem: the clash between their stated desire for a deep-reaching transformation of the region and their underlying interest in maintaining the useful relations they have with the present governments of many nondemocratic states there.[40]

Yet if foreign democracy promotion initiatives failed to catalyze systemic change, they did have a palpable effect on the dynamics of political contestation in the Arab world, particularly in Egypt. As a major recipient of U.S. military and economic aid and a close ally of the West, Egypt was singled out by President Bush in his National Endowment for Democracy speech as a target of high expectations: "The great and proud nation of Egypt has shown the way toward peace in the Middle East, and now should show the way to democracy in the Middle East." Heightened scrutiny of the authoritarian practices of the Mubarak regime produced a twofold effect. First, it encouraged all sectors of the opposition, including the Muslim Brotherhood, to accelerate their demands for political reform. Second, it tilted the calculus of the regime in favor of a more accommodative approach to opposition forces and raised the cost of any direct moves to suppress them. Of most immediate relevance here, such trends encouraged the Brotherhood's senior leadership to reassert the group as a central actor in public affairs.

THE MUSLIM BROTHERHOOD'S REFORM INITIATIVE

On March 3, 2004, at a conference at the headquarters of the journalists' syndicate in downtown Cairo, the Muslim Brotherhood seized the public spotlight by announcing its own comprehensive program for reform. Mohammad Mahdi 'Akef led off by condemning the U.S.-sponsored Greater Middle East Initiative, noting that the Brotherhood "denounces foreign interference in the affairs of Egypt or any other Arab or Islamic country."[41] Muhammad Habib, first deputy to the Supreme Guide, proceeded to read the Brotherhood's reform program.[42] Interestingly, apart from a new introduction rejecting foreign meddling in the region, the text of the initiative was identical to the campaign platform of Mamoun Hudeibi, the former Supreme Guide, in the 2000 parliamentary elections.[43] What was new about the 2004 proposal was not its content but the Brotherhood's high-profile intervention at a time that external pressure for reform had reached new heights. Predictably, the regime denounced the Brotherhood's salvo, arguing that as an illegal organization, it had no right to offer its opinions on state affairs. Further, the minister of the interior chastised the journalists' syndicate for allowing the Brotherhood to hold a press conference in its halls.[44]

The Brotherhood offered its initiative as a direct alternative to proposals emanating from the West. As it observed, "The Arab and Islamic world today have seen repeated attempts to impose change from the outside," yet the goal of such efforts "is not genuine reform in the interests of the peoples of the region, but rather above all to maintain the hegemony of the United States and intensify its control of the region's resources and capacities, as well as to entrench the Zionist entity occupying the land of Palestine and cultivate other governments more amenable to its broader strategy."[45] The initiative framed comprehensive reform as "a national Egyptian, Arab and Islamic demand" and defined the peoples (shuʿub) of the region as the only ones authorized to lead it. Drawing directly on Hudeibi's 2000 electoral campaign statement, it offered a thirteen-point reform program, beginning with "the Construction of the Egyptian Person" and proceeding to a discussion of political, electoral, judicial, economic, social, and cultural matters.

The Brotherhood's initiative integrated democratic themes into a broader project of Islamic reform. In the political domain, many of its demands echoed those of secular opposition groups and conformed with the thrust of the very foreign reform proposals it rejected out of hand. For example, it asserted that the people are the source of all authority and have the right to select their political representatives in free and fair elections. It called for the separation of the presidency from any political party and the restriction of the holder of that office to two consecutive terms. Further, it called for lifting the state of emergency and replacing the country's restrictive party and syndicate laws with new legislation that "affirms the freedom of the citizen and his dignity and right to participate in public life." The statement also called for a release of political prisoners, an end to torture, and limiting the security establishment to "the protection of the state and society, rather than protecting the government or being used to repress the opposition." Likewise, it advocated strengthening judicial independence, abolishing all exceptional courts, and using military courts exclusively for those accused of military crimes.

Yet in the Brotherhood's reform program, such demands were couched within—and inseparable from—a broader religious agenda. The introduction of the program asserts that the Brotherhood's vision of reform stems from "[o]ur conviction that our mission is the call to God. . . . And we believe that the whole world in general and we in particular are in need of this call, and of everything which paves the way toward it." Further, it states that "the ultimate goal of our mission is a genuine and comprehensive reform, which we all must work for together, through constitutional and legal channels, to establish the Law of God [*Shar' Allah*]."[46]

The purpose of reform was not to establish a framework providing equal representation to all sectors of opinion in Egyptian society but to promote Islamic values and behavior as the Brotherhood defined them. This thrust is revealed in the opening section of the program, titled "Constructing the Egyptian Human Being" (Bina' al-Insan al-Misri). "While the Egyptian people as a whole are religious by nature," it opined, "this religiosity has been eroded in recent years by selfishness and materialism, adversely affecting the Egyptian character, and hence "anyone seeking reform must strive to purify the core of this personality and rebuild it, especially among the new generations, on the basis of faith and morals." To this end, the proposal called for "Consolidating respect for the fixed values of the nation [*thawabet al-umma*] represented in the faith in God and His Books and His Prophets and His Laws," "Raising the young in theory and in practice on the principles of the faith and proper manners," "Giving the proponents of the *da'wa* the freedom to explain the principles and characteristics of Islam, the most important of which is its comprehensiveness as a guide to all aspects of life," "Prompting the people to abide by worship and good morals and upright actions," and "Purifying the media of everything which violates the rulings of Islam and established norms."

Islam and the "fixed values of the nation" would hence serve as the ultimate reference point for the new political order, setting the outer limits of free expression and assembly. Consider, for example, the passages in the section on political reform, in which such references have been placed in italics: "We affirm our support for a state system which is a republican, parliamentary, constitutional and democratic system *in the framework of the principles of Islam*" and "affirm freedom of opinion and the right to promote ideas peacefully *in the framework of the public order and public morals and the constitutive foundations of society*." In the section on judicial reform, the proposal calls for "adjusting the laws and cleansing them to hasten their conformity with the principles of Shari'a, considering it the primary source of legislation based on Article 2 of the Constitution." In the domain of education, it calls for the "spread of religious values and moral principles and good examples and national belonging." Finally, the program calls for the reform of public culture and its methods of transmission, including newspapers, journals, and television broadcasts, to ensure that they are free of indecent content and deepen the public's commitment to Islamic values and principles.

As these passages indicate, the Brotherhood's reform program was shot through with tensions and ambiguities. First and most obvious was the contradiction between its assertion that the people are the source of all authority and its indirect allusion to the higher sovereignty of God entailed by the call for Shari'a rule.[47] Second, the Brotherhood's claim that Egyptians are "religious by nature" appears distinctly at odds with its observation that the religious commitments of Egyptians have been eroded by secularism, materialism, and Western cultural influences. To "rebuild the Egyptian person," it suggests, the levers of the state—such as its control over education, the media, and the mosques—must be employed to spread Islamic beliefs and values.[48] One cannot escape the conclusion that the freedom of expression and assembly supported by the initiative was first and foremost the freedom of the Brotherhood to pursue its *da'wa* mission, not the freedom of others to oppose or defy it.

References to "the principles and values of Islam" (*mabadi wa qiyam al-Islam*), the "enduring constants of the nation" (*thawabet al-umma*), and the constitution are invoked in the program to limit the scope of public freedoms. *But how much and in what ways such freedoms should be restricted pivot on how those terms are defined.* The practical implications of the Brotherhood's reform initiative thus hinged on *what interpretation of Islam operated as its point of reference*, an issue on which it was silent.

If the Brotherhood's reform initiative contained an uneasy mix of religious and democratic elements, it chose to emphasize the latter in the closing years of the Mubarak era when it joined secular groups to mobilize bottom-up pressure for democratic reform. Beginning in December 2004 and continuing through the summer of 2005, an unprecedented wave of democracy protests broke out across Egypt. It was spearheaded by a loose network of individual activists, many with roots in the Arab nationalist and leftist opposition. Called the "Egyptian Movement for Change," the network became known as "Kefaya" (Enough), its chief slogan and rallying cry. How the Brotherhood responded to the new dynamic Kefaya set in motion is examined next.

KEFAYA AND THE MUSLIM BROTHERHOOD: PARTNERS OR RIVALS?

The Kefaya movement did not emerge out of thin air. It built on the foundation of the Egyptian Popular Committee in Solidarity with the Intifada (EPSCI), a network of leftist activists formed in 2000 that later organized protests against the U.S.-led invasion of Iraq, including a large demonstration at Tahrir Square on March 20, 2003, the day American air strikes commenced. The focus of these protests quickly turned to domestic issues, and in July a predominantly leftist group calling itself the March 20 Popular Campaign of Change raised the slogan "No to Extension, No to Hereditary Succession" ("la lil-tamdid, la litawrith"), which would become one of Kefaya's chief slogans one year later.[49]

The genesis of Kefaya dates to a meeting of more than twenty people held at the end of the month of Ramadan in November 2003 at the home of Aboul 'Ela Madi, an ex-Brother and founder of the Wasat party. As Madi recalled, "Every year I would invite guests to an *Iftar* [evening meal] at my home. These were social gatherings, but they were also an opportunity to discuss broader issues; this year we focused on political reform." Guests at the *Iftar* included individuals with a wide range of backgrounds and orientations, including Coptic Christians, liberals, Nasserists, Marxists, and Islamists, the latter encompassing several members of the Brotherhood. In December, six leaders who would later emerge as key figures in the Kefaya movement met to discuss the issues raised at the *Iftar* in greater depth: George Ishaq, a Coptic Christian and a leftist activist; Ahmad Baha' Sha'ban, a Marxist; Amin Iskandar, a Nasserist; Muhammad Sayyid Idris, an independent; Sayyid Abd al-Sattar, a member of the Muslim Brotherhood; and Aboul 'Ela Madi.

As George Ishaq recalled,

> We talked about the fact that all these reform proposals were coming from the outside; why was there no Egyptian agenda? Also, we were looking ahead to the presidential and parliamentary elections scheduled for 2005, and said, "Do we want to end up with the same ideas, the same people, and the same mismanagement, or can we do something to change the dynamic?" We decided that we should try to reach a minimal consensus, identifying points on which we could all agree.[50]

Ishaq noted that it was difficult at first reach an agreement "because we belong to different ideologies." Indeed, it took eight months of intensive discussion to iron out a common set of principles.[51] In July 2004 the group released their first statement to the Egyptian press, signed by more than three hundred civic and political leaders. The statement posited a vital link between the defense of Arab sovereignty and the imperative of democratic reform. In order to "confront Zionist-American hegemony in the region," Egypt needed a state built on strong civic institutions. Hence it called for the peaceful alternation of power, the direct election of the president, strengthening the independence of the judiciary and the media, the abolition of the country's Emergency Laws, and the imposition of strict limits on presidential power.[52]

The establishment of the "Egyptian Movement for Change" ("al-haraka al-misriyaa lil-taghyir") was formally announced at its inaugural conference on September 22, 2004. Known as the Upper Egypt Conference, the meeting was attended by some five hundred people and was timed to coincide with the ruling National Democratic Party's annual conference.[53] As Aboul 'Ela Madi recalled, "We spoke of the 'death of politics' and the problems of corruption and dictatorship in the country, and someone shouted *Kefaya*! [Enough]. From then on it became the movement's main slogan."[54] A Coordinating Council was elected, encompassing thirty-five public figures from across the ideological spectrum, eleven of whom were appointed to the Steering Committee charged with managing the movement's day-to-day affairs. George Ishaq was chosen as the executive director, and a website was launched that quickly received tens of thousands of hits.

The leaders of Kefaya characterized it as a "movement of conscience" (harakat damir), which Egyptian citizens joined as individuals rather than as representatives of organized groups and parties. Distinctly cross-partisan in character, it reflected the shared political consciousness and experience of the "70s generation" (jil al-sab'inat), individuals who had been active in the student movement in the Sadat era and had initially sought a role in the country's established parties and political organizations, only to find their advancement blocked by the autocrats at their helm. Over time they became increasingly disillusioned with such groups, which they saw as co-opted into the very system they allegedly sought to change.[55] Some "70s generation" activists retreated from the field of politics altogether, others channeled their energies into the NGO sector, and others set out to form new parties of their own. As Diya' Rishwan observed,

> Most of the leaders of Kefaya were members of the 70s generation: we had different political views, but one experience [tajriba]. Most are not members in parties, or they left politics for a long period and are reentering it now.[56]

The deepening of connections among political activists of the "70s generation" in the 1980s and 1990s set the stage for Kefaya's formation. As 'Esam Sultan, a lawyer who left the Brotherhood and helped form the Wasat party, explained,

> Kefaya was the result of a sustained process of deliberation and dialogue; we had many discussions that took place over a long period of time; this helped create trust [thiqa] so that no side was afraid of the other.[57]

The Kefaya movement held its first street protest on December 12, 2004, in front of the High Court of Justice in downtown Cairo. As Aboul 'Ela Madi recalled:

> We held up signs that read "No to Extension, No to the Inheritance of Power" [la lil-tamdid, la lil-tawrith]. We agreed not to shout but rather placed tape over our mouths as a sign that this dictatorship was preventing its citizens from speaking. This was the first time that a popular demonstration ever dared to say no to the Mubarak regime.[58]

Kefaya held additional demonstrations at the Cairo International Book Fair on February 4 and at the entrance to Cairo University on February 21. According to Mustafa Kamal al-Sayyid, a political scientist and member of Kefaya, the movement's strategy of civil disobedience drew inspiration from grassroots democracy movements in Eastern Europe, particularly Georgia's Revolution of the Roses and Ukraine's Orange Revolution.[59] Additional rallies by Kefaya and various spin-off groups continued through the spring.

The demonstrations organized by Kefaya were small, with groups of five hundred to two thousand protestors typically outnumbered by the riot police surrounding them. Yet as the first movement to launch an open protest against the Mubarak regime, Kefaya broke a powerful taboo and provided a new model of civil resistance, amplified by the extensive coverage it received in the Arab and foreign press. Even more defiant language and tactics were brought into play by some of the younger demonstrators, particularly Marxists and Communists, who shouted, "Down with Mubarak!" and "Get Out! [Irhal]." That the regime did not respond more harshly to such demonstrations was undoubtedly due in part to their small size but also likely reflected a concern about its public image at a time of intense foreign scrutiny. The reluctance of the security establishment to crush the demonstrations with brute force also arguably stemmed from Kefaya's insistence on a strategy of nonviolence, as well as the public visibility of the leaders associated with it. As 'Esam Sultan observed: "The security have a heavier burden going after Kefaya. It's one thing to go after terrorists, but it's another to confront public figures calling peacefully for democracy. The path of peaceful protest is more effective than the path of violence."[60]

Kefaya's bold debut as a force on the Egyptian street caught the Brotherhood off guard. Having featured for decades as the largest and most influential sector of the opposition, the Brotherhood found itself upstaged by a small network of mostly secular activists who had suddenly seized the initiative and the media spotlight. It is not that Kefaya was unknown to the Brotherhood. Some Brotherhood members, primarily from its middle-generation cohort, joined the Kefaya movement as individuals, and Sayyid Abd al-Sattar, a Brotherhood activist, served on its executive board.[61] But Kefaya had its own cross-partisan leadership, was dominated numerically and in spirit by leftists, Nasserists, and Arab nationalists, and, in stark contrast to the Brotherhood's seeming timidity, had the audacity to confront the regime head-on.[62] This contrast was pointedly emphasized in the Arab media, triggering protests within the Brotherhood, especially among its activist youth.[63] As Aboul 'Ela Madi recalled,

> There was a lot of criticism of the Brotherhood on Arabic satellite TV stations, noting that the Brotherhood had been conspicuous by its absence. Some members of the Brotherhood asked the leadership, "Why aren't we holding any demonstrations?"[64]

As internal pressure to act mounted, the senior leaders of the Brotherhood confronted a dilemma. They knew that mobilizing their members into the street would likely trigger a harsh response from the regime, exposing the group to further arrests and imprisonments as well as other intrusive measures, such as new efforts to disrupt its financial networks. Given the vast network of social, religious, and educational institutions under its control, and the numerous individual and group interests tied up in them, the Brotherhood had more to lose than Kefaya did. And because the Brotherhood was viewed as a greater threat, the likelihood of repression was higher. Once again, the Brotherhood's superior organization and mass appeal increased the risks of calling its supporters into the streets. Yet Brotherhood leaders did not want to alienate their own rank and file by remaining on the sidelines, nor did they want to be eclipsed as the leading edge of the opposition when other groups were agitating for reform.

Ultimately the latter considerations prevailed, though the Brotherhood did not abandon its habits of self-restraint completely. Before staging its first rally in Cairo on March 27, it attempted to obtain a government permit and only moved without one after its request was denied.[65] Further, in statements to the media, Brotherhood leaders emphasized that its demonstrations were merely "symbolic," an apparent attempt to signal that it was not seriously pushing for the regime's downfall.[66] Further, unlike radical leftists who shouted "Down with Mubarak!" at some of Kefaya's rallies, the Brotherhood refrained from attacking the president himself.[67] Perhaps most tellingly, the Brotherhood's antigovernment rallies involved only a small fraction of its supporters, compared with the hundreds of thousands who had amassed at the funerals of its last two Supreme Guides, suggesting that it chose not to flex its full mobilizing power.

Nevertheless, as a result of its superior organization and discipline, as well as its larger base, the Brotherhood's protests quickly outstripped those of Kefaya in size. As noted earlier, Kefaya demonstrations tended to involve a few thousand people at most. The Brotherhood's rallies were at least five times that size and in some instances were much larger. For example, a demonstration on April 22, 2005, in the town of Tanta was reportedly attended by twenty thousand people, and its largest demonstration, on May 4, involved as many as fifty to seventy thousand.[68] As Egyptian journalist Omayma Abdel-Latif observed, such demonstrations exhibited "a radical shift in the group's thinking, a clear break from its long-standing tradition (and conscious choice) of avoiding direct confrontation with the state during Hosni Mubarak's rule."[69]

The upsurge in grassroots democratic protest, dubbed the "Cairo Spring," reached its height in April and May, with both Kefaya and the Brotherhood staging demonstrations, in some instances in multiple cities at the same time.[70] A central focus of the protests was an amendment to Article 76 of the constitution, proposed by President Mubarak in a speech and letter to parliament on February 26, ratified by parliament on May 10, and scheduled for a popular referendum on May 25. Heralded by the regime as an important step on the path to democracy, the amendment and the new elections laws associated with it established a framework for the direct election of Egypt's president for the first time. Yet Kefaya, the country's legal opposition parties, and the Brotherhood all rejected the amendment because of the restrictions it placed on who could compete against Mubarak or his handpicked successor. Any leader affiliated with a legal opposition party would be allowed to run in 2005, but in all future elections, parties would be able to field candidates only if they had won at least 5% of the seats in both the People's Assembly and the Shura Council (the lower and upper houses of parliament). The problem, as the International Crisis Group observed, was that

> [n]ot one of them has anything like 5% of the seats in either of the two houses of parliament and there is no reason to assume that this will be significantly changed by the next legislation elections. The Wafd, which among legal opposition parties won the highest tally of People's Assembly seats (6) in the 2000 legislative elections, would need to have more than quadruple this in the 2010 legislative elections to field a candidate in the 2011 presidential election.[71]

Independent candidates for the presidency faced an ever higher bar, as they would have to be supported by at least 250 members of the country's representative bodies, including 65 members of the People's Assembly, 25 members of the Shura Council, and 10 members of local councils in 14 governorates (140 members in total), with the remaining 20 drawn from any of the above.[72] Given that both houses of parliament and most local councils were dominated overwhelmingly by the government-affiliated NDP, the ability of any independent to qualify as a candidate was limited in the extreme. As the date of the referendum neared, Kefaya and several opposition parties called for a boycott, and the Muslim Brotherhood followed suit. The referendum passed with an official turnout figure of 53.6%, with 82% voting in favor, though opposition leaders questioned the turnout rate and claimed that many people "did not know what they were voting for."[73]

Although the Brotherhood was not the first or boldest group to challenge the Mubarak regime, it was the largest and best organized, making it both a greater threat and an easier target. Hence as the referendum neared and the regime resorted to more aggressive tactics to contain the protests, it was the Brotherhood that bore the brunt of its wrath. By the summer, according to official figures, eight hundred Brotherhood leaders had been arrested, with the Brotherhood claiming the real number exceeded two thousand. Further, several key leaders of the group were arrested in May, most notably Secretary-General Mahmoud 'Ezzat, the most senior figure arrested since 1996, and 'Esam al-'Aryan, a prominent spokesman for the group.[74] In addition, the independent daily al-Masri al-Yawm quoted Brotherhood sources as saying that "high-ranking security officials had threatened to 'squash the group' if it did not stop taking its demands to the streets."[75] Despite such threats, the Brotherhood refused to be cowed. As 'Ali Abd al-Fattah, a Brotherhood activist, noted, "'The price we are willing to pay shows that the Brotherhood cannot be ignored"; as Supreme Guide Mohammed Mahdi 'Akef declared, "We have become fearless."[76]

With calls for reform gaining momentum, the Brotherhood tried to overcome its historic isolation from other sectors of the opposition. First, its leaders took pains to emphasize the demands the Brotherhood and secular groups shared in common and to downplay those on which they remained divided. As Muhammad Mahdi 'Akef declared: "For the Brotherhood, the issue of freedom is at the top of our agenda now."[77] Further, when a group of demonstrators at the Brotherhood's first anti-government rally in March raised up copies of the Quran, triggering an outcry in the press, Abd al-Mun'im Abu al-Futouh urged the group's rank and file to refrain from holding up the Quran at future demonstrations. As Abu al-Futouh explained:

> I told them to put the copies of the Quran down. The Quran is a text that is too holy to be used in political demonstrations. Further, it gives the false impression that I am agitating as a believer against the infidel [kafir]. Our disagreements with others are not about the mushaf [the text of the Quran] but about the policies of the current government. The slogans of the democratic movement—"No to the Extension of Power," "No to Inheritance" [la li'l-tamdid; la li'l-tawrith]—are supported by Islam. Islam in fact is the first to demand freedom and social justice.

According to Diya' Rishwan, 'Esam al-'Aryan made a similar argument on Orbit, an Arabic-language television channel, a few days after the demonstration.[78]

Moreover, in public statements at the time, Muhammad Habib emphasized that the Brotherhood was "a Society of Muslims" rather than "*the* Society of Muslims," and Abu al-Futouh declared that the Brotherhood offered a "human interpretation of Islam" (the latter formulation, Wasat party leaders claimed, "he took from us!").[79] Such statements stood in sharp contrast with previous statements depicting the Brotherhood as a movement representing all Muslims and as embodying the principles of Islam itself, echoes of which had appeared in the Brotherhood's reform initiative as recently as the year before.[80]

In a parallel shift, Brotherhood leaders stressed that all sectors of the opposition were victims of an oppressive political system and that only by pooling their energies and resources could they mobilize effective pressure for change. As Muhammad Habib observed,

> We are all in the same jail cell; even if we differ in our philosophies and objectives, we can agree on our right to more sleep, better food, more decent living conditions. If you live inside a prison, you try to get a bit more freedom and a bit more comfort which will benefit everyone. Otherwise, you will remain isolated, stuck inside "a prison within the prison."

Accordingly, Habib argued, all of the country's political forces "should agree on a minimal consensus rather than focus on our differences," and what they could agree on was a general framework for reform based on "democracy and the peaceful alternation of power."[81]

Yet for all of Habib's talk of extending a hand across the country's partisan divide, the Brotherhood was unwilling to defer to a movement led by others. As Gasir Abd al-Raziq, a leftist human rights activist, put it, "This new juncture is confusing to the Muslim Brotherhood. It wants to be seen as part of the wider movement for democratic reform but still wants to maintain its own separate identity."[82] Despite the fact that several middle-generation Brothers had joined Kefaya as individuals, the Brotherhood itself kept its distance. According to George Ishaq, Kefaya and Brotherhood leaders met three times in the spring of 2005 to coordinate strategy. Each time, Ishaq recalled, "We asked the Brotherhood to join our demonstrations. 'Esam al-'Aryan asked, 'How many people do you want?' and we answered, 'As many as you'd like to bring.' Three times they accepted our invitation, but none of them showed up."[83] Abu al-Futouh tells the story differently, claiming the Brotherhood deliberately sent only a few members to Kefaya demonstrations so as not to overwhelm them: "We only participated in a symbolic way so we wouldn't dominate their events. They can bring out five hundred people. We can bring out five thousand if we wanted to, but if we did that, it would dilute the presence of Kefaya."[84]

During the same period, the Brotherhood took the lead in establishing a new cross-partisan alliance. Known as al-Tahaluf al-Watani Min Ajl al-Islah wa al-Taghyir (The National Coalition for Reform and Change), it was announced at the journalists' syndicate headquarters on June 30, 2005, and encompassed the Muslim Brotherhood, several Nasserist and Marxist figures who joined as individuals, and the communists and Revolutionary Socialists, who joined as blocs.[85] Though the Brotherhood was by far the largest group in the coalition, it deliberately limited its representation to just nine of the thirty-six seats on its Steering Committee, leaving the remaining seats to its partners. Likewise, though Muhammad Habib, a senior Brotherhood leader and one of the chief architects of the alliance, was appointed its first chairman, it was agreed that the position would rotate every two months.[86] In such ways, the Brotherhood sought to downplay its role as the coalition's prime instigator and largest bloc and to buoy its credentials as an inclusive national front.

The formation of the Tahaluf was not preceded by the type of sustained dialogue and deliberation between Islamists and secularists that paved the way for the Kefaya movement. As 'Esam Sultan observed:

> The long discussions which laid the foundations for Kefaya helped create relationships of trust across ideological boundaries. The experience of the Tahaluf is exactly the opposite. The Brotherhood joined to give the impression that it was part of a "national consensus," while the Revolutionary Socialists are very small and they wagered that they could appear stronger if they allied with the Brotherhood. But they have no real dialogue. If they talked for just ten minutes, they would reach an impasse! The Brotherhood established a coalition with groups that it still sees as kuffar [infidels]![87]

More broadly, during the period of democratic protests that became known as the Cairo Spring, the Brotherhood and the secular opposition made a conscious decision to table their differences and articulate a shared demand for constitutional and political reform. As Diya' Rishwan noted:

> The Brotherhood doesn't talk about Shari'a, and the communists don't make attacks on private property, etcetera. The opposition has not reached a total consensus on everything, but we've reached an agreement on the basic principles of reform, and the feeling is "let's not focus now on the differences between us."[88]

Despite such efforts to forge a common agenda, the Muslim Brotherhood and the secular opposition failed to establish the type of robust and enduring cross-partisan alliance that contributed to many "third wave" democratic transitions from the 1970s forward. Why is this the case?

First, the structural imbalance between the large and well-organized Brotherhood and Egypt's wide assortment of Lilliputian secular groups and movements, some of which had virtually no popular following at all, diminished the strategic benefit of such an alliance for the Brotherhood while prompting secular leaders to worry that the Brotherhood would end up dominating any coalition it joined. Second, unlike the Wasat Islamists, who had interacted closely with secular activists for years, the Brotherhood's old-guard leadership had remained more aloof, and their motives continued to be regarded with suspicion in secular circles. When George Ishaq was asked whether the Islamist and secular leaders in Kefaya had resolved their differences on the issue of Shari'a, he replied that the issue "never came up" (*lam tutrah*), since a decision was made to postpone the discussion of contentious issues for a later time. While conceding that the views of the ex-Brothers and Brotherhood reformists in Kefaya differed from those of their secular counterparts, Ishaq stressed that such Islamists had moved toward support of the concept of equal citizenship rights for all and could be trusted to respect the rules of the democratic game. By contrast, Ishaq and other secular activists continued to question the democratic commitments of the Brotherhood old guard, noting the "vagueness" and "ambiguity" of their public statements, as well as the striking gap between the ideas they were now espousing and the illiberal views they had expressed in the not-so-distant past. As Ishaq observed,

> If you look at the Tahaluf platform, it is a purely liberal democratic agenda. There is nothing in it about Islamic law. Did they just suddenly give up their goals? All of their long heritage—has it all been forgotten? I don't think you become a liberal democrat overnight.[89]

Likewise, Hisham Qasim, a liberal publisher and activist, noted,

> The Brotherhood says they are for democratic reform, but I don't buy it. The development in their thought and discourse doesn't show where they saw the light. The Brotherhood used to say it's Islam versus everything else, but they bit off more than

they could chew so they had to backtrack. So now they speak in a democratic language, but their goals are the same.[90]

Some Brotherhood figures, like Sayyid Abd al-Sattar, 'Esam al-'Aryan, and Abd al-Mun'im Abu al-Futouh, were seen by Kefaya leaders as more open-minded, but they were viewed as forced to defer to prevailing opinion within the Brotherhood, which remained quite conservative. As Hisham Qasim noted, "'Esam [al-'Aryan] has called for a complete revisiting of everything, but he refuses to say so in public; it is the outcome of an apparatchik mentality."[91] Likewise, George Ishaq recalled, "Last year Abd al-Mun'im Abu al-Futouh said it was fine with him if a Copt became president, and the Guidance Bureau protested, 'How can you say that?' The course the Brotherhood takes hinges on the instructions of the old guard." Ishaq also noted that the Brotherhood's culture of obedience, of "Sit down! Stand up!" was inimical to democratic values, as was their claim to possess a monopoly on the truth. As he stated in July 2005:

> Some members of the Brotherhood seek a genuine dialogue with us, but others want only a monologue. At our last meeting with them, it was the monologue trend which prevailed. When a group claims to speak for Islam, that is monologue. When they say, "I have the absolute truth," that is a monologue. No one has access to the absolute truth![92]

Ishaq and other secular leaders in the Kefaya movement supplied further anecdotes demonstrating the Brotherhood's "snobbery" and "arrogance." For example, Ishaq recalled, "I met the *murshid* [Supreme Guide] and told him: 'You must reassure the people; the Copts for example, are extremely afraid of you!' And one of the conservatives in his entourage looked at me and said, 'You are going to tell us what to do? Who do you think you are?'"[93] Finally, secular leaders emphasized, for the Brotherhood to be fully accepted as a partner in the democratic process, it must transform itself into a political party with a clear program and a membership base open to all. Yet Ishaq noted, "When you tell them they should transform into a political party, they get angry and accuse you of interfering in their internal affairs."[94]

In addition to questioning the Brotherhood's motives, secular activists were reluctant to associate with the group for other reasons. First, they were trying to crystallize their own distinctive identity. As Ishaq noted, Kefaya was attempting to build a "third bloc," a civil democratic project representing an alternative to both the Brotherhood and the state. Second, the regime employed a combination of carrots and sticks to induce secular groups to stay clear of the Brotherhood. As Muhammad Habib, a deputy to the Supreme Guide, noted:

> The regime uses the various mechanisms at its disposal to isolate the Brotherhood from all the other political forces in the field. It can meddle in their internal affairs, freeze its assets, or provoke internal conflicts. The legal parties know that if they get too close to the Brotherhood the government will increase its intervention in their

affairs. In addition, the regime offers them benefits. For example, it will say to a secular party, "I'll give you a few seats in parliament if you keep your distance from the Brotherhood." When Ayman Nur was trying to establish the al-Ghad party, we wanted to have a meeting with him to discuss possible forms of cooperation. And Safwat Sharif, a senior government official, called him in and said, "If you want a party, stay away from those people."[95]

Hisham Qasim agreed with this assessment, noting that many secular activists were convinced that "the Brotherhood is trouble; if you bring them into anything it will only cause problems for you."[96] Brotherhood leaders claimed the Mubarak regime had deliberately cultivated this impression in order to prevent secular and religious elements of the opposition from joining forces against it. As Habib observed, "The regime aims to keep the Brotherhood isolated, as it serves their broader interests."[97]

THE MUSLIM BROTHERHOOD IN THE 2005 PARLIAMENTARY ELECTIONS

The democracy protests of the Cairo Spring waned by the summer as civil and political leaders turned their attention to the presidential and parliamentary elections scheduled for the fall. With the outcome of the presidential election in September viewed as a foregone conclusion, the only element of uncertainty was the level of voter turnout. When Kefaya and three of the country's secular opposition parties called for a boycott of the presidential election, the Brotherhood initially signed on, with Abd al-Mun'im Abu al-Futouh serving as its chief liaison. But a few weeks before the elections, the Brotherhood suddenly reversed course and encouraged the Egyptian public to participate, though it advised them not to support "repression and corruption," an implicit signal to vote against Mubarak. Flouting the thrust of internal opinion (according to one report, over two-thirds of Brotherhood members supported a boycott), the group's senior leaders presumably changed gears to avoid provoking government officials in the weeks leading up to the parliamentary elections.[98] Hence a principled stand against the regime yielded to short-term considerations of political advantage, as the Brotherhood set it sights on the electoral contest coming up in November.

The Brotherhood's campaign in the parliamentary elections of 2005 demonstrated the tension between its impulse toward self-assertion and its ingrained habits of self-restraint. Seeking to capitalize on the political opening created by external pressure, the Brotherhood ran 161 candidates, more than double the number it had run in 2000. Yet the Brotherhood also announced that it would not contest seats in districts where senior government candidates were running and, most important, would not contest more than one-third of the seats so as not to challenge the NDP's two-thirds majority.[99] That this restraint was a strategic choice is suggested by a Brotherhood study conducted at the time that showed the group could have run as many as 250 successful candidates. With input from the group's Central Elections Commission, which oversaw the nomination of candidates through the Brotherhood's regional administrative offices, the Guidance Bureau selected 161 candidates, with a list of alternates including members on the security establishment's "black list."[100]

This time around, the Brotherhood did not form an electoral coalition with secular opposition groups. Instead it ran its own list and revived its old slogan "Islam Is the Solution," which, though a flashpoint of controversy, continued to resonate among members of its base and conservative religious voters more generally.[101] Likewise, Brotherhood campaign workers chanted, "It's not for position, nor for power, not for money, nor for party . . . it's for Islam and for God."[102] As Noha Antar observed, the appeal to religion remained a valuable trump card:

> Those affiliated with the Muslim Brotherhood, members and sympathizers, often saw it as a religious duty to vote for a candidate of the movement. This gave them the courage to challenge the regime's security forces and to cast their vote within the authoritarian system—preachers reminded them that a good Muslim only need fear his creator, Allah.[103]

Yet the Brotherhood also took pains to stress that it was not trying to shut out the secular opposition. Invoking the slogan "Partnership, Not Domination," it ordered its candidates to leave certain districts to secular candidates rather than compete against them.[104]

Under a new law mandating full judicial oversight of the elections, the balloting occurred in three rounds to ensure the presence of a judge at every polling station. The first round of voting proceeded with a minimum of government interference, but the Brotherhood's early gains triggered a dramatic increase in the harassment and intimidation of opposition campaign agents and supporters in the second and third rounds. In some districts, security officials blocked the entrance to polling stations, and thugs hired by the NDP attacked voters. According to a report by an independent Egyptian monitoring group, there were 2,271 arrests, 819 people wounded, and 14 deaths.[105] In some districts, the government's efforts to prevent Brotherhood victories in the latter rounds of the elections included the arrest of Brotherhood campaign agents and outright electoral fraud.[106]

Despite the regime's aggressive tactics in the last two rounds of the elections, the Brotherhood won a total of eighty-eight seats, or nearly ten times the number of seats (nine) won by all of the country's legal opposition parties combined. Even more telling, the Brotherhood won roughly two-thirds of the seats they contested.[107]

Against a backdrop of sensationalist reporting on its stunning gains in the Arab and Western media, the Brotherhood launched a public relations campaign to reassure its critics. For example, on November 23, Khayrat al-Shatir, the second deputy to the Supreme Guide and one of the group's most influential members, gave an interview to the British newspaper *The Guardian* in which he underscored the Brotherhood's commitment to a course of pragmatic self-restraint. Under the title "No Need to Be Afraid of Us," al-Shatir stressed,

> We are not seeking more than a small piece of the parliamentary cake. This decision is dictated by political realities, both locally and internationally, in other words, the possible reaction of a repressive government backed to the hilt by the U.S. and other Western governments.[108]

Further, at a "meet the deputies" conference in December introducing the members of its new parliamentary bloc, the Brotherhood focused on the qualifications of its representatives and shouted "Reform!" rather than Islamist slogans.[109] The Brotherhood also initiated a dialogue with leaders in the Coptic Christian community and in January 2006 promised a "white paper" on the issue of Coptic citizenship rights.[110] In an article in *al-Hayat* on January 11, 2006, Muhammad Habib, first deputy to the Supreme Guide, took aim at the alarmist media reports. "This terror of the Brotherhood exceeds the bounds of logic," he opined, noting that with only 20% of the seats, the Brotherhood was hardly in a position to upend the political system. He said with no small measure of exasperation:

> We have been forced—up against this manufactured terror—to send letters assuring all groups of the nation, even though the NDP has a majority large enough to achieve total dominance of the decisions made by parliament, and the only risk was of serious discussions and fruitful deliberations and a strengthening of parliament's effectiveness and skill, and an increase in the people's confidence in it.[111]

Despite the Brotherhood's efforts to downplay the significance of its strong showing in the 2005 parliamentary elections, the results shocked regime officials. In the wake of the elections, the regime launched a new campaign against the Brotherhood, which helped consolidate the power of the group's conservative factions at the expense of the reformists. Thus repression led not to radicalization but to retrenchment, as well as to the postponement of any normalization in the group's relations with the state and other forces in society. It is to these developments that we now turn.

CHAPTER SIX

Repression and Retrenchment

From 2005 to 2010 the Mubarak regime took new steps to contain the Brotherhood, and in response the group ramped up its calls for constitutional and political reform. But heightened security pressure strengthened the hand of Brotherhood conservatives at the expense of those advocating fundamental change in the Brotherhood itself. Further, for all their complaints about the regime's dictatorial practices, the Brotherhood's senior leaders were unwilling to confront it head-on. Frustrated by the old guard's excessive caution, some younger members of the group urged them to adopt a bolder stance against Mubarak. But until the outbreak of the Egyptian popular uprising in 2011, it was the risk-averse stance of the old guard that prevailed.

A Victim of Its Own Success

The Brotherhood's strong showing in the 2005 parliamentary elections shocked the regime and strengthened its resolve to contain it. As Prime Minister Ahmad Nazif noted the following spring:

> Islamists who say they belong to an illegal organization have been able to go into parliament and in a format that would make them seem like a political party. . . . We need to think clearly about how to prevent this from happening.[1]

Nazif later described the Brotherhood as a "secret cell" and vowed that the government would not "allow them to form a parliamentary bloc in the future nor to assume any role in the political arena."[2] Such ominous rhetoric soon turned into action when the regime launched what the International Crisis Group described as "the most widespread campaign against the group since the 1960s, even if the level of repression is far less and its aim is to control and contain rather than eradicate the group."[3] According to regional experts, the victory of

Hamas in the Palestinian legislative elections of January 2006, Israel's war with Hizbollah in Lebanon that summer, and the escalation of sectarian conflict in Iraq increased concern within the Bush administration and other foreign governments about the growing influence of Islamist groups in the region, prompting them to tone down their calls for democratic reform. Against this backdrop, the Mubarak regime felt emboldened to move more aggressively against the Islamist opposition at home.[4]

The regime's strategy to rein in the Muslim Brotherhood entailed a wide range of coordinated political and security measures, beginning with a sustained campaign against the group in the official media, where it was described as a "secret" and "illegal" organization seeking to undermine the public order. These accusations escalated after a demonstration by Brotherhood students at Al-Azhar University on December 10, 2006, to protest government interference in student union elections. At the al-Azhar event, about fifty Brotherhood students dressed in black military fatigues, their faces covered by black hoods, staged a martial arts demonstration reminiscent of similar displays by Hamas and Hizbollah in Palestine and Lebanon, respectively.[5] The demonstration triggered a firestorm of criticism in the government-controlled media as well as in secular opposition newspapers. The Brotherhood was accused of establishing a paramilitary group modeled after the "secret apparatus" of the interwar era, and parallels were drawn with the movements of fascism and Nazism. As the editor of the government-owned daily *al-Gumhuriyya* charged:

> It appears that the Muslim Brothers looked at history and found that the best way to express themselves was through black shirts and through resembling Fascists and Nazis, for a very simple reason: Fascism and Nazism are compatible with the Muslim Brotherhood's aims of toppling the regime, spreading out, and using violence and blood as a way of resolving disagreements.[6]

In what was roundly depicted as a public relations disaster for the Brotherhood, the "Al-Azhar militia" incident placed the group on the defensive.[7] The students issued an apology, and Mohammad Mahdi 'Akef, the Brotherhood's Supreme Guide, gave a series of public interviews in which he stressed that the group had no military wing and opposed the use of violence to solve problems, while statements on the group's website accused the media of blowing the event out of proportion. Nevertheless, the incident helped the regime frame the Brotherhood as a threat to the public order. As Muhammed Abd al-Fattah 'Umar, former head of the state security apparatus, put it, "The Muslim Brotherhood represents the framework for future violence."[8] Likewise, President Mubarak stated in a public interview in January 2007:

> The Muslim Brotherhood movement, which is banned in Egypt, is a danger to security because it adopts a clear religious path. . . . [Should this movement come to

power], many will take their money and flee the country; investment will come to a halt; unemployment will increase; and worse yet, Egypt will be irrevocably isolated from the world.[9]

In addition, the regime moved decisively against the group whenever it tried to contest an election or mobilize its supporters into the street. For example, 850 Brotherhood members were detained in the spring of 2006 when the Brotherhood and secular opposition groups staged a series of demonstrations supporting the Judges' Club's demands for greater judicial independence. Further, hundreds of Brotherhood members were arrested ahead of elections for the Shura Council (the upper house of parliament) in June 2007 and in the weeks before municipal elections were held in April 2008.[10]

The regime's assault on the Brotherhood included the arrest and long-term detention of some of its most influential leaders and financiers. After the al-Azhar demonstration, the security police rounded up more than 140 Brotherhood leaders, including Khayrat al-Shatir, who supervised the Brotherhood's financial networks, and his business partner Hasan Malik. The regime also froze more than seventy of the Brotherhood's companies and other assets. The cases of al-Shatir, Malik, and thirty-eight other detainees were transferred to a military tribunal, where they were charged with "belonging to and funding an illegal organization, money laundering and financing terrorism" (though the latter charge was later dropped). On April 15, 2008, al-Shatir and Malik were sentenced to stiff prison terms of seven years each.[11] The regime's efforts to contain the Brotherhood thus entailed a new strategy: targeting its main sources of funding. According to 'Amr al-Chobaki, the arrest of al-Shatir and his colleagues "dried up about one third of the Society's funding streams, forcing it to rely on the two other main streams, membership dues and revenue from small businesses it operates."[12] One source estimated the cost to the Brotherhood at half a billion Egyptian pounds, or $88 million.[13] Al-Shatir's imprisonment also deprived the group of a critical intermediary between the organization's old guard and younger reformist cadres.[14]

Due in large part to regime interference, the Brotherhood failed to win a single seat in the Shura Council elections of April 2007. In the lead-up to the April 2008 municipal elections, which had been postponed for two years, more than 800 Brotherhood candidates and supporters were arrested. In addition, only 498 of the 5,754 candidates they fielded were permitted to register, and according to Muhammad Habib, only 10 were eventually accepted, prompting the Brotherhood to pull out of the elections altogether.[15] Further, the regime impeded the efforts of Brotherhood deputies in parliament to serve the members in their districts. As Saber Abul Futuh, a Brotherhood MP from Alexandria, complained, "They tell everyone in government offices not to deal with us, and even those government officials who know us very well are afraid to help us because they can be punished."[16]

The regime consolidated its grip in a final move by introducing thirty-four amendments to Egypt's constitution, which were approved by parliament and ratified by popular referendum on March 26, 2007. Two amendments were particularly devastating for the Muslim Brotherhood. Although the Political Parties Law of 1977 already prohibited the formation of parties on a religious basis, the amended version of Article 5 enshrined this ban in the constitution itself. In addition, Article 62 was amended to omit wording permitting citizens to directly elect their representatives in parliament, paving the way for the reversion to a strict party-list system or a hybrid system in which only a limited number of seats would be reserved for independents. As Shehata and Stacher noted, the "real purpose" of these reforms was to "reduce significantly the ability of the Brotherhood to compete in elections." In addition, amendments to Article 88 stipulated that future elections would be supervised by an electoral commission of active and retired judges, some of whom would be regime appointees, effectively removing future elections from independent judicial control.[17]

The connection between the Brotherhood's strong showing in the 2005 parliamentary elections and the wave of repression that followed was not lost on Brotherhood leaders. As Muhammad Habib ruefully observed in 2007, if he could change one thing that had happened over the previous few years, it would be for the group to have "won 50 seats instead of 88."[18] Yet the Brotherhood responded to the crackdown with a striking degree of self-restraint. As Muhammad Saʿd al-Katatni, the head of the Brotherhood's bloc in parliament, noted, the regime wanted to "provoke the Brothers so that they abandon their peaceful methods,"[19] but they would not take the bait. As Muhammad Habib put it, "we do not function by an action and reaction policy."[20] The Brotherhood's refusal to be prodded in the direction of radicalization—for example, by reactivating its armed wing or mobilizing thousands of supporters into the streets—reflected the hard lesson its leaders had learned from the Nasser era, namely that they could not win in a direct confrontation with the state.

The Brotherhood's subdued response to the measures taken against it was also a direct consequence of its strategic choice to pursue a path of nonviolence in the early 1970s. Since that time, the Brotherhood had developed a vast infrastructure of branch offices, charitable associations, health clinics, and businesses that gave it a large stake in the existing order, and that multiplied the personal and institutional interests at risk. Further, having trained its cadres for more than three decades to engage in peaceful social and political activism, it would have been very difficult for the group to suddenly reverse course. As Issandr El-Amrani put it, "their [nonviolent] strategy doesn't allow them to react—it doesn't allow an escalation."[21] Indeed, from the Cairo Spring of 2005 to the Arab Spring of 2011, the Brotherhood rarely mobilized large numbers of supporters into the streets; the one major exception was the demonstrations it organized to protest Israel's incursion into Gaza in January 2009, which led to 1,200 arrests.[22]

Yet the post-2005 repressive turn did have a profound effect on the Brotherhood's relationship to the political order as well as the balance of power among its competing factions. In particular, the reformist trend lost much of its momentum. From 2005 to 2010, several of the Brotherhood's most prominent reformist figures spent time in prison, allowing conservative leaders to consolidate their dominant position in the Guidance Bureau and their control over the group's day-to-day affairs. In addition, Brotherhood conservatives took the lead in drafting a new platform for a Brotherhood political party, which was distributed to Egyptian intellectuals and analysts in late summer 2007. We now turn to that platform and the sharp internal dispute it generated.

THE BROTHERHOOD's 2007 DRAFT PARTY PLATFORM

The draft party platform released by the Brotherhood in 2007 was but the latest in a series of proposals that had been circulated internally at various points in the 1980s and 1990s. As in the past, the Brotherhood did not submit the proposal to the government, since they knew in advance that it would be rejected. Instead it released the platform as a means to present its agenda to the Egyptian public, as well as to clarify its positions on hot-button issues about which it had been criticized for being too vague and ambiguous in the past.

The draft platform envisioned a Muslim Brotherhood party as a "civil party with an Islamic frame of reference" (*marja'iyya islamiyya*) and declared its support for a constitutional order based on the peaceful alternation of power through popular elections, as opposed to a system of clerical rule. Like earlier proposals, it expressed support for political pluralism, the rule of law, judicial independence, and strengthening the role of civil society. But the platform also contained a number of controversial elements that reflected the orientations of the Brotherhood's conservative wing. First, it stressed the Brotherhood's commitment to the eventual application of Shari'a, which was a departure from the Brotherhood's efforts to downplay the issue during the democracy protests of 2005. Second, while affirming its support of the principle of popular sovereignty, the platform called for the establishment of a council of religious scholars to vet executive and legislative bills for conformity with Shari'a principles. Finally, while affirming the citizenship rights of women and Coptic Christians, the platform barred them from running for president.[23]

The draft party platform touched off a burst of criticism in the media. Secular figures accused the Brotherhood of seeking to establish a clerical authority, akin to the Council of Guardians in Iran, which could veto laws passed by a democratically elected parliament; in addition, they pointed to the exclusion of Copts and women from the position of head of state as evidence of the group's failure to support the equal rights of all citizens. Such negative commentary took the Brotherhood leadership by surprise. In public statements following the release of the platform, Muhammad Mahdi 'Akef and Muhammad Habib stressed that the envisioned council of religious scholars would serve a purely advisory function.[24] Further, they argued, the conformity of legislation with the principles of Shari'a was already demanded by Article 2 of the constitution.

The draft platform also triggered a critical response from reformist leaders in the Brotherhood itself. Prominent figures such as Abd al-Mun'im Abu al-Futouh, Gamal Hishmat, and 'Esam al-'Aryan insinuated that the platform had been drafted by a few senior leaders without the proper consultation of group members and that its call for the establishment of a religious council and the disqualification of Copts and women from the presidency did not reflect a wider consensus.[25] In addition, they challenged the Islamic validity of these provisions. For example, Abu al-Futouh cited the opinion of the prominent Islamist scholar Yusuf al-Qaradawi in arguing that only the Supreme Constitutional Court was authorized to determine whether existing legislation violated the Shari'a.[26] Critics also described the platform as violating the principles of democracy, noting that the exclusion of Copts and women from the presidency violated the principle of equal rights for all citizens.[27] A new cadre of outspoken, Internet-savvy Brotherhood youth weighed in as well, criticizing the manner in which the platform was drafted and the regressive character of its provisions in their blogs and statements to the press, as did Islamist thinkers and activists outside the Brotherhood's fold.[28]

In February 2009, senior Brotherhood leaders met with a small group of secular activists to discuss the platform. According to Diya' Rishwan, who attended the meeting, they were met by a barrage of objections and concluded the meeting promising to omit any references to a religious council in future drafts and reaffirming the exclusive authority of the Supreme Constitutional Court to vet existing laws for conformity with Shari'a principles.[29] Likewise, in statements to the media, Muhammad Habib promised to form a committee to revise the draft platform. However, Brotherhood leaders turned down subsequent invitations to discuss the platform, apparently concerned that such meetings would only compound their embarrassment. As Abd al-Mun'im Mahmoud, a young Brotherhood blogger, observed, "they wanted to close the file and aren't likely to revive it anytime soon."[30]

What is particularly interesting is that a very different party program had been in the works in the months before the platform was released.[31] Drafted under the supervision of 'Esam al-'Aryan, head of the Brotherhood's political bureau, the earlier program was both much shorter and more progressive in tone. It made no mention of a religious council and placed no restrictions on the eligibility of Copts and women for senior government positions. Among those consulted in the drafting of the early platform were prominent Islamist and secular intellectuals outside the Brotherhood. According to Abd al-Mun'im

Mahmoud, the conservative majority in the Guidance Bureau rejected the early draft, which they deemed "too secular," and when 'Esam al-'Aryan was sent to prison in May, they jettisoned the draft he had been working on and composed a new one under the supervision of Muhammad Mursi, former head of the Brotherhood's bloc in parliament. Mahmoud recalled al-'Aryan's astonishment and indignation when he saw the new platform, which, al-'Aryan stressed, "was not the program we were working on!" One of the most glaring differences was that the new conservative platform cited extensively a source called *Ahkam al-Sultaniyya*, a text written by Islamic medieval scholar al-Mawardi.[32] Like other reformist leaders, al-'Aryan shared his consternation with the media, telling a reporter from the *Wall Street Journal* that the program distributed by the Brotherhood was so wrong it had probably "been exposed to a virus."[33]

The critical response of reformist leaders in the Brotherhood to the 2007 draft platform revealed the existence of profound differences of opinion within the group about how Shari'a rule should be defined and converted into practice, as well as about the citizenship rights of non-Muslims and women. Brotherhood leaders also disagreed about the proper relationship of a Brotherhood political party to the Brotherhood *jama'a* (association), discussion of which was conspicuous in its absence from the 2007 draft party platform. While reformist figures supported converting the *jama'a* into a political party, conservative leaders insisted that any party function alongside the *jama'a* in order to preserve the latter's broader *da'wa* and social service activities. In early 2008 the Guidance Bureau voted on whether to convert the *jama'a* into a political party. According to one source, only two members, Abd al-Mun'im Abu al-Futouh and Muhammad Bishr, voted in favor of the proposal.[34]

The new cadre of young Brotherhood bloggers, most of whom identified with the reformist wing of the movement, were especially blunt in their criticism of the party platform, provoking the ire of some of the group's senior leaders. For example, conservative stalwart 'Ali Abd al-Fattah posted an article titled "Islam Marja'iyyatuna" (Islam Is Our Frame of Reference) on the Brotherhood's official website accusing critics of the platform of "ideological defeatism" (*inhizam fikri*) and insisting that the *da'wa* and political functions of the Brotherhood could never be separated. "He didn't name names, but it was clear that he was talking about us [the young bloggers]," recalled Abd al-Mun'im Mahmoud. "He called us secularists; it almost reached the point of *takfir* [calling someone a *kafir*, or infidel]."[35] Mahmoud replied to the article on his blog. Another blogger, Ibrahim Hudeibi, submitted a response to the Brotherhood's official website, but they refused to publish it, prompting him to take the matter directly to Muhammad Mahdi 'Akef, the Supreme Guide: "I said to him, 'I have a question. Does 'Ali Abd al-Fattah speak for the Brotherhood or not? If so, OK. But if not, then his opinion is just one among many and I have a right to respond to it.'" 'Akef eventually intervened and Hudeibi's response was posted on the group's website.[36]

The Brotherhood's Disputed Internal Elections, 2008–10

The power monopoly of the old guard was reinforced by the outcome of Guidance Bureau elections in 2008 and 2009, as well as by the election of a new Supreme Guide in January 2010. But these elections were sharply criticized by some members of the Brotherhood, not just behind closed doors but also in statements to the press. Let us look more closely at these developments.

As a technically illegal organization subject to ongoing government surveillance and control, the Brotherhood was understandably reluctant to share information about its internal operations. According to Brotherhood sources, sometime in the early 1990s, the Brotherhood's charter (la'iha) underwent a number of important revisions. For the first time, members of the Guidance Bureau were to be chosen by the Shura Council in a secret ballot, according to a formula distributing seats to each region based on the number of Brotherhood members active within it. In addition to its sixteen elected members, the Guidance Bureau was collectively authorized to appoint three additional members. If a position opened up as a result of the death, illness, or incapacitation of a current member, his seat would be allocated to whichever losing candidate had won the most votes in the previous elections, as long as he received a minimum of 40%; otherwise, new elections would be called. Further, positions on both the Guidance Bureau and the Shura Council would be limited to four-year terms.

The Shura Council consisted of approximately 105 members, including 90 members elected to represent its regional branches and up to 15 additional members appointed by the Guidance Bureau on the basis of their particular technical qualifications and expertise. A new Shura Council was elected in 1995, but mounting security pressures blocked it from meeting for ten years. In 2005, against the backdrop of the political opening created by the Cairo Spring, calls for holding a new round of Shura Council elections gained steam. Under the radar of the security apparatus, a new Shura Council was elected, and several ideas were floated about how it might elect a new Guidance Bureau. For example, Abd al-Mun'im Abu al-Futouh suggested that the Brotherhood seek government permission to hold a meeting of the Shura Council. Muhammad Mahdi 'Akef proposed renting a large conference room in a hotel or conducting elections during the Brotherhood's annual *Iftar* celebration at the end of Ramadan; when security officials caught wind of the latter idea, they banned the holding of *Iftar* meetings.[37] In order to evade the security establishment, Brotherhood leaders decided that members of the Shura Council should meet in small groups across the country to get to know one another and establish the ground rules for future Guidance Bureau elections. Government security forces raided one such meeting at the home of businessman Nabil Muqbil in Giza and arrested sixteen Shura Council members, including 'Esam al-'Aryan, head of the Brotherhood's Political Office, and Dr. Mahmoud Hussein, a member of the Guidance Bureau. Following these arrests, the Guidance Bureau elections were again postponed. As Abd al-Mun'im Abu al-Futouh observed, "The Egyptian regime has blocked every effort of the Brotherhood to renew its blood through arrests and military trials."[38]

The Brotherhood faced an ongoing dilemma: how could its legislative assembly elect a new executive board when it had not been free to meet as a group since 1995? By 2008 the situation had become acute: two acting Guidance Bureau members were in prison, one had died, and two more were frequently absent because of their advancing age and health problems. In May, limited elections (intikhabat takmiliyya) ended up adding five members to the Guidance Bureau on a provisional basis. In order to stay under the radar of state security, the elections were conducted by tamrir, that is, with election committee members passing by the homes of Shura Council members to collect their votes. How many Shura Council members participated in these elections, and whether they were truly free and fair, is unclear. Yet in a controversial article, "How Does the Brotherhood Choose Its Leaders?" published shortly after the elections concluded, Abd al-Mun'im Mahmoud, a prominent young Brotherhood blogger, alleged that senior Guidance Bureau members had "instructed" Shura Council members to vote for the list of candidates they favored.[39] As he elaborated in an interview a month later, "Because of these irregularities, the elections maintained a facade of democracy but were far from democratic in practice."[40] At the same time, senior Guidance Bureau members indicated their adamant opposition to the election of 'Esam al-'Aryan, an obvious contender for a seat, because of his liberal positions on the status of women and Coptic Christians, as well as some controversial statements he had made in support of a two-state solution to the Israeli-Palestinian conflict.[41] When al-'Aryan came in sixth in the elections, the Guidance Bureau decided to limit new members to the five candidates who had received the highest number of votes.

Strikingly, all five of the new Guidance Bureau members—Muhammad Sa'd al-Katatni and Sa'd al-Husseini, both of whom represented the Brotherhood in parliament, as well as Muhi Hamid, Osama Nasr, and Muhammad Abd al-Rahman—were identified with the conservative wing of the movement. After the results were announced, several Brotherhood insiders publicly challenged the manner in which the new members had been selected. As Abd al-Mun'im Abu al-Futouh noted, under exceptional circumstances, the Guidance Bureau can assume the technical functions of the Shura Council but cannot arrogate the right to choose its members, that is, it cannot "elect itself," an allusion to the influence exerted by Guidance Bureau members in support of their favored candidates.[42]

The issue of al-'Aryan's candidacy—and conservative leaders' fierce resistance to it—resurfaced when it was proposed that al-'Aryan be appointed to the

Guidance Bureau post vacated by the death of Muhammad Hilal at the age of ninety in October 2009, according to a provision in the charter stipulating that a vacancy created by death or incapacitation should be filled by whichever losing candidate won the most seats in the previous elections. According to Abd al-Mun'im Mahmoud, a number of "second- and third-tier members" (a reference to the Brotherhood's younger cadres) warned of an open rebellion if al-'Aryan were denied the seat. In addition, the Supreme Guide, Muhammad Mahdi 'Akef, who had long sought to achieve a balance among the group's internal factions and who strongly supported al-'Aryan's nomination, walked out of a Guidance Bureau meeting at which objections to al-'Aryan's appointment were raised.[43] Nevertheless, Hilal's seat remained unoccupied.

A few months before this incident, in August 2009, Muhammad Mahdi 'Akef announced that he would step down as Supreme Guide when his term expired in January 2010; this would be the first time in the organization's history that the *murshid* did not remain in the position until his death. 'Akef's decision raised the question of whether an entirely new Guidance Bureau should be elected right away or whether the elections should be postponed until a new Shura Council had been elected. The conservative faction, dominated by Secretary-General Mahmoud 'Ezzat, insisted on holding elections for the Guidance Bureau as quickly as possible, allegedly in order to exploit their influence among the members of the existing Shura Council to ensure the victory of their chosen candidates. Another group, headed by Muhammad Habib, wanted to postpone the elections until June 2010, after a new Supreme Guide and a new Shura Council had been elected.[44] In the end, 'Ezzat's recommendation prevailed, and elections for a new Guidance Bureau were held in December 2009.

The elections generated a great deal of controversy. As Brotherhood youth blogger Ibrahim Hudeibi recalled, "Mahmoud 'Ezzat went on Al-Jazeera on a Thursday to announce the elections; they were held on Friday and Saturday, and the results were announced on Sunday. The Brotherhood hadn't conducted elections in ten years, saying it was impossible due to security pressures. So how could they hold such elections so quickly?"[45] Several Guidance Bureau candidates lodged formal complaints, alleging that the integrity of the elections had been compromised by haste and disorganization.[46] Since surveillance by government security agents made it impossible for the Shura Council to convene as a group, the elections took place in small groups or by visiting the homes of Shura Council members to collect their votes. According to Hudeibi and other internal sources, some members were not at home, and others were not given a ballot. Aboul 'Ela Madi, an ex-Brotherhood member, claimed that the election commission deliberately avoided passing by the homes of members with known reformist orientations (he estimated a quarter of the council members were reformers), skewing the results.[47] Further, there was no independent body to vet such complaints and determine whether the procedures used in the elections were fair. As Hudeibi recalled, "I proposed that Tariq Bishri or Mohammad Salim al-'Awa [two independent Islamist lawyers] be brought in to offer their opinion, but they [the Brotherhood leadership] refused."[48]

When the results of the elections were announced, both Abd al-Mun'im Abu al-Futouh, the Guidance Bureau's most outspoken reformist, and Muhammad Habib, a pragmatist who had helped mediate between the conservative and reformist wings, lost their seats. The four new Guidance Bureau members included three leaders associated with the conservative da'wa wing of the movement—plus 'Esam al-'Aryan. Although al-'Aryan's victory can be seen as a concession to reformist pressures, it was widely alleged that he gained the support of the old guard only after agreeing to "dissociate himself from his reformist colleagues."[49] Following the elections, Muhammad Habib questioned the integrity of the elections in an interview with Al-Jazeera. Shortly thereafter, 'Esam al-'Aryan published a response on the Brotherhood's website in which he stressed that Abu al-Futouh had decided not to seek another term on the Guidance Bureau and that the conduct of the elections had proceeded as fairly as possible under existing security constraints. While al-'Aryan admitted that the timing and the conduct of the elections had raised some hackles, "consensus is impossible because of the divergence in the viewpoints and personal preferences" of Brotherhood members.[50]

One of the most important aspects of the Guidance Bureau elections of 2008 and 2009 was the emergence of the group's charter (la'iha) as a central point of contention. Prominent reformist figures and young bloggers insisted that the elections be held in strict conformity with the charter's rules. More generally, they argued that fidelity to the charter was necessary to ensure that the principles of democratic representation and accountability, which the Brotherhood supported in the broader political system, were also applied in the Brotherhood itself. The appeal to the charter can be seen as an effort to limit the ad hoc authority of the Supreme Guide and the Guidance Bureau by insisting that they make important decisions in consultation with the Shura Council and its subunits in the provinces. It is not surprising that such attempts generated resistance. As Abd al-Mun'im Mahmoud observed, the revised version of the charter was not readily available to Brotherhood members, and when someone asked to see it, some senior leaders responded by questioning his loyalty to the organization, sometimes even accusing him of working for the security police.[51] It was not until late December 2009, after the conclusion of the Guidance Bureau elections, that the charter was finally posted on the Brotherhood's official website.

The Brotherhood held a third round of elections in January 2010, this time to select a new Supreme Guide. The victory of Muhammad Badi', a sixty-seven-year-old professor of veterinary medicine who had been arrested with Sayyid Qutb in 1965 and spent nine years in prison under Nasser, further consolidated the position of the conservative da'wa wing at the apex of the group. Having spent most of his political career working within Brotherhood circles, Badi' was a quintessential insider. He had served two terms as the secretary-general of the veterinarians' syndicate in the late 1980s, but according to others active in syndicate politics at the time, he continued to prioritize his work within the *jama'a* over cooperation with other social and political groups. As Aboul 'Ela Madi observed:

> Those of us coordinating the Brotherhood's strategy in the syndicates decided that Badi' was the appropriate choice as the Brotherhood's candidate for the secretary-general of the veterinarians' syndicate, given his position as a senior professor in the field. But as secretary-general he didn't spend much time at the syndicate office and did not play an active role in the organization. It became clear that he wasn't convinced of the value of public work and that he didn't like it; for example, he did not initiate any successful programs during his tenure. This is one of the major reasons why the Brotherhood was voted out of power in the syndicate in the early 1990s.[52]

Not only was the new Supreme Guide a veteran leader closely aligned with the *da'wa* wing of the group, but so were three of the four individuals appointed as his deputies. Rashad Bayoumi, Gum'a Amina, and Mahmoud 'Ezzat (the former secretary-general) were all staunch conservatives; only Khayrat al-Shatir, the fourth deputy, can be considered an intermediary figure with ties to the reformist camp. As Ibrahim Hudeibi recalled:

> When the names of the deputies were announced, I said, "This is organizational suicide." All four of them are from the conservative wing. There is no balance, and this is not healthy for the organization.[53]

While the *da'wa* faction managed to achieve a virtual monopoly over the Brotherhood's executive branch, the ad hoc authority historically exercised by the Supreme Guide and his deputies became a target of heightened scrutiny and debate. From the outset, Badi', as a less charismatic and influential figure than previous Supreme Guides, adopted a more low-key approach, running the Brotherhood in close consultation with other group members rather than launching any bold initiatives of his own. Badi''s authority was further compromised by allegations that the old guard had secretly engineered his election in clear violation of the rules.[54] As Egyptian analyst Khalil al-Anani observed, "Although Badi' attempted to draw a veil over any procedural irregularities surrounding his election, the shadow of suspected illegitimacy will lurk behind every decision he makes."[55]

Finally, the new Supreme Guide and Guidance Bureau faced greater pressure to respond to demands for broader democratic oversight of their executive functions than at any previous period in the Brotherhood's history. As blogger Mustafa al-Naggar observed,

> The calls for transparency after the recent elections have forced the old guard to accede to these internal pressures, to the idea that decisions must be made in con-

formity with the laws. Before 2007 no one talked about these things, but now, with Brotherhood members using blogs, Facebook, and independent websites, there is open information, and people can know what is going on. The new media has become a tool of pressure, and taboos have been broken. As a result, the old model of "Listen and Obey" doesn't work anymore. The old guard can't simply say, "Who are you to question our authority?" They have to respond.[56]

In addition to invoking the charter as a constraint on executive power, reformist leaders in the Brotherhood began to push for its revision. For example, some argued that in future elections, candidates should be permitted to nominate themselves and be required to circulate their programs to voters. Others proposed that women, who had come to play an increasingly active role in the group, particularly during elections when they helped bring out the vote, be given full membership and voting rights. Independent Islamists weighed in as well. For example, in a controversial article published in June 2008, Heba Raouf Ezzat, a prominent independent female Islamist scholar, proposed fundamental changes in the charter, including a stipulation that the Supreme Guide should be no older than fifty and be limited to one three-year term, and that the Brotherhood appoint two official spokesmen, a woman and a youth under the age of thirty.[57] Though the Brotherhood's senior leaders did not follow up on any of these proposals, they were no longer in a position to ignore them. As al-Naggar observed in 2010, "What the old guard says now is, 'We acknowledge that the charter has some problems, and we will look into them.' They have opened new lines of communication with the youth and, unlike in the past, the advice being offered goes in both directions."[58] If true, this would constitute a significant departure from the past.

Mapping the Brotherhood's Internal Leadership Divisions

By the end of the Mubarak era, the Brotherhood encompassed a broader range of viewpoints, orientations, and interests than ever before. Of particular relevance are three important vectors of differentiation among its leaders. First is whether they spent the bulk of their time working within movement circles— for example, in the socialization and training of new members and the administration of its branch offices—or participated in the wider political system with other social and political groups. Second is whether they subscribed to more conservative or progressive interpretations of Islam, and third is whether they supported change in the group's internal norms and practices. At the same time, Brotherhood leaders had different personalities. For example, some were more opportunistic, prioritizing their own advancement within the ranks of the organization and willing to adjust their positions when expedient, while others, whether conservative or progressive, were motivated more consistently by ideological conviction, even if this diminished their influence within the group's ranks. The general point is that Brotherhood leaders were—and remain—complex and unique individuals with different life experiences, personalities, and motivations, not one-dimensional stand-ins for the movement they represent.

Such internal differentiation is difficult to capture along a single continuum, as the positions taken by individual leaders varied with the issue in question and were open to change over time. Nevertheless, on the eve of the uprising, the Brotherhood's leadership arguably encompassed three distinct trends or factions.

THE DAʿWA FACTION

The first faction in the Brotherhood consisted of its aging leaders, the "old guard," by this time in their seventies, eighties, and nineties. Having devoted long years of service to the *jamaʿa* and survived the persecution of the Nasser era, they were a close-knit group whose authority derived from the traditional respect accorded to the group's elders, as well as the personal sacrifices they had made on the movement's behalf. Members of the old guard occupied a majority of seats in the Guidance Bureau, as well as the position of the Supreme Guide and most of his deputies. Their influence was augmented by their control over the distribution of resources and appointments in the *jamaʿa's* branch offices, as well as the training of new recruits. Though its members were aging, and several key figures had died or been incapacitated by poor health,[59] the old guard retained the support of local functionaries, particularly in provinces of the Delta, like Daqhaliyya and Sharqiyya, where their ties with branch leaders were especially strong.

The old guard favored the continuation of the Brotherhood as a multipurpose organization rather than its conversion into a legal party subject to tighter state control. Although they endorsed the Brotherhood's participation in electoral politics, they remained wary of the liberal values associated with democratic systems in the West. Further, with a more limited history of interacting with figures outside movement networks, they were less careful in their rhetoric and more apt to express views out of sync with the Brotherhood's alleged commitment to democratic norms.

THE PRAGMATIC CONSERVATIVES

A second group within the Brotherhood leadership at the end of the Mubarak era were the "pragmatic conservatives." Compared to the old guard, their views were more flexible, they were generally less advanced in age, and they had wider political experience. Many of them had served as Brotherhood deputies in parliament. Leaders in this group included Khayrat al-Shatir, Muhammad Habib, Muhammad Mursi, and Sa'd al-Katatni (with some, like Mursi, viewed as more conservative, and others, like Habib, as somewhat closer to the reformists). Such figures were more adept than the old guard at explaining the Brotherhood's mission to outsiders and more disposed to adjusting the group's rhetoric and strategy to the demands of its environment. For example, shortly after the 2005 parliamentary elections, Khayrat al-Shatir wrote an open letter to *The Guardian* titled "No Need to Be Afraid of Us," in which he sought to reassure a Western audience of the group's benign intentions. Al-Shatir's pragmatic bent arguably reflected, at least in part, his status as a wealthy entrepreneur with multiple businesses and a large network of contacts in the private sector and the government.[60]

As noted previously, some of the Brotherhood's leading pragmatic conservatives had broad experience in the public domain. For example, both Muhammad Mursi and Sa'd al-Katatni headed the Brotherhood's bloc in parliament during the Mubarak era. As public figures, they developed new political competencies and skills. For example, they became adept in the use of parliamentary rules and procedures, whether to challenge state policy or develop bills of their own. Residing in the Maadi Hotel in Cairo when parliament was in session, Brotherhood deputies met regularly and typically served in two or three of the bloc's nineteen committees, which focused on such areas as education, health, and the economy. In addition, the bloc established a "parliamentary kitchen," which, as Stacher and Shehata observed, was "divided into specialized teams that gather information about issues the MPs deal with in the Assembly." These teams regularly consulted with experts outside the movement for technical assistance in drafting their own positions on national social and economic issues.[61]

Indeed, during the last decade of Mubarak's rule, the Brotherhood was the most active force in parliament. The regular attendance of its deputies at parliamentary committee meetings and general assembly sessions forced members of the NDP, whose attendance was sporadic at best, to show up in force lest the Brotherhood achieve a quorum in their absence. As 'Ali Fath al-Bab, a three-term Brotherhood member of parliament, observed, "the NDP now has to have 100 people in parliament at all times to maintain their majority."[62] Further, Brotherhood deputies took the lead in reviving parliament's long-dormant oversight authority, as indicated by their frequent interpellations of government ministers, published on the Brotherhood's official website. One researcher estimated that from December 2005 to July 2006, the Brotherhood was responsible for 80% of all parliamentary initiatives.

Of course, the Brotherhood's ability to initiate legislation was blocked by the NDP's large majority in parliament. In addition, the NDP prevented Brotherhood deputies from assuming leadership posts in parliamentary committees.[63] Hence the role of the Brotherhood was largely confined to commenting on bills sponsored by the NDP and the regime. But even within these constraints, Brotherhood deputies articulated positions on a wide range of national issues, including the avian flu, housing shortages, unemployment, and corruption, which extended far beyond the moral and religious issues that they had focused on in the past. The determination of Brotherhood MPs to weigh in on broad matters of public policy, and their growing technical capacity to do so, can be seen in their response to the government's annual statement on budgetary and policy priorities in February 2006. As Fath al-Bab recalled,

> MPs only get five minutes each to respond to the statement. This is a document that includes among other matters economic, agricultural, social, foreign, domestic and youth affairs. So we decided to write and publish a response. Our response was 300 pages.[64]

Did the Brotherhood's participation in the People's Assembly contribute to the group's "democratic habituation"? If we restrict our focus to its deputies in parliament, the answer is yes, if we define such "habituation" as increased familiarity with—and competent exercise of—the norms and procedures of representative politics. But when we turn to the impact of participation on the ideological orientations of Brotherhood deputies, the results are more mixed. In many cases, their rhetoric shifted toward a greater emphasis on democratic constitutional and political reforms. But this shift did not necessarily entail a readiness to grant the country's elected leaders unrestricted authority to fashion laws of their own choosing or an endorsement of the full range of civil and political rights associated with democratic systems in the West. For example, Muhammad Mursi, a longtime Brotherhood MP, took the lead in formulating the draft party agenda released in 2007, which envisioned the establishment of a council of religious scholars to vet legislation for conformity with the Shari'a and which limited eligibility for the presidency to a Muslim male. Likewise, Muhammad Sa'd al-Katatni vigorously objected to a proposal introduced in parliament in 2007 to amend Article 1 of the Egyptian Constitution to include a provision guaranteeing the equal rights of all citizens and stormed out of the session in which the bill had been raised. When asked about this incident, al-Katatni explained:

> The concept of citizenship [al-muwatana] is too broad and diffuse; it requires definition. [The problem is that] everything is subject now to the concept of citizenship. If I say that the position of the president should not be occupied by a woman or a Copt, I am accused of discrimination. The critics say, "You are against citizenship." They use it as a weapon against us. . . . The problem with the concept of citizenship is that the rights it entails have not been clearly specified [lam tuhaddad].[65]

Brotherhood deputies also persisted in demanding the stricter regulation of public life to defend the religious foundations of Egyptian society. For example, they opposed government efforts to modernize the curricula in public schools, framing such moves as a concession to foreign pressure and a threat to the country's Islamic values. In November 2006 'Ali Laban, a Brotherhood MP, condemned the education minister's decision to appoint an American education expert to aid in the process of curricular reform as "an act of treason for which the minister should be executed."[66] In addition, Brotherhood deputies favored tighter state control of the media and the censorship of artistic, intellectual, and cultural works deemed offensive to Islam and the conservative sensibilities of Egyptian society. Some deputies were more outspoken on such issues than others, but their positions were arguably consistent enough to suggest a shared conservative outlook within the bloc as a whole. Indeed, a study of the Brotherhood's interpellations during the 2000–2005 parliament found that approximately 80% of them pertained to issues in the fields of culture, media, and education.[67] Until a comparable study is conducted for the 2005–10 parliament, it is difficult to gauge whether this focus on moral and cultural issues subsequently declined. As a general rule, however, the Brotherhood's positions in parliament during the last years of the Mubarak era exhibited an uneasy mix of support for the expansion of public freedoms in some instances and calls for their restriction in others.

Yet in assessing the impact of electoral participation, we must consider not only whether it prompted *change* in the ideology of Brotherhood deputies but also whether it altered the *relative weight* of ideology versus other considerations as a driver of their behavior. Here there is some evidence of a shift: Brotherhood deputies began to attach a higher priority to demonstrating effectiveness in the delivery of services and the representation of the citizens in their districts than to ideological posturing in the People's Assembly. For example, when asked in 2010 about the Brotherhood bloc's biggest achievements in parliament over the previous decade, al-Katatni replied:

> The biggest achievement has been training a large number of Brotherhood deputies in parliamentary practices, and the second is the Brotherhood's opening to society through the activities of the deputies' offices in their respective districts. The regime treats us an illegal organization, but having offices in our districts enables us to interact with the mass public in an official capacity. When a person wants to move to another place, it is very difficult, because he faces a lot of bureaucratic red tape. We have an opportunity to help him. We can also help people find jobs and provide support to the poor by collecting donations from the rich.[68]

Al-Katatni's description of his work as a deputy revealed the extent to which pragmatism trumped ideology as the order of the day. He expressed pride in the fact that a visitor to his district office would find Coptic Christians as well as Muslims seeking assistance: "I told an American journalist to see for himself, and he did. When he saw Christians waiting in the reception hall to speak with someone, he asked them, 'Why did you come here?' and they answered, 'al-Katatni does not discriminate.'"[69]

Perhaps just as significant, when asked whether he supported demands for the immediate application of Shari'a, al-Katatni replied:

> This is not the time for it. We want freedom first! How can I ask for the application of Shari'a when the people can't make their demands, when there is no freedom? One year under the reign of 'Umar Ibn al-Khattab [an early caliph] there was a famine, so for that period he did not implement the *hudoud* laws. How can a robber be punished when he is stealing to eat?[70]

More generally, al-Katatni noted, the main criterion for determining whether a specific Shari'a ruling should be applied was whether it served the public interest (*al-maslaha al-'amma*). Al-Katatni exhibited a similar pragmatic bent when asked if he favored the expansion of the role of women in the Brotherhood:

> At present it is difficult to include women in the *jama'a's* decision-making bodies because their deliberations take place in small meetings behind closed doors. Involving women in these sessions would be awkward; it is an issue of modesty [*hishma*] [rather than any principled opposition to their inclusion]. In addition, security pressures make some leaders reluctant to include women out of fear for their safety. But it is possible that the participation of women will increase in the future, especially if the Brotherhood gains legal recognition and its meetings can be held in public. The door is open.[71]

Within Brotherhood circles, pragmatic conservatives served as a bridge between their more conservative and more progressive counterparts. Indeed, more than any other faction within the Brotherhood's leadership, they can be said to represent the "new mainstream" of the *jama'a*—ideologically more conservative than the reformists but more flexible than the old guard and more experienced in, adept at, and committed to representing the Brotherhood in wider spheres of public life.

The reformist trend was the third main faction in the Brotherhood on the eve of the uprising. As discussed earlier, what distinguished the reformists from their counterparts was their embrace of more progressive interpretations of Islam, their support of greater engagement with other forces in Egyptian society, and their push for fundamental changes in the policy orientations and internal practices of the Brotherhood itself. How did the spike in repression against the Brotherhood after 2005 affect the status of the reformist trend within its ranks? It is to this question that we now turn.

THE WANING OF THE REFORMIST IMPULSE

The influence of the reformist faction waxed and waned with the fortunes of the Brotherhood. In times of political opening, the reformist impulse gained traction, but in times of repression, it lost its resonance as the focus of the group shifted to surviving under siege.

As noted in previous chapters, the reformist faction was closely associated with the middle generation in the Brotherhood, that is, with former Islamist student leaders who joined the group in the late 1970s and early 1980s. But the reformist trend was not a strictly generational phenomenon. First of all, not all members of the "70s generation" evinced a reformist orientation. Particularly in the provinces, many of this age cohort remained fiercely loyal to the movement's old guard. Second, some of the Brotherhood's veteran leaders, such as 'Umar al-Tilmisani, were early proponents of reformist ideas. Third, by the end of the Mubarak era, a new cadre of Brotherhood activists in their twenties and thirties, including an outspoken group of young male and female bloggers, had embraced the reformist agenda of the middle generation as their own.

During the Mubarak era, reformists were represented in the Brotherhood's legislative assembly (the Shura Council) as well as in several of its specialized units, particularly those responsible for its relations with the media and the wider society. The reformists were more receptive than leaders in other factions to interviews with Western journalists and academics (who typically gravitated to them). They were also more open to, and skilled at, representing the Brotherhood at conferences and workshops organized by Egyptian and Western civil society organizations, where they engaged in discussions with secular activists, journalists, and academics not just external to—but often highly suspicious of—the Brotherhood and the Islamic movement more generally. The positions taken by the reformists were often profoundly out of sync with the views of more conservative members of the group's leadership and base. Indeed, some of them, like Abd al-Mun'im Abu al-Futouh, appeared to have changed so much that it was unclear whether they could still be described as Islamist at all. In a provocative article, Egyptian researcher Hossam Tammam highlighted Abu al-Futouh's "absolute acceptance of democracy as a means of decision-making at all levels, seeing it as a common human legacy reflecting the achievements of human development." Tammam continued,

> Nowhere does Abu al-Futouh talk of the "particularities of Arab-Islamic culture" as a constraint on democracy, nor does he cite religious texts and verses, nor does he make any distinction between *shura* and democracy, which Islamists typically cite to justify things which depart from democratic norms. . . . According to Abu al-Futouh, democracy means the rule of the people, and this is not limited to rule of the people according to the Laws of God, but rather it is an absolute commitment to the rule of the people, supporting whatever the people choose, even if it contradicts Islam or rejects it in principle.

Such views, Tammam observed, which were nearly indistinguishable from those of a secular liberal, were "astonishing to the extreme," leading us to wonder, "how can this discourse be Islamic?" Noting the stark gap between Abu al-Futouh's views and those of the Brotherhood's mainstream, Tammam wondered why he hadn't pushed harder to spread his views internally, and if that didn't work, why he didn't resign and bring like-minded members with him, since things had continued as though nothing had changed.[72]

Tammam's comments highlight the dilemma facing reformist leaders. Though they had become increasingly marginalized within the Brotherhood, they had nowhere else to go. In part, the waning of the reformist impulse was a by-product of the increased security pressures facing the group after 2005. During periods of political opening, when restrictions on the Brotherhood's participation eased, the reformist impulse gained resonance. By contrast, calls for progressive ideological and institutional reforms lost currency during periods of repression, which shifted the group's focus to matters of organizational unity and survival.

But the failure of the Brotherhood's reformist wing to cultivate a strong internal following also stemmed from the ways in which its leaders allocated their energies and resources. As Aboul 'Ela Madi observed, by concentrating on "outside activities," the reformists lost the battle for the hearts and minds of the group's base. As he admitted in a moment of frank self-criticism:

> We [middle-generation activists] were all professionals, oriented toward establishing a wider base [jumhur]. We worked with students, professionals, and leaders from other political forces. This was our priority and it took up a lot of time, that is, representing the Brotherhood in the public domain and reaching out to other groups. In the meantime, the conservatives worked to influence the base of the Brotherhood from inside. We were stronger [than the conservatives] in the 1980s and 1990s, but we channeled our energies in the syndicates, in conferences and workshops on matters of national reform, while viewing work in the shu'ab and the usar [the small, local-level units of the Brotherhood] as a waste of time. This was a strategic mistake, which we realized too late. While we were working for the Egyptian people, their [the old guard's] primary interest was in the internal organization. They were socializing the youth of the jama'a to be loyal to them. As a result, the majority of the new leadership cadres are men like they are and we became increasingly marginalized over time.[73]

In what Madi described as the "Great Theft," the old guard succeeded in "stealing" the bulk of the Brotherhood's new recruits.

In sum, while Brotherhood reformists developed friendly ties with a wide range of Egyptian civil and political leaders and were actively courted by Arab and Western journalists and researchers, they never developed an institutional platform from which to mobilize support for their agenda among members of the group's base. Veteran conservatives like Mahmoud 'Ezzat and Rashad Bayoumi—and the tandhimi ("organization") men loyal to them in the group's local branches—retained control over the religious education and training of new recruits. Further, insiders claim that some Guidance Bureau members, Mahmoud 'Ezzat in particular, attempted to inoculate the group's members against reformist ideas by undertaking a systematic campaign to tarnish the reputation of Abu al-Futouh, its most iconic figure. As Ibrahim Hudeibi noted, "If Abu al-Futouh makes a statement about women or Copts, 'Ezzat says nothing about it in public. But within the organization, he sends a message to the provinces that Abu al-Futouh does not represent the Guidance Bureau and has apologized for his comments. This distorts his image among members of the base."[74] Likewise, Abd al-Mun'im Mahmoud observed, "They say he is not *multazim* [committed]. And some have said truly awful things, claiming that he works for the CIA or sells drugs. I told him you will be the first to lose in the Guidance Bureau elections, and I was right." By contrast, Mahmoud said, the conservatives supported al-'Aryan, who, though also identified as a reformist, "holds the stick in the middle"; this was a way to "show they were not excluding the reformists altogether."[75] Abu al-Futouh's defeat in the 2009 Guidance Bureau elections was in a sense a mutual decision, reflecting his growing disillusionment with the Brotherhood's conservative leadership as much as the latter's opposition to him. In sum, Abu al-Futouh remained true to his progressive convictions even when it led to the erosion of his status within the Brotherhood itself.

Although leaders in the reformist trend were becoming increasingly isolated within the Brotherhood, the risk was that in leaving the group they would consign themselves to political irrelevance. The experience of the Wasat party (which, in 2010, fourteen years after its initial bid, had still not received party status) served as a cautionary tale. Defecting from the Brotherhood had enabled Madi and his partners to develop their ideas free of the Brotherhood's disciplining pressures, but it had also diminished their influence within society at large. This trade-off was viewed as too costly by some of the Brotherhood's progressive youth. As Ibrahim Hudeibi observed,

> I have a lot of respect for their platform and I read it with pride. But they have failed as a political experiment. First, they became very confrontational with the Brotherhood and devoted a lot of energy to distinguishing themselves from it. We can all agree that the Brotherhood is immature—it has institutional issues, as well as problems relating to its relationship with other social forces, willingness to abide by the laws, and developing the capacity to address the real-life needs of the country. But what about a mature party like the Wasat? What has it done in the past fourteen years to convince me that it is in my interest to defend its existence?[76]

Mustafa al-Naggar struck a similar tone:

> Their conflict with the Brotherhood takes up all their energies. They don't do anything constructive. What have they done in the past fifteen years to indicate that we should support them? Ideas are not enough. They need to go into the street and mobilize support.[77]

When I relayed such criticisms (without revealing their source) to Madi, he conceded their validity but chose to adopt a longer time horizon: "We are patient, and we made a decision: no organization building until we have a license. I will set my own pace."[78]

THE BROTHERHOOD'S REFORMIST YOUTH

By the eve of the uprising, the reformist cause had been taken up by a new type of Brotherhood activist: young, urban, hip, technologically savvy, and in regular contact with other members of their generation through social networking sites like Facebook and Twitter. In their twenties and thirties, such activists, both male and female, began to articulate their own proposals for Islamist "auto-reform." Some of the most prominent bloggers were offspring of the Brotherhood's elite. For example, Ibrahim Hudeibi is the grandson of Mamoun Hudeibi, the former Supreme Guide, while Asma al-'Aryan is the daughter of 'Esam al-'Aryan. Self-confident, assertive, poised, and well connected, such bloggers helped force the issue of reform onto the agenda of the Brotherhood's inner circle. As Marc Lynch observed,

> With their high visibility and (often) their family ties to the senior leadership, they clearly represent an elite among the youth, one with unusual access to decision-makers. . . . Reformists punch above their weight because they are intellectually engaged, take-charge personalities who have gained the confidence of the leadership.[79]

With the bloggers gaining attention in the Arab and Western media, their demands became harder for senior leaders to ignore. By 2007, Khalil al-Anani observed:

> Some Brotherhood leaders began holding meetings with the youth bloggers, both on general occasions devoted to discussing issues of freedom of opinion and in private meetings, like the one organized between Dr. Muhammad Mursi, the head of the Brotherhood's political division, and a group of young Brotherhood bloggers, which was specifically devoted to an airing of the youths' opinions and criticisms.[80]

The old guard's response to the recommendations of the young bloggers generally took the form of assuring them that their input was welcome, promising to "study the issues," and ultimately setting their proposals on the back burner. In the meantime, some bloggers became even more outspoken in their criticism, denouncing what they saw as the Brotherhood's ideological rigidity, lack of internal democracy and transparency, continued isolation from other social and political forces, and excessive restraint in defending itself from the predatory behavior of an increasingly despotic regime.[81] They reserved their harshest criticism for conservative leaders at the apex of the organization whom they saw as unable or unwilling to break away from outmoded beliefs and practices inherited from the past. As Abd al-Mun'im Mahmoud bluntly put it in an interview with the Associated Press, "those in charge aren't connected with today's world."[82]

Yet some of the Brotherhood's activist youth were also critical of the middle-generation reformists, who, they claimed, took pride in being seen as a progressive force without working hard enough to articulate a clear vision of what they stood for.[83] In addition, they did not devote sufficient time and energy to winning over members of movement's base. As Mahmoud noted:

> The reformists have historically not been courageous enough to present their views clearly and openly to challenge the conservatives, who enjoy greater legitimacy in the *jama 'a* and maintain a stranglehold over the ideological formation of its mass base. The reformists simply have not tried hard enough to absorb these youth.[84]

Indeed, Mahmoud argued, the reformers should be promoting value-change not just in the Brotherhood but within the public at large:

> When the Brotherhood says, "Islam Is the Solution," that is a pragmatic stance, as is their objection to a woman running for president, since the Egyptian people themselves would reject it. It is a form of deference to the public culture and sensibilities. In fact, the Egyptian State Council recently refused to appoint a woman to their bench, and these are the same judges who call for democracy, the judicial supervision of elections, etcetera. That's Egypt! But we say to the reformists, "You must be influential, you must work to change your society."[85]

The results of the Brotherhood's internal elections in 2009 and 2010 only deepened the alienation of progressive youth, but their options were few. As al-Anani observed,

> Many younger members of the organization are in a state of shock following the elimination of reformists from a hierarchy now dominated by elderly, conservative hardliners. A good many young reformers would now love to leave the Brotherhood, their problem being that there is nowhere for them to go.[86]

Such youth signaled their disillusionment by not attending Brotherhood meetings and events and, in some cases, by freezing their memberships.[87] For example, Ibrahim Hudeibi decided to leave the Brotherhood in 2007 and formally submitted his resignation in 2008. As he put it, "I realized that this is not where I fit. The organizational problems go beyond my ability to solve them; I am not a politician."[88] Abd al-Mun'im Mahmoud froze his membership in 2008,[89] and Mustafa al-Naggar followed suit in 2009. As al-Naggar explained, "I got fed up, so I decided to take a vacation. I froze my membership after what happened to 'Esam al-'Aryan [in the 2009 Guidance Bureau elections]." Al-Naggar, however, later returned to the Brotherhood, claiming that the establishment of a genuine "two-way dialogue" between the senior leadership and younger members had renewed his optimism in the potential for change from within.[90]

Activist youth were quick to point out that their views were out of sync with mainstream opinion in the Brotherhood. As Abd al-Mun'im commented,

> There are those within the Brotherhood that use technology and are open-minded about the world. I am with [this] group, but we are a minority. The problem with those analysts attracted to our language is that they fell in love and started running behind us. That is not the Brothers.[91]

Likewise, he told me, "The number of Brotherhood youth who share our progressive ideas you can count on one hand. We are very few, maybe a hundred people, and that's it. And remember, I myself am not a member of the Brotherhood anymore."[92]

Indeed, while a handful of hip, worldly youth articulated bold visions of reform on their blogs, the composition of the Brotherhood's senior leadership cadres was becoming increasingly rural and conservative. As Hossam Tammam observed in 2010, the locus of power and initiative was shifting from Cairo and Alexandria to branch offices in the provinces:

> In recent Muslim Brotherhood elections, five members of the group's Shura Council won seats in the Guidance Bureau. Most of those were either from rural areas or people with a pronounced rural lifestyle. . . . Over the past decade or so most of the newcomers to the Guidance Bureau were from the countryside: Mahmoud Hussein from Assiut, Sabri 'Arafat Komi from Daqahliya and Muhammad Mursi from Sharqiyya. Rural governorates, such as Assiut, Minya, Daqahliya and Shariya, are now in control of much of the Muslim Brotherhood, especially middle-ranking posts, while Cairo and Alexandria have seen their status gradually erode.

This trend was encouraged by the Brotherhood's old guard, Tammam noted, because "rural people are less prone to challenging their leaders." Tammam highlighted the "ruralization" of the group's internal norms and practices:

> Over the past few years, the Muslim Brotherhood has been infused with rural elements. Its tone is becoming more and more patriarchal, and its members are showing their superiors the kind of deference associated with countryside traditions. You hear them referring to their top officials as the "uncle hajj," "the big hajj," "our blessed one," etc. Occasionally, they even kiss the hands and heads of the top leaders. Not long ago, a Muslim Brotherhood parliamentarian kissed the hand of the Supreme Guide in public.[93]

Other manifestations of this trend included a greater emphasis on ritual, a reaffirmation of the duty of absolute loyalty and obedience to the group's elders, and growing intolerance of self-criticism. Tammam concluded, "It is my belief that the countryside is affecting the Muslim Brotherhood more than the Muslim Brotherhood is affecting it."[94]

Brotherhood insiders, as well as other researchers who have studied the group closely for many years, also noted the growing influence of Salafi ideas and practices among members of the Brotherhood's rank and file. The Salafi movement, which bore the imprint of Wahhabi ideas imported from the Gulf, embraced a highly literalist and puritanical reading of Islam's sacred texts and urged strict conformity with Islamic codes of behavior, such as praying five times a day and the veiling and seclusion of women. The cultural gap between the progressive bloggers based in Cairo and the Salafi youth of the provinces could not have been more stark. As Marc Lynch observed:

> While the politically engaged *shabab* [youth] of Cairo peruse the columns of liberals, nationalists and the Islamist-leaning intellectual Tariq al-Bishri, the Salafi youth restrict their attention to Islamic pamphlets and proselytizing. Where the bloggers think nothing of discussing movies or music, the Salafis cultivate a spartan aesthetic that radiates disdain for popular culture. Indeed, the gap between the stylishly dressed, clean-shaven blogging Brothers and their bearded Salafi counterparts can seem as wide as that between the Salafis and Western-oriented youth.[95]

Some observers have suggested that the growing influence of Salafi ideas— transmitted by Salafi preachers, mosques, and satellite television stations— among younger, poorer Egyptians, and among Brotherhood members in particular, reflected their growing disillusionment with *siyasa* (high politics) and their subsequent retreat into private piety and observance.[96] Whatever the cause of the Salafi trend's growing influence, it prompted intensely religious individuals to insulate themselves from the wider culture. As Abd al-Mun'im Mahmoud put it,

> The Salafis are very conservative, they go to the mosque, they don't watch TV, they remain within their own small circles. It is like they live inside a box. They don't know how to leave the box and they can't imagine life outside it. And when they do step out of the box, they feel alienated and want to return to it.[97]

PARTICIPATION AS A STRATEGIC CHOICE

The consolidation of the old guard's monopoly on executive power in the internal elections of 2009 and 2010 triggered predictions in the Arab and Western media that the Brotherhood would retreat from the political stage and redirect its energies back to the *da'wa* and social service activities it had prioritized in the past.[98] However, the Brotherhood gave no indication that it intended to withdraw from the field of electoral politics. Participation was no longer a tactic but a strategic choice perceived by Brotherhood leaders as serving the group's long-term interests, regardless of which faction was at the helm. As Khalil al-Anani noted: "Any suggestion that the Muslim Brotherhood will withdraw from engagement in political life because of the conservatives' control over the organization is logically flawed. Political involvement is vital to the MB if it is to score political gains, sustain its connection with the public and . . . recruit new members."[99]

While the Brotherhood remained committed to participation as a matter of principle, whether to run candidates in a particular national or local election, and for how many seats, would be determined on a case-by-case basis. As Gamal Nassar, the Brotherhood's director of public relations, explained:

> Participation is the foundation [*asl*]. That is, as a matter of principle we participate in all elections. But each election has its own circumstances, and the number of candidates we run depends on the situation.[100]

Yet the strengthening of the conservative faction subtly altered the *character* of the Brotherhood's participation. First, it reinforced the group's habit of pragmatic self-restraint. As the organization's new Supreme Guide, Badi' toned down its oppositional rhetoric. For example, in his first statements to the media, Badi' struck a conciliatory note, alleging that the Brotherhood had not been "for one day an adversary of the regime" and emphasizing its commitment to gradual reform.[101] Further, when President Mubarak traveled to Germany in March 2010 for medical treatment, Badi' and other Brotherhood leaders issued statements to the media wishing him a speedy recovery. Appealing to Mubarak as "the father of all Egyptians," Badi' implored him to look at what was happening in the country's prisons, such as the brutal mistreatment of political prisoners. Such statements provoked the ire of some youth activists. As Abd al-Mun'im Mahmoud remarked:

> Badi' says Mubarak should come see how political prisoners are being treated, but he is the one who imprisoned them! The leaders claim to want change, but they are unwilling to launch demonstrations. So what does change mean for them? They say it means change in the behavior and values of the people, but they refuse to confront the system [*nidham*]. You are the largest political opposition in the Arab world. Why don't you act like one?[102]

In a second shift, the conservatives at the helm of the Brotherhood were less inclined to downplay the traditional Islamist elements of its platform in a bid for social acceptance. As Tammam observed,

> The conservative faction is more interested in working from within to cultivate a strong disciplined movement than in engaging with other political forces and intellectual currents in Egyptian society. They place a higher premium on the spiritual

education and social upbringing of the movement's base than on developing a comprehensive reform program that would appeal to a broader audience.[103]

In the run-up to the fall 2010 parliamentary elections, Brotherhood leaders held a series of meetings with secular opposition parties, coordinating their campaigns to avoid competing for the same seats. Yet they did not attempt to articulate a common agenda that would have required a compromise of their principles.

Third, while the idea of submitting a formal application for legal party status continued to surface every now and then, in private discussions in the spring of 2010 the new leadership made it clear that it would not push to form a party if doing so required the dissolution of the *jama'a* or the stricter regulation of its public outreach activities. In the view of its senior leaders, the costs of legality, which would subject the Brotherhood to tighter state control, exceeded its benefits.

Abu al-Futouh's Gambit

In early 2010, with a new round of parliamentary elections set to begin in the fall, a few members of the Brotherhood began to openly question whether the group should continue to run candidates in a system manipulated by the regime to its own advantage. "Participation as usual" became harder to justify in light of the maneuvers undertaken by the regime since 2005 to control the outcome of elections. Constitutional amendments introduced in 2007 eliminated the previous requirement that a standing judge be present at every polling station and granted a new body, the Higher Electoral Commission (HEC), full oversight over the conduct of elections and vote counting. Seven of the HEC's eleven commissioners were appointed by the NDP-controlled lower and upper houses of parliament, undermining its alleged status as an "independent and neutral" body.[104] Moreover, the regime appeared resolved to prevent the Brotherhood from repeating its strong performance in the 2005 elections. The more energy and resources the Brotherhood invested in any future electoral campaigns, the more likely it would face a new round of repression.

Interestingly, it was Abd al-Mun'im Abu al-Futouh who first proposed that the Brotherhood break from the strategy of participation it had pursued in the past. Since the 1980s, the reformists had urged the Brotherhood to take full advantage of the opportunities for participation available under authoritarian constraints. Yet by early 2010 a striking shift had occurred. In February, Abu al-Futouh issued a provocative statement calling on the Brotherhood to abstain from contesting parliamentary elections for the next twenty years, an idea quickly and categorically rejected by the Supreme Guide and the Guidance Bureau.[105] In a seeming reversal of roles, it was the old guard who framed participation as a inviolable right, while Abu al-Futouh appeared to be crumbling under duress. Abu al-Futouh's proposal was condemned as defeatist by the old guard, but a closer look at his reasoning suggests that it was anything but. Abu al-Futouh did not ask the Brotherhood to withdraw from political life but to abstain from running its own candidates and instead back whatever party or candidate could serve as an effective catalyst for reform. In this way, Abu al-Futouh argued, the Brotherhood could rob the regime of its running excuse for blocking any meaningful change in the political system and enable the Brotherhood and other groups to forge a united democratic front.[106]

Abu al-Futouh's proposal was even shocking to Brotherhood youth who shared his outlook. Abd al-Mun'im Mahmoud questioned his claim that the Brotherhood's participation was an impediment to reform:

> Since when has the Brotherhood ever competed for power since the 1970s? Has the Brotherhood ever had a strategy of contesting for power in Egypt, taking into account that parliamentary contestation is not a competition for power since the Egyptian parliament is nothing more than an arm of the regime itself?[107]

He argued that what Abu al-Futouh should have done instead was persuade the Brotherhood to confront the regime head-on:

> We would have expected Dr. Abd al-Mun'im Abu al-Futouh to call on the Brotherhood to make its political participation commensurate with its actual power as the largest force on the field. We would have thought he would call on the jama'a to break out of its organizational cocoon into the field of open public work to confront the dictatorial regime and not to content itself with denunciations, and to assume its rightful position as the leader of the people, enlightening them and inciting them against the conditions of dictatorship in which they live.[108]

Both Abd al-Mun'im Abu al-Futouh and Abd al-Mun'im Mahmoud, his younger and more defiant counterpart, urged the Brotherhood to become a more effective catalyst for change, albeit in different ways. But neither of their proposals gained much traction among the group's senior leaders, who had, in a sense, resigned themselves to the role they had been allotted by the regime. A conversation between Abd al-Mun'im Mahmoud and Abd al-Rahman al-Barr, a member of the Guidance Bureau and the Brotherhood's new mufti (senior religious authority), was particularly revealing in this regard. As Mahmoud recalled, "I said to al-Barr, 'You are an opposition movement! Why don't you act like one?' And he replied, 'No, we are not just a political force, our involvement in politics is only one part of our broader da'wa mission.'" As Mahmoud elaborated, "They feel that if they engage in religious outreach, and provide services, and build up the organization, that in itself is a form of success. We tell them, 'We want you to move [yuharrik] the masses. Don't you see, you are just playing a role in the system as it is!'"[109]

The key point is that the Brotherhood's senior leaders did not measure the group's achievements in terms of how many seats it won in parliament or in terms of how much immediate pressure it was able to mobilize for regime change. Adopting a longer time horizon, they defined progress as the spread of Islamic values and norms of behavior, paving the way for that time in the future when the people would demand the application of Shari'a themselves. In sum, their accommodation to the narrow margin of participation allowed to them under Mubarak reflected their commitment to the Brotherhood's broader mission, the success of which did not hinge on political gains alone.

THE LAST ELECTION OF THE MUBARAK ERA

By 2010 a new dynamic had emerged in Egypt with the rise of Muhammad Baradei, former chief of the International Atomic Energy Agency (IAEA), as a leading advocate of reform. With parliamentary elections approaching in the fall and presidential elections expected the following spring, Baradei forged a network called the National Association for Change (NAC) and urged the opposition to unite behind a seven-point reform agenda. Among other things, the agenda called for an end to the state of emergency, a lifting of restrictions on independent candidates for president, and the resumption of full judicial supervision of all future elections. Baradei hinted that he might run for president if the integrity of the election process was ensured. To mobilize pressure for reform, the NAC launched an online petition, hoping to secure a million signatures. As Baradei told a crowd of supporters in August, "that will be a message to the regime that it is time to pack your bags and go."[110]

The government's refusal to meet the NAC's demands prompted Baradei to call for a boycott of the fall parliamentary elections to deny what was expected to be a deeply compromised process any shred of legitimacy. As Baradei explained at an NAC meeting in September: "If nobody but the national party runs, then the regime will have to give in to us," noting on his Twitter page that "Total boycott of elections & signing petition R first steps 2 unmask sham 'democracy.'"[111]

Two liberal parties, al-Ghad (Tomorrow) and the National Democratic Front, quickly endorsed the boycott, but as marginal parties unlikely to win more than a few seats they arguably did not have much to lose. Egypt's older and better-organized groups, including the Brotherhood, the Wafd, and the Tagammu' party, faced a harder choice. Like Baradei and the NAC, they fully expected the Mubarak regime to intervene in the elections, and they supported Baradei's calls for reform. But they were reluctant to give up their representation in parliament. While a vocal contingent in each group urged their leaders to join the boycott, others insisted that they run. Within the Brotherhood, those in the latter camp framed participation as an exercise of the group's legitimate rights. As ʿEsam al-ʿAryan declared, "The lesson is not to be absent, not be out of the scene. We are living in this society. We are a popular power. We must present our popularity as a whole and in the system." In addition, al-ʿAryan argued, participation would enable the opposition to hold the government accountable for its actions: "When we boycott, the regime can say that there was no fraud; that the election was free and fair. When we participate, the regime has to face us."[112]

After much debate, all three groups decided to move forward with their election campaigns, much to the dismay of those who had wanted the opposition to present a united front against the regime. In an indication of the controversy surrounding this decision, the Brotherhood's Guidance Bureau conducted a poll of Shura Council members before announcing its decision to run in October. While Brotherhood spokesmen claimed the survey indicated "overwhelming support" for participation, later reports indicated that the proposal won by a narrow majority.[113] Further, just days before the Brotherhood's decision was announced, a new bloc calling itself the Brotherhood Reformers issued a public statement urging the Guidance Bureau to boycott the elections, which they described as "farcical." Twenty current and ex-leaders of the Brotherhood signed the statement, including Ibrahim al-Zaʿfarani; his wife, Jehan al-Halafawi (the first woman to run for parliament as a Brotherhood candidate, in 2000); Kamal al-Halabawi, the Brotherhood's longtime representative in Europe; Mukhtar Nuh, a prominent Islamist lawyer; Haitham Abu Khalil, an engineer; Khaled Dawoud, a journalist; and Abd al-Hayy al-Faramawy, a professor.[114] Such figures had criticized the Guidance Bureau in the past, but this was the first time they weighed in as a group—and in public—on an important policy issue. Further, Haitham Abu Khalil, whose membership in the Brotherhood had been frozen earlier that year, circulated an online petition in support of the boycott, which had reportedly gained five hundred signatures by October, mostly from Brotherhood youth.[115]

The Brotherhood entered the parliamentary elections in 2010 fully expecting to lose many of the 88 seats it had won in 2005, with some leaders predicting it would win as few as 15 seats. The Brotherhood fielded 135 candidates, or roughly 25% of the 508 seats open to contestation (increased from 444 in 2005 with the addition of 64 seats reserved for women). The Ministry of the Interior disqualified many of the Brotherhood's candidates, however, after which just over 100 remained.[116]

The elections proceeded in two rounds, beginning on November 28 and December 5, respectively. Government intervention in the polling process was even more aggressive than anticipated. By the end of the first round, numerous reports had surfaced of security agents blocking voters' access to polling stations in hotly contested districts, as well as multiple instances of vote buying and ballot stuffing.[117] The Brotherhood reported that more than 1,200 members and supporters had been arrested, and Muhammed Saʿd al-Katatni, the head of the Brotherhood's parliamentary bloc, claimed that he was assaulted when campaigning in his home district in Minya.[118] The official results of the first round of balloting indicated that the NDP had won 208 of 221 seats and the Brotherhood had won none. Protesting what it described as a systematic pattern of vote rigging and fraud, the Brotherhood pulled out of the elections altogether before the runoff on December 5. In the end, the NDP won 420 seats, or 83% of the total, with most of the remainder going to independents aligned with the ruling party. Opposition parties combined won just 15 seats, or 3% of the total.[119]

The 2010 elections all but eviscerated the opposition in parliament and left the Brotherhood with no representation at all. Intended to consolidate the regime's grip on power ahead of the presidential race in the spring, the fraudulent elections ended up eroding the legitimacy of the political system as a whole. In addition, the elections encouraged the opposition, long divided by partisan and personal rivalries, to unite. After the results were announced, Brotherhood leaders met with representatives of the NAC, the Kefaya movement, the Wafd, and the Democratic Front Party to coordinate strategy. On December 13, as parliament opened its first session, a diverse mix of opposition leaders, including a number of former MPs, held a vigil outside the State Council Court in Cairo, vowing to spearhead a legal battle to nullify the election results and dissolve parliament. As Akram al-Sha'ir, one of the eighty-eight Brotherhood deputies who lost his seat, declared at the rally: "We seek the establishment of a genuine parliament, a representative parliament, as opposed to the falsified parliament that exists today."[120] Further, approximately twenty opposition figures announced their plan to form a "parallel parliament" that would monitor the activities of the legislature and hold it accountable to the people's will.[121] By early January 2011 the Brotherhood, the Wafd, and several smaller opposition parties had signed on. As Muhsin Radi, a former Brotherhood MP, explained, the Brotherhood's participation was required to unite the country's patriotic forces and serve the public interest. In addition to monitoring the work of the official legislature, he noted, the parallel parliament would formulate its own proposals for reform and begin work on a new constitution.[122] For the Brotherhood, the 2010 parliamentary race was a defining moment. Up to that point it had opted to participate according to the regime's rules so as not to be shut out of the political system altogether. But the 2010 elections exposed this strategy as an exercise in futility. By the start of the uprising, the Brotherhood had joined with other sectors of the opposition to push for systemic change.

REVISITING THE PARTICIPATION-MODERATION THESIS: THE LESSONS OF THE EGYPTIAN CASE

A review of the Brotherhood's arc of participation during the Mubarak era yields some interesting findings. Operating without legal standing and at chronic risk of repression, the Brotherhood adopted a strategy of pragmatic self-restraint, deliberately not calling its supporters into the streets or mobilizing them for sweeping electoral victories for fear that flexing their political power too aggressively would trigger a direct confrontation with the state. More broadly, the Brotherhood accepted a limited role in the country's political life and refrained from mobilizing its considerable resources and mass support to push for regime change.

How did participation under authoritarian constraints shape the evolution of the Brotherhood's goals, strategies, and internal practices? As suggested by the foregoing analysis, the question "Did participation lead to moderation?" does not lend itself to a simple "yes" or "no" answer. Different aspects of participation had different effects on the Brotherhood, and these effects were experienced in various ways by the members of different factions. That being said, some broader trends can be discerned.

After thirty years of participation in the formal political system, the Brotherhood had become habituated to the norms and procedures of competitive politics, as indicated by its refusal to be goaded into violence and its support for the alternation of power through free and fair elections. Further, the focus of Brotherhood deputies in parliament shifted away from calls for the immediate application of Shari'a toward engagement with a wider array of national issues and a greater emphasis on the need for democratic reform. This shift in priorities was not limited to the reformist faction of the Brotherhood but extended to its more conservative factions as well. For example, in an interview I conducted in May 2010, Muhammad Mursi echoed the reformists in stressing that the Brotherhood supported the people's right to choose their leaders through free and fair elections. As he elaborated, "Our motives might differ from others, but the mechanisms we support are the same."[123] Likewise, when asked to identify the Brotherhood's highest priorities, Rashad Bayoumi, a staunch conservative and Guidance Bureau member, spoke of repealing the country's Emergency Laws, confronting the climate of corruption, creating space for free expression, and supporting the democratic alternation of power.[124] When asked how such priorities could be harmonized with the application of Shari'a, Bayoumi explained with no small degree of impatience to an apparently obtuse Western researcher that the expansion of public freedoms *was* the call for Shari'a.

The Brotherhood's growing emphasis on freedom and democracy exhibited a clear strategic logic. First, its leaders came to realize that the expansion of public freedoms would make it easier to advance their long-term agenda. That is, lifting authoritarian constraints on public life came to be seen as a prerequisite for progress toward the establishment of Shari'a rule. Second, Brotherhood leaders were confident that a large sector of the Egyptian public shared their views and hence that a shift toward free and fair elections would redound to their advantage.

At the same time, as suggested by Bayoumi's remarks by the eve of the uprising, even conservative members of the Brotherhood had come to embrace a
definition of Islamic rule that, by endorsing strict limits on state power and
making its exercise contingent on the people's consent, represented a sharp
break from the absolutist models of Islamic governance supported by Salafi Islamists and by some of the Brotherhood's own ideologues in the past. Yet by
supporting democracy *with an Islamic frame of reference* and by *equating its
own agenda with the mandates of Islam itself*, the Brotherhood positioned itself
as religiously and morally superior to its rivals. The contradictions between the
religious and democratic elements of its agenda were most pronounced for
members of the Brotherhood's *daʿwa* faction and least pronounced among the
reformists, with the pragmatic conservatives occupying a space in between. Yet
even the reformists were apt to invoke the "fixed values" of Islam and the nation
to justify constraints on freedom of expression, as well as to regulate the behavior of private citizens. *Participation hence prompted the Brotherhood to embrace
the procedural norms of democracy without fully embracing its tolerant and inclusive spirit.*

The impact of participation on the Brotherhood's internal norms and practices was also protracted and uneven. During the Mubarak era, the Brotherhood's administrative structure was expanded to include numerous specialized
bureaus headed by professionals with relevant expertise. In addition, the appointment of the Brotherhood's top leaders gave way to their election by secret
ballot, and term limits were established for members of the Guidance Bureau
and the Supreme Guide. Further, calls for the strict application of the Brotherhood's internal charter (*laʾiha*) challenged the broad powers traditionally exercised by the Supreme Guide and his close advisors. Nevertheless, the evolution
of the Brotherhood into a more professional, routinized, transparent, and internally democratic organization was stunted by the nature of the environment
within which it was embedded, the balance of power among its competing factions, and the nature of its institutional culture.

Stuck in a near chronic state of siege, the Brotherhood was understandably
reluctant to publish information on its structures, activities, finances, and membership rolls. In addition, it was blocked from holding public meetings and
since 1995 had been unable to convene its legislative assembly to elect the
group's executive officers and approve or veto the policy decisions they made on
the group's behalf. The restrictive environment within which it operated hence
impeded the Brotherhood's transformation into a "normal" political actor. Further, the old-guard leaders who dominated the Brotherhood's executive board
were ill disposed—by age, personality, experience, and self-interest—to support
any radical departure from the group's longstanding norms and practices. Finally, as Ibrahim Hudeibi observed, the group's institutional culture, including
its methods of recruitment, training, and advancement, continued to reward
expressions of religious piety and obedience over critical thinking and debate.[125]

While Brotherhood leaders became outspoken proponents of democracy at the level of national politics, the culture of democracy remained weakly developed within the Brotherhood itself.

The uprising that broke out January 25, 2011, dramatically changed the course of Egyptian politics, not least by catapulting the Brotherhood to the center of public life. What role did the Brotherhood play in the protests, and how did it navigate the opportunities and challenges that emerged in its wake? We turn to these questions in the next chapter.

CHAPTER SEVEN

The Brotherhood and the Egyptian Uprising

THE MASSIVE POPULAR UPRISING that erupted in Egypt on January 25, 2011, produced a sea change that no one could have predicted just a few weeks earlier. President Hosni Mubarak, who had ruled the country without any serious challenge for thirty years, resigned from his post after just eighteen days of protest. Yet the success of the uprising was not a function of "people power" alone; it hinged on the support of the Egyptian military, the only institution in the country capable of forcing Mubarak to step down. Though hailed as a "revolution" (*thawra*) in Egypt and in the global media, the uprising did not lead to a dismantling of the authoritarian state nor to the assumption of power by the uprising's leaders. Instead, the Supreme Council of the Armed Forces (SCAF) assumed control of the country's affairs and arrogated to itself the task of supervising the transition to a new political order. The concentration of power in the hands of an institution formerly allied with the Mubarak regime, together with the fragmentation and disorganization of the uprising's leaders, exposed the gap between the aspirations of the protestors and their capacity to translate them into results. Indeed, Egypt's uprising can be said to have produced a "change of regime" without a "regime change,"[1] postponing any fundamental restructuring of the state to some shadowy point in the future.

One outcome of the uprising is indisputable, however, and that is the unprecedented boost it gave to the Muslim Brotherhood, which quickly emerged as the country's most powerful civilian actor. Glimmers of the Brotherhood's dramatic turn of fortune appeared as early as mid-February when one of its members was appointed to the committee formed by the SCAF to amend the constitution, and became even clearer a few months later when the Brotherhood was granted a license to form its own party. But Egypt's sudden political opening also presented the Brotherhood's senior leaders with a host of new challenges. One was to reassure others that they did not seek to dominate the new political order or to push for the immediate application of Shari'a provisions at odds with the uprising's democratic spirit. Another was to manage growing calls for the reform of the Brotherhood that emanated from within the group itself.

Let us look more closely at the origins of the uprising, the Brotherhood's role within it, and the new circumstances in which the Brotherhood found itself after Mubarak stepped down.

THE SEEDS OF CHANGE: THE RISE OF A CROSS-PARTISAN YOUTH NETWORK

The mass protests that began on January 25, 2011, were but the latest in a string of demonstrations staged by Egyptian activists in support of democratic reform. Indeed, in retrospect, the street protests launched by the Kefaya movement in 2004–5 loom as a dress rehearsal for the much larger protests that took place seven years later. During the intervening period, several new groups emerged, including the April 6 movement and Muhammad Baradei's National Association for Change (NAC), that adopted Kefaya's democratic agenda as their own. Such groups shared some common characteristics. First, they were independent of Egypt's political parties. Second, many of them were headed by urban, educated, technically savvy youth, mostly from secular leftist or liberal backgrounds, who utilized Facebook, YouTube, Twitter, and other new social media to coordinate activities and attract new members.[2] For example, the April 6 movement began on Facebook and used it to mobilize support for workers' strikes in the public sector factories of the town of Mahalla al-Kubra in the spring of 2008.[3]

In the years preceding the uprising, a cadre of activist Brotherhood youth began to forge ties of friendship and trust with their counterparts in secular human rights networks at a time when the senior leadership of the Brotherhood remained largely isolated from—and was viewed with suspicion by—other opposition groups. Further, while the Brotherhood's top leaders continued to act in accordance with deeply ingrained habits of caution and self-restraint, such Brotherhood youth were willing—indeed, eager—to confront the Mubarak regime head-on.

Like their middle-generation counterparts, this new generation of activist youth (shabab) typically began their political activity as students, particularly in the large universities of Greater Cairo. During the early 1990s, Brotherhood-affiliated youth were the largest and best-organized faction of the student movement, but their relationship with secular youth leaders was strained. As Islam Lutfi, a former Islamist student leader who went on to become a key figure in the January 25 uprising, explained,

At the time there was a lot of mutual distrust among the various political forces. They [secular groups] saw us as backward, and we saw them as opportunists, not real patriots.... The roots of the animosity were historical, dating back to events that happened thirty or forty years ago.[4]

Some Brotherhood student leaders became convinced that they would be more effective as part of a wider coalition than they would be acting alone. This would provide them with some measure of protection from the security police and encourage students who were reluctant to associate with the Brotherhood to participate in campus politics. As Ahmad Abd al-Gawwad, another Brotherhood student activist and future leader of the uprising, noted:

> Some of the students might be afraid to get involved if we asked them in the name of the Brotherhood. We realized we would be more effective coordinating an event with others; we didn't need to put the Brotherhood slogan on it.[5]

Muhammad Qassas, a Brotherhood student leader a few years Lutfi's senior, proposed that they reach out to their contacts in secular groups at Cairo University to form a coordinating council (lajna tansiqiyya) for political activities on campus. This council was established and later replicated at other universities in the Greater Cairo region, expanding the opportunities for cross-partisan cooperation. As Qassas observed,

> The formation of these committees, which included student leaders from different groups, was unprecedented, at least for our generation. They gave us the new experience of working together and enabled us to get to know each other on a personal level, establishing a pattern of cooperation that continued over the next fifteen years.[6]

Indeed, as Qassas and Lutfi pointed out, the Cairo University student council included several figures who would later emerge as key organizers of the January 2011 uprising.[7]

After they graduated, Qassas, Lutfi, Abd al-Gawwad, and others helped coordinate Brotherhood activities in the universities through their work in the group's student division (qism al-tullab), which included separate units for the media and politics. Though technically under the supervision of the Guidance Bureau, the youth in charge of the Brotherhood's student division exercised a considerable degree of autonomy in practice. For example, together with Nasserist and socialist student leaders, they organized a series of protests against the U.S. occupation of Iraq. Further, in March 2003 they cosponsored a three-day conference called "Against Imperialism and Zionism." Similar conferences focused on resistance to foreign domination were held annually through 2007.[8]

Struck by the decline in cross-partisan cooperation among university students in the mid-2000s, Qassas, Lutfi, and others in the Brotherhood's student division took the lead in establishing new student councils in the universities of Greater Cairo, including those of Helwan, Cairo, 'Ayn Shams, and Al-Azhar. As

Lutfi recalled: "Qassas and I believed in the idea. . . . By now we were the 'older generation,' and through these councils we introduced younger activists of different backgrounds to each other."[9] Hence Brotherhood activists in their thirties used their skill and experience to foster new cross-partisan networks among students in their teens and twenties.

The Brotherhood's activist youth were more inclined than the group's elders to participate in anti-regime protest. For example, when secular youth activists organized a rally in support of a workers' strike in the textile town of Mahalla al-Kubra on April 6, 2008, the Brotherhood's senior leadership held back, uncertain about the identity of the organizers and the scope of their demands. But several young Brothers lobbied the Guidance Bureau for permission to join the rally, not as official representatives of the Brotherhood but in the name of *shabab al-Ikhwan* (Brotherhood youth). After getting the green light, they joined the demonstration and participated in subsequent protests held on the same day in 2009 and 2010. As Abd al-Gawwad observed, "As young people we were not afraid, and we did not face the same risks [as those at the Brotherhood's helm]."[10]

The January 25 uprising exhibited several striking similarities with other protests staged in the years since the Cairo Spring. Like these earlier protests, it was organized by a loose network of youth activists who utilized cell phones, Facebook, YouTube, and Twitter to expose the regime's brutality and to organize activities "offline." The decentralized nature of these networks, as well as the anonymity of their online coordinators, made it more difficult for the security establishment to identify and infiltrate them. In addition, at least initially, such features diminished the extent to which they were perceived as a threat by regime officials.

Yet the January 25 protest was distinguished by two features that set it apart from similar events in the past. First was the success of its organizers in "waking the sleeping giant," that is, in mobilizing huge numbers of ordinary citizens, and second was the rapid escalation in the protesters' demands to include the call for Mubarak's immediate resignation.

THE BACK STORY OF THE UPRISING

The history of Egypt's uprising is still being written, and new details are emerging that will undoubtedly deepen our understanding of its origins and dynamics.[11] My aim here is not to attempt a comprehensive account of the uprising but to offer a brief sketch of some of the key factors that triggered it and document the way it unfolded, focusing on the early contributions of Brotherhood youth, the eventual decision of the Brotherhood to join the protests en masse, and, from that point forward, the group's involvement as a critical actor behind the scenes.

Several developments set the stage for the uprising, a few of which were especially important. First, the regime's blatant interference in the 2010 parliamentary elections convinced the country's opposition groups that the path to reform through formal institutional channels was blocked. As an Egyptian diplomat remarked:

> The situation could have been contained if the past months hadn't been so badly mismanaged. When you force the opposition—all the opposition—onto the streets, that's where they will act. The elections showed an enormous regression, not progress. They seemed to definitively close the door on any opening of the system and prepared the ground for Gamal to succeed his father.[12]

Second, events in neighboring Tunisia galvanized Egyptian youth by demonstrating the efficacy of nonviolent protest as an instrument of political change. The "Jasmine Revolution" in Tunisia began when Mohamed Bouazizi, a twenty-six-year-old street vendor, set himself on fire on December 17 to protest the confiscation of his license, leaving him unable to support his family. Bouazizi's dramatic self-injury, which led to his death on January 3, triggered a huge outpouring of anger in Tunisian cities and towns against longstanding conditions of economic hardship and repression. The protests eventually expanded to include the country's independent trade unions and lawyers' and teachers' associations. On January 14, after twenty-eight days of massive civil disobedience that his security forces were unable to snuff out, President Zine el-Abdine Ben Ali fled to Saudi Arabia and his twenty-three-year dictatorship collapsed. The Tunisian uprising served as a model and source of inspiration for young political activists in other Arab states, including Egypt. On Facebook and other social networking sites, Egyptian youth featured the Tunisian flag and posted messages urging Egyptians to emulate the courage and determination of their Tunisian counterparts. On January 14, about one hundred youth activists from the April 6 movement, Kefaya, and Baradei's NAC demonstrated outside the Tunisian Embassy in Cairo. Some returned to the site the following day but were quickly encircled and outnumbered by rows of heavily armed riot police. As Seif al-Ghadban, a radio announcer affiliated with the NAC, observed, "those people who have the courage to cross the police barriers to come here are few."[13]

Egyptian youth activists learned some valuable tactical lessons from the Tunisian experience, which they applied at home. In an interview with the International Crisis Group on February 3, an Egyptian activist "ticked off specific tactics he had learned, via internet, from the protests in Tunisia: spray-painting the windows of security vehicles and sticking a rag in their exhaust pipes to disable them; and applying vinegar to a scarf to counter the effects of tear gas."[14]

Why did Egyptian youth choose to launch a protest on January 25, a national holiday honoring the Egyptian police who battled the forces of the British occupation in 1952? Here we must trace an arc of events dating back to June 2010, when a young man from Alexandria was apprehended and beaten to death by Egyptian security agents.

Khaled Sa'eed, a twenty-eight-year-old with a job in the import-export business and no ties to any opposition group, was suspected by the police of posting a video on his blog showing police officers divvying up illegal drugs after a bust. The video eventually spread to YouTube, where it joined other clips and photos posted by Egyptian youth on police corruption. On June 6, 2010, two plainclothes officers, one of whom was implicated in the video, tracked Sa'eed down at an Internet café and, according to eyewitnesses, dragged him to a nearby building and subjected him to a savage beating, banging his head repeatedly against an iron door, the steps of the staircase, and the building walls, causing his death. During his family's visit to the morgue, Khaled's brother snapped a photo of the young man's mangled face on his cell phone and posted it on the Internet. The image quickly went viral, and the story of Khaled's short life and violent death was repeated in scores of YouTube videos, where images of Khaled as a boy and young man smiling for the camera were juxtaposed with the photo from the morgue. In addition, a Facebook memorial page for Sa'eed was established anonymously by Wael Ghoneim, a young Egyptian Google executive based in Dubai.[15] As many posts on the Facebook page observed, Khaled's death proved that every Egyptian was a potential victim of police brutality; as the headline of the page declared, "We Are All Khaled Saeed." By the start of the uprising, Khaled's memorial page was the largest human rights website in the country, encompassing close to four hundred thousand members and serving as a distribution point for articles, video clips, and photos documenting other instances of police abuse.[16]

As Jillian York, a Harvard professor, noted: "Prior to the murder of Khaled Sa'eed, there were blogs and YouTube videos that existed about police torture, but there wasn't a strong community around them. This case changed that."[17] Beginning in late June, youth activists utilized the tribute page to coordinate silent protests against police brutality and corruption and demand the punishment of Sa'eed's assailants. Demonstrators dressed in black stood five meters apart along the Nile River, first in Alexandria and later in Cairo and other cities; by spacing out the demonstrators, the organizers sought to circumvent emergency legislation banning the congregation of more than five individuals for political purposes in one place.[18] The protests were staged every week through the summer and continued more sporadically in the fall, when a verdict in the case was postponed pending further inquiry.

The uprising of January 25, 2011, was not the first time that activists had chosen Police Day to protest police brutality. For several years running, the April 6 network had "celebrated" the holiday by uploading the photos of officers accused of torture on the Internet.[19] Yet the outrage over the death of Khaled Sa'eed and the unfolding of the uprising in Tunisia made this Police Day unique. In the weeks leading up to the protest, youth activists involved in the April 6 movement, the Khaled Saʿeed tribute page, and the NAC, as well as youth leaders from the Brotherhood, the liberal Ghad party, and other groups, issued calls on Facebook and Twitter for a massive demonstration on January 25. For example, the administrator of the Khaled Saʿeed tribute page created a Facebook "event" that functioned as an invitation to the protest. When the event showed up on his Twitter feed, Mahmoud Salem, a young blogger, recalled wondering if it was real: "Who does a Facebook event for a revolution, you know?" Yet within a few days more than eighty thousand people had received the invitation and clicked "yes."[20]

To reach as wide an audience as possible, the organizers of the January 25 protest not only spread word of the event online but also distributed flyers on the street and called on others to join them by text message and word of mouth.[21] Initially intending the event as a symbolic protest against police abuses, the organizers added a number of broader demands at the last minute, including the immediate resignation of the minister of the interior, an increase in the minimum wage, the abolition of the Emergency Laws, and a two-term limit on the presidency.[22]

The Role of Brotherhood Youth in the Uprising

A number of Brotherhood youth leaders, already in direct communication with their counterparts in the April 6 movement and other secular youth networks, were involved in planning the January 25 demonstration from the very beginning. A few days before it was scheduled to occur, they asked the Guidance Bureau for permission to participate in the name of shabab al-Ikhwan (Brotherhood youth), but their request was turned down. As Abd al-Gawwad recalled, "It was going to focus on a very sensitive issue, condemning the police and demanding the resignation of the minister of the interior, so they didn't want us to get involved." But the youth leaders persisted. For example, Abd al-Gawwad called ʿEsam al-ʿAryan, a Guidance Bureau member, and told him that it would be embarrassing for the Brotherhood youth to pull out and that doing so would anger their partners in other groups. Abd al-Gawwad and other youth made it clear that they intended to move forward with or without the blessing of the Guidance Bureau; as Abd al-Gawwad recalled, "We told them we're not going to stay home." The Guidance Bureau eventually acquiesced, but only after extracting a promise from the youth not to attack any government official by name. The Brotherhood itself would maintain a position of neutrality, neither supporting the protest nor opposing it. However, the stance taken by the group's branch offices (makatib idariyya) varied. While some instructed their members not to attend the protest, others, like the branch office in the satellite city October 6 on the outskirts of Cairo, announced they would send a contingent to participate.[23]

The Brotherhood's initial reluctance to join the January 25 demonstration reflected the special circumstances it faced as the largest and best-organized sector of the opposition. In an attempt to justify the group's decision not to participate, 'Esam al-'Aryan, in his role as the Brotherhood's official spokesman, explained to al-Dustour that it was a public call launched through Facebook directed at the Egyptian people, not political groups. Further, coordination and planning with other groups was necessary before a decision could be made to call the Brotherhood's supporters into the streets. Moreover, as al-'Aryan told the Daily News Egypt, "we have reservations on the January 25 date, as it isn't just a police holiday, it's a national holiday that honors the Egyptian resistance against the British occupation."[24] The sensitive timing and focus of the protest clearly increased the risks facing the Brotherhood if it decided to participate. At the same time, however, the Brotherhood did not want to remain on the sidelines during a major protest event. As Egyptian researcher Nabil Abd al-Fattah observed: "The Brotherhood is afraid of aggravating security forces against them and are at the same time afraid of missing the opportunity to participate in this widely anticipated protest against the regime."[25] The Brotherhood's decision to support the general demands of the protest and permit its members to participate in it as individuals, without granting the event their official endorsement, reflected such conflicting priorities.

While the Brotherhood's senior leaders remained aloof from the protest, several of the group's activist youth were on the ground from the start. Together with youth from other groups, they spread out across the city of Cairo, setting out from multiple departure points at the same time in order to avoid a massive security crackdown. Further, "they misled the police by announcing and then quickly changing locations, alerting participants to new sites via Twitter, text message and mobile phone."[26] As Abd al-Gawwad recalled, his group initially planned to meet at a cross-section of Gami'at al-Duwal al-'Arabiyya Street, a major thoroughfare in the upscale neighborhood Mohandiseen. But to head off police intervention, they changed plans at the last minute and congregated instead in the nearby area of Nahiyya, part of the densely populated sha'bi ("popular," that is, lower class) neighborhood of Imbaba, whose narrow streets would make it more harder for security officers to pursue them. Nevertheless, they expected the police to catch up with them eventually. As Abd al-Gawwad noted, "Our goal was to march to Tahrir Square, a distance of five or six kilometers, but we didn't expect to make it all the way."

The posters and chants used by the demonstrators made no reference to any partisan agenda. As Abd al-Gawwad stressed, "We didn't raise the slogan 'Islam Is the Solution' or anything like that." Instead, organizers from various groups "wrote the slogans together," which focused on police abuse and demanded the resignation of the minister of the interior. The demonstrators were aided by the booster club of the local Zamalek soccer team, whose members shouted from loudspeakers and beat large drums, much as they did during soccer matches against Zamalek's rivals.[27] Such booster clubs, known as "ultras," helped stir up the crowds in other locations as well.

The organizers of the protest were stunned by the number of people who decided to join them. As Ahmad Mihran, a Brotherhood youth activist, recalled, "We thought we'd attract five hundred people here, and five hundred people there, but five hundred quickly became five thousand. It became clear to us that the people in the street were waiting for something like this."[28] As the International Crisis Group reported:

> The result was unprecedented; for the first time in most protestors' memory, they outnumbered police. Even more shocking, in some places no police were in sight, as protesters paused before apartment buildings and called on those watching to join. Many did.

By day's end, tens of thousands of people had joined the protests in Cairo, many of whom eventually amassed in Tahrir Square. Demonstrations also took place in Alexandria, Suez, and other cities.[29]

THE BROTHERHOOD STEPS IN

Over the next few days as the protests grew in magnitude, the Brotherhood apparently reached the conclusion that its own fate hung in the balance, knowing that it would be the first target of the regime's wrath if the uprising failed. As one leader put it, "Our only card is the mobilization in Tahrir Square. It has been our life insurance against the swing of the pendulum if the regime gets back on its feet."[30] Indeed, just hours after the protests began on January 25, the minister of the interior issued a statement blaming the Muslim Brotherhood for the unrest, and the following day, Guidance Bureau members were warned that they would be arrested if the protests continued.[31] The Brotherhood abandoned its earlier caution and ordered its members into the streets after noon prayers on Friday, January 28, billed by protest organizers as the "Day of Rage." According to one estimate, more than one hundred thousand Brotherhood members joined the demonstrations, most of them in Cairo.[32]

In the days that followed, Brotherhood youth served as a critical liaison between the Brotherhood and other groups, building on the ties of friendship and trust they had established with members of secular youth networks. For example, just days into the uprising, a number of "second-tier" Brotherhood youth in their twenties helped set up the Revolutionary Council of Youth (RCY), which included youth leaders from different political backgrounds.

In addition, Brotherhood youth activists engaged in direct outreach to lower-income residents in the sha'bi neighborhoods of Greater Cairo. As Muhammad Qassas recalled: "I was part of a group that went to Bulaq, while others went to Talbiyya, Imbaba, Shubra, and Dar al-Salaam. We spoke to the people about police brutality but mostly we talked about bread, food, and jobs, about the rise in the cost of a kilo of meat or a kilo of lentils, and the desire to live a free life."[33] Brotherhood youth thus helped connect the political demands of the protestors with the socioeconomic grievances of Egypt's poor.

More generally, Brotherhood youth replaced their elders as the prime movers of events, exhibiting an unprecedented degree of operational autonomy as they tracked new developments and adjusted their tactics in consultation with other youth activists on the ground. As Ibrahim al-Za'farani, a prominent Brotherhood reformist, observed: "They [Brotherhood youth] were on the ground mixing with others and this gave the Brotherhood legitimacy. The Guidance Bureau was forced to depend on them [whether they wanted to or not]."[34]

The Escalation of Protest and the Collapse of the Mubarak Regime

President Mubarak initially hoped to crush the protests in the same way that he had confronted unrest in the past: by deploying the ranks of his vast security apparatus against them. On January 25, security forces opened fire on demonstrators in the town of Suez, leading to several deaths and injuries, and beginning in the early hours of January 26, riot police entered Tahrir Square and used teargas, water cannons, and grenades in an attempt to disperse the crowds.[35] But instead of deterring the protesters, the security crackdown increased their defiance. As one activist observed, "The speed with which people suddenly confronted the security forces and the violence that they used against them came not just as a shock but as an inspiration to all of us who were on the ground, and that fear barrier was within the span of three days taken down."[36] The "Police Day" protest quickly escalated into something much larger, as calls for reform morphed into the demand for Mubarak's immediate resignation, with crowds across the country shouting, "Irhal!" (Get out!) The determination of the organizers to continue the protests until Mubarak stepped down, no matter what the cost, was powerfully expressed by Mustafa al-Naggar, a former Brotherhood activist who joined Muhammad Baradei's NAC in 2010 and, during the uprising, served as one of its main coordinators and spokesmen. On January 27, al-Naggar delivered a message to the Egyptian nation and the world on Al-Jazeera that burned with quiet force and conviction:

> The Egyptians have shattered the barrier of fear. There is nothing for them to be afraid of anymore. That's it. They have broken our bones, and opened fire on us, piercing our bodies with bullets. This did not and will not stop us. Regarding the threats and oppression of the security agencies—what more can they do to us? We want one of two positive things: freedom or martyrdom. Our lives will be a small

price to pay for this country. Continuing the current tyranny means a cruel and slow death for us. . . . We know that the people who used bullets and tear gas against us were acting against their will. We hope that their conscience will prevent them from shooting at us, and from repeating what they did on January 25. At the same time, we emphasize that bullets will not deter us. None of the things they are doing will frighten us. We have nothing left to lose. We will defend our freedom, our beliefs and the peaceful nature of our revolution, to the end. Let them kill the Egyptian people in its entirety. . . . If they want to persist, they must kill the entire Egyptian people, if they can.[37]

On January 28, with the protests continuing to grow in size, Mubarak declared a curfew in Cairo, Alexandria, and Suez and ordered troops into the streets. But the military confined its mission to maintaining the public order and did not fire on the protesters, who welcomed their presence and appealed for their support. As the International Crisis Group reported, citizens in central Cairo treated the soldiers as friends and brothers, "exchanging smiles and embraces, proffering cigarettes, offering sweets, posing for photos, and dressing their children in army fatigues when taking them to protests."[38] In addition, the protestors portrayed the military as an ally of their cause, chanting, "the people and the military are one hand" (al-sha'b wi'l-geysh 'id wahid). Determined to quash the protests once and for all, Mubarak reportedly convened an urgent face-to-face meeting with the commanders of the Egyptian armed forces and asked for their help. Aboul 'Ela Madi, the founder of the Wasat party, who was monitoring developments by the hour with other activists from his office on Kasr al-'Aini Street, close to Tahrir Square, was in touch with contacts close to the army, who told him what happened at that meeting. According to Madi's sources:

> Mubarak asked them to respond with force. Tantawi [Defense Minister Muhammad Hussein Tantawi, chief of the Egyptian Armed Forces] was shocked, and told the president that this was impossible. Then Mubarak turned to the chief of the air force, and he, too, shook his head. Their answer was no.[39]

On January 31, in a televised address to the nation, a military spokesman declared that the army supported the "legitimate demands" of the people and would not use force against them. Emboldened by the military's neutral stance, the organizers of the uprising called for a "million-man march" on February 1. Hundreds of thousands participated in both Cairo and Alexandria, and tens of thousands came out in other cities as well. Having failed to gain the military's backing, on February 2 the regime sent bands of plainclothes thugs (baltagiyya), allegedly hired by the NDP, to attack the demonstrators at Tahrir Square, some of whom sowed terror by riding into the crowds on horses and camels. Armed with "fists, rocks, sticks, pipes, knives, machetes, brass knuckles and tear gas canisters," the *baltagiyya* fought the protestors in hand-to-hand clashes that continued through the following day.[40]

In addition to trying to contain the uprising by force, the regime attempted to defuse it by offering a series of concessions to the protestors' demands. On January 29, Mubarak sacked his cabinet and, for the first time since taking office, appointed a vice president, choosing Omar Suleiman, the director of state intelligence and a trusted ally. On February 1, Mubarak announced that he would not run for another term and promised constitutional reforms. He also "pulled at the nation's heart-strings when he expressed his desire to die on the soil of his homeland."[41] On February 6, Mubarak authorized Suleiman to talk with the leaders of various opposition groups, including the Muslim Brotherhood and six of the uprising's organizers, hoping to secure a way out of the impasse.

But the concessions offered by Mubarak amounted to too little, too late. As the International Crisis Group noted, "the grudging, limited and piecemeal way in which carrots were offered undermined their intended purpose." In sum, Mubarak's response to the uprising contributed to his own demise. As a former Egyptian diplomat observed:

> He did it as if it were a gesture as opposed to his responsibility. He didn't own up to mistakes and put forward a case that things could change. He was neither convincing nor credible and didn't offer anything substantive until it was far too late to matter.[42]

On the evening of February 10, Mubarak addressed the nation for the last time, promising to transfer some of his powers to the vice president but refusing to step down. But with his security forces in retreat, the ruling NDP in disarray, and the military pursuing its own agenda, Mubarak could no longer rely on the powerful institutions that had shored up the regime in the past.[43] Earlier that day, the Supreme Council of the Armed Forces (SCAF), the military's highest authority, which had met only twice before (during Egypt's wars with Israel in 1967 and 1973), took the unprecedented step of convening a meeting during peacetime that was chaired not by the president but by Defense Minister Tantawi. It issued a communiqué expressing its support of "the people's legitimate demands."[44] The following day, February 11, Vice President Omar Suleiman delivered a statement on television announcing Mubarak's resignation and transferring his authority to the military, triggering a euphoric response among the crowds thronging Tahrir Square, who chanted "We have brought down the regime!" Ayman Nur, a liberal opposition figure who had stood against Mubarak in the presidential elections of 2005, proclaimed it "the most important day in Egypt's history." Muhammad Baradei described it as a "dream come true," adding, "You cannot comprehend the amount of joy and happiness of every Egyptian at the restoration of our humanity and our freedom."[45]

The success of Egypt's popular uprising in bringing down a long-entrenched dictator was one of the defining moments of our times. The organizers must be credited for presenting a united front that transcended ideological, generational, and class divisions and for confining themselves to the use of peaceful methods, when a descent into violence could have easily prompted events to take a very different turn. Another source of the uprising's success was the decision of its organizers to focus on broad issues that resonated with citizens from all walks of life, anchored around the demand for a restoration of Egyptians' human dignity (*karama*), as well as their determination to remain in the street until Mubarak stepped down. In the final analysis, however, it was the military's support of the uprising that tipped the scales against the regime most decisively, and it was the military—and not the "revolutionaries"—who assumed power after Mubarak resigned.

One of the first steps taken by the military was to acknowledge the sacrifice of those who had been killed or wounded during the uprising. Eighteen days of protest had produced an estimated 846 deaths and more than 6,000 injuries.[46] A few hours after Mubarak's resignation was announced, Major General Muhsin al-Fingari, deputy minister of defense and the SCAF's official spokesman, issued a televised statement in which he praised Mubarak for stepping down "in the interests of the nation," acknowledged the people's demands for radical change, and then, after a brief pause, raised his hand in solemn salute to the "martyrs" of the uprising, an iconic moment captured for posterity in thousands of video clips and photos and replicated on placards later sold at Tahrir Square.

On February 13, the SCAF issued a communiqué declaring that it had dissolved parliament, had suspended the constitution, and would assume responsibility for managing the country for six months or until new parliamentary and presidential elections were held. Further, it announced that a committee was being formed to propose interim amendments to the old constitution, which would be presented to the people in a public referendum.[47] In sum, while expressing support for the uprising's demands, the SCAF arrogated to itself the authority to oversee the transition to a new political order at a time when its intentions remained opaque and its commitment to democracy and transparency unclear at best. Attuned to these concerns, the SCAF assured the public that it would transfer authority to an elected civilian government once stability was restored and the constitutional framework for an orderly transition had been put in place.

Assessing the Brotherhood's Contribution to the Uprising

When it ordered its members into the streets on January 28, the Brotherhood became a vital part of the uprising. In addition to providing extra manpower, it marshaled its considerable discipline and expertise in operations and logistics to help maintain order on Tahrir Square and protect the crowds amassed there and elsewhere from attacks by the police and hired thugs. Brotherhood members, many of the men with untrimmed beards and calloused foreheads (caused by frequent prayer) and the women in veils, helped run security checkpoints at various entrance points to the square, politely frisking new arrivals and checking their bags for weapons. In addition, during the notorious "Battle of the Camel" on February 2, Brotherhood members manned the frontlines in clashes with those hired by the regime to attack the crowds. As one protestor who was pulled into an impromptu lesson offered by the Brotherhood on how to use a slingshot said, "I didn't like how aggressive the Brotherhood was, but I have to admit that they were more organized and ardent and their efforts were very important in protecting the Square."[48] Other protesters likewise praised the courage of the Brotherhood cadres and their skill in outmaneuvering the attackers; as a Coptic Christian protestor put it, "They were at the forefront. They defended all of us. This is a fact."[49] In addition, the Brotherhood smuggled food and water past the police blockades, strung up plastic sheeting for tents, distributed wool blankets, and set up makeshift medical clinics to provide first aid to the injured. They were also reportedly the first to set up microphones and speaker towers on the square, and some of their leaders, such as Muhammad al-Baltagui, a powerful orator, used them to deliver stirring speeches to the crowds.[50]

But the Brotherhood was also careful to avoid being seen as exploiting the uprising for its own ends. For example, its members refrained from holding up copies of the Quran and posters with slogans like "Islam Is the Solution," adhering to the instructions of the organizers to keep the protest areas free of any overt signs of partisan affiliation. Instead, they joined with other citizens in raising the Egyptian flag as a powerful visual symbol of patriotism and national unity. The Brotherhood also took pains to assure other groups that it did not seek to lead or control the uprising. As a Brotherhood statement issued during the protests asserted, "The blessed revolution . . . is one of all the Egyptian people and is not driven by any party, group or faction." In addition, the Brotherhood emphasized that it did not seek to establish a religious state akin to the Islamic republic of Iran but "a civil state and an Islamic democracy, where the people are the source of authority and sovereignty."[51] Likewise, Brotherhood members involved in the protests stressed that they were there not as Islamists but as Egyptians. As Shadi Hamid, an Egyptian American researcher, recalled: "During my time in Cairo, I met with Brotherhood activists and leaders to try to get a better read of their role in the revolution. They were careful to say, and repeat over and over, that the revolution had nothing to do with Islam and everything to do with being Egyptian."[52]

The Brotherhood's eagerness to present itself as part of a united front was underscored one week into the uprising when it announced that it was backing

Muhammed Baradei, the leader of the NAC, as a spokesman for the uprising's demands and the potential head of a new transitional government.[53] More broadly, its efforts to remain in the background reflected an awareness of the acute suspicion and anxiety with which its participation was viewed by powerful actors, including senior members of the Egyptian military and governments in the West. As Mohammad al-Biltagi explained on January 31, "The Brotherhood realizes the sensitivities, especially in the West, toward the Islamists, and we're not keen to be in the forefront." According to Shadi Hamid and Steven Brooke, "Islamists even have a phrase for this—the 'American veto'—the notion that the United States, and the world at large, is not yet ready for Islamists in government."[54] When on February 4, Ayatollah Ali Khamenei, Supreme Leader of the Islamic Republic in Iran, saluted the Egyptian uprising as "an Islamic liberation movement," the Brotherhood was quick to correct him. As Khaled Hamza, the editor in chief of the Brotherhood's English website, noted the following day, "The Egyptian protests are not an 'Islamic' uprising, but a mass protest against an unjust, autocratic regime, which includes Egyptians from all walks of life, all religions and all sects."[55]

The Brotherhood's efforts to dissociate itself from Khameinei occurred at a time that an intense debate was raging within the American media on whether Egypt could become "another Iran"; some commentators asserted that the Brotherhood aimed to hijack Egypt's transition, while others argued with equal vehemence that it did not.[56] Against this backdrop, two senior Brotherhood leaders, 'Esam al-'Aryan and Abd al-Mun'im Abu al-Futouh, submitted op-ed articles published in the *New York Times* and the *Washington Post*, respectively, to rebut allegations made by the group's detractors. As al-'Aryan explained in his piece:

> We come with no special agenda of our own—our agenda is that of the Egyptian people. We aim to achieve reform and rights for all: not just for the Muslim Brotherhood, not just for Muslims, but for all Egyptians.[57]

Likewise, in a piece titled "Democracy Supporters Should Not Fear the Muslim Brotherhood," Abu al-Futouh wrote that "contrary to fear-mongering reports, the West and the Muslim Brotherhood are not enemies" and that "it is a false dichotomy to posit, as some alarmists are suggesting, that Egypt's choices are either the status quo of the Mubarak regime or a takeover by 'Islamic extremists.'" On the contrary, Abu al-Futouh argued, over the past three decades the Brotherhood had exhibited a clear pattern of moderate and responsible behavior:

> We have embraced diversity and democratic values. In keeping with Egypt's pluralistic society, we have demonstrated moderation in our agenda and have responsibly carried out our duties to our electoral base and Egyptians at large. Our track record

of responsibility and moderation is a hallmark of our political credentials, and we will build on it.

Directly addressing the Brotherhood's controversial call for the application of Shari'a, Abu al-Futouh noted that "this is not on anyone's immediate agenda" and that in any case, Shari'a is not a route to theocracy but "a means whereby justice is implemented, life is nurtured, the common welfare is provided for, and liberty and property are safeguarded" and that "any transition to a Shari'a-based system will have to garner a consensus in Egyptian society."[58] Such statements were quickly dismissed on conservative American Internet, television, and radio sites as an effort to mask the Brotherhood's radical intentions behind a moderate veneer. For example, a post on the Jihad Watch website commented: "They're just waiting in the wings, like vultures. . . . [But] their face for the media is always benign."[59]

The Brotherhood's efforts to downplay its role in the uprising reflected above all its intense desire for it to succeed and for its long decades of marginalization and exclusion to come to an end. Hence its leaders were intent to avoid any move that might place its outcome at risk. But the Brotherhood's support of the protestors' demands for constitutional and political reform was not a function of strategic calculation alone. As the largest and most popular opposition group in the country, the Brotherhood clearly understood that a transition to democracy was in its own best interest. At the same time, however, working through the constitutional order—rather than against it—had become both a habit for the Brotherhood over the preceding decades and—just as important—a powerful group norm. How exactly the Brotherhood would reconcile its religious mission with its alleged support for an inclusive and pluralistic democratic order was yet to be determined when President Mubarak stepped down and a new era commenced.

THE MUSLIM BROTHERHOOD IN EGYPT'S TRANSITION

Although the Brotherhood did not lead the uprising, it ended up as one of its greatest beneficiaries. After nearly sixty years of operating under the watchful eye of a hostile authoritarian state, the Brotherhood was suddenly invited to participate in shaping the country's future. In an early sign of this shift, the Brotherhood was among those invited to meet with Vice President Omar Suleiman on February 6. The Brotherhood's participation in these talks was sharply criticized by Brotherhood youth at Tahrir Square, who, together with Muhammad Baradei and other protest leaders, insisted that no negotiations were possible as long as Mubarak remained in power. Such criticism highlighted the conflict between the pragmatic approach of the Brotherhood's senior leaders, who welcomed the opportunity to meet with regime officials, and the hard-line position taken by its activist youth, whose commitment to the goals of the "revolution" had come to supersede their loyalty to the Brotherhood itself.[60] Under growing pressure, the Brotherhood ultimately pulled out of the talks, but it was quick to assume a leading role in the transition once Mubarak stepped down.

Like other segments of the Egyptian opposition, the Brotherhood welcomed the military's assumption of power as the first step toward the creation of a new political order, knowing full well that no transition could succeed without the military's support. For its part, the SCAF included the Brotherhood in the transition process from the start. For example, on February 15, the SCAF appointed an eight-member committee to reform the constitution, headed by Tariq Bishri, a well-respected Egyptian judge with known Islamist orientations. While most of the committee's members were Egyptian constitutional law experts, it also included Subhi Salih, a Brotherhood lawyer and former MP, raising objections in some circles that the Brotherhood had been granted a privileged status denied to other groups. As Aboul 'Ela Madi of the Wasat party put it, "Why does the Brotherhood get a representative on the committee while other political forces do not?"[61] In addition, the military permitted Yusuf al-Qaradawi, an independent Egyptian Islamic scholar based in Qatar with close ties to the Brotherhood, to return to Cairo and deliver the Friday sermon to a crowd of hundreds of thousands of worshipers at Tahrir Square on February 18.[62] Further, the SCAF did not balk when the Brotherhood announced on February 21 that it planned to establish a political party.

The Brotherhood's special standing was underscored when 'Esam Sharaf, appointed by the military to head up the transitional government, addressed a large crowd at Tahrir Square on March 4 with Muhammad al-Biltagi, a former Brotherhood MP and one of its leading figures in the uprising, at his side.[63] But the fall of the Mubarak regime also presented the Brotherhood with a host of new challenges. Arguably its most immediate concern was to assure other groups that it did not seek to monopolize power in the new political order. As Supreme Guide Muhammad Badi' and other Brotherhood leaders repeatedly emphasized, "we seek to participate, not dominate," and to advance the interests of the nation as a whole.[64] Before Mubarak's resignation, the Brotherhood had already promised not to pursue any positions in the new transitional government or to run a candidate for president. In an attempt to further reassure its critics during the transition period, the Brotherhood promised that its new party, the Freedom and Justice Party (*hizb al-hurriyya wa al-'adala*), would not contest more than 50% of the seats in the coming parliamentary elections, with the goal of obtaining a third of the seats.[65]

Ongoing debates about the Brotherhood's intentions intensified in the lead-up to the March 19 popular referendum, when the constitutional amendments recommended by the SCAF-appointed committee would be put to a vote. Among the proposed revisions was a time line for the transfer of power from the military to a civilian elected government. Elections for a new parliament would take place in six months, after which the members of parliament would select the members of a hundred-person commission to draft a permanent constitution. Once this document was approved, presidential elections would be held. Opponents of this time line argued that it did not give new parties sufficient time to establish themselves and cultivate mass support in advance of the parliamentary elections, with some voicing fear that the new groups—including those being formed by leaders of the uprising—could be shut out of parliament altogether. More broadly, opponents of the proposed amendments argued that the drafting of a new constitution should precede the holding of elections and involve a process of broad popular consultation rather than be left to a commission chosen by a parliament in which better-organized groups were likely to be overrepresented. Implicit—if not always directly stated—in the position taken by those calling for a "no" vote in the referendum was the concern that the Brotherhood, acting in concert with conservative rural MPs, would select a constitutional commission likely to produce a document in which the protection of civil and political freedoms would be diluted in the name of preserving the country's Islamic values.

The Brotherhood strongly supported a "yes" vote in the referendum, arguing that the proposed time line offered the fastest and most direct route to the restoration of stability and the transfer of authority to a civilian government. But the Brotherhood's support of the proposed constitutional amendments reflected a more partisan set of considerations as well, as some members worried that the redrafting of the constitution by a nonparliamentary body could pave the way for the removal of Article 2, which identifies the principles of the Shariʿa as the primary source of legislation. In the days leading up to the referendum, the Brotherhood, together with more conservative Salafi groups, gave speeches and distributed flyers implying that a vote against the amendments was a vote against Islam. Such tactics triggered a chorus of protest from activists in the opposing camp, who accused the Brotherhood of exploiting religion for its own ends. In response, Brotherhood leaders argued that they were simply exercising their freedom of speech and deemed the accusations insulting. As one Brotherhood activist put it:

> It is true that we distributed brochures and pamphlets calling on people to vote yes and it is also true that we worked with other Islamist forces through mosques and charities to support this call. But this does not mean that we hijacked the revolution, it means we are resorting to democracy.[66]

More broadly, Brotherhood leader Muhammad al-Biltagi observed, a problem in the debate leading up to the referendum was a tendency in both camps to demonize those advocating a different outcome than the one they supported: "Those who framed a vote against the referendum as a vote against religion were wrong, but so were those on the opposing side who framed a vote in favor of the amendments as a betrayal of the revolution. Both exhibited a lack of tolerance when in fact either view can be construed as a patriotic [*watani*] position."[67]

Held on March 19, the referendum attracted an impressive turnout of eighteen million voters and resulted in a 77% vote in favor of the amendments, with 23% against. Many observers read the results as indicating a desire for stability and a swift transition to civilian rule, but the impact of the religious campaign in favor of a "yes" vote cannot be discounted.

On March 28, the SCAF issued a revised political parties law that outlined the rules for the formation of new parties. Interestingly, the law retained the preexisting ban on parties established on the basis of religion and social class, presumably to stem the rise of sectarian and socioeconomic conflict. In addition, the law required that new parties register five thousand members from at least ten governorates and publish their names in two daily newspapers. The cost of purchasing large advertisements in the daily papers, together with the expenses associated with renting an office, printing and distributing party literature, and related tasks, would require a substantial sum of money, estimated by civil society activists to be at least $100,000 and more likely to reach $250,000, triggering complaints that the new law privileged well-financed groups over those with more limited resources.[68] Here, too, an implicit concern was that the Brotherhood, with its strong grassroots organization and deep pockets, would be far better equipped to establish a party than would democracy activists seeking to join the political fray for the first time.

The Wasat party, whose numerous bids for legal status had been rebuffed over the previous fifteen years, was the first new party to gain legal recognition, on February 19. But they, too, faced the challenge of quickly establishing branch offices and building a mass constituency in the few months preceding the start of parliamentary elections in the fall. When I met with Madi in his Cairo office in April, he had just returned from Hurghada, a town on the Red Sea, and was expected in another town the following day; when I returned to Cairo in July, he was unavailable to meet because he was attending a party conference in Ismailiyya. Madi remained optimistic that the Wasat party would gain seats in parliament in the fall and that the new parties being formed during the transition period would develop greater institutional capacity over time. But he emphasized that building a party required a massive commitment of time and effort and could not be accomplished by activists unwilling to give up the comfort of their routines in Cairo:

> The new parties will grow stronger day by day, but through effort [*guhuud*]. There are some good leaders with some good platforms, but they need to reach out directly to the people. I tell them, "Please don't stay in Cairo and whine and complain. Don't spend all your time on television. You need to go down to the cities and villages and get organized."[69]

A key demand of the parties seeking to compete with the Brotherhood in the coming parliamentary elections was a shift in the electoral rules from a system in which citizens voted for individual candidates to a proportional representation system in which they would vote for candidates aggregated into lists (*qawa'im*). As many civil and political activists observed, the individual system in place in Egypt's most recent parliamentary elections augmented the influence of religion, family, clan affiliation, and wealth in the election process. For example, it enabled a prominent businessman to "buy" votes through the distribution of monetary incentives, the scion of a prominent rural family to mobilize the support of his kinsmen, and the preacher at a local mosque to lobby voters from the pulpit.[70] Further, the shift to a party-list system would force candidates to clarify their positions on various issues and hence present voters with a choice among different programmatic alternatives. As one civil society activist put it:

> When candidates run as independents, they are not forced to develop political programs. By contrast, a list system will force candidates to articulate clear agendas, it will encourage real politics and transparency. Now everyone says they support "social justice," but there is a difference in the approach, say, of the Wafd and leftist groups. Such differences will become manifest in a list system.[71]

Others noted that a list system would enable smaller parties to gain seats and hence ensure a truly representative parliament.[72] More broadly, the introduction of party lists would help consolidate Egypt's transition to democracy. As Mona Zulfiqar, a lawyer and human rights activist, observed:

> You cannot have real political development in Egypt unless you have strong political parties based on programs. We have to move away from the influence of tribal leaders and businessmen who buy votes, and [this is one way] to build strong democratic institutions.[73]

Not only would a proportional representation (PR) system foster the emergence of robust parties, democracy activists claimed, but it would also increase the representation of women and Coptic Christians, who were far more likely to win seats as part of a broader list than to be elected as individuals in a conservative, Muslim-majority environment. Though the exact type of PR system advocated by democracy activists varied, all of them agreed that a continuation of the individual system would seriously undermine the democratic character of the new political order.[74] As Sayyid al-Badawi, president of the Wafd party, warned:

> There is no alternative to the list system. If the SCAF insists on the individual system, all of the parties will boycott the elections, we have already agreed on that. Because in this case it will be as if the revolution never happened, and the martyrs will have died in vain.[75]

With its long history of grassroots outreach and large popular base in Cairo and the towns of the Delta, the Brotherhood was positioned to do well in the parliamentary elections whatever the electoral system in place. Yet in a nod to the concerns of other civil and political groups, Brotherhood leaders stressed they would endorse whatever electoral rules were supported by the majority. When I asked Muhammad al-Biltagi if the Brotherhood would support the shift to a PR system, even if this had the effect of strengthening its rivals, he replied in the affirmative. "This may be hard for some people to understand," he conceded, "but the goal of the Brotherhood is to build up the entire society."[76]

While the Brotherhood had less at stake in the nature of the country's electoral rules, it faced a different set of challenges emanating from within its own ranks. Beginning in the spring of 2011 and continuing through the summer, the Brotherhood confronted a string of defections by some of its most prominent reformist leaders, as well as by many Brotherhood youth who had played a leading role in the uprising. At the same time, the group's senior leaders faced unprecedented pressures to enact long-delayed institutional reforms. Interestingly, one of the main triggers of internal criticism was the manner in which the Guidance Bureau proceeded to establish a Brotherhood political party. The Brotherhood's party initiative and the controversy it generated are discussed next.

The Formation of the Freedom and Justice Party

Mubarak's departure created an unprecedented opening for the Brotherhood to establish a political party of its own. On February 21, Muhammad Badi', the Brotherhood's Supreme Guide, delegated longtime MP Muhammad Sa'ad al-Katatni to supervise the formation of the Freedom and Justice Party (FJP). According to Brotherhood spokesmen, the FJP would be "a civil party with an Islamic frame of reference"—terminology borrowed verbatim from the Wasat party—and would be open to citizens of all faiths who supported its objectives. In April, at its first meeting in more than sixteen years, the Brotherhood's Shura Council approved the formation of the party and selected its top leadership. At a press conference in front of the Brotherhood's lavish new headquarters in the Muqattam area of Cairo on April 30, Muhammad Mursi was announced as the party's president, 'Esam al-'Aryan as vice president, and Muhammad Sa'ad al-Katatni as secretary-general.[77] The party was reported to have close to nine thousand founding members, of whom approximately 80% were affiliated with the Brotherhood. Although women were historically barred from full membership in the Brotherhood, roughly a thousand of the FJP's founding members were female.[78] Further, in a demonstration of the party's openness to citizens of all faiths, the Brotherhood selected Rafiq Habib, a Coptic Christian, as one of its deputy chairmen. Brotherhood spokesmen stressed that the party would be fully independent of the movement organization (*jama'a*) but would consult with it on important policy decisions. Touted as a sign of the new party's autonomy, it was announced that Mursi, al-'Aryan, and al-Katatni would step down from their posts in the Guidance Bureau before assuming their new roles in the party.

The Brotherhood submitted its party proposal to the government's Political Parties Committee in May, and on June 6 the FJP achieved legal status—a watershed moment in the Brotherhood's history. On June 10, the FJP held its first public conference in the Delta province of Qalubiyya, reportedly attended by more than ten thousand people. At the conference, 'Esam al-'Aryan emphasized that the FJP did not seek to obtain a parliamentary majority but sought to gain 30–35% of the seats. In addition, he stressed that the FJP was open to working with other political parties in pursuit of common goals. As he stated: "We are willing to form an alliance with the political forces that agree to our principles; whether they are socialists, liberals, or other Islamist forces and all forces concerned about this homeland."[79]

From the outset, the manner in which the Brotherhood's senior officials handled the party initiative generated intense criticism from leaders in the group's reformist camp. In February, they challenged Badi''s authority to delegate al-Katatni to begin the process of forming a party without consulting the Shura Council or the group's membership at large. Over the following months, additional objections were raised, most vigorously by Abd al-Mun'im Abu al-Futouh, who argued against the formation of a Brotherhood party on principle. As Abu al-Futouh stressed, no one but the Prophet Muhammad had the right to fuse religious and political authority. Such domains must be kept separate, he explained, to "prevent tyranny." Hence the Brotherhood should remain a *da'wa* organization, operating in the domain of civil society, and its members should be free to support any party they wanted.[80]

Other reformists did not oppose the establishment of a Brotherhood party per se but objected to the manner in which its leaders were chosen, noting that the FJP's leadership should have been elected directly by its members, not by the Brotherhood. Further, they argued that ongoing consultation between the Guidance Bureau and the party's leadership raised serious doubts about the extent to which the FJP would exercise any real autonomy in practice.[81] Youth activists who had left the Brotherhood before the uprising were particularly outspoken in their criticism of the party initiative on both counts. For example, Abd al-Mun'im Mahmoud, an ex-Brotherhood journalist and blogger, offered this assessment of the Brotherhood's new venture:

> The religious discourse of the Brotherhood is centrist [*wasati*]; they are conservative but they are not extremist; they are not like the Salafis. But their political horizons are still narrow, and the Brotherhood is still a closed [*munghalaq*] organization. Its senior leadership handpicked the president, vice president, and secretary-general of

the FJP, and its founders were selected by the Brotherhood's regional offices, who picked individuals known for their religious commitment and discipline. Hence there is no real separation between the Brotherhood and the FJP. Rather, the FJP is the political arm of the Brotherhood. The Guidance Bureau, which governs the movement organization, will also run the party. For example, when the party wanted to raise its own funds, the Guidance Bureau replied: "No, when you need money, come to us."[82]

At this juncture, the exact contours of the relationship between the Brotherhood and the FJP are difficult to pin down. The two organizations are likely to remain joined at the hip for some time, but it is possible that the latter will acquire greater institutional, financial, and operational autonomy in the future. For now, the path chosen by the Brotherhood appears to approximate the model adopted in Jordan, where the Islamic Action Front (IAF) is formally independent of the Brotherhood but serves in practice as its political wing. Further, my reading of such developments is that an agreement was reached between the Brotherhood's *da'wa* and pragmatic conservative factions, in which the former would retain its dominant position in the movement organization and the latter would represent the Brotherhood in the sphere of electoral politics. This division of labor would enable the old guard to safeguard the movement's ideological uniformity while allowing the Brotherhood's more politically experienced and media-savvy figures to serve as the movement's primary interlocutors with Egyptian society at large.

Although some members of the reformist camp have gravitated to the Brotherhood's new party, it is unclear whether they will be able to carve out a meaningful leadership role within it. However, Egypt's political opening has presented reformist leaders with another option: to leave the Brotherhood and form new groups of their own. Indeed, in the months after the uprising, the Brotherhood confronted a series of defections by middle-generation and youth leaders associated with the group's reformist wing. Such defections received extensive coverage in the Arab and Western media, fueling claims of mounting discord in an organization that had long prided itself on its internal discipline and unity. Why did some of the Brotherhood's most prominent reformists abandon the group in the wake of the Arab Spring? It is to this question that we now turn.

The Incipient Fragmentation of the Muslim Brotherhood

For many years, members of the Brotherhood's reformist faction confronted two distasteful options: either accept a marginal role in the organization or leave the group and consign themselves to political irrelevance. The experience of the Wasat party founders, who broke from the Brotherhood in 1996 and had failed to gain legal status more than a decade later, served as a cautionary tale for those tempted to leave the Brotherhood's fold. But the uprising and the transitional period that followed created space for new groups seeking to enter the political scene. As noted earlier, the Wasat party gained legal status on February 19, and shortly thereafter, several groups with leftist and liberal backgrounds announced that they, too, were forming parties of their own.[83]

In the freewheeling climate of the transitional period, the pent-up frustrations of the reformists were finally matched with opportunity. After years of pushing for changes in the Brotherhood's agenda and internal practices only to encounter stiff resistance from the old guard, several high-profile reformists were ready to strike out on their own. For Ibrahim al-Za'farani, a former Brotherhood MP from Alexandria, the turning point came in March, when Muhammad Badi' stated that members of the Brotherhood would not be allowed to join any party other than the FJP. As al-Za'farani explained to reporters, Badi''s attempt to infringe on Brotherhood members' political freedoms spurred his decision to resign from the group and form the Nahda (Renaissance) party. Although the Nahda party, like the FJP, had an Islamic frame of reference, the majority of its founding members were not affiliated with the Brotherhood. In an interview with me on July 17, 2011, al-Za'farani highlighted the marginalization of the reformist current in the Brotherhood over the preceding decades and identified the key elements of their dispute with the old guard:

> The ideas of the reformist trend have been in circulation among members of the Brotherhood for a long time, at least since the early 1990s. But we were not organized. We had our convictions, but we did not have any institutional connection ['itisal] with the Brotherhood's wider ranks. By contrast, the conservatives were well organized internally. They formed a network of members who coordinated with each other and put forward their own list of candidates in internal elections. This network had no name, but it included many influential figures, like Mahmoud 'Ezzat, Khayrat al-Shatir, Muhammad Badi', Muhammad Mursi, and Rashad Bayoumi.
>
> On many issues, our point of view differed from theirs. For example, we called for greater transparency in our dealings with the wider society and placed a greater priority than they did on obtaining legal status. We also supported a clearer separation between the group's da'wa and party activities. In the domain of internal affairs, we called for a stricter separation of power between the executive branch (the Supreme Guide and Guidance Bureau) and the legislative branch (the Shura Council). For example, we felt that the Shura Council should have the authority to withdraw its confidence from the Guidance Bureau, as without this, it has no means to hold the Guidance Bureau accountable for its actions. At present the Shura Council simply offers advice, and that's it.

When I asked if there was a parallel between the limited oversight capacity of the Shura Council and that of the People's Assembly during the Mubarak era, al-Za'farani responded: "Yes, it is exactly like that!" Al-Za'farani noted a further parallel with the Mubarak regime: the absence of an independent judicial authority in the Brotherhood that could investigate and prosecute the misconduct of group leaders.[84]

Al-Za'farani noted that the Nahda party, the Wasat party, and other new groups with an Islamist orientation would engage in "honorable competition" with the FJP in the coming parliamentary elections. While sharing a common frame of reference, he explained, such parties had different priorities and would focus on different issues. Noting that "no one party can do everything," al-Za'farani said that the Nahda party would concentrate on the development of education, science, and technology:

> We want to nurture creativity and innovation, by introducing new educational methods that will enable people to function in a changing world. We are asking Egyptians who are leaders in their fields and went abroad to return to the country and assist us in our efforts. We also want to confront the problem of illiteracy, building new schools in poor neighborhoods and in regions of the country that have been historically neglected, like Upper Egypt. While the Wasat party focuses on issues of political reform, the Nahda party adopts a longer time horizon. Our goal is to ensure that dictators will not ever return by equipping citizens with the knowledge and skills to remain active in public life.

In July, the Nahda party gained a boost when Muhammad Habib, a former deputy Supreme Guide of the Brotherhood, joined the party and took charge of its Education Committee.

Al-Za'farani expressed his confidence that the Nahda party would win some seats in the new parliament but acknowledged that it would initially rely on the good reputation of its candidates and their track record of providing services to attract voters, since introducing citizens to the party's ideas would take time:

> Our candidates have distinguished themselves by providing services to voters in their districts. For example, one of our candidates in Menoufiyya [a town in the Delta] has paved roads, funded health care initiatives, and recently set up a soccer competition involving teams from thirty different villages. This shows he can mobilize people. In Upper Egypt, our candidates come from well-known and respected families. In the beginning, people will vote for our candidates on the basis of the services they provide, the trust people have in them, and the strength of their family reputations. But gradually they will become aware of the party's agenda. For example, we have set up training centers, in which party members explain our ideas, discussing the meaning of the constitution and the basic ideas of democracy. We now have offices in thirteen governorates, and each office has a training center of this kind.[85]

After the uprising, other prominent Brotherhood reformists launched new initiatives as well. Most notably, Abd al-Mun'im Abu al-Futouh announced in the spring that he was considering a run for the presidency. Brotherhood spokesmen quickly denounced the plan, stressing that it conflicted with the Brotherhood's promise not to field a candidate for president. As with al-Za'farani, Abu al-Futouh's decision to pursue an independent path was preceded by a longer history of growing independence from—and conflict with—conservative members of the Guidance Bureau. Even before losing his seat on the Guidance Bureau in December 2009, Abu al-Futouh had become known as a maverick unwilling to toe the party line and was openly critical of the old guard's parochial mind-set. Further, in the last years of the Mubarak era, Abu al-Futouh's views had come to appear closer to the tenets of secular liberalism than to mainstream Islamist opinion. A profile of Abu al-Futouh in the *New York Times* on June 19, 2011, noted that:

> Dr. Abou el-Fotouh [*sic*] cites verses of the Koran to support the right of Muslim women to reject the veil, the freedom of Muslims or Christians to ignore Islam's prohibition on alcohol, the right of a woman or non-Muslim to hold the office of Egypt's president, the separation of the Brotherhood's religious mission from politics, and his own opposition to the Brotherhood's recent proposals to require Muslims to pay 2.5 percent of their income to a state-sponsored charity in fulfillment of the Islamic charitable duty known as *zakat*.
>
> "Allah told our Prophet, 'You cannot control or strongly influence people, you can only advise them,'" Abu al-Futouh stated, adding that "The people must have a free will."[86]

Although Abu al-Futouh alienated conservative figures in the Guidance Bureau, he became a model and source of inspiration for activist Brotherhood youth like Islam Lutfi and Muhammad Qassas, who played a leading role in the uprising. In May 2011, Abu al-Futouh announced that he was considering a run for the presidency in order to fulfill his "duty to the youth of the revolution" and to serve the nation as a whole. In comments to the media, Abu al-Futouh stressed that he had halted all of his activities with the Brotherhood on February 11 to clear the way for a presidential campaign. Further, he would run as an independent "because I would represent Egypt and not the Brotherhood," noting that he would "always feel fondly for the group" nonetheless.[87]

Of all the Brotherhood's reformists, Abu al-Futouh appeared to have proceeded the furthest in shedding his former partisan affiliations and recasting himself as a trustee of the public interest who could bridge the country's deep ideological divides. Commenting on the rise of sectarian violence in Egypt after the uprising, he noted:

> Such sectarian strife makes me more determined to pursue the presidency. As elements of religious extremism creep up in the transition period, the country needs someone who is well connected to the Muslim, Christian, and liberal sides of the political spectrum.[88]

As he explained in a press interview in June, Abu al-Futouh's program would focus on four overarching priorities: (1) the deepening of freedoms; (2) the independence of the judiciary; (3) economic development; and (4) education and health. Conspicuous in its absence was any reference to the Shari'a, underscoring Abu al-Futouh's efforts to articulate a reform agenda backed by a national consensus.[89]

Abu al-Futouh's decision to run for president was the last straw in his increasingly strained relationship with the Brotherhood. As 'Esam al-'Aryan stated: "He has nothing to do with us now. We cannot support anyone violating our decisions." In a move Abu al-Futouh must have anticipated, the Shura Council expelled him from the Muslim Brotherhood on June 19.

The departures of al-Za'farani, Habib, and Abu al-Futouh were part of a broader trend. Even before the uprising, some of the Brotherhood's most outspoken reformist leaders had resigned from the Brotherhood, frozen their memberships, or been expelled after publicly criticizing its senior leadership one too many times. Since the uprising this has accelerated, with more reformists leaving the Brotherhood and forming new groups of their own. While some defectors joined the Wasat and the Nahda parties, others helped establish new parties encompassing Islamist and secular democracy activists. Such latter parties reveal another important outcome of the uprising: the emergence of new political identities and commitments transcending older ideological divides. For example, in March, Mustafa al-Naggar, an ex-Brotherhood blogger and activist who joined Baradei's NAC, helped found the 'Adl (Justice) party, which positioned itself "at the center between the liberal and religious forces of the Egyptian political scene."[90] The Justice party supports the civil equality of all Egyptians irrespective of faith and gender, and, al-Naggar proudly pointed out, more than half of its members are women.

Likewise, several Brotherhood youth leaders who figured prominently in the uprising, including Islam Lutfi, Muhammad Qassas, and Ahmad Abd al-Gawwad, announced on June 21, two days after Abu al-Futouh's expulsion, that they were forming the al-Tayyar al-Misri (Egyptian Current) party, which would include youth activists from the Muslim Brotherhood, the April 6 movement, Kefaya, and other groups, as well as independents.

Both the Justice and Egyptian Current parties framed their agendas as moving beyond older ideological projects that had divided the nation and failed to meet the needs of ordinary Egyptians. As Mustafa al-Naggar observed, "The Egyptian people don't care about ideologies and they don't characterize themselves as adopting a certain political ideology. On the contrary, they reject and sometimes fear these ideologies." Hence the Justice party offered "a new ideology beyond ideologies" that sought to promote the interests of the nation as a whole. Members of the Egyptian Current party agreed that the time for narrow ideological projects had passed. As Abd al-Gawwad explained:

We concluded that society is bigger than the Ikhwan. Egypt is the main locus of our identity and our loyalty. Our goal is the renewal of our country, and this stands above the priorities of any narrow group or faction. Many of those who joined us are independents with no formal ideological affiliations. And our program takes ideas from different groups—the idea of social justice from the leftists, the idea of freedom from liberals, and the concept of identity from the Islamic trend. My behavior is still a reflection of my religious convictions, but my main priority is to address the needs of the Egyptian street. I'm not going to say, "Islam is the Solution," since the people can't eat Islam. . . . By 2030 we want Egypt to be a leader in culture, economics, and politics. And the imposition of a particular ideology is not the way to achieve this.[91]

The founders of the Egyptian Current party saw no contradiction between their cooperation with secular activists and the duties of their faith. As Qassas put it: "I am still committed to religion in my personal life, and our party is not against Islam. But it brings together Islamists, liberals, and independents. For example, Abd al-Rahman Faris, a well-known liberal, is with us."[92]

The youth who broke from the Brotherhood also contrasted the Brotherhood's emphasis on reform (islah) with their call for change (taghyir), that is, a radical democratic transformation of the basic institutions of Egyptian society and state. As Abd al-Gawwad observed:

The revolution demonstrated that the idea of reform is outdated, and that there is another approach which is more successful. We want root change. By contrast, the Brotherhood wants stability. They say, let's focus on preparing for the elections, let's open a new headquarters. It is a matter of priorities.[93]

In a clear sign of this clash, the Egyptian Current party actively participated in what came to be known as the "second wave of the revolution"—the sit-ins, strikes, and demonstrations that occurred during the spring and summer of 2011. The banners, posters, and chants at these events demanded the swift prosecution of Mubarak and other high-ranking officials guilty of corruption and responsible for the deaths of protesters during the uprising, as well as cleansing (tathir) the state apparatus of associates of the old regime. By contrast, the Muslim Brotherhood remained aloof from the second-wave protests, directing its energies to establishing a new party and preparing for parliamentary elections in the fall.

Brotherhood youth leaders also exhibited their new sense of agency by reviving calls for the reform of the Brotherhood itself. On March 26, a group of youth members convened an unofficial conference in Cairo, at which several hundred young professional men and women listened to a series of speakers detailing a series of proposals for change in the Brotherhood's charter.[94] Echoing earlier calls for reform, they recommended expanding the authority of the Shura Council and, by extension, reducing the ad hoc decision-making power of the Supreme Guide and his advisors. In addition, they called for greater representation of women and youth at all levels of the group's leadership, with some going so far as to demand quotas to redress their marginalization in the past. Again and again, speakers highlighted the gap between the Brotherhood's calls for democracy, transparency, and pluralism in the broader political arena and the autocratic practices of the group's senior leadership. They also criticized prevailing norms that demanded unquestioning obedience and submission to the group's elders and asserted their right to participate in shaping the group's future.

According to Abd al-Gawwad, when the idea of the conference was first raised, the Guidance Bureau was receptive: "The Guidance Bureau welcomed the idea in light of new realities, agreeing that we must be more transparent now and more willing to discuss our issues out in the open." But as plans for the conference progressed, al-Gawwad recalled, the Guidance Bureau's apprehensions increased: "They worried that the organizers were adopting the views of their critics, like Abd al-Mun'im Abu al-Futouh and Muhammad Habib. So they became uncomfortable with the idea of the conference, imagining that it would embarrass them and undermine their authority." The Guidance Bureau twice asked the organizers to postpone the conference, but when they asked for it to be postponed a third time, the organizers balked. Abd al-Gawwad recalled, "I got involved as a mediator, and I asked members of the Guidance Bureau 'What do you want?' They said, 'We don't want the organizers to invite Abu al-Futouh and Habib; and we want to see the lists of the guests and attendees.'" The organizers agreed to these terms and attempted to allay the apprehensions of the Guidance Bureau's members by giving them the conference papers in advance. In addition, they called Abu al-Futouh and Habib, as well as other reformist figures like Haytham Abu Khalil and Khaled Dawoud, asking them not to attend (Dawoud did attend the conference but only as an observer). Nevertheless, the Guidance Bureau refused to endorse the event. As Muhammad Mursi stated on March 24, "the Guidance Bureau does not and did not approve of this conference and does not know anything about its details."[95] Further, when the conference was held, not a single Guidance Bureau member attended. Nevertheless, Abd al-Gawwad stressed, "there were no attacks on the Guidance Bureau at the conference. On the contrary, it was an objective discussion of some very developed ideas."[96]

The growing assertiveness of the Brotherhood activist youth after the uprising triggered a series of punitive reprisals. Youth leaders involved in the March conference and the formation of the Egyptian Current party were placed under internal investigation, and by July, seven of them had been expelled.[97] Among them was Islam Lutfi. As he recalled,

The investigation [tahqiq] was a farce. They asked me, "Did you help to establish a new party?" And I said yes. That was the extent of it. I thought they might freeze my membership, but I didn't see what grounds they had for my expulsion. The Brotherhood charter stipulates a process, they need to specify what rules you broke, but this did not happen. As I see it, the formation of the Egyptian Current party was just a pretext. The main issue was that we dared to challenge the will of the old guard.[98]

Other Brotherhood youth were warned that if they associated with Abu al-Futouh or any of the Egyptian Current party's founders, they would face expulsion as well. As Muhammad Ghuzlan, a Guidance Bureau member, explained in a press interview in July, Brotherhood members "cannot be all over the political spectrum and at the same time claim to support the Brotherhood's conservative Islamic values."[99] To some observers, the expulsions were tantamount to a witch-hunt, exposing a darker side of the Brotherhood at odds with its democratic pretensions. As Abd al-Mun'im Mahmoud confessed,

> Some have said they fear what will happen if the Brotherhood comes to power, and now I am afraid, too. Look at their treatment of their youth, who were called into interrogations for writing something on Facebook or meeting with Islam Lutfi. If they do this to their own youth, what will they do some day to the communists and the secularists? There was recently an election for a branch [*shu'ba*] of the Brotherhood in Mohandiseen [an upper-class district in Cairo]. They wouldn't let some people vote, accusing them of associating with Islam Lutfi and Muhammad Qassas. We said, "You people are acting like *Amn al-Dawla* [State Security]!"

THE SOURCES OF THE BROTHERHOOD'S ORGANIZATIONAL DISCIPLINE AND COHERENCE

The rift between the Brotherhood's senior leaders and its activist youth was described in some press reports as a "schism" or "split" within the group's ranks, but this overstates the impact of the defections on the Brotherhood as a whole. First, though the exact figures are unknown, the youth involved in such initiatives appeared to number in the hundreds and at most a few thousand in an organization with tens of thousands of active members. Second, and just as important, senior leaders in the Guidance Bureau retained control over the Brotherhood's Education Unit (*qism al-tarbiya*), through which they supervised the recruitment and socialization of new members.

Here it is worth noting that individuals did not join the Brotherhood by choice but had to be invited into the group and pass through successive phases of evaluation and training before they obtained full membership rights. Hence by the time a new recruit achieved full membership status, his commitment to the values and norms of the Brotherhood had already been vetted over a period of several years. A prospective member started out as a *muhibb* (sympathizer), then proceeded to become a *mu'ayyid* (supporter), *muntasib* (appointee), *muntadhim* (member), and finally an *'udw 'amil* (active member) with full rights to vote and run for office. At each stage the individual enrolled in a religious and cultural study program (*barnamig thaqafi*) specifically designed for members of that level, and his behavior was scrutinized to ensure conformity with group norms. When I asked a young activist what, for example, would happen if an individual at an early stage of this process was discovered to be having a premarital sexual relationship, he replied that such a person might be permitted to participate in Brotherhood activities but would not be invited to become a full member.[100]

This process of gradual promotion to higher tiers of membership status helped promote a certain degree of ideological and behavioral conformity within the group's ranks. Further, as an individual proceeded through the socialization process, not only his political career but also his social life became more deeply embedded within movement networks. Colleagues, friends, and even marriage partners were more likely to be chosen from within such networks, raising the costs of leaving the group behind. Indeed, reformist leaders emphasized how difficult it was to break with the organization, their primary focus of allegiance for all of their adult lives. Ibrahim al-Za'farani told a reporter that on the eve of his resignation, "I could not sleep all night, and neither could my wife." As he recalled, "For two weeks, we received thousands of calls from Brothers and Sisters inside and outside Egypt. They begged me to change my mind. These phone calls used to kill us emotionally on a daily basis."[101] Youth members who resigned from the group or were expelled from it emphasized the psychological and emotional stress associated with leaving the Brotherhood. As Muhammad Qassas observed: "Resigning from the Muslim Brotherhood is a very tough decision, because the group is a society that engulfs your social and familial relations, as well as your intellectual and political activities." Likewise, Khaled Dawoud, a reformist from Alexandria who was married to two Muslim Sisters and whose eight children were all Brotherhood members, noted: "When a Brother leaves the group, he is uprooting himself from a milieu with which he has organic, emotional and fateful ties. Your friends boycott you. They may not even say hello if they bump into you in the street. Your wife's friends, who are usually from the Muslim Brotherhood, may boycott her as well."[102] Dawoud was shunned after publicly supporting Abd al-Mun'im Abu al-Futouh's progressive views. As he recalled, "I was subjected to moral assassination. I have not been allowed to attend certain events held by the group. They fear my attendance because they do not want me to express my views." As he emphasized, any Brotherhood member who chooses to part ways with the group's leadership must be "capable of bearing the psychological cost" of his decision.[103]

Yet characterizing tensions in the Brotherhood as a conflict between conservative elders and progressive youth is problematic.[104] The Brotherhood youth activists who pursued an independent path after the uprising were in many respects a special case, since they had spent years involved in cross-partisan networks agitating for democratic reform. By contrast, the majority of Brotherhood youth remained enmeshed in the group's insular communities, with limited exposure to activists from other political backgrounds, especially in towns and villages geographically and culturally removed from the largely urban, educated, secular, and middle-class democracy and human rights activists based in Cairo. According to Egyptian experts like Hossam Tammam, most youth in the provinces remained deeply conservative in their outlook. Indeed, many of them had begun to gravitate toward Salafi groups that subscribed to a much stricter and literalist interpretation of Islam.[105] For such members, the issues raised at the March youth conference did not resonate all that much. Indeed, scores of Brotherhood youth posted comments on Facebook and social media sites lambasting the conference organizers for speaking out of turn and affirming their loyalty to the Guidance Bureau and the Supreme Guide.[106]

At the same time, the Brotherhood's senior leaders attempted to seize the initiative by presenting their own plans for the group's administrative overhaul. As Mahmoud Ghuzlan, a Guidance Bureau member and official spokesman for the group, stated in July, the Brotherhood was responding to changes in the country's political environment by launching new programs to facilitate the group's "development" (*tatwir*)—a term conspicuously substituted for "reform" (*islah*). Heading up such initiatives was Khayrat al-Shatir, one of the Brotherhood's most powerful figures behind the scenes.[107] During the summer of 2011, al-Shatir embarked on a series of "listening tours" to Brotherhood branches around the country and collected various proposals for change. As Mahmoud Ghuzlan noted:

> Al-Shatir is now in the process of collecting suggestions for ways to develop the Brotherhood after the revolution. So far he has received over ten thousand suggestions from individuals inside the Brotherhood and outside it. There will likely be many changes in the structure, the rules, and the procedures. The proposals will be studied and then presented to the Shura Council for a vote.[108]

Additional initiatives launched in the spring and summer of 2011 included the formation of a Brotherhood satellite television channel and the establishment of Brotherhood-affiliated NGOs focused on economic and social development. As al-Shatir elaborated in an interview published in the Kuwaiti Islamist journal *al-Mujtama'* in July, such projects aimed to facilitate a renaissance of the nation, building on an Islamic frame of reference. The problem with existing developmental models, he noted, is that all of them are rooted in Western rather than Islamic modes of thought. Nevertheless, the Brotherhood could learn from the experience of other countries, such as the successful partnership between the government and private sector in Taiwan. Indeed, al-Shatir stressed, one of the main objectives of the Brotherhood's new projects was to expand the participation of the private sector and civil society in the nation's development and challenge the prevailing mentality among Egyptians that the government alone should bear responsibility for everything.[109]

Efforts to "develop" the Brotherhood were arguably intended to serve a number of different goals. In addition to laying the groundwork for a broader national renewal, they can also be seen as a means to increase the Brotherhood's visibility and influence and to channel the energies of its members into projects under its senior leaders' direct control.

The Tensions between Shari'a and Democracy

Egypt's political opening also pushed the Brotherhood to clarify its long-term objectives. In particular, the Brotherhood faced mounting pressure to specify whether—and how—its alleged commitment to pluralism and democracy could be reconciled with its call for Shari'a rule. This question became more pressing after some of the Brotherhood's conservative leaders made statements at public rallies and meetings of Brotherhood supporters that cast doubt on the group's democratic pretensions.

For example, at a public rally in the Cairo neighborhood of Imbaba in March, Sa'd al-Husseini, a member of the Guidance Bureau, talked about "preparing society for Islamic rule." Shortly thereafter, Mahmoud 'Ezzat, another Guidance Bureau member, made a public statement anticipating the eventual implementation of the *hudoud* punishments mentioned in the Quran for such crimes as theft, murder, and adultery. Under a firestorm of criticism, 'Ezzat backpedaled, claiming that his comments had been taken out of context and that Egypt was still a long way from becoming the kind of society in which the *hudoud* punishments could be applied. Such efforts at damage control notwithstanding, Egyptian democracy activists were nonplussed. As George Ishaq, a Copt and leading member of the Kefaya, warned, "These are grave statements. Every time we try to reassure public opinion about the desire of the Muslim Brotherhood to join a civil movement, we get shocked by [these] statements from here or there."[110]

Did such comments by elderly leaders—who spent their entire professional lives within the Brotherhood, rarely spoke to outsiders, and came across in their public statements as either defiant or inept—represent the "real" objectives of the Brotherhood? Such a question is difficult to answer because there is simply no smoking gun or "aha" moment when the "true" nature of the Brotherhood is suddenly revealed. That is because the group encompasses a wide range of opinions, and we do not have much information on which views prevail in which corners of the organization and why. Hence when a figure like Mohammed al-Biltagi makes a reassuring statement or Mahmoud 'Ezzat makes an alarming one, it is hard to gauge whether they are voicing a personal opinion, representing the views of a particular faction, or speaking on behalf of the Brotherhood as a whole.

While we must guard against inferring the Brotherhood's "real intentions" from individual statements, a broader examination of the evolution of the Brotherhood's rhetoric on Shari'a reveals some interesting trends. First, when I asked Brotherhood leaders directly whether the Brotherhood supported the application of Shari'a, they answered in the affirmative but framed their response as a defense of the constitution and the rule of law, highlighting the fact that Article 2 of the Egyptian Constitution refers to the principles of the Shari'a as the primary source of legislation. Second, they emphasized that the number of Egyptian laws that must be adjusted to conform with the Shari'a was actually quite small. When asked prior to the uprising which laws should receive priority, their answer was the Emergency Laws and other laws of "bad reputation," such as those permitting government interference in the formation and activities of political parties, nongovernmental associations, and media outlets.

Since the uprising, Brotherhood leaders have continued to advocate the application of Shari'a. As Subhi Salih noted in May, "Terms like 'civil' or 'secular' state are misleading. Islamic Shari'a is the best system for Muslims and non-Muslims."[111] Likewise, Mahmoud Ghuzlan, the Brotherhood's official press spokesman, confirmed in July that the FJP called for the application of Shari'a:

We created a party to serve our ideas and our wider mission [risala]. This is a matter of belief ['aqida] and we can never abandon it. The Shari'a is what God handed down to the people as a source of guidance. It is a system for all dimensions of life—the organization of the family, the economic system, relations between Muslims and non-Muslims in a Muslim society, relations with non-Muslims around the world, the punishment of crimes—the Shari'a has organized all this. In addition, it establishes a link between behavior and morals in the political domain. Many politicians are opportunistic, self-serving, and lie for political advantage. But in Islam this is forbidden [haram]; behavior must conform to morals and principles.[112]

The Brotherhood's call for the application of Shari'a has continued to provoke apprehension and concern among secular political and civil leaders in Egypt, and rightly so. As experts inside and outside Egypt have observed, the Brotherhood speaks in a "discourse of generalities," simultaneously persisting in vague calls for Shari'a rule that resonate with its base while invoking ideas of freedom and democracy in a bid for wider social acceptance. The result is a hybrid discourse in which the tensions and contradictions between the Brotherhood's religious and democratic commitments have yet to be fully acknowledged, let alone resolved.

Most important, the Brotherhood has yet to clearly define how the application of Islamic law would translate into practice. For example, would it entail the imposition of traditional rulings, or ahkam, inherited from the past, or the application of general Shari'a principles, or mabadi', such as freedom and justice, which correspond with laws that vary considerably across time and place? When asked this question, senior Brotherhood leaders demurred, noting only that the number of definitive rulings (*ahkam qat'iyya*) that demand universal application is quite small.[113] Of course, this only begs the question of which rulings should be characterized as "definitive" and on what basis, an issue on which the Brotherhood has remained silent.

Brotherhood leaders have also begun to frame their call for the application of the Shari'a as a means to safeguard the public interest (*al-maslaha al-'amma*). However, the public interest is invoked in favor of democratic norms and institutions in some cases and against them in others. For example, in statements to the press and in their interviews with me, senior Brotherhood leaders have cited the public interest in support of free and fair presidential elections, the establishment of sharp limits on the power of the president and the security establishment, and the right of political parties and civil society groups to operate free of government intervention. Yet on moral, cultural, and social issues, these same leaders have invoked the public interest to justify stricter controls on the expression of ideas and lifestyle choices deemed at odds with *thawabet al-umma*, that is, the fixed and enduring values of the Egyptian people.

For example, in an interview I conducted with him in May 2010, Muhammad Mursi argued that an individual is free to question the basic precepts of Islam as a matter of private conscience, but once he or she begins to promote those ideas in the public domain, they cause harm (*darar*) to the public interest, and therefore the right to free expression can be legitimately curtailed.[114] Likewise, a citizen is free to drink alcohol, eat during the holy month of Ramadan, or engage in homosexual practices in the privacy of his or her home, but such behaviors must be prohibited in the public domain to safeguard the collective interests of society. The public interest has also been invoked by Brotherhood leaders to justify the censorship of intellectual, creative, and artistic works; regulate the content of the media and school curricula; and oppose legal reforms that infringe on male prerogatives in matters of marriage, divorce, and inheritance. Even "liberal" Islamists, such as those associated with the Wasat party, have invoked *thawabet al-umma* as a constraint on freedom of expression, differing only in defining the range of permissible ideas and behaviors more broadly.

A surprising aspect of the Brotherhood's discourse is that at times the "public interest" is invoked as a constraint on the Shari'a itself. For example, several senior Brotherhood leaders have argued that the *hudoud* punishments for capital crimes, while mandated by the Shari'a, should not be applied under current circumstances because they would cause harm to society. What is most interesting here is that the defense of the "public interest" trumps the application of fixed rulings (*ahkam*) revealed by God.

A final point is that the gap between the Brotherhood's call for the application of Shari'a and the preferences of the Egyptian electorate is not as wide as

Western observers might predict. Few Egyptians support the strict separation of religion and state. Indeed, a 2010 Pew Research Center poll indicated that 85% of respondents view Islam as a positive force in the political life of their country and that large majorities supported the enforcement of traditional Shari'a punishments for adultery, theft, and apostasy.[115] A call for the repeal of the Shari'a provision in Egypt's constitution, then, is unlikely to gain much traction in the wider public. Even within liberal and leftist circles, it is generally understood that any call for a repeal of Article 2 is a nonstarter, and the new secular parties that have formed since the uprising have not raised the issue, knowing that to do so would cost them dearly at the polls.[116]

Certainly within the Islamist movement, few individuals publicly call for the repeal of Article 2 and the transition to a secular state.[117] Where more progressive Islamists diverge from their conservative counterparts is not on whether they support Shari'a rule but in how they define it. In particular, the former endorse the application of the *general principles* (*al-mabadi' al-'amma*) of Shari'a rather than insist on the imposition of specific *rulings* (*ahkam*) inherited from the past. As Aboul 'Ela Madi, the founder of the Wasat party, explained, "No one can say they are against Shari'a. The people are conservative and they would not accept this. But from within the Shari'a we can find ways to reassure others [that we respect their rights]." He elaborated, "The program of our party inspires broad trust and confidence, as it supports full democracy and full citizenship rights, consistent with our own interpretation of the Shari'a."[118] Likewise, Islam Lutfi, a leader in the Egyptian Current party (which does not have an explicit Islamic frame of reference), supports the application of Shari'a but stresses its broader philosophical and ethical underpinnings:

> There is something called the higher objectives [*maqasid*] of the Shari'a. What are these? They are the protection of the human spirit, intellect, religion, property, and physical integrity. The range of permitted things is very wide, indeed everything is permitted unless a particular text prohibits them. But privacy is a sacred thing. There is a story about 'Umar Ibn al-Khattab, who was out walking at night and heard some people talking, and suspected that they were drunk. So he followed them to their home, where he climbed over a wall to see what they were doing, and he ended up breaking their wine bottles and beating them up. They complained to the authorities—"We made one mistake, we were drinking, but he made two mistakes—he spied on us, and he violated our property." Likewise, the Shari'a does not allow for the punishment of adultery unless there are four adult witnesses, meaning that the act occurred in public.

"I feel as if I'm selling the Shari'a to you!" Lutfi concluded with a laugh.[119]

While the Shari'a interpretations advanced by reformists in the Islamic movement are relatively expansive, those supported by conservative figures in the Muslim Brotherhood are decidedly less so. This reflects the long history of the Brotherhood as both a political and religious outreach organization that sought to expand the freedoms available to citizens under authoritarian rule at the same time that it sought to promote Islamically correct values and behavior. Consistent with this pattern, the Brotherhood has continued to invoke the application of Shari'a for contradictory purposes, to support the expansion of pluralism and civic and political freedoms in some instances, and to justify their restriction in others.

THE DEBATE OVER CONSTITUTIONAL PRINCIPLES

In the summer of 2011, a heated debate broke out over whether a binding set of "higher principles" should be formulated by the country's political elites and endorsed by the SCAF to guide the writing of the constitution. According to the schedule approved in the March referendum, the newly elected parliament would select a hundred-member commission to draft a permanent constitution. Those supporting a prior agreement on the "higher principles" of the constitution argued that it was needed to ensure that the document reflected a broad consensus among the country's different political and civil society groups. Such principled arguments were intertwined with the interests of small democratic parties and civil society organizations that sought a voice in shaping the constitution but were likely to be weakly represented in the parliament and hence would have little say in choosing its drafters.

For their part, the Muslim Brotherhood and other Islamist groups, including the Wasat party, argued that the articulation of "higher principles" by any group not chosen directly by the people's elected representatives constituted an infringement on the public will.[120] In addition, they argued, the project smacked of elitism. As Muhammad Hamza, a Brotherhood youth activist involved in the uprising, put it:

> Who led the revolution? The people. Some say as many as twenty million people took part in the events. They caused Mubarak to fall, and they have the right to decide on the political system which will replace him. What's the alternative? Some say the people are not mature enough to choose their leaders. But who gets to determine the maturity of the people? This is the same kind of argument that Mubarak used. He'd say the people aren't ready for democracy; if they are allowed to choose their leaders, they will vote the Brotherhood into power. Now we have these new political forces saying the same thing. . . . The real motivation behind the demand for constitutional principles is an effort by some political leaders to participate in power. But I'd ask Osama Ghazzali Harb or Muhammad Baradei, who delegated you to draft the articles of the constitution? . . . A constitution is a social contract. We are eighty million people, and these eighty million are the ones who have the right

to decide on the articles of the constitution, not Osama Ghazzali Harb, not the Brotherhood, and not any other group.[121]

While the Brotherhood opposed any deviations from the time line laid out in the March referendum, it was sensitive to fears that the Brotherhood would exploit its power at the ballot box to shape the composition of the Constitutional Commission and dominate the constitution writing process. To defuse such anxieties, the Brotherhood's FJP joined the Wafd and twenty-three other political parties in an alliance known as al-Tahaluf al-Dimuqrati Min Ajl Misr (Democratic Coalition for Egypt), whose representatives met at the FJP's new headquarters in the Cairo neighborhood of Roda on a regular basis to iron out their differences and articulate a common agenda. In a concession to its coalition partners, the FJP agreed that the commission formed by parliament to draft the constitution should include figures from a wide range of political and civil society groups to ensure that the constitution reflected a broad consensus among all national forces.

While demonstrating some flexibility with respect to the composition of the Constitutional Commission, the Brotherhood and the FJP took a strong stand against the articulation of a binding set of "higher principles" as the foundation of the constitution itself. As Mahmoud Ghuzlan explained,

> Some say there should be "higher principles," but this idea is rejected by us and many others. There is no such thing as principles which stand "above the constitution." This would constitute an infringement on the freedom of the commission. One can certainly offer suggestions and recommendations, but these cannot be binding. The constitution is a document which the people give to itself. Hence it must be drafted by individuals elected by the people and then approved by the people in a popular referendum.[122]

Although the Brotherhood cast itself as a defender of the people's will, its position in the debate was not so straightforward. The Brotherhood's support of the principle of popular sovereignty was not absolute, given their belief in the necessity of establishing a political system consistent with the mandates of divine guidance. Rather, their stress on the people's will reflected their confidence in the conservative religious values of the Egyptian people. Were a majority of Egyptian citizens to support a strict separation of religion and state, the Brotherhood would be far less likely to defend their final say in determining the constitution's content.

By contrast, more progressive Islamists, such as those affiliated with the Wasat and Egyptian Current parties who opposed the formulation of "higher principles" for the constitution were arguably motivated less by considerations of partisan advantage, given that their representation in parliament was likely to be negligible at best. As Islam Lutfi explained, he had no problem with the content of the "higher principles" proposed by liberal politicians but objected to the formation of such a document outside regular democratic channels:

> We can all agree that the Islamists have a problem with democracy. But we'd expect the liberals to have a more robust commitment to democratic principles. Instead, they say, "The people are illiterate, and we must direct them." This is fascist. They don't trust the people, and the people don't trust them. If you look at the articles proposed by Baradei and others, you'll find that ten of eleven of them come straight out of the UN's Universal Declaration of Human Rights. I'm a human rights activist so I have no problem with them. But I object to framing them as "above the constitution."

The eleventh article, Lutfi noted, contained a reference to the Shari'a as the primary source of legislation. This, too, is appropriate, he argued, given that an overwhelming majority of Egyptians, "including Muslims and Christians," are devout and believe that religion should play a role in public life.[123]

Lutfi's comments hinted at the emergence of a new consensus in the wake of the heated debates of the summer. The first element of this consensus was that that drafting of the constitution should be an inclusive process involving a wide cross-section of political and civil groups. Second, the final document should balance the guarantee of individual freedoms with the preservation of the distinctive values and identity of the Egyptian people. To this end, the Democratic Coalition for Egypt issued a charter purporting to identify the "general and foundational principles upon which there is wide agreement in Egyptian society" as the basis for a "free, just and democratic" political order.

A close reading of this document reveals an uneasy mix of liberal democratic and Islamist themes. For the most part, its section on "the political system and public freedoms" reads as a blueprint for liberal democracy, among other things, calling for an alternation of power through free and fair elections, affirming the right of citizens to form political parties and civil society organizations, and supporting an independent judiciary and a free press. But the document also exhibits clear signs of the Brotherhood's influence. In language borrowed almost verbatim from earlier Brotherhood statements, the charter leads with a section titled "The Construction of the Individual and the Basic Values of Society," which begins with the affirmation of Islam as *din wa dawla*, religion and state, and of the principles of the Islamic Shari'a as the primary source of legislation, though it adds a provision recognizing the right of non-Muslims to adhere to their own religious rulings in family matters. Further, the charter asserts that "moral values and principles are the foundation of the construction of the person" and calls for adherence to "the agreed-upon enduring values of the nation and its identity and its spiritual values as defined by the Semitic religions." In addition, it asserts that the freedom of the press must be balanced against its *"obligation to respect the general values and morals and norms of society according to the law"*; likewise, it calls for "respect for human rights according to international documents and conventions, *in so far as they do not contradict the principles of Islamic Shari'a and the preservation of Arab identity*" (emphasis added). Along the same lines, the section on social issues advocates "the protection of the public morality and religious values in society" and "a focus on the family and its defense."[124]

The charter arguably exhibited concessions by both the Muslim Brotherhood and its secular counterparts. For their part, the Muslim Brotherhood agreed to support existing language defining the *principles* of the Shari'a as the primary source of legislation rather than lobby for more specific and robust Shari'a provisions, as Salafi groups have done. On the other end of the spectrum, the Wafd and other secular parties decided not to fight for the repeal of Article 2 or to insist on a strict separation of religion and state.[125]

Yet by speaking in general terms instead of specifics, the Democratic Coalition's charter papered over the tensions between Islamist and liberal principles rather than resolving them. For example, it provided no indication of when and how "Shari'a principles" should be invoked to censor political, intellectual, and artistic expression, block the formation of parties and civil society groups perceived as anti-Shari'a and hence unconstitutional, and discriminate between the rights of men and women in matters of marriage, divorce, and inheritance.

While the Brotherhood and secular parties were working to forge a national consensus on the shape of the new constitution, Salafi Islamists weighed in on the street. On July 29, Tahrir Square, the epicenter of the uprising, became the scene of a massive demonstration calling for the establishment of an Islamic state. A few days earlier, a number of ultraconservative Salafi groups had called for a "million-man march" against the document of "higher principles" that had been presented for the SCAF's review, and the Muslim Brotherhood and the FJP decided to join the demonstration as well. In response, secular groups planned a counterdemonstration, portending an outbreak of open conflict along the country's Islamist-secular divide. In the days preceding the planned demonstrations, leaders from the Wasat party and the Muslim Brotherhood stepped in to mediate. As Muhammad al-Biltagi noted on July 26: "Several meetings have been held between [the two sides] where everybody spoke about reaching national consensus, while stressing that nobody should monopolize the revolutionary scene." In a veiled critique of those supporting the "higher principles" document, he added, "Neither does anyone have the right to play the role of the guardian of the revolution and the people."[126] Representatives from different factions, including Salafi groups, signed an agreement promising to focus on shared goals and avoid the use of controversial slogans.[127]

Ultimately such negotiations failed. On July 29, tens of thousands of bearded men in gallabiyas and women dressed in black amassed on Tahrir Square in a stunning display of Islamist force. While speakers at the edges of the square appealed for unity, Salafi protestors held up banners declaring "The Quran Is Our Constitution" and "Egypt's Identity Is Islamic," while organizers led the crowds in chanting, "Islamic, Islamic, neither secular nor liberal."[128] Other slogans turned the themes of the uprising on their head. For example, protesters chanted, "Raise your head high, you're a Muslim," instead of "Raise your head high, you're an Egyptian," and altered another well-known slogan of the uprising, "The people want to topple the regime" to "The people want to apply God's law." Islamist protestors at the square expressed pride in the large turnout and insisted that their demands were backed by a majority of the Egyptian people. As a twenty-eight-year-old accountant declared, "It's simple. We're stronger than any other force in the country, and we've made that clear on this day." In addition, they emphasized their right to a voice in shaping the country's future. As a twenty-six-year-old student put it: "If democracy is the voice of the majority and we as Islamists are the majority, why do they want to impose on us the views of minorities—the liberals and the secularists?"[129]

Secular leaders responded with indignation and outrage, accusing the Salafis of hijacking the demonstration. In particular, they accused the Salafis of breaking their pledge to avoid divisive chants and slogans. Watching the Islamist demonstration unfold, small groups of secular activists, who had been camped out on Tahrir Square for weeks, huddled in their tents and expressed dismay at the direction events had taken. "Welcome to the infidel section," a young woman said in a wry greeting to reporters. "I'm upset. We, the youth, did the revolution. We didn't say it should be Islamic or whatever. The people felt good. They felt relaxed here. And then suddenly these Islamic liars came, and they want us to go back 300 years." Or as Lina Wardani, a secular journalist and activist, tweeted in midmorning, "Confused when did Taliban take over?"[130]

The demonstration at Tahrir Square on July 29 was the first time since the start of the uprising that a mass protest was dominated by those calling for the establishment of an Islamic state. More broadly, it reflected the growing influence of the country's Salafi groups, which had entered the political fray in earnest by the summer. Over the objections of secular and liberal groups, the leaders of newly organized Salafi parties insisted on the strict application of Shari'a law, and some went so far as to demonize their critics as infidels. "Whoever opposes the implementation of Shari'a is not Muslim," noted Adel 'Afifi, one of the founders of the Salafi Asala (Authenticity) party. Unlike the Brotherhood, Salafi leaders were not satisfied with the current language of Article 2, arguing that the constitution should be modified so that it referred not just to the "principles" of the Shari'a but more specifically to its "commandments."[131] As 'Esam Dirbala, a founder of the Salafi-based Construction and Development party, observed: "The way secularists interpret the word 'principles' empties Shari'a of its content. The reduction is a way of circumventing the true meaning of implementing Shari'a."[132]

The growing assertiveness of Salafi groups placed the Brotherhood in an awkward position. On the one hand, the Brotherhood and the Salafis were part of the same broad ideological current, and any stand taken by the Brotherhood against the Salafis would open it to the charge of having abandoned the Islamic cause. On the other hand, identifying too closely with the Salafi movement would undermine the credibility of the Brotherhood's democratic commitments and threaten the fragile cross-partisan alliances it had forged with secular groups. The Brotherhood's response to the July 29 protest reflects the push and tug of such conflicting pressures. While quick to acknowledge that the Salafis, like all Egyptian citizens, were entitled to express their views, Brotherhood spokesmen criticized their behavior at Tahrir Square. For example, writing on its party website, 'Esam al-'Aryan stressed that the FJP opposed the efforts of some Islamists to impose their vision on the Egyptian people, since it "rejects dictatorship in all its forms." Yet al-'Aryan also sought to downplay the provocative nature of the Friday protest, casting the Islamist slogans raised at Tahrir Square as "individual and emotional" demands that were likely chosen in reaction to some of the slogans raised by secular groups over the preceding weeks. Finally, in a skillful act of deflection, al-'Aryan emphasized that it was up to the Egyptian people to adjudicate among different groups' agendas and "decide who they will trust to manage their affairs."[133]

As elections for a new parliament approached, the Brotherhood simultaneously sought to assure secular groups of its democratic commitments and assure the members of its base that it remained faithful to the group's historic da'wa mission. As we will see in the concluding chapter, the Brotherhood would emerge as the clear victor in the parliamentary elections, gaining over 40% of the seats on its own and, with Salafi Islamist groups, ending up with control of two-thirds of the seats in the assembly. In addition, Muhammad Mursi, a senior Brotherhood leader, would be appointed Egypt's new president. While these electoral victories have handed the Brotherhood unprecedented power, they have also imposed a much heavier burden of responsibility than any the group has faced in the past.

Before considering the new challenges confronting the Brotherhood, let us take a step back for a moment and consider its evolution in broader perspective. How does the Brotherhood's trajectory compare with those of its counterparts in other Arab states? That is, to what extent does its path reflect a broader pattern of Islamist movement change that transcends the particulars of any single country case? It is to these questions that we turn in the next chapter.

CHAPTER EIGHT

Egypt's Islamist Movement in Comparative Perspective

To WHAT EXTENT DOES THE EVOLUTION of the Muslim Brotherhood in Egypt reflect a wider pattern of Islamist movement change? This chapter places the Brotherhood in comparative perspective by considering the paths taken by its counterparts in Jordan, Kuwait, and Morocco. My aim is not to offer a full account of the development of such groups. Rather, drawing on research I conducted in each country in the mid-2000s and building on the work of other scholars, I sketch the broad outlines of Islamist movement change in Jordan, Kuwait, and Morocco, highlighting key parallels with—and divergences from—the Egyptian case.

THE ORIGINS OF SUNNI REVIVALIST GROUPS IN JORDAN, KUWAIT, AND MOROCCO

The three organizations I focus on here—the Islamic Front Party (IAF) in Jordan, the Islamic Constitutional Movement (ICM) in Kuwait, and the Parti de Justice et Developpement (PJD) in Morocco—are rooted in the movement of Sunni revivalist Islam that first took organized expression with the formation of the Egyptian Muslim Brotherhood more than eighty years ago. In Egypt, the *da'wa* and political functions of the Muslim Brotherhood remained fused within one movement organization until the formation of the Freedom and Justice Party in 2011. By contrast, the Brotherhood's counterparts in Jordan, Kuwait, and Morocco developed separate political arms much earlier, permitting a functional division of labor. While the movement association (*jama'a*) focuses on religious outreach and social services, the party (or, in Kuwait, bloc) represents the movement in the formal political arena. Let us begin by examining the origins of the Sunni Islamist movement associations (*jama'at*, the plural of *jama'a*) in each country and the circumstances under which they established separate political arms to represent the movement in electoral contests for political power.

THE MUSLIM BROTHERHOOD IN JORDAN

The Muslim Brotherhood Society in Jordan was founded by Sheikh Abd al-Latif Abu Qurah in November 1945 and was formally registered as a charitable society in January 1946. A fervent admirer of Hasan al-Banna, especially his call for a jihad to expel the Jewish community in Palestine, Abu Qurah met with Brotherhood leaders in Cairo and decided to establish a branch of the group in Jordan.[1] The society's inaugural meeting was attended by King Abdullah, reflecting the close relationship between the monarch and the East Bank merchants and property owners who headed the group at the time. While adopting the Egyptian Brotherhood's broad conception of Islam as *din wa dawla*, the Jordanian branch avoided calling directly for Islamic rule so as not to alienate regime authorities.[2] In 1953, just a year before the Egyptian Brotherhood was disbanded and forced underground, the Jordanian government elevated its counterpart from a charitable society to a "general multi-function Islamic group," allowing it to spread its ideas in mosques and public places and open new branches free of security interference.[3] As a supplement to its *da'wa* and social service activities, the Brotherhood fielded several candidates for parliament as independents in 1951 and 1954, and under its own banner in 1956. In both 1954 and 1956 the group won four seats out of forty. Though Abu Qurah opposed the decision to participate on the grounds that the "time was not yet ripe for a strong performance," most of the group's members favored the move as a means to "spread the group's ideas and introduce its activists to the public."[4]

The Brotherhood chose not to challenge the Hashemite monarchy positioned at the apex of the Jordanian state. This stemmed in part from their acknowledgment of the special status of the Hashemite rulers, whose lineage could be traced back to the family of the Prophet. In addition, it reflected the conservative religious values and personal and family ties linking the Brotherhood's East Bank leaders with regime officials. During the 1950s and 1960s, the Brotherhood sided with the regime against the Arab nationalist and leftist opposition, despite its growing discomfort with the regime's pro-West orientation. Whatever the monarchy's flaws, Brotherhood leaders understood that their fate under an Arab nationalist government would likely be far worse. As Yusuf al-'Azm, a Brotherhood leader, explained:

> The Muslim Brotherhood did not rise against the King because it was not possible for us to open fronts with all the sides all at once. We stood by the King in order to protect ourselves, for if it were left to Abdel Nasser to enter Jordan . . . he would have eliminated us as he did to the *Ikhwan* in Egypt.[5]

The Brotherhood was rewarded for its loyalty. For example, when political parties were banned in 1956, the Brotherhood, as a nonparty association, was exempt from the restrictions imposed on its secular counterparts and was able to expand its support base at a time that other groups were suppressed. As Ellen Lust-Okar observed,

> When political parties were banned and venues of participation were shut down, the Brotherhood was allowed to act as a charitable association, given ministers with socially oriented portfolios (particularly in Education and Religious Affairs) and enjoyed the freedom to establish and build a large network of social organizations—including schools, hospitals, health clinics, etc.[6]

Among the institutions established by the Brotherhood was the Islamic Center Charity Society (ICCS), licensed in 1963, which in later decades would channel donations by those who had made their fortunes in the Gulf into clinics and schools under the Brotherhood's control.[7] As Quintan Wiktorowicz noted, the financial resources of the ICCS eventually exceeded those of any other NGO in the country except those under royal patronage.[8]

Israel's victory in the June War of 1967 dealt a lethal blow to Arab nationalism and fueled the expansion and radicalization of Islamist groups across the region. In the war's aftermath, Palestinian guerrilla forces (fida'iyyiin) based in Jordan launched attacks on Israel in which several Brotherhood members participated. Tensions between the Hashemite regime and Palestinian militants came to a head in the early 1970s, when Jordanian troops expelled the Palestinian Liberation Organization from Palestinian refugee camps in Jordanian territory. But the Brotherhood remained on the sidelines in this conflict, presumably out of concern for its own survival.

During the 1970s and 1980s, the Brotherhood expanded its role in public life. Some of its leaders assumed positions in the Ministry of Education, where they helped set the country's educational curriculum and, through their control over school budgets and appointments, channeled patronage to their supporters.[9] Further, a few individuals accepted senior posts in the government. For example, in 1970, Ishaq Farhan accepted a joint appointment as minister of education and minister of religious endowments, and Abd al-Latif 'Arabiyyat was appointed director general of the Amman Department of Education (1981–82) and later served as the Ministry of Education's secretary-general (1982–85).[10] During the same time period, in a direct parallel with Egypt, the Brotherhood emerged as the dominant force in Jordan's student unions and professional associations. Further, when parliament was restored after a fourteen-year hiatus in 1984, the Brotherhood won three of the eight vacant seats.[11]

By the 1980s, several distinct trends had coalesced within the Jordanian Brotherhood, reflecting profound differences of opinion on the group's proper relationship with the regime and other sectors of society. As Mansour Moaddel observed, one trend, associated with such figures as Yusuf al-'Azm, Ahmad Azaideh, and Ishaq Farhan, favored "closer interaction with political trends in society and dialogue with the government," while a second trend, represented by hard-liners such as Muhammad Abu Faris and Hammam Sa'eed, "took a more puritan and politically isolationist approach."[12] In addition, the Brotherhood was internally divided on the priority to be given to the liberation of Palestine over domestic affairs. Such discord reflected the diversification of the Brotherhood's base, which now included a mix of East Bank Jordanians and Palestinians. While East Bank, ethnically Jordanian leaders had a history of cordial relations with the Hashemite regime, the Palestinians who entered the group in 1948 and 1967 injected a new strain of radical activism into the group's ranks. Indeed, over time the Brotherhood became the primary vehicle for the incorporation of Palestinians into the Jordanian polity and the most important venue for the articulation of their demands. The Brotherhood's eventual adoption of a hard-line stance against any accommodation with the "forces of Zionism and imperialism" created new tensions with the regime and strained the pattern of cohabitation they had forged in the past.

But unlike in Egypt, both the regime and the Brotherhood sought to prevent these strains from reaching a breaking point. Periods of tension were typically followed by periods of rapprochement, with each side anxious to avoid the trauma of an open conflict. Though increasingly outspoken in its opposition to regime policy, the Brotherhood stopped short of challenging the legitimacy of the monarchy itself. In return, the regime allowed the Brotherhood to function in the open and maintain a large network of mosques and charitable and social service organizations, enabling it to build a mass base far exceeding that of any secular group. The Brotherhood was thus uniquely positioned to benefit from the opening that ushered in a new era of Jordanian politics in the early 1990s.

The Muslim Brotherhood in Kuwait

Less is known about the history of the Muslim Brotherhood in Kuwait, and published studies of the group, whether in English or Arabic, are few in number and difficult to access. Nevertheless, piecing together bits of information from different sources, a picture emerges that exhibits numerous parallels with the Jordanian case. In Kuwait, the Muslim Brotherhood first took organized expression as the Islamic Guidance Society in 1952 and was relaunched after Kuwait gained independence from Britain in 1962 as the Social Reform Society.[13] As in Jordan, the Kuwaiti branch looked to the Egyptian Brotherhood for inspiration and guidance. In addition, it was directly influenced by Brotherhood teachers and other professionals who fled Nasser's Egypt in the 1950s and 1960s and established new lives in the Gulf. In contrast with the Jordanian Brotherhood, the Kuwaiti branch was not formally registered but operated informally, conducting its affairs away from the public eye.[14]

Like its counterparts in Egypt and Jordan, the Kuwaiti Social Reform Society directed the bulk of its energies to grassroots outreach, establishing a network of mosques and social service organizations funded by donations from private individuals and Brotherhood-affiliated companies and investment banks. In its early years, the Kuwaiti Brotherhood's understanding of Islam was influenced by radical Egyptian ideologues like Sayyid Qutb, as well as by the ultrapuritanical Wahhabi strand of Islam that prevailed in Saudi Arabia. But from the outset, it eschewed violence and avoided direct confrontation with the Sabah monarchy, opting to promote Islamization within—rather than against—the institutions of Kuwaiti society and state.[15]

During the 1960s and 1970s, the Brotherhood remained aloof from conflict between the Sabah regime and Arab nationalist and leftist groups in parliament, whose demands for greater oversight of regime policy led the emir to suspend the legislature in 1976. The Brotherhood did not challenge the emir's decision and was rewarded with the appointment of its chairman, Yusuf al-Hajji, as the minister of religious endowments. Other Brotherhood members were appointed to positions in the state bureaucracy, particularly in the Ministries of Education and Communication, where they pushed for a greater focus on religious themes in school textbooks and television programs.[16]

Emboldened by the Iranian Revolution in 1979, the Brotherhood extended its reach into new domains in the 1980s. Like its counterparts in Egypt and Jordan, it ran candidates for the boards of student unions and professional associations and scored striking gains, particularly in the scientific and technical fields.[17] When parliament was restored and elections were held in 1981, the Brotherhood, together with Salafi groups, outperformed leftist and liberal forces for the first time. In part, this was a result of the government's decision to expand the country's electoral system by adding several new districts in tribal areas outside the country's main urban centers.[18] Ostensibly intended to boost the representation of pro-regime tribal deputies in parliament, the addition of the new districts was a boon for Islamist groups as well. Beginning in the early 1980s, the Brotherhood tapped into the economic grievances of the Bedouin population, who resented city dwellers' privileged access to government benefits and services, and exploited their anxiety about the loosening of traditional patriarchal authority structures in a period of rapid social change.

By appealing to the country's newly naturalized Bedouin tribes, the Brotherhood was able to expand its base of support. At the same time, its close association with the Bedouin community reinforced its conservative positions on social and moral issues. As Ghanim al-Najjar, a Kuwaiti political scientist, observed, the incorporation of the Bedouin tribes contributed to the "desertization" of Kuwaiti politics, eroding the cosmopolitan norms and values associated with the country's urban merchant, professional, and intellectual elites.[19]

Islamist and secular deputies in parliament were deeply divided on social and moral issues. For example, after the elections in 1981 and 1985, the Brotherhood and Salafi groups introduced a series of bills that called for elevating the status of the Shari'a in the constitution from a *primary source* to *the* source of legislation.[20] In another controversial move, they demanded the stricter segregation of men and women in public places. Yet on other matters, Brotherhood deputies cooperated with their liberal and leftist counterparts. After the 1985 elections, they joined forces to assert the right of parliament to greater oversight of the executive functions of the ruling family.[21] For example, they both participated in the aggressive interpellation (*istijwab*) of individual cabinet members, eventually leading the prime minister (per tradition, the Crown Prince) and his cabinet to resign on July 1, 1986, claiming that parliament's relentless interference had made it impossible for them to govern.[22]

During the next four years, the emir ruled the country by decree. Against this backdrop, a pro-democracy movement emerged, encompassing merchants, professionals, and intellectuals from across the ideological spectrum. To circumvent the government's ban on political meetings, the opposition revived the Kuwaiti tradition of holding informal gatherings or salons (*diwaniyyaat*) in private homes. As the movement coalesced, it developed a common set of demands, "focused on the restoration of parliament, the full implementation of the 1962 constitution, and the lifting of restrictions on free speech and on the right to peaceful assembly."[23] In January 1990, opposition leaders organized a demonstration calling for the reopening of parliament, which, in a move uncharacteristic for a regime that had rarely resorted to outright repression in the past, was forcibly dispersed by baton-wielding riot police. In an effort to defuse the situation, the emir invited the opposition to participate in a national dialogue and, in April, established a new advisory body to "study the advisability and feasibility of a restoration of parliament." Leaders of the pro-democracy movement rejected these moves as a stalling tactic and remained firm in their demand for the immediate restoration of parliament and the 1962 constitution.[24] Though cut short by the Iraqi invasion of Kuwait on August 2, 1990, the democracy movement exerted a defining influence on the priorities and objectives of the new political blocs formed after the end of the Iraqi occupation in 1991, including the Islamic Constitutional Movement (ICM).

THE SHABIBA MOVEMENT AND ITS SUCCESSORS IN MOROCCO

As in Jordan, the Moroccan state is headed by a monarchy that traces its lineage back to the Prophet Muhammad, but the authorities of the Moroccan king were even more expansive. Defined by the constitution as the "supreme representative of the nation," he served not only as the highest political authority and commander of the army but also as the country's supreme religious authority, as indicated by his designation as "commander of the faithful" (*amir al-mu'minin*). This double political and religious authority, rooted in both tradition and the Moroccan constitution, distinguishes the Moroccan king from other rulers in the Arab world.[25] Hence Islamist groups in Morocco are forced to contend with a powerful state religious establishment that claims to possess the ultimate authority to adjudicate on all matters pertaining to Shari'a and Islam.

During the 1960s, under the reign of King Hassan II, a Sunni revivalist movement with clear ideological affinities to the Muslim Brotherhood began to coalesce in Morocco with a base in the country's universities and secondary schools. Jam'iyyat al-Shabiba al-Islamiyya (The Association of Islamic Youth) was founded by 'Abdelkrim Muti'. Though independent of the Muslim Brotherhood, the Shabiba movement drew on its ideas and was particularly influenced by the ideas of Sayyid Qutb. As 'Abdalla Bagha, a PJD leader who was a member of al-Shabiba at the time, recalled:

> We were revolutionary in our outlook, reflecting the view of Sayyid Qutb and our own radical interpretation of the Quran and the Hadith. The cultural atmosphere at the time encouraged radical thinking among all groups—a rejection of reality—not just by Islamists but also on the left.[26]

When al-Shabiba was implicated in the 1975 assassination of 'Umar Ben Jalloun, a prominent leftist trade union leader, the group was dissolved, several leaders were arrested, and Muti' fled into exile.[27] Such events triggered a process of soul-searching within al-Shabiba's ranks. As Abd al-Qadir 'Umara, a member of the PJD Executive Council, explained:

> The assassination of Ben Jalloun was a critical juncture for the movement. It raised a number of fundamental questions that became a focus of heated internal debate: Who are we? What do we want? What is our relationship with the political system, the king, and other groups? Is it possible to impose Islam by force? When we arrived at answers to these questions, we advanced.[28]

In the early 1980s, a group of Shabiba leaders based in Rabat broke from Muti'and formed a new association, Al-Jama'a Al-Islamiyaa (Islamic Group).[29] Its founding leaders, then in their thirties, included 'Abdalla Bagha, Muhammad Yatim, and 'Abdalla Benkirane. This group set the movement on a new course. As Michael Willis observed:

> From the outset, it was apparent that the new grouping was intent on breaking not only with Abdelkrim Mouti's leadership, but also with his whole approach when seeking the application of Islamic values and doctrines in Morocco. Whereas Al-Shabiba under Mouti's leadership had been renowned for its belligerence and criticism of the regime and had even been implicated in violence against its opponents, al-Jama'a adopted a very different approach. It both explicitly accepted the legitimacy of the Moroccan regime—fundamentally the monarchy—and renounced the use of violence. Emphasis was, instead, placed on the promotion of Islamic values through gradualist and peaceful means.[30]

Over the next ten years, this evolution progressed. As Muhammad Tozy noted, "They asked themselves, 'Is our interpretation of Islam the only one? Is it the right one?'"—moving from a stress on absolutes toward greater ideological flexibility and openness to dialogue with other groups.[31]

As part of this wider shift, the Islamic Group attempted to normalize its relationship with the regime and acquire a legal foothold in the political system. After their bid for legal status was denied in 1983, Islamic Group leaders wrote a series of letters to government officials emphasizing their loyalty to the king and the Moroccan state. Soon after, they moved to create a party that would function alongside the movement association and represent the latter in the political system. In 1992, their application to form Hizb al-Tajdid al-Watani (The National Renewal Party) was denied. As Muhammad Darif observed, the regime was determined to avoid what had happened in Algeria, where the stunning victory of the Islamic Salvation Front (known by its French acronym, FIS) in parliamentary elections in December 1991 prompted the army to intervene and declare martial law.[32] In an effort to distinguish itself from the FIS and defuse the allegation that it claimed the exclusive right to represent Islam, the Islamic Group changed its name to al-Islah was al-Tajdid (Reform and Renewal).

It also began to explore other ways to enter the political arena. After an attempt to merge with the large and well-established Moroccan nationalist Istiqlal party failed, it reached out to the Mouvement Populaire Democratique and Constitutionnel (MPDC), a small Berber party close to the palace led by Abdelkrim Khatib. The MPDC was such a marginal group that it had not won a seat in parliament in over twenty years. Negotiations between al-Islah wa al-Tajdid and the MPDC began in 1992 and culminated in the holding of an extraordinary Party Congress in 1996, when several movement leaders were appointed to the MPDC's executive committee. This was a watershed moment for al-Islah wa al-Tajdid. As Willis observed, "[T]he objective of finding a party political vehicle had been achieved and the perceived isolation of the Islamist movement from the formal political process had been broken."[33] Later that year, the group merged with a smaller Islamist association, Rabitat al-Mustaqbal al-Islami, and changed its name to Harakat al-Tawhid wa al-Islah (Movement of Unity and Reform, or MUR).[34] The MPDC, which was renamed the Justice and Development Party (Parti de Justice et Developpement, or PJD) in 1998, would function from then on as the political arm of the MUR.

Morocco experts emphasize that the Islamist trend could not have gained a legal foothold in the political system without the king's blessing. As noted earlier, movement leaders set the stage for this breakthrough by attempting to persuade the king, for the better part of a decade, that they sought to work within the existing order rather than against it. This helped soften the regime's perception of the group as a threat. More generally, Muhammad Darif explained, al-Islah wa al-Tajdid's willingness to join the party system via a pro-palace party, and the monarchy's acquiescence to it, can be understood as an effort by both sides to manage their relationship in such a way that the Algerian experience could be avoided.[35]

What is most striking is that *the political inclusion of al-Islah wa al-Tajdid (later, the MUR) was preceded by the self-conscious break of its leaders from the radical ideas associated with the movement's anti-system past.* In Jordan and Kuwait, where the relationship of Sunni revivalist groups with reigning monarchs was less antagonistic to begin with, there was less external pressure on group leaders to critically reexamine the movement's absolutist foundations, such as their claim to speak for all Muslims and the definition of their ideas as the "correct" interpretation of Islam. In Egypt, younger members in the Brotherhood began to call for progressive changes in the group's agenda beginning in the mid-1980s, but they were blocked from assuming top leadership positions by the old guard. By contrast, the split of current MUR and PJD leaders from the Shabiba movement in the mid-1970s set the stage for a qualitative shift in the movement's core ideology. As Abd al-Qadir 'Umara put it,

> Over a period of more than ten years, through a process of ongoing discussion and debates, what started out as a closed and insular movement characterized by a belief in absolutes was transformed into a participatory movement characterized by an acceptance of the Other [*qubuul bi'l-'akhar*]. This shift was solidified by 1990.[36]

Longtime observers of Moroccan politics agree that the ideological orientations of MUR and PJD leaders changed significantly over time. The early onset of this shift, and the extent to which it shaped the PJD's later evolution, make the Moroccan group something of a special case.

In recent decades, the Jordanian, Kuwaiti, and Moroccan groups, like the Brotherhood in Egypt, expanded their participation in electoral politics. Let us look at the impact of participation on each group below.

The Trajectory of Islamist Participation in Jordan

In April 1989, riots broke out in the southern Jordanian city of Maan that quickly spread to other parts of the country. The immediate trigger of the protests was a set of austerity measures implemented by the regime under pressure from the International Monetary Fund, including cuts in subsidies that led to sharp increases in the cost of food and other staple items. The riots came as a shock to the regime, which was amplified by the fact that they originated in tribal areas of the south, historically a strong base of regime support. As Curtis Ryan observed, the regime of King Hussein responded by launching a process of "defensive liberalization," through which it "attempted to mollify its domestic critics and open the system to more meaningful levels of political participation than had been the case thus far."[37]

Jordan's political opening began with the holding of parliamentary elections in November 1989, the first general elections since 1967. With the country's secular groups in disarray, the Muslim Brotherhood was virtually the only organized group capable of running an effective campaign. Yet in a pattern that would repeat itself in future elections, the Brotherhood opted not to run for all eighty seats, fielding candidates for less than a third. As Ishaq Farhan observed, participation in elections was not a high priority for the group at the time, and moreover if the Brotherhood had sought and won a larger number of seats, "the dose would have been too heavy" for the Jordanian polity to bear.[38] Mobilizing the base it had cultivated over the preceding decades, the Brotherhood won twenty-two seats, 85% of the seats it contested and more than a quarter of the eighty seats in total. An additional twelve Islamist candidates won seats as independents. Arab nationalist and leftist groups won a total of thirteen seats, with the remainder going to pro-regime candidates.

Brotherhood leaders interpreted the group's strong showing as a sign of widespread support for its agenda. After the elections, they issued a statement declaring that the group's "most important duty" was to "exert every possible effort to revise all laws and regulations in Jordan so that they completely conform with the Islamic Shari'a."[39] The Brotherhood stressed that it would pursue such goals through the legislative process rather than outside it. In addition, it participated in negotiations to establish a framework for the new political order. In April 1990, six Brotherhood leaders joined a sixty-member commission appointed by the king to draft a National Charter (*mithaq watani*). Formally adopted in June 1991, the charter represented a compromise between the king and the country's main political trends. While defining Jordan's system of government as a hereditary monarchy, it enshrined the principle of political pluralism by affirming the right of citizens to form parties, as long as their methods were peaceful and their objectives did not violate the constitution. While stressing the pluralistic character of the new system, the charter acknowledged the special status of Islam as the religion of the state and of the Shari'a as the primary source of legislation.[40] Hence the charter incorporated a mix of democratic and religious elements, leaving the question of how they should be reconciled open to interpretation.

In 1992, after martial law was lifted and a new political parties law was passed, the Brotherhood established the Islamic Action Front party (Jabha al-'Amal al-Islami), or IAF. Though the party initially included a number of Islamist independents, it became clear early on that who would run it and what positions it would take were subject to Brotherhood direction. Though formally independent, the IAF hence functioned in practice as the Brotherhood's political arm, reflecting a division of labor in which the *jama'a* retained control of the movement's *da'wa* and social service networks while the IAF represented the movement in electoral politics.

Less than a year after the IAF was established, the regime changed the country's electoral laws to limit its presence in parliament. Further, to contain growing opposition to the country's 1994 peace treaty with Israel and, later, to U.S.-led military operations in Afghanistan and Iraq, the monarchy imposed new restrictions on freedom of expression and assembly and increased the powers of the state security establishment (*mukhabarat*). Such deliberalizing measures triggered a striking shift in the IAF's discourse away from calls for the immediate application of Shari'a toward an emphasis on the urgent need for constitutional and political reform. This shift is examined in greater detail next.

The IAF's Rhetorical Shift to Democracy

The Brotherhood's strong showing in the 1989 parliamentary elections came as a surprise to the regime, which had predicted that it would gain about ten seats, less than half the number it actually won. From the viewpoint of regime officials, the electoral system in place at the time, in which citizens chose candidates for all of the seats in their multimember districts, with each seat won by a simple plurality, had enabled the Brotherhood to achieve a level of representation greater than its support in society at large. The election tally backs up this claim, since the Brotherhood won 12% of the popular vote but managed to gain 27% of the seats in parliament.[41] Before the next round of parliamentary elections in 1993, the regime altered the country's electoral laws: citizens would be permitted to vote for only one candidate in each multimember district. In a society where tribal and clan loyalties ran strong, the "one person, one vote" law essentially forced voters to choose between their favored tribal candidate and candidates fielded by the IAF and other parties. In addition, the regime adjusted the number of seats allocated to each district, padding the representation of historically pro-regime rural areas and limiting that of large urban centers like Amman and Zarqa where support for the Brotherhood and other opposition parties was concentrated.

The IAF denounced the electoral reform as a flagrant instance of government intervention in the democratic process in order to limit Islamist gains. As Ishaq Farhan stated:

> The government says this is a one-person, one-vote system, but the weight of individual votes are not the same. . . . The government knows that we have considerable popular support, which is why they have corrupted the democratic process in order to prevent us from achieving a majority.[42]

In 1993 the Brotherhood's share of seats in parliament dropped from 28% to 20%, even though its share of the popular vote increased.[43] The following year, the Jordanian government signed a peace treaty with Israel over the vigorous objections of the IAF and secular nationalist parties. Soon after, these groups launched an "anti-normalization" campaign within Jordan's professional syndicates. To contain growing opposition to the treaty as well as the grievances triggered by a new round of economic reforms, the regime imposed new restrictions on freedom of expression and assembly, including the establishment of a controversial press and publications law in 1997. In July of that year, the IAF and several secular parties called for a boycott of the parliamentary elections scheduled for the fall. Further, the IAF shifted its attention from religious matters to the regime's dictatorial practices. As Schwedler observed, other than opening and closing with brief verses from the Quran, the IAF's statement made no references to Islam and stressed the urgent need for political reform.[44]

In sum, by the mid-1990s, we see a clear shift in the IAF's discourse toward a new emphasis on public freedoms and democracy. This shift was clearly grounded in self-interest since the Brotherhood, as the largest and best-organized sector of the opposition, would benefit most from a lifting of the restrictive laws then in place. As Shadi Hamid put it, "As the Muslim Brotherhood and IAF were fighting for, literally, their very freedom, they were forced to prioritize and redefine their focus."[45] Yet what began as a tactical adjustment yielded a broader and more lasting ideological shift, in which the call for Shari'a rule was redefined as consistent with the strengthening of democratic rules and procedures.

Developments in Jordan after the ascension of King Abdallah II to the throne in 1999 reinforced this trend. The breakdown of the Israeli-Palestinian peace process and the onset of the U.S.-led occupation of Iraq created new flashpoints of conflict between the Brotherhood and the regime. At the same time, a new round of economic reforms triggered unrest around the country. With opposition growing on multiple fronts, King Abdallah suspended parliament in 2001 and ruled by decree until 2003, when long-delayed elections were finally held in June. Although more elections followed in 2007 and 2010, the "one person, one vote" election law prevented the IAF from achieving any meaningful gains.

Further, beginning in the mid-2000s, the Brotherhood's public endorsement of violent acts of resistance in Palestine and Iraq prompted a number of senior figures in the state establishment to conclude that the group had begun to pose a threat to national security. In 2004, the government arrested several Brotherhood preachers for "excessive criticism of the regime," and in 2005 it sought to rein in the Brotherhood-dominated professional syndicates by banning the holding of any event, meeting, or gathering without the government's approval.[46] The bombing of three luxury hotels in Amman by an affiliate of al-Qa'ida in November 2005 on the orders of Abu Musab al-Zarqawi, a former Jordanian national, prompted new restrictions on preaching in mosques and the introduction of a new anti-terrorism law that expanded the powers of the state security and police.[47] Although the Brotherhood and the IAF were not directly implicated in the bombings, some of their leaders saw Zarqawi as an icon of resistance. After Zarqawi's death in 2006, IAF hard-liner Muhammad Abu Faris lauded him as a "martyr" and several IAF parliamentarians paid a condolence call to his family.

Further, the victory of Hamas in the Palestinian legislative elections of January 2006 raised fears that a newly triumphant Hamas would exert a radicalizing influence on its sister movement in Jordan. Emboldened by Hamas's success, 'Azzam Huneidi, head of the IAF's bloc in parliament, declared that the IAF could win as much as 50% of the vote in free and fair elections, and urged the regime to stop trying to "downsize" the movement by manipulating the country's electoral laws to reduce their electoral weight.[48]

The IAF participated in the 2003 and 2007 parliamentary elections, but its margin of representation continued to erode. In 2003, it won seventeen of the thirty seats it contested, a respectable success rate of 57%. But in an expanded parliament of 110 members, its share of seats declined to 16% (compared with 20% in 1993 and 28% in 1989). In 2007, with tensions between the regime and the Brotherhood at a new height, the IAF only contested twenty-two seats and avoided running pro-Hamas and anti-government candidates.[49] Amid widespread allegations of vote rigging and fraud, the IAF won six seats, just 27% of the seats it contested and less than 6% of the total, its worst performance yet. Bitter recriminations among the group's internal factions ensued, with each side seeking to deflect blame for the party's losses onto their rivals.[50] More broadly, the results underscored the regime's determination to block the Brotherhood from achieving an effective presence in parliament, triggering growing cynicism and frustration with the electoral process.

By the time a new round of elections approached in 2010, an internal poll indicated that over 70% of IAF members favored a boycott. As IAF secretary-general Hamza Mansour explained, the boycott was "a political act and a logical consequence of the political impasse," as well as a means to signal the group's protest against the country's rising poverty levels.[51] The most notable feature of the Brotherhood's call for a boycott of the November 2010 elections was that it was led by leaders of the "moderate" or "dovish" wing of the party who had strongly endorsed participation in the past. In an effort to "transform the boycott into a political platform," prominent "moderates" joined with counterparts from secular parties and civil society organizations to call for the transformation of the system into a parliamentary monarchy in which the powers of the king would be sharply circumscribed.[52] In sum, in a direct parallel with Egypt, by 2010 the reformist wing of the Brotherhood had concluded that participation by the regime's rules had reached a dead end and that future participation would not be productive unless those rules were fundamentally revised.

The Scope and Limits of the IAF's Democratic Shift

Like the Brotherhood in Egypt, the Jordanian Brotherhood and its political arm, the IAF, began to challenge the rules and practices of authoritarian leaders by joining the call for democratic reform. Though glimmers of this trend surfaced as far back as the mid-1990s, it became even more pronounced in the years that followed. As Shadi Hamid observed, the IAF's 2003 electoral program prominently featured two democratic concepts—the "alternation of power" and "the people are the source of authority"—for the first time, and they have become a Brotherhood rallying cry ever since.[53] Likewise, the detailed reform program released by the IAF in 2005 endorsed a wide range of civic and political freedoms.[54]

This striking rhetorical shift, and the fact that Brotherhood and IAF leaders have remained "surprisingly on-message,"[55] has been pointed to by experts as proof that the Brotherhood has embraced the democratic cause as its own. As Juan Stemman observed, "[D]eclarations that democracy was anathema to Islam and calls for an Islamic state ruled solely by Shari'a are a thing of the past." Or as Hamid put it,

> The fact that the IAF was arguing in favor of popular as opposed to divine sovereignty could only be taken as an implicit retreat from advocating the creation of an actual Islamic state. . . . Democracy is assumed to be compatible with the Shari'a, *a priori*. . . . In effect, liberal democracy has absorbed Islamist thought, proving the ideological power of the democratic ideal.[56]

Indeed, Hamid argued,

> It is true that Islamic movements in certain countries have been guilty of political equivocation on the issue of democracy. This, however, is not the case in Jordan. An objective analysis of what the Muslim Brotherhood and the IAF have said and written in recent years should put alarmist concerns to rest.[57]

The IAF's ideological shift was less coherent and encompassing than such comments suggest, however. In a parallel with the Brotherhood in Egypt, the IAF's commitment to democracy continues to be tempered by its opposition to individual freedom and equality when they are seen as conflicting with the Shari'a and the fixed values of Jordanian society as they define them. Let us look at such tensions in greater detail.

First, although Brotherhood leaders repeatedly emphasized their commitment to political pluralism in statements to the press, a closer look at their discourse suggests that this commitment was not absolute. For example, IAF leader Abd al-Latif 'Arabiyyat argued that the Brotherhood's commitment to pluralism is proven by its endorsement of the National Charter of 1991.[58] But the charter is in fact an ambiguous document. In addition to affirming the principle of party pluralism, it asserts that Islam is the religion of the state and the Shari'a is the primary source of legislation. According to the terms of the charter, then, whether or not Jordanian parties must accept the privileged status of the Shari'a is open to interpretation. That the charter can be invoked as a *constraint* on political pluralism can be seen in the comments of 'Azzam Huneidi, who at the time of our interview in 2004 was the head of the IAF's parliamentary bloc. When asked if he supported the right of communists to form their own party, Huneidi replied:

> The communists can participate according to the terms of the National Charter. But every country has its limits, don't they? Can one be a member of the Communist Party in the United States? In Turkey, those who criticize Ataturk are considered criminals, and the U.S. considers Turkey a democracy. So why can't we say that those who attack Islam are rejected?[59]

Second, although all of the IAF leaders I interviewed in 2004 stressed that the "people are the source of all authority," they did so with the full expectation that a parliament formed through free elections would be dominated by members of their own party, along with conservative tribal MPs who shared their agenda. When asked if the IAF would respect the outcome of an election that brought a communist party to power, the leaders I interviewed said that they would because they respect the people's will. As Hamza Mansour (secretary-general of the IAF for two terms, 2002–6 and 2010–present) said:

> If there were free elections based on just and fair electoral laws, we would respect the outcome no matter what. If a leftist party won a majority, we would sit in the opposition [and pursue our objectives from there]. We respect the will of the citizens.[60]

Yet IAF leaders also stressed that such an outcome would never happen because the people favor a political system based on Islam. As Mansour observed,

> If we gave Jordanian citizens complete freedom they would choose Islam. This is because it is in harmony with human conscience [damir insani] and with human nature as God created it. The government knows that the people respect the authority of God and want a system based on submission to God [al-taqwa li-llah]. That is why the government will not permit free and fair elections and the real alternation of power.[61]

Third, all of the IAF leaders I interviewed opposed extending the unbridled freedoms available in the West to citizens in Jordan, arguing that this would undermine public morals and weaken the institution of the family. Every society, they stressed, should have the right to strike its own balance between respect for individual rights and deference to public sensibilities, noting that even in the West people cannot walk in the street naked or have sex in public. *While advocating the expansion of citizens' rights in the political domain, the IAF simultaneously supported the stricter regulation of their private behavior.* IAF leaders saw no contradiction here; on the contrary, they framed such positions as complementary. As Mansour noted: "One of our main goals is to overcome corruption of all types—political, financial, economic, and moral. We seek to put an end to the marketing of values and behavior that are not in harmony with our own Arab and Islamic values."[62] When asked to give some examples of what the

IAF opposed, Mansour mentioned the spread of nightclubs, mixed-gender swimming pools, and deviant forms of massage.

IAF leaders were quick to stress that they did not seek to impose conformity with Islamic standards of behavior by force. Noting that there is "no coercion in religion" (la ikrah fi'l-din), the only way to promote correct behavior was through persuasion (iqna'). For example, although all of the IAF leaders I interviewed regarded veiling (wearing the hijab) as a religious requirement for all Muslim women, they stressed that their goal was to convince women to adopt it by choice.

But from a civil rights perspective, two problems persisted in the IAF's efforts to promote the veil and, by extension, other types of Islamically correct behavior. First, it remained unclear whether the IAF was willing to grant those with conflicting opinions—including different views of Islam—the same access to the media, the schools, and the mosques they sought for themselves. Second, IAF leaders differed on whether the state should legally mandate veiling at some point in the future. While some IAF leaders I interviewed, like Raheel Gharibeh, stressed that whether or not a woman veiled should be left to her individual conscience, others disagreed. For example, both Hamza Mansour and 'Azzam Huneidi suggested that after an initial phase of consciousness-raising (taw'iya) to educate women of their duties in Islam, a bill requiring veiling should be proposed, to be converted into law by popular vote. Just as Mansour claimed that "the people want Shari'a," so too he insisted that "the vast majority of Jordanian women, as believing Muslims, are already receptive to the hijab by their very nature (bil-fitra)."[63]

More broadly, IAF leaders emphasized that they did not oppose women's rights but sought to advance them within an Islamic framework. For example, while Westerners might see the veil as a hardship, 'Azzam Huneidi noted, "To us, it is a form of respect [takrim] for women."[64] The IAF's stance on women's rights cannot be simply framed as based on "Islam," since, like all religions, Islam is open to multiple and conflicting interpretations. Indeed, the IAF's selective reading of Islam exhibited the influence of conservative tribal norms and customs, particularly on matters concerning women's sexual and personal autonomy. The IAF's opposition to two reform bills proposed by the Jordanian government in recent years exhibits in sharp relief the limits of its support for women's rights.

THE IAF'S OPPOSITION TO THE REFORM OF GENDER-DISCRIMINATORY LAWS

Over the past decade, IAF deputies in parliament have repeatedly blocked efforts to reform provisions of Jordan's criminal and civil status codes that discriminate against women. For example, they opposed changes in the penal code that would have stiffened the penalties for "honor crimes," cases in which one family member injures or kills another in order to restore the family's honor. According to Article 340, a man who kills or attacks his wife or any female relative in the act of committing adultery or in an "unlawful bed" is granted an exemption from punishment. In 1998, the Jordanian National Commission for Women, headed by Princess Basma, the sister of King Hussein, urged the government to change the law, and later that year, a group called the Campaign for the Elimination of So-Called "Crimes of Honor" led by Rana Husseini and other women's rights activists drafted a reform petition that gained over 15,000 signatures.[65] In 1999 the government issued a temporary law repealing the article, which was sent to parliament twice, in November 1999 and again in January 2000. Both times the lower house rejected it. In 2001, when parliament was suspended, the government issued another temporary law that amended Article 340 in two ways. First, rather than fully exonerate defendants in honor crimes cases, it treated such circumstances as the basis for a reduction in punishment; second, it granted women who attacked their husbands the same consideration. After the parliamentary elections of 2003, the amended law was brought to a vote several times and each time it was rejected.[66]

Although adultery (al-zina), defined broadly as sexual relations outside the framework of marriage, is considered a crime according to Shari'a, IAF leaders acknowledged that Islam does not allow an individual to take the law into his hands. As Abd al-Latif 'Arabiyyat, then president of the IAF's Shura Council, noted:

> Killing people in this way is against the Shari'a. No one is authorized to apply the law himself. Everything must go through the courts and follow proper procedures, for example, there must be four witnesses to the event. It can't be based on rumors.[67]

Nevertheless, IAF leaders denounced the proposed reforms as buckling to foreign pressure and claimed they would ease the way to adultery.[68]

The IAF also opposed the reform of Jordan's civil status code to grant women the unrestricted right to divorce their husbands. According to the rules of standard divorce (talaaq) in Jordan, a woman can only appeal for a divorce on a number of specific grounds; if the judge rules in her favor, she is granted the divorce with no financial penalty. Under the new bill, a woman could initiate a divorce without justification if she returned the dowry she had received at the time of marriage, a type of divorce known as khul'. Like the penal code reform, the khul' provision was introduced as a temporary law when parliament was suspended.[69] Issued in 2001, it was presented to parliament in August 2003 and was rejected by the elected lower house. In June 2004, the lower house once again voted against the khul' provision, this time by a margin of five votes.

Islamist and tribal MPs who voted against the bill claimed that it "would encourage immorality, is against Islamic Shari'a and disintegrates family values."[70] Yet the claim that *khul'* divorce was against the Shari'a was strongly challenged by women's rights activists, as well as by a number of prominent Jordanian religious scholars who argued that it was supported by extensive Islamic sources, including a well-known Hadith in which the Prophet himself allowed a woman who was unhappy in her marriage to divorce without her husband's consent. While Muhammad Abu Faris argued that this was "an exceptional case," other IAF leaders conceded that *khul'* was in fact supported by the Shari'a. They rejected the bill, they explained, because it eliminated the role of the judge in the process. Without an independent authority to assess the validity of a woman's case, the bill opened the door to baseless petitions for divorce, putting the family at risk. As Abd al-Latif 'Arabiyyat explained,

> *Khul'* is permitted in the Shari'a. Our disagreement with the law concerns the role of the judge, which is eliminated in the new law. Some women want the authority to divorce at will. But some of them have no justification. The judge must share in the decision; it's not enough for a woman to say she's unhappy and give no reason. Maybe she just wants to be with someone else. The interests of the children and the family must also be taken into consideration.[71]

IAF and tribal deputies opposed two other provisions of the reform bill as well. They opposed increasing the minimum age of marriage from sixteen for boys and fifteen for girls to eighteen for both sexes, claiming this would encourage promiscuity, as young men would resort to extramarital sex. Likewise, they objected to a provision authorizing the court to inform a woman if her husband took another wife, arguing that this was a matter that should be left to the husband's discretion. Women's rights activists noted that the IAF's stance against progressive changes in Jordan's penal and civil status codes was in part a means to embarrass the new king and demonstrate that its support could not be taken for granted. But it also exposed the fact that many IAF members viewed women as weaker in mind and judgment and hence believed that their behavior must be subject to patriarchal control. As Rana Husseini noted, "When we called attention to the plight of women at risk of being killed by their own families for so-called honor crimes, the IAF argued that anyone who defends these women is defending adultery, defending prostitutes."[72]

To undermine the credibility of women's rights advocates, IAF leaders accused them of exaggerating the problems in Jordanian society and promoting Western ideas at odds with its culture. As Rana Husseini noted, "I've been accused of everything, of being a Western agent, a Zionist agent, of encouraging sexual liberation. They say the West is using me, as if I don't have a brain of my own. It's insulting." More generally, Husseini observed, IAF and tribal deputies do not like people criticizing deeply entrenched social practices. "They say, 'This is our tradition, this is our culture.' They say, 'This is a perfect society.' That is a problem. We can't accept self-criticism, we can't admit to our mistakes. Instead we always blame everything on Israel and the United States."[73]

While many IAF leaders retain a deeply conservative outlook on social and moral issues, others have begun to gravitate toward more progressive interpretations of Islam that entail a more robust commitment to pluralism and civil rights. In a parallel with the fissures that emerged in the Brotherhood in Egypt, several of the IAF's most progressive figures eventually broke from the party, either to become independents or to form new groups of their own. For example, in 2000 about twelve leaders, all from the Salt branch of the IAF, tendered their resignations and joined with independent Islamists in 2001 to form the Islamic Center (Wasat) party as an explicit alternative to the IAF.[74]

Why did these leaders leave the IAF? It is to this question that we now turn.

The Reformist Trend in Jordan

Senior IAF leaders explain the defection of those involved in the Wasat initiative as a dispute over tactics, most notably over the IAF's's boycott of the parliamentary elections in 1997, which they opposed. Yet the causes of their alienation were far deeper. As Marwan Fawri, a founder of the Wasat party, noted:

> It is claimed that the IAF is independent from the Brotherhood, but this is independence in form only. In terms of financing, membership, and decisions, the IAF remains under the Brotherhood's control. . . . We reached the conclusion that there is a big need for an Islamic political party which can represent the Islamic trend that is independent of the Brotherhood.

Among other things, Fawri explained, the continued influence of the Brotherhood on the IAF created powerful pressures for ideological and behavioral conformity:

> The Brotherhood concentrates on guiding the behavior of the individual through proper religious instruction, or *tarbiya*. If anyone has Islamic tendencies but is not as strict in his Islamic behavior, they will feel very uncomfortable. The Brotherhood has specific regulations: no beer, no cigarettes, all the women must veil, and more. Most of the leaders and members of the IAF are members of the Brotherhood, so those who do not share the Brotherhood's orientations feel isolated.[75]

In a striking parallel with developments in Egypt, the departure of Fawri and his associates was preceded by efforts to reform the IAF from within. As Fawri recalled,

> Since the 1980s we tried to achieve changes in the structure of the IAF, in the system and its laws, for example, insisting that the position of secretary-general only be for two years and renewable once, to achieve a real alternation of power. Some of the Brotherhood leaders supported this, but others opposed it.[76]

Moreover, they questioned the wisdom of the IAF's confrontational stance toward the regime, as well as the diversion of its energy and focus to regional issues at the expense of national development. In addition, they opposed IAF hard-liners' rigid interpretation of Islam. As Bassam 'Emoush, another Wasat founder, explained,

> I was in the Brotherhood for thirty years, and represented them in parliament from 1993 to 1997. But I became put off by their ideological rigidity [jumud]. The hard-liners in the group favor confrontation and don't accept the legitimacy of the state. A lot of them are Palestinians, people like Abd al-Mun'im Abu Zant, Muhammad Abu Faris, and Hammam Sa'eed. They don't have useful ideas. For example, they call for jihad against Israel when we don't have the ability to wage war, so this is not realistic. In addition, they don't accept the views of others, they have a problem with pluralism. They say those who are not with us are against us and they want to impose their views. But Islam accepts fiqhi [jurisprudential], political, and religious pluralism. Creation is pluralistic, so God must have wanted it that way. It is very revealing of the hawks' mind-set that they don't criticize repressive Islamic systems in the Sudan or Iran where people are forced to submit to Islamic rule.[77]

Further, 'Emoush and other Wasat party leaders openly criticized prevailing tribal norms as at odds with the progressive and egalitarian spirit of Islam. For example, 'Emoush stressed that he personally supported raising the minimum age of marriage and granting women the option of a khul' divorce, noting that "marriage should not be a prison."

The Wasat party founders also diverged from mainstream opinion in the IAF in supporting the "real participation of women and youth" in the party's decision-making structures. The IAF's platform acknowledges the right of women to participate in public life "within the framework of Islamic virtues and values."[78] Since its founding in 1992, women have played a central role in fundraising and mobilizing voters during elections. In addition, they have occupied leadership positions in Brotherhood-affiliated schools and charitable associations, and contributed to the Brotherhood's impressive victories in Jordan's student unions and professional associations.[79] Yet as Janine Clark and Jillian Schwedler observed, the participation of women was channeled into a parallel women's sector, reflecting "the efforts of party leaders to ghettoize women's activities rather than envision meaningful gender equality within the party."[80] Whether it was appropriate for women to serve in the party's central decision-making bodies and represent the IAF in parliament were matters of dispute. For example, while Ishaq Farhan advocated the participation of women in the IAF's Shura Council (legislative assembly) and the nomination of women as IAF candidates for parliament, Muhammad Abu Faris and Hammam Sa'eed adamantly opposed such moves. Nawal Fawri (unrelated to Marwan Fawri), a respected school administrator and female activist in the town of Madaba, was the first woman elected to the Shura Council in 1993. In the 2002 Shura Council elections, six women were elected, and by 2008 the number of women had increased to nine.[81] Further, in 2003 the IAF included a few women on its list of candidates for parliament for the first time. While none of them won an open seat, Hayat al-Misimi, a pharmacist from al-Zarqa, won one of the six seats reserved for women according to the new women's quota established shortly before the elections commenced.[82]

According to Hayat al-Misimi, women could have achieved an even greater presence in the IAF's central decision-making bodies had they wanted to. As she noted, "We decided to run seven candidates for the Shura Council in 2002 and six won. If we had wanted more seats, we would have run more candidates." Yet, al-Misimi noted, IAF women were in agreement that it was still early to expand their role, not because they were incapable but "due to the nature of the work," which entailed long meetings and diverted time and energy away from their responsibilities at home.[83] By contrast, those who broke from the IAF to form the Wasat party argued that the underrepresentation of women in the IAF's leadership structures, and the continued expectation that they defer to their male counterparts within them, deprived women of a meaningful role in the conduct of party affairs. As 'Emoush observed, "The norm is that they sit far away from the men, and they are told it is better for them not to speak, because a woman's voice is 'awra [a source of sexual temptation]." Hence, he noted, the IAF's commitment to women's participation is more superficial than real.[84] Nawal Fawri, the first woman elected to the IAF's Shura Council and another founding member of the Wasat party, recalled her long struggle to overcome internal resistance to women's involvement in party affairs:

> In 1993, no one even imagined having women on the Shura Council; the leaders said, "It is not suitable for women to participate." [But] I didn't look at Islam as they envisioned it in their minds, I took my understanding of Islam from the sacred texts. I have long experience as an activist in the Brotherhood, which I joined when I was fourteen. When I entered the Shura Council, it wasn't easy for some people to accept me. The conservatives didn't want women to assume leadership positions, they said, "This is kufr [unbelief]." I told them to let women acquire the skills and experience needed to be effective leaders, but from their point of view, this would have been a revolution [inqilab]! They rejected all my ideas; even the IAF women didn't agree with me. Hayat al-Misimi said to me, "Why do you insist [on pushing for women's involvement in the IAF's leadership bodies]? We need to organize ourselves first." And I said, "I would have to wait ten years, and I refuse to wait that long!"[85]

Though difficult and frustrating, Fawri noted, her experience paved the way for other women to assume a greater role in the party.

When Fawri left the IAF, she initially considered forming a women's party that would encompass Islamist and secular gender activists. But in the end she decided "that it was a good thing to have a party in which men and women worked together" and helped establish the Wasat party. At the time, King Abdallah was promoting a moderate image of Islam, which she and other Wasat party founders endorsed. While at odds with conservative Islamist opinion, she stressed, "Our interpretation of Islam is also based on the sacred texts. They have their methods of interpretation, and we have ours." What distinguished the Wasat party's vision, she noted, was that "it rejects working in the realm of idealism [*mithaliyya*] and instead seeks to work in the realm of the possible, starting from an understanding of the realities of our society."[86]

Like its counterpart in Egypt, the Jordanian Wasat party was a small organization, with limited name recognition and support. Further, though Wasat party leaders forged close ties with secular democracy activists, their relationship with the Brotherhood and the IAF was strained. As Marwan Fawri noted, "There is a debate within the Brotherhood about us. More moderate leaders support our presence, but others think that any gains on our part come at their expense."[87] IAF leaders criticized the Wasat party for accepting financial support from the government for an expensive and well-publicized international conference called "Moderation in Islam," which their leaders hosted in June 2004,[88] and boycotted its proceedings. But the real reason the IAF shunned the Wasat party, Marwan Fawri argued, was that "They don't want another party which speaks from an Islamic perspective and is not under their control."[89] Or as Nawal Fawri put it, "They want to be the only ones."[90]

As in Egypt, the departure of some of the IAF's most progressive figures diluted the influence of the reformist trend within the IAF itself. Nevertheless, the IAF continued to encompass a wide range of factions, which largely replicated those present in the Brotherhood, and none of them managed to achieve full control of the party's agenda.[91] Rather than representing different positions along a single ideological spectrum, such factions were fluid and shifting, depending on the issue at hand. Hence leaders might adopt a "moderate" position on some issues and a "hard-line" position on others. As a result of these shifting alliances and coalitions, a known religious conservative or Palestinian hardliner would be elected as the Brotherhood or IAF secretary-general in one election, only to be replaced by a "moderate" or "centrist" in the next. This alternation of power among the Jordanian Brotherhood's internal factions stands in sharp contrast to the Brotherhood in Egypt, where aging leaders associated with the conservative wing of the movement have retained a dominant position on the executive board.

Nevertheless, the advance of progressive ideas within the IAF is blocked by a number of hard constraints. First, the Brotherhood's continued influence within IAF circles creates powerful pressures for ideological and behavioral conformity, limiting the space for unorthodox self-expression within its ranks. Second, progressive figures like Raheel Gharaibeh, whose views do not differ substantially from those who broke from the IAF to form the Wasat party, must compete with ideological conservatives and Palestinian hard-liners in shaping the party's agenda. Third, any progressive changes in the IAF's positions on social and moral issues expose party leaders to the charge that they have strayed too far from Shari'a mandates. As Hani Hourani, a Jordanian researcher, noted, IAF leaders "don't want to be criticized for not being Islamic enough, of supporting something that violates this or that *aya* [verse] of the Quran."[92] As Jordanian political analysts have observed, the Brotherhood's mass appeal derives largely from its reference to the Shari'a and its calls for resistance to "Western and Zionist domination," including the spread of ideas seen as threatening Arab-Islamic values and culture. Against this backdrop, the ideas of progressive leaders do not have much traction among the party's supporters. Indeed, while the IAF has exhibited an impressive record of fidelity to democratic procedures in selecting leaders and setting policy by majority vote, *the very responsiveness of the IAF's leaders to the views of its base has impeded progressive reform in the group's agenda.*

The participation of the Muslim Brotherhood in electoral politics in Jordan prompted a shift in its discourse toward a new emphasis on the merits of democratic institutions and procedures, but its internalization of the cultural values of democracy has been partial and incomplete. Persistent ideological divisions within the Brotherhood and the IAF, as well as the continued influence of conservative tribal norms and values in Jordanian society at large, have limited the IAF's embrace of more progressive interpretations of Islam that are closer in spirit to the ethos of pluralism and toleration associated with democracy in the West. Indeed, as I have argued, such a shift would likely alienate IAF hard-liners and dilute the party's mass appeal.

That said, some of the most ideologically conservative leaders in the IAF have shifted their positions over time. A case in point is Muhammad Abu Faris, who vigorously opposed the election of women to the Shura Council and the nomination of women candidates for parliament. At a party conference in December 2001, which included a brief speech by a representative of the IAF's women sector, Abu Faris led a walkout by some members who "rejected the idea of a woman speaking before a public gathering of men."[93] Abu Faris was similarly nonplussed when Hayat al-Misimi joined the IAF's parliamentary bloc after the 2003 elections. As al-Misimi recalled, he was visibly uncomfortable with her presence in the group's first meetings. Yet over time Abu Faris came to admire al-Misimi's dedication and seriousness of purpose and eventually acknowledged her effectiveness, both in conversations with her and with other IAF leaders. As al-Misimi observed, "Even some of those who were most opposed to us in the beginning have come around to accepting our presence."[94] Though Abu Faris is hardly an advocate of full gender equality, this shift highlights the ways that life experience can fundamentally alter an Islamist actor's values and beliefs.

THE ISLAMIC CONSTITUTIONAL MOVEMENT IN KUWAIT

The trajectory of the Islamic Constitutional Movement (ICM) in Kuwait exhibits some striking parallels with that of the IAF in Jordan. At the same time, it bears the imprint of distinctive features of Kuwaiti politics and society. The Iraqi occupation of Kuwait from 1990 to 1991 weakened the position of the Sabah royal family, which fled into exile. When Kuwait's sovereignty was restored, those who had stayed in Kuwait and participated in the resistance movement assumed an active role in public life. Forming parties was not an option, since they were prohibited under Kuwait law. Instead, like some of Kuwait's secular groups, the Brotherhood took advantage of the country's political opening by forming a separate bloc to represent the group in future elections, called the Islamic Constitutional Movement. The ICM joined Arab nationalists and liberals in demanding a strengthening of the oversight functions of parliament vis-à-vis the state administration and the royal family. Further, some ICM leaders began to gravitate toward more progressive interpretations of Islam. However, as was the case in Jordan, the scope and pace of movement reform were limited by pushback from ideological hard-liners, as well as by fears that adopting positions out of sync with the conservative values of the ICM's base would be costly at the polls. Let us look more closely at such developments.

The Iraqi occupation of Kuwait, which lasted from August 2, 1990, to February 28, 1991, tilted the balance of power between state and society, emboldening Kuwaiti activists demanding the restoration of parliament and the implementation of broader political reforms. While members of the royal family sat out the occupation in Saudi Arabia, many of those who remained in Kuwait risked their lives as part of a resistance network operating under the nose of the Iraqi authorities. When the Sabah royal family returned to Kuwait, members of the resistance "had to be convinced that their sacrifices would not be in vain" and that "the ousting of Iraqi troops would not be followed by a return to 'politics as usual.' "[95]

During the occupation, the emir also faced intense pressure from the United States, which led a major military operation to liberate Kuwait. As Thomas Friedman noted in the *New York Times*, the United States should not go to war "to make the world safe for feudalism."[96] Against this backdrop, the emir organized a three-day conference in Jeddah, Saudi Arabia, in October 1990, involving 1,200 figures from a broad cross-section of Kuwaiti society. The conference produced a deal between the ruling family and the opposition: "The latter agreed to stand by the emir, reaffirm its loyalty toward him and acknowledge him as the legitimate ruler of the country. In exchange, the emir promised that liberation would be followed by far-reaching political reforms that would include the restoration of parliament."[97]

After the occupation ended, leaders from various sectors of the opposition began to assert themselves. On March 2, 1991, the Kuwait Democratic Forum (*al manbar al-dimuqrati al-kuwayti*), or KDF, was formed, representing an alliance between two Arab nationalist groups dating back to the 1960s. Shortly thereafter, on March 31, the Islamic Constitutional Movement (*al haraka al-dustouriyya al-islamiyya*) was established by leaders of the Muslim Brotherhood. During the occupation, a younger generation of Brotherhood activists with roots in the Islamist student movement on university campuses played a leading role in the resistance, "gaining stature at the expense of the older generation and those who had fled."[98] These younger activists spearheaded the formation of the ICM as an organization independent of the Brotherhood. As indicated by its name, the ICM emphasized its fidelity to the Kuwaiti constitution and, by extension, the Kuwaiti state. As Muhammad Dalal, an ICM leader, noted, by affirming its commitment to the existing constitutional framework, the ICM laid to rest any fears that the Brotherhood would exploit the instability created by the occupation to undermine the regime. With the formation of the ICM, he observed, "No one could question our commitment to the interests of the nation."[99] In addition, the ICM publicly broke its ties with the international Muslim Brotherhood because the latter supported Saddam Hussein during the occupation of Kuwait.

Unlike its counterparts in Egypt and Jordan, the ICM was but one of several Islamist groups active on the political scene, each with its own distinct agenda. In addition to the ICM, two other major Islamist blocs emerged in the wake of the occupation, the Islamic Popular Alliance (IPA), a conservative religious Salafi bloc, and the National Islamic Coalition (NIC), a Shi'ite bloc encompassing religious and secular figures who sought to advance the interests of Kuwait's Shi'ite community, which represented about 30% of the population.[100] Other Islamists ran for parliament as independents. Kuwait's diverse political landscape also included Arab nationalist groups like the KDF, liberal activists, and members of the country's prominent merchant families. Further, in parliamentary elections, the ICM competed not only with other political blocs but also with pro-regime "service deputies" and independent tribal candidates, particularly in outlying Bedouin districts. As a result, the ICM's representation in the fifty-member Kuwaiti parliament, while exhibiting some fluctuation, never exceeded more than a handful of seats. It won four in 1992, five in 1996, four in 1999, two in 2003, six in 2006, three in 2008, and one in 2009, a share ranging from 2% at its lowest to 12% at its height.[101]

During the 1990s, the ICM joined secular nationalist and liberal MPs in an effort to strengthen parliamentary control over the use of public funds, including the government's overseas investments.[102] In addition to demanding the investigation of high-level corruption and financial mismanagement, deputies in parliament called individual ministers to the assembly for interpellation, in which ICM leaders played a leading role. Accusing parliament of making it impossible for the cabinet to govern, the emir suspended the assembly in 1999 (but did so constitutionally by promptly calling for new elections).[103]

At the same time, the ICM allied with Salafi and tribal deputies in a push for social and moral reforms. In December 1991 the government established a higher consultative committee to complete the harmonization of Kuwaiti laws with Shari'a mandates, but it was given no enforcement powers and progress was slow.[104] In addition to criticizing the government for its sluggish response, ICM and Salafi deputies demanded that the reference to the Shari'a in Article 2 of the Kuwaiti Constitution be elevated from "a principle source of legislation" to "*the* source of legislation" (*masdar al-tashri'*). In 1994, a bill to that effect was signed by thirty-five of the fifty members in parliament and delivered to the emir. Although supported by a majority of *elected* MPs, the bill did not pass. In what Nathan Brown and 'Amr Hamzawy describe as "a Kuwaiti constitutional oddity," non-elected government ministers are also granted a vote in parliament on most issues.[105] This typically adds sixteen or seventeen votes on important bills, with ministers tending to vote en bloc in support of the government. For a bill to become law, it must gain the support of a two-thirds majority of parliament (including government ministers), as well as the approval of the emir, a bar the Islamists failed to cross.[106]

In the early 1990s, the ICM and other Islamist deputies also circulated a bill to establish a public authority to "direct the public to do good and refrain from evil" (*al-'amr bi'l-ma'arouf wa'n-nahy 'an il-munkar*), a phrase derived from the Quran. With offices in every district, the commission would promote religiously correct behavior through lectures, pamphlets, and books, and report on "any phenomena contradicting public decency." Sharply criticized by secular and liberal figures in the media, the bill was ultimately defeated.[107]

Yet as part of a wider coalition of Islamists and conservative tribal deputies, the ICM also scored some important gains. A bill mandating the gender segregation of Kuwait University was narrowly defeated in 1994 but passed in 1996, based on a compromise that gave the university five years to segregate its classes and facilities and ensured government noninterference in co-ed private schools.[108] The bill was portrayed in the media as a major victory for the Islamists, who favored the stricter supervision of Kuwaiti teenagers in order to prevent the formation of illicit sexual relationships. As Mubarak Duwaileh, an ICM MP who supported the bill, explained:

> Adolescence is a sensitive age, and students arriving at the university are pushed from a conservative atmosphere into a free atmosphere. This can lead to bad results, that is, to sexual relations outside marriage. Before coming to university, the girl is controlled by her father, she goes out with a driver and comes home with a driver. We know everything that goes on. But now all of a sudden she is out from 8:00 A.M. to 4:00 P.M. with no supervision, and no one knows what she is doing between classes. . . . The bad students can influence the good students. A lot of

accidents happened, unwanted pregnancies and things like that. Once she graduates, it is a very different situation. If she becomes an employee, she must punch a time clock and must wear respectable clothes. Also she is older, more mature, and is likely to get married. So the period of study at the university is especially sensitive.[109]

The logistical and financial challenges created by the gender segregation law were noted by several Kuwaiti professors I interviewed in 2004. As Ghanim al-Najjar observed, Kuwait University must now maintain separate buildings, libraries, and courses for male and female students: "About 70% of courses are now segregated. Remember that about two-thirds of students are women, and sometimes you don't have enough men enrolled in a course so you have to cancel it. Both male and female students are complaining that they can't get enough courses."[110]

Islamist deputies in parliament also sought to censure Kuwaiti scholars and writers accused of offending Islamic values. For example, they condemned 'Alya Shu'ayb, a professor of philosophy at Kuwait University, for "spreading degenerative ideas" when she stated in an interview that lesbian relationships were widespread among university students. Likewise, in January 1997, under pressure from Islamists, a female writer was hauled to court for a book of short stories describing love relationships, prompting liberals to protest that the Islamists were leading "an organized campaign against freedom of thought."[111] Further, Islamist deputies accused Ahmad al-Baghdadi of insulting the Prophet Muhammad. In an interview with a Kuwaiti newspaper, al-Baghdadi observed that the Prophet had "failed" in Mecca and hence was forced to move to Medina. As Shafiq Ghabra observed:

> The word "failed" became an issue. Several Islamists took it to parliament and called for punishment and resignation. Others threatened al-Baghdadi's life, and some sued him in court, while others wanted to force him to divorce his wife.[112]

Al-Baghdadi was arrested and spent two weeks in prison before he was released.[113]

The role of the ICM—as distinct from that of Salafi groups—in the drive to censor Kuwaiti intellectuals and writers is unclear because media reports described its instigators generically as "Islamists." At a minimum, I found no evidence of ICM deputies actively defending those targeted in the campaigns. Further, in interviews I conducted in 2004, it became evident that ICM leaders' commitment to political and intellectual pluralism did not extend to supporting free speech that violated the core values and principles of Islam as they defined them.

ICM leaders framed calls for censorship, especially on matters of religion, as consistent with the mandates of the Kuwaiti Constitution, which asserts that "[t]he State protects the freedom of practicing religion *in accordance with established customs, provided that it does not conflict with public policy or morals* [emphasis added]." Among those who invoked the constitution in this way was Muhammad Dalal, a member of the ICM political bureau:

> We respect all opinions, even those which oppose our views. We criticize each other, and that is not a problem. But on matters of religious belief, it is different. Attacks on religion destroy the higher values of society—faith [*iman*] and respect for God, the Prophet, and his Companions. These are things all citizens must respect. Everyone can say what he wants, but if he goes against the high values, that means he is against the constitution, and we can take him to court.[114]

The ICM and the Debate over Women's Political Rights in Kuwait

In November 1999, ICM leaders in parliament, together with conservative Salafi and tribal deputies, voted down a bill that would have granted women the right to vote and run for parliament. The bill was one of sixty-three temporary laws issued by the emir after he had suspended parliament and before new elections had occurred. When the bill was put to a vote in parliament, forty-one members voted against it and twenty-two in favor. The bill's defeat provoked an outcry from Kuwaiti women's rights groups, which had been urging the government to move on the issue for a long time. As Rola Dashti, a prominent activist, noted with exasperation, "We have scored a first in history. A parliament votes to limit democracy—what a farce."[115]

ICM leaders explained that their vote against the bill was, in part, a protest against the issuing of laws by decree. As Badir al-Nashi' noted, "We rejected all of the laws proposed by the government during that period [when parliament was suspended]."[116] But the ICM's position also reflected the fact that some ICM leaders opposed the decree on principle. As ICM deputy Mubarak Duwaileh stated in 1996, "Politics is not a right for women; it is a man's right only."[117] During group meetings held by the ICM after the decree's announcement in May 1999, it became clear that its leaders were sharply divided on the issue, with some opposing both women's voting and candidacy rights, some supporting women's right to vote but not to run for elected office, and others supporting the extension of rights to women on both counts. Nasser al-Sani' recalled such internal discussions:

> Before the vote in 1999 we held a series of meetings to discuss these issues, to which we invited members of the 'ulema, social scientists, and women activists from within the ICM. The women sat in another room, rather than talking face-to-face with the men, because the culture of the ICM prevented men and women from sitting together. But the women offered their opinions using microphones.

ICM leaders also conducted an internal poll, which indicated that a majority of its members opposed the bill. One of the main concerns, al-Sani' explained, was that the extension of political rights to women without clear rules and regulations could lead to inappropriate contact between women and unrelated men. Some ICM leaders, he noted, were willing to grant women political rights but only if measures were taken to prevent social harm. By framing the bill as an "up or down" vote on voting and candidacy rights, al-Saniʿ argued, its liberal supporters doomed it to failure. "Like President Bush," al-Saniʿ wryly observed, "supporters of the bill said, 'You are either with us or against us'; there was no middle ground. I spoke with some of the women's rights activists later and told them, 'It's because of your arrogance that you lost.' "[118]

THE ICM'S NEW LEADERSHIP

During the mid-2000s the ICM underwent a major administrative overhaul that catapulted a new cadre of leaders in their thirties and forties into top positions at its helm. The turnover was prompted in part by the ICM's poor showing in the 2003 parliamentary elections, when the number of its deputies dropped from four to two, triggering a wave of self-critical reflection. Younger activists like Badir al-Nashiʾ, Muhammad Dalal, and Saʿd al-Dafiri, many of whom were former leaders in the Kuwait Student Union, argued for greater transparency in the organization, more clarity in its programs, and greater cooperation with other forces in Kuwaiti society, including those with whom it had clashed in the past. As Muhammad Dalal noted, before the 2003 elections, "the situation had deteriorated to the point that all the trends were fighting each other, putting each other down. This made all of us look bad in front of the voters." Though younger-generation leaders led the call for change, it was supported by some older leaders as well. For example, ʿIsa Shahin, a veteran ICM leader, opened the door to turnover in the group's leadership by deciding not to run for the position of secretary-general. In 2004, Badir al-Nashiʾ was elected as the ICM's secretary-general, and a new Political Bureau (*maktab siyasi*) was formed, dominated by younger leaders who sought to give the movement a more "modern" cast. As Dalal noted in 2004, "We are trying to put a new face on the movement, to be more open to other trends, and to make more of an effort to find common ground."[119]

As part of this general reorientation, the ICM called for reforms to strengthen parliament, legalize parties, and expand press freedoms. It also joined liberal and leftist groups and the youth-led Orange Movement in demanding a reduction in the number of the country's electoral districts from twenty-five to five. Creating larger districts was viewed as a means to limit the corruption and vote buying that gave an edge to local tribal leaders and wealthy businessmen. The ICM also called for greater transparency in government decision making, reducing waste and corruption, upgrading educational technology and curricula, and economic development and job creation.[120]

The ICM's positions on political and economic reform differed little from those of its secular counterparts. As Nasser al-Saniʿ noted, "On political reform we share the same priorities—we all want to change electoral laws and party laws to expand rights of assembly, we all want to fight corruption, and we all want to strengthen parliament so that it can hold the government accountable for its actions." However, the ICM and secular groups continued to disagree on social and moral issues. In addition to supporting political and economic reform, al-Saniʿ noted, the ICM sought to "protect and strengthen Kuwait's Islamic heritage, identity, culture, and traditions."[121] By the mid-2000s, rather than continue to push for change in the wording of Article 2 of the constitution, the ICM opted for a more "practical" approach, advocating the Islamization of individual laws that violated Shariʿa precepts. In addition, they proposed revising Article 79, which makes the passage of new legislation contingent on the approval of parliament and the emir, to include a provision that it must also conform with the Shariʿa.

According to al-Saniʿ, the primary point of difference between the ICM and the liberal opposition in Kuwait is in "how they view the social structure." Liberals, al-Saniʿ observed, "don't mind the existence of relations between the sexes, even if that takes the form of 'girlfriends' and 'boyfriends' as you have in the West, with sex before marriage. But Kuwait is a conservative society. They [the liberals] are trying to push society in the direction of Westernization."[122] While liberals objected to stricter controls on private speech and behavior as a "civil liberties" issue, the ICM viewed such controls as necessary to prevent social harm (akin, one might say, to the rationale for laws restricting gambling, pornography, and drug use in the West).

Likewise, the ICM framed its objection to the extension of political rights to women as a defense of the public interest (al-maslaha al-ʿamma). Conceding that Shariʿa scholars disagreed on whether the participation of women in elections was religiously permissible, the ICM leaders I interviewed in 2004 emphasized that the group's position on the matter was not a question of halal and haram (what is religiously permitted and forbidden) but reflected its concerns about the adverse consequences that might result from women mixing with unrelated men. As Muhammad Dalal observed,

> There are different Shariʿa opinions on these matters, and since they are subject to religious dispute, we are free to take any position. It is not a matter of Shariʿa but what is good for society, is the timing right, are the conditions appropriate or not. Some members argue that women's participation will damage society.[123]

Mubarak Duwaileh, an ICM deputy in parliament who noted with a wry laugh that he is considered a hard-liner (mutashaddid) on the issue, elaborated on such concerns:

> Let's say that parliament grants political rights to women in my district. Its composition is half urban and half Bedouin. Let's say I have a campaign rally with speeches

that go on from 9–12 P.M. The ladies will be busy with such meetings and campaigns and will not return home until midnight. First of all, they will have neglected their families, and second, it will cause problems between them and their husbands. The husband will say, "Where you have been?" The older child has an exam tomorrow and his dinner is not ready; another child is sick and needs attention. In addition, this will give bad girls and wives an opportunity to do something wrong. She can say she was at a campaign meeting but who knows where she really went? Also, let's say a man is sitting with his wife and there is a knock at the door. It's me and my campaign staff, and we say that we want to speak with his wife—that is an abnormal situation. For the sake of our community, for the interests of our families, for the sake of social relations, we oppose granting women political rights.[124]

Several ICM leaders I interviewed, including Badir al-Nashi', Isma'il al-Shati', and Nasser al-Sani', stressed that they personally supported women's political rights but that this position was rejected by a majority of the ICM's members when the matter was put to an internal vote. As Isma'il al-Shati' observed, the ICM has performed an important social function by integrating members of the country's recently naturalized Bedouin tribes into the Kuwaiti polity. But such inclusion has come at a price, in forcing the ICM to harmonize its positions with conservative tribal values. To underscore this point, al-Shati' offered an example:

Muhammad al-Basiri is from the Ijma' tribe, which is a big tribe. He believes in women's political rights on the inside but cannot say that to his voters because they still believe in their traditions. He says, "Look, everything can succeed if you do it gradually. If you do it quickly, you'll cause a shock, and it may have the opposite effect by triggering an even harsher reaction."

Other ICM leaders, al-Shati' noted, said the same thing: "The people inside our districts won't accept it." He went on, "If we drive the vehicle at a hundred kilometers per hour we will alienate our base, so we can only drive it at fifty kilometers per hour. If you want to influence them, you should expect that they will also influence you." But al-Shati' also highlighted the contradiction between the ICM's opposition to women's political rights and its historic reliance on women's votes to win elections in the country's student unions and professional associations.[125]

Secular political leaders agreed that fear of alienating its base had blocked the ICM from evolving in a more progressive direction. As Ahmad al-Baghdadi observed: "If they vote in favor of women's rights, they will lose the votes of their tribal supporters, and they don't want this." While Salafi Islamists opposed the extension of political rights to women on principle, he argued, the ICM based its positions on political interests. Yet ironically, al-Baghdadi predicted, if women are granted voting rights, "a majority of them will likely vote for Islamist groups and we liberals will lose."[126]

A bill extending voting and candidacy rights to women was presented to parliament several times in the six years after the first vote in 1999, and each time the ICM voted against it. In May 2005 the bill was raised in parliament once again, and this time it won by a vote of thirty-five to twenty-three (with one abstention). The bill passed *despite the fact that a majority of elected members of parliament voted against it*, with government ministers voting en bloc enabling its approval. According to press reports at the time, to pick up the additional votes needed to ensure that the bill passed, the government "bought off" a number of deputies, though it was not clear exactly what, if anything, was promised to whom. Further, the vote was preceded by nine hours of debate, during which ICM deputies managed to attach a rider to the bill requiring that "women adhere to the rules and provisions of Islamic law when it comes to voting and candidacy." As Badir al-Nashi' explained, this was "to ensure that the law did not violate the Islamic identity of Kuwaiti society." For example, it would require the establishment of separate polling centers for men and women, as well as a law to regulate women's participation in elections.[127] Women voted in parliamentary elections in 2006, 2008, and 2009. In addition, women candidates have run for seats since 2006. In 2009, four women were elected to the parliament for the first time, all in mostly urban districts. This breakthrough was all the more significant because they won their seats without the benefit of a women's quota.

While celebrated as a major victory for women's rights groups in Kuwait, the extension of political rights to women was also a boon to the ICM. Once the bill became law, the ICM launched a major effort to mobilize women voters. Two months after the bill passed, Muhammad al-Basiri, an ICM leader, explained this seeming shift of course:

> We have already closed this chapter and are looking forward to women's active participation in political life but according to the limits and laws given by our religion. The ICM is thinking seriously about future issues, including ways to ensure society's maximum participation in the electoral system and currently we are targeting the women vote bank. We aim to launch political awareness programs directed mainly at women to attract their votes.[128]

The ICM benefited significantly from the women's vote in 2006. As Brown and Hamzawy observed, "Members recount how one of their leading parliamentarians, Nasser al-Sani', was going down to defeat . . . until the women's ballots (cast separately in gender-segregated polling) were counted."[129]

THE SCOPE AND LIMITS OF ISLAMIST MOVEMENT CHANGE IN KUWAIT

The ICM's administrative overhaul in 2004 brought a new generation of leaders into top posts in the Political Office (*al maktab al-siyasi*), the body responsible for running the group's day-to-day affairs. Most of these leaders were urban professionals in their thirties and forties, and many had roots in the Kuwaiti student movement. Both in terms of their life experience and wider outlook and sensibilities, they bore a close resemblance to middle-generation reformists in the Muslim Brotherhood in Egypt. The ICM's new leadership pushed the organization toward greater transparency. For example, in 2004 they publicly identified the members of the Political Office for the first time and launched the publication of a bulletin laying out the group's priorities and explaining its positions on key issues. According to Kuwaiti analysts, the leaders at the ICM's helm aimed to give the group a more "modern" image and to overcome the suspicion and hostility that had marred its relations with other groups in the past. After 2004, the ICM participated in several cross-partisan initiatives, including a campaign to reduce the number of Kuwait's electoral districts. Supported by a wide range of political factions and civil society groups, the redistricting bill was approved by parliament in 2006. The ICM also joined secular opposition figures in pushing for the legalization of political parties and asserting parliament's right to select the country's prime minister.

Further, the ICM attempted to position itself as a bridge between the country's urban and tribal communities, and between Kuwaiti liberals and hard-line Salafi conservatives. As Badir al-Nashi' observed, "One of the main strengths of our movement is that we are in the center [wasat] and can build bridges with the other trends."[130] Yet in attempting to forge a "middle" path, the ICM opened itself up to criticism from both sides of the ideological spectrum. Arab nationalists and liberals complained that the ICM's positions on key issues were marked by a lack of clarity and consistency. As Ahmad Bishara, a leader in the National Democratic Front (al-Tajammu' al-Watani al-Dimuqrati) and one of the ICM's most outspoken critics, observed,

> I find it really difficult to know where they stand. You have to read between the lines and cross-reference their statements. Their double-talk and slippery statements are often accepted because people aren't paying close attention. I try to expose the contradictions in their statements and make them public, and they don't like that. They try to discredit me, calling me an Americanized liberal, trying to find something to kill me politically, but they can't.[131]

According to Khalil Haydar, a progressive Shi'ite Kuwaiti writer, the problem is that:

> They confuse Islam with the Islamic movement, and when they assert that something is required by Islam, you don't have the right to discuss it or reinterpret it. For the Islamists to absorb human rights principles, they will need to overcome many barriers. Most leaders in the ICM are not ready to support freedom of religion, the equality of men and women, and the equality of Muslims and non-Muslims.

According to Haydar, the views of some figures in the ICM, like Isma'il al-Shati', appeared to have genuinely changed, but they lacked a coherent approach (minhaj) to the reinterpretation of religious texts that would allow them to justify their positions according to the principles of Islamic jurisprudence (*fiqh*).[132]

Likewise, secular analysts claimed, a lot was revealed by what ICM leaders *didn't say* when they discussed issues of political reform. As Ahmad al-Diyyan, a journalist affiliated with the Arab nationalist trend, noted:

> When you look at the discourse of the ICM since 1992, you will see references to the constitution, parliamentary life, elections, popular participation, and the right of women to vote. But they don't mention freedom of belief, personal freedoms, or gender and religious equality.[133]

At the same time, the ICM was portrayed by Salafi hard-liners and tribal leaders as having strayed too far from Islamic mandates. The ICM's losses in the parliamentary elections of 2008 and 2009 were due in part to fierce competition from Salafi and tribal candidates, especially in outlying Bedouin districts. From a high point of six deputies in 2006, the ICM's representation dropped to three in 2008 and one in 2009. As Brown and Hamzawy observed, the reasons for the ICM's electoral decline after 2006 were varied and complex. It stemmed in part from tactical errors, such as the ICM's attempt to form electoral alliances with Salafis, only to have them defect at the last minute. But even more decisive was the conversion of two of Kuwait's five electoral districts into "the exclusive preserve of tribal candidates, selected before the election in illegal but increasingly sophisticated tribal primaries." Voters in such primaries "opted for candidates who generally combined intense social conservative views with fierce loyalty to the tribal population—and an insistence on securing government benefits."[134]

Although the ICM's electoral losses were caused in part by factors outside its control, they made it more difficult for younger-generation leaders to push the organization in a more progressive direction. Shortly after the May 2009 election results were announced, Badir al-Nashi' submitted his resignation as secretary-general, as did all the members of his Political Office.[135] In September, Nasser al-Sani' was elected as al-Nashi''s replacement, and over the ensuing months he launched an inquiry into "what went wrong."[136] In a May 2010 interview al-Sani' noted that the ICM had erred by fielding candidates from smaller tribes who could not compete against members of larger tribes in outlying districts. Looking ahead, he said, the group would launch a new phase of "institution-building" to strengthen its presence at the grassroots level. In addition, al-Sani', who chose a new team for the Political Office that month, said he wanted the ICM "to re-focus on 'Islamist issues'"—such as the gradual implementation of Shari'a—that he believed were the root of its previous successes, before it was "politicized." As he stressed: "This is what our followers and members traditionally love, this is the mainstream, I would say. Some people think we have shifted a little bit away from that so we have to get it back."[137]

In sum, as the new secretary-general saw it, the ICM's shift away from the social and moral issues it had prioritized in the past had cost it at the polls. Like the IAF in Jordan, the more attuned ICM leaders were to the views of its base, the more difficult it was to adopt progressive positions out of sync with the conservative values of its supporters. Such constraints were amplified by the fact that the ICM's main electoral competitors were Salafis and tribal leaders who outflanked it on the right.

ICM leaders who subscribed to a more progressive interpretation of Islam were quick to categorize their views as "personal opinions," highlighting the gap between such views and mainstream opinion within the ICM's ranks. In recent years, some observers argue, the progressive wing of the ICM has become increasingly marginalized; for example, Isma'il al-Shati', one of its most iconic figures, has left the group altogether. Meanwhile, in response to pressure from below, the new Political Office has moved to revive the group's conservative religious agenda. As Khalil Haydar observed:

> Some of the ICM's leaders are more open but their base [jumhur] is very conservative. The base places limits on the extent of change that is possible. In the end, the ICM is a populist movement [haraka sha'biyya] so they say things to make the people happy. Populism is a big problem for the Islamic movement.[138]

To be clear, the primary constraint on the progressive reform of the ICM's agenda was not "Islam" per se but a particular reading of Islam inflected by deeply rooted conservative social norms and customs. As Kuwaiti liberals were the first to admit, such ideas as gender equality and civil rights have yet to gain much traction beyond the country's urban educated elite. As Ahmad al-Baghdadi observed, "Kuwait has liberals, but there is no liberalism. There is a big difference between the two. You will find liberal individuals, but liberalism as a concept in society remains weak. This is the main problem."[139]

Certainly such broader conditions are open to change, as is the ICM's agenda. Yet in the future, as now, the ICM's development will be shaped by the values and interests of its constituents.

THE JUSTICE AND DEVELOPMENT PARTY IN MOROCCO

Likes its counterparts in Egypt, Jordan, and Kuwait, the Parti de Justice et de Developpement (PJD) in Morocco joined the political system to change it. Like the IAF in Jordan and the ICM in Kuwait, it serves as the political arm of a "parent" da'wa association, representing the movement in the field of electoral politics. Like the Muslim Brotherhood in Egypt and the IAF in Jordan, the PJD has exercised self-restraint in parliamentary elections, deliberately fielding a limited number of candidates in order to avoid achieving "too large" a victory that might alarm the regime and jeopardize its own survival. Indeed, it was not until 2007 that the PJD ran a full complement of candidates for parliament, comparable to that of its main competitors, for the first time.

Yet despite these similarities, the PJD is something of a special case. Of the Islamist groups included in this study, the PJD has gone the furthest to downplay its call for Shari'a rule and has been the most restrained in pursuit of its conservative social and moral agenda. Further, the PJD has evolved further than its counterparts into a professional, routinized, and transparent political organization. Of the groups under study here, the PJD exhibits the greatest shift away from the Sunni revivalist movement's anti-system past.

The PJD's trajectory bears the imprint of the political and social environment in which it is embedded. It conceded early on to the supreme religious authority of the Moroccan king and the official religious establishment rather than claim to possess the exclusive right to speak in Islam's name. In addition, its evolution has been shaped by the presence of secular parties and civil society organizations with sufficient resources and mass support to serve as an effective counterweight to—and constraint upon—the PJD's power.

The PJD's restrained approach to controversial social and moral issues also reflects the relative strength of pragmatic and ideologically flexible figures within the group's leadership ranks. Indeed, most "older generation" PJD leaders are closer in outlook to reformist figures in the Egyptian Brotherhood than to members of the Brotherhood's old guard. Nevertheless, like the Egyptian Brotherhood and its affiliates in Jordan and Kuwait, the PJD has yet to fully reconcile its new commitments to democracy and pluralism with older Islamic precepts carried over from the past.

Joining the System in Order to Change It

In the mid-1970s, what now counts as the older generation of PJD leaders broke from the radical Shabiba organization and set the movement on a new course. Unlike the Justice and Charity (al-'Adl wa al-Ihsan) movement, a parallel Islamist organization led by Abd al-Salam Yasin, the ex-members of al-Shabiba publicly acknowledged the supreme authority of the king as the Commander of the Faithful and the guardian of the Islamic character of the Moroccan state. Further, while Justice and Charity denounced the political order as un-Islamic, the ex-Shabiba leaders decided to join it. In 1996 they finally gained a foothold in the system by merging with a small legal party, the MPDC, which was renamed the PJD in 1998.

The PJD initially emphasized the Islamist character of its platform. When a new government with secular and progressive leanings was appointed in 1998, the PJD was sharply critical of its policies. Known as the "alternance" government, the new cabinet was headed by Abdel Rahman Youssefi, the leader of the Union Socialiste des Union Nationale des Forces Populaires (USFP), and included other ministers from the Kutla, an alliance of the USFP, Istiqlal (a nationalist party with roots in the country's fight for independence), and a few other secular parties that had together gained a plurality of seats in the last elections. The alternance government, which included prominent opposition figures in the cabinet for the first time, was heralded as a sign of the king's commitment to democratic reform. Yet as Marina Ottaway and Meredith Riley observed, it "did not in any way limit royal power or change the balance between the palace and elected officials."[140]

In the domain of social policy, however, the alternance government launched a bold new course. In March 1999, with the backing of the World Bank and Moroccan women's rights groups, Sa'd Saadi, the minister of childhood and family issues, rolled out a major new initiative to improve the legal and social status of women. The National Action Plan for the Integration of Women in Development (hereafter, the Plan) identified four main priorities: (1) expanding education and combating illiteracy; (2) promoting the health of women and children; (3) integrating women into economic development; and (4) raising the status of women in the legal, political, and public institutional spheres.[141] The most controversial element of the Plan was its call for the reform of the Mudawwana, Morocco's personal status code. It called for:

> Abolishing the perpetual guardianship of women, which would, among other things, allow them to marry and work without permission; raising the official minimum marriage age from 15 to 18; abolishing polygamy; equalizing the right of divorce and making it subject to the courts . . . ; conferring half of the husband's wealth on the wife in the event of divorce or the husband's death; and giving women the right to retain custody of her children in the event she remarried.[142]

Such provisions directly undermined the authority historically granted to male heads of households in Morocco under the provisions of Shari'a. Not surprisingly, they were quickly denounced by senior members of the religious establishment, including the minister of Islamic affairs and the Moroccan League of 'Ulama, an official state body that "declared that the plan would denigrate Islamic jurisprudence" and, "by unjustly interfering in the affairs of the family," would "deter men from marriage and encourage prostitution and the loosening of morals."[143] The PJD also expressed strong objections to the Plan. Indeed, it took the lead in forming a large umbrella group, L'Instance National Pour le Protection de la Famille Moroccaine, comprising forty-one associations, to oppose it. In March 2000, women's rights groups together with secular civil society organizations and parties staged a mass rally in support of the Plan in Rabat, while in Casablanca, the PJD and other Islamist groups simultaneously held a much larger demonstration against it. At the latter event, signs carried by marchers framed the Plan as a sell-out to foreign pressure and an effort by secular politicians to impose a radical social agenda rejected by a majority of the Moroccan people.[144]

That the PJD felt free to voice its objections to the Plan reflected the fact that it emanated from liberal and leftist-leaning figures in the government rather than the monarchy itself. Further, according to Moroccan analysts, the death of King Hassan II and the succession of his son Muhammad VI to the throne in July 1999 created an opening for Islamist groups to assume a larger role in public affairs.[145] Confronted by a strong outpouring of Islamist opposition, the Youssefi government shelved the reform project and appealed to the king to arbitrate among its supporters and its critics.

As the 2002 parliamentary elections approached, the PJD, with a more robust party organization and a larger base of support, was in a much stronger position to compete than it had been in the past. In addition to its deputies in parliament, it now had more than a hundred local councillors and six local commune presidents. As Sa'd al-Din 'al-Uthmani, the party's deputy secretary-general, observed, the party had made the transition from "being a small party to a medium-sized one."[146] Further, as Willis noted, the party stood to gain from its conservative stance on social and moral issues and the reputation of its local representatives for honesty and hard work.[147] The disappointing performance of the alternance government in addressing the country's social and economic problems, as well as growing popular anger over the U.S. "war on terrorism" and growing violence in Palestine and Iraq, further enhanced the PJD's appeal.

THE PJD'S ELECTORAL SELF-RESTRAINT

Yet as the party's electoral prospects improved, so too did the pressures it faced to limit its gains to acceptable levels. As Willis noted, the party confronted a dilemma when it came to contesting elections: "The party clearly wanted to increase its representation in local and national government but did not want to be seen to do well and raise the fear of an Islamist run or dominated government." Indeed, in candid statements before the election, PJD leaders "acknowledged that massive gains, or even victory, for the PJD in the elections was not in its own interest."[148] The risks of "performing too well" were accentuated by the Algerian experience, which weighed heavily on the minds of regime authorities and the PJD alike. As Sa'd al-Din al-'Uthmani explained in 2000, "We are frightened of frightening people."[149]

Hence in the 2002 parliamentary elections, the PJD fielded candidates in just fifty-five, or roughly 60%, of the country's ninety-one electoral districts. Although this represented an increase from 1997, when it ran in 43% of the districts, it still diverged significantly from the strategy of the country's main secular parties. For example, the USFP and the Istiqlal both ran candidates in 100% of the districts. Despite these self-imposed limitations, the PJD won a respectable forty-two seats, emerging as the third-largest party in parliament after the USFP and the Istiqlal.[150] Further, as some Moroccan analysts observed, the PJD's gains would have been even greater were it not for regime intervention in the vote counting. Yet rather than protest such interference, Willis noted, the PJD appeared "quite content to have a reduced presence in the parliament and thus reduce the risk of the sort of backlash that [had] occurred in Algeria against the FIS after its strong electoral performance."[151]

The PJD came under even greater pressure after a series of bombings wracked Casablanca on May 16, 2003. In what came to be known as "Morocco's 9/11," the attacks, waged by an underground Islamic militant cell, caused thirty-seven deaths and traumatized the country. Though not directly implicated in the bombings, the PJD was deemed guilty by association by its rivals. As Willis observed, opponents of the party accused it of "having helped prepare the ground for the attacks through their sustained and intemperate rhetoric against the West and Israel (all of the targets of bombings had been Western or Jewish establishments) in the party's newspaper and official statements." For example, the deputy secretary-general of the USPF, Muhammad al-Yazigh, publicly called on the PJD to "apologize to the Moroccan people" for creating an environment in which Islamic extremism thrived. In addition, rumors circulated that senior figures in the security establishment were urging the party's dissolution.[152]

While seeking to defend itself against such criticism, Willis noted, the PJD also "understood that the atmosphere was sufficiently hostile . . . to necessitate some sacrifices."[153] Under direct pressure from the Ministry of the Interior, the party's senior leadership drastically cut back the number of candidates it fielded in the September 2003 municipal elections.[154] This decision triggered protest from local party activists, who viewed the leadership's approach as "too compromising." Further, unlike in the 2002 parliamentary elections, in which 90% of the PJD's candidates were chosen by its base, the party's Executive Council intervened directly in the selection of candidates in the 2003 municipal elections, favoring candidates with technical and professional expertise over more popular, and politically assertive, candidates.[155] Later that year, when the PJD's parliamentary bloc elected Mustafa Ramid, a prominent regime critic, as its president, the Ministry of the Interior warned the party that this choice was unacceptable. Under pressure from senior leaders in the party, Ramid resigned rather than risk being forced out.[156]

Pragmatism over Ideology

From the mid-2000s forward, the PJD moved toward greater self-restraint in its approach to social and moral issues as well. In October 2003, King Muhammad VI presented parliament with a bill replacing the Mudawwana with a new "modern Family Law." Unlike the "Plan d'Integration," the bill was drafted by a royal commission that included prominent members of the Moroccan ulema.

In announcing the reform bill, the king situated himself above the fray of partisan conflict:

> As the King of all Morocco, I do not make legislation for a given segment of the populace or a specific party. Rather, I seek to reflect the general will of the Nation.[157]

The king announced that the bill "meant to free women from the injustices they endure, in addition to protecting children's rights and safeguarding men's dignity." With numerous references to the Quran and Shari'a jurisprudence, the king emphasized that the bill was in harmony with the "tolerant aims of Islam." Further, he framed it as a legitimate exercise in *ijtihad* (human interpretation), a standard method used by Islamic jurists to apply the constants of the sacred texts to changing times.[158] Though the bill was depicted as in full accord with the values of the Moroccan people and the religion of Islam, its provisions differed little in substance from those that the PJD and other Islamist groups had vigorously opposed four years earlier.

When the bill was put to vote in parliament in January 2004, the PJD supported it. When I asked about this seeming about-face in an interview two years later, Abd al-Qadir 'Umara, a member of the PJD's Executive Council, explained that unlike the earlier reform, the 2004 bill was an outcome of broad consultation with a wide range of civic and religious leaders and was anchored within an Islamic frame of reference. In addition, it was not narrowly focused on the rights of women but sought to advance the well-being of the family as a whole.[159]

But according to Moroccan analysts, the main reason the PJD acquiesced to the Mudawwana reform was that it had been placed on the defensive by the May 2003 bombings and was no longer in a position to oppose it, particularly once the reform acquired the imprimatur of the king. As Abu Bakr al-Jami'i recalled, when PJD deputies expressed some reservations about the bill in parliamentary committee, the minister leading the session bluntly told them, "I'm here to tell you what the Commander of the Faithful has decided, not to debate this with you." Nevertheless, the PJD managed to introduce some qualifications to the bill before it received parliamentary approval. As al-Jami'i noted, "On each contentious point, they inserted an exceptionality clause, for example, marriage before the age of eighteen is prohibited *except* in the following circumstances; judges will apply the law *except* in such and such cases, etcetera." Similarly, though the bill restricted the practice of polygamy, it was not completely banned, allowing judges to approve it in certain cases. Having succeeded in adding these clauses, al-Jami'i observed, "the PJD could say, 'We won.'"[160]

In sum, the PJD's support of the Mudawwana reform was less the result of a systemic shift in the party's core ideology than a concession to external pressures. In particular, it reflected the fact that the party's senior leadership prioritized averting a direct confrontation with the regime over advancing the group's conservative social agenda. Indeed, in the interviews I conducted with PJD leaders in 2006, it became clear that many of them still had reservations about the new family code, which, they believed, would cause more harm than good if it failed to take into account social realities on the ground. As 'Aziz Rbah, a member of the Executive Council, noted:

> The law allows a woman when she reaches the age of majority to get married without the permission of her *wali* [male guardian]. I am from the countryside, near Kneitra. For a girl to do this in my district would go against our traditions. It would be difficult for the head of the household, because it would cause a loss of face. Further, if a young woman marries without her parents' authorization, it could cause problems for her as well. If there is a problem in the marriage, where will she turn? Who will support her? She needs her family. People often assume that parental controls on children are a form of persecution, but this is not true. Such controls are a way to protect their well-being.[161]

At its fifth Party Congress in April 2004, figures associated with the PJD's more "accommodationist" wing were elected to senior positions in the party.[162] Such leaders have attempted to balance the party's bid for social acceptance with continued responsiveness to the views of its base. As Muhammad Tozy observed, party leaders have struggled with the question, "How can we maintain a popular base which has been mobilized through a *da'wa* project which is traditional, Islamic, and conservative, while at the same time managing to coexist with other political forces who are critical of such ideas?"[163]

The evolution of the PJD's discourse on Shari'a is instructive here. In September 2002, Mustafa Ramid, a charismatic hard-liner, declared in a press interview that in the long term, the PJD wanted Shari'a applied completely, including the application of the *hudoud* punishments, such as cutting off a hand as punishment for theft, that are stipulated in the Quran. This triggered an outcry in the secular press, and other PJD leaders quickly distanced themselves from Ramid's remarks. Further, Ramid himself declared that his views had been misinterpreted and that the Shari'a would be applied only when the people themselves supported it.[164] In an interview with Reuters in the midst of the controversy, 'Abdalla Benkirane, a senior PJD leader, noted that though the party favored the gradual implementation of Shari'a in Moroccan daily life, such as by banning alcoholic drinks, casinos, and lotteries, radical change was not on its agenda. As he stressed, "what we want is to give a job to the millions of unemployed, not cut the hand of thieves."[165]

A few years later, none of the PJD's senior leaders was openly calling for the implementation of Shari'a, which, as Abu Bakr al-Jami'i observed, would be "ostentatious." Instead, al-Jami'i noted, to demonstrate their moderation, PJD leaders now "emphasize that they are *not* asking for the Shari'a to be the primary source of legislation," claiming that such matters should be decided by the country's elected representatives in parliament. As Moroccan academic Muhammad Darif explained:

> They know they can't lead off with a call for Shari'a rule. In a country where a lot of people don't pray and don't wear the hijab, the application of Shari'a is not a possible goal and they know it. In today's climate that would never be accepted. So they emphasize that Shari'a will only be applied once it has the support of the people. This is the main difference between the Salafis and the PJD; for the PJD, you can only apply the Shari'a if the people and their representatives agree to it.[166]

In a different vein, 'Aziz Rbah argued that it is neither the party nor the masses but qualified Islamic jurists who should harmonize the country's laws with the principles of Shari'a. As he explained,

> This is not a party issue [*qadiyat hizb*], it is a matter to be left to the *ijtihad* of the jurists and the ulema. The Moroccan Constitution stipulates that Morocco is an Islamic state. This is enough. We say that laws should not contradict Islam, but thank God most of our laws are already consistent with Islam. There are some outstanding issues in the Shari'a, like the *hudoud* punishments, which require further study. In addition, there are such issues as the prohibition on the charging of interest and the sale and consumption of alcohol. But it is not my job as a party to interpret Islam; the party is not a *faqih* [Islamist jurist]! This is the duty of the Constitutional Assembly, the Council of 'Ulema, and the Council of Jurists.[167]

Other PJD leaders have worked to rehabilitate the concept of Shari'a by defining it as a set of general principles rather than a cluster of fixed rulings inherited from the past. As 'Abdalla Bagha, deputy secretary-general, noted:

> What does this mean, "Shari'a"? We apply it now, when we apply the principle of transparency and make our party conferences open to all, that is Shari'a. When we confront corruption, that is Shari'a. When we call for social justice, that is Shari'a. For something like the *hudoud* punishments, there must be conditions under which certain rulings are applied, and if society doesn't accept them, that's OK. We apply the divine rules through our own practice, not by force. We are against dictatorship [*istibdad*] in the name of Islam, like the system of *vilayet i-faqih* in Iran. For us, an Islamic state is a civil state.[168]

Muhammad Yatim, a progressive PJD intellectual and activist, went even further, arguing that the Shari'a contains a set of higher objectives (*maqasid*) that constrain the act of human legislation, including the application of rulings (*ahkam*) contained in the Quran. As Yatim noted:

> The rulings in the Quran don't get adjusted; what changes is our interpretation [*tafsir*] and application [*tatbiq*] of them. There is a Hadith which exhorts us not to apply a ruling if the results will violate Islam's higher objectives. Sometimes the

Shariʻa says not to apply the Shariʻa. That is, don't apply rulings if they go against Islam's higher principles or against the public interest.[169]

Yatim's views cannot be said to represent the PJD as a whole, but they demonstrate that the party encompasses leaders who have self-consciously re-jected the literalist and absolutist ideas that characterized the movement in the past.

The PJD's reluctance to articulate a strong stand in support of Shariʻa rule reflected the constraining influence of other forces in Moroccan society. To a greater extent than in Egypt, Jordan, or Kuwait, the political scene in Morocco encompasses robust secular political parties, media outlets, and civil society organizations that serve as a counterweight to the PJD and limit its freedom of maneuver. As Muhammad Hafid, editor in chief of *al-Sahifa*, observed:

> The PJD's discourse is limited by the situation they are in, which places restrictions [*quyud*] on what they can say and do. Most human rights and women's organizations in Morocco are not Islamist, and we have a strong independent press, strong civil society groups, a long experience of leftist activism, and prominent secular cultural figures. There are countervailing blocs of power that limit the PJD's capacity to do what they wanted, even if they had mass support.[170]

Rather than call for the application of Shariʻa, PJD leaders have campaigned in recent years for the "moralization" (*takhliq*) of public life. For example, PJD leaders have called for restrictions on the sale and consumption of alcohol, sought to prohibit open-air evening musical concerts that encourage drunken-ness and the open mixing of the sexes, called for the censorship of films, books, and art deemed offensive to public morals and religion, and demanded the stricter regulation of Morocco's tourism industry to combat the scourge of pe-dophilia and prostitution. As a general rule, the PJD leaders I interviewed in 2006 argued that greater social controls were necessary to achieve a proper bal-ance between individual freedoms and the protection of Morocco's religious values and identity. But they differed significantly in the priority they attached to social and moral issues, as well as on how stringently art, entertainment, and culture, as well as the private behavior of Moroccan citizens, should be regu-lated by the state.

While senior leaders of the PJD calibrated their public statements to avoid controversy, the MUR, its parent movement association, was less circumspect. For example, in December 2004, the MUR's newspaper, *al-Tajdid*, published a front-page article describing the tsunami that had ravaged the coast of South-east Asia as God's punishment for the acts of moral depravity that had taken place on its shores. Likewise, in 2006 it condemned the distribution of *Le Ma-rock*, a provocative film about a love affair between a Muslim teenage girl and Moroccan Jewish teenage boy, and demanded that its license be withdrawn.

The functional separation of the MUR and the PJD permitted the PJD to distance itself from the MUR's inflammatory rhetoric. As Abu Bakr al-Jami'i observed, the PJD "uses the framework of the MUR to say things they couldn't say otherwise," and when a backlash occurs, party leaders deny responsibility, saying, "That was the newspaper of the MUR, not the PJD."[171] But many PJD leaders also occupy top positions in the MUR. For example, in 2006, Benkirane served both as president of the PJD's parliamentary bloc and as general director of al-Tajdid. Moreover, some of the movement's most assertive hard-liners, like Mustafa Ramid, were based in the PJD rather than the MUR. Hence the different opinions expressed through MUR and PJD channels actually signaled ideological disagreement within the PJD itself. Senior PJD leaders were quick to acknowledge such dissension. For example, in 2006 Benkirane told me that while he agreed with Sa'd al-Din al-'Uthmani, the party's secretary-general, on most issues, there were instances when he felt al-'Uthmani was too "soft," adding, "'Uthmani is very progressive, too much, in my opinion." Benkirane also opposed al-'Uthmani's decision to accept an invitation from a U.S.-based group to visit America at a time when the U.S. administration was supporting Israeli aggression in Palestine and engaging in systematic violence against Muslims as part of the "war on terrorism" and the military occupation of Iraq. While the PJD's Executive Council approved al-'Uthmani's visit, Benkirane noted, "I personally would not have gone." Such disagreements, Benkirane opined, have fueled allegations that the PJD "speaks in a double language," when, in fact, they reflect genuine differences in party leaders' convictions.[172]

Although some PJD leaders favor the stricter regulation of private citizens' behavior, the public expression of such views routinely triggers a firestorm of criticism from the country's secular parties, media outlets, and human rights groups, which carefully scrutinize everything that party leaders do and say. As Benkirane noted, "We are constantly being criticized, and our adversaries are always trying to provoke suspicions against us."[173] Jamal Hashim, a professor of philosophy, described himself as part of a network of Moroccan democracy activists who oppose the Islamist project for society "au fond" (at the core) and are unafraid to confront it in the public domain:

> We are the avant-garde. I write about them [the PJD] almost every day. I challenge them, by asking "Why did you say this? Why did you do that?"

For example, when al-Tajdid called for a ban on the film Le Marock, Hashim was quick to respond. "They say, 'We are moderate,'" Hashim observed, "but when you say that the producer of a film is outside the frame of morals, you are indirectly abetting violence against her." Hashim noted that he and other Moroccan democrats are committed to humanistic values (qiyam insaniyya) and want Morocco to be "a modern, democratic, and secular society." If the PJD gains power, he warned, "they will decide what film I can watch, whether I can drink alcohol, whether a woman can wear a bathing suit on the beach." Further, Hashim criticized the PJD for categorizing films, music, and literature as *halal* or *haram* rather than judging them on the basis of their artistic merit. More broadly, Hashim noted, "PJD leaders say, 'We have an Islamic frame of reference,' and hence by definition those who disagree with them are placed outside the Islamic framework. [By contrast], we say that religion belongs to society."[174]

The effect of such external pressures can be seen in the PJD's discourse on the hijab. To a greater degree than their counterparts in Egypt, Jordan, and Kuwait, PJD leaders are quick to emphasize that whether or not a woman covers her hair and body should be left to the dictates of her own conscience. Whether this reflects an ideological shift or a response to existing constraints is difficult to determine and likely varies from one leader to another. But what is striking is that the PJD, unlike its counterparts, counts unveiled women among its members, and PJD leaders often point to their presence as a sign of the party's tolerance and enlightenment.

Another spur to pragmatism was the PJD's effort to demonstrate its capacity for effective governance. For example, when a PJD leader was elected mayor of Kneifra, a small, impoverished town on the coast where many women earn a living through prostitution, he did not ban the practice but sought to attract investment to the area to create other job opportunities for its residents. Likewise, the PJD mayor of Temara focused his energies not on moral issues but on infrastructure and economic development. As 'Aziz Rbah proudly exclaimed:

> Go to Temara if you can so you can see the mayor's wonderful achievements. He didn't impose the veil on anyone, and while he didn't authorize the opening of any new bar, he didn't close down the existing ones. His work has focused on creating jobs, infrastructure, electricity, and addressing the needs of the citizens.[175]

Further, to a greater degree than any other party in Morocco, the PJD has established strict performance standards for its representatives in parliament and local government. While Moroccan parliamentarians are notorious for their absenteeism, as indicated by the sparsely attended legislative sessions broadcast on television, the PJD requires its deputies to attend all general assembly meetings and publishes their attendance record in the party's newspaper. In addition, PJD deputies are required to pose at least one oral question per week, one written question per month, and one bill per legislative year.[176] Such measures have enhanced the PJD's reputation as a party that takes its electoral mandate seriously and is working hard to address the country's problems.

The PJD's General Secretariat also monitors the work of party delegates at the municipal level. As Eva Wegner observed, whether in parliament or local government, PJD deputies deemed to be underperforming risk being left off the party's list in subsequent elections. This has minimized PJD members' use of public office for private gain and has enhanced the party's image as serious, honest, and responsive to the needs of their constituents.

Since the mid-2000s, the General Secretariat has also required PJD deputies in parliament to vote the party line and has intervened in the selection of the parliamentary bloc's key appointments. Further, the Forum du Developpement (FDD), a technical commission headed by a member of the Secretariat, has weighed in on important legislative bills, cutting into the authority of the party's elected deputies. Such measures, Wegner observed, represent an effort by the pragmatic wing of the PJD that dominates the party's Executive Council to dictate party policies, whether or not they are supported by the party's base. The PJD's pragmatic leadership has imposed strict party discipline in part to prevent members from acting in ways that could place the group in jeopardy. As Wegner put it, the risk of the discontentment of the base was judged to be less important than the risks deriving from the environment within which the party was embedded.[177]

The Limits of the PJD's Progressive Shift

Though the PJD refrains from calling for the strict application of Shariʻa, it has yet to call for fundamental change in the patriarchal structure of Moroccan society. For example, PJD leaders claim to support the rights of women and children, but they have not taken a proactive stance against domestic violence, incest, or child abuse, or in favor of expanding access to contraception and abortion and equalizing the rights of men and women in matters of marriage, divorce, and inheritance. Further, though PJD leaders claim to endorse a "relativistic" approach to religion involving the ongoing (re)interpretation of sacred texts, such flexibility has its limits. For example, Mustafa Abu Bindi, a professor of Semitic religions, was shunned by his PJD colleagues after he published a book in the early 1990s that challenged the validity of several Hadith attributed to Abu Ghayra, a companion of the Prophet. As Abu Bindi recalled, "I said that his view didn't represent the will of the Prophet, but rather reflected the political context of the time." As a result, Abu Bindi became a persona non grata in Islamist circles. As he noted, "There was a vicious campaign against me in *al-Tajdid* and other Islamist papers, and in the mosques I was called a *kafir* [infidel]."[178]

Abu Bindi eventually left the PJD, but he has continued to write and speak publicly in an effort to influence the movement's direction. In 2006 I had an opportunity to interview him. Though PJD leaders profess their support for pluralism and democracy, he observed, such concepts "require an important cultural change in mind-set. You can't just roll them off your tongue and that's it." What is needed, Abu Bindi argued, is a "break from a certain cluster of ideological precedents [*kasr min majmuʻa min al-musabaqat al-fikriyya*]," something he and other like-minded Islamist intellectuals are trying to promote.[179]

Certain figures in the PJD's leadership are committed to deepening the values of democracy, both within the party and in Moroccan society as a whole.

According to secular democracy activists, Muhammad Yatim stands out in this regard. He frames the PJD's mission as an effort to "build a democratic culture, not just in the domain of political institutions and elections but also in the family, in relations between husbands and wives, parents and children, and in the workplace." According to Yatim, this mission reflects the centrality of the principle of *shura* (consultation) in Islam, "which pertains not just to affairs at the level of the nation but also to relations in the family and daily behavior."[180] What is far from clear, however, is the extent to which Yatim's views resonate with—and are shared by—wider sectors of the PJD's leadership and mass base.

PRAGMATISM AS A CONSTRAINT ON THE PJD'S SUPPORT FOR DEMOCRATIC REFORM

Like the Egyptian Brotherhood under Mubarak, the PJD has endorsed calls for constitutional and political reforms but has been unwilling to push too hard on their behalf. Indeed, over the past decade, while a number of small leftist parties and civil society groups have begun to agitate for change in the constitution to strengthen parliament and reduce the power of the unelected king, the PJD has remained conspicuously accommodating of the king's authority to set the agenda of the Moroccan state. By limiting themselves to supporting a gradual process of reform contingent on the king's consent, al-'Uthmani, Benkirane, and other senior figures have positioned the PJD as a pillar of the existing order rather than a challenge to it. As Muhammad Hafid observed, "The leftists want a system in which the king reigns but does not rule. By contrast, the PJD has taken no pivotal positions in favor of a fundamental change in the character of the system."[181]

The PJD's deferential approach to the king and the state establishment has triggered internal criticism. Most notably, Mustafa Ramid and his supporters have taken a more confrontational stance, arguing that real progress is impossible unless and until the country's elected representatives break the king's monopoly on power. As Abu Bakr al-Jami'i observed,

> Ramid says, look, we weren't elected to be disciplined parliamentarians, we were elected to solve the people's problems. Now when we go back to our constituents, what have we done for them? Why haven't we accomplished more? The constitution must be changed, the parliament must be given more authority.[182]

The parliamentary elections of 2007 and the municipal elections of 2009 signaled voters' growing alienation from all of the country's established parties, including the PJD. In 2007 the PJD decided to run candidates for nearly all of the seats in parliament for the first time, with leaders anticipating that it would win 25–30% of the vote and sixty to seventy seats. Some sources predicted even larger gains. For example, a report by the U.S.-based International Republican

Institute, based on two opinion polls, indicated that the PJD could win as much as 50% of the popular vote, fueling widespread fears of a resounding Islamist victory.

Yet the PJD did not come close to meeting these predictions, winning just 11% of the votes cast and forty-six seats. As Willis noted, two features distinguished the 2007 parliamentary elections from previous polls: the conspicuous low turnout (officially estimated at 37%, down from 52% in 2002) and the high number of spoiled or invalid ballots, which included over a million ballot papers and 19% of the votes cast, "more than the score of the two leading parties, the PJD and the Istiqlal, combined."[183] Such results appeared to indicate voters' growing frustration with the seeming inability of any of the country's political parties to address the urgent problems of unemployment, urban overcrowding, dilapidated infrastructure, and rising prices that concerned them most. As Brown and Hamzawy observed, "Wide segments of the population have come to see the parliament as a failed institution that can do little to solve their pressing economic and social problems."[184] A study carried out by the U.S.-based National Democratic Institute after the election to determine why turnout was so low appeared to confirm these impressions, as did anecdotal evidence collected by journalists and researchers during the campaign period: "Derogatory comments about politicians and the political parties were matched by observations that the parliament was a waste of time and could change nothing in the country . . . because all meaningful power was in the hands of the King."[185]

The PJD's "failure" in the 2007 elections was a relative one. Though its gains fell short of expectations, the party nevertheless increased its presence by four seats and went from being the third largest party (after the Istiqlal and USFP) to the second largest (having outperformed the USFP).[186] But the PJD's accommodative approach to the monarchy undermined its ability to present itself as an agent of systemic change. The PJD's seeming complicity in a political system incapable of addressing the most urgent problems of Moroccan citizens arguably helps explain its disappointing showing at the polls. In a continuation of this trend, the PJD contested approximately 40% of the sears in the municipal elections of June 2009, winning just 1,509, or 13.6%, of the seats it contested and 5.43% of the seats in total.

A PJD Prime Minister

Just two years later, the PJD's fortunes experienced a sudden and dramatic improvement as a result of events largely beyond its control. With mass protests leading to the ouster of President Zein el-Abidine Ben Ali in neighboring Tunisia in January 2011 and demonstrations breaking out in Egypt and other Arab states, the convulsions of the Arab Spring quickly spread to Morocco as well. Beginning on February 20, thousands of demonstrators poured into the streets in several Moroccan towns and cities chanting slogans such as "Down with Autocracy" and "The People Want to Change the Constitution." While not calling for the king's ouster, protestors demanded stricter constitutional limits on his power. In addition, they called for more jobs; better health care, education, and housing; and an investigation into government corruption and mismanagement. As in Egypt, the main instigator of the demonstrations was not the PJD or any other organized group but a loose network of Moroccan youth groups and civil society organizations encompassing individuals from a wide range of political and ideological backgrounds. Although those who founded the "February 20 Movement" were mostly middle-class students and graduates of Muhammad V University in Rabat, the movement eventually attracted supporters from poorer areas of such cities as Casablanca and Tangiers as well.[187]

In response to the protests, King Muhammad V delivered a televised address on March 9 in which he promised constitutional reforms. On June 17 he outlined the proposed changes, and on July 1 they were approved via popular referendum by an overwhelming majority. As critics pointed out, the new constitution fell short of endorsing the principle of popular sovereignty. While requiring the king to appoint the leader of the largest party in parliament as prime minister, increasing the powers of parliament, and strengthening the independence of the judiciary, it also confirmed the position of the king as the spiritual and political head of the Moroccan state. Leaders of the February 20 Movement rejected the reforms as insufficient and called for a boycott of the referendum. After the new constitution was approved, many activists vowed to continue agitating for a "truly democratic constitution and a parliamentary monarchy."[188]

By contrast, the majority of the country's political parties, including the PJD, endorsed the new constitution and urged their members to support it. While smaller pro-democracy demonstrations continued through the fall, the PJD and other political parties focused on preparing for the upcoming parliamentary elections, which took place in November. In a sign of some measure of renewed faith in the political system, voter turnout increased to 45.4% in 2011 from 37% in 2007, though once again, about 20% of the ballots were invalid. As in 2007, the PJD decided to run candidates in nearly every district, as did its closest competitors. According to the official results, the PJD achieved its best showing yet, winning 107 seats, more than double the number it had won in 2007 and far ahead of the Istiqlal party, which, with sixty seats, came in second.

Moroccan analysts interpreted the PJD's gains as a vote for change and as stemming more from the party's populist economic orientation than from its conservative social agenda. Further, Muhammad Tozy noted, voters cast their ballots for the PJD to punish the current government as well to signal their disenchantment with established parties, like the USPF, which they felt had let them down.[189]

On November 30, 2011, in keeping with the provisions of the new constitution, King Muhammad V appointed 'Abdalla Benkirane, who had replaced Sa'd al-Din 'Uthmani as secretary-general of the PJD in 2008, as prime minister. Though known as a staunch defender of the king, Benkirane had sparked controversy in the past because of his blunt personality and his conservative take on social and moral issues. For example, Benkirane was still remembered for his verbal lashing of a scantily dressed camerawoman during a session of parliament in 2001. Recalling this incident after the elections, sociologist Samira Kassimi noted that "there is a fear that the new head of government could meddle in Moroccans' private lives, and particularly women's lives."[190] Attuned to such concerns, Benkirane and other senior PJD leaders stressed that the party would focus on addressing the country's urgent social and economic problems rather than on citizens' private behavior. As Benkirane stated at a press conference in Rabat on November 27, the PJD "would not touch Moroccans' civil liberties," noting, for example, that "his party had no intention of attacking those who drink alcohol or dictating to women what they should wear."[191] Likewise, in a public interview in December, Benkirane attempted to reassure Morocco's European trading partners of his benign intentions: "Let Europeans be assured that I will not interfere in people's private lives. Don't count on me to go around checking the length of women's skirts."[192]

Regardless of the PJD's intentions, it is hardly in a position to dictate government policy on its own. Because of the fragmented nature of the Moroccan political system and the allocation of seats in parliament by proportional representation, it is virtually impossible for any party to gain a resounding majority. Although the PJD emerged from the November 2011 elections as the largest bloc in parliament, it still controlled less than 25% of the seats, forcing it to enter into a coalition with other parties in order to form a government. The PJD not only will have to compromise with its coalition partners in order to govern effectively but, even more consequentially, will have to share power with the king, who retains control over the country's defense and internal security and continues to claim ultimate authority on matters pertaining to Islam. For example, in the negotiations preceding the announcement of the new government, Benkirane acceded to the king's control over the portfolios of Defense and Religious Affairs.[193]

The protests of the Arab Spring did not produce democratic regime change in Morocco. Instead they prompted a gradual opening of the political system, which enabled the monarchy to retain its privileged position while rewarding the PJD for its self-restraint. Even though the PJD's secretary-general became head of the new government in January 2012, its freedom to maneuver will remain limited by other centers of power, as well as by an electorate that is apt to judge the PJD above all on its ability to address the country's dire economic woes. Further, the Moroccan political environment has favored the ascension of

more pragmatic leaders to top posts in the PJD's leadership, as well as a conspicuous softening of its positions on sensitive social and moral issues.

Of course, the balance of power among the PJD's internal factions could
change over time, but a dramatic radicalization of its agenda is unlikely. As
noted earlier, the PJD's evolution hinged on its leaders' critical examination of
the absolutist foundations of the Sunni revivalist movement, a process that
began earlier, and has proceeded further, than it has in Egypt, Jordan, or Kuwait. As a result, the PJD's senior leadership is generally more progressive than
its counterparts, as indicated by their more elastic conception of Shari'a rule
and their tolerance of behaviors—such as women choosing not to veil or people
consuming alcohol—which violate traditional Islamic norms. Such views are
likely out ahead of those that prevail among members of the party's base, whom
Moroccan analysts describe as more traditional and conservative in orientation.
What distinguishes the PJD is not the existence of a progressive ideological
consensus extending across the party's ranks but the stronger position of more
pragmatic and more ideologically flexible leaders at its helm. It is such figures—
rather than movement hard-liners—who are likely to set the party's course as it
adjusts to the new influence it has gained in the wake of the Arab Spring.

CHAPTER NINE

The Muslim Brotherhood in (Egypt's) Transition

WHAT PATH HAS THE MUSLIM BROTHERHOOD taken in the wake of the Egyptian uprising, and what role will it play in shaping the country's new political order? This chapter leads off with an effort to address these questions, focusing on the Brotherhood's stunning victories in recent parliamentary and presidential elections and the pushback it has encountered from other forces in Egyptian society. As we will see, the Brotherhood's actions exhibit the same uneasy mix of self-assertion and self-restraint that marked its behavior during the Mubarak era, albeit under a very different set of circumstances. Which of these impulses will prevail at any juncture is hard to predict, but one thing is clear. Despite its success at the polls, the scope of the Brotherhood's authority and the purposes to which it is directed will be contested for a long time to come. And how the Brotherhood handles the opposition its choices inspire will serve as a signal test of its commitment to an open and inclusive political order.

At the end of the chapter, I summarize the book's core analytic findings, highlighting the broad features of Islamist movement change in the Arab world and explaining why observable shifts in Islamist actors' rhetoric and behavior cannot be attributed to a single strand of cause and effect. By demonstrating that the processes of change within Islamist groups encompassed strategic and ideational components and proceeded unevenly across their internal factions, I highlight the value of complexity over parsimony in the analysis of Islamist movement politics and, by extension, in the study of social movements and contentious politics more generally.

THE BROTHERHOOD ASCENDANT

The Muslim Brotherhood has achieved a level of influence virtually unimaginable before the Arab Spring. It emerged as the resounding victor in the parliamentary elections of November 2011 to January 2012, and five months later

Muhammad Mursi, a senior figure in the group, became Egypt's first democratically elected president.

Yet the Brotherhood's climb has been a rocky one. As indicated by the tortuous series of constitutional and political crises that wracked the country in the spring and summer of 2012, the Brotherhood's advances have triggered significant pushback from high-ranking officials in the state establishment. Such tensions reached a peak in mid-June. First, the SCAF, acting on a ruling by the Supreme Constitutional Court (SCC), dissolved the Brotherhood-led parliament. Second, the SCAF issued a "supplement" to the March 2011 Constitutional Declaration, arrogating legislative authority to itself, stripping the president of control over matters of national defense and security, and granting the military and the judiciary veto power over the terms of the new constitution. Denounced as a "soft coup," such measures highlighted the determination of senior members of the military and the judiciary to retain control over the terms of Egypt's transition and prevent the Brotherhood from monopolizing power. At the same time, the Brotherhood has confronted ongoing pressure from secular and liberal forces to honor the democratic and inclusive spirit of the uprising that toppled Mubarak and set the stage for its own meteoric rise. Indeed, the struggle over the fate of Egypt's transition, far from being over, appears to have just begun.

Having languished on the sidelines for decades, it is not surprising that the Brotherhood has sought to capitalize on the momentum created by the uprising to secure a leading role for itself in Egypt's new political order. The Brotherhood's decision to contest more than 50% of the seats in parliament and to run its own candidate for president in violation of previous commitments, as well as its efforts to stack the Constitutional Assembly with an Islamist majority, exhibit the group's eagerness to "seize the moment," that is, to maximize its influence at a crucial early phase in the transition process. Yet in the face of pushback from the institutions of the "deep state," the Brotherhood will not be able to govern effectively without earning the trust and confidence of other sectors of Egyptian society. In particular, the Brotherhood will need the support of its rivals to bolster the country's fragile democratic institutions, reform the state apparatus, and address the economic issues of greatest concern to Egyptian voters.

Let us look more closely at the Brotherhood's recent electoral victories and the pushback they have engendered.

The Freedom and Justice Party in Egypt's 2011–12 Parliamentary Elections

Egypt's first parliamentary elections since the fall of Mubarak began in late November 2011. They were overseen by the Higher Electoral Commission (HEC), a mixed body of judges and government officials established by the SCAF in

July to coordinate the voting process and ensure the integrity of its results. In order to meet the requirement that a judge preside over the voting and counting of ballots in each of the more than fifty thousand polling stations set up across the country, the elections were held in three phases, with different regions proceeding to the polls on November 28, December 14, and January 3. According to the election rules chosen by the SCAF, two-thirds (332) of the representatives would be elected through a closed-list PR system in forty-six multiseat constituencies, and the remaining third (166) would be elected as individuals in eighty-three two-seat local districts. In addition to the 498 seats open to contestation, the SCAF, acting as the country's interim executive authority, exercised the right constitutionally granted to the president to appoint an additional ten members, raising the total number of seats to 508.[1]

Well ahead of the elections, the Brotherhood's Freedom and Justice Party (FJP) decided not to run a separate campaign but to field candidates as part of a wider coalition with other groups. In June 2011, the FJP allied with the Wafd and several smaller secular parties to form the Democratic Alliance, the first electoral coalition established after the uprising. In a June 14 statement, the Alliance declared that it sought to "mobilize political forces that are committed to the principles of democracy and a civil state" and "secure a representative parliament that will lead to a government of national unity." As noted in a joint study by Al-Ahram Online and *Jadaliyya*, the primary factor driving the formation of the Alliance was the fear that figures associated with the old regime and the former ruling party could dominate the new parliament without effective coordination among the country's opposition groups.[2]

At its height, the Alliance included more than forty parties across the ideological spectrum, ranging from secular democrats to conservative Salafi Islamists. But this broad coalition quickly fell apart. A few small secular parties, including the Democratic Front and Tagammu' parties, broke away first. Shortly thereafter, several leaders in the Wafd, who had criticized the Alliance from the outset on the grounds that it placed the party in a subordinate position to the Brotherhood and forced it to compromise its longstanding commitment to a secular state, defected to the Egyptian Bloc, a rival coalition of secular parties formed in August. In October, the Wafd officially withdrew from the Alliance, citing its objections to the FJP's domination of the coalition's electoral lists. (The relatively small size of the closed lists, which averaged only seven seats, exacerbated tensions within all of the country's electoral coalitions by limiting the number of positions available for distribution among their members.)

By late October, only eleven parties remained in the Alliance, including just two significant secular parties, al-Ghad and al-Karama. Hence what was initially intended as a broad national front devolved into a much narrower partnership dominated by the FJP.[3] Indeed, when the elections commenced, FJP candidates topped more than 60% of the Alliance's forty-six closed lists, and the FJP was running candidates for 70% of the individual seats in local districts.[4] To signal its commitment to a consensus agenda, the FJP did not campaign under the slogan "Islam Is the Solution," which had stirred controversy in the past. Instead, together with its partners in the Democratic Alliance, it ran under the slogan "We Bring Good for Egypt."

Once it became clear that the Brotherhood was fielding candidates for most of the seats up for election, it found itself in the awkward position of having to explain why it had violated its earlier promise not to run for more than 45–50% of the seats, which it had emphasized over the spring and summer as a sign of its commitment to "participation, not domination." According to Muhammad Sa'd al-Katani, the FJP's secretary-general, the party had violated its earlier pledge "out of necessity." As he explained at a press conference on October 25,

> The Shura Council set that [ceiling] when elections were still based on a single-winner system. When the system became list-based, we were obliged to fill the lists with names so that they get accepted. However, names that appear on the second half of any list have very little chance of making it into the parliament.

Hence, al-Katani insisted, the FJP members "who had a real chance of success made up only 35–40% of the total number of the coalition's nominees."[5]

The parliamentary elections took place at a time of heightened tension between the SCAF and its critics. On November 18, a new round of large-scale protests broke out following the release of a government draft document that appeared to give the SCAF a controlling role in the drafting of the new constitution, a process scheduled to begin once the new parliament was seated.[6] Security forces responded with force, and forty people were reportedly killed in the week preceding the elections alone, including two members of the Egyptian Current party. In response to the violence, several liberal parties suspended their campaigns and demanded that the elections be postponed, while protestors at Tahrir announced they were boycotting the elections, which would only "legitimize the rule of the Military Council they sought to remove."[7]

However, the SCAF insisted that the elections proceed on schedule. Defying predictions of further chaos, the voting went smoothly, despite delays in the opening of some polling stations and huge lines of citizens waiting, in some cases up to seven hours, for their turn to vote. Indeed, in what can be read as a strong show of confidence in the election process, about twenty-eight million people, 54% of the country's eligible voters, participated in the elections.

In the pre-election period, many parties had launched energetic campaigns to attract voters, plastering the streets with poster and banners, distributing fliers, and using mobile loudspeakers to pitch their candidates. Nevertheless, the Brotherhood's superior organizational machine was evident from the start. With a well-established infrastructure in "popular" (*sha'bi*) lower-middle-class and poor neighborhoods in Cairo, Alexandria, and towns in the Delta and Upper Egypt, and the help of a vast army of campaign volunteers, the Brotherhood was able to canvass voters more effectively than its rivals could. Further, as Yasmine El Rashidi, an eyewitness to the election process, reported, the

Brotherhood also maintained a strong presence during the voting process itself:

> At the polling stations themselves, the Brotherhood representatives were the most efficient. They were easily identifiable by the FJP caps and pins . . . and were on hand to answer any questions people might have had about their party or candidates. Even inside the voting stations, their members stood in corners tallying the numbers of people coming in to vote. "It's to calculate voter turnout," one of them told me.[8]

El Rashidi's interviews with voters indicated that the Brotherhood's long experience providing social services in economically disadvantaged areas was a key source of its appeal:

> At an election rally hosted by the FJP a few weeks ahead of the vote in the impoverished neighborhood of Imbaba [in Cairo], I spoke to dozens of men and women who had stories to share of how the Muslim Brotherhood had helped alleviate some of their basic struggles (selling meat at wholesale prices, offering subsidized school supplies, offering afterschool lessons, helping with medical treatment). One woman, the 48-year-old mother of five, told me: "One of the biggest costs for a mother is after-school lessons. The public schools are very bad, and the only hope for our children is in private lessons, which are extremely expensive. No one can afford them without being a millionaire. God bless the Brotherhood for helping us with these, and for providing our children with better futures."[9]

Until a finer-grained analysis of the election results becomes available, it is difficult to know exactly who voted for the Brotherhood and why. However, anecdotal evidence suggests that supporters of the Brotherhood were not limited to poor neighborhoods but included middle- and upper-class civil servants and professionals as well. For example, as El Rashidi observed, preliminary reports indicated that the Brotherhood outperformed its secular rivals in the district of Zamalek, an affluent, leafy neighborhood in central Cairo.

In total, the Brotherhood-led Democratic Alliance won a staggering 10,138,134 votes, or over a third of the total. Of even greater concern to secular democracy activists, the Islamic Alliance, a coalition of three hard-line Salafi parties led by the al-Nur party, came in second with 7,534,266 votes. Political novices unfamiliar with the electoral process, the Salafis nevertheless benefited from their reputation as "clean" and "untainted" figures attuned to the daily struggles of the poor. For example, the Nur party was affiliated with al-Daʿwa al-Salafiyya (Islamic Call), Egypt's largest Salafi movement, which provides services and engages in religious outreach in marginalized urban areas, especially in Alexandria, where it is based. As Ashraf al-Sharif, a professor at the American University in Cairo, observed:

> People voted for them for religious reasons and because they are very local. They have accessibility in local networks and a local vocabulary that can be easily under-

stood. Politics is about visibility and presence, which you get with the FJP and Nour and not with the liberal parties.[10]

Salafi candidates emphasized that they represented a sector of Egyptian society that the country's established parties had long neglected. As Alaa El Bahaei, a physician and the first candidate on the Salafi list in Port Saʿid, noted, "Other parties look from high up, but we are right there in the bottom of the community."[11]

According to the complex rules converting votes into seats, the FJP emerged as the largest bloc in parliament by far, with 216, or 43.4%, of the seats, and the Islamic Alliance placed second with 125, about 25% of the total. Coming in third and fourth were the Wafd party and the Egyptian Bloc (a coalition of three secular parties: the Tagummuʿ party, the Social Democratic Party, and the Free Egyptians), with 41 (8.2%) and 34 (6.8%) seats, respectively. The remaining seats were distributed among parties that individually won no more than 10 seats. These included the Reform and Development party, dominated by figures associated with the former regime (10 seats); the Wasat party (9 seats); the Revolution Continues party (8 seats); the Karama party (6 seats); and a total of 24 seats won by small parties, each of which won 5 seats or fewer. In addition, 25 seats went to independents.[12]

Parties with a clear secular democratic orientation, like the Wafd and the new parties formed by key figures in the uprising, altogether captured about 20% of the seats in parliament—roughly the same proportion occupied by the Brotherhood in the NDP-dominated parliament from 2005 to 2010. Much to the disappointment of women's rights groups, very few seats went to female candidates, due in large part to the removal of the women's quota, which had guaranteed women 64 seats in the 2010 parliamentary elections. The Constitutional Declaration of March 2011 required all parties to include at least one woman on their closed lists. But most parties placed women candidates toward the bottom of their lists, making it less likely that they would be elected. In total, only 9 women won seats. Three additional women were appointed by the SCAF, increasing the number to 12, but even with that boost women occupied just 2.3% of the seats in total.

The Brotherhood quickly parlayed its strong showing in the parliamentary elections into control of the assembly's most important leadership posts. On January 23, 2012, the FJP's secretary-general, Muhammad Saʿd al-Katatni, was elected Speaker of the House (though not before ex-Brother ʿEsam Sultan, an MP for the Wasat party, launched a symbolic run against him). Shortly thereafter, the heads of the parliament's nineteen committees were announced; twelve of them, including the most high-profile posts, went to leaders in the FJP. These included the Foreign Affairs Committee, the Defense and National Security Committee, the Budget and Planning Committee, and the Religious Affairs Committee. Deputies from the Salafi al-Nur party were elected to the chairmanships of three committees, raising the number of committees headed by Islamist parties to fifteen, or nearly 80% of the total. Non-Islamist parties, by contrast, headed up just four committees. Indeed, both the Wafd and the Justice parties ended up boycotting the committee elections to protest the FJP's efforts to monopolize the assembly's most strategic posts.[13]

The FJP and Salafi parties also took the lead in selecting the one-hundred-member Constituent Assembly (CA) charged with writing the new constitution. The composition of the CA was approved by parliament on March 25. Half of the seats were allocated to members of parliament, with the other half encompassing constitutional law experts and representatives of various civil and political groups. Secular and liberal deputies in parliament cried foul, noting that sixty-six of the CA's members were associated with the Islamist trend, while other sectors of opinion were conspicuously underrepresented. For example, the CA included only six women (three of whom were affiliated with Brotherhood) and five Coptic Christians. In addition, critics argued, the criteria for selecting CA members were unclear and appeared subject to political bias, as indicated by the fact that a young, inexperienced member of the Nur party was included in the mix while a number of prominent constitutional scholars under consideration were not.[14] In the midst of the controversy, twenty-five secular and liberal members of the CA decided to boycott its proceedings. When the assembly met for the first time on March 28, a quarter of its members were absent, and the boycott camp later increased to include nearly a third of the CA's members.[15]

The power struggle over the composition of the CA reflected a conflict of interests between Islamist and secular groups in parliament, with both sides seeking to maximize their influence over Egypt's new constitution. Yet both sides wrapped their interests in a cloak of principle. FJP and Salafi deputies argued that the composition of the CA should reflect the distribution of political forces in the democratically elected parliament, in which Islamists occupied the majority of seats. As Subhi Salih, an Islamist lawyer and FJP deputy, noted, it was unreasonable for secular and liberal groups to demand a share of seats on the CA far exceeding their modest electoral gains; as he put it, parliament must "not fall hostage to the dictatorship of the minority."[16] Secular deputies argued just as vehemently that the CA should reflect the full range of views and opinions in Egyptian society rather than the makeup of parliament, which, by definition, was open to change over time. As Muhammad Abu al-Ghar, head of the Social Democratic Party, who resigned from the CA, explained:

> Who knows what the next election will bring? Maybe the liberals and leftists will be the majority. So how can Egypt's constitution be written by a group of people who happen to be elected at one point in history?[17]

In a provocative statement, the Revolutionary Youth Union, a group of activists, accused the Brotherhood of "putting its interests before those of the country," as the NDP had done under Mubarak.[18] In the midst of the controversy, a group of lawyers and political activists filed a suit with the Higher Administrative Court asserting that the assembly was unrepresentative and demanding that it be dissolved.[19]

Brotherhood leaders in parliament found their authority challenged by others as well. Most important, their efforts to form a new government were rebuffed by the SCAF, which interpreted the March 2011 Constitutional Declaration as reserving that right for the president. In practice, this meant that the SCAF would retain control over cabinet appointments until a new president was elected.

The Brotherhood's Bid for the Presidency

Once the Brotherhood was blocked from using its base in parliament to form a new government, its stakes in the upcoming presidential race increased. After attempting—and failing—to convince several independent figures to run with its backing, the Brotherhood revisited its earlier promise not to field a presidential candidate from within its own ranks. Opinion within the Brotherhood on the matter was sharply divided.[20] Viewing the other contenders in the race less as partners than as rivals, some of the group's top leaders apparently concluded that the Brotherhood had no choice but to run a candidate of its own. But several figures in the group's reformist wing, including Muhammad al-Biltagi and a number of outspoken activist youth, opposed the move, contending that violating the Brotherhood's original promise would tarnish its reputation and cast doubt upon its sincerity. As one member put it, "The Brotherhood can't come out now and refute its promise not to nominate one of its members. No one will trust us anymore."[21]

When the issue of whether to nominate a Brotherhood candidate for president was put to a vote in the Shura Council it passed by a narrow margin, 56 to 52. On March 31, the Brotherhood identified Khayrat al-Shatir, one of the group's most powerful figures behind the scenes, as its nominee for the post. Brotherhood leaders were quick to justify the move as a response to the SCAF's intransigence. As Mahmoud Hussein, a senior member of the Guidance Bureau, explained, the decision was taken in the face of "attempts to abort the revolution," namely, the SCAF's rejection of numerous Brotherhood requests to appoint a new prime minister and cabinet.[22] Likewise, Muhammad Mursi, head of the FJP, stressed, "We have chosen the path of the presidency not because we are greedy for power but because we have a majority in parliament which is unable to fulfill its duties."[23]

The choice of Khayrat al-Shatir was no surprise. Technically, he served as one of four deputies to Muhammad Badi', the Brotherhood's Supreme Guide, but the scope of his influence was far greater than any authority vested in that position alone. A multimillionaire businessman, al-Shatir played a key role in managing the Brotherhood's financial networks. Ideologically he could be placed within the pragmatic conservative mainstream of the group, positioned between the group's hard-line and reformist poles. While close to the old guard, al-Shatir also maintained good relations with leaders in the Brotherhood's reformist wing and served as a critical liaison between the two groups. Although he had been arrested and imprisoned twice, first in 1995 and again in 2007, al-Shatir was also was rumored to possess contacts at high levels of the state establishment. Indeed, in the years prior to the uprising, several of the Brotherhood and ex-Brotherhood activists I spoke with contended that only al-Shatir could have brokered a détente between the Brotherhood and the Mubarak regime. A large bear of a man who controlled a deep well of resources and was respected for his political savvy, managerial skill, and strategic vision, al-Shatir commanded considerable authority within the Brotherhood, though he avoided the public spotlight. In the months before the uprising, al-Shatir held weekly meetings with Brotherhood youth who came to visit him in prison. They provided al-Shatir with written reports on the group's activities and relayed his advice to those on the outside.[24]

Al-Shatir was released in March 2011, shortly after Mubarak resigned. As the transition got under way, he emerged as the principal architect of the Brotherhood's Nahda (Renaissance) Project, a comprehensive program of political, economic, and social reform with an "Islamic frame of reference." In the early months of 2012, when the Brotherhood still had hopes of using parliament as the springboard for forming a new government, al-Shatir was widely rumored to be its top choice for prime minister.

The Brotherhood's nomination of Khayrat al-Shatir for president, like its push for an Islamist majority in the CA, exacerbated longstanding suspicions that it sought to monopolize power in the new political order. Whatever the Brotherhood's intentions, such moves triggered significant pushback from state officials held over from the Mubarak era. On April 1, a higher administrative court suspended the CA, ruling that parliament had erred by allocating half the seats in the assembly to its own members. As Mara Revkin and Yussef Auf observed, although the court's "decision to suspend the assembly took a procedural rather than political angle," it was also clearly addressed "to the broader issue of Islamists' domination of the Constitutional Assembly."[25] Sa'd al-Katatni, the Brotherhood's Speaker of parliament, denounced the ruling as politically motivated, but in the face of mounting external pressure he eventually dismissed the existing CA and tasked parliament with forming a new one in its place.

Just four days later, the Brotherhood faced a second challenge when the Presidential Election Commission (PEC), a panel of senior judges appointed by the SCAF to oversee the upcoming presidential race, disqualified ten candidates, including three front-runners: Khayrat al-Shatir, the Brotherhood's nominee; Hazim Abu Isma'il, an ultraconservative Salafist; and Omar Suleiman, a former director of intelligence and a close Mubarak ally. All ten candidates were banned on the basis of "legal irregularities," the particulars of which varied in each case. Al-Shatir was banned because of his conviction in a 2007 military trial, when he received a prison sentence of seven years. The Brotherhood protested that the charges against al-Shatir in the case were political and hence did not warrant his exclusion. But it had no legal recourse other than to appeal the decision to the PEC, the same body that had issued the ban in the first place. Predictably, on June 17, the PEC rejected the appeals submitted by al-Shatir, Abu Isma'il, and several other disqualified candidates.

The PEC claimed that it was simply upholding the legal criteria for candidacy and had been even-handed in applying them to allies as well as opponents of the old regime. But Brotherhood leaders cited the ruling as evidence of a coordinated effort by the SCAF and the PEC to eliminate strong Islamist candidates from the race.[26] The PEC could not be viewed as an impartial body, the Brotherhood charged, since its chairman, Farouq Sultan, was a former army officer and military court judge, and not just Sultan but nearly all of the PEC's members were "sympathizers with the old regime."[27] Shortly after his appeal was rejected, al-Shatir called on the Egyptian people to "protect the revolution," implying that those attempting to undermine it included high-ranking officials in the state itself.[28]

Despite such defiant rhetoric, the Brotherhood was unwilling to push matters to the brink. The opportunity to field a candidate for president was simply too valuable to pass up, so once again, principle yielded to pragmatic self-interest, and the Brotherhood announced that it would run its backup candidate, Muhammad Mursi, in al-Shatir's place. Mursi, an engineer with a Ph.D. from the University of Southern California, had served on the Guidance Bureau since 2000 and had been head of the Brotherhood's bloc in parliament from 2000 to 2005. Like al-Shatir, Mursi was a pragmatic conservative, but his views arguably veered further to the right than al-Shatir's, that is, closer in thinking to the old guard. Notably, Mursi played a leading role in drafting the controversial 2007 party platform that the Brotherhood later shelved in the face of public criticism. More generally, Mursi was seen as a quintessential organization man who was loyal to the old guard and faithful in carrying out their directives. As Ibrahim Hudeibi, a blogger and ex-Brother, put it, "He does not challenge any organizational decision . . . he is not an independent leader."[29] Though Mursi had nothing akin to al-Shatir's power base and commanding presence, he had extensive experience representing the Brotherhood in parliament. In the spring of 2011, Mursi was chosen as the head of the FJP and resigned from the Guidance Bureau in order to assume that new post.

Mocked in the press and on the street as the Brotherhood's "spare tire," Mursi was a less-than-ideal candidate for president. He was visibly stiff and uncomfortable in front of the cameras, and his public statements came across as shrill.

Hence the Mursi campaign relied less on its candidate's personal appeal than on the backing of the Brotherhood's nationwide organizational network. In public appearances ahead of the first round of the presidential elections on May 23–24, 2012, Mursi was often accompanied by al-Shatir and surrounded by banners associating his campaign with the Nahda Project that al-Shatir had pioneered. Though Mursi could count on the Brotherhood's support, his association with the more conservative wing of the movement and his rigid public persona arguably limited his crossover appeal.

The First Round of the Presidential Elections

The initial round of Egypt's first competitive elections for president took place on May 23 and 24. Judges presided over the balloting in each of the 13,099 polling stations set up for the event, and despite reports of minor procedural irregularities in some places (such as delayed openings, improper layout of the voting cabins, a failure to check entrants for ink on a finger), the process was generally observed to be free of external interference. Further, according to the Carter Center, which deployed international election witnesses to 909 polling stations in twenty-five governorates, candidate agents were present at the vast majority of the polling stations it visited. Such agents witnessed not only the process of voting but the counting of the ballots as well. Further, in thirty-six of the thirty-seven polling stations where the Carter Center team witnessed the counting process at the close of polls on the second day of balloting, the judge provided the candidate agents in attendance with an official copy of the results, which the Carter Center commended as an important step toward transparency.[30]

With an official turnout of 46% of eligible voters, the first round of the presidential elections revealed the fragmented nature of the Egyptian electorate, as none of the candidates came close to winning an absolute majority. According to the PEC's official tally, Mursi came in first with 24.7% of the vote, closely followed by Ahmad Shafiq, a former air force commander and the last prime minister to serve under Mubarak, with 23.6%. In an unanticipated turn, Hamdeen Sabahi, a secular Nasserist who pitched himself as "a man of the people" (running under the slogan "One of Us") and who focused his campaign on issues of social justice, higher wages, and better living conditions, came in third with 20.7%. Abd al-Mun'im Abu al-Futouh, a progressive Islamist who had broken his ties with the Brotherhood the previous year, followed with 17.4%. 'Amr Musa, who had once served as foreign minister and had been seen as a leading contender for the post, came in a distant fifth, with 11.1% of the vote, while the remaining eight candidates won 1% or less. According to the two-tiered election system in place, the results would trigger a runoff between the top two vote getters, Mursi and Shafiq, the following month.

A few aspects of the results are worth remarking upon. First, Sabahi and Abu al-Futouh, two top contenders who represented a clear alternative to both the Brotherhood and the old regime, together won close to 40%, more than either Mursi or Shafiq. But they split the vote between them, eliminating them both from the race. Referring to Sabahi, Abu al-Futouh, and Khaled ʿAli (another revolutionary candidate), Ahmad Mahir, founder of the April 6 movement, opined: "They made a mistake by not unifying. We said it from the beginning: We need one candidate for the revolution, not two or three."[31] Second, support for Sabahi was concentrated in urban centers; he came in first in Cairo (with 27.8% of the vote), in Alexandria (31.6%), and in Port Saʿid (40.4%).[32] By contrast, support for Shafiq and Mursi was highest in the provinces, where local organizational and family networks helped bring out the vote. In particular, it was reported that Shafiq had mobilized networks associated with the formally dissolved NDP to outflank his rivals in the Delta,[33] winning 30% of the vote in Qalyubiyya, 31% in Gharbiyya, 37.2% in Sharqiyya, and 53.4% in Menoufia.[34] Likewise, Brotherhood networks helped Mursi gain the lead in the transitional urban-rural governorate of Giza, where he won 27.9% of the vote, and in the impoverished provinces of Upper Egypt in the south, where he gained 32.6% of the vote in Asyut, 41.8% in Beni Suef, 42.2% in Minya, and 47% in Fayoum. Support for Abu al-Futouh exhibited less of a regional tilt. Further, his supporters encompassed a highly disparate mix of "modern" Islamist youth, conservative Salafi groups (which backed Abu al-Futouh despite their discomfort with his progressive reading of Islam, in a move against Brotherhood domination), and various secular, liberal, and politically unaffiliated voters who were drawn to him on the strength of his charisma and his reputation as a man of principle, as well as his vision of bridging the country's Islamist-secular divide.

Another striking feature of the results was a pronounced decline in support for the Brotherhood. While the Brotherhood-dominated Democratic Alliance for Egypt had gained over ten million votes in the 2011–12 parliamentary elections, Mursi won 5.4 million votes, roughly half that number, in the first round of the presidential race. Observers attributed this decline to the Brotherhood's lackluster performance in parliament over the preceding months, as well as the perception that the group had overreached by pushing for a large Islamist majority in the Constituent Assembly and deciding to run a candidate for president in violation of its earlier promise not to do so.

A final point worth noting is that Shafiq's progression to the runoff was subject to challenge on two grounds. First, on April 12, the Brotherhood-dominated parliament had passed a new political isolation law that banned top officials in the old regime from running for public office for ten years. The PEC initially disqualified Shafiq but on appeal put him back in the race, referring his case to the SCC for a final decision. With Shafiq's case pending, his standing as a presidential candidate remained a matter of dispute, and in the weeks leading up to the runoff, protesters at Tahrir Square shouted, "Batil! Batil!" (Invalid! Invalid!)

and demanded he be removed from the race. Second, the campaigns of Sabahi, Abu al-Futouh, and Khaled 'Ali submitted complaints to the PEC alleging that hundreds of thousands of active duty military and police officers (who, under Egyptian law, are not permitted to vote) had cast ballots in the first round, ostensibly tipping the results in Shafiq's favor.[35] But they failed to provide any solid evidence and the PEC rejected their appeals, with Farouq Sultan, the PEC chairman, declaring such rumors false.[36]

With Mursi and Shafiq advancing to the runoff, many began to question whether the huge sacrifices people had made on behalf of the "revolution" had been in vain. Rather than enabling the country to transcend the political polarization of the Mubarak era, the results of the May elections appeared to have reproduced it. Particularly devastated were those who were banking on the rise of a civil democratic "third bloc" that could serve as a viable alternative to both the Brotherhood and the *fuloul* (remnants) of the old regime. As Issander el-'Amrani, an Egyptian analyst, observed: "A substantial number of people who are 'pro-evolution' had hoped for an outcome that wouldn't be this binary choice. A lot of people were hoping for a wider opening."[37] In Cairo and other urban centers where support for third bloc candidates was particularly strong, many voters regarded both of the top contenders with disgust, framing the runoff, in an oft-repeated phrase, as "a choice between cholera and the plague."[38] According to liberal activist Hisham Kassem, the advance of Mursi and Shafiq to the runoff created "one of the most difficult political situations that Egypt has even known," since "we [now] face the risk of maintaining the Mubarak regime, or Islamizing the country."[39] Unable to stomach either of the two leading candidates, some pro-revolution groups urged voters to boycott the runoff or invalidate their votes, while Muhammad Baradei, who had from the beginning advised against holding elections before a new constitution was in place, called for the runoff to be canceled.[40]

As the date of the runoff approached, both top contenders reached out to broader sectors of the electorate. Shafiq pitched himself as the law-and-order candidate, promising to return the country to normalcy and stability after eighteen months of nearly constant turmoil and disruption. In addition, he presented himself as a bulwark against an Islamist takeover, warning that a Mursi victory would "take Egypt back to the Dark Ages."[41] In particular, Shafiq urged Coptic Christian and women voters to support him in order to safeguard their civil and political liberties.

For its part, the Mursi campaign framed their nominee as "the candidate of the revolution," calling on all Egyptians to unite against the remnants of the old regime; as Mursi campaign banners declared, "Our Strength Lies in Our Unity" ("Quwwatuna fii Wihdatuna"). Further, the Mursi campaign took pains to emphasize that the Brotherhood did not seek to dominate the political order. As Mursi declared at a press conference on May 30, the era of the autocratic president was over. Indeed, he promised, his presidential team would "include deputies, assistants and advisers encompassing all national forces, including youth, women, Salafis, Copts and patriotic former presidential candidates."[42] Further, Mursi stressed, he supported the creation of a new Constitutional Assembly acceptable to all sectors of opinion and would ensure that the constitution reflected "all hues of Egyptian political and social life."[43]

Mursi also made a conscious effort to assure women that he had no intention of infringing on their rights, though his efforts in this regard were not wholly successful. At a press conference on June 5, Mursi emphasized that "legally women have the same rights as men in Egypt." Yet when pushed to explain how he would address such issues as underage marriage, women's limited access to divorce, and the widespread practice of female genital mutilation, Mursi insisted that no legal reforms were necessary since "laws protecting women are already in place." Likewise, in a speech aired on Al-Jazeera's satellite television network the same day, Mursi claimed that child abuse and sexual violence did not exist in Egypt and that "marital relations adhere to social norms," triggering an outcry from women's rights advocates who accused Mursi of whitewashing reality and urged him to acknowledge that serious rights abuses occurred in Egypt as well.[44]

The contenders who had been defeated in the first round took different positions on the choice between Mursi and Shafiq. As the runoff neared, Abu al-Futouh's campaign announced that it would back Mursi. As Muhammad ʿUsman, head of the campaign's political committee, explained, this endorsement was "not necessarily a vote for the Muslim Brotherhood but a vote for a total break with the Mubarak regime." At the same time, Abu al-Futouh, as well as a number of independent Islamist intellectuals and thinkers, including Fahmi Howeidy, Heba Raouf Ezzat, and Ibrahim Hudeibi, proposed various outlines of a charter for Mursi to sign ahead of the runoff to reassure voters of his commitment to a civil democratic state.[45] While Sabahi and most of the country's other secular party and youth leaders chose not to endorse either candidate, some of them hinted that they might be persuaded to support Mursi if he committed to some sort of democratic charter in advance. Though Mursi held numerous meetings with a wide range of political and civil leaders, including Abu al-Futouh, Sabahi, and several prominent revolutionary youth, he stopped short of committing himself to any substantive guidelines that would limit his room to maneuver as president.

The "Deep State" Strikes Back

In the weeks leading up to the runoff, Egyptian observers began to contemplate the very real possibility that the Brotherhood could end up in control of the presidency as well as both houses of parliament. On June 14, just two days before the runoff was scheduled to begin, the SCC issued a ruling that underscored the determination of the institutions of the "deep state" to prevent such a scenario from being realized. First, the SCC ruled that the Political Isolation Law passed by parliament was unconstitutional, clearing the way for Shafiq to participate in the runoff. Second, and more controversially, the SCC challenged the legal standing of the parliament itself. In particular, the SCC nullified the election results for a third of the seats in the assembly, those reserved for independents, because party candidates (most of whom belonged to the FJP) had competed for those seats as well. On the basis of the SCC's ruling, the SCAF immediately dissolved the parliament, locking the gates to the building and posting guards at its entrance. Further, the SCAF declared that it would assume legislative authority until elections for a new parliament were held. Muhammad Sa'd al-Katatni, the Speaker of the Assembly, denounced the SCAF's move as unconstitutional and urged the military council to "respect the will of the people"; FJP deputy Muhammad al-Biltagi went even further, describing the move as a "full-fledged coup."[46] Several figures outside the Brotherhood, including Abd al-Mun'im Abu al-Futouh and secular human rights activist Husam Bahgat, echoed al-Biltagi's assessment. As Bahgat tweeted: "Egypt has just witnessed the smoothest military coup. We'd be outraged if we weren't so exhausted."[47]

The motives behind the SCC ruling remain opaque, but it was undoubtedly shaped by the mounting tensions that had caused relations between the parliament and the judiciary to deteriorate over the preceding months. For example, many senior judges vigorously opposed the proposals being floated in parliament to reform the judicial establishment, seeing them as an affront to their independence.[48] Further, many judges were shocked by the harsh criticism expressed in parliament against the June 2 verdict issued by a Cairo criminal court in the trial of President Hosni Mubarak and other high-ranking figures in the old regime. The court sentenced Mubarak and Habib 'Adli, his minister of interior, to life in prison, but the judge did not apply the death penalty, arguing that the prosecution had presented no evidence that either Mubarak or 'Adli had directly ordered the killing of the protestors. Instead they were deemed accessories to murder, not guilty of ordering the killings but of having failed to stop them.[49] Further, the court acquitted six of Mubarak's chief security officers and dismissed the corruption charges against the former president and his sons. The verdicts triggered an outcry from individuals and groups across the political spectrum who saw the sentences as too light. More specifically, the presiding judge was faulted for exonerating the security officers directly responsible for the death of protesters, and the prosecution team was accused of having failed to undertake a thorough investigation of the corruption charges involved in the case. In an acrimonious meeting of the People's Assembly, Brotherhood deputies openly condemned the verdict, which al-Katatni described as "a shock to the families of the victims of the revolution, to the protesters and to all Egyptians who had expected justice." Al-Katatni concluded the session by announcing that parliament would establish a committee to investigate judicial corruption.[50]

While criticism of the verdict emanated from many quarters, the Brotherhood-dominated parliament was the principal target of the judges' ire. Describing it as "a thorn in the side of Egypt," Ahmad al-Zand, the outspoken head of the Judges' Club, accused parliament of slandering the judiciary and opined that the country's judges would never have agreed to supervise the parliamentary elections had they known the results.[51] While other judges distanced themselves from al-Zand's remarks, the public exchange of insults and recriminations indicated that tensions between the judiciary and parliament had reached a new height. Technically speaking, the SCC ruling of June 14 only invalidated the results for a third of the seats in parliament, those reserved for independents. Nevertheless, outgoing SCC chair Farouq Sultan noted on state TV that, in practice, the ruling required "the full dissolution of parliament."[52] Hence in suspending the assembly the SCAF could argue that it was simply enforcing the court's decision. This was not the first time the SCC had challenged the legal standing of parliament because election rules had been violated; indeed, it had issued similar rulings in 1987 and 1990.[53] What differed this time was the strong impression that the SCC's ruling, coming two days before the presidential runoff, was driven by politics rather than by principle and, more specifically, sought to contain the Brotherhood's power. Doubts concerning the neutrality of Egypt's judicial institutions would cast a shadow over the presidential runoff as well, since the outgoing head of the SCC, Farouq Sultan, also chaired the PEC, which was entrusted with the final say over the conduct of the elections and the determination of their results.

The Presidential Runoff

The runoff between Muhammad Mursi and Ahmad Shafiq for the presidency began under a rather unpropitious set of circumstances. With no parliament, no constitution, and no formal checks on the authority of the PEC, whose capacity to serve as a neutral arbiter of the proceedings was open to dispute, the polls opened on the morning of June 16 under a cloud of heightened tension and uncertainty. Nevertheless, in the vast majority of the polling stations, the voting proceeded in a calm and orderly manner without any egregious instances of government interference. As reported by the Carter Center, which sent international election witnesses to nearly a thousand polling stations across the country, as in the first round, proper procedures were generally followed, despite reports of minor irregularities. Further, the judges who supervised the proceedings allowed agents from both campaigns to witness the balloting and the counting of votes.

As a short-term observer with the Carter Center, I had the opportunity to witness the runoff firsthand. Together with Muhammad Musbih, an Iraqi election expert who had witnessed Egypt's first post-uprising parliamentary elections and the first round of the presidential race, I visited twenty polling stations in the Governorate of Giza on the western edge of Greater Cairo over the two days of polling. Our area of deployment included densely populated "transitional" rural-urban areas like Bulaq al-Dakrur, al-Mu'tamadiyya, and Kerdassa, the latter of which was known as an important Brotherhood stronghold. Our direct observations confirmed media reports on the Brotherhood's impressive organizational reach and efficiency. At several of the polling stations we visited, there were no Shafiq agents on-site; at others, they were present but visibly distracted, talking on their cell phones, chatting with poll workers, and ducking out on occasion to buy a soda or smoke a cigarette. By contrast, at least one Mursi agent was present in every polling station we visited, keeping a close eye on the ballot box. One Mursi agent showed me the ticker he kept concealed in his hand, which he used to keep track of voter turnout. At the entrance to a polling center in Kerdassa, veiled female voters could be seen disembarking from vans emblazoned with Mursi's face. And at every polling station we visited on the first day of voting, Mursi agents informed us that a campaign volunteer would spend the night guarding the room in which the sealed ballot boxes would be stored until the following morning. As one Mursi agent wryly observed, "Tonight it will be just us and the army." The vigilance of the Mursi campaign clearly reflected its concern about the risk of electoral fraud, an issue apparently of less concern to Shafiq supporters, perhaps because any malfeasance on the part of government poll workers would likely work to their advantage. At the close of the polls on the second day of voting, we witnessed the counting of the ballots in a female polling station in an urban neighborhood of Giza. The presiding judge at the station permitted agents from both campaigns to double-check the vote tallies and gave them a signed copy of the results. We then proceeded to the district's aggregation center,[54] an open-air tent set up on the main road leading to the pyramids. We arrived to find a panel of senior district judges seated on a dais, waiting for the judges from adjacent polling stations to arrive with their results. In addition to the judges and our small Carter Center team, the tent was packed with over a hundred male Mursi campaign agents. At around 3:30 A.M., the Mursi agents lined up in orderly rows at the side of the tent to pray. About an hour later the final judge arrived, and shortly thereafter the presiding judge announced that Mursi had won the district with 82,615 votes, against 73,113 for Shafiq. The Mursi agents immediately broke into applause, congratulating each other with bear hugs and high fives, then proceeded to launch into a brief victory chant.

Despite predictions of a lower turnout, the percentage of eligible voters who cast a ballot actually increased to 51.9%, up from 46.4% in the first round. The Brotherhood kept close track of the turnout and the results at polling stations and aggregation centers around the country. Though campaign agents were not permitted to witness the final stage of the counting at the PEC's headquarters, by dawn on June 18 the Brotherhood's own records indicated that Mursi had won, by their count, with 52.5% of the vote (a figure that would turn out to be just 0.8% off from the official results).[55] The Brotherhood's ability to keep an independent tally of the vote count, a formidable undertaking given the large number of polling stations that required monitoring, arguably made it more difficult for government election officials to manipulate the final results.[56]

On June 24, after several days of delay, the PEC announced the results of the presidential runoff. According to official figures, Mursi won with 13.2 million votes, or 51.7% of the valid ballots, against 12.3 million, or 48.3%, for Shafiq. The total number of invalid ballots was 843,242, 3.2% of the total, up from 406,720, or 1.7%, in the first round. While some of the invalid ballots were spoiled inadvertently, such as those in which a check had been placed just outside the box for Mursi or Shafiq, others were clearly intended as a form of political protest. For example, in the stack of invalid ballots I was allowed to look over at one polling station during the counting process, several ballots had an X over the faces of both Mursi and Shafiq, and others were left blank except for the phrase *al-thawra mustamirra* (the revolution continues) or *Hasbu Allah* (may God punish them).

Mursi's victory was a watershed event. For the first time in Egypt's history— as some Mursi supporters put it, "for the first time in seven thousand years"— the Egyptian people had selected their ruler in free and fair elections. In another precedent, an Islamist had become the democratically chosen president of a modern Arab state. Yet the presidential race was nearly overshadowed by the SCAF's abrupt announcement on June 17, the second day of the runoff, of a "supplement" to the Constitutional Declaration of March 2011. In anticipation of a Mursi victory, the supplement stripped the president of his authority over matters of national defense and security. Until a new constitution was written, Article 53 of the supplement noted, the SCAF would retain full authority over the armed forces, including control of the Ministry of Defense and all military appointments and promotions. The supplement also gave senior state officials effective veto power over the provisions of the new constitution. According to Article 60, both the head of the SCAF and the president of the Supreme Judicial Authorities Council could require the Constituent Assembly to reconsider any provisions that "contradict the goals and basic principles of the revolution by which the higher interests of the country are accomplished, or the principles which have been set in previous constitutions." If no agreement could be reached, the disputed provisions would be referred to the SCC. Finally, Article 60 stated that if the Constituent Assembly failed to fulfill its duties, the SCAF would appoint a new one in its place. The new body would draft a new constitution within three months, which would be subjected to a popular referendum within fifteen days of its completion. New elections for parliament would be held within a month from the passage of the new constitution.[57]

At a press conference on June 18, Mamdouh Shahin, an SCAF spokesman, noted that the supplement would "ensure a balance of power" between the country's legislative and executive authorities, with the former assumed by the SCAF after the dissolution of parliament, and the latter vested in the president. Shahin emphasized that the SCAF would not be able to pass laws except with the president's approval and that the SCAF would have no authority to interfere in state affairs other than in matters related to the armed forces.[58]

But the supplement also indicated that the SCAF had no intention of fulfilling its pledge to hand over the full range of its powers to a civilian government by June 30. There is little evidence that the country's senior military officers sought to bear the burden of governing the country indefinitely. Rather, the supplement can be seen as an effort by Egypt's senior military officers to safeguard their vital interests, in the short term, by removing the military establishment from immediate presidential oversight and, in the longer term, by demanding a voice in drafting the constitution. As a mid-ranking army officer, speaking on condition of anonymity, told the *Egypt Independent* a few days before the supplement was announced, the military would return to the barracks only after it had been guaranteed a safe exit, that is, had secured control over its own affairs.[59]

On June 12, less than a week before the supplement was issued, parliament had elected a new Constituent Assembly following several days of intense negotiations between Islamist and secular deputies in an effort to reach a consensus on the allocation of seats within it. The new assembly elected on June 12 included twenty figures from the Muslim Brotherhood and ten members of the Salafi Nur party. Together with representatives from the Wasat party and Al-Azhar, as well as several Salafi sheikhs and Islamist independents, the Islamic bloc encompassed fifty-seven members in total. While this was smaller than the size of the Islamic bloc in the first assembly (which included sixty-six members), it nevertheless gave the Islamists an absolute majority. This time around, secular and liberal figures appointed to the new assembly were divided. While some supported the new body, others protested that, like its predecessor, it overrepresented the Islamist trend at the expense of the country's artists, writers, Coptic Christians, Nubians, and women, and decided to withdraw.[60] Citing the lack of consensus on the composition of the new assembly, the representatives of the SCC pulled out as well.[61]

The new assembly began work on a new constitution despite the controversy that dogged its formation. But the SCC ruling of June 14 that led to the dissolution of parliament also placed the legal status of the Constitutional Assembly in doubt. Indeed, the fate of the body would remain uncertain pending a court ruling scheduled for the fall.

In granting state officials effective veto power over the terms of the new constitution, the SCAF could portray itself as preventing the document from being hijacked by the Islamists, who occupied a majority of the assembly seats. However, the SCAF was arguably less concerned about the democratic and inclusive character of the constitution than about safeguarding its own prerogatives. As

Michael Wahid Hanna, a fellow at the Century Foundation in New York, observed:

> The SCAF doesn't trust civilians and definitely doesn't trust the political class, and it thinks the Muslim Brotherhood's overreach gives it a platform to position itself as the balance. So the SCAF will generally cloak its actions under the pretext of national interest but of course, part of that is to serve its interests.[62]

AN ISLAMIST TAKEOVER?

The inauguration of Muhammad Mursi as Egypt's president on June 30, 2012, constituted a stunning breakthrough for a group that had spent most of its existence under siege. But it would be too much of a stretch to characterize Mursi's victory as an "Islamist takeover." The Mursi presidency is just one vector in a complex system with multiple sites of contending power. With a new constitution yet to be written, Mursi assumed the presidency at a time when the exact nature of the authority vested in that position remained ill defined and open to conflicting interpretations. Against this backdrop, Mursi has clashed repeatedly with other arms of the state establishment. He balked when the SCAF insisted that he take his presidential oath before the SCC (in line with the provisions of the constitutional addendum) rather than before parliament. While Mursi ultimately gave in, the day before he took the oath of office he gave a speech at Tahrir Square in which he emphasized that his authority derived from the people and, in an oblique reference to the SCAF and the SCC, declared that "no institution can be above the people's will."[63] Likewise, in the inaugural speech he gave at Cairo University after being sworn in, Mursi noted that his first task was to be "an arbiter between the authorities and a patron of the Constitution and the law, after the people placed their trust and confidence in me in free and fair elections." Mursi also promised to honor the sacrifices of the martyrs of the revolution by working to ensure that Egypt never goes back to "the loathsome times of repression and tyranny." As Mursi observed, the people themselves had "succeeded in correcting the path of power [by] toppling an unjust repressive regime in a peaceful and civilized manner." In an effort to dispel fears that the Brotherhood would exploit its control over the levers of the state to impose a narrow partisan agenda, Mursi emphasized that the people themselves would not permit this to happen:

> I say to those who have lingering concerns about the Egyptian state changing paths: the people have chosen me to march on the path of civilization of the modern Egyptian state, and the people will not accept, and I would not want them to accept, any deviation from that path.[64]

On July 8, Mursi invoked his role as guardian of the people's will when he issued a decree reinstating the dissolved parliament. The move triggered a furious response from senior figures in the judicial establishment. On July 9, a sharply worded statement signed by the SCC, the State Council, the Judges Club, and the lawyers' syndicate demanded that Mursi annul the decree.[65] On July 10, the "rogue parliament" convened, though most of the assembly's secular deputies chose not to attend. During the brief session, which lasted only a few minutes, Sa'd al-Katatni announced that the status of the parliament would be referred to the Court of Cassation, Egypt's highest appeals court. Brotherhood lawyers insisted that they respected the SCC ruling but questioned the way it had been applied, arguing that since the ruling invalidated only a third of the seats in parliament, it did not constitute grounds for dissolving the entire assembly. That afternoon, the SCC ordered the dissolution of parliament for a second time, and Mahir Sami, an SCC spokesman, warned that the president could face criminal charges if he refused to comply. On July 11, Mursi issued a statement that affirmed his respect for the rule of law and the SCC but fell short of meeting the judges' demands.[66] Throughout the crisis, senior figures in the military and the judiciary framed the SCC as a "supraconstitutional authority" whose decisions were above the law. As Muhammad Hamid al-Jamal, the former president of the State Council, argued: "By law, this court's rulings are categorical and final. These rulings are binding on all state authorities and officials, including the head of state."[67] In sum, in the absence of a constitution, senior figures in the state establishment sought to rein in the Brotherhood by giving the SCC powers that were virtually absolute.

Despite a good deal of grandstanding, Mursi ultimately gave in and conceded that the parliament would have to go. Indeed, his decree of July 8, billed as an act of defiance, actually represented a concession to the SCC ruling, since Mursi stated that new parliamentary elections would be held sixty days after the ratification of a new constitution. Further, during the short meeting of parliament on July 10, al-Katatni made it clear that they "would not be holding any further wildcat parliamentary sessions while their appeal was pending."[68]

In the broadest sense, the dispute over the fate of the suspended parliament can be seen as a power struggle between the elected and unelected arms of the Egyptian state, with the Brotherhood-dominated presidency and parliament at odds with state institutions headed by Mubarak-era appointees. Yet under closer scrutiny, the realities of the situation become more complex, since neither the state establishment nor the Brotherhood is a unified entity with a coherent overarching agenda. Though the SCAF and the SCC took a joint stand in dissolving parliament, the motivations of their key decision makers, and the degree of active coordination between them, are unclear. Further, opinion within the judiciary establishment was divided. While the SCC and the State Council framed Mursi's July 8 decree as openly flouting the rule of law, other senior judges disagreed. For example, Ahmad Mekki, a former deputy chief of the Court of Cassation, argued that the president "had the full right to practice his power and cancel the SCAF's decision to dissolve parliament." In fact, he insisted, Mursi's move

[d]id not violate the court ruling, and even confirmed its respect of it. What the president cancelled was Tantawi's decision and not that of the court. Mursi said let us look into how to implement the SCC ruling, and hold new elections for parliament as soon as a new constitution has been drafted.[69]

Treating the Brotherhood as a single entity is equally problematic. The expansion of the Brotherhood's involvement in public affairs since the uprising has engendered the rise of separate entities with different institutional interests. What we might now refer to as the "Brotherhood sector" encompasses the *jama'a*, the original movement organization; the Freedom and Justice Party, the Brotherhood's political arm; and the Mursi presidency. The Brotherhood is a disciplined cadre organization; by contrast, the FJP, as a party open to all citizens, is more diverse, including members with varying levels of ideological commitment as well as women and Christians, and Mursi was elected president of all Egyptians. Hence the Brotherhood sector encompasses three distinct institutional entities that are answerable to different constituencies, occupy different roles in the political system, and are subject to different norms and expectations. The degree of coordination between these different wings of the movement—in particular, the extent to which the FJP and the president are subject to directives from the Guidance Bureau—is difficult to assess at this juncture. This is because of the newness of the Brotherhood's auxiliary arms, whose relations with its "mother organization" are still evolving, as well as our limited access to meetings and discussions removed from the public eye. What is clear is that the Brotherhood, like the state establishment, is not a monolith but a complex institutional network with different moving parts.

The Brotherhood's Double Dilemma

At this phase of Egypt's transition, the actors and institutions of the Brotherhood sector face two major challenges that are closely intertwined, what I refer to here as the Brotherhood's "double dilemma." The first challenge is to exercise the public mandate it won at the polls without pushing so hard as to trigger a major backlash from the institutions of the "deep state" carried over from the Mubarak era. The second challenge for the Brotherhood is to advance its own partisan agenda without alienating other sectors of society to the point that they actively mobilize against it. Both of these challenges will be exceedingly difficult to navigate, with the potential for miscalculations and missteps at every turn. But if the Brotherhood fails to give its opponents a stake in the new political order, it could end up being seen as having hijacked the democratic process for its own ends, placing the transition—and its own gains—at risk.

With the Brotherhood-dominated parliament dissolved, the primary burden for setting, and defending, the Brotherhood's policy agenda has fallen to Egypt's new president, Muhammad Mursi. How far Mursi should go to assert his authority in the face of resistance from other quarters appears to be something that has been decided on an ad hoc basis, but if there has been a general trend, it has been one toward greater assertiveness, not less. For example, when FJP leader Muhammad al-Biltagi condemned the SCAF's dissolution of parliament in June 2012 as a "full-fledged coup," Mursi swiftly distanced himself from this interpretation. As he said in a television appearance the evening the decree was announced, "I don't see what is going on as a military coup," adding, "I love the armed forces."[70] Yet Mursi appeared to reverse course on July 8, a week after his inauguration as president, when he reinstated the dissolved parliament. According to Samer Shehata, Mursi's about-face reflected pressure emanating from the Brotherhood, as indicated by the fact that the decree was announced after the Shura Council held a meeting on the matter the night before.[71] This sequence of events appears to indicate Mursi's continued deference to the organization he has faithfully represented over the entire course of his political career.

On August 12, Mursi went even further to consolidate his authority. In his boldest move yet, he announced the retirement of Field Marshal Muhammed Hussein Tantawi, the minister of defense, and Sami Anan, the army chief of staff, and named their replacements. Other senior military commanders, including the heads of the navy, the air force, and the air defense forces, were also replaced. In addition, Mursi canceled the SCAF's June 17 addendum to the constitution, reclaiming the executive powers the SCAF had arrogated to itself.[72] Whether Mursi acted on his own or at the prompting of the Brotherhood's senior leadership is unclear. Either way, his actions represented a dramatic rebuke of those military commanders most resistant to the idea of being held accountable to a civilian government.

The sudden reshuffle of the country's top military leaders caught observers by surprise, and reactions were mixed. Many celebrated the move as an important step toward establishing effective civilian control over the military establishment, while others denounced it as an effort by Mursi—and, by extension, the Brotherhood—to assume dictatorial powers. But both of these interpretations miss a crucial point, namely that the reshuffle was apparently supported by senior figures in the military itself. According to Hesham Sallam, a series of defiant actions and statements by Tantawi and other senior military figures over the summer signaled that they were in for a long fight with the Brotherhood and might even be preparing for a coup d'état. Other military leaders viewed such a confrontational posture as unnecessary and unwise, arguing that it would antagonize the country's anti-SCAF forces and put the military's core interests at risk. Hence far from being a united entity, the military establishment was itself split, with some leaders more willing to support the new president than others. The lack of much outcry from the military establishment powerfully suggests that Mursi had secured support for the shake-up in advance. As Sallam observed,

The way these events have unfolded further suggest[s] it is highly unlikely that Mursi or the Brotherhood could have led this initiative single-handedly without the support, if not the leadership, of senior military officials. For starters, SCAF member General Muhammad al-Assar, who was rewarded in the recent reshuffle, was quick to tell media outlets shortly after Mursi's decision was announced that the president had in fact consulted with military leaders before retiring Anan and Tantawi.[73]

Further, despite forcing some turnover at the top, Mursi has made no serious move to assert control over the military budget, to prosecute military officers for human rights violations they are accused of committing before, during, and after the uprising, or to threaten the military's vast economic empire, which, by conservative estimates, accounts for as much as 15% of Egypt's GDP. Though Mursi's future actions are difficult to predict, it is unlikely that he will launch a frontal assault on the military's vital political and economic interests. Nevertheless, we should expect the struggle between Mursi and state officials carried over from the Mubarak era to continue, if not intensify, as long as the proper division of authority between them remains open to dispute.

As noted earlier, the first challenge the Brotherhood faces is asserting its authority vis-à-vis the institutions of the "deep state." At the same time, the Brotherhood confronts a second and equally daunting challenge: gaining the trust and confidence of wider sectors of Egyptian society without losing the support of its base.

In the months following the uprising, the Brotherhood alienated potential allies by packing the Constitutional Assembly with an Islamist majority and breaking earlier promises not to contest more than half of the seats in parliament and to run its own candidate for president. Indeed, such "overreach" reinforced the impression that the group sought to dominate the political order. Pressure on the Brotherhood to exhibit greater tolerance and flexibility is especially acute for Muhammad Mursi. Mursi won the presidency by a narrow margin; indeed, roughly half of those who supported him in the runoff had voted for someone else in the first round. Mursi's ability to credibly portray himself as "the president of all Egyptians" will require that he make good on his pledge to work closely with political and civic leaders outside the Islamist camp. Despite the inclusive tone of his rhetoric, Mursi has yet to translate that commitment into practice. Mursi's new cabinet, announced on August 2 after weeks of delay, was dominated by technocrats, disappointing those who had hoped it would include several secular and liberal public figures. Further, as Shehata observed in mid-July, Mursi appears to be receiving most of his advice from members of the Brotherhood and the FJP, who have positioned themselves as "gatekeepers," limiting other groups' access to the president and hence making it more difficult for him to hear and evaluate their ideas.[74]

Yet no matter how impressive its recent electoral gains, the Brotherhood has neither the power nor the technical know-how to govern the country on its own. In order to consolidate the country's fragile democratic institutions, reform the state apparatus, and address the urgent social and economic problems of greatest concern to voters, the Brotherhood will need the support of other civic and political forces. Whether it manages to elicit that support will hinge in part on its willingness to compromise on social and moral issues on which Islamist and secular opinion remains sharply divided. The problem for the Brotherhood is that any concessions on such issues not only are opposed by ideological hard-liners in the group but could also open it to the charge that it has betrayed the Islamic cause and prompt the defection of some of its members to Salafi groups on the right. To win over its opponents without losing its supporters, the Brotherhood will need to walk a fine line, affirming its fidelity to the Islamic cause while honoring the democratic and inclusive spirit of the uprising that brought it to power.

During the summer of 2012, such conflicting pressures came into sharp focus in the Constitutional Assembly. Figures involved in the group's proceedings have noted that some of the most contentious issues under discussion concerned whether and how the rulings of the Shari'a should be invoked as the basis for legislation. The wording of Article 2 of the constitution currently refers to "the principles of Shari'a" as the primary source of legislation. Brotherhood leaders have repeatedly assured secular and liberal groups that they would support the replication of this wording in the new constitution, which represents a compromise between those seeking the strict enforcement of traditional Shari'a provisions and those calling for the full separation of religion and state. However, Salafi members of the assembly have demanded that the constitution's reference to the "principles" of the Shari'a be changed to the "rulings" of the Shari'a, and/or be supplemented by more definitive and robust references to the Shari'a in other sections of the document. In the assembly's heated debates on these issues, Brotherhood figures have found themselves between a rock and a hard place, seeking to placate their secular counterparts while protecting themselves from the charge that, in a bow to public pressure, they have diluted their commitment to Shari'a rule. Whatever the wording of any references to the Shari' in the new constitution, disagreements over how they should be interpreted and enforced are sure to persist, both between the Brotherhood and the Salafis and among different factions of the Brotherhood itself.

In the struggle over Egypt's new constitution, the two sides of the Brotherhood's "double dilemma" converged. On the one hand, the Constituent Assembly was at risk of being dissolved—and any document it produced annulled—by a hostile judiciary; on the other, the assembly, dominated by Islamists, was deemed unrepresentative by secular parties and civil society groups, which vowed to reject any draft constitution that restricted civil rights in religion's name. Against this backdrop, the Brotherhood will confront a difficult trade-off, as the harder it pushes to get its version of the constitution ratified, the more resistance it will provoke from its opponents. Indeed, though the Brotherhood can claim a public mandate on the strength of its showing at the polls, the overzealous exercise of that mandate could trigger a backlash in which Mubarak-era state officials and secular groups that faced off during the uprising unite against it.

The Muslim Brotherhood and Egypt's Unfinished Transition

It is still too early to define the broad themes of the Mursi presidency. Nevertheless, it is striking that his first major policy initiatives have focused on alleviating economic and social hardships rather than regulating citizens' private behavior. Shortly after assuming office, Mursi mandated a 15% increase in the bonuses for public sector workers and boosted the social insurance benefits for the country's poorest families from \$33 to \$50 per month.[75] In addition, he announced an ambitious "100 day plan" to achieve immediate improvement in five areas: security, fuel, bread, garbage collection, and traffic. As part of this plan, Mursi launched the Clean Homeland Initiative, mobilizing local community and youth volunteers to remove piles of accumulated garbage from the streets, refurbish sidewalks and pavements, plant trees, and improve public hygiene.[76] Along a parallel track, Hatim Abd al-Latif, a professor of traffic engineering at 'Ayn Shams University, was tasked with developing a plan to alleviate the traffic congestion in Greater Cairo and other urban areas. Proposed changes include improvements to road and bus networks and the deployment of a large number of foot police to enforce traffic laws.[77] Meaningful progress in each of the five areas of Mursi's plan will require a much longer time horizon, especially in light of the acute budgetary constraints facing the government and the sluggish response rate of Egypt's vast and inefficient bureaucracy. Nevertheless, a good-faith effort to alleviate the daily hardships of ordinary citizens could help expand Mursi's following beyond the Brotherhood's traditional base of support.

The agenda Mursi will pursue over the longer term is harder to pin down. During his presidential campaign, Mursi made constant reference to the Nahda (Renaissance) Project—the Brotherhood's comprehensive program of development "within an Islamic frame of reference." But it is unclear how Mursi and Brotherhood deputies in parliament define this frame of reference and intend to translate it into practice.

A Mursi campaign conference on tourism, held at a luxury hotel near the pyramids just days before the presidential runoff commenced, may offer a glimpse of what the group's broader development agenda will look like. The decision to convene a high-profile conference on tourism, which Mursi attended and which was covered by a large phalanx of reporters and cameramen, underscored the importance of the tourist industry as a source of foreign currency, as well as widespread concerns that a Brotherhood-led government might implement new restrictions, such as a ban on the sale of alcohol, that would drive tourists away. The conference, which I attended, gave Brotherhood leaders the opportunity to emphasize their commitment to the tourism industry and to share some "out of the box" thinking about how it could be developed in the years to come. Numerous innovative proposals were put forward, including the construction of a distinctive brand for Egyptian tourism and using social media as a marketing tool; expanding religious tourism to Muslim and Christian pilgrimage sites; boosting ecotourism and introducing measures to prevent the environmental degradation of Egypt's coral reefs; and developing medical tourism. Further, one Brotherhood leader announced that he had recently visited the United States to promote Egypt as an American tourist destination and to stress that "the Brotherhood after the revolution is open to the whole world." Speakers also noted that the Egyptian government could increase revenues by charging more for tourist services. As one speaker noted, "I just returned from Geneva and I paid a fortune! It is time for us to increase our visa price." More generally, another speaker observed, "The rates for tourists in Egypt are very cheap, so we're not getting the full value for what we have to offer."

Struck by the absence of any reference to the "Islamic" dimension of the Brotherhood's tourism strategy, I raised the issue with one of Mursi's campaign agents. The Brotherhood's approach, he explained, sought to achieve a balance between development (*tatwir*) and wise management (*rashd*), the latter a reference to harmonizing practices in the tourism field with the values of Egyptian society. For example, he noted, some hotels could establish a barrier in the middle of a pool, reserving one section for men and another for women, or could open the pool to them at different hours.[78]

The focus of the conference on measures to expand tourism rather than to regulate tourists' behavior can be interpreted in different ways—that is, as a strategic decision to downplay the more controversial elements of the Brotherhood's agenda or as evidence that such elements no longer figured at the top of its priorities. My own reading falls somewhere in between. While the Brotherhood remains committed in principle to the Islamic reform of society and state, Egypt's urgent social and economic problems have tilted its immediate strategy toward a focus on creative problem-solving within existing social and political constraints.

Without a doubt, one of the Brotherhood's highest priorities since Mursi's election as president is to demonstrate its capacity for effective governance, most notably in the domain of the economy. The new cabinet formed by Mursi in the summer of 2012 is headed by Hisham Qandil, a former irrigation minister, and dominated by technocrats who, according to Mursi aides, were selected on the basis of their ability to implement the president's agenda.[79] Though improving the state of the economy is not the only challenge facing the new government, its performance in this area will arguably be most decisive in determining how it is judged by the Egyptian public at large.

There is no denying that Egypt's economy is in dire shape, with the country struggling to adjust to the harsh conditions of a global economic recession and recover from the disruption and uncertainty produced by the uprising and the dramatic political changes that have followed. Unlike Iran and Saudi Arabia, Egypt does not have massive oil revenues to finance social benefit programs and spur economic growth.[80] In the last half of 2011, Egypt reported zero growth in its economy.[81] Further, unemployment has reached a ten-year high, with some analysts estimating a "real" (as opposed to "official") rate of 20%, with an additional 175,000 people flooding the job market each year. Moreover, the demographic pressures facing the Egyptian economy are likely to intensify. As Geoffrey Kemp of the Center for the National Interest observed, with a population growth rate of about 2%, Egypt's population could reach 115 million in fifteen years. Since most of Egypt's terrain is desert, such growth will place an even greater strain on the densely populated strip along the Nile and the fertile northern region of the Delta, all told, a land area smaller than the Netherlands.[82] Rapid population growth will also make it more difficult for Egypt to feed its population. As Kemp observes, Egypt is the world's largest importer of wheat and the second-largest importer of maize, staple products whose prices have soared sky-high and must be paid for in foreign currency. Without a massive infusion of loans from world financial institutions, Kemp warns, "Egypt will go bankrupt unless it instigates rigorous reforms."[83] Yet any moves toward greater financial discipline are likely to aggravate unemployment and trigger a further spike in the price of basic consumer items at a time when an estimated 40% of the population lives on less than $2 per day.[84] In the face of such harsh realities, the SCAF reopened talks with the International Monetary Fund (IMF) in early 2012 over the terms of a $3.2 billion loan, though it had earlier rejected IMF guidance as "an affront to national sovereignty."[85]

President Mursi and Brotherhood deputies in parliament are keenly aware of the enormity of Egypt's economic problems and have no desire to shoulder the responsibility for addressing them alone. Looking ahead, we can expect them to seek the backing of a wider coalition before launching any bold measures to stimulate the economy, particularly those, like the reform of Egypt's costly and inefficient subsidy system, that will cause short-term "social pain." Further, Brotherhood leaders understand that accessing the capital needed for economic growth will hinge on gaining the trust and confidence of foreign investors, as well as the support of key financial and political institutions in the global economy. Indeed, in what the *New York Times* portrayed as a "stunning reversal after eight decades of denouncing Western colonialism and dependency," the FJP held its own meeting with the IMF at the start of 2012.[86] As Khayrat al-Shatir told Thomas Friedman, "It is no longer a matter of choice whether one can be with or against globalization. It is a reality. From our perspective, we favor the widest possible engagement with globalization through win-win situations."[87] The Brotherhood's awareness of the daunting problems facing Egypt has also increased its incentive to govern in concert with—rather than against—other social and political forces at home. As Khayrat al-Shatir told the Egyptian daily *al-Ahram*:

> We know that the challenges facing Egypt are too large and complex for any party or faction to face alone. In the coming period, there must be as much integration and cooperation as possible, with alliances and coalitions among the various political stakeholders and actors in the Egyptian arena.... There is no possibility of a power monopoly. It simply is not part of our strategy or our culture.[88]

Pragmatic, Not Progressive

For all of the Brotherhood's talk about national unity and consensus, there is still a legitimate worry that it will exploit its newfound power to pursue a conservative social agenda based on Islamic precepts as it defines them. Brotherhood leaders claim to favor a balance between respecting individual freedoms and preserving the religious norms and values of Egyptian society. Yet where Brotherhood leaders will draw the line between acceptable and unacceptable speech and behavior is unclear. As I have noted repeatedly throughout this book, Brotherhood leaders share a vague commitment to reform within "an Islamic frame of reference" but lack a common vision of what that would entail in practice. Many members of the Brotherhood's *da'wa* wing, including some of the most powerful figures in the Guidance Bureau, adhere to a highly conservative version of Islam, while those in the group's reformist wing have gravitated toward interpretations that privilege ideas of gender equality, pluralism, and human rights. Mursi and the top leaders in the FJP can be characterized as occupying a middle position between these two poles. While their outlook on social and moral issues can be found wanting from a secular humanist standpoint, they are unlikely to push aggressively for the strict implementation of Shari'rulings inherited from the past. First, this would trigger intense opposition from other figures in the Brotherhood itself, threatening the group's unity and diminishing its capacity to respond effectively to external challenges. Second, it would directly undermine the efforts of Mursi and the FJP to portray themselves as respectful of Egypt's cultural and social diversity. Indeed, since his election as president, Mursi has repeatedly assured Egyptian citizens that he has no intention of infringing on their rights. As one Brotherhood member explained: "We know that people are afraid that we are going to [attack] their lifestyles and we are trying very hard in every way possible to dispel these concerns."[89] As an indication of this trend, during his first week in office Mursi told a group of editors and TV anchors, including unveiled women, that "no particular dress code would be imposed on women," and in his victory speech a few weeks earlier he sought to assure the country's Coptic Christians that he would serve as "a president for all Egyptians—Muslims and Christians alike."[90]

In sum, at a time when Mursi and the FJP are under considerable pressure to demonstrate their fidelity to the tolerant and inclusive spirit of the "revolution" that brought them to power, they are unlikely to pursue a radical agenda that would play into the hands of their detractors and enable powerful actors in the "deep state" to intervene in the political process in the name of democracy and the rule of law. At the same time, however, they are unlikely to support the type of progressive reforms sought by secular rights groups, such as moves to rectify the blatant gender discrimination embedded in Egypt's Shari'a-based family laws or to safeguard the rights of homosexuals. Such reforms not only are at odds with the ideological convictions of top Brotherhood leaders but would open them to the charge of having betrayed the Islamic cause. While Mursi may have no intention of imposing the veil on Egyptian women, he is also unlikely to figure as a champion of gender equality. More broadly, his social agenda will likely qualify as "pragmatic" but not "progressive," endeavoring to avoid being seen as pushing Shari'a rule too aggressively on the one hand and as abandoning it on the other.

Further, given the different pressures facing the Brotherhood presidency, the Brotherhood bloc in parliament, and the Brotherhood movement organization, as well as the disagreement contained within them, we should expect the positions staked out by Brotherhood leaders on sensitive cultural and moral issues to be marked by a high degree of inconsistency. Brotherhood leaders have a history of making conflicting statements, and what they say to the media often differs from what they say to members of their base. Such incoherence is, if anything, likely to increase in the coming era. Hence the Brotherhood will remain vulnerable to the charge that it speaks in a "double language" and that its commitments to pluralism and democracy cannot be trusted.[91]

The contradictory statements that have emanated from the Brotherhood since the uprising are striking. While spokesmen for the FJP have talked in measured tones about the merits of an inclusive democratic order, some leaders in the *da'wa* wing of the movement have struck a triumphalist note, invoking themes of domination carried over from the movement's anti-system past. For example, in December 2011, following the Brotherhood's strong showing in the early rounds of Egypt's parliamentary elections, Muhammad Badi', the Supreme Guide, declared,

> The Brotherhood is getting closer to achieving its greatest goal as envisioned by its founder, Imam Hasan al-Banna. This will be accomplished by establishing a righteous and fair ruling system, with all its institutions and associations, including a government evolving into a rightly guided caliphate and mastership of the world.[92]

Predictably, Badi''s statement was posted on conservative websites in the United States as damning proof of the Brotherhood's radical intentions.

Yet even the Brotherhood's Supreme Guide does not speak for the movement as a whole. On the contrary, those representing the Brotherhood in the domain of electoral politics are answerable to different constituencies and subject to different external pressures. There is certainly a chance that the latter will propose measures to preserve the country's "public morals," such as new restrictions on the sale and consumption of alcohol, or to ban "un-Islamic content" in the media, entertainment, art, and public scholarship. But they strike me as too savvy and too pragmatic to pursue a radical agenda that would place their own gains at risk. Indeed, several Brotherhood leaders have expressed hope that the enormity of the challenges facing the country will push the country's hard-line Salafis toward greater pragmatism as well. As 'Esam al-'Aryan noted in January 2012, "We hope that we can pull the Salafists—not that they pull us—and that both of us will be pulled by the people's needs."[93]

A similar pragmatic shift can be seen in the Brotherhood's positions on sensitive matters of foreign policy, including Egypt's peace treaty with Israel. The Brotherhood is well-known for its hostility toward Israel, which has long extended beyond the defense of Palestinian rights to include a fundamental rejection of the legitimacy of the Zionist state, which it has denounced as based on the illegal foreign occupation of Arab-Islamic territory. Further, Brotherhood leaders have frequently resorted to anti-Semitic vitriol that blurs the distinction between Israelis and Jews and depicts the latter as an existential adversary of all Muslims and Islam itself. During its years in opposition, the Brotherhood faced little accountability for such rhetoric. But now that its leaders have assumed key roles in public office, the costs associated with such positions have increased. While continuing to express deep reservations about Egypt's peace treaty with Israel, Mursi and his counterparts in parliament have stressed that they will respect the treaty as a commitment of the Egyptian state, leaving the door open to its revision through constitutional means, such as a popular referendum, at some point in the future.

Egypt's new Islamist government will likely be more forceful than the Mubarak regime in holding Israel to account for its actions and protesting any moves on its part that violate the spirit or the letter of international agreements, such as the expansion of Israeli settlements or the initiation of new military strikes on Palestinian targets. Further, just as there are hard-liners in the Brotherhood who advocate the strict application of Islamic law, there are those who favor a more aggressive posture toward Israel and who are likely to resort to inflammatory anti-Israel rhetoric at times of heightened tension. Nevertheless, in matters of foreign policy, as on the contentious issue of Shari'a, real-world constraints and responsibilities create powerful incentives for pragmatism. As Martin Indyk observed after meetings with Brotherhood leaders in Cairo in January 2012:

Newly-elected Egyptian politicians—the Muslim Brotherhood first and foremost—understand that they have to make a choice between feeding the people and fighting

Israel, and for the time being they have made a conscious choice of bread over bombs.[94]

Likewise, Khayrat al-Shatir, one of the Brotherhood's most powerful figures, describes politics as "the art of the possible."[95] When asked in June 2012 by Matthew Kaminski of the *Wall Street Journal* about Egypt's peace treaty with Israel, al-Shatir replied: "Egypt is a constitutional country. It's not possible with each ruler to rethink our obligations and conventions. This will lead to a lack of confidence in dealing with Egypt." Moreover, he stressed, the Brotherhood's priority at this juncture is to develop a strategic partnership with the United States, which, Kaminski observed, the group "expects to help unlock credit markets and gain international legitimacy."[96]

The Brotherhood's pragmatism will not necessarily translate into support for liberal or pro-Western policies. First, the Brotherhood's insistence on devising a policy agenda "consistent with Islamic values" will limit the range of options it is willing to consider. As al-Shatir put it, "We will follow the homeland's interests wherever they point, unless they conflict with Islamic principles, which set the general basic rules."[97] Yet how such "Islamic principles" will shape Brotherhood policy is difficult to predict, since they remain only vaguely defined.

Second, as noted earlier, the Brotherhood will be judged simultaneously by different audiences for its commitment to democracy and its fidelity to the Islamic cause. In the face of such conflicting pressures, the strategic calculations of Brotherhood leaders will likely tilt in favor of liberal or pro-Western policies in some instances and against them in others.

Finally, when the Brotherhood's vital interests are at stake and the opportunity exists to realize them, the group's impulse toward self-assertion may trump its impulse toward self-restraint. The Brotherhood's decision in spring 2012 to run a candidate for president after promising not to do so, in reaction to the SCAF's obstruction of the efforts of its parliamentary bloc to form a new government, is a case in point, as is Mursi's shake-up of the senior military command a few months later. Likewise, in the ongoing battle over Egypt's new constitution, in which the stakes are high and public opinion is sharply divided, the Brotherhood has demonstrated that it is willing to move forward over the objections of its opponents, insisting all the while that it has the public mandate to do so. In sum, in order to push the transition in the direction it favors, the Brotherhood may throw caution to the wind at critical junctures and deal with the fallout later.

The Unfulfilled Promise of Egypt's "Revolution"

Whether or not the Brotherhood will attempt to hijack Egypt's democratic transition for illiberal purposes remains an open question. But the sober reality is that the democratic promise of Egypt's "revolution" has yet to be fulfilled. The uprising succeeded in decapitating the old regime, but the institutions of the "deep state" carried over from the Mubarak era remain largely intact. Protesters at Tahrir Square demanded *tathir al-dawla* ("cleansing" the state of Mubarak appointees), but so far no more than a few officials have been removed from their positions, and the internal culture of the bureaucracy has yet to be revised. Further, any democratic restructuring of Egypt's state institutions will face powerful resistance from those with a vested interest in a continuation of the corrupt and cronyistic practices that have pervaded all levels of the administration for decades. Looking ahead, the consolidation of Egypt's transition to democracy will arguably require progress on three fronts simultaneously. First, it will require the country's newly elected leaders to overcome their differences and mobilize the tremendous political will and capacity needed to reform the country's state institutions and subject them to greater public scrutiny and control. Second, if Egypt's transition is to entail more than a shift to majority rule, the new constitution must include robust guarantees of individual rights, and the country's judicial institutions must have the power and the will to defend them. Third, a democratic system is unlikely to flourish if any group is in a position to monopolize power over the long term. Hence it will be vital that secular and Islamist progressive groups cultivate stronger ties with the mass public, a process that will require a major investment of time, resources, and effort. Whether such groups will ever match the organizational reach of the Brotherhood and the Salafis remains to be seen. But without the backing of broader constituencies, secular and progressive Islamist groups will not be able to function as an effective counterweight to the conservative Islamist trend.

Will Egypt succeed in establishing a democratic system of rule? Perhaps, but it will take time, and it will be an outcome of political struggle. The formative stage of a new democracy tends to be marked by intense disagreements among various groups, whether with respect to the new system's founding principles and/or the rules for contestation within it.[98] And the effective resolution of such conflicts is not guaranteed. On the contrary, it is apt to hinge on the work of leaders with exceptional judgment and political acumen who are willing to compromise with their opponents in the interest of the public good. The problem, of course, is that many of the leaders who rise to the fore in new democracies lack these critical attributes. It is too early to determine how the Brotherhood's public officials and their secular rivals rate on this score. But their inability to date to reach a consensus on the broad contours of Egypt's new political order is not encouraging.

The Muslim Brotherhood in a New Egypt

The Brotherhood's forty-odd years of participation in electoral politics before the Arab Spring can be seen in retrospect as a long period of incubation, during which its leaders developed new competencies and skills and adjusted to the "pursuit of the possible" under existing constraints. During the same time frame, a critical mass of reformist leaders emerged within the Islamist movement and began to agitate for progressive changes in the goals, strategies, and internal practices of the Brotherhood itself. But the impact of the reformist trend was more muted than it might have been under a different leadership and in a less forbidding political environment. The dominance of conservative stalwarts in the Brotherhood's highest decision-making bodies diminished the scope and pace of reform, as did the group's chronic vulnerability to state repression. Although the Brotherhood managed to survive its long years under siege intact, it did so without making a decisive break with its anti-system past. Indeed, the very features of internal unity, discipline, and obedience that helped the Brotherhood survive in the shadow of a hostile authoritarian state have stunted its development into a professional, transparent, and internally democratic organization suited to operating in an open political environment.

Further, although the Brotherhood's agenda contains numerous references to freedom, pluralism, and democracy, it has yet to consciously abandon—or radically reinterpret—its historic *da'wa* mission. As a result, its commitment to democracy remains bounded by a set of ideological tenets inherited from the past. Though Brotherhood leaders now call for a "civil state" headed by elected public officials, their insistence on the state's "Islamic frame of reference" injects an authority that supersedes the preferences of the electorate. For the Brotherhood, as for any group that bases its agenda on Islam, some crucial questions come to the fore. Who has the right to define Islam for the rest of society? More specifically, who decides which of the infinitely diverse interpretations of its mandates should form the basis of positive legislation? Having historically arrogated this right to itself, the Brotherhood has yet to acknowledge the prerogative of other civil and political actors to define Islam for themselves and of private citizens to live according to values of their own choosing, whether or not their behavior conforms with Islamic guidelines as the Brotherhood understands them.

A crucial issue going forward is how the Brotherhood will interpret the articles of Egypt's new constitution, in particular, the Shari'a references contained within them. Will the Brotherhood seek to enforce the application of traditional Shari'a rulings, which are clearly illiberal and discriminatory in many aspects, or will it focus instead on adherence to Shari'a principles, such as the duty of the state to pursue justice, evince accountability, and guarantee freedom? For years the Brotherhood has framed its commitment to Shari'a rule in vague and abstract terms, but it will become increasingly difficult for them to do so in the future. In particular, the Brotherhood will be pressed to clarify its positions in three issue areas. First, it will need to specify its stance on the citizenship rights of Coptic Christians and women, not just in terms of their eligibility for political office but in the domains of society and culture, where the expansion of their rights will necessarily dilute the privileges historically enjoyed by the country's

Muslim majority and diminish male authority in the home. Will the Brotherhood support the right of Egyptian Copts to build churches without restriction and hold large public celebrations on Christian holidays? Will it support the full equality of women in matters of marriage, divorce, and inheritance? Brotherhood leaders disagree on such matters, and any position they take will satisfy certain audiences and alienate others. But when such issues cross the desk of the president or are raised in parliament, they will be forced to take a stand.

Second, the Brotherhood will face growing pressure to define the extent of its support for free political, intellectual, and artistic expression, as well as its willingness to allow citizens to make their own choices with respect to styles of dress, leisure activities, gender relations, and sexual orientation. Will the Brotherhood permit the public dissemination of ideas that contradict its understanding of Islam? Will it permit women to wear bathing suits on the beach, restaurants to sell beer, and civil society groups to celebrate the Christian, Jewish, and Greek elements of Egypt's national heritage? Will it permit individuals to choose their sexual partners and conduct their sexual relationships free of governmental constraints? Taking a clear stand on such issues will inevitably open the Brotherhood to criticism. Yet here, too, it will become increasingly difficult to invoke broad slogans as a substitute for detailed policy positions and programs.

A third challenge facing the Brotherhood is that of accountability to a wider global audience. For years Brotherhood leaders were free to engage in radical posturing that played well with their supporters. Examples include the embrace of jihad, the defense of suicide terrorism as a legitimate form of resistance in Palestine and Iraq, the rehabilitation of anti-Semitic diatribes like the Protocols of the Elders of Zion, and the portrayal of the Jews as rejected by God and enemies of Islam. But now the Brotherhood's allies as well as its opponents are scrutinizing its every word. In this context, the Brotherhood will be under pressure to exercise greater judiciousness and restraint if it wants to distinguish itself from militant Islamist groups that are vilified in the West and encourage the United States and the European Union to back its efforts to reform the state and achieve economic growth.

Finally, the Brotherhood will face the challenge of adapting its organizational structures and practices to the demands of a new political environment. Despite all the references to pluralism and equality in its official statements, the Brotherhood remains a highly traditional and parochial organization. New recruits must undergo a long vetting process before they are granted full membership rights, and members who openly challenge the decisions of the senior leadership are subject to expulsion. While women play an active role in the group, they lack formal rights and have little say over its direction. Further, the aging leaders who dominate the Guidance Bureau continue to exercise considerable ad hoc authority, and robust mechanisms have yet to be established to ensure the transparency of the policy decision-making process and to hold the group's senior leaders accountable to the Shura Council and the membership at large. The rapid pace of events since the uprising has pushed the Brotherhood into an immediate response mode and, in doing so, postponed the onset of any serious reform. Senior leaders in the Brotherhood claim to support the group's "institutional development," but it is far from clear whether they are ready to endorse fundamental changes in the group's core norms and practices, such as the inclusion of women and youth in top leadership positions, the empowerment of the Shura Council, and establishing two-way lines of communication between the group's leadership and its base.

At the broadest level, the Brotherhood faces a tough existential question that strikes at the very heart of its identity: What does it strive to be? A missionary organization that seeks to remake society in its own image, or a group content to be one voice among many, on an equal footing, that respects the rights of individuals who do not share its vision to answer to their own conscience? The Brotherhood has demonstrated that it is exceptionally good at providing services and mobilizing supporters at the ballot box. But it has yet to develop the habit of cooperating with other groups as equal partners, to establish a robust democratic culture, or to embrace self-criticism as a catalyst for growth. Whether or not the Brotherhood moves in this direction remains to be seen. For now, the state of Egypt's political transition—and of the Brotherhood itself—remains in flux.

THE BROADER PATTERN OF ISLAMIST MOVEMENT CHANGE IN THE ARAB WORLD

This book has analyzed the evolution of the Muslim Brotherhood in Egypt over more than eighty years, focusing on the ways it has been shaped by its participation in a political process warped by authoritarian rule. Further, by comparing the Egyptian Brotherhood's trajectory to those of similar Islamist groups in Jordan, Kuwait, and Morocco, it has sought to discern the features it shares in common with other groups, as well as the particularities that set it apart. More broadly, the book seeks to contribute to the literature on Islamist group evolution in four ways. First, it analyzes the scope *and* limits of Islamist movement change, highlighting elements of continuity as well as transformation. Second, it distinguishes between adjustments in Islamist group rhetoric and behavior that exhibit a clear strategic logic and those that appear to reflect deeper changes in their members' core values and beliefs. Third, it addresses the crucial problem of aggregation: whether, when, and how changes at the level of individual actors spread across the movement organizations of which they are a part. Fourth, by exploring the microdynamics of Islamist movement change at close range, it is able to establish finer-grained patterns of cause and effect than do studies that address the subject more schematically and from a greater distance. Here I recap my main analytic findings.

None of the Islamist groups under study can be characterized as having undergone a linear, unidirectional, and internally consistent process of "moderation," however the term is defined. This is because the scope and pace of the changes implied by the term have been protracted and uneven within Islamist groups, proceeding further in some issue areas than in others and occurring more deeply within subunits of each group than within the group as a whole. *Yet defining the essential character of Islamist groups as fixed and unchanging, and hence resistant to adaptation, is equally flawed.* Those who claim that observable changes in Islamist group rhetoric and behavior—including their recent calls for the expansion of democracy and public freedoms—are just "for show" are as guilty of minimizing the changes that have occurred as those at the opposite end of the spectrum are of exaggerating them. The objective of this book is not to align with either pole in the current debate about whether the Egyptian Muslim Brotherhood and other mainstream Islamist groups are "moderate" or "moderating" but to expose the gross simplifications and overgeneralizations that permeate the discussion on both sides.

The Muslim Brotherhood in Egypt and its counterparts in Jordan, Kuwait, and Morocco joined the formal political system in order to change it, but they ended up being changed by it themselves. Such groups initially entered the fray of electoral politics to advance their historic *da'wa* mission, that is, to facilitate the comprehensive Islamic reform of society and state, their conception of which flowed from a conservative reading of Islam's sacred texts and juristic precedents. However, instead of "going for broke" and risking a backlash that could threaten their own survival, the Brotherhood and its counterparts adjusted to the narrow space available to them under conditions of authoritarian rule.

As participants in political systems subject to regime manipulation and control, Islamist groups sought to balance the advancement of long-term objectives with such short-term considerations as avoiding repression, gaining (and retaining) a legal foothold in the system, and overcoming the distrust of their secular opponents. These latter considerations prompted Islamist leaders to exercise increasing self-restraint in both rhetoric and practice.

In the domain of rhetoric, they toned down their calls for the application of Shari'a by postponing it far into the future and/or redefining it in terms of general principles rather than juristic rulings inherited from the past. Further, in contrast to their previous expressions of contempt for democracy as an "alien" system imported from the West, they began to frame the expansion of democracy and public freedoms, as well as the establishment of strict limits on state power, as essential components of an Islamic order. In the domain of practice, Islamist groups exercised self-restraint by running for some, but not all, seats in parliament, regional and municipal councils, and professional syndicates to limit their gains to acceptable levels. In a related move, they took pains to emphasize that they wanted to "participate, not dominate," and joined secular groups in the push for constitutional and political reforms.

The ascent of "freedom" and "democracy" to the top of Islamist group agendas reflected, at least in part, the dawning recognition of their leaders that strengthening democratic institutions and procedures would work to their own advantage. As the largest, best-organized, and most popular sector of the opposition, Islamist groups were in a strong position to benefit from any political opening, and this fact was not lost on those at their helm. Indeed, both conservative and progressive figures in the Egyptian Brotherhood and other Islamist groups have come to embrace the procedural aspects of democracy, noting that *shura* (consultation) is mandated by Islam and was practiced by the Prophet Muhammad himself.

Yet the claim that Islamist groups have fully embraced the tolerant and inclusive ethos of democracy goes too far. Rather, they have developed a hybrid discourse in which ideas of popular sovereignty, pluralism, and freedom coexist uneasily with older, more traditional conceptions of Islam that are decidedly less liberal in tone and content. The vagueness and ambiguity of this discourse indicate that the contradictions between the democratic and religious themes contained within it have yet to be acknowledged, let alone resolved. But speaking in terms of broad generalities rather than specifics has allowed Islamist leaders to address multiple audiences at the same time rather than satisfy some of them at the expense of alienating others.

The record of observable changes in Islamist rhetoric and behavior conforms, at least in part, to an instrumental logic. But a strategic explanation of Islamist movement change does not capture its full range of causes and dynamics. In particular, it fails to offer a persuasive theoretical account of the robust empirical evidence offered in the preceding chapters that the ideological commitments—and not just the material and organizational interests—of some Islamist actors have changed over time.

As candidates for, and occupants of, elected seats in parliament, local government, and professional syndicates, Islamist leaders were motivated to conform with new behavioral norms in order to be effective in new institutional environments. They developed new competencies and skills and became habituated to new rules and procedures for selecting power holders and setting policy. Further, as elected public officials, they negotiated with government officials and rival parties, worked closely with secular individuals and groups, and were expected to respond to the needs and interests of their constituents, whether the latter voted for them or not. Such experiences encouraged the gradual transformation of some Islamist actors into increasingly professionalized and pragmatic politicians, whose bearing, sensibilities, dispositions, and ways of relating to others evinced a sharp break from the past. This process of habituation proceeded further for some individuals in the movement than for others. It was certainly more pronounced among those who participated the longest and the most intensively in national representative institutions than among those who remained encapsulated within movement networks for most of their political careers.

The gradual, reflexive, and largely unconscious adaptation of Islamist actors to the norms of electoral politics is difficult to explain if we confine ourselves to models that characterize political behavior as driven solely by the self-conscious pursuit of individual and group interests. Such models are also ill equipped to explain when, why, and how the ideological commitments of political actors change over time. When we enter the domain of human motivations—as opposed to observable changes in rhetoric and behavior—the claims we make are not susceptible to a definitive "proof" because we do not have direct access to what lies within an individual's mind and heart. In cases where changes in the rhetoric and behavior of political actors are open to a "double interpretation," that is, to being characterized as strategic posturing or as reflecting change in their underlying values and beliefs, we are forced to make a subjective judgment about which interpretation is better supported by the evidence at hand. As I have shown in the preceding chapters, the evidence strongly suggests that the values and beliefs of some Islamist actors were fundamentally transformed by their experience as participants in the political process. Breaking out of the movement's insular networks and engaging in sustained dialogue and cooperation with secular civil and political leaders, journalists, and researchers had a profound effect on how such individuals viewed the world and their place within it. In particular, their experiences augmented the resonance of more progressive interpretations of Islam that privileged ideas of pluralism, equality, and human rights.

Although value-change occurred first and foremost at the level of individuals, it came to assume a collective dimension as well, as indicated by the rise of a reformist trend within the Brotherhood and other Islamist groups, fueled by middle-generation and youth leaders with shared sensibilities and concerns. In recent years, figures associated with the reformist trend have called for far-reaching change in the Islamist movement itself. Among other things, they have called for progressive revisions in the agendas of Islamist groups and the application of democratic rules and procedures in the management of their internal affairs.

Yet we cannot equate the reformist trend with the movement associations, parties, and blocs from which it sprung. The Brotherhood in Egypt, and its counterparts in Jordan, Kuwait, and Morocco, remain large umbrella organizations that encompass a wide range of opinion, including different views on how the broad objectives of the movement should be defined. In all four groups under study, progressive actors compete with hard-liners for power and influence, as well as with those situated between these poles. We also must guard against exaggerating the value shift that has occurred within the reformist trend itself. Though leaders affiliated with this trend have proceeded further than their peers toward the embrace of democratic values, their belief system is still grounded within an Islamic framework that requires that they justify their positions by reference to Islamic historical precedents and sacred texts. Further, like their more conservative counterparts, reformist leaders support a balance between respect for individual freedoms and protection of the religious character and identity of society. They differ from conservatives in how much social diversity they are willing to tolerate, but the difference is a matter of degree.

Variations on a Theme

If the trajectories of mainstream Islamist groups in Egypt, Jordan, Kuwait, and Morocco exhibit some important commonalities, the scope and pace of progressive change within them has varied, reflecting differences in the balance of power among their competing factions, the social profile of their base, and the nature of the political environment in which they are embedded.

All of the Islamist groups included in this study encompass a wide range of views and opinions. However, those who support more progressive interpretations of Islam have achieved greater influence and authority in some groups than in others. In Egypt, leaders affiliated with the reformist trend have never gained more than a marginal presence in the Guidance Bureau, the group's highest decision-making body. While the Brotherhood's new political arm, the Freedom and Justice Party, includes some reformist figures, its top positions are occupied by "pragmatic conservatives" situated between the reformists and the Brotherhood's old guard. Further, since the uprising, several prominent reformist leaders have left the Brotherhood to pursue new initiatives of their own.

The leadership ranks of the Islamic Action Front in Jordan and the Islamic Constitutional Movement in Kuwait also encompass different factions, but unlike in Egypt, none of them has managed to monopolize power at the expense of its rivals. In both countries, ideological hard-liners continue to call for the strict application of traditional Shariʿa rulings, while others, variously described as "moderates," "reformists," and "centrists," have moved toward new and more progressive readings of Islam.

It is in the Justice and Development Party (PJD) in Morocco that the reformist trend appears to have achieved the greatest influence. This reflects the early break of its veteran leaders from the radical al-Shabiba movement and the sustained process of self-reflection and self-criticism that occurred thereafter. Yet progressive figures like Saʿd al-Din al-ʿUthmani and Muhammad Yatim still remain one set of voices among many in the PJD, and competition persists among different factions for positions in the movement association and party leadership.

In addition, the Islamist groups under study face a common dilemma in seeking to bolster their democratic credentials while assuring supporters of their continued fidelity to the Islamic cause. In all four countries, mainstream Islamist leaders have sought to gain wider social acceptance and ward off accusations of extremism from secular parties, civil society organizations, and media outlets. Yet any softening of their positions on social and moral issues risks alienating members of their base. The costs of "moderation" are particularly steep in Jordan and Kuwait, where Islamist groups rely in part on the support of deeply conservative tribal constituencies. In such cases, the more responsive movement leaders are to the values and interests of their supporters, the less free they are to adjust their platforms. *Here strategic considerations work against progressive reform.*

The external pressures facing Islamist groups also vary from one country to the next. In all four countries, secular parties, civil society organizations, and media outlets perform an important "watchdog function"—exposing and censuring Islamist rhetoric and behavior perceived as violating democratic norms. Yet here, too, Morocco sets the curve. It is in Morocco where secular civil society groups are the best organized and where secular parties have sufficient resources, cadres, and mass support to function as viable competitors in national elections. Though secular democracy and human rights groups are also active in Egypt, Jordan, and Kuwait, they lack strong ties to the mass public and hence are less able to pose an effective counterweight to Islamist groups.

In sum, differences in the pace and scope of progressive reform among Islamist groups are due, in part, to differences in the social environments within which they are embedded. Although not included in this study, the Nahda party in Tunisia can be highlighted as an Islamist party that is even more progressive than its counterparts in Egypt, Jordan, Kuwait, and Morocco, emerging in the context of an even more secular, urban, and cosmopolitan society. The trajectories of Islamist groups in Egypt, Jordan, Kuwait, and Morocco exhibit a complex mix of departures from—and continuities with—the ideological and institutional features that characterized them in the past. All of them continue to call for the application of Shari'a, but what "Shari'a rule" would mean in practice and how aggressively it should be pursued have become a pivot of internal debate, and the resonance of conservative and progressive opinion on such matters differs from one group to another.

The pattern of Islamist movement change described in this book resists easy categorization. Islamist groups cannot be said to be "moderating" or "not moderating," any more than they can be characterized as "for" or "against" democracy. Such facile generalizations gloss over the internal complexity of Islamist groups and understate the profound tensions and contradictions that permeate their agendas. Likewise, changes in the rhetoric and behavior of Islamist leaders over time cannot be attributed to a single strand of cause and effect. Social scientists often seek parsimonious explanations for social and political change, but such explanations risk exaggerating the impact of some causal factors while missing or underestimating others. And these risks are even greater when we seek to capture changes in large, complex organizations that encompass many moving parts.

Finally, given the limited information available to us at this juncture, any claims we make about Islamist groups in the Arab world must be tempered by a healthy dose of humility. Over the course of more than twenty years of research on the Egyptian Muslim Brotherhood, the more I have learned, the more struck I've become by how little we know about its internal operations. For example, we have yet to fully understand the Brotherhood's methods for recruiting and socializing its members; the size and regional, generational, occupational, and class composition of its base; the sources of its financing; the activities of its local cells and branch offices; and the mechanisms available to its leaders to promote conformity and limit the expression of dissent. Further, though we have become more attuned to the existence of different ideological factions within the group's leadership, we still don't know which factions are supported by which constituencies and why. Similar gaps in our knowledge persist for Islamist groups in Jordan, Kuwait, and Morocco.

In the wake of the Arab Spring, Islamist groups are emerging from the shadows and beginning to offer journalists and researchers greater access to their affairs. Yet systematic research on such groups remains at an early stage. This book has sought to provide some insight into the nature of Islamist group dynamics, but there is far more work to be done. It is my hope that this book will inspire others to undertake the research needed to illuminate such dynamics in all their nuance and complexity in the years to come.

Endnotes

Preface

1. Wickham 2004b.

Chapter One
Conceptualizing Islamist Movement Change

1. For a similar argument, see Clark and Schwedler 2003.
2. Jupille, Caporaso, and Checkel 2003, 12.
3. Checkel 1999b, 546–49.
4. For a discussion of the causal mechanisms of preference change, see Checkel 2003.
5. See Johnston 2005, 1021–23.
6. Zürn and Checkel 2005, 1058.
7. Ibid.
8. I thank Suzanne Hoeber Rudolph for this insight, which she offered in a discussion of a paper I presented at the Halle Institute Faculty Seminar Workshop on Religion and Global Civil Society, Emory University, September 2002, titled "Modernizing Islam/Islamizing Modernity: Globalization and the Islamist Alternative" (see also Wickham 2005).
9. For a discussion of the causal mechanisms of preference change, see Checkel 2003.
10. Bermeo 1992; Roberts 1995; McCoy 2000.
11. Such independent Islamist thinkers include Yusuf al-Qaradawi, Mohammed al-Ghazzali, Muhammad Salim al-'Awa, Tariq Bishri, and Fahmi Howeidi.
12. Charles C. Ragin, *The Comparative Method: Moving Beyond Qualitative and Quantitative Strategies* (Berkeley: University of California Press, 1987), 20.
13. Peter A. Hall, "Aligning Ontology and Methodology in Comparative Research," in *Comparative Historical Analysis in the Social Sciences*, ed. James Mahoney and Dietrich Rueschemeyer (New York: Cambridge University Press, 2003), 394.
14. Zürn and Checkel 2005, 1047, 1056–58.

Chapter Two
The Brotherhood's Early Years

1. The epigraph is from the published proceedings of the Fifth Conference of the Muslim Brotherhood, cited in Mitchell 1969, 5n11. The first section of this chapter draws heavily on Mitchell's work, which still represents the most comprehensive and incisive treatment of the Brotherhood's ideology, organization, and relationship with other social and political forces in the period before 1952. For a more recent analysis of the Brotherhood's development as a mass Islamic movement, see Lia 1998.

2. Mitchell 1969, 1–2.

3. Ibid., 2.

4. Mitchell 1969, 4.

5. Ibid., 8.

6. Ibid., 9.

7. Ibid., 328.

8. Cleveland 2004, 196–204.

9. Mitchell 1969, 223–24.

10. See, for example, al-Banna's *risala* "Our Mission":

We believe that Islam is an all-embracing concept which regulates every aspect of life, adjudicating on every one of its concerns and prescribing for it a solid and rigorous order. . . . Some people mistakenly understand by Islam something restricted to certain types of religious observances or spiritual exercises . . . but we understand Islam—as opposed to this view—very broadly and comprehensively as regulating the affairs of men in this world and the next. (Wendell 1978, 46–47)

11. Mitchell 1969, 320–27; Brown 2000, 146–47. See also Rashid Rida, "Renewal, Renewing and Renewers," in Kurzman 2002, 77–85.

12. Mitchell 1969, 233.

13. Hasan al-Banna, "Toward the Light," in Wendell 1978, 106.

14. Hasan al-Banna, "Between Yesterday and Today," in Wendell 1978, 36.

15. Mitchell 1969, 245.

16. See, for example, Brown 2000, 146–48.

17. Mitchell 1969, 308.

18. Ibid., 235.

19. Ibid., 325–26. See also his thoughtful discussion of the Brotherhood's "sense of group exclusiveness" (319).

20. Mitchell 1969, 32–33, 309.

21. Hasan al-Banna, "On Jihad," in Wendell 1978, 150.

22. As Maye Kassem notes, "In addition to the Muslim Brotherhood, other extremist organizations of the national-social variety also appeared in the 1930s. . . . The emergence of political violence under the monarchy was [hence] not an exclusive Islamist pursuit, but rather was connected to an attitude of desperation born out of wider socioeconomic and political discontent" (2004, 136).

23. Ziyad Abu Amr, *Islamic Fundamentalism in the West Bank and Gaza* (Bloomington: Indiana University Press, 1994), 2–3.

24. Mitchell 1969, 63–64.

25. Ibid., 62–71.

26. Ibid., 105–6.

27. Ibid., 96.

28. Ibid., 126. In the original decree of January 16, 1953, abolishing all political parties, the Brotherhood had been spared (ibid., 109).

29. Ibid., 150–51.

30. Zollner 2007, 414.

31. Initially fifteen members were sentenced to death, but nine of the sentences were commuted. Among those whose initial death sentence was commuted was the new Supreme Guide, Hasan al-Hudeibi.

32. Most Brotherhood members were interred in the Al-Wahat prison camp in the Western Desert and in Liman al-Tura prison outside Cairo. Zollner 2007, 413.

33. Kepel 1993, 41. Qutb was sentenced on July 13, 1955; briefly released in 1964, he was re-arrested and sentenced to death in 1966.

34. Ibid., 37. On the radicalization of Qutb's thought, see also Kassem 2004, 139.

35. Zollner 2007, 418.

36. Kepel 1993, 43; Zollner 2007, 419.

37. Zollner 2007, 420. See also Haydar 1998, 13.

38. Zollner 2007, 420.

39. According to Kepel (1993, 63), Qutb's iconic status made him "virtually untouchable."

40. Zollner 2007, 422–23.

41. Ibid., 423. On the absolute division Qutb made between the "rule of God" and man-made systems, see Mubarak 1995, 51.

42. Zollner 2007, 426.

43. The "correction of the revolution" was announced on May 15, 1971; for a discussion of the broader dimensions of this shift, see Mustafa 1995, 145–49 and Hinnebusch 1988, 50–51.

44. For further discussion of Sadat's use of religious themes and symbols as a source of political authority, see Esposito 1984, 236–37; Guenena 1986, 35–36; and Kassem 2004, 141.

45. Kassem 2004, 141–42.

46. Ramadan 2004. The year of al-Tilmisani's appointment as Supreme Guide is disputed in the sources. Some date it to 1973 (Haydar 1998, 16; Beinin 2005, 118; Auda 1994, 380); while others date it to 1974 (Mustafa 1995, 204) or 1977 (El-Ghobashy 2005, 377). Al-Tilmisani was in prison from 1954 to 1971 (Mustafa 1995, 205).

47. According to Ramadan (2004), the owner and publisher of *al-Da'wa* was its editor in chief and al-Tilmisani was in charge of its "management and supervision." However, other sources identify al-Tilmisani as its editor in chief. See, for example, Kepel 1993, 105; Baker 1990, 243; Hinnebusch 1988, 201; Esposito 1984, 237; and Gorman 2003, 101.

48. Ramadan 2004, 166.

49. Hinnebusch 1988, 205; Esposito 1984, 237; Gorman 2003, 101.

50. Kepel 1993, 125.

51. Ibid.

52. Hinnebusch 1988, 159–60.

53. Kepel 1993, 127.

54. See, for example, Ramadan 2004, 166.

55. Interview with al-Tilmisani in *The Masses*, September 29, 1982, cited in Baker 1990, 245. As al-Tilmisani noted, if the Brotherhood were granted legal recognition as an association, the Ministry of Social Affairs would "then have the right to dissolve the society at any time, to change its board of directors, and to submit it to administrative, technical and financial supervision." See also Ramih 1997, 203 and Haydar 1989, 108.

56. Lombardi 2006, 125–29, 132; see also Mustafa 1995, 150.

57. Al-Khatib 1990, 39.

58. Mustafa 1995, 206.

59. Ibid., 206, 212–13.

60. Ibid., 218. See also Lombardi 2006, 126–27.

61. Al-Khatib 1990, 41.

62. Mustafa 1995, 212.

63. On Jehan's law and Islamist opposition to it, see Esposito 1984, 244 and Mustafa 1995, 213–14.

64. Lombardi 2006, 133; Mustafa 1995, 214.

65. For the Brotherhood's views on the Jews and the State of Israel, see Kepel 1993, 111–16. See also Baker 1990, 255–56.

66. Quoted in Kepel 1993, 113.

67. Baker 1990, 244; Esposito 1984, 244–45.

68. *Al-Da'wa*, November 1979, cited in Baker 1990, 258. On Sadat's call for the separation of religion and politics, see Guenena 1986, 38.

69. Ramadan 2004, 172; Hinnebsuch 1988, 77; Kepel 1993, 271.

70. Kepel 1993, 92–102; Ramadan 2004, 381–82; Auda 1994, 397–98. See also Mustafa 1995, 225–29.

71. Guenena 1986, 37.

72. Ramadan 2004, 159.

73. Kepel 1993, 194–204. See also Mustafa 1995, 229–31.

74. Hinnebsuch 1988, 203.

75. See Kepel 1993, 91–92, 125; Ramadan 2004, 167. For example, in July 1978 *al-Da'wa* described the murder of Sheikh Dhahabi as "an awful crime, forbidden by religion and repugnant to custom" (cited in Ramadan 2004, 167–68).

76. Badr 1989, 11.

77. Mubarak 1995, 131.

78. Ibid., 131–32; Mustafa 1995, 151–52; Esposito 1984, 237.

79. Abdalla 1985, 226; Kepel 1993, 134; Haydar 1998, 16; Wickham 2002, 116.

80. Kepel 1993, 139. Kepel (1993, 138) claims that the first university-wide summer camp, held by the Islamic student group at Cairo University, occurred in 1973; Badr (1989, 11) dates it to the summer of 1972.

81. Mubarak 1995, 133.

82. Kepel 1993, 143–44.

83. Ibid., 141, 150.

84. Wickham 2002, 116.

85. Wickham 2002, 117; Kepel 1993, 149, 151; Abdalla 1985, 227.

86. As Sayyid Abd al-Sattar, a former Islamist student leader, explained: "Our sources were not books published by the Brotherhood, but Salafi books, many of which

were imported from Saudi Arabia." Interview with Sayyid Abd al-Sattar, July 10, 2005. See also Ramih 1997, 149; Kepel 1993, 152–56; and Mubarak 1995, 139.

87. See Hinnebusch 1988, 205–6.

88. Kepel 1993, 151. See also Haydar 1998, 21 and Abdalla 1985, 227–28.

89. Mubarak 1995, 139.

90. Badr 1989, 25. Other prominent Islamist student leaders included Khaled Dawoud, Muhammad Zamzam, and Muhammad Abd al-Fattah at Alexandria University; Sayyid Abd al-Sattar at 'Ayn Shams University; and Karam Zuhdi, Osama Hafez, Tal'at Fu'ad Qasim, and Muhyiddin 'Isa in the Sa'id. Mubarak 1995, 134; interview with 'Esam Sultan, March 8, 2004.

91. Interview with Diya' Rishwan, November 10, 2000.

92. Cited in al-Awadi 2004, 91.

93. "Dialogue with the Muslim Youth," al-Sha'b, March 27, 1984, cited in Abdalla 1985, 280n10.

94. Abdalla 1985, 228; Badr 1989, 86.

95. Badr 1989, 87.

96. Ibid. Also cited in Abdalla 1985, 280n12. See also Wickham 2002, 117, 193.

97. Kepel 1993, 147–48, 152.

98. Baker 1990, 249. For more on al-Tilmisani's efforts in 1978 and 1979 to help "calm down" Islamist student groups, see Abdalla 1985, 227, 280n9, citing an interview with al-Tilmisani in al-Ahali, September 29, 1982, and Ramih 1997, 143.

99. Kepel 1993, 148–49.

100. Baker 1990, 249. See also Mubarak 1995, 135.

101. Mubarak 1995, 136–37.

102. Ibid., 137.

103. Interview with Aboul 'Ela Madi, November 11, 2000.

104. Ibid.

105. Ibid.

106. Interview with Aboul 'Ela Madi, Sawt al-Umma, September 1, 2003. Madi describes al-Tilmisani in the article as a sheikh fadil (eminent leader) who "was the best to lead the Brotherhood since Hasan al-Banna."

107. Ramih 1997, 143; Mubarak 1995, 137–38. Ramadan (2004, 171) observes that some jama'at leaders continued to regard the Muslim Brotherhood as an enemy.

108. Ramih 1997, 143.

109. Mubarak 1995, 139.

110. Ibid., 140.

111. Baker 1990, 246.

112. For further discussion of the Brotherhood's exclusion from the formal political order as a strategic choice, see Tammam 2006, 7–9.

113. Al-Khatib 1990, 40.

114. Al-Chobaki 2006, 14, 15.

Chapter Three
The Brotherhood's Foray into Electoral Politics

1. Springborg 1989, 215.

2. In 1976, six candidates with personal ties to the Muslim Brotherhood won seats

in parliament but they ran as independents. See Ramadan 2004, 174 and Aboul 'Ela Madi, "Hakayati Ma'a al-Ikhwan wa Qisat al-Wasat" [My Narrative with the Brotherhood and the Story of the Wasat], January 2, 2006 (hard copy given to the author by Aboul 'Ela Madi).

3. El-Ghobashy 2005, 378 and Makram-Ebeid 1989, 431; Hussein 1990, 42; Abed-Kotob 1995, 328. See also Rabi 2005, 79.

4. El-Ghobashy 2005, 378.

5. Ibid. Note that the reported number of seats won by the Muslim Brotherhood varies slightly across published sources; al-Chobaki (2006, 20) and Abu Talib (2007, 435) cite seven; El-Ghobashy (2005, 378), Aly (2007, 3), and Norton (2004, 136) cite eight; Springborg (1989, 206) and Haydar (1989, 93 cite nine; Auda (1994, 387) and al-Sayyid (2003, 10) cite twelve.

6. Makram-Ebeid 1989, 433.

7. As Springborg observes, during the 1987 parliamentary elections, "the Brotherhood demonstrated that it possessed the most broadly based, lavishly financed and well organized opposition electoral machine in the country" (1989, 184). See also Hussein 1990, 49.

8. Springborg 1989, 218. See also Makram-Ebeid 1989, 433–34.

9. El-Ghobashy 2005, 379. Here, too, the exact numbers are contested, with respect to both the number of seats won by Brotherhood candidates and the number won by the Islamic Alliance in total. Like El-Ghobashy, Aly (2007) and Abu Talib (2007, 435) set the number of seats won by the Brotherhood in 1987 at thirty-six; according to Springborg (1989, 218), the Brotherhood gained thirty-eight; according to al-Chobaki (2006, 20) it gained thirty-five; and according to Yasin (1990, 419), it gained thirty-four. Further, according to al-Chobaki (2006, 20), Norton (2004, 136), and Abu Talib (2007, 435), the Islamist Alliance gained a total of sixty seats, not fifty-six. According to Norton (2004, 136), this included thirty-six seats for the Brotherhood and four for Islamist independents.

10. 'Umar al-Tilmisani, *Dhikrayat la Mudhakkarat* [Memories not Memoirs] (Cairo: Islamic Publication and Distribution Company, 1985), 12, cited in El-Ghobashy 2005, 378.

11. Salah Abd al-Maqsud, "Ten Charges against the Society [Muslim Brotherhood]," *Liwa' al-Islam*, February 1989, cited in Abed-Kotob 1995, 330.

12. Quoted in Haydar 1989, 91–92.

13. Quoted in ibid., 97.

14. Ibid., 94–95.

15. The text of the article is reprinted in al-Khatib 1990, 24–28, but no date is given. Since Mashhour refers to the 1987 elections and al-Khatib's book was published in 1990, it is clear that it appeared sometime between 1987 and 1990.

16. Yasin 1990, 418–19; Ramadan 2004, 174.

17. Yasin 1990, 418; Makram-Ebeid 1989, 433.

18. Springborg 1989, 206.

19. Ramadan 2004, 173.

20. On al-Banna's opposition to partyism, see Norton 2004, 140; al-Chobaki 2006, 9; and al-Sayyid 2003, 10.

21. Al-Sayyid 2003, 10.

22. Haydar 1989, 91.

23. Al-Awadi 2004, 83.

24. Haydar 1989, 99; Dalal 2006, 297–98; interview with Aboul 'Ela Madi, Louisville, Kentucky, October 10, 2004.

25. *Al-Mukhtar al-Islami*, no. 30, November 1984, cited in Dalal 2006, 296. See also al-Tilmisani's statement to *al-Qubs* on November 16, 1985, cited in Haydar 1989, 106.

26. Haydar 1989, 107.

27. Aly 2007, 3; Stacher 2002, 420.

28. See, for example, Hudeibi's statements to *al-Qubs*, March 29, 1989, cited in Dalal 2006, 298.

29. Dalal 2006, 298–99. See Dalal for a fuller elaboration of such reservations about forming a Brotherhood party, which he shared.

30. See, for example, the objections raised by Abd al-Rahman Banna, the brother of Brotherhood founder Hasan al-Banna, in *al-Anba'*, June 28, 1986, cited in Haydar 1989, 117.

31. Tammam 2006, 8.

32. Interview with Aboul 'Ela Madi, Louisville, Kentucky, October 10, 2004.

33. El-Ghobashy 2005, 380–81; see also Rishwan 2006, 41–42.

34. Yasin 1986, 342.

35. Ibid., 343.

36. Interview with *al-Qubs*, November 16, 1985, cited in Dalal 2006, 165. On al-Tilmisani's call for a gradualist approach, see also his comments in *al-Mujtama'*, April 9, 1985, cited in ibid.

37. Dalal 2006, 166.

38. Yasin 1990, 21.

39. For a detailed examination of the Islamic reorientation of the Labor Party and its mouthpiece *al-Sha'b*, see Yasin 1990, 419–29. See also El-Ghobashy 2005, 379; Haydar 1998, 54–55; Ramadan 2004, 175–76; and Springborg 1989, 230.

40. Ramadan 2004, 176–77; see also the International Crisis Group 2004, 12; Haydar 1998, 55; and Springborg 1989, 221.

41. See, for example, references to the slow pace of Shari'a reforms in the speeches delivered in parliament by Muhammad Habib, June 25, 1987 (al-Khatib 1990, 86–87); Ahmed Saif al-Islam al-Banna, June 24, 1987 (al-Khatib 1990, 91); Muhammad Ahmad Abd al-Hamid Nafi', January 10, 1988 (al-Khatib 1990, 130); Muhyiddin 'Isa Muhsab, 1987 (al-Khatib 1990, 148–49); and Muhammad Hussein Muhammad 'Isa, January 25, 1988 (al-Khatib 1990, 209–10).

42. Al-Khatib 1990, 73.

43. Cited in Haydar 1989, 135.

44. See, for example, the transcript of Hudeibi's speech before parliament on January 9, 1988, in which the Speaker admonished Hudeibi several times for straying off topic and exceeding his time limits, noting at one point that he had been speaking continuously for twenty-eight minutes; al-Khatib 1990, 71–83.

45. Cited in al-Khatib 1990, 86–87.

46. El-Ghobashy 2005, 380.

47. See the transcripts of the speeches of Brotherhood MPs in al-Khatib 1990; see also Yasin 1991, 429–30.

48. From the proceedings of a seminar published in the Kuwaiti newspaper *al-Anba'*, November 21, 1987, cited in Haydar 1989, 128.

49. Cited in al-Khatib 1990, 74. See also the speech by Mukhtar Nuh on June 24, 1987 (al-Khatib 1990, 118) and El-Ghobashy 2005, 380.

50. Cited in al-Khatib 1990, 72. As other examples, see the speech by Muhammad Abd al-Hamid Nafi before parliament on January 10, 1988 in which he declared that "the masses all aspire to the application of Shar'a" (ibid., 130), and similar comments by Mustafa Mashhour in an article published in the same period in *Liwa' al-Islam*, vol. 37, and reprinted in al-Khatib 1990, 27.

51. From a speech before parliament on June 24, 1987, in al-Khatib 1990, 91.

52. On the Brotherhood's decision to boycott the 1990 parliamentary elections, see Yasin 1991, 427; El-Ghobashy 2005, 381; Abed-Kotob 1995, 328, 331; Haydar 1998, 55; and Campagna 1996, 285–86.

53. Middle East Watch, "Egypt: Elections Concerns," November 15, 1990, 8, cited in Campagna 1996, 286.

54. Abed-Kotob 1995, 331.

55. El-Ghobashy 2005, 374–75.

56. For a clear exposition of the distinction between democracy and *shura*, see the article by Sheikh Salah Abu Isma'il, who represented the Brotherhood in parliament in the mid-1980s, originally published in *Liwa' al-Islam* and reprinted in al-Khatib 1990, 41 (the date of publication is not given).

57. Qasim's speech before parliament on January 12, 1988, cited in al-Khatib 1990, 144; see also Hudeibi's speech before parliament on January 9, 1988, cited in al-Khatib 1990, 72.

58. For further information on the history of Egypt's professional syndicates, see Bianchi 1989 and al-Sayyid 2003. See also Wickham 2002, 179–80.

59. Interview with Aboul 'Ela Madi, November 11, 2000. See also al-Awadi 2004, 92.

60. On the electoral rise of the Brotherhood in Egypt's professional syndicates, see Wickham 2002, 183–89; International Crisis Group 2004, 12–13; Yasin 1990, 432–33; El-Ghobashy 2005, 380; and Ramih 1997, 156.

61. Al-Awadi 2004, 123; Abed-Kotob 1995, 329; International Crisis Group 2004, 12.

62. Wickham 2002, 178–79, 183–89.

63. Interview with Salah Abd al-Karim, cited in Stacher 2002, 419.

64. Wickham 2002, 191–92. See also al-Awadi 2004, 95–98.

65. See Ramih 1997, 157–59.

66. Ramih 1997, 157. Madi recalls that Milad Hanna, a Coptic Christian engineer and prominent public figure, defied the security agents and marched up the steps of the headquarters and entered the building despite their warnings. Ramih claims that the conference was scheduled to take place in October 1989 while Madi says it was set for January 1990. See Wickham 2002, 262n27.

67. "Al-Niqabat al-Mihniyya wa Qadaya al-Mujtama' al-Misri" 1995, 3–4.

68. Ibid., 273; see also El-Ghobashy 2005, 382 and Ramih 1997, 159–60.

69. Interview with Aboul 'Ela Madi, November 11, 2000. Madi also mentioned with some pride that he received the highest grades.

70. Wickham 2002, 262n29.

71. Interview with Abd al-Mun'im Abu al-Futouh, March 14, 2004, July 12, 2005.

72. Wickham 2002, 193. For similar observations, see al-Awadi 2004, 90–91.

73. Interview with Muhammad Siman, March 9, 2004.

74. Interview with Sayyid Abd al-Sattar, July 10, 2005.

75. For a discussion of the impact of participation on middle-generation leaders' values and beliefs, see Ramih 1997, 160.

76. Interview with 'Esam Sultan, March 8, 2004.

77. Interview with Sayyid Abd al-Sattar, July 10, 2005.

78. Interview with Aboul 'Ela Madi, July 13, 2005.

79. Interview with Ibrahim Bayoumi Ghanim, March 10, 2004.

80. Interview with Abd al-Mun'im Abu al-Futouh, March 14, 2004.

81. Interview with Aboul 'Ela Madi, November 11, 2000.

82. Misbah Qutb, *Majalla al-Yasar*, no. 2, April 1995, cited in Ramih 1997, 161. The Brotherhood later opened its new headquarters in an apartment on a side street in Manyal, a residential neighborhood of Cairo. Based on my own observations during the 1990s, the contrast described by Qutb still applied.

83. Madi, "My Narrative with the Brotherhood"; 'Esam Sultan, "Fasl Ma'moun al-Hudeibi Min al-Ikhwan Fi Waqi'at Tazwir" [The Separation of Mamoun Hudeibi from the Ikhwan in an Incidence of Fraud], *Sawt al-Umma*, September 8, 2004.

84. Hazem Saghiya, "Profile of Abu Ayla Madi," *al-Hayat*, December 25, 1996.

85. See Ramih 1997, 169–71.

86. For a discussion of the middle generation's critique of the Brotherhood's old-guard leadership, see Ramih 1997, 169–72.

87. Interview with Ibrahim Bayoumi Ghanim, March 10, 2004.

88. Interview with Aboul 'Ela Madi, July 2, 1997. See also Muhammad Salah, "Aboul 'Ela Madi Yakshif Tafasil al-Azma Dakhil Jama'at al-Ikhwan al-Muslimin" [Aboul 'Ela Madi Reveals the Details of the Crisis within the Muslim Brotherhood Association], *al-Hayat*, April 5, 1997.

89. Interview with Aboul 'Ela Madi, November 11, 2000.

90. On the "reformist trend" and its calls for change in the Brotherhood's agenda, see Rishwan 2006, 32–36, especially 35.

91. Interview with Ibrahim Bayoumi Ghanim, March 9, 2004.

92. Tariq Bishri, Muhammad 'Imara, and Abd al-Wahhab al-Masiri, as well as the *Sha'b* editor in chief, 'Adil Hussein, all switched to the Islamic Trend after experience in the left.

93. On the New Islamic Discourse and its influence on the thinking of the middle generation, see Ramih 1997, 181–86.

94. El-Ghobashy 2005, 383.

95. "Al-Mar'a al-Muslima fi'l-Mujtama' al-Muslim, al-Shura wa Ta'addud al-Ahzab" [The Muslim Woman in Muslim Society, Consultation and Party Pluralism] 1994, p. 31.

96. El-Ghobashy 2005, 384–85. On the 1994 and 1995 statements, see also Abd al-Fattah 1996, 169–70; Hamid 2007, 4; and Abd al-Fattah, n.d., 3.

97. El-Ghobashy 2005, 386.

98. Interview with Aboul 'Ela Madi, July 2, 1997.

99. Rishwan 2006, 32. See also Yasin 1996, 165–67.

100. Yasin 1996, 167.

101. Ibid., 167.

102. Ibid., 170.

103. Interview with Aboul 'Ela Madi, July 2, 2007. See also Madi, "My Narrative with the Brotherhood."

104. 'Esam Sultan, *Sawt al-Umma*; September 8, 2004.

CHAPTER FOUR
THE WASAT PARTY INITIATIVE AND THE BROTHERHOOD'S RESPONSE

1. Abu Talib 2003, 435.

2. Abdalla 1993, 29, cited in Campagna 1996, 284.

3. "Extremists 'Secret' Arm of Muslim Brotherhood," Agence France Presse, April 17, 1989, as reported by FBIS, April 18, 1989, 11, quote cited in Campagna 1996, 285n13.

4. Ami Ayalon, ed., *Middle East Contemporary Survey*, vol. 15 (Boulder, CO: Westview Press, 1991), 351–52, cited in Campagna 1996, 286.

5. Al-Awadi 2004, 148–49.

6. Interview with 'Esam al-'Aryan, December 19, 2000, cited in al-Awadi 2004, 149.

7. Campagna 1996, 286–87.

8. Ibid., 293–94; Rishwan 2006, 45.

9. Campagna 1996, 292–93; Wickham 2002, 203; al-Awadi 2004, 149–51.

10. Quoted in Campagna 1996, 292–93n47.

11. *New York Times*, October 21, 1992, cited in Wickham 2002, 203. See also Stephen Hubbell, "Tremors after the Earthquake," *Middle East International*, October 23, 1992, 9, in which Musa complained that "some people are trying to use the disaster for their own political ends"; cited in Campagna 1996, 293.

12. Al-Awadi 2004, 152–53.

13. Wickham 2002, 200; see also al-Awadi 2004, 153 and Campagna 1996, 294–95.

14. Al-Awadi 2004, 153.

15. Wickham 2002, 200–201.

16. Campagna 1996, 295–96.

17. Ibrahim 1995, 6.

18. Ibid.

19. Ibid.

20. Abd al-Fattah 1998, 219.

21. Campagna 1996, 296–97.

22. Mary Ann Weaver, "The Novelist and the Sheikh," *New Yorker*, January 30, 1995, cited in Campagna 1996, 297–98; El-Ghobashy 2005, 384; Yasin 1986, 177. See also the similar charges levied against the Brotherhood by President Mubarak in an interview with *Der Spiegel*, May 16, 1994, cited in Yasin 1986, 176.

23. Rishwan 2006, 45–46; Kassem 2004, 155. As Kassem notes, changes to the Penal Code in 1992 expanded the definition of terrorism to include "spreading panic" and "obstructing the work of authorities." In addition, a military law dating to 1966 empowered the president "to refer to the military judiciary any crime punishable under the Penal Code or under any other law." The president's right to refer cases to military courts was reaffirmed in a Supreme Constitutional Court ruling in 1993.

24. Al-Awadi 2004, 174.

25. Wickham 2002, 215; see also Dalil 2006, 46; Campagna 1996, 298–301; and Yasin 1986, 180.

26. Al-Awadi 2004, 172.

27. Ibid., 173.

28. Ibid., 171.

29. Egyptian Organization of Human Rights, "Democracy Jeopardized: The Egyptian Organization of Human Rights Account of Egypt's 1995 Parliamentary Elections" (Cairo, 1996), 14, cited in Campagna 1996, 299. See also International Crisis Group 2004, 12.

30. Wickham 2002, 225; El-Ghobashy 2005, 384; Haydar 1998, 55; Campagna 1996, 279. Al-Awadi claims the Brotherhood ran 170 candidates (2004, 172).

31. Abd al-Fattah 1998, 209–10; see also the interview with Mustafa Mashhour in al-Safir, March 30, 1995, cited in Campagna 1996, 301.

32. Campagna 1996, 302.

33. Stacher 2002, 422; for a list of the names of the founders, see Awraq Hizb al-Wasat al-Misri 1996, 118–23.

34. Wickham 2002, 218. See also Mohammad Salah, al-Hayat, May 21, 1996, and Norton 2004, 142.

35. Norton 2004, 141–42; Abd al-Fattah 1998, 208; Wickham 2002, 218.

36. See, for example, the interview with Ma'moun Hudeibi published in al-Hayat, February 20, 1996. See also references to Mashhour's and Hudeibi's comments on the Wasat party initiative in Qadaya Dawliyya, June 24, 1996.

37. Wickham 2002, 218, citing Salah 1996; see also Wickham 2004b, 223; Stacher 2002, 422; and Norton 2004, 142.

38. Qadaya Dawliyya, June 24, 1996. The lawyers who signed the party's petition included 'Adil 'Iid, Ahmad al-Hilali, Sami Jamal al-Din, and Farid Abd al-Karim.

39. Interview with 'Esam Sultan, March 8, 2004.

40. For the text of one of their letters of resignation, see Ramih 1997, 235–37.

41. On al-Qaradawi's endorsement, see Abd al-Fattah 1998, 228; see also al-Ahali, October 16, 1996.

42. Quote by Salah 'Isa on the back cover of Ramih 1997. For a fuller elaboration of his argument, see Salah 'Isa, "The Brotherhood Effort to Fool Us," al-Yasar, February 1996, and 'Isa, "This Laughable Coalition," al-'Aalam al-Yawm, December 3, 1996.

43. See the text of the High Administrative Court Decision, May 9, 1998 (hard copy of text given to author by Aboul 'Ela Madi).

44. Interview with Aboul 'Ela Madi, November 11, 2000.

45. Stacher 2002, 422–23; Simon Apiku, "Moderate Islamist Party Rebuffed Again," Middle East Times, June 10–16, 1999.

46. Awraq Hizb al-Wasat al-Misri 1998. In an interview with the author on March 8, 2004, 'Esam Sultan emphasized that the drafting of both the 1996 and 1998 platforms was a collaborative project, a point emphasized by Salah Abd al-Karim as well in an interview with the author on March 18, 2004.

47. See Wickham 2005.

48. Awraq Hizb al-Wasat al-Misri 24.

49. Ibid., 24–29.

50. For a fuller elaboration of these arguments, see Wickham 2005, 153–58.

51. In interviews I conducted with them from 1997 to 2004, Aboul 'Ela Madi, 'Esam Sultan, and Salah Abd al-Karim all cited Muhammad Salim al-'Awa first and Tariq Bishri second as the Islamist intellectuals with the greatest influence on the Wasat party platform. On the influence of such thinkers on the development of the Wasat founders' thinking, see Ramih 1997, 181–90 and Badr 1996.

52. See, for example, the lengthy profile on Aboul 'Ela in *al-Hayat*, December 26, 1996. Early Arab media coverage of the Wasat party initiative and the reactions of the regime and the Muslim Brotherhood to it include articles in *al-Hayat*, January 18, 1995; *al-Wasat*, January 22, 1996; *al-Mujtama'*, January 23, 1996; *al-Hayat*, February 20, 1996; *al-Anba'*, March 17, 1996; *al-Sha'b*, May 31, 1996; *Qadaya Dawliya*, June 24, 1996; *al-Hayat*, July 2, 1996; *al-Ahrar*, September 30, 1996; *al-Wasat*, November 18, 1996; *al-Ahali*, November 27, 1996; *al-'Aalam al-Yawm*, December 1996; and *al-Anba'*, February 16, 1997. In English, see, for example, Andre Hammond, "Reconstructing Islamism," *Middle East Times*, September 29–October 5, 1996; and Nabil Abd al-Fattah, "Politics and the Generations' Battle," *Al-Ahram Weekly*, October 17–23, 1996.

53. One such workshop was held at the Ibn Khaldun Center; see *al-Ahali*, November 27, 1996. Aboul 'Ela Madi also discussed the Wasat initiative at a workshop titled "The Freedom of Forming Political Parties and Associations in Egypt," sponsored by the Center for Legal Aid on November 10, 1996. For a summary of the proceedings, see *al-Yasar*, December 1996.

54. Interview with Salah 'Isa, March 17, 2004.

55. See, for example, Osama 'Urabi, "The Wasat Party under Formation: Where Do They Stand on Democracy?" *al-Nada' al-Jadid*, May 1997. Aboul 'Ela Madi responded to the criticism of Salah 'Isa and other secularists in *al-Qahira* on June 27, 2000, noting that he objected to the polarization of the discussion around the issues of freedom and the *thawabet* and, affirming the party's position, "which could well be shared by everyone," that "freedom of expression must not contradict the values and *thawabet* of the *umma*," claiming that "differences of opinion are limited to small details, such as how this should be decided and who has the authority to determine such matters, etc."

56. Aboul 'Ela Madi, "Political Forces . . . and the Freedom of Opinion and Belief," *al-Sha'b*, October 25, 1996.

57. See, for example, Muhamad al-Shibh, "This Laughable Wasat," *al-'Aalam al-Yawm*, December 5, 1996, a sharp critique of Salah 'Isa's article in support of the Wasat party published in the same journal two days earlier (see note 42). See also al-Shibh's comments as reported in *al-Ahali*, November 27, 1996. Another outspoken critic of the Wasat initiative was Rif'at al-Sa'eed, chairman of the leftist Tagammu' party, who portrayed it as a Brotherhood ruse. See Abd al-Fattah 1998, 229 and al-Sayyid's article in *al-Ahali*, January 31, 1996.

58. Interview with Sayyid al-Naggar, November 21, 2000.

59. Ibid.

60. Yasin 1996, 171; interview with Aboul 'Ela Madi, July 2, 1997.

61. Aboul 'Ela Madi, *Sawt al-Umma*, September 1, 2003. On Hudeibi's behavior as a source of grievance, see also Abd al-Fattah 1998, 215–16; 'Esam Sultan, *Sawt al-Umma*, September 8, 2004; an interview with Mamoun Hudeibi published in *al-Hayat*, February 20, 1996; and the text of the resignation letter submitted to the Supreme Guide by a founding member of the Wasat party in Ramih 1997, 235–37.

62. Aboul 'Ela Madi, *Sawt al-Umma*, September 1, 2003. See also Madi, "My Narrative with the Brotherhood."

63. Interview with Aboul 'Ela Madi, November 11, 2000.

64. Yasin 1996, 179–80; interview with 'Esam Sultan, March 8, 2004.

65. Abd al-Fattah 1998, 215.

66. Karim al-Gawhary, "We Are a Civil Party with an Islamic Identity': Interview with Abu 'Ila Madi Abu 'Ila and Rafiq Habib," *Middle East Report* (April–June 1996): 39; *al-Sha'b*, July 16, 1996.

67. Aboul 'Ela Madi, *al-Anba'*, March 17, 1996.

68. Sartori 1966, 31, cited in Anderson 1997, 28. See also the argument that "the hegemonic regime creates a self-fulfilling prophecy" in Dahl 1973, 13, cited in Anderson 1997, 29.

69. Anderson 1997, 28–29.

70. Madi, "My Narrative with the Brotherhood."

71. Stacher 2002, 421.

72. Madi 2008.

73. Interview with Aboul 'Ela Madi, July 2, 1997; such ideas were reiterated by 'Esam Sultan in my interview with him on March 8, 2004. See also Rafiq Habib's comments in al-Gawhary, "We Are a Civil Party with an Islamic Identity.'"

74. Ramih 1997; see also the review of the book in *al-Takaful*, February 20, 1997.

75. Cited in Ramih 1997, 176–77. The translation is my own, and I have tried to be as faithful as possible to the Arabic original while making some minor adjustments for clarity and ease of expression in English.

76. Muhammad Salah, interview with Mamoun Hudeibi, *al-Hayat*, February 20, 1996.

77. Salah 1996.

78. The text of "Fawa'id 'an al-Shada'id" is reproduced in Ramih 1997, 237–44. In the index, it is described as "a statement distributed by the Brotherhood leadership to members, warning them about the *Wasat* party." The date and authorship of the statement are not listed. See also Abd al-Fattah 1998, 228–29 for a summary of the document.

79. Hudeibi 1997. See also Wickham 2004b, 208–9.

80. Hudeibi 1997, 24, cited in Wickham 2004b, 209.

81. Hudeibi 1997, 21.

Chapter Five
The Brotherhood's Seesaw between Self-Assertion and Self-Restraint

1. Wickham 2002, 225, see also El-Ghobashy 2005 and interview with Michele Dunne, "'Very Dramatic' Achievement for Muslim Brotherhood in Egyptian Parliamentary Elections," http://www.cfr.org/, November 30 2005.

2. Wickham 2002, 225; Makram-Ebeid 2001, 36.

3. Abu Talib 2003, 435.

4. Ibid.

5. Wickham 2002, 223; Kassem 2004, 63; Thabet 2006, 14.

6. El-Ghobashy 2005.

7. Thabet 2006, 19. See also Kassem 2004, 66–67.

8. El-Ghobashy 2005; Kassem 2004, 69; Makram-Ebeid 1989, 35; Thabet 2006, 19.

9. The Wafd party won seven seats, the Tagammu' six, the Nasserists three, and the Liberal Party one; in addition, independents elected to parliament included two non-Brotherhood Islamists and five Nasserists (Thabet 2006, 17).

10. The NDP bloc included 388 of 454 seats (including ten seats allocated to government appointees). However, official NDP candidates won only 175 seats; the other 213 members of the NDP bloc were independents who joined the NDP after the elections. Thabet 2006, 17; Makram-Ebeid 1989, 32, 38; Kassem 2004, 81; Wickham 2002, 224.

11. *Al-Hayat*, December 2, 2000, cited in Wickham 2002, 225.

12. Interview with Abd al-Mun'im Abu al-Futouh, November 16, 2000.

13. Abu Talib 2003, 435–36; see also Wickham 2002, 225; El-Ghobashy 2005, 12.

14. Dan Murphy, "Egypt Keeps Muslim Brotherhood Boxed In," *Christian Science Monitor*, June 7, 2005.

15. Hossam El-Hamalawy, "Closer to the Street," *Cairo Times*, February 6–19, 2003.

16. Ibid.

17. "A Year of Challenge and Promise," *Al-Ahram Weekly*, December 26, 2002–January 1, 2003.

18. El-Hamalawy, "Closer to the Street"; Ashraf Khalil, Paul Schemm, and Issandr El-Amrani, "Boiling Point," *Cairo Times*, April 4–10, 2002; Hossam El-Hamalawy, "Whose Fight Is It Anyway?" *Cairo Times*, April 11–17, 2002.

19. El-Hamalawy, "Closer to the Street"; Hossam El-Hamalawy, "Street Protests," *Cairo Times*, September 26, 2002.

20. El-Hamalawy, "Whose Fight Is It Anyway?"

21. "Cairo in Action," *Al-Ahram Weekly*, January 23–29, 2003; Amira Howeidy, "A Chronology of Dissent," *Al-Ahram Weekly*, June 23–29, 2005.

22. Glen C. Carey and Hossam el-Hamalawy, "Protests Endure," *Cairo Times*, February 27–March 5, 2003.

23. The Brotherhood launched another regime-approved antiwar protest on March 28; Paul Schemm, "Hard Times," *Cairo Times*, January 1–7, 2004.

24. Tamir Moustafa, "Protests Hint at New Chapter in Egyptian Politics," *Middle East Report*, April 9, 2004; Schemm, "Hard Times"; Yasmine El-Rashidi, "Tahrir: One Year On," *Al-Ahram Weekly*, March 25–31, 2004; interview with Gasir Abd al-Raziq, July 10, 2005.

25. Moustafa, "Protests Hint at a New Chapter in Egyptian Politics."

26. Amira Howeidy, "Stepping into a Burgeoning Gap," *Al-Ahram Weekly*, January 23–29, 2003.

27. El-Hamalawy, "Closer to the Street."

28. Tammam 2006, 106.

29. Rishwan 2006, 29; Tammam 2006, 82.

30. Paul Schemm, "The Old Man Passes," *Cairo Times*, January 15–22, 2004.

31. Tammam 2006, 82.

32. Ibid., 80–81.

33. Ibid., 81.

34. Mona Salem, "Muslim Brotherhood Old Guard and Reformers Compromise on

New Leadership," *Agence Presse*, January 14, 2004; "New Head of Egypt's Muslim Brotherhood Calls for Dialogue with Government," Al-Jazeera TV, Doha, BBC Monitoring International Reports, January 14, 2004; "The Old Man Passes."

35. Joseph S. Nye, "A Whole New Ball Game," *Financial Times*, December 28, 2002.

36. See http://www.ned.org/ for a transcript of the George W. Bush speech, November 6, 2003.

37. The G-8 nations are Great Britain, Canada, France, Germany, Italy, Japan, Russia, and the United States. On U.S. democracy promotion efforts, see Marina Ottaway and Thomas Carothers, "The Greater Middle East Initiative: Off to a False Start," Policy Brief #29, Carnegie Endowment for International Peace, March 2004, http://carnegie endowment.org/; Tamara Cofman Wittes, "The New U.S. Proposal for a Greater Middle East Initiative: An Evaluation," Saban Center for Middle East Policy, Brookings Institution, May 10, 2004, http://www.brookings.edu/; "The Broader Middle East and North Africa Initiative: Imperilled at Birth," Briefing No. 14, Middle East and North Africa Briefing, International Crisis Group, June 7, 2004, http://www.crisisgroup.org/; and Jeremy M. Sharp, "The Broader Middle East and North Africa Initiative: An Overview," Congressional Research Report for Congress, February 15, 2005, http://fpc.state.gov/.

38. Sharp, "The Broader Middle East."

39. For a thoughtful analysis of these issues, see Abdsalem Maghraoui, "The Broader Middle East and North Africa Initiative: Potential and Limitations" (paper presented at the Woodrow Wilson Center, Washington, DC, June 4, 2004).

40. Ottaway and Carothers, "The Greater Middle East Initiative."

41. This statement also appears in the introduction of the Brotherhood's reform initiative. Hamdy al-Husseini, "Muslim Brotherhood Submits Own Initiative for Reform," *Islam On-Line*, March 4, 2004. For a more detailed discussion of the Islamist critique of U.S. democracy promotion efforts, see Wickham 2004c.

42. Magid Fayez and Muhammad Mursi, "Islamist Initiative," *Cairo Times*, March 11–17, 2004.

43. See Mamoun Hudeibi's campaign statement, Dokki District, Cairo, November 2000 (in author's possession), and compare it with "The Initiative of the Supreme Guide of the Muslim Brotherhood on the General Principles of Reform in Egypt" (in Arabic), http://www.ikhwanonline.com/, March 3, 2004.

44. Fayez and Mursi, "Islamist Initiative."

45. "The Initiative of the Supreme Guide of the Muslim Brotherhood."

46. As Elad-Altman (2006a) observed: "This unambiguous restatement of the MB's traditional goals within the Reform Initiative makes it clear that these goals remain a central part of the MB's current formal position."

47. As one Egyptian critic of the Muslim Brotherhood, Sayed Mahmoud al-Qumni (2004), observed: "They talk about 'establishing God's rule'; this is where the initiative becomes a total mystery, because the concept of Islamic law totally collides with rights in the democratic system. In Islamic law, rights don't reflect the people's will, unlike in a democracy."

48. As al-Qumni (2004) argued: "the most obvious aspect of their plan is that they see no one else. They don't see citizens with full rights choosing the life they want to lead, and choosing the media they want to browse, and having the right to listen to music, have a good time, and pursue individual happiness." For another secular critique of the Brotherhood's initiative, see Khalil 2006.

49. Amira Huweidy, "A Chronology of Dissent," *Al-Ahram Weekly*, no. 748, June 23–29, 2005.

50. Interview with George Ishaq, July 11, 2005.

51. Interview with George Ishaq, *World Peace Herald*, May 25, 2005. During this period, the group invited three others to join them: 'Esam al-Islambouli, a Nasserist affiliated with the Karama party; Abd al-Ghaffar Shukr, a Marxist from the Tagammu' party; and Gamal Fahmi, a Nasserist. Interview with George Ishaq, July 11, 2005.

52. Interview with George Ishaq, July 11, 2005.

53. Interview with Aboul 'Ela Madi, July 9, 2005; see also Oweidat et al. 2008, 10,and International Crisis Group 2005, 11n72.

54. Interview with Aboul 'Ela Madi, July 9, 2005.

55. As George Ishaq told the International Crisis Group, "You want frank speaking? I don't believe in the parties; they are rubbish!" Crisis Group Interview, April 18, 2005, cited in International Crisis Group 2005, 11n70.

56. Interview with Diya' Rishwan, July 12, 2005. As Aboul 'Ela noted, "All the people at my *Iftar* were from the 1970s generation" (interview, July 9, 2005). See also Oweidat et al. 2008, 12.

57. Interview with 'Esam Sultan, July 12, 2005.

58. Interview with Aboul 'Ela Madi, July 9, 2005. The tape Aboul 'Ela was referring to were yellow stickers with the word "Kefaya"; Howeidy, "A Chronology of Dissent."

59. Oweidat et al. 2008, 14.

60. Interview with 'Esam Sultan, July 12, 2005.

61. Interview with Aboul 'Ela Madi, July 9, 2005; interview with Sayyid Abd al-Sattar, July 10, 2005. According to Abd al-Sattar, the thirty-six-member Executive Committee included six or seven members of the Muslim Brotherhood.

62. As Diya' Rishwan observed, the leftist activists involved with Kefaya were known for their courage (*garaa'a*); interview with Diya' Rishwan, July 12, 2005. A key Kefaya figure widely admired for his bold opposition to the Mubarak regime was Abd al-Halim Qandil, editor of the Arab nationalist newspaper *al-'Arabi*. After publishing a series of vitriolic attacks on the president, his wife, and his sons, Qandil was kidnaped by government security forces, beaten up, and left naked in the desert outside Cairo in November 2004. According to Qandil, the attack generated "700 articles in support of me" in the Arab press. Interview with Abd al-Halim Qandil, July 11, 2005.

63. As El-Hamalawy observed, "A middle-ranking Muslim Brotherhood activist spoke of the increasing frustration among the group's cadres at the leadership's 'leaving the street empty for the leftists'. When Kefaya came onto the scene, some Brotherhood youth wanted to follow suit." Hossam El-Hamalawy, "Comrades and Brothers," *Middle East Report* 37, no. 242 (Spring 2007). And Gasir Abd al-Raziq, a leftist human rights activist, noted: "The Brotherhood decided to act as a result of pressure coming from their younger members. They said—'We're the oldest and best organized, but these lefties are on the street, and on Al-Jazeera getting all the attention. Why are we, the strongest movement, absent?'" Interview with Gasir Abd al-Raziq, July 10, 2005. See also Elad-Altman 2006a, 8.

64. Interview with Aboul 'Ela Madi, July 9, 2005.

65. Omayma Abdel-Latif, "Fighting for Turf," *Al-Ahram Weekly*, May 12–18, 2005. According to a report cited by Elad-Altman (2006a, 32n67, 32n80, 26, 28), the Brotherhood told the government in advance about all of its demonstrations except one.

66. Omayma Abdel-Latif, "The Shape of Things to Come," *Al-Ahram Weekly*, no. 736, March 31–April 6, 2005; Abdel-Latif, "Fighting for Turf."

67. Elad-Altman 2006a, 8.

68. On the May 4 demonstrations, see Antar 2006, 13n27. According to Noha Antar, almost 128,000 people participated in the Brotherhood's demonstrations between March and May 2005, "showing the movement's mobilization capacity" (13).

69. Abdel-Latif, "Fighting for Turf."

70. International Crisis Group 2005, 3n18, 19n141.

71. Ibid., 5.

72. Ibid., 4.

73. Ibid., 6. Indeed, Muhammad Habib of the Muslim Brotherhood claimed that the actual turnout did not exceed 10% of eligible voters. Mona El-Nahhas, "Opposition Cries Foul," *Al-Ahram Weekly*, June 2–8, 2005.

74. International Crisis Group 2005, 3n19.

75. Abdel-Latif, "Fighting for Turf."

76. Daniel Williams, "Banned Group Leads Dissent in Egypt," Washington Post Foreign Service, May 23, 2005; Omayma Abdel-Latif, "The Shape of Things to Come," *Al-Ahram Weekly*, March 31–April 6, 2005.

77. Murphy, "Egypt Keeps the Muslim Brotherhood Boxed In." The same point was stressed to the author by Muhammad Habib and Abd al-Mun'im Abu al-Futouh in interviews in July 2005.

78. Interview with Abd al-Mun'im Abu al-Futouh, Cairo, July 12, 2005; interview with Diya' Rishwan, July 12, 2005. The "Quran incident" was also emphasized as a seminal event by 'Esam Sultan, Gasir Abd al-Raziq, George Ishaq, and Abd al-Halim Qandil in my interviews with them in summer 2005. See also Vivian Salama, "Sending Mixed Signals," *Daily Star*, February 8, 2005, http://www.ikhwanweb.com/.

79. For Habib's statement, see International Crisis Group 2005 and interview, July 13, 2005. For Abd al-Mun'im Abu al-Futouh's statement, see his 2004 collection of essays and the author's interview, July 12, 2005. 'Esam Sultan's statement is from the author's interview, July 12, 2005; as Sultan elaborated, "we [in the Wasat party] were the first to say this."

80. Whether such formulations were supported by others in the movement is unclear; they were certainly never officially endorsed by the group as a whole. See Elad-Altman 2006a.

81. Interview with Muhammad Habib, July 13, 2005.

82. Interview with Gasir Abd al-Raziq, July 10, 2005.

83. Interview with George Ishaq, July 11, 2005.

84. Interview with Abd al-Mun'im Abu al-Futouh, July 12, 2005.

85. Interview with Diya' Rishwan, July 12, 2005; interview with Sayyid Abd al-Sattar, July 10, 2005. A key representative of the Brotherhood in early talks with Revolutionary Socialists and leftists leading to the formation of the Tahaluf was 'Ali Abd al-Fattah; El-Hamalawy, "Comrades and Brothers," 5. See also International Crisis Group 2005.

86. Interview with Diya' Rishwan, July 12, 2005; interview with Sayyid Abd al-Sattar, July 10, 2005. In addition to Kefaya and the Tahaluf, a third cross-partisan group, called al-Tagammu' al-Watani, was established in May 2005 under the leadership of 'Aziz Sidqi, an eighty-five-year-old former prime minister. This group did not engage in

street protests, but the prestige of its founders, who included former senior state officials, writers, professors, and former diplomats, gave it a certain weight.

87. Interview with 'Esam Sultan, July 12, 2005; interview with George Ishaq, July 11, 2005.

88. Interview with Diya' Rishwan, July 12, 2005.

89. Interview with George Ishaq, July 11, 2005.

90. Interview with Hisham Qasim, July 10, 2005.

91. Ibid.

92. Interview with George Ishaq, July 11, 2005.

93. Ibid.

94. Ibid.

95. Interview with Muhammad Habib, July 13, 2005. Abd al-Mun'im Abu al-
Futouh offered similar observations in my interviews with him in the summer of 2005.

96. Interview with Hisham Qasim, July 10, 2005.

97. Interview with Muhammad Habib, July 13, 2005.

98. Elad-Altman 2006a, 33.

99. Ibid., 34; Hamzawy and Brown 2010, 13; Antar 2006, 13.

100. Antar 2006, 14.

101. Ibid., 14, 16. See also Salah 2005.

102. "Parliamentary Election Assessment in Egypt" 2005, 14.

103. Antar 2006, 15.

104. Ibid., 13; Hamzawy and Brown 2010, 15.

105. Antar 2006, 15n43; Sharp, "The Broader Middle East," 5. According to Sharp,
1,600 people were arrested and 13 people were killed during the elections. See also Muhammad Habib, "Li-Madha al-Khawf min Al-Ikhwan al-Muslimin? Al 'Ra'ab' Minna . . .
Tujawiz Hudoud al-Mantiq" [Why the Fear of the Muslim Brotherhood? This Terror
Regarding Us . . . Exceeds the Bounds of Logic], al-Hayat, January 11, 2006, on regime
intervention in the latter two rounds of the voting.

106. International Crisis Group 2008; Habib, "Why the Fear of the Muslim
Brotherhood?"

107. By comparison, NDP candidates won only a third of the seats they contested.

108. International Crisis Group 2008, 5.

109. Ibid., 6.

110. International Crisis Group 2008, 4–5. However, this paper never materialized.

111. Habib, "Why the Fear of the Muslim Brotherhood?"

CHAPTER SIX
REPRESSION AND RETRENCHMENT

1. Jonathan Wright, "Egypt's PM Wants No Brotherhood Block in Parliament," Reuters, May 20, 2006.

2. A. Othman and M. Almesryoon Rashid, "Analysts: Egyptian Government to
Curb MB Further Political Gains," http://www.ikhwanweb.com/, May 30, 2006.

3. International Crisis Group 2008, 9.

4. See, for example, Samer Shehata and Joshua Stacher, "Boxing in the Brothers,"

Middle East Report, August 8, 2007, http://www.merip.org/; Yaroslav Trofimov, "Muslim Brothers Failing as Egypt Outflanks Islamists," *Wall Street Journal*, May 15, 2009; and Ellen Knickmeyer, "Cairo Moving Aggressively to Cripple Muslim Brotherhood," *Washington Post*, October 1, 2007. As Shehata and Stacher observed, "Washington has remained silent as the Mubarak regime has arrested hundreds of Brothers and transferred dozens to military courts."

5. See Shehata and Stacher, "Boxing in the Brothers."

6. Azuri 2007.

7. On the government's negative press campaign in the wake of the "al-Azhar militia" incident, see Shehata and Stacher, "Boxing in the Brothers."

8. Knickmeyer, "Cairo Moving Aggressively."

9. *Al-Usbu'*, January 12, 2007, cited in Azuri 2007.

10. International Crisis Group 2008, 10.

11. Ibid., 19. See also Shehata and Stacher, "Boxing in the Brothers" and Knickmeyer, "Cairo Moving Aggressively."

12. International Crisis Group 2008, 11n61. According to Noha Antar, the Brotherhood received an average monthly income of 11 million Egyptian pounds from membership dues. In addition, it received donations from charitable associations and businesses, though the amounts are not known. According to Antar, the Brotherhood had 60,000–70,000 active members, each of whom paid monthly dues of 23 Egyptian pounds. The accuracy of such figures requires additional verification. Antar 2006, 15.

13. Azuri 2007, 3.

14. International Crisis Group 2008, 11. See also Stacher 2009.

15. International Crisis Group 2008. Stacher (2009) provides somewhat different figures: over 6,000 Brothers filed papers to register as candidates, and 2,664 of them obtained court orders allowing them to compete after they were rejected by the security arm of the state. According to Stacher, 20 candidates made it onto the ballot.

16. Trofimov, "Muslim Brothers Failing." See also Shehata and Stacher, "Boxing in the Brothers."

17. Shehata and Stacher, "Boxing in the Brothers."

18. Lynch 2008, 4.

19. International Crisis Group 2008, 10, citing "Muslim Brotherhood Says Egypt Aims to Provoke Violence," Agence France-Presse, February 10, 2007.

20. Knickmeyer, "Cairo Moving Aggressively."

21. Trofimov, "Muslim Brothers Failing."

22. Stacher 2009; Steven Brooke, "Muslim Brotherhood Faces Growing Challenges in Egypt," *Combating Terrorism Center Sentinel*, May 31, 2009.

23. See Brown and Hamzawy 2008 and Lynch 2008, 5–6.

24. They also argued that the purpose of this provision was to replace an existing advisory body of Islamist jurists affiliated with Al-Azhar University (Majma' al-Buhuth al-Islami) with an elected body of religious experts independent of state authority. Interview with Mahmoud 'Ezzat, July 3, 2008.

25. Brown and Hamzawy 2008, 7–8; Lynch 2008, 6.

26. Brown and Hamzawy 2008, 9.

27. "A Division within the Muslim Brotherhood?" *Political Islam*, October 8, 2007.

28. For example, one Islamist female activist and political science professor de-

clared that the platform "has no connection to Islamic political thought or even to political thought at all." 'Amr al-Chobaki, "The Religious Association and the Political Organization . . . The Decisive Problem of the Muslim Brotherhood" (in Arabic), *al-Hayat*, October 25, 2007.

29. Interview with Diya' Rishwan, July 2008.

30. Interview with Abd al-Mun'im Mahmoud, April 30, 2010.

31. Interview with Abd al-Mun'im Mahmoud, July 3, 2008; Trofimov, "Muslim Brothers Failing."

32. Interview with Abd al-Mun'im Mahmoud, July 3, 2008. On the regressive character of the party platform and its reliance on al-Mawardi, see Khalil al-Anani, "Backing into the Future," http://weekly.ahram.org.eg/, May 1, 2008.

33. Trofimov, "Muslim Brotherhood Failing."

34. Interview with Aboul 'Ela Madi, July 1, 2008.

35. Interview with Abd al-Mun'im Mahmoud, April 30, 2010.

36. Interview with Ibrahim Hudeibi, April 28, 2010.

37. Ahmad 'Uthman, "Official Announcement at the End of the Week . . . Expected Changes in the Membership of the Guidance Bureau Confirm the Influence of the First Deputy of the Association's Guide" (in Arabic), *al-Misriyun*, June 2, 2008.

38. Mahmoud 2008b.

39. Ibid.

40. Interview with Abd al-Mun'im Mahmoud, July 3, 2008.

41. Ibid.

42. Ibid.

43. "Dispute Hints at Rift in Egypt's Muslim Brotherhood," Egypt News, October 20, 2009; Alaa Bayoumi, "Muslim Brotherhood's Testing Time," http://www.aljazeera .com/, October 24, 2009.

44. Khalil al-Anani, "Survival Is Not Enough," *Al-Ahram Weekly*, February 3, 2010; interview with Ibrahim Hudeibi, April 28, 2010; interview with Mustafa al-Naggar, April 29, 2010.

45. Interview with Ibrahim Hudeibi, April 28, 2010.

46. "Muslim Brotherhood Rigs Their Own Elections," *The Spittoon*, December 22, 2009.

47. Interview with Aboul 'Ela Madi, May 1, 2010.

48. Interview with Ibrahim Hudeibi, April 28, 2010.

49. Tammam 2010a. See also Marc Lynch, "Conservative Gains in Muslim Brotherhood Elections," http://lynch.foreignpolicy.com/, December 21, 2009. According to Lynch, al-'Aryan joined the slate of the group's conservative secretary-general, Mahmoud 'Ezzat.

50. 'Esam al-'Aryan, "Egypt: New Phase in the Muslim Brotherhood," Brotherhood website, January 5, 2010.

51. Interview with Abd al-Mun'im Mahmoud, April 30, 2010.

52. Interview with Aboul 'Ela Madi, May 1, 2010.

53. Interview with Ibrahim Hudeibi, April 28, 2010.

54. Al-Anani 2010; Amro Hassan, "Egypt: New Leader Won't Advance Muslim Brotherhood on Political Stage, Critics Say," *Los Angeles Times*, January 17, 2010; Fawaz Gerges, "The Muslim Brotherhood: New Leadership, Old Politics," http://www.guard ian.co.uk/.

55. Al-Anani, "Survival Is Not Enough"; see also al-Anani 2010.

56. Interview with Mustafa al-Naggar, April 29, 2010.

57. 'Ezzat 2008.

58. Interview with Mustafa al-Naggar, April 29, 2010.

59. In May 2010 I had the opportunity to visit the Brotherhood's headquarters in Cairo just before a Guidance Bureau meeting. As the members assembled in the reception area, I was struck by their advanced age and physical frailty; several were bent over or using walkers.

60. Khairat El-Shatir, "No Need to Be Afraid of Us," The Guardian, November 22, 2005; interview with Abd al-Mun'im Mahmoud.

61. Stacher and Shehata 2006.

62. Ibid. See also Azarva 2007.

63. Habib, "Why the Fear of the Muslim Brotherhood?"

64. Stacher and Shehata 2006.

65. Interview with Muhammad Sa'd al-Katatni, May 2, 2010.

66. Azarva 2007, 3.

67. Ibid.

68. Interview with Muhammad Sa'd al-Katatni, May 2, 2010.

69. Ibid.

70. Ibid.

71. Ibid.

72. "Tahawwulat al-Ikhwan al-Muslimin . . . Tafakkuk al-Idiulujiyya wa Nihayat al-Tandhim" [The Evolutions of the Muslim Brotherhood . . . Ideological Fragmentation and the End of the Organization], al-Badil, July 2, 2008. See also "Tayyar al-Wasat Dakhil al-Ikhwan al-Muslimin Yutalib bi-Tasfiyat al-Jam'iyya wa al-Insihab Min al-Tandhim al-Duwali li-Tatahawwal ila Hizb 'Alani" [The Centrist Trend within the Muslim Brotherhood Demands the Dissolution of the Association and Withdrawal from the International Organization in Order to Change into a Transparent Party], al-Qahira, March 16, 2004.

73. Interview with Aboul 'Ela Madi, May 1, 2010.

74. Interview with Ibrahim Hudeibi, April 28, 2010.

75. Interview with Abd al-Mun'im Mahmoud, April 30, 2010.

76. Interview with Ibrahim Hudeibi, April 28, 2010. Abd al-Mun'im Mahmoud offered a similar assessment of the Wasat party in my interview with him on April 30, 2010.

77. Interview with Mustafa al-Naggar, April 29, 2010.

78. Interview with Aboul 'Ela Madi, May 1, 2010.

79. Lynch 2007.

80. Al-Anani 2010.

81. Khalil al-Anani, "Silent Revolution within the Brotherhood," Daily News Egypt, October 15, 2008. See also al-Anani 2010.

82. Hadeel al-Shalchi, "Powerful Islamic Movement Sees Leadership Struggle," Associated Press, October 30, 2009.

83. Abd al-Mun'im Mahmoud, "Wa Madtha 'An Mashru' al-Islahiyin Dakhil al-Haraka al-Islamiyya?" [And What about the Reformists' Project inside the Islamic movement?], Ana Ikhwan (online blog), March 25, 2009.

84. Ibid.

85. Interview with Abd al-Mun'im Mahmoud, April 29, 2010.

86. Khalil al-Anani, "Opposite Effects," *Al-Ahram Weekly*, March 3, 2010.

87. Al-Anani, "Silent Revolution within the Brotherhood."

88. Interview with Ibrahim Hudeibi, April 28, 2010.

89. Interview Abd al-Mun'im Mahmoud, April 30, 2010.

90. Interview with Mustafa al-Naggar, April 29, 2010.

91. "Sisters in the Muslim Brotherhood," *Daily News Egypt*, April 15, 2009.

92. Interview with Abd al-Mun'im Mahmoud, April 30, 2010.

93. Hossam Tammam, "MB Goes Rural," *Ikhwan Scope*, February 15, 2010.

94. Ibid. On the growing influence of leaders with a rural background, see Ibrahim Hudeibi, "Brotherhood Faces Leadership Challenge," *Arab Reform Bulletin*, Carnegie Endowment for International Peace, November 2009.

95. Lynch 2007.

96. Nathan Field and Ahmed Hamem, "Salafism Making Inroads," *Arab Reform Bulletin*, Carnegie Endowment for International Peace, March 2009.

97. Interview with Abd al-Mun'im Mahmoud, July 3, 2008.

98. See, for example, "Conservatives Dominate Brotherhood," BBC News, Cairo, February 10, 2010.

99. Al-Anani, "Survival Is Not Enough."

100. Interview with Gamal Nassar, May 2, 2010.

101. Heba Saleh, "Egypt's Muslim Brotherhood Picks New Leader," *Financial Times*, January 17, 2010; Shadi Hamid, "A Radical Turn for the Muslim Brotherhood?" Up Front Blog, Brookings Institution, January 26, 2010, http://www.brookings.edu/.

102. Interview with Abd al-Mun'im Mahmoud, April 30, 2010.

103. Tammam 2010a. See also Lindsey Ursula, "Egypt's Muslim Brotherhood: Widening Split between Young and Old," *Christian Science Monitor*, December 21, 2009. See also Abd al-Mun'im Mahmoud, "Ma al-Farq Bayn Tashrihat Murshid al-Ikhwan 'an Mubarak wa Ughniyat Ra'isna lil-Mutriba Shirin?" [What Is the Difference between the Statements of the Brotherhood's Supreme Guide on Mubarak and the Song "Our President" by the Musical Artist Shirin?], *al-Dustour*, April 16, 2010.

104. See Michele Dunne, 'Amr Hamzawy, and Jennifer Windsor, "Egypt's Political Future: The Parliamentary Elections and Beyond," Carnegie Endowment for International Peace, November 18, 2010, http://carnegieendowment.org/; see also Bahey Eldin Hassan, "Egypt's Electoral Commission: Who's Running the Show?" *Arab Reform Bulletin*, Carnegie Endowment for International Peace, November 22, 2010.

105. See the full-page article on Abu al-Futouh's decision in *al-Dustour*, February 11, 2010, p. 8, and the follow-up article by Iman Abd al-Mun'im in *al-Dustour*, February 13, 2010, p. 1.

106. Abu al-Futouh's proposal and the Brotherhood's adamant rejection of it are covered in detail in a series of articles in *al-Dustour*, February 11, 2010, February 13, 2010, February 14, 2010.

107. Abd al-Mun'im Mahmoud, "Insihab al-Ikhwan Brajmatiyya Tandhimiyya," *al-Dustour*, February 19, 2010, reprinted in *Ana al-Ikhwan*, February 19, 2010.

108. Ibid.

109. Interview with Abd al-Mun'im Mahmoud, April 30, 2010.

110. "Egypt's Muslim Brotherhood to Enter Parliament Elections—Slogan, 'Islam Is the Solution,'" *Wall Street Journal*, October 11, 2010; Nadia Abou el-Magd, "Call for

Muslim Brotherhood Boycott Grows," http://www.xn--kgbdb1a2ipam.net/, August 23, 2010.

111. Quoted in Mona El-Naggar, "New Call for Election Boycott in Egypt," *New York Times*, September 7, 2010.

112. Abigail Hauslohner, "Egypt's Opposition Splits on Election Boycott," *Time*, October 15, 2010.

113. 'Amr Hamzawy and Michele Dunne, "Brotherhood Enters Elections in a Weakened State," Carnegie Commentary, Carnegie Endowment for International Peace, November 15, 2010, http://carnegieendowment.org/. The Wafd and the Tagammu' party also conducted internal polls, and in the Wafd as in the Brotherhood, the decision to participate won by a narrow majority, 54 to 46. Dunne, Hamzawy, and Windsor, "Egypt's Political Future."

114. Mounir Adib and Nesma Abdel Qader, "In About-Face, MB Leaders Urge Boycott of November Elections," *al-Masry al-Youm*, October 5, 2010; Hamzawy and Dunne, "Brotherhood Enters Elections in a Weakened State."

115. Noha El-Hennawy, "Muslim Brotherhood to Run, Despite Calls for Election Boycott," *al-Masry al-Youm*, October 9, 2010.

116. Dunne, Hamzawy, and Windsor, "Egypt's Political Future"; Michele Dunne and 'Amr Hamzawy, "The Egyptian Parliamentary Elections: Facts and Figures," Carnegie Endowment for International Peace, November 28, 2010, http://egyptelections.carnegie endowment.org/.

117. For instance, a video posted on YouTube and allegedly captured on a cell phone showed election workers filling out ballots and handing them to someone beyond the camera's range. Soraya Sarhaddi Nelson, "Furor Grows Over Egypt's Election Results," *All Things Considered*, November 30, 2010, http://www.npr.org/. See also Evan Hill, "Election Day in Mansoura," Al-Jazeera Blogs, November 29, 2010, http://blogs.alja zeera.com/.

118. Yolande Knell, "Egypt's Muslim Brotherhood Campaigns through Crackdown," BBC News Middle East, November 26, 2010.

119. One Brotherhood candidate won a seat in the second round but only after defying the boycott and losing the group's backing.

120. "Opposition MPs Pledge to Egyptians to Overthrow Fraud Parliament," http://www.ikhwanweb.com/, December 14, 2010.

121. Muhammad Mahmoud, "Egyptian Parliament Convenes as Opposition Members Form 'Parallel Parliament,'" http://www.Al-Shorfa.com/, December 17, 2010.

122. "Experts: Brotherhood's Participation in the People's Parliament Ensures Its Survival," http://www.ikhwanweb.com/, January 5, 2011.

123. Interview with Muhammad Mursi, May 1, 2010.

124. Interview with Rashad Bayoumi, May 2, 2010.

125. Hudeibi, "Brotherhood Faces Leadership Challenge."

Chapter Seven
The Brotherhood and the Egyptian Uprising

1. I thank Peter Jones for this prescient observation. Workshop, "Change in the Arab World," Centre for International Policy Studies, University of Ottawa, April 29, 2011.

2. Many sources highlight the role of the social media in the Egyptian uprising. See, for example, Ghoneim 2012 and Howard and Hussain 2011.

3. For more on the April 6 movement, see Samantha Shapiro, "Revolution, Facebook-Style," *New York Times*, January 22, 2009, and Sarah Carr, "April 6: Genealogy of a Youth Movement," http://www.jadaliyya.com/, April 5, 2012.

4. Interview with Islam Lutfi, July 19, 2011.

5. Interview with Ahmad Abd al-Gawwad, July 18, 2011.

6. Interview with Muhammad Qassas, July 18, 2011.

7. These figures included Qassas and Lutfi from the Brotherhood, and Ziyat al-'Alimi and Khaled Abd al-Hamid from nationalist and leftist groups.

8. Interview with Islam Lutfi, July 19, 2011.

9. Ibid.

10. Interview with Ahmad Abd al-Gawwad, July 18, 2011.

11. Early studies of the uprising include International Crisis Group 2011.

12. Interview with Egyptian diplomat, January 2011, cited in ibid., p. 2.

13. Eric Trager, "After Tunisia, Is Egypt Next?" *Atlantic Monthly*, January 17, 2011, http://www.theatlantic.com/.

14. International Crisis Group 2011, 2n14.

15. Ghoneim 2012.

16. Mike Giglio, "We Are All Khaled Said: Will the Revolution Come to Egypt?" *Daily Beast*, January 22, 2011.

17. Jennifer Preston, "Movement Began with Outrage and a Facebook Page That Gave It an Outlet," *New York Times*, February 5, 2011.

18. Noha El-Hennawy, "We Are All Khaled Saeed: Redefining Political Demonstration in Egypt," http://www.egyptindependent.com/, August 4, 2010; see also John D. Sutter, "The Faces of Egypt's 'Revolution 2.0,'" http://www.cnn.com/, February 21, 2011, and Preston, "Movement Began with Outrage."

19. Interview with Islam Lutfi, July 19, 2011; "Revolution in Cairo: The April 6 Movement," *Frontline*, PBS.

20. International Crisis Group Report 2011, 3; Sutter, "The Faces of Egypt's 'Revolution 2.0.'"

21. Giglio, "We Are All Khaled Said."

22. International Crisis Group Report 2011, 3.

23. Interview with Ahmad Abd al-Gawwad, July 18, 2011.

24. Heba Fahmy, "Muslim Brotherhood Reconsiders Refusal to Participate in January 25 Demo," *Daily News Egypt*, January 20, 2011.

25. Ibid.

26. International Crisis Group Report 2011, 4.

27. Interview with Ahmad Abd al-Gawwad, July 18, 2011.

28. Interview with Ahmad Mihran, July 18, 2011. See also Rami El-Amine and Mostafa Henawy, "A People's History of the Revolution," *LeftTurn*, July 7, 2011, http://www.leftturn.org/.

29. International Crisis Group Report 2011, 3; "Timeline: Egypt's Revolution," http://www.al-jazeera.net/.

30. Hossam Tammam and Patrick Haenni, "Islam in the Insurrection," *Al-Ahram Weekly*, no. 1037, March 3–9, 2011, http://weekly.ahram.org/.

31. "Timeline: Egypt's Revolution."

32. Tammam and Haenni, "Islam in the Insurrection."

33. Interview with Muhammad Qassas, July 18, 2011.

34. Interview with Ibrahim al-Za'farani, July 17, 2011.

35. "Timeline: Egypt's Revolution."

36. El-Amine and Henaway, "A People's History of the Egyptian Revolution."

37. Al-Jazeera (Qatar), January 27, 2011. Translation provided by the Middle East Media Research Institute (MEMRI) and by the author.

38. International Crisis Group Report 2011, 16.

39. Interview with Aboul 'Ela Madi, April 5, 2011.

40. International Crisis Group Report 2011, 7.

41. Ibid., 8.

42. International Crisis Group Report, 2011, 6.

43. Ibid., 7.

44. International Crisis Group Report 2011, 13–14; Galal Nassar, "The Army's Revolutionary Mission," http://weekly.ahram.org.eg/, February 17–23, 2011.

45. Craig Whitlock, "Mubarak Steps Down, Prompting Jubilation in Cairo Streets," *Washington Post*, February 12, 2011; "Post-Mubarak Era Dawns on Egypt," http://www.aljazeera.net/, February 12, 2011; "Egypt Crisis: President Hosni Mubarak Resigns as Leader," BBC News Middle East, February 12, 2011. The SCAF has eighteen members, selected on the basis of rank.

46. These estimates appeared in a five-hundred-page report had prepared by a fact-finding committee headed by Judge 'Adil Qoura investigating the acts of violence against unarmed demonstrators. Mohamed Abdel-Baky, "Blood on Their Hands," *Al-Ahram Weekly*, no. 1044, July 5–8, 2011.

47. Text of Communiqué No. 5 Issued by the Egyptian Military, http://www.mcclatchydc.com/, February 13, 2011.

48. International Crisis Group report, 2011, 24.

49. Dina 'Ezzat, "Tactical Gains," *Al-Ahram Weekly*, no. 1034, 2011.

50. Charles M. Sennott, "Inside the Muslim Brotherhood: Part I," http://www.GlobalPost.com, February 21, 2011; interview with Muhammad Hamza, July 16, 2011.

51. International Crisis Group 2011, 25.

52. Shadi Hamid, "The New Egypt and the Muslim Brotherhood," blog post, Up-Front, Brookings Institute, March 8, 2011, http://www.brookings.edu/.

53. Margaret Coker, "Muslim Group Backs Secular Struggle," *Wall Street Journal*, January 31, 2011.

54. Shadi Hamid and Steven Brooke, "The Muslim Brotherhood's Role in the Egyptian Revolution," *CTC Sentinel* 4, no. 2 (2011): 1–3. The quote from al-Biltagi, cited in the article, is from Jack Shenker, "Egypt Protesters Play Down Islamist Party's Role," *The Guardian*, January 31, 2011.

55. "Egypt's Revolution Is a People's Revolution with No Islamic Agenda," http://www.ikhwanweb.com/, February 5, 2011.

56. Such ripostes are too numerous to mention them all here. By way of example, see Bruce Reidel, "Don't Fear Egypt's Muslim Brotherhood," *Daily Beast*, January 27, 2011; Andrew McCarthy, "Fear the Muslim Brotherhood," *National Review*, January 31, 2011; Catherine Herridge, "Just What Is the Muslim Brotherhood?" http://www.foxnews.com/, January 31, 2001; and Steven Emerson, "Egypt's Future and the Chameleon Muslim Brotherhood," IPT News, January 2011. See also my own intervention in this

debate, "The Muslim Brotherhood after Mubarak: What the Brotherhood Is and How It Will Shape the Future," http://www.foreignaffairs.com/, February 3, 2011.

57. Essam El-Errian ['Esam al-'Aryan], "What the Muslim Brothers Want," *New York Times*, February 9, 2011.

58. Abd al-Mun'im Abu al-Futouh, "Democracy Supporters Should Not Fear the Muslim Brotherhood," *Washington Post*, February 9, 2011.

59. http://www.jihadwatch.org/, February 5, 2011.

60. International Crisis Group 2011, 25.

61. Interview with Aboul 'Ela Madi, April 5, 2011.

62. International Crisis Group 2011, 25.

63. Hamid, "The New Egypt and the Muslim Brotherhood."

64. "MB Chairman: We Seek to Participate, Not Dominate Elections," http://www.ikhwanweb.com/, April 20, 2011.

65. Interview with Muhammad al-Biltagi, April 6, 2011; Noha El-Hennawy, "Egypt's Muslim Brotherhood Selects Hawkish Leaders," *al-Masry al Youm*, March 30, 2011; Mohammed Abu Zaid, "El-Erian to Political Parties: Win Votes Then Discuss Power," http://www.ikhwanweb.com/, June 13, 2011; Dina 'Ezzat, "A Justified Fear?" *Al-Ahram Weekly*, no. 1040, March 24 –30, 2011.

66. 'Ezzat, "A Justified Fear?"

67. Interview with Muhammad al-Biltagi, April 6, 2011.

68. Interview with Sally Sami, April 5, 2011; interview with Rif'at al-Sa'eed, April 6, 2011; interview with Magid Surour, April 6, 2011.

69. Interview with Aboul 'Ela Madi, April 5, 2011.

70. Interview with Mona Zulfiqar, April 5, 2011; interview with Ahmad Fawzy, April 7, 2011; interview with Sayyid al-Badawi, April 8, 2011.

71. Interview with Ahmad Fawzy, April 7, 2011.

72. Interview with Sally Sami, April 5, 2011; interview with Magid Surour, April 6, 2011.

73. Interview with Mona Zulfiqar, April 5, 2011.

74. Interview with Rif'at al-Sa'eed, April 6, 2011; interview with Ahmad Fawzy, April 7, 2011; interview with Sayyid al-Badawi, April 8, 2011.

75. Interview with Sayyid al-Badawi, April 8, 2011.

76. Interview with Muhammad al-Biltagi, April 6, 2011.

77. Ahmed Eleiba, "Muslim Brotherhood Announces Future Plans after Two-Day Meeting," *Al-Ahram Weekly*, April 30, 2011.

78. Ahmed Eleiba, "Muslim Brotherhood Supreme Guide Praises Egypt's Revolution for Bringing about Fair Elections," *Al-Ahram Weekly*, August 6, 2011.

79. Abu Zaid, "El-Erian to Political Parties."

80. Salah al-Din Hasan, "Abul Fotouh: I Reject the Existence of a Muslim Brotherhood Party in Egypt," http://www.islamonline.net/, March 16, 2011.

81. Hanan Solayman, "Muslim Brotherhood Young Members Dismayed at New Leadership Appointments," http://www.thedailynewsegypt.com/; Amani Maged, "Not Without Squabble," *Al-Ahram Weekly*, May 5–11, 2011, http://weekly.ahram.org/.

82. Interview with Abd al-Mun'im Mahmoud, July 14, 2011.

83. Kathy Lally, "Egyptian Parties Take First Steps toward Democracy," *Washington Post*, February 23, 2011.

84. Interview with Ibrahim al-Za'farani, July 17, 2011.

85. Ibid.

86. David Kirkpatrick, "Egypt Elections Expose Divisions in Muslim Brotherhood," *New York Times*, June 19, 2011.

87. Hany El Waziry and Mahmoud Ramzy, "Muslim Brotherhood Member Mulls Running for Presidency," *Egypt Independent*, April 5, 2011.

88. Noha El-Hennawy, "Brotherhood Reformist Launches Campaign, Reveals Divisions," *Egypt Independent*, May 13, 2011, http://www.egyptindependent.com/.

89. *Al-Masry al-Youm*, June 22, 2011.

90. Rana Khazbak, "Adl Party Seeks to Displace Brotherhood from Center Ground of Egyptian Politics," *Egypt Independent*, May 24, 2011, http://www.egyptindependent.com/.

91. Interview with Ahmad Abd al-Gawwad, July 18, 2011.

92. Interview with Muhammad Qassas, July 18, 2011.

93. Interview with Ahmad Abd al-Gawwad, July 18, 2011. See also Salma Shukrallah, "Egypt's Muslim Brotherhood Struggles to Contain Cracks," http://english.ahram.org.eg/, July 19, 2011.

94. "Young Members of Egyptian Muslim Brotherhood Call for Revolution Within," MEMRI (Special Dispatch No. 3654), March 9, 2011, http://www.memri.org/; Noha El-Hennawy, "Brotherhood Youths Broach Reformation at Conference Denounced by Group's Vanguard," *al-Masry al-Youm*, March 26, 2011, http://www.almasryalyoum.com; Amira Howeidy, "Message from the Young Brothers," *Al-Ahram Weekly*, March 31, 2011–April 6, 2011, http://weekly.ahram.org.

95. Noha El-Hennawy, "Political Freedom, Competition Drive Rifts between Muslim Brotherhood Factions," *al-Masry al-Youm*, March 24, 2011.

96. Interview with Ahmad Abd al-Gawwad, July 18, 2011.

97. These seven were Islam Lutfi, Muhammad Qassas, Ahmad Abd al-Gawwad, Hani Mahmoud, Musab al-Gaml, Abd al-Rahman Khalil, and Abd al-Rahman Haridi.

98. Interview with Islam Lutfi, July 19, 2011.

99. Soray Sarhaddi Nelson, "Rifts Develop in Egypt's Muslim Brotherhood," http://www.npr.org/, July 13, 2011.

100. Interview with Muhammad Hamza, July 16, 2011.

101. Noha El-Hennawy, "A Split in the Muslim Brotherhood? Not So Easy," *al-Masry al-Youm*, April 17, 2011.

102. Ibid.

103. Ibid.

104. For an example of this tendency, see "In Egypt, Youth Wing Breaks from Muslim Brotherhood," *New York Times*, June 22, 2011.

105. For example, see Hossam Tammam, "The Brotherhood Embraces Salafism," *Marased* (a periodical published by the Future Studies Unit of the Biblotheca Alexandrina) (in Arabic), vol. 1, 2010. For a summary of Tammam's findings, see Basant Zaineddin, "Study: Salafism a Strong Influence in Brotherhood," *al-Masry al-Youm*, December 1, 2010, http://www.almasryalyoum.com, and Galal Nassar, "Egypt: Down the Salafi Road," *Al-Ahram Weekly*, December 16–22, 2010, http://weekly.ahram.org/.

106. Interview with Abd al Mun'im Mahmoud, July 14, 2011.

107. Ahmad 'Izz al-Din, interview with Khayrat al-Shatir, *al-Mujtama'*, no. 1962, July 23–29, 2011.

108. Interview with Mahmoud Ghuzlan, July 19, 2011.

109. 'Izz al-Din, interview with Khayrat al-Shatir (n. 107).

110. Muhammad Hasan Sha'ban, "Panic in Egypt over Muslim Brotherhood's Call for Islamic Rule," *al-Sharq al-Awsat*, April 20, 2011, http://www.asharq-e.com/.

111. Khalaf Ali Hassan, "Brotherhood Leaders: We Shall Apply Islamic Shar'a," *Egypt Independent*, May 25, 2011, http://www.egyptindependent.com/.

112. Interview with Mahmoud Ghuzlan, July 19, 2011.

113. Interview with Muhammad Mursi, May 1, 2010.

114. Ibid.

115. "Most Embrace a Role for Islam in Politics, Muslim Publics Divided on Hamas and Hezbollah," Pew Research Global Attitudes Project, December 2, 2010, http://www.pewglobal.org/.

116. For example, see Noha El-Hennawy, "Islamists and Secularists Battle for the Heart of the Nation," *al-Masry al-Youm*, May 26, 2011, http://www.almasryalyoum.com.

117. One exception to this rule is Gamal al-Banna, the younger brother of the Hasan al-Banna, the founder of the Muslim Brotherhood, who advocates a strict separation of religion and state. However, al-Banna's views have limited traction within Islamist circles, and he is viewed as an iconoclast at best, a heretic at worst.

118. Interview with Aboul 'Ela Madi, May 1, 2010.

119. Interview with Islam Lutfi, July 19, 2011.

120. Interview with Mahmoud Ghuzlan, July 19, 2011; Sami Magdi, "El-Erian to Masrawi: The Brotherhood Would Oppose the Army if It Adopts the Notion of 'Constitution First,'" http://www.ikhwanweb.com/, June 29, 2011.

121. Interview with Muhammad Hamza, July 16, 2011.

122. Interview with Mahmoud Ghuzlan, July 19, 2011.

123. Interview with Islam Lutfi, July 19, 2011.

124. "Wathiqat al-Tahaluf al-Dimuqrati min Ajl Misr" [Charter of the Democratic Coalition for Egypt], August 2, 2011.

125. Magdi, "El-Erian to Masrawi."

126. Marwa al-A'asar , "Islamists, Political Forces Negotiate Stance on Friday Protest," *Daily News Egypt*, July 26, 2011.

127. Ibid.; Hasan Nafa', "An Islamist Threat?" *al-Masry al-Youm*, July 31, 2011.

128. Anthony Shadid, "Islamists Flood Square in Cairo in Show of Strength," *New York Times*, July 29, 2011; "Cairo: Muslim Brotherhood Call for Islamist State," *Global Post*, July 29, 2011; Abigail Hauslohner, "Islamist Show of Strength Shows Egypt's Liberals What They're Up Against," *Time*, July 29, 2011.

129. Shadid, "Islamists Flood Square in Cairo in Show of Strength."

130. Hauslohner, "Islamist Show of Strength."

131. Noha El-Hennawy, "After Show of Force, Islamists Debate Role of Religion in Politics," *al-Masry al-Youm*, August 2, 2011.

132. Ibid.

133. Hany El Waziry, "Freedom and Justice Party Rejects Islamist Slogans in Tahrir," *al-Masry al-Youm*, July 29, 2011.

Chapter Eight
Egypt's Islamist Movement in Comparative Perspective

1. Ali Abdul Kazem, "The Muslim Brotherhood: The Historic Background and the Ideological Origins," in Hourani 1997, 15.

2. Ibid., 15–16.

3. Ibid., 17; Robinson 1997, 380.

4. Ibrahim Gharaibeh, "The Muslim Brotherhood: Political and Organizational Performance," in Hourani 1997, 47–48.

5. Moaddel 2002, 104–5.

6. Ellen Lust-Okar, "Divergent Experiences of the Muslim Brotherhood in Syria and Jordan" (paper presented at Eastern Michigan State University, 2007), 2.

7. Ryan 2008.

8. Wiktorowicz 1999, 7.

9. Robinson 1997, 381.

10. Moaddel 2002, 108.

11. Gharaibeh, "The Muslim Brotherhood," 48.

12. Moaddel 2002, 109.

13. Brown and Hamzawy 2010; Moaddel 2002, 110.

14. Indeed, several Kuwaiti scholars and journalists I interviewed referred to the Muslim Brotherhood at this time as a "secretive" organization.

15. Moaddel 2002, 111.

16. Shafeeq N. Ghabra, "Balancing State and Society: The Islamic Movement in Kuwait," *Middle East Policy* 5, no. 2 (1997): 59.

17. Ibid., 60.

18. Baaklini, Denoeux, and Springborg 1999, 182.

19. Interview with Ghanim al-Najjar, July 5, 2004.

20. Interview with Ahmad al-Baghdadi, July 8, 2004.

21. Baaklini, Denoeux, and Springborg 1999, 183–84.

22. Ibid.

23. Ibid., 185.

24. Ibid., 185–86.

25. Kristina Kausch, "An Islamist Government in Morocco?" FRIDE Democracy Backgrounder No. 11 (July 2007): 3.

26. Interview with ʿAbdalla Bagha, May 19, 2006.

27. According to Muhammad Darif, an expert on the Moroccan Islamist movement, Kamal Ibrahim, one of Mutiʾs top deputies, was arrested and tied to the murder.

28. Interview with Abd al-Qadir ʿUmara, May 14, 2006.

29. Eva Wegner (2004, 7) notes that the group was created informally in 1981 and officially in 1983.

30. Willis 1999, 46.

31. Interview with Muhammad Tozy, May 22, 2006.

32. Interview with Muhammad Darif, May 18, 2003.

33. Willis 1999, 49.

34. Ibid.; Wegner 2004, 7.

35. Interview with Muhammad Darif, May 18, 2003.

36. Interview with Abd al-Qadir ʿUmara, May 14, 2006.

37. Ryan 2002, 15.

38. Mufti 1999, 110.

39. Hamid 2005, 2.

40. The Jordanian National Charter, December 1990, http://www.kinghussein.gov.jo/.

41. On the Brotherhood's share of the popular vote, see Ahmad Jamil Azm, "The Islamic Action Front Party," in Hourani 1997, 98.

42. Schwedler 2006, 165.

43. Azm, "The Islamic Action Front Party," 98. Azm notes that in 1993 IAF candidates won about 150,000 votes, or about 18% of the total number of votes cast, compared with 250,000 votes, or 12% of the total, which the Islamic movement won in 1989. See also Ryan 2002, 28.

44. Schwedler 2006, 175; see also Hamid 2005, 9.

45. Hamid 2005, 9.

46. Ibid., 12.

47. Ryan 2008, 6.

48. Ibid., 7.

49. Shadi Hamid, "The Islamist Response to Repression: Are Mainstream Islamist Groups Radicalizing?" Brookings Doha Center Publications, no. 5, August 9, 2010.

50. Ryan 2008, 8.

51. Muhammad Abu Rumman, "Jordan's Parliamentary Elections and the Islamist Boycott," *Arab Reform Bulletin*, Carnegie Endowment for International Peace, October 20, 2010.

52. Ibid.

53. Hamid 2005, 11–12.

54. Juan J. E. Stemmann, "The Crossroads of Muslim Brothers in Jordan," *MERIA Journal*, March 4, 2010.

55. Hamid 2005, 16.

56. Stemmann, "The Crossroads of Muslim Brothers in Jordan," 4; Hamid 2005, 11, 13, 17.

57. Hamid 2005, 15.

58. Interview with Abd al-Latif ʿArabiyyat, June 29, 2004.

59. Interview with ʿAzzam Huneidi, June 29, 2004.

60. Interview with Sheikh Hamza Mansour, July 1, 2004. The same argument was made, in different words, by Abd al-Latif ʿArabiyyat (interview, June 29, 2004) and Raheel Gharaibeh (interview, June 30, 2004) as well.

61. Interview with Sheikh Hamza Mansour, July 1, 2004. Likewise, ʿAzzam Huneidi averred that "most of the people want a system based on Shariʿa" (interview, June 29, 2004).

62. Interview with Sheikh Hamza Mansour, July 1, 2004.

63. Ibid.

64. Interview with ʿAzzam Huneidi, June 29, 2004.

65. Warrick 2009, 77–78.

66. Ibid., 76. See the section titled "Jordan" in Amnesty International Annual Report 2004 and "Honoring the Killers: Justice Denied for 'Honor' Crimes in Jordan," http://hrw.org/, April 20, 2004. Women's rights activists stress that the proper target of reform should have been Article 98 of the penal code, which permits a reduction in the penalty for crimes committed in a "fit of rage" caused by an unrightful and dangerous act by the victim. It is Article 98, rather than Article 340, that is most frequently invoked by judges in "honor crimes" cases. Interview with Rana Husseini, June 29, 2004. See also Amnesty International's 2004 Annual Report.

67. Interview with Abd al-Latif ʿArabiyyat, June 29, 2004. The same point was made

by Raheel Gharaibeh in an interview on June 30, 2004. See also the interview with Abd al-Latif 'Arabiyyat in Human Rights Watch, "Honoring the Killers."

68. Interview with Raheel Gharaibeh, June 30, 2004.

69. "House Rejects Khuloe Law by a Narrow Margin," *Jordan Times*, June 28, 2004.

70. Rana Husseini, "House Rejection of Khuloe Law Dismays Human Rights Activists," *Jordan Times*, June 29, 2004.

71. Interview with Abd al-Latif 'Arabiyyat, June 29, 2004. Hayat al-Misimi, 'Azzam Huneidi, Hamza Mansour, and Raheel Gharaibeh expressed similar concerns about the bill in my interviews with them, and Reem Abu Hasan, a lawyer and women's rights activist, highlighted the nature of the IAF's objections to the bill in an interview on July 3, 2004.

72. Interview with Rana Husseini, June 29, 2004.

73. Ibid.

74. Interview with Marwan Fawri, July 3, 2004.

75. Ibid.

76. Ibid.

77. Interview with Bassam 'Emoush, June 29, 2004.

78. Hasan Abu Hanieh, *Women and Politics: From the Perspective of Islamist Movements in Jordan* (Amman, Jordan: Friedrich-Ebert-Stiftung, 2008), 98.

79. Ibid., 113–14. See also Lisa Taraki, "Jordanian Islamists and the Agenda for Women: Between Discourse and Practice," *Middle Eastern Studies* 32, no. 1 (January 1996): 155–56.

80. Clark and Schwedler 2003, 301–2.

81. Abu Hanieh, *Women and Politics*, 102.

82. In 2007, the Brotherhood's list of twenty-seven candidates for parliament included two women, though neither of them won a seat. In 2010 the IAF boycotted the parliamentary elections.

83. Interview with Hayat al-Misimi, June 30, 2004.

84. Interview with Bassam 'Emoush, June 29, 2004.

85. Interview with Nawal Fawri, July 4, 2004.

86. Ibid.

87. Interview with Marwan Fawri, July 3, 2004.

88. The conference was formally sponsored by the International Assembly for Moderation in Islam, a nongovernmental association affiliated with the Jordanian Wasat party.

89. Interview with Marwan Fawri, July 3, 2004.

90. Interview with Nawal Fawri, July 4, 2004.

91. See Brown and Hamzawy 2010, 55.

92. Interview with Hani Hourani, July 4, 2004.

93. Abu Hanieh, *Women and Politics*, 101–2.

94. Interview with Hayat al-Misimi, June 30, 2004.

95. Baaklini, Denoeux, and Springborg 1999, 187.

96. Ibid.

97. Ibid., 188.

98. Brown and Hamzawy 2010, 111.

99. Interview with Muhammad Dalal, July 8, 2004.

100. Baaklini, Denoeux, and Springborg 1999, 189–90.

101. Michael Herb, Georgia State University, Kuwait Politics Database, http://www2
.gsu.edu/.

102. Baaklini, Denoeux, and Springborg 1999, 192.

103. Brown and Hamzawy 2010, 114.

104. Ghabra, "Balancing State and Society," 64.

105. Brown and Hamzawy 2010, 114–15.

106. Ibid., 66.

107. Ghabra, "Balancing State and Society," 65; Baaklini, Denoeux, and Springborg
1999, 195.

108. Ghabra, "Balancing State and Society," 66.

109. Interview with Mubarak Duwaileh, July 8, 2004.

110. Interview with Ghanim al-Najjar, July 5, 2004.

111. Ghabra, "Balancing State and Society," 67–68.

112. Ibid., 68.

113. Interview with Ahmad al-Baghdadi, July 8, 2004.

114. Interview with Muhammad Dalal, July 8, 2004.

115. Phil Reeves, "Hardliners Defeat Votes for Kuwait's Women," *The Independent*,
November 24, 1999.

116. Interview with Badir al-Nashi', July 10, 2004; this point was also made by Nasser
al-Sani' during my interview with him on July 10, 2004.

117. Huda Fawzi, "Al Ghabra Stirs a Hornet's Nest," *Gulf News*, February 22, 2002.

118. Interview with Nasser al-Sani', July 10, 2004.

119. Interview with Muhammad Dalal, July 8, 2004.

120. Confidential cable from the U.S. Embassy in Kuwait to the Department of State,
April 18, 2004, http://wikileaks.org/.

121. Interview with Nasser al-Sani', July 10, 2004.

122. Ibid.

123. Interview with Muhammad Dalal, July 8, 2004.

124. Interview with Mubarak Duwaileh, July 8, 2004.

125. Interview with Isma'il al-Shati', July 7, 2004.

126. Interview with Ahmad al-Baghdadi, July 8, 2004. A similar argument was made
by 'Abdalla Nubairi in an interview on July 10, 2004.

127. "Kuwait: Interview with Dr. Badr al-Nashi, President of the Islamic Constitutional Movement," *Arab Reform Bulletin* 4, no. 3 (April 2006), http://carnegieendow
ment.org/.

128. "Kuwaiti Islamists Launch Campaign to Enlist Support of Women," AMAN
News Center, July 5, 2004.

129. Brown and Hamzawy 2010, 125.

130. "Kuwait: Interview with Dr. Badr al-Nashi."

131. Interview with Ahmad Bishara, July 7, 2004.

132. Interview with Khalil Haydar, July 8, 2004.

133. Interview with Ahmad al-Diyyan, July 9, 2004.

134. Brown and Hamzawy 2010, 118–19. Most press reports note that the ICM won
only one seat in 2009; see, for example, Mary Ann Tétreault and Mohammed Al-
Ghanim, "The Day after 'Victory': Kuwait's 2009 Election and the Contentious Present,"
http://www.merip.org/, July 8, 2009. Brown and Hamzawy contend that the group won

two seats. Nevertheless, they note that one of the two deputies owed his seat more to his success in his district's tribal primary than to his ICM affiliation.

135. "Kuwait HADAS to Choose Its New Leader on August 1st," http://www.ikhwan web.com/, July 13, 2009.

136. "Humbled by Voters, Kuwait's Islamists Regroup," *The National*, May 26, 2010.

137. Ibid.

138. Interview with Khalil Haydar, July 8, 2004.

139. Interview with Ahmad al-Baghdadi, July 8, 2004.

140. Ottaway and Riley 2006, 6.

141. Maddy-Weitzman 2005, 402.

142. Ibid., 403.

143. Ibid.

144. Harrak 2009, 5.

145. Interview with Abu Bakr al-Jami'i, May 17, 2006.

146. Willis 2004b, 57.

147. Willis 2004a, 9.

148. Willis 2004b, 60.

149. Willis, 2004a, 10.

150. Ibid.

151. Ibid., 12.

152. Ibid.

153. Ibid., 13.

154. Wegner 2004, 18. According to Wegner, the PJD ran candidates in less than 10% of the districts. See also Willis 2004a, 13.

155. Wegner 2004, 18–19.

156. Interview with 'Abdalla Benkirane, May 23, 2006.

157. Maddy-Weitzman 2005, 406.

158. Ibid., 404.

159. Interview with Abd al-Qadir 'Umara, May 14, 2006.

160. Interview with Abu Bakr al-Jam'i, May 17, 2006

161. Interview with 'Aziz Rbah, May 19, 2006.

162. Willis 2004a, 13–14.

163. Interview with Muhammad Tozy, May 22, 2006.

164. Interview with Abu Bakr al-Jami'i, May 17, 2006.

165. Ali Bouzerda, Reuters, September 29, 2002.

166. Interview with Muhammad Darif, May 18, 2006.

167. Interview with 'Aziz Rbah, May 19, 2006.

168. Interview with 'Abdalla Bagha, May 19, 2006.

169. Interview with Muhammad Yatim, May 23, 2006.

170. Interview with Muhammad Hafid, May 20, 2006.

171. Interview with Abu Bakr al-Jami'i, May 17, 2006.

172. Interview with 'Abdalla Benkirane, May 23, 2006.

173. Ibid.

174. Interview with Jamal Hashim, May 20, 2006.

175. Interview with 'Aziz Rbah, May 19, 2006.

176. Wegner 2004, 15.

177. Ibid., 19.

178. Interview with Mustafa Bu Hindi, May 20, 2006.

179. Ibid.

180. Interview with Muhammad Yatim, May 23, 2006.

181. Interview with Muhammad Hafid, May 20, 2006.

182. Interview with Abu Bakr al-Jami'i, May 17, 2006.

183. Willis 2008, 12.

184. Brown and Hamzawy 2010, 101.

185. Willis 2008, 14.

186. Ibid., 8.

187. Zahir Rahman, "Morocco's Bottom-Up Movement for Reform," http://mideast.foreignpolicy.com/, December 13, 2011.

188. Siham Ali, "Moroccans Approve New Constitution," http://magharebia.com/, July 4, 2011.

189. Mawassi Lahcen, "Morocco Vote Reveals Changing Electorate," http://magharebia.com/, December 2, 2011.

190. Siham Ali, "Benkirane to Head New Moroccan Government," http://magharebia.com/, November 30, 2011.

191. Hassan Benmehdi and Siham Ali, "Morocco Reflects on Election Results," http://magharebia.com/, November 29, 2011.

192. Omar Brouksy, "Moroccan King Unveils Islamist-Led Government," Agence France Presse, January 4, 2012.

193. "Morocco's New Cabinet Held Up Over Key Jobs," Reuters, December 30, 2011.

CHAPTER NINE

THE MUSLIM BROTHERHOOD IN (EGYPT'S) TRANSITION

1. "Preliminary Report on All Three Phases of the People's Assembly Elections," Carter Center Election Witnessing Mission, Egypt 2011/2012 Parliamentary Elections, January 24, 2012, http://www.cartercenter.org/.

2. "Democratic Alliance for Egypt," Egyptian Elections Watch, November 18, 2011, http://www.jadaliyya.com/.

3. Ibid.

4. "Freedom and Justice Party," http://www.jadaliyya.com/, February 2, 2011.

5. Noha El-Hennawy, "Brotherhood Contests over 50 Percent of Parliamentary Seats," Egypt Independent, October 25, 2011.

6. Yasmine El Rashidi, "Choosing Egypt's Future," New York Review of Books blog, December 3, 2011, http://www.nybooks.com/.

7. Ibid.; Carter Center, "Carter Center Preliminary Statement on the First Round of Voting in Egypt's People's Assembly Elections," http://www.cartercenter.org/, December 2, 2011.

8. El Rashidi, "Choosing Egypt's Future."

9. Ibid.

10. Nadine Marroushi, "Against Expectations, Salafis Score High," Egypt Independent, February 7, 2012. See also Ursula Lindsey, "Ultraconservative Islamist Party Reshapes Egypt's Politics," Daily Beast, December 8, 2011.

11. David D. Kirkpatrick, "In Egypt, a Conservative Appeal Transcends Religion," *New York Times*, December 10, 2011.

12. "Results of Egypt's People's Assembly Elections," Guide to Egypt's Transition, Carnegie Endowment for International Peace, http://egyptelections.carnegieendow ment.org/.

13. Zeinab El Gundy, "Freedom and Justice Party Heads Most of Egypt's Parliamentary Committees," http://english.ahram.org.eg/, January 31, 2012; Gamal 'Esam El-Din, "Islamist Takeover at the People's Assembly," *Al-Ahram Weekly*, no. 1083, February 2–8, 2012.

14. Kristen Chick, "Egyptian Court Ruling Raises Stakes in Presidential Race," *Christian Science Monitor*, April 11, 2012.

15. Eric Trager, "Egypt's Muslim Brotherhood Pursues a Political Monopoly," Policywatch Brief No. 1918, April 4, 2012, http://www.washingtoninstitute.org/; Chick, "Egyptian Court Ruling"; Mara Revkin and Yussef Auf, "Beyond the Ballot Box: Egypt's Constitutional Challenge," Atlantic Council, Rafik Hariri Center for the Middle East, June 12, 2012.

16. Trager, "Egypt's Muslim Brotherhood Pursues a Political Monopoly."

17. Leila Fadel, "Liberals and Leftists Resign from Constitution-Writing Panel in Egypt," *Washington Post*, March 25, 2012.

18. Ibid.

19. Bradley Hope, "Egyptian Constitution Suspended," *The National*, April 11, 2012.

20. "Egypt's Muslim Brotherhood Faces Sharp Internal Divisions over Presidential Race," *Washington Post*, March 26, 2012; Kristen Chick, "In Major Reversal, Muslim Brotherhood Will Vie for Egypt's Presidency," *Christian Science Monitor*, April 1, 2012.

21. "Muslim Brotherhood Split on Fielding a Candidate in Egypt's Presidential Election," *Los Angeles Times*, March 27, 2012.

22. "Brotherhood to Run for Egypt's Presidency," http://www.aljazeera.com, April 1, 2012.

23. "In Major Reversal, Muslim Brotherhood Will Vie for Egypt's Presidency."

24. David D. Kirkpatrick, "Keeper of Islamist Flame Rises as Egypt's New Decisive Voice," *New York Times*, March 12, 2012.

25. Revkin and Auf, "Beyond the Ballot Box," 3.

26. Leila Fadel, "Disqualified Candidate Says Egypt's Military Rulers Have No Intention of Ceding Power," *Washington Post*, April 18, 2012.

27. Jon Leyne, "Egypt Election Bans Threaten Fresh Political Turmoil," BBC News, April 17, 2012.

28. Paul Armstrong, "Ban on Egyptian Presidential Candidates Upheld," http://www.cnn.com, April 20, 2012.

29. Kristen Chick, "Egyptian Presidential Candidate: Mohamed Morsi of the Muslim Brotherhood," *Christian Science Monitor*, June 1, 2012.

30. Carter Center 2012b, 1–8. However, the Carter Center emphasized that no candidate agents, international or domestic observers, or media personnel were allowed to witness the aggregation of the national vote at the Cairo headquarters of the PEC.

31. Nancy A. Youssef and Hanna Allam, "Revolutionaries Dismayed by Apparent Result of Egyptian Presidential Vote," http://www.miamiherald.com/, May 25, 2012,

32. Statistics from "Judges for Egypt" (http://www.egyptpresident2012.com/). For

further analysis of Sabahi's success, see Dina K. Hussein and Hesham Sallam, "Roundtable: The Presidential Poll, Unpacked," http://www.jadaliyya.com/, June 8, 2012; Ekram Ibrahim, "Why Did Sabahi—'One of Us'—Do So Well?" http://english.ahram.org.eg/, May 25, 2012.

33. Speaking of Shafiq's second-place showing, Egyptian political analyst Issandr al-Emrani observed, "There still remain patronage networks that we didn't see at work in the parliamentary elections, where the old NDP—the former ruling party—networks did not perform well. But they seem to have come back with a vengeance in this election." Sharif Abdel Kouddous, "Egypt's Polarizing Presidential Elections," *The Nation*, June, 1, 2012. On Shafiq's mobilization of NDP patronage networks in the Delta, see Rana Khazbak and Mohamed Elmeshad, "Tried and True: Shafiq Campaign Takes a Few Pages from the NDP Handbook," *Egypt Independent*, June 14, 2012.

34. "Judges for Egypt"; see also "Egypt's Run-Off Scenarios," *Democracy Digest*, June 6, 2012.

35. "Egypt's Third Runner-Up Seeks Election Suspension," http://www.alarabiya .net/, May 26, 2012; "Eliminated Candidates Sabahi, Aboul-Fotouh and Ali Complain of Electoral Violations," http://english.ahram.org.eg/, June 4, 2012. The number of military and police officers rumored to have voted illegally ranged from 600,000 to 1.5 million.

36. "Commission Confirms Results of Egyptian Presidential Vote," *Los Angeles Times*, May 28, 2012, http://latimesblogs.latimes.com/.

37. Abdel Kouddous, "Egypt's Polarizing Presidential Elections."

38. "The Failings of Egypt's Arab Spring Revolution," http://www.dw.de/, June 17, 2012; David Ignatius, "In Egypt, a Sense of Dread," *Washington Post*, June 14, 2012.

39. "Egypt's Third Runner-Up Seeks Election Suspension."

40. "Boycott Camp Hopes to Lower Turnout, Strip Vote's Legitimacy," *Egypt Independent*, June 6, 2012; "El Baradei: The Real Battle Is to Write Constitution, Cancel Election," *Egypt Independent*, June 5, 2012; Dina 'Ezzat, "Countdown to the Unknown," *Al-Ahram Weekly*, June 14–20, 2012.

41. "Egypt's Run-Off Scenarios: Prospect of Chaos 'Should Be Alarming Policymakers,'" *Democracy Digest*, June 6, 2012.

42. "Morsy Makes 15 Pledges to Egyptians," *Egypt Independent*, June 13, 2012.

43. "Morsi: Presidential Institution, Egypt's New National Charter and New Cabinet Are for All Egyptians," http://www.ikhwanweb.com/, May 30, 2012.

44. Sara El-Rashidi, "Brotherhood Presidential Candidate Mursi Attempts to Mollify Women's Fears," http://www.awid.org/, June 5, 2012; see also Mursi's June 15 speech on Al-Jazeera, available on http://www.memri.org/.

45. 'Ezzat, "Countdown to the Unknown."

46. "Dissolution of Parliament 'Unconstitutional' El-Katatni Tells SCAF," http:// www.english.ahram.org.eg, June 14, 2012; Hamza Hendawi and Sarah el-Deeb, "Egypt Court Dissolves Islamist-Led Parliament," Associated Press, June 14, 2012.

47. Nancy A. Youssef, "Egyptian Court Rulings Seen as Reversal of Last Year's 'Revolution,'" http://www.mcclatchydc.com/, June 14, 2012.

48. Nathan Brown, "Judicial Turbulence Ahead in Egypt, Fasten Your Seatbelts," *Commentary*, Carnegie Endowment for International Peace, June 6, 2012.

49. David D. Kirkpatrick, "Egyptian Court Sentences Mubarak to Life in Prison," *New York Times*, June 2, 2012.

50. Mara Revkin, "Egypt's Injudicious Judges," http://mideast.foreignpolicy.com/,

June 11, 2012. On the Brotherhood's reaction to the verdict, see also "Freedom and Justice Party Statement on Shocking Verdict in Martyr Killers' Case," http://www.ikhwan web.com/, June 2, 2012.

51. Revkin, "Egypt's Injudicious Judges."

52. Youssef, "Egyptian Court Rulings."

53. Brown, "Judicial Turbulence Ahead."

54. Haram-Giza Aggregation Center #7.

55. At the aggregation center, Mursi agents told us that with 97% of the vote counted, Mursi had won by 1.2 million votes. According to the official results, the difference was 900,000 votes.

56. "Muslim Brotherhood Claims Victory in Egyptian Presidential Vote," http://www.cnn.com/, June 17, 2012. See also "Relive the Intense Vote-by-Vote Count in Egypt's 1st Post-Mubarak Presidential Race," http://english.ahram.org.eg/, June 18, 2012, and "Live Updates: Morsy Leads in Upper Egypt, Shafiq in Lower Egypt," http://www.egyptindependent.com/, June 18, 2012.

57. English text of the June 17 supplement appended to the "Media Brief Update" of June 18, 2012, Carter Center, Atlanta, Georgia. These media updates were prepared by the Carter Center for members of the center's international election observation team during the presidential runoff.

58. "Egypt's New President Won't Be a Cipher, Claims Ruling Junta," http://english .ahram.org.eg/, June 18, 2012.

59. Abdel-Rahman Hussein, "Too Many Chefs," *Egypt Independent*, June 14, 2012.

60. Fadel, "Liberals and Leftists Resign from Constitution-Writing Panel in Egypt."

61. Hussein, "Too Many Chefs."

62. Ibid.

63. Ramadan al-Sherbini, "Mursi Woos Tahrir Crowd with Symbolic Oath before Inauguration," http://gulfnews.com/, June 29, 2012; Dina 'Ezzat, "Mursi's First Messages," http://weekly.ahram.org.eg/, July 5–11, 2012.

64. President Mohamed Morsi's speech at Cairo University, Saturday, June 30, after taking oath of office, http://www.ikhwanweb.com/, July 1, 2012.

65. Gamal 'Esam El Din, "Inching Towards a Showdown?" *Al-Ahram Weekly*, July 12–18, 2012, no. 1106.

66. Ibid.

67. Abdul Sattar Hatitaa, "Mursi and Al-Katatni Could Be Imprisoned—Egyptian Judge," http://www.asharq-e.com/news, July 31, 2012.

68. Ashraf Khalil, "Egypt's Overhyped Parliamentary Showdown," *Daily Beast*, July 11, 2012.

69. Khaled Dawoud, "Turned Down," http://weekly.ahram.org.eg/, July 12–18, 2012.

70. Youssef, "Egyptian Court Rulings."

71. Samer Shehata, "President Morsi under Brotherhood Siege," http://english .ahram.org.eg/, July 15, 2012.

72. Kareem Fahim, "In Upheaval for Egypt, Morsi Forces Out Military Chiefs," *New York Times*, August 12, 2012; Marc Lynch, "Lamborghini Morsi," http://www.foreign policy.com/, August 13, 2012.

73. Hesham Sallam, "Morsy, the Coup and the Revolution: Reading between the Red Lines," http://www.jadaliyya.com/, August 15, 2012.

74. Ibid.

75. Rana Mamdouh, "Egypt: Keeping Tabs on Mursi's Promises," http://english
.al-akhbar.com/, July 3, 2012.

76. "'Clean Homeland' Campaign Launched Today in Cairo and Other Governorates," http://www.ikhwanweb.com/, July 27, 2012.

77. Jon Donnison, "Egyptian President Mursi's 100-Day Plan Hits Traffic," BBC
News Middle East, August 8, 2012.

78. Interview with 'Ali Shari'i, Mursi campaign agent, "With the Tourism Sector"
conference, Meridien Pyramids Hotel, Cairo, June 14, 2012. See also "Morsy Aims to
Increase Number of Tourists Visiting Egypt to 20 Million," http://www.ikhwanweb
.com/, June 15, 2012.

79. "Egypt PM to Announce Cabinet on Thursday," ArabNews, July 28, 2012.

80. For a sharp analysis of Egypt's economic challenges, see Thomas L. Friedman,
"Political Islam without Oil," New York Times, January 10, 2012.

81. Sennott, "Inside the Muslim Brotherhood: Part I."

82. Geoffrey Kemp, "Egypt's Demographic and Environmental Time Bombs," National Interest, July 6, 2012.

83. Ibid.

84. Sherine Tadros, "Time for Egypt's Economic Revolution," http://blogs.aljazeera
.com/, January 12, 2012.

85. David D. Kirkpatrick and May el Sheikh, "Economic Crisis Adds Dangers on
Egypt's New Political Path," New York Times, January 24, 2012.

86. Ibid.

87. Friedman, "Political Islam without Oil."

88. Susie al-Juneidi, "Khairat al-Shater to Al Ahram: We Are Not at War with Any-
one," http://www.ikhwanweb.com/, January 29, 2012. See also the similar statements by
'Esam al-'Aryan as reported in Yolande Knell, "Egypt's Muslim Brotherhood Faces
Fresh Political Fight," BBC News, Cairo, September 8, 2011.

89. 'Ezzat, "Mursi's First Messages."

90. Ibid.

91. See, for example, David Pollock, "Egypt's Muslim Brotherhood and Its Record
of Double Talk," Washington Post, January 26, 2012.

92. Raymond Ibrahim, "Muslim Brotherhood Declares 'Mastery of the World' as
Ultimate Goal," Jihad Watch, January 12, 2002, http://www.meforum.org/; "Muslim
Brotherhood Leader: We Are Getting Closer to Reaching Banna's Greatest Goal of Es-
tablishing the Caliphate," http://www.copticsolidarity.org/, January 10, 2012.

93. Friedman, "Political Islam without Oil."

94. Martin S. Indyk, "Prospects for Democracy in Egypt" (Foreign Policy Trip Report no. 19, Brookings Institution, January 23, 2012).

95. See, for example, al-Juneidi, "Khayrat al-Shater" and Matthew Kaminski's interview with him, "Khayrat al Shater: The Brother Who Would Run Egypt," Wall Street
Journal, June 22, 2012.

96. Kaminski, "Khayrat al Shater."

97. "Khayrat al Shater: The Brother Who Would Run Egypt."

98. Jack Goldstone, "Cross-Class Coalitions and the Making of the Arab Revolts of
2011," Swiss Political Science Review 17, no. 4 (December 2011): 457–62.

List of Interviews

Egypt

All interviews took place in Cairo unless otherwise stated. All interviews cited in the book took place during 2000–2011, except for a 1997 interview with Aboul 'Ela Madi.

Abdalla Rozza, Ahmad. March 12, 2004
Abd al-Gawwad, Ahmad. July 18, 2011
Abd al-Karim, Salah. March 18, 2004
Abd al-Latif, Muhammad. July 10, 2005
Abd al-Magid, Wahid. March 15, 2004
Abd al-Raziq, Gasir. March 10, 2004, July 10, 2005
Abd al-Sattar, Sayyid. July 10, 2005
Abu al-Futouh, Abd al-Mun'im. November 16, 2000, March 14, 2004, July 12, 2005,
    July 5, 2008, April 5, 2011
'Ali, Abd al-Rahman. March 7, 2004
Al-'Aryan, 'Esam. March 14, 2004
Bayoumi, Rashad. May 2, 2010
Al-Badawi, Sayyid. April 8, 2011
Al-Biltagi, Muhammad. April 6, 2011
'Ezzat, Mahmoud. July 3, 2008
Fawzy, Ahmad. April 7, 2011
Ga'far, Hisham. March 14, 2004
Ghanim, Ibrahim Bayoumi. March 10, 2004
Ghuzlan, Mahmoud. July 19, 2011
Habib, Muhammad. July 13, 2005
Al-Hamami, Hisham. July 1, 2008
Hamza, Muhammad. July 16, 2011
Harb, Osama Ghazzali. November 5, 2000
Al-Hawwari, Anwar. November 5, 2000, March 11, 2004
Hilmi, Mustafa Kamal. November 18, 2000

Hudeibi, Ibrahim. April 28, 2010

'Isa, Salah. March 17, 2004

Ishaq, George. July 11, 2005

Al-Katatni, Muhammad Saʿd. May 2, 2010

Lutfi, Islam. July 19, 2011

Madi, Aboul 'Ela. July 2, 1997, November 11, 2000, March 16, 2004, June 26, 2004 (in Amman, Jordan), October 10, 2004 (in Lexington, Kentucky), July 13, 2005, July 1, 2008, July 5, 2008, May 1, 2010, April 5, 2011

Mahmoud, Abd al-Munʿim. July 3, 2008, April 30, 2010, July 14, 2011

Mihran, Ahmad. July 18, 2011

Mursi, Muhammad. May 1, 2010

Musa, ʿAmr. April 7, 2011

Al-Naggar, Mustafa. April 29, 2010

Al-Naggar, Sayyid. November 21, 2000

Nassar, Gamal. May 2, 2010

Qandil, Abd al-Halim. July 11, 2005

Qasim, Hisham. March 10, 2004, July 10, 2005, July 5, 2008, April 7, 2011

Qassas, Muhammad. July 18, 2011

Qodmani, Basma. March 15, 2004

Rishwan, Diya'. November 10, 2000, March 17, 2004, July 12, 2005, July 2008

Saʿeed, Muhammad Sayyid. March 10, 2004

Al-Saʿeed, Rifʿat. April 6, 2011

Sami, Sally. April 5, 2011

Shaʿban, Ahmad Baha'. March 15, 2004

Al-Shirbini, Mahmoud. July 16, 2011

Siman, Muhammad. March 9, 2004

Sultan, ʿEsam. March 8, 2004, July 12, 2005

Surour, Magid. April 6, 2011

Tammam, Hossam. July 2, 2008, April 28, 2010

Al-Zaʿfarani, Ibrahim. July 17, 2011

Zahran, Farid. March 13, 2004

Zulfiqar, Mona. April 5, 2011

Jordan

All interviews took place in Amman.

Abu Hasan, Reem. July 3, 2004

'Arabiyyat, Abd al-Latif. June 29, 2004

'Emoush, Bassam. June 29, 2004

Fawri, Marwan. July 3, 2004

Fawri, Nawal. July 4, 2004

Gharaibeh, Raheel. June 30, 2004
Hourani, Hani. July 4, 2004
Huneidi, 'Azzam. June 29, 2004
Husseini, Rana. June 29, 2004
Khawaldeh, 'Ali. June 26, 2004
Mansour, Hamza. July 1, 2004
Al-Misimi, Hayat. June 30, 2004
Al-Nimri, Jamil. June 28, 2004
Rintawi, 'Uraib. July 4, 2004

KUWAIT

All interviews took place in Kuwait City.

Al-'Ali, Khalida Muhammad. July 7, 2004
Al-Baghdadi, Ahmad. July 8, 2004
Bishara, Ahmad. July 7, 2004
Dalal, Muhammad. July 8, 2004
Al-Diyyan, Ahmad. July 9, 2004
Duwaileh, Mubarak. July 8, 2004
Haydar, Khalil. July 8, 2004
Mubarak, Masouma. July 8, 2004
Al-Mulla, Lulwa. July 6, 2004
Al-Najjar, Ghanim. July 5, 2004, July 10, 2004
Al-Nashi', Badir. July 10, 2004
Nubairi, 'Abdalla. July 10, 2004
Al-Sani', Nasser. July 10, 2004
Al-Shati', Isma'il. July 7, 2004

MOROCCO

All interviews took place in Casablanca and Rabat, unless otherwise stated.
Al-Jami'i, Abu Bakr. May 17, 2006
Bagha, 'Abdalla. May 19, 2006
Benkirane, 'Abdalla. May 23, 2006
Benrahman, Jamal. May 17, 2006, May 22, 2006
Bu Hindi, Mustafa. May 20, 2006
Darif, Muhammad. May 18, 2006
Hafid, Muhammad. May 20, 2006
Al-Haqqani, Bassima. May 22, 2006
Hashim, Jamal. May 20, 2006

Khalfi, Mustafa. May 5, 2006 (Washington, D.C.)
Mu'tasim, Mustafa. May 20, 2006
Rbah, 'Aziz. May 19, 2006
Tozy, Muhammad. May 22, 2006
'Umara, Abd al-Qadir. May 14, 2006
Yassin, Nadia. May 23, 2006 (Sale, Morocco)
Yatim, Muhammad. May 23, 2006

Selected Bibliography

ENGLISH SOURCES

Abdalla, Ahmad. 1985. *The Student Movement and National Politics in Egypt, 1923–1973*. London: Al-Saqi Books.

———. 1993. "Egypt's Islamists and the State: From Complicity to Confrontation." *Middle East Report*, July–August.

———. 2003. "Democratization in Egypt." Visiting Research Fellow Monograph Series, No. 380. Institute of Developing Economies, Japan External Trade Organization, September.

Abed-Kotob, Sana. 1995. "The Accommodationists Speak: Goals and Strategies of the Muslim Brotherhood of Egypt." *International Journal of Middle East Studies* 27, no. 3 (August): 321–39.

"Abou-Fotouh: Reform According to Hassan Al Banna." 2006. http://www.ikhwanweb.com/.

Al-Anani, Khalil. 2008. "Brotherhood Bloggers: A New Generation Voices Dissent." *Arab Insight* 2, no. 1 (Winter 2008): 29–38.

———. 2009. "The Young Brotherhood in Search of a New Path." *Current Trends in Islamist Ideology*, vol. 9. http://www.current trends.org/.

Al-Awadi, Hisham. 2004. *In Pursuit of Legitimacy: The Muslim Brothers and Mubarak, 1982–2000*. London: Tauris Academic Studies.

Al-Sayyid, Mustapha Kamel. 2003. "The Other Face of the Islamist Movement." Democracy and Rule of Law Project, Carnegie Paper no. 33 (January): 1–28.

Albrecht, Holger, and Eva Wegner. 2006. "Autocrats and Islamists: Contenders and Containment in Egypt and Morocco." *Journal of North African Studies* 11, no. 2 (June).

Aly, Abdel Monem Said. 2007. "Understanding the Muslim Brothers in Egypt." Middle East Brief 27, Crown Center for Middle East Studies, Brandeis University, December.

Amghar, Samir. 2007. "Political Islam in Morocco." Centre for European Policy Studies, CEPS Working Document No. 269. June.

Anderson, Lisa. 1997. "Fulfilling Prophecies: State Policy and Islamist Radicalism." In *Political Islam: Revolution, Radicalism or Reform?*, ed. John Esposito. Boulder, CO: Lynne Reinner Publishers.

———, ed. 1999. *Transitions to Democracy*. New York: Columbia University Press.

Antar, Noha. 2006. "The Muslim Brotherhood's Success in the Legislative Elections in Egypt 2005: Reasons and Implications." Euro-MeSCo Paper, No. 51. October.

Asbeek Brusse, Wendy, and Jan Schoonenboom. 2006. "Islamic Activism and Democratization." *ISIM Review* 18, no. 1 (Autumn): 8–9.

Auda, Gehad. 1994. "The 'Normalization' of the Islamist Movement in Egypt from the 1970s to the Early 1990s." In *Accounting for Fundamentalisms: The Dynamic Character of Movements*, ed. Martin E. Marty and R. Scott Appleby, 374–412. The Fundamentalism Project. Vol. 4. Chicago: University of Chicago Press.

Azarva, Jeffrey. 2007. "The Problem of the Egyptian Muslim Brotherhood." AEI Outlook Series, November. http://www.aei.org/.

Azuri, L. 2007. "The Egyptian Regime vs. the Muslim Brotherhood." http://archive.front pagemag.com/, February 5.

Baaklini, Abdo, Guilain Denoeux, and Robert Springborg. 1999. *Legislative Politics in the Arab World: The Resurgence of Democratic Institutions*. Boulder, CO: Lynne Rienner.

Baker, Raymond William. 1990. *Sadat and After: Struggles for Egypt's Political Soul*. Cambridge, MA: Harvard University Press.

Barsalou, Judy. 2005. "Islamists at the Ballot Box: Findings from Egypt, Jordan, Kuwait, and Turkey." United States Institute of Peace, Special Report 144. July.

Beinin, Joel. 2005. "Political Islam and the New Global Economy: The Political Economy of an Egyptian Social Movement." *CR: The New Centennial Review* 5, no. 1: 111–39.

Bermeo, Nancy. 1992. "Democracy and the Lessons of Dictatorship." *Comparative Politics* 24, no. 3: 273–92.

———. 1997. "Myths of Moderation: Confrontation and Conflict during Democratic Transitions." *Comparative Politics* 29, no. 3: 305–22.

Bianchi, Robert. 1989. *Unruly Corporatism: Associational Life in Twentieth Century Egypt*. New York: Oxford University Press.

Browers, Michaelle L. 2009. *Political Ideology in the Arab World: Accommodation and Transformation*. New York: Cambridge University Press.

Brown, L. Carl. 2000. *Religion and State: The Muslim Approach to Politics*. New York: Columbia University Press.

Brown, Nathan J. 2008. "Do Islamists Have a Commitment Problem? Islamic Political Parties and Signaling Democratic Sincerity." Paper presented at Stanford University Freeman Spogli Institute for International Studies. February 12.

———. 2012. *When Victory Is Not an Option: Islamist Movements in Arab Politics*. Ithaca: Cornell University Press.

Brown, Nathan J., and ʿAmr Hamzawy. 2008. "The Draft Party Platform of the Egyptian Muslim Brotherhood: Foray into Political Integration or Retreat into Old Positions?" *Middle East Series*, no. 89 (January).

Brown, Nathan J., and ʿAmr Hamzawy. 2010. *Between Religion and Politics*. Washington, DC: Carnegie Endowment for International Peace.

Brown, Nathan J., ʿAmr Hamzawy, and Marina Ottaway. 2006. "Islamist Movements and the Democratic Process in the Arab World: Exploring the Gray Zones." Carnegie Paper no. 67, Carnegie Endowment for International Peace. March.

Brown, Nathan J., et al. 2011. "Roundtable: How Do Scholars Study Islamist Movements and How Should We Be Studying Them?" *International Journal of Middle East Studies* 43, no. 1 (February): 133–34.

Campagna, Joel. 1996. "From Accommodation to Confrontation: The Muslim Brotherhood in the Mubarak Years." *Journal of International Affairs* 50, no. 1 (Summer): 278–304.

Capoccia, Giovanni, and Daniel Ziblatt. 2010. "The Historical Turn in Democratization Studies: A New Research Agenda for Europe and Beyond." *Comparative Political Studies* 43, no. 8–9 (August/September): 931–68.

Carter Center. 2012a. "Carter Center Preliminary Statement on Egypt's Presidential Election." May 26. http://www.cartercenter.org/.

———. 2012b. "The Carter Center Releases Preliminary Statement on the Second Round of Egypt's Presidential Election." June 19.

Checkel, Jeffrey T. 1998. "The Constructivist Turn in International Relations Theory." *World Politics* 50, no. 2 (January): 324–48.

———. 1999a. "Sanctions, Social Learning and Institutions: Explaining State Compliance with the Norms of the European Human Rights Regime." ARENA Centre for European Studies, ARENA Working Paper 99/11. March 15.

———. 1999b. "Social Construction and Integration." *Journal of European Public Policy* 6, no. 4: 545–60.

———. 2001. "Why Comply? Social Learning and European Identity Change." *International Organization* 55, no. 3 (Summer): 553–88.

———. 2003. "'Going Native' in Europe?: Theorizing Social Interaction in European Institutions." *Comparative Political Studies* 36, no. 1–2 (February–March): 209–31.

———. 2005. "International Institutions and Socialization in Europe: Introduction and Framework." *International Organization* 59, no. 4 (2005): 801–26.

Al-Chobaki, 'Amr. 2006. "The Future of the Muslim Brotherhood in Egypt." Cairo: Al-Ahram Center for Political and Strategic Studies.

Choucair, Julia. 2006. "Illusive Reform: Jordan's Stubborn Stability." Carnegie Paper no. 76, Democracy and Rule of Law Project, Carnegie Endowment for International Peace. December.

Clark, Janine A. 2006. "The Conditions of Islamist Moderation: Unpacking Cross-Ideological Cooperation in Jordan." *International Journal of Middle East Studies* 38, no. 4 (November): 539–60.

Clark, Janine A., and Jillian Schwedler. 2003. "Who Opened the Window? Women's Activism in Islamist Parties." *Comparative Politics* 35, no. 3: 293–312.

Cleveland, William. 2004. *A History of the Modern Middle East*. 3rd ed. Boulder, CO: Westview Press.

Cook, Scott D. N., and Dvora Yanow. 1993. "Culture and Organizational Learning." *Journal of Management Inquiry* 2, no. 4 (December): 373–90.

Dahl, Robert, ed. 1973. *Regimes and Oppositions*. New Haven: Yale University Press.

Democracy Reporting International. 2012. "Egypt: Assessment of the Legal Framework for Presidential Elections." Briefing Paper 26. February.

Diamond, Larry, Marc F. Plattner, and Daniel Brumberg, eds. 2003. *Islam and Democracy in the Middle East*. Baltimore: Johns Hopkins University Press.

Egyptian Organization of Human Rights. 1996. "Democracy Jeopardized: The Egyptian Organization of Human Rights Account of Egypt's 1995 Parliamentary Elections." Cairo, Egypt.

Ehrenfeld, Rachel, and Alyssa A. Lappen. 2007. "The Muslim Brotherhood's Propaganda Offensive." *American Thinker*, August 29.

El-Ghobashy, Mona. 2005. "The Metamorphosis of the Egyptian Muslim Brothers." *International Journal of Middle East Studies* 37 (August): 373–95.

El-Said, Sabah. 1995. *Between Pragmatism and Ideology: The Muslim Brotherhood in Jordan, 1989–1994.* Washington Institute Policy Paper no. 39, Washington Institute for Near East Policy.

Elad-Altman, Israel. 2005. "Currents Trends in the Ideology of the Egyptian Muslim Brotherhood." http://www.hudson.org/, December 28.

——. 2006a. "Democracy, Elections and the Egyptian Muslim Brotherhood." *Current Trends in Islamist Ideology* 3 (February 16). http://www.currenttrends.org/.

——. 2006b. "The Egyptian Muslim Brotherhood after the 2005 Elections." *Current Trends in Islamist Ideology* 4 (November 1).

——. 2007. "The Crisis of the Arab Brotherhood." *Current Trends in Islamist Ideology* 6 (November 26).

[Ellis]. 2012a. "Political Conflict and Legal Maneuvering." *Nisralnasr: Occasional Thoughts on Middle Eastern and US Politics,* July 9. http://nisralnasr.blogspot.com/.

——. 2012b. "Round Two: A Quick Look at the Presidential Run-Off." *Nisralnasr: Occasional Thoughts on Middle Eastern and US Politics,* June 21. http://nisralnasr.blogspot.com/.

Esposito, John L. 1984. *Islam and Politics.* 4th ed. Syracuse: Syracuse University Press.

Finnemore, Martha, and Kathryn Sikkink. 1998. "International Norm Dynamics and Political Change." *International Organization* 52, no. 4 (Autumn): 887–917.

George, Alexander L., and Andrew Bennett. 2005. *Case Studies and Theory Development in the Social Sciences.* Cambridge, MA: MIT Press.

Ghabra, Shafeeq. 1994. "Democratization in a Middle Eastern State: Kuwait, 1993." *Middle East Policy* 3, no. 1: 102–19.

Ghoneim, Wael. 2012. *Revolution 2.0: The Power of the People Is Greater than the People in Power.* New York: Houghton Mifflin Harcourt.

Glennie, Alex, and David Mepham. 2007. "Reform in Morocco: The Role of Political Islamists." Institute for Public Policy Research, September.

Gorman, Anthony. 2003. *Historians, State and Politics in Twentieth Century Egypt: Contesting the Nation.* London: Routledge.

Guenena, Nemat. 1986. "The 'Jihad': An 'Islamic Alternative' in Egypt." *Cairo Papers in Social Science* 9, Monograph 2, Summer.

Guenena, Nemat, and Nadia Wassef. 2003. *Unfulfilled Promises: Women's Rights in Egypt.* Cairo: Population Council.

Guitta, Olivier. 2010. "Muslim Brotherhood Parties in the Middle East and North Africa (MENA) Region." Policy Brief, Centre for European Studies. September.

Hamid, Shadi. 2005. "New Democrats? The Political Evolution of Jordan's Islamists." Paper presented at "Democracy and Development: Challenges for the Islamic World." CSID Sixth Annual Conference, Washington, DC, April 22–23.

——. 2007. "Parting the Veil." *Democracy: A Journal of Ideas.* http://www.democracyjournal.org/.

Hamzawy, ʿAmr, and Nathan Brown. 2010. "The Egyptian Muslim Brotherhood: Islamist Participation in a Closing Political Environment." Carnegie Paper no. 19, Carnegie Endowment for International Peace. March.

Hamzawy, ʿAmr, and Marina Ottaway. 2009. "When Islamists Go into Politics." *Fletcher Forum of World Affairs* 33, no. 2 (Fall): 37–46.

Hamzawy, ʿAmr, Marina Ottaway, and Nathan J. Brown. 2007. "What Islamists Need to Be Clear About: The Case of the Egyptian Muslim Brotherhood." Policy Outlook, Carnegie Endowment for International Peace. February. http://www.carnegieendow ment.org/.

Harrick, Fatima. 2009. "The History and Significance of the New Moroccan Family Code." Working Paper No. 09-002, Roberta Buffett Center for International and Comparative Studies, Northwestern University.

High Administrative Court Decision (Rejecting the Wasat Party's Appeal). May 9, 1998. Copy in author's possession.

Hinnebusch, Raymond A., Jr. 1988. *Egyptian Politics under Sadat: The Post-Populist Development of an Authoritarian-Modernizing State*. Boulder, CO: Lynne Rienner.

Hourani, Hani, ed. 1997. *Islamic Movements in Jordan*. Amman, Jordan: Al Urdun- Al-Jadid Research Center.

Howard, Philip N., and Muzammil M. Hussain. 2011. "The Upheavals in Egypt and Tunisia: The Role of Digital Media." *Journal of Democracy* 22, no. 3 (July): 5–19.

Hudeibi, Muhammad Maʾmoun. 1997. *Politics in Islam*. 10th Ramadan City, Egypt: Islamic Publishing and Distribution House.

Huntington, Samuel. 1991. *The Third Wave: Democratization in the Late Twentieth Century*. Norman: University of Oklahoma Press.

Hurd, Ian. 1999. "Legitimacy and Authority in International Politics." *International Organization* 53, no. 2 (Spring): 379–408.

Ibrahim, Saad Eddin. 1995. "The Changing Face of Islamic Activism." *Civil Society* (May).

International Crisis Group. 2004. "Islamism in North Africa II: Egypt's Opportunity." Middle East and North Africa Briefing No. 13. April 20.

———. 2005. "Reforming Egypt: In Search of a Strategy." Middle East/North Africa Report No. 46. October 4.

———. 2008. "Egypt's Muslim Brothers: Confrontation or Integration?" Middle East/North Africa Report No. 76. June 18.

———. 2011. "Popular Protest in North Africa and the Middle East (I): Egypt Victorious?" Middle East/North Africa Report No. 101. February 24.

Johnson, James. 1993. "Is Talk Really Cheap? Prompting Conversation between Critical Theory and Rational Choice." *American Political Science Review* 87, no. 1: 74–86.

Johnston, Alastair Iain. 2001. "Treating International Institutions as Social Environments." *International Studies Quarterly* 45, no. 4 (December): 487–515.

———. 2005. "Conclusions and Extensions: Toward Mid-Range Theorizing and Beyond Europe." *International Organization* 59, no. 4: 1013–44.

Jupille, Joseph, James A. Caporaso, and Jeffrey T. Checkel. 2003. "Integrating Institutions: Rationalism, Constructivism, and the Study of the European Union." *Comparative Political Studies* 36, no. 1–2 (February): 7–40.

Kalyvas, Stathis N. 1998. "Democracy and Religious Politics: Evidence from Belgium." *Comparative Political Studies* 31, no. 3 (June): 292–320.

———. 1996. *The Rise of Christian Democracy in Europe*. Ithaca: Cornell University Press.

Kassem, Maye. 2004. *Egyptian Politics: The Dynamics of Authoritarian Rule*. Boulder, CO: Lynne Reinner.

Katznelson, Ira, and Barry R. Weingast, eds. 2002. *Preferences and Situations: Points of Intersection between Historical and Rational Choice Institutionalism*. New York: Russell Sage Foundation.

Kepel, Gilles. 1993. *Muslim Extremism in Egypt: The Prophet and Pharaoh*. Berkeley: University of California Press.

Khalil, Magdi. 2006. "Egypt's Muslim Brotherhood and Political Power: Would Democracy Survive?" *Middle East Review of International Affairs* 10, no. 1 (March).

Kienle, Eberhard. 1998. "More than a Response to Islamism: The Political Deliberalization of Egypt in the 1990s." *Middle East Journal* 52, no. 2 (Spring).

Knopf, Jeffrey W. 2003. "The Importance of International Learning." *Review of International Studies* 29, no. 2 (April): 185–207.

Kramer, Martin. 1997. "The Mismeasure of Political Islam." In *The Islamism Debate*, ed. Martin Kramer. Tel Aviv: Moshe Dayan Center for Middle Eastern and African Studies.

Kurzman, Charles, ed. 2002. *Modernist Islam: 1840–1940*. New York: Oxford University Press.

Langohr, Vickie. 2001. "Of Islamists and Ballot Boxes: Rethinking the Relationship between Islamisms and Electoral Politics." *International Journal of Middle East Studies* 33, no. 4 (November): 591–610.

Laskier, Michael M. 2003. "A Difficult Inheritance: Moroccan Society under King Muhammad VI." *Middle East Review of International Affairs* 7, no. 3 (September).

Leiken, Robert S., and Steven Brooke. 2007. "The Moderate Muslim Brotherhood." *Foreign Affairs* 86, no. 2 (March/April): 107–21.

Lewis, Jeffrey. 2003. "Institutional Environments and Everyday EU Decision Making: Rationalist or Constructivist?" *Comparative Political Studies* 36, no. 1–2 (February): 97–124.

Lia, Brynjar. 1998. *The Society of the Muslim Brothers in Egypt: The Rise of an Islamic Mass Movement, 1928–1942*. Reading, UK: Ithaca Press.

Lombardi, Clark B. 2006. *State Law as Islamic Law in Modern Egypt: The Incorporation of the Shari'a into Egyptian Constitutional Law*. Studies in Islamic Law and Society. Leiden: Brill.

Lynch, Marc. 2005. "Transnational Dialogue in an Age of Terror." *Global Society* 19, no. 1 (January): 5–28.

———. 2007. "Young Brothers in Cyberspace." *Middle East Report* 37, no. 245 (Winter). http://www.merip.org/.

———. 2008. "The Brotherhood's Dilemma." Middle East Brief No. 25, Crown Center for Middle East Studies, Brandeis University. January.

Madi, Aboul 'Ela. 2008. "The Wasat Party and Egyptian Politics." Unpublished manuscript, Sophia University, Tokyo. February 23.

Maddy-Weitzman, Bruce. 2005. "Women, Islam, and the Moroccan State: The Struggle over the Personal Status Law." *Middle East Journal* 59, no. 3 (Summer): 393–410.

Mahoney, James, and Dietrich Ruseschemeyer, eds. 2003. *Comparative Historical Analysis in the Social Sciences*. New York: Cambridge University Press.

Mainwaring, Scott. 1992. "Transitions to Democracy and Democratic Consolidation: Theoretical and Comparative Issues." In *Issues in Democratic Consolidation: The New South American Democracies in Comparative Perspective*, ed. Scott Mainwaring,

Guillermo O'Donnell, and J. Samuel Valenzuela. Notre Dame: University of Notre Dame Press, 1992.

———. 2003. "Party Objectives in Authoritarian Regimes with Elections or Fragile Democracies: A Dual Game." In *Christian Democracy in Latin America*, ed. Scott Mainwaring and Timothy R. Scully. Stanford: Stanford University Press.

Makram-Ebeid, Mona. 1989. "Political Opposition in Egypt: Democratic Myth or Reality?" *Middle East Journal* 43, no. 3 (Summer): 423–36.

———. 2001. "Egypt's 2000 Parliamentary Elections." *Middle East Policy* 8, no. 2 (June): 32–44.

Masoud, Tarek. 2008. "Islamist Parties: Are They Democrats? Does It Matter?" *Journal of Democracy* 19, no. 3 (July).

McAdam, Doug, Sidney Tarrow, and Charles Tilly. 2001. *Dynamics of Contention.* New York: Cambridge University Press.

McCoy, Jennifer L., ed. 2000. *Political Learning and Re-Democratization in Latin America: Do Political Leaders Learn from Political Crises?* Coral Gables: North-South Center Press, University of Miami.

Mecham, R. Quinn. 2004. "From the Ashes of Virtue, a Promise of Light: The Transformation of Political Islam in Turkey." *Third World Quarterly* 25, no. 2 (April): 339–58.

Mitchell, Richard P. 1969. *The Society of the Muslim Brothers.* New York: Oxford University Press.

Moaddel, Mansour. 2002. *Jordanian Exceptionalism: A Comparative Analysis of State-Religion Relationships in Egypt, Iran, Jordan and Syria.* New York: Palgrave.

Moussalli, Ahmed. 1999. *Moderate and Radical Islamic Fundamentalism: The Quest for Modernity, Legitimacy and the Islamic State.* Gainesville: University of Florida Press.

Mufti, Malik. 1999. "Elite Bargains and the Onset of Political Liberalization in Jordan." *Comparative Political Studies* 32, no. 1 (February).

"Muslim Brotherhood Initiative: On the General Principles of Reform in Egypt." 2004. Cairo: Muslim Brotherhood. March.

Nasira, Hani. 2011. "The Internal Crisis of the Muslim Brotherhood in Egypt." *Terrorism Monitor* 9, no. 16 (April 22).

Nasr, Vali. 2005. "The Rise of Muslim Democracy." *Journal of Democracy* 16, no. 2 (April): 13–27.

Norton, Augustus Richard. 2004. "Thwarted Politics: The Case of Egypt's Hizb Al-Wasat." In *Re-Thinking Muslim Politics: Pluralism, Contestation, Democratization*, ed. Robert Hefner. Princeton: Princeton University Press.

Olson, Joel. 2008. "Democratic Extremism: Abolitionists, Abortionists, and the Democratic Uses of Fanaticism." Paper presented at "Democracy and Extremism: An International Conference." Georgia State University, Atlanta. June 11–13.

Ottaway, Marina, and Meredith Riley. 2006. "Morocco: From Top-Down Reform to Democratic Transition?" Carnegie Paper no. 71, Carnegie Endowment for International Peace. September.

Oweidat, Nadia, et al. 2008. *The Kefaya Movement: A Case Study of a Grassroots Reform Initiative.* Santa Monica, CA: National Defense Research Institute, Rand Corporation.

Pargeter, Alison. 2010. *The Muslim Brotherhood: The Burden of Tradition.* London: Saqi Books.

"Parliamentary Election Assessment in Egypt, November 15–21, 2005." 2005. Washington, DC: International Republican Institute.

Pearse, Hilary. 2007. "Majoritarian Parties in Multi-Party Parliaments." Paper presented at the Canadian Political Science Association Annual Conference, May 30–June 1.

Pioppi, Daniela. 2011. "Is There an Islamist Alternative in Egypt?" IAI Working Papers 11/03, Istituto Affari Internazionali.

Pipes, Daniel. 1995. "There Are No Moderates: Dealing with Fundamentalist Islam." *The National Interest*, no. 41 (Fall).

Piscatori, James, and John L. Esposito. 1991. "Democratization and Islam." *Middle East Journal* 45, no. 3: 427–40.

Prentice, Patricia. "Article 2 of the Egyptian Constitution." Arab-West Academic Papers. http://www.arabwestfoundation.com/.

"The Primacy of Values: A Conversation with Ibrahim al-Houdaiby." 2010. *Currents Trends in Islamist Ideology* 10 (June 9). http://www.currenttrends.org/.

Pruzan-Jørgensen, Julie E. 2010. "The Islamist Movement in Morocco: Main Actors and Regime Responses." DIIS Report 2010:05, Danish Institute for International Studies.

Przeworski, Adam. 1985. *Capitalism and Social Democracy*. New York: Cambridge University Press.

Przeworski, Adam, and John Sprague. 1988. *Paper Stones: A History of Electoral Socialism*. Chicago: University of Chicago Press.

Al-Qumni, Sayed Mahmoud. 2004. "The Muslim Brotherhood's Initiative as a Reform Program: A Critical Review." Conference on Islamic Reform, Saban Center for Middle East Policy, Brookings Institution, Washington, DC. October 5–6.

Qutb, Sayyid. 1978. *Milestones* [English translation of *Ma'alim Fii al-Tariq*]. Salimiah, Kuwait: International Islamic Federation of Student Organizations.

Rabi, Amre Hashem. 2005. "Electoral Systems and Parliamentary Elections in Egypt." In *Building Democracy in Egypt: Women's Political Participation, Political Party Life and Democratic Elections*, ed. Hala Mustafa, Abd al-Ghaffar Shukor, and Amre Hashem Rabi. IDEA and Arab NGO Network for Development. http://www.idea.int/.

Ramadan, Abdel Azim. 2004. "Fundamentalist Influence in Egypt: The Strategies of the Muslim Brotherhood and the Takfir Groups." In *Fundamentalisms and the State: Remaking Polities, Economies, and Militance*, ed. Martin E. Marty and R. Scott Appleby, 152–83. The Fundamentalism Project. Vol. 3. Chicago: University of Chicago Press.

Rapp, Laurel. 2008. "The Challenges and Opportunities Moroccan Islamist Movements Pose to Women's Political Participation." Center for the Study of Islam and Democracy. May 14.

Raymond, Gregory A. 1997. "Problems and Prospects in the Study of International Norms." *Mershon International Studies Review* 41, no. 2 (November): 205–45.

Revkin, Mara, and Yussef Auf. 2012. "Beyond the Ballot Box: Egypt's Constitutional Challenge." Issue Brief. Atlantic Council, Rafik Hariri Center for the Middle East. June 12.

Roberts, Kenneth M. 1995. "From the Barricades to the Ballot Box: Re-Democratization and Political Re-Alignment in the Chilean Left." *Politics and Society* 23:495–519.

Robinson, Glenn E. 1997. "Can Islamists Be Democrats?: The Case of Jordan." *Middle East Journal* 51, no. 3 (Summer).

Rubin, Barry. 2007. "Comparing Three Muslim Brotherhoods: Syria, Jordan, Egypt." *Middle East Review of International Affairs* 11, no. 2 (June).

Rutherford, Bruce K. 2006. "What Do Egypt's Islamists Want? Moderate Islam and the Rise of Islamic Constitutionalism." *Middle East Journal* 60, no. 4 (Autumn): 707–31.

———. 2008. *Egypt after Mubarak: Liberalism, Islam and Democracy in the Arab World.* Princeton: Princeton University Press.

Ryan, Curtis R. 2002. *Jordan in Transition: From Hussein to Abdullah.* Boulder, CO: Lynne Rienner.

———. 2008. "Islamist Political Activism in Jordan: Moderation, Militancy, and Democracy." *Middle East Review of International Affairs* 12, no. 2 (June).

Said, Muhammad al-Sayed. 1995. *The Arab Strategic Report of 1994.* Cairo: Al-Ahram Center for Political and Strategic Studies.

Salamé, Ghassan, ed. 1994. *Democracy without Democrats? The Renewal of Politics in the Muslim World.* London: I. B. Tauris.

Salih, M. A. Mohamed, ed. 2009. *Interpreting Islamic Political Parties.* New York: Palgrave Macmillan.

Sartori, Giovanni. 1966. "Opposition and Control: Problems and Prospects." *Government and Opposition* 1, no. 1 (Winter).

Schwedler, Jillian. 2004. "Is Moderation a Myth? Islamist Parties in Comparative Perspective." Paper presented at "Roots of Radicalism," Yale University. May 7–9.

———. 2006. *Faith in Moderation: Islamist Parties in Jordan and Yemen.* New York: Cambridge University Press.

———. 2007. "Democratization, Inclusion and the Moderation of Islamist Parties." *Development* 50, no. 1 (March): 56–61.

———. 2011. "Can Islamists Become Moderates? Rethinking the Inclusion-Moderation Hypothesis." *World Politics* 63, no. 2 (April): 347–76.

Schwedler, Jillian, and Janine A. Clark. 2006. "Islamist-Leftist Cooperation in the Arab World." *ISIM Review* 18, no. 1 (Autumn): 10–11.

Share, Donald. 1985. "Two Transitions: Democratization and the Evolution of the Spanish Socialist Left." *West European Politics* 8 (January).

Al-Sharnoubi, Abdul Galil. 2008. "Interview with Muslim Brotherhood Chairman Mohamed Mahdy Akef." http://www.ikhwanweb.com/, November 27.

Sharp, Jeremy M. 2006. "Egypt: 2005 Presidential and Parliamentary Elections." Congressional Research Service, Order Code RS22274. Updated January 15.

Shehata, Samir, and Joshua Stacher. 2006. "The Brotherhood Goes to Parliament." *Middle East Report* 36, no. 240 (Fall).

Skocpol, Theda, and Margaret Somers. 1980. "The Uses of Comparative History in Macrosocial Inquiry." *Comparative Studies in Society and History* 22, no. 2 (April): 174–97.

"Speech by Mr. Mohamed Mahdi Akef General Guide of the Muslim Brotherhood Group to Cairo 3rd Rally for International Campaign against American and Zionist Occupation." 2005. March.

Springborg, Robert. 1989. *Mubarak's Egypt: Fragmentation of the Political Order.* Boulder, CO: Westview Press.

Stacher, Joshua. 2002. "Post-Islamist Rumblings in Egypt: The Emergence of the Wasat Party." *Middle East Journal* 56, no. 3 (Summer): 415–32.

———. 2009. "The Brothers and the War." *Middle East Report* 39, no. 250 (39). http://www.merip.org/.

Stowasser, Barbara Freyer. 1987. "Liberated Equal or Protected Dependent? Contemporary Religious Paradigms on Women's Status in Islam." *Arab Studies Quarterly* 9, no. 3: 260–83.

Tammam, Hossam. 2010a. "Egypt's New Brotherhood Leadership: Implications and Limits of Change." *Arab Reform Bulletin*, Carnegie Endowment for International Peace. February 17. http://carnegieendowment.org/.

———. 2010b. "The Muslim Brotherhood and the Egyptian Regime: The Test of Parliamentary Elections as a Condition for Political Transition." Arab Reform Brief No. 38, Arab Reform Initiative. March.

Tezcur, Gunes Murat. 2010. "The Moderation Theory Revisited: The Case of Islamic Political Actors." *Party Politics* 16 (January): 69–88.

Thabet, Hala G. 2006. "Egyptian Parliamentary Elections: Between Democratisation and Autocracy." *Africa Development* 31, no. 3: 11–34.

Tozy, Mohammed. 1993. "Islam and the State." In *Polity and Society in Contemporary North Africa*, ed. William I. Zartman and William Mark Habeeb. Boulder, CO: Westview Press.

Warrick, Catherine. 2009. *Law in the Service of Legitimacy: Gender and Politics in Jordan*. London: Ashgate.

Wegner, Eva. 2004. "The Contribution of Inclusivist Approaches towards the Islamist Opposition to Regime Stability in Arab States: The Case of the Moroccan Parti de la Justice et du Développement." EUI Working Paper RSCAS No. 2004/42, European University Institute.

———. 2007. "Authoritarian King and Democratic Islamists in Morocco." In "The Challenge of Islamists for EU and US Policies: Conflict Stability and Reform," ed. Muriel Asseburg and Daniel Brumberg. SWP Research Paper 2007/RP 12, Stiftung Wissenschaft und Politik. November.

Weingast, Barry R. 2002. "Rational Choice Institutionalism." In *Political Science: The State of the Discipline*, ed. Ira Katznelson and Helen V. Milner. New York: W. W. Norton.

Wendell, Charles, trans. 1978. *Five Tracts of Hasan al-Banna (1906–1949)*. Berkeley: University of California Press.

Werenfels, Isabelle. 2005. "Between Integration and Repression: Government Responses to Islamism in the Maghreb." SWP Research Paper S 39, Stiftung Wissenschaft und Politik. December.

Wickham, Carrie Rosefsky. 2002. *Mobilizing Islam: Religion, Activism and Political Change in Egypt*. New York: Columbia University Press.

———. 2004a. "Interests, Ideas, and Islamist Outreach in Egypt." In *Islamic Activism: A Social Movement Theory Approach*, ed. Quintan Wiktorowicz. Bloomington: Indiana University Press.

———. 2004b. "The Path to Moderation: Strategy and Learning in the Formation of Egypt's Wasat Party." *Comparative Politics* 36, no. 2 (January): 205–28.

———. 2004c. "The Problem with Coercive Democratization: The Islamist Response to the U.S. Democracy Reform Initiative." *Muslim World Journal of Human Rights* 1, no. 1 (October).

———. 2005. "The Islamist Alternative to Globalization." In *Religion in Global Civil Society*, ed. Mark Juergensmeyer. New York: Oxford University Press.

——. 2011a. "The Muslim Brotherhood after Mubarak." http://www.foreignaffairs
.com/, February 3.

——. 2011b. "The Muslim Brotherhood and Democratic Transition in Egypt." *Middle
East Law and Governance Journal* 3, no. 1–2 (October): 204–23.

——. 2011c. "Uprising: Were the Events in Egypt This Year a 'Revolution'?" *Academic
Exchange* 14, no. 1.

——. 2011d. "What Would Hasan al Bana Do?: Modern (Re-) Interpretation of the
Brotherhood's Founding Discourse." In *The Muslim Brotherhood in Europe*, ed. Roel
Meijer and Edwin Bakker. London: Hurst and Company.

Wiktorowicz, Quintan. 1999. "Islamists, the State and Cooperation in Jordan." *Arab
Studies Quarterly* 21, no. 4 (1999): 1–17.

——. 2001. *The Management of Islamic Activism: Salafis, the Muslim Brotherhood and
State Power in Jordan*. New York: State University of New York Press.

Willis, Michael J. 1999. "Between Alternance and the Makhzen: At-Tawhid wa Al-Islah's
Entry into Moroccan Politics." *Journal of North African Studies* 4, no. 3: 45–80.

——. 2004a. "Islamism in Morocco: The End of the Moroccan Exception?" Paper presented at the Middle East Studies Association (MESA) of America Annual Meeting,
San Francisco, California. November.

——. 2004b. "Morocco's Islamists and the Legislative Elections of 2002: The Strange
Case of the Party That Did Not Want to Win." *Mediterranean Politics* 9, no. 1 (Spring):
53–81.

——. 2008. "Islamism, Democratization and Disillusionment: Morocco's Legislative
Elections of 2007." Research Paper No. 1, Mohammed VI Fellowship in Moroccan
and Mediterranean Studies, St Antony's College, Oxford. http://www.sant.ox.ac.uk.

Wittes, Tamara Cofman. 2008. "Islamist Parties: Three Kinds of Movements." *Journal of
Democracy* 19, no. 3 (July): 7–12.

Zeghal, Malika. 2008. "Participation without Power." *Journal of Democracy* 19, no. 3
(July): 31–36.

Zollner, Barbara. 2007. "Prison Talk: The Muslim Brotherhood's Internal Struggle
during Gamal Abdel Nasser's Persecution, 1952 to 1971." *International Journal of
Middle East Studies* 39:411–33.

Zürn, Michael, and Jeffrey T. Checkel. 2005. "Getting Socialized to Build Bridges: Constructivism and Rationalism, Europe and the Nation-State." *International Organization* 59, no. 4 (Fall): 1045–79.

Arabic Sources

Abd al-Fattah, Nabil, ed. 1996. *Taqrir 'an al-Hala al-Diniyya fii Misr* 1995 [Report on
Religious Conditions in Egypt]. Cairo: Al-Ahram Center for Political and Strategic
Studies.

——, ed. 1998. *Taqrir 'an al-Hala al-Diniyya fii Misr* [Report on Religious Conditions
in Egypt]. 2nd ed. Cairo: Al-Ahram Center for Political and Strategic Studies.

——. N.d. "Al-Ikhwan al-Muslimun: Mulahadhat Hawl Mashahid al-Tahawwul" [The
Muslim Brotherhood: Comments on the Signs of an Evolution]. Unpublished paper.

Abd al-Jawwad, Jamal. 1998. *Al-Tahawwul al-Dimuqrati al-Muta'athir fii Misr wa Tunis* [The Stumbling Democratic Change in Egypt and Tunisia]. Cairo: Cairo Institute for the Human Rights Studies.

Abd al-Maqsud, Salah. 1990. "Al-Ikhwan al-Muslimun fii Misr wa al-I'tirafat al-Qanuni" [The Muslim Brotherhood and Legal Recognition]. *Liwa' al-Islam*, March 28.

Abu Talib, Hassan. 2003. *Al-Taqrir al-Istratiji al-'Arabi, 2002–2003* [Arab Strategic Report]. Cairo: Al-Ahram Center for Political and Strategic Studies.

Abu al-Futouh, Abd al-Mun'im. 2004. *Al-Mafhoum al-Islami lil-Islah al-Shamil: Muqaddimat Jadida* [The Islamic Concept of Comprehensive Reform: New Indicators]. [Cairo:] Noon Publishing and Distribution.

———. 2005. *Mujaddidoun la Mubaddidoun* [Renewers, Not Squanderers]. [Cairo:] Tatwir Publishing and Distribution Company.

Al-'Adwi, Mustafa. 1987. *'Umar al-Tilmisani: Bayn Hamas al-Shabab wa Hikmat al-Shuyukh* ['Umar al-Tilmisani: Between the Zeal of Youth and the Wisdom of the Elders]. Giza, Egypt: Jerusalem House for Books and Studies.

'Akef, Muhammad Mahdi. 2004. *Mubadarat al-Ikhwan al Muslimin Hawl Mabadi' al-Islah fii Misr* [The Muslim Brotherhood's Initiative on the Principles of Reform in Egypt]. Cairo: The Muslim Brotherhood.

Al-Anani, Khalil. 2007. *Al-Ikhwan al-Muslimun fii Misr: Shaykhukha Tusari' al-Zaman* [The Muslim Brotherhood in Egypt: A Gerontocracy Confronts Time]. Cairo: Shuruk Publishers.

———. 2010. "Hal Intahat Salahiyyat al-Mashru' al-Ikhwani?" [Has the Usefulness of the Brotherhood Project Ended?]. *Al-Hayat*, January 26.

Al-'Aryan, 'Esam. 2002. "Al-Tajdid wa al-Muraja'at wa al-Naqd al-Dhati" [Renewal, Review, and Self-Criticism]. *Al-Mujtama'*, November 9.

'Ali, Haydar Ibrahim. 1994. "Hawl Darourat al-Hiwar Bayn al-Harakat al-Islamiyya wa al-Quwa al-Siyasiyya al-Ukhra" [On the Necessity of Dialogue between Islamist Movements and Other Political Forces]. *Al-Tariq*, no. 5 (September): 7–17.

"Al-Mar'a al-Muslima fi'l-Mujtama' al-Muslim, al-Shura wa Ta'addud al-Ahzab" [The Muslim Woman in Muslim Society, Consultation and Party Pluralism]. 1994. Islamic Center for Studies and Research.

"Al-Radd 'ala As'ilat Jaridat *Al-'Arabi* al-Warida min al-Ustadh Abd al- Fattah Abd al-Mun'im ila al-Muhandis Aboul 'Ela Madi, Wakil Mu'assisi Hizb al-Wasat" [The Reply to the Questions of *Al-Arabi* Newspaper from Mr. Abd al-Fattah Abd al-Mun'im to the Engineer Aboul 'Ela Madi, Representative of the Founders of the Wasat Party]. 1996. Mimeograph given to the author by Aboul 'Ela Madi. May 11.

Awraq Hizb al-Wasat al-Misri [The Papers of the Egyptian Wasat Party]. 1996. Cairo: Wasat Party.

Awraq Hizb al-Wasat al-Misri [The Papers of the Egyptian Wasat Party]. 1998. Cairo: Wasat Party.

Badr, Badr Muhammad. 1989. *Al-Jama'a al-Islamiyya Fii Jami'at Misr, Haqa'iq Wa Watha'iq* [The Islamist Associations in Egypt's Universities: Facts and Documents]. Self-published.

———. 1996. "Qissat Awwal Hizb Siyasi Yu'assisuhu Shabab al-Ikhwan al-Muslimin" [The Story of the First Political Party Founded by the Youth of the Muslim Brotherhood]. *Al-Mujtama'*, January 23.

"Bayan lil-Naas" [Statement to the People]. 1995. The Muslim Brotherhood. Mimeograph.

Al-Chobaki, 'Amr. 2006. *Mustaqbal Jama'at al-Ikhwan al-Muslimin* [The Future of the Muslim Brotherhood Society]. Cairo: Al-Ahram Center for Political and Strategic Studies.

Dalal, 'Abdallah Sami Ibrahim. 2006. *Al-Islamiyyun wa al-Dimuqratiyya Fii Misr* [The Islamists and Democracy in Egypt]. Cairo: Madbuli Publishers.

Ezzat, Heba Raouf . 2008. "Ahlam al-'Asafir" [The Dreams of the Birds]. Parts 1–4. *Al-Dustour*, June 8, 15, 22, 29.

Haydar, Khalil 'Ali. 1989. *Al-Ikhwan al-Muslimun: Sujal al-Ahdath* [The Muslim Brotherhood: Documentation of Events]. Kuwait: Kazima Company for Publishing, Translation and Distribution.

———. 1998. *Al-Haraka al-Islamiyya fi'l-Duwal al-'Arabiyya* [The Islamic Movement in the Arab States]. Abu Dhabi: Emirates Center for Strategic Studies and Research.

Hussein, Ashraf. 1990. *Al-Musharaka al-Siyasiyya wa al-Intikhabat al-Barlmaniyya* [Political Participation and Parliamentary Elections] in *Al-Intikhabat al-Barlmaniyya fii Misr: Dars Intikhabat 1987* [Parliamentary Elections in Egypt: A Study of the 1987 Elections], ed. Ahmad Abdalla. Cairo: Sinai Publishers.

'Id, Samih. 2000. *Al-Ikhwan al-Muslimoun: Al-Hadir wa al-Mustaqbal* [The Muslim Brotherhood: Present and Future]. Cairo: n.p.

Al-Ikwhan al-Muslimun: Bayanat wa Tasrihat Khilal 'Am 2003–2004 [The Muslim Brotherhood: Documents and Statements during the Year 2003–2004]. N.d., n.p.

Al-Khatib, Muhammad 'Abdallah. 1990. *Al-Ikhwan al-Muslimun Taht Qubbat al-Barlaman* [The Muslim Brotherhood under the Dome of Parliament]. Cairo: Islamic Distribution and Publishing House.

Madi, Aboul 'Ela. 2004. "Numudhaj li'l-Fikr al-Islami al-Siyasi fii Misr" [A Model of Islamist Political Thinking in Egypt]. Paper presented at the seminar "Changing Knowledge and Authority in Islam." Japan Association for Middle East Studies, Tokyo. March 25–26.

Madi, Aboul 'Ela, Farid Zahran, Amin Askandar, and Wahid Abd al-Magid, eds. 1999. *Misr wa al-Namudhaj al-Dimuqrati* [Egypt and the Democratic Model]. Hiwarat al-Mustaqbal [Conversations of the Future] Series. Vol. 1. Cairo: Mahrousa Center for Publishing.

Mahmoud, Abd al-Mun'im. 2008a. "Madha Yajri Dakhil Jama'at al-Ikhwan al- Muslimin" [What Is Going On inside the Muslim Brotherhood Association]. Ana Akhwan (online blog). May 27.

———. 2008b. "Kayf Takhtar Jama'at al-Ikhwan al-Muslimin Qiyadiha" [How Does the Muslim Brotherhood Association Choose Its Leaders?]. Copy of article given to author. July 3.

Al-Mar'a al-Muslima fii al-Mujtama' al-Muslim wa al-Shura wa al-Ta'addudiyya al-Hizbiyya [The Muslim Woman in Muslim Society and *Shura* and Party Pluralism]. 1994. Islamic Center for Studies and Research.

Mubarak, Hisham. 1995. *Al-Irhabiyyun Qadimun!: Dirasa Muqarana Bayn Mawqif al-Ikhwan al-Muslimin wa Jama'at al-Jihad min Qadiyat al-'Unf, 1938–1994* [The Terrorists Are Coming!: A Comparative Study of the Positions of the Muslim Brotherhood and the Jihad Organization on the Issue of Violence, 1938–1994]. Cairo: Mahrousa Center for Publishing and Media Services.

Muhammad, Ihab Kamal. 2006. *Al-Tariq lil-Qimma: Su'oud al-Ikhwan al-Muslimin* [The Path to the Top: The Rise of the Muslim Brotherhood]. Cairo: Huriyya Publishing and Distribution.

Mursi, Fu'ad, ed. 1990. *Al-Intikhabat al-Barlmaniya fii Misr: Dars Intikhabat 1987* [Parliamentary Elections in Egypt: The Study of the 1987 Elections]. Cairo: Sina Publishers.

Mustafa, Hala. 1992. *Al-Islam al-Siyyasi fii Misr: Min Harakat al-Islah ila Jama'at al-'Unf* [Political Islam in Egypt: From Reform Movement to Organizations of Violence]. Cairo: Al-Ahram Center for Political and Strategic Studies.

———. 1995. *Al-Dawla wa al-Haraka al-Islamiyya al-Mu'arida: Bayn al-Muhadana wa al-Muwajaha fii 'Ahday al-Sadat wa Mubarak* [The State and the Islamic Opposition Movement: Between Truce and Confrontation in the Sadat and Mubarak Eras]. Cairo: Mahrousa Center for Publishing and Media Services.

Al-Niqabat al-Mihniyya wa Qadaya al-Mujtama' al-Misri [The Professional Syndicates and the Issues Facing Egyptian Society]. 1995. Cairo: Coordinating Committee of the Professional Syndicates.

Nuh, Mukhtar. N.d. "Al-La'iha al-Dakhiliyya li'l-Ikhwan Tu'ani min Khamsat 'Uyoub Khatira Taj'aluha Mukhalifa lil-Dimuqratiyya wa al-Shura wa al-Tashri'" [The Internal Charter of the Brotherhood Suffers from Five Dangerous Flaws That Make It Opposed to Democracy, Consultation, and Lawmaking]. http://www.mokhtarnouh.com/.

Qandil, Amani. 2000. *Al-Mujtama' al-Madani fii Misr fii Matla' Alfiyya Jadida* [Civil Society in Egypt at the Dawn of a New Millennium]. Cairo: Al-Ahram Center for Political and Strategic Studies.

Ramih, Tal'at. 1997. *Al-Wasat wa al-Ikhwan* [The Wasat and the Brotherhood]. Cairo: Jaffa Center for Studies and Research.

Rishwan, Diya', ed. 2006. *Dalil al-Harakat al-Islamiyya fi'l-'Aalam* [Directory of Islamist Movements in the World]. Cairo: Al-Ahram Center for Political and Strategic Studies.

Salah, Muhammad. 1996. "Al Ikhwan al-Muslimun Yuwajihun Akhtar Azma Dakhiliyya" [The Muslim Brotherhood Confronts the Most Dangerous Internal Crisis]. *Al-Wasat*, no. 251, November 18.

———. 2005. "Ba'ad Fawz bi-34 Maq'ad fi Dawratayn al-'Ula wa al-Thaniya wa Tahawulihim ila Munafis li'l-Hizb al-Hakim . . . Tunafis Bayn Shabab 'al-Ikhwan' al-Misriyin wa Shuyoukhihim . . . wa al-Nidham Yantadhiruhum 'la Haffat Hiwarihim ma'a al-Gharb" [After Winning by 34 Seats in the First and Second Rounds and Their Evolution into a Competitor to the Ruling Party . . . The Egyptian Youth of the Muslim Brotherhood Compete with Their Elders . . . and the Regime Awaits Them on the Brink of Their Dialogue with the West]. *Al-Hayat*, November 17.

Salama, Osama. 2004. "The Rulings of the Brotherhood in Declaring Parties Apostate and the Oppression of Women and Copts." *Ruz al-Yusuf* 3953, no. 13 (March 19).

Shubaki, 'Amr, ed. 2006. *Islamiyyun wa Dimuqratiyyun* [Islamists and Democrats]. 2nd ed. Cairo: Al Ahram Center for Political and Strategic Studies.

"Al-Tahaluf al-Watani min Ajl al-Islah wa al-Taghyir: Mashru' al-Nidham al-Siyasi" [The National Coalition on Behalf of Reform and Change: A Plan for the Political System].

Tammam, Hossam. 2006. *Tahawwulat al-Ikhwan al-Muslimin: Tafakkuk al-Idiulujiyya wa Nihayat al-Tandhim* [The Evolutions of the Muslim Brotherhood: The Fragmentation of Ideology and the End of the Organization]. Cairo: Madbouli Publishers.

Yasin, al-Sayyid, ed. 1986. *Al-Taqrir al-Istratiji al-'Arabi* 1985 [Arab Strategic Report]. Cairo: Al-Ahram Center for Political and Strategic Studies.

———. 1987. *Al-Taqrir al-Istratiji al-'Arabi* 1986 [Arab Strategic Report]. Cairo: Al-Ahram Center for Political and Strategic Studies.

———. 1989. *Al-Taqrir al-Istratiji al-'Arabi* 1988 [Arab Strategic Report]. Cairo: Al-Ahram Center for Political and Strategic Studies.

———. 1990. *Al-Taqrir al-Istratiji al-'Arabi* 1989 [Arab Strategic Report]. Cairo: Al-Ahram Center for Political and Strategic Studies.

———. 1991. *Al-Taqrir al-Istratiji al-'Arabi* 1990 [Arab Strategic Report]. Cairo: Al-Ahram Center for Political and Strategic Studies.

———. 1992. *Al-Taqrir al-Istratiji al-'Arabi* 1991 [Arab Strategic Report]. Cairo: Al-Ahram Center for Political and Strategic Studies.

———. 1996. *Al-Taqrir al-Istratiji al-'Arabi* 1995 [Arab Strategic Report]. Cairo: Al-Ahram Center for Political and Strategic Studies.

Zahran, Farid, ed. *Al-Hiwar*. Cairo: Mahrousa Firm for Publishing and Services.

Index

'Abd al-Mun'im, Abu al-Futouh, 37, 38, 59, 63, 66, 72, 87, 97, 100, 113, 114, 116, 125, 126, 130, 140, 168, 184, 261; backing of Mursi in the presidential election, 260; on the Brotherhood's political action, 98–99; on the Brotherhood's relationship with the syndicates, 99; as candidate for the presidency of Egypt, 257, 258, 259; change in political beliefs of, 138; on the changed thinking concerning Islamist Trend, 65; on the climate of repression faced by the Brotherhood, 102, 128; confrontation of with Sadat, 38–39; as liaison with Kefaya, 117; as member of the National Charter drafting committee, 85–86; objections of to the formation of a Brotherhood political party, 175; political gambit of, 146–48; as a political maverick, 178–80; political priorities of, 180; and the Shura Council, 127, 128

'Abd al-Salam, 'Arif, 28

'Abd al-Salam, Yasim, 231

'Abdalla, Ahmed, 38, 76

'Abdalla al-Khatib, Muhammad, 54

Abduh, Muhammad, 23

Abdullah (king of Jordan), 197

Abdullah II (king of Jordan), 207

Abed-Kotob, Sana, 57

'Abd (Justice) Party, 180

'Adli, Habib, 261

Afghanistan, 205

'Afifi, Adel, 194

"Against Imperialism and Zionism" conference, 156

Ahmad, Makram Mohammad, 80

'Akef, Mohammed Mahdi, 102, 104–5, 112, 113, 121, 125, 126, 127; resignation of as Supreme Guide, 129

al-'Adl wa al-Ihsan (Justice and Charity) movement, 3

Al-Ahram, 33

Al-Ahram Center, 71

al-Anani, Khalil, 131, 141, 142, 145

al-'Aryan, Asma, 141

al-'Aryan, 'Esam, 37, 38, 76–77, 87, 97, 112, 113, 114, 116, 125, 126, 149, 168, 175, 195; arrest of, 127–28; as contender for a seat on the Guidance Bureau, 128–29, 130; and the role of youth in the Egyptian uprising, 160, 161; on the Salafi movement, 277; as vice-president of the Freedom and Justice Party, 174

al-'Awa, Muhammad Salim, 68, 82, 84, 300n51

al-Awadi, Hisham, 51, 79

Al-Azhar University, 31, 265, 307n24; and the "Al-Azhar militia" incident, 121

al-'Azm, Yusuf, 197, 198

al-Bab, 'Ali Fath, 134, 135

al-Badawi, Sayyid, 173

al-Baghdadi, Ahmad, 222, 226, 230

al-Banna, Gamal, 316n117

al-Banna, Hasan, 20–21, 37, 64, 68, 197, 276; assassination of, 26; as candidate for parliament, 25, 49; on the decline of Western civilization, 23; education of, 20; first public message (*risala*) of, 24; on Islam, 290n10; motivations of for starting the Muslim Brotherhood, 21; rejection of *hizbiyya* (partyism) by, 42, 50; stress of on *tarbiya* (bottom-up spiritual formation of society), 42

al-Barr, Abd al-Rahman, 147
al-Basiiri, Muhammad, 227
al-Biltagi, Muhammad, 168, 170, 171–72, 174, 186, 193, 261, 269
al-Chobaki, ʿAmr, 44, 122
al-Dafiri, Saʿd, 224
al-Daʿwa, 30, 31, 33, 39, 291n47; on the murder of Sheikh Dhahabi, 292n75
al-Daʿwa al-Salafiyya (Islamic Call), 251
al-Din, Fuʾad Siraj, 47
al-Din al Khatib, Muhibb, 23
al-Diyyan, Ahmad, 229
Alexandria University, 37, 41, 293n90
al-Faraj, Muhammad Salim, 41
al-Faramawy, Abd al-Hayy, 149
Al-Farida al-Ghaʾiba (The Hidden Imperative [Faraj]), 34
al-Fatah, Misr, 22
al-Fattah, ʿAli Abd, 112, 126, 305n85
al-Fattah, Muhammad Abd, 293n90
al-Fattah, Nabil Abd, 161
al-Fingari, Mushin, 166
al-Gawwad, Ahmad Abd, 156, 160, 180; role of in the Egyptian uprising, 161–62
Algeria, 80, 89, 203, 234
al-Ghad (Tomorrow) Party, 148, 249
al-Ghadban, Seif, 158
al-Ghar, Muhammad Abu, 253
al-Ghazzali, Muhammad, 39, 68
al-Hajji, Yusuf, 200
al-Halabawi, Kamal, 149
al-Halafawi, Jehan, 149
al-Hayat, 92
al-Hudeibi, Hasan, 29, 37, 42, 43, 291n31
al-Husseini, Saʿd, 128, 186
ʿAli, Khaled, 258, 259
Al-Ikhwan al-Muslimin That Qubbat al-Barlaman (The Muslim Brotherhood Under the Dome of Parliament [ʿAbdalla al-Khatib]), 54
al-Isla was al-Tajdid (Reform and Renewal), 203, 204
al-Islambouli, ʿEsam, 304n51
al-Islambuli, Khaled, 33
al-Islambuli, Muhammad, 33
al-Jamaʿa Al-Islamiyya (Islamic Group), 202; name change of, 203
al-Jamal, Hamid, 267
al-Jamiʿi, Abu Bakr, 235, 236–37, 239, 242
al-Jihad, 34
al-Karama Party, 249

al-Karim, Salah Abd, 60, 89, 300n51; drafting of the Wasat Party's platform, 83
al-Katani, Muhammad Saʿd, 128, 134, 149–50, 174, 175, 250, 252, 255, 267; on the application of Shariʿa law, 137; on the Brotherhood's major achievement in parliament, 136; denouncement of the SCAF, 261; reaction of to the verdicts in the Mubarak and ʿAdli trials, 261–62
al-Latif, Mahmud Abd, 27
al-Mahgoub, Rifʿat, 55, 78
al-Mawardi, 126
al-Mawdudi, Alaʾ, 28
al-Messiri, Abd al-Wahhab, 68
al-Misimi, Hayat, 216, 218, 319n71
al-Mujtama, 185
al-Musawwar, 80
al-Nadwi, Abu Hasan, 28
al-Naggar, Mustafa, 163, 180; on the calls for transparency in the internal elections of the Brotherhood, 131–32; criticism of the Wasat Party, 140; freezing of his membership in the Brotherhood, 142–43
al-Naggar, Sayyid, 86
al-Najjar, Ghanim, 200, 222
al-Nashiʾ, Badir, 223, 224, 226, 227, 228, 229
al-Qahira, 84
al-Qaʿida, 3
al-Qaradawi, Yusuf, 68, 82, 125
al-Qudus, Muhammad Abd, 33
al-Qumni, Sayed Mahmoud, criticism of the Brotherhood, 303nn47–48
al-Rahman, Muhammad Abd, 128
al-Raziq, Gasir, 113–14, 304n63, 305n78
al-Saniʿ, Nasser, 223, 225, 226, 229
al-Sattar, Sayyid Abd, 64, 87, 116, 292–93n86, 293n90, 304n61
al-Sayyid, Mustapha Kamal, 50
al-Shaʿb, 53
a-Shadaʾid, Fawaʾid ʿan, 301n78
al-Shaʿir, Akram, 150
al-Sharif, Ashraf, on reasons people voted for the Brotherhood candidates, 251–52
al-Shatiʾ, Ismaʿil, 226, 228, 230
al-Shatir, Khayrat, 71, 103, 119, 122, 131, 134, 185–86; arrest and imprisonment of, 255; on the necessity of globalization, 274–75; as nominee for president of Egypt, 254–56; on politics as the "art of the possible," 278
al-Shibh, Muhamad, 300n57

al-Tagammu' al-Watani, 305–6n86
al-Tahaluf al-Dimuqrati Min Ajl Misr (Democratic Coalition for Egypt), 191
al-Tahaluf al-Watani Min Ajl al-Islah wa al-Taghyir (The National Coalition for Reform and Change), 114
al-Tajdid, 238, 239, 241
al-tayyar al-ishahi (the reformist trend among Muslim Brotherhood activists), 46
al-Tayyar al-Misri (Egyptian Current) Party, 191; formation of, 180; goals of, 180–81; role of in the "second wave of the revolution," 181
al-Tilmisani, 'Umar, 33, 39, 40, 42, 47, 59, 138, 291n47; arrest of, 43; on the Brotherhood as a legal association, 292n55; confidence of in the Brotherhood's message to secure votes, 49; death of, 51; decision to enter electoral politics, 47–48; explanation of for the Brotherhood's entry into politics, 48–49; gradualist approach to the Islamic reform of society and the application of Shari'a law, 30, 53; idea of to form a Muslim Brotherhood political party, 31, 51; on the legitimacy of political parties, 50–52; as Supreme Guide of the Brotherhood, 30, 291n46
'al-Uthmani, Sa'd al-Din, 233, 239, 242, 286
Al-Wasat wa al-Ikhwan (The Wasat and the Brotherhood [Ramih]), 90
al-Yasar, 65
al-Yazigh, Muhammad, 234
al-Za'farani, Ibrahim, 37, 87, 149, 163, 177–78, 184
al-Zand, Ahmad, 262
al-Zarqawi, Abu Musab, 207
al-Zayyat, Muhyiddin, 37
Amini, Gum'a, 131
Anan, Sami, 269
Anderson, Lisa, 88
Antar, Noha, 118, 307n12
'Aqif, Muhammad Mahdi, 66, 67
"Arab socialism," 29
Arab Socialist Union, 30, 35; platforms (manaber) of, 30–31
"Arab Spring," the, 1–2, 123, 176, 243–44, 245, 246, 247, 279, 288
'Arabiyyat, Abd al-Latif, 198, 209; on adultery and Islamic law, 212
Asyut University Faculty Club, 60
Auf, Yussef, 255

'Ayn Shams University, 40, 41
Azaideh, Ahmad, 198

Badi', Muhammad, 130–31, 145, 170, 174; on the primary goal of the Brotherhood, 276
Badr, Badr Muhammad, 39
Badr, Zaki, 76
Bagha, 'Abdalla, 202, 237
Bahgat, Husam, 261
Bahrain, 20
Baker, Raymond, 39, 40, 43
Baradei, Muhammad, 148, 155, 163, 165, 168, 169, 259. See also National Association for Change (NAC)
Battalions (kata'ib), 26
"Battle of the Camel," 167
Bayat, Asef, 4
Bayoumi, Rashad, 131, 139, 151
Bedouins, in Kuwait, 200
Benkirane, 'Abdalla, 202, 236, 239, 242; as prime minister of Morocco, 244–46
Bermeo, Nancy, 12
Bindi, Mustafa Abu, 241
Bishara, Ahmad, 228
Bishr, Muhammad, 126
Bishri, Tariq, 68, 84, 170, 300n51
Bouazizi, Mohamed, 158
Brooke, Steven, 168
Brotherhood/Brothers. See Muslim Brotherhood (in Egypt)
Brotherhood Reformers, 149
Browers, Michelle, 4
Brown, Nathan, 4, 221, 227, 229, 243, 320–21n134
Bush, George W., 103; National Endowment for Democracy speech of, 104

Cairo Spring, 111, 114–15, 117
Cairo University, 37, 38, 41, 100, 109, 156, 292n80; Faculty Club of, 60
Campaign for the Elimination of So-Called "Crimes of Honor," 212
Carothers, Thomas, 104
Carter Center, 262, 263, 325n57; overseeing of Egypt's presidential election by, 257, 323n30
Checkel, Jeffrey T., 12
citizenship, 56, 189; citizenship rights for Coptic Christians, 70, 119, 124, 280–81; citizenship rights for women, 68, 84, 92, 124, 126, 280; concept of, 135; and equal rights, 6, 10, 45, 55, 115

Clark, Janine, 4, 215
comparative historical analysis, value of, 15–17; and "double interpretation," 16; and "multiple conjunctural causation," 16; and "systematic process analysis," 16
Constituent Assembly (CA), 258, 264, 265, 270, 271; elected members of, 253
Constitutional Assembly, 237, 248, 255, 260, 265, 270, 271
"Constructing the Egyptian Human Being" (opening section of the Brotherhood's reform program), 106
Consultation Party (Hizb al-Shura), 51
Coptic Christians, 59, 78, 258, 265, 276; citizenship rights for, 70, 119, 124, 280–81
Court of Cassation, 267

Dalal, Muhammad, 220, 223, 224, 225
Daqhaliyya, 133, 143
Dar al-'Ulum, 21
Darif, Muhammad, 203, 203, 237
Dashti, Rola, 223
Dawoud, Khaled, 149, 184, 293n90
democracies, "bourgeois," 9
democracy, 10, 13, 46, 56, 102, 103, 151, 280, 287; in the Arab world, 5; democracy movements in Eastern Europe, 109–10; distinction between democracy and a political system based on *shura*, 58; Islamist view of, 32, 152; liberal democracy, 44; tensions between democracy and Shari'a law, 186–90. *See also* "democracy promotion," as a factor in Egyptian public life
"democracy promotion," as a factor in Egyptian public life, 103–4; and the "Broader Middle East and North Africa Initiative" (BMENA), 103–4; and the "Greater Middle East Initiative," 103
"Democracy Supporters Should Not Fear the Muslim Brotherhood" (Abu al-Futouh), 168–69
Democratic Alliance, 249, 251, 258; decline in member parties of, 249–50
Democratic Front, 249
"democratic habituation," 9, 135, 284–85
democratic values, hybridization of, 13
Du'ah La Qudah (Preachers, Not Judges), 29
Duwaileh, Mubarak, 221, 223, 225–26

Egypt, 1, 11, 15, 17, 199, 238, 286, 287; aping of Western ways in, 22; "deep state" institu-tions of, 18, 248, 261, 268, 270, 276, 279; display of Islamist force in, 193–94; economic weakness of, 273–75; police brutality in, 158–60; political development in, 173; political infighting (*hizbiyya* [partyism]) in, 22; post-Mubarak presidential election in, 254–66. *See also* Egyptian Constitution; Egyptian uprising; Muslim Brotherhood
Egyptian Bloc, 249, 252
Egyptian Constitution, 154, 170–71, 250, 280; amendments to Article 5 and Article 62 of (2007), 123; Article 1 of, 135; Article 2 of, 31, 32, 56, 86, 97, 99, 106, 125, 171, 187, 189, 193, 194, 221, 225, 271; Article 53 supplement, 264; Article 60 supplement, 264–65; Article 79 of, 225; Article 88 of, 123; Article 340 of, 212, 318n66; "higher principles" debate concerning constitutional principles, 190–95; proposed amendment to Article 76 of, 111–12
Egyptian Current Party. *See* al-Tayyar al-Misri (Egyptian Current) Party
Egyptian Movement for Change, 107, 108
Egyptian Organization for Human Rights, 80, 85
Egyptian Penal Code: Article 98 of, 318n66; Article 340 of, 212, 318n66; changes to, 211–12, 298n23
Egyptian People's Committee for Support of the Palestinian Intifada (EPC-SPI), 99–100
Egyptian Popular Committee in Solidarity with the Intifada (EPSCI), 107
Egyptian Reform Party. *See* Hizb al-Islah al Misri (Egyptian Reform Party)
Egyptian Student Union Charter, 36
Egyptian Universities Act (1994), 78
Egyptian uprising, 154–55; attacks on demonstrators by thugs (*baltagiyya*) hired by the NDP, 164–65; backstory of the uprising, 157–60; deaths and injuries as a result of, 166, 313n46; escalation of the protests and subsequent collapse of the Mubarak regime, 163–66; launching of by youths on national holiday (Police Day) to protest police brutality, 158–60; role of soccer booster clubs ("ultras") in, 162; role of social media in, 155, 159, 160, 312n2; success of, 166; unfulfilled promise of, 278–79. *See also* Muslim Brotherhood, and the Egyptian uprising
'Ela Madi, Aboul, 129, 296n66, 296n69, 300n51; opinion of Muhammad Badi', 131;

response to the criticism of Salah 'Isa, 300n55; self-criticism of the middle-generation Brotherhood activists, 139

el-Abdine Ben Ali, Zine, 158

Elad-Altman, Israel, 303n46, 304n65

El-Amrani, Issandr, 123, 259

El Bahaei, Alla, 252

El-Ghobashy, Mona, 4, 47, 52, 55, 57, 69

El-Hamalawy, Hossam, 304n63

El Rashidi, Yasmine, 250–51

'Emoush, Bassam, 215, 216

Europe, 22, 26, 88, 90; eastern Europe, 109–10; "third-wave" democratic transitions in southern Europe, 4, 12, 115; western Europe, 4

Ezzat, Heba Raouf, 132, 260

'Ezzat, Mahmoud, 66, 112, 129, 131, 139–40, 186

Fahmi, Gamal, 304n51

Faith in Moderation (Schwedler), 4

Faraj, Muhammad Abd al-Salam, 34

Farhan, Ishaq, 198, 204, 206, 215

Faris, Abd al-Rahman, 181

Faris, Muhammad Abu, 199, 207, 213, 215, 218

"Fawa'id Min al-Shada'id" (The Virtues of Hardship, statement of the Muslim Brotherhood), 93–94

Fawri, Marwan, 214, 217

Fawri, Nawal, 215–16; struggle of for women's involvement in political affairs, 216–17

Forum du Developpement (FDD), 241

Fouda, Farag, 78

Free Officers' coup, 27

Freedom and Justice Party (*hizb al-hurriyya wa al-'adala* [FJP]), 170, 177, 178, 191, 193, 195, 196, 250–51, 252–53, 270, 276, 286; in Egypt's 2011–12 parliamentary elections, 248–54; formation of, 174–76; meetings with the IMF, 274; as a party open to all citizens, 268

"Freedoms and Civil Society" conference, 85

Friedman, Thomas, 219

"Fulfilling Prophecies: State Policy and Islamist Radicalism" (Anderson), 88

Futuh, Saber Abul, 122

G-8 nations, 103, 303n37

Gazzar, Hilmi, 35, 37, 59

General Egyptian Students' Union, 36; national information and publishing committee (*jama'at*) of, 36, 37, 40, 41

Ghab, Shafiq, 222

Ghanim, Ibrahim Bayoumi, 65, 67, 68

Gharibeh, Raheel, 211, 217–18, 319n71

Ghay, Abu, 241

Ghoneim, Wael, 159

Ghuzlan, Muhammad, 183, 185; on the application of Shari'a law, 187; on the "higher principles" concept of constitutional law, 191

globalization, 274–75

Guidance Bureau, 66, 67, 71, 81, 102, 126, 133, 139–40, 143, 175, 177, 179, 275, 286; aging old guard of, 133, 309n59; calls for transparency in the internal elections of the Brotherhood, 131–32; choosing members of by the Shura Council, 127; and the Egyptian uprising, 157, 160; elections of (2008 and 2009), 127–32; influence wielded by aging members of, 281–82; and the youth conference, 182; youth division of, 156

Habib, Muhammad, 54–55, 103, 105, 113, 114, 122, 123, 125, 129, 130, 134; as head of the Nahda Party's Education Committee, 178; on the Mubarak regime's attempts to isolate the Brotherhood, 116–17; on the terror of the Brotherhood, 119

Habib, Rafiq, 174

habituation. *See* "democratic habituation"

Hadith, the, 25

Hafez, Osama, 293n90

Hafid, Muhammad, 238, 242

hakimiyyat Allah (absolute sovereignty of God), 28, 29, 107, 209

Hall, Peter, 16

Hamas, 3, 79, 121, 208

Hamid, Muhi, 128

Hamid, Shadi, 167, 168, 207; on the IAF's shift toward democracy, 209

Hamza, Khaled, 168

Hamza, Muhammad, on the drafting of a new Egyptian Constitution, 190–91

Hamzawy, 'Amr, 4, 221, 227, 229, 243, 320–21n134

Hanna, Michael Wahid, 266

Hanna, Milad, 296n66

Harakat al-Tawhid wa al-Islah (Movement of Unity and Reform [MUR]), 3, 203, 204, 238–39

Hasan, Reem Abu, 319n71
Hashim, Jamal, 239–40; criticism of the PJD by, 240
Hassan II (king of Morocco), 202, 233
Haydar, Khalil, 228, 230
Hilal, Muhammad, 129
Hinnebusch, Raymond, 34
historical analysis. *See* comparative historical analysis, value of
Hizb al-Islah al Misri (Egyptian Reform Party), 51
Hizb al-Tajdid al-Watani (National Renewal Party), 203
Hizb al-Wasat al-Jadid (New Wasat Party), 82
Hizb al-Wasat al-Misri (Egyptian Center Party), 82
hizbiyya (partyism), 42, 50
Hizbollah, 3, 79, 121
Hourani, Hani, 218
Howeidy, Fahmi, 260
Hudeibi, Ibrahim, 126, 129, 130, 131, 140, 141, 260; on the Brotherhood's turn toward democracy, 152–53; decision to leave the Brotherhood, 142
Hudeibi, Mamoun, 48, 54–55, 56, 76, 81, 92, 93, 94, 105, 141, 295n44; criticism of his arrogance and strong personality, 86–87; death of, 102; as member of the National Charter drafting committee, 85–86; as a political candidate, 98; return of from exile, 66
hudoud punishments, 31, 44, 137, 186, 188, 236, 237
human rights, 13, 14, 46, 59, 68, 103, 159, 228, 275, 285; violations of, 270
human rights organizations, 59, 100, 238, 239, 287
Humanitarian Relief Committee, 77
Huneidi, 'Azzam, 208, 209–10, 211, 319n71
Huntington, Samuel, 4, 8
Hussein (king of Jordan), 204, 212
Hussein, 'Adil, 53, 68
Hussein, Mahmoud, 128
Husseini, Rana, 212, 213
Huweidi, Fahmi, 68
hybridization: democratic, 13; ideological, 14

Ibn Taymiyya, 34
Ibrahim, Kamal, 317n27
Ibrahim, Sa'd al-Din, 78
Idris, Muhammad Sayyid, 108
Ikhwan. See Muslim Brotherhood

'Imara, Muhammad, 68
Indyk, Martin, 277–78
international relations theory, constructivist views of, 11–12
Iraq, 15, 20; invasion of by the United States, 107, 205
'Isa, Muhyiddin Ahmad, 41, 293n90
'Isa, Salah, 82, 300n55, 300n57
Ishaq, George, 108, 109, 114, 115, 186; on the arrogance of the Brotherhood, 116
Iskandar, Amin, 108
Islah (Reform) Party, 72
Islam, 228, 280, 290n10; principles of, 106, 107; vision of as both state and religion (*din wa dawla*), 14, 23, 92
"Islam Is the Solution" banner, 47, 53, 64, 77, 97, 118, 142, 161, 167, 250
"Islam Marja'iyyatuna (Islam Is Our Frame of Reference [Abd al-Fattah]), 126
Islamic Action Front (Jabha al-'Amal al-Islami [IAF]), 3, 176, 196, 205, 206, 217, 230, 286; blocking of progressive ideas in, 217–18; influence of the Brotherhood on, 217–18; loss of progressive members in, 217; number of votes for IAF candidates in the 1993 elections, 318n43; opposition to the reform of gender-discrimination laws, 211–14; promotion of the veil and other Islamically correct behavior, 211; representation of women in, 215–17; scope and limits of its shift to democracy, 208–11; shift of to democracy, 206–8
Islamic Alliance (al-Tahaluf al Islami), 47, 53, 305n86; banner of ("Islam Is the Solution"), 47, 53, 64, 77, 97, 118, 142, 161, 167, 250
Islamic Center Charity Society (ICCS), 198
Islamist Constitutional Movement (*al haraka al-dustouriyya al-islamiyya* [ICM]), 3, 196, 201, 286; and the debate over women's political rights in Kuwait, 223–24; in Kuwait, 219–23, 227–30; new leadership of, 224–27; poor showing of in the 2003 parliamentary elections, 224, 320–21n134; support of women's rights among ICM leaders, 226–27
Islamic Group (*al-jama'a al-islamiyya*), 35
Islamic Guidance Society (later the Social Reform Society), 199
Islamic law. *See* Shari'a law
Islamic Popular Alliance (IPA), 220
Islamic Salvation Front (FIS), 89, 203
Islamist groups, 5, 202, 286–88, 290n22; ascent

of freedom and democracy in their agendas, 284; challenges to broad generalizations concerning, 2–3; common dilemma of, 287; defining the essential character of, 283; expansion of their participation in electoral politics, 4, 285; external pressures facing, 287; hybrid discourse of, 284; as leading actors in Arab politics, 2; moderation of goals and strategies of, 5–6; movement of away from illiberal features that characterized them in the past, 2; national resistance movements, 3; in new institutional environments, 284–85; reformist trends in, 13–14, 105–6, 285; Salafi Islamist groups, 3–4, 144; Shi'ite Islamist groups, 3; Sunni revivalist groups, 3, 22–23. See also Islamist student associations (during the Sadat era)

Islamist militants, 34, 78–79

Islamist movement change, analysis of, 6–8, 282–88; adjustments in ideology and considerations of strategic advantage, 9; broader pattern of movement change in the Arab world, 282–88; casual mechanisms of movement change, 8–9; characterization of movement change, 5–8; and disaggregating participation, 8; ideational dimensions of, 9–10; movement change as a process of strategic adaptation, 9–12; political engagement and value-change, 12–15, 285–86; progressive dimensions of, 7–8. See also Islamist movement change, Wickham's analysis of; "rational actors"

Islamist movement change, Wickham's analysis of, 10–11, 17; whether they have deepened their commitment to the legal guarantee of individual rights, 6; whether they have embraced the principle of equal citizenship rights, 6; whether they have moved toward a greater toleration of the expression of values and perspectives that conflict with their own, 6; whether they have moved toward a more relativistic approach to religion, 6

Islamist student associations (during the Sadat era), 34–36; and the formation of Shura Councils, 35; outreach of the Muslim Brotherhood to student associations, 39–42; student leaders who joined the Muslim Brotherhood, 41; support of, 35–36; worldview of Islamist student leaders, 37–39

Islamist Trend (al-tayyar al-islami), 60, 72; accountability of to syndicate members, 61; concern of with domestic and regional issues, 61–62; distancing of itself from its initial insular networks, 63–64; interaction with individuals outside the movement, 64–65; and programs dealing with national issues, 62

Islamist Voice (as-sawt al-islami), 59–60

Isma'il, Hazim Abu, 256

Isma'il, Muhammad 'Uthman, 35

Isma'il, Nabawy, 39

Isma'il, Salah Abu, 31, 40, 44, 296n56; on democracy, 32

Ismailiyya, 21

Israel, 32, 33, 35, 36, 55, 58, 100, 121, 205, 206, 215, 234, 277–78; Arab confrontations/wars with, 165, 198; creation of, 101

jahiliyya (from jahl [ignorance], referring to Arabia before the advent of Islam), 28, 29

Jalloun, 'Umar Ben, 202, 317n27

jama'a (movement association), 51, 72, 73, 76, 89, 93, 126, 133, 196; "new mainstream" of, 137; threat to, 92; unity of, 94; and women, 137

Jam'iyyat al-Shabiba al-Islamiyya (The Association of Islamic Youth), 202

"Jehan's law," 32, 53

jihad, 25–26, 39, 42, 281; against Israel, 100, 197, 215; against the Soviets in Afghanistan, 78; jihadist groups, 33–34; primary targets of, 26

jizya (tax on minority religious groups), 70

Jordan, 3, 4, 11, 15, 17, 20, 196, 238, 286, 287; "anti-normalization" campaign in, 206–7; the Muslim Brotherhood in, 197–99, 282, 285; questions concerning the move to pluralism and democracy in, 209–11; reformist trend in, 214–18; trajectory of Islamist participation in, 204–6

Jordanian National Commission for Women, 212

Justice and Charity (al'Adl wa al-Ihsan) movement, 231

Justice and Development Party (JDP). See Parti de Justice et Developpement (PJD)

Kalyvas, Stathis N., 4, 8

Kassem, Hisham, 259

Kassem, Maye, 290n22, 298n23

Kassimi, Samira, 245

Kefaya (Enough) network, 150, 155; leftists involved in, 304n62. *See also* Kefaya (Enough) network, and the Muslim Brotherhood

Kefaya (Enough) network, and the Muslim Brotherhood, 107–17; attempts of to build a "third bloc," 116; boycott of the 2005 elections, 117; genesis of Kefaya, 108–9; as a "movement of conscience," 108; refusal of the Brotherhood to defer to the Kefaya movement, 113–14

Kemp, Geoffrey, 274

Kepel, Gilles, 33; on Islamic student organizations, 35, 36

Khalil, Haitham Abu, 149

Khamenei, Ayatollah Ali, 168

Khatib, Abdelkrim, 203

Kuwait, 3, 4, 11, 15, 17, 20, 196, 238, 286, 287; censorship of intellectuals in, 222–23; and the "desertization" of Kuwaiti politics, 200; Islamic Constitutional Movement (ICM) in, 219–23; the Muslim Brotherhood in, 199–201, 282, 285; scope and limits of the Islamist movement in, 227–30

Kuwait Democratic Forum (*al manbar al-dimuqrati al-kuwayti* [KDF]), 220

Kuwait University, gender segregation in, 221–22

Laban, 'Ali, 136

Latin America, "third-wave" democratic transitions in, 4, 12

Law 114 (1983), 47

Law to Guarantee Democracy in the Professional Alliances (1993), 78

Lebanon, 121

Le Marock (2005), 239

Liberal (Ahrar) Party, 47, 53, 302n9

L'Instance National Pour le Protection de la Famille Moroccaine, 232

Liwa' al-Islam, 49

Lust-Okar, Ellen, 198

Lutfi, Islam, 155, 156, 157, 179, 180, 189; on the concept of "higher principles" in the new Egyptian Constitution, 191–92

Lynch, Marc, 141; on the Salafi movement, 144

Ma'alim fii al-Tariq (Signposts Along the Path [Qutb]), 28, 36

Madani, Abd al-Harith, 79

Madi, Aboul 'Ela, 37, 40–41, 52, 59, 71, 72–73, 164, 170, 189; activity of in the professional syndicates, 62–63; on the changed thinking within Islamist Trend, 64–65; criticism of Hudeibi, 87; criticism of the Wasat Party, 140; and the formation of Kefaya, 108, 109; and the formation of the Wasat Party, 81, 82, 85, 88; as member of the National Charter drafting committee, 85–86; optimism of concerning the Wasat Party, 172; on the tensions between the middle generation and the old guard of the Brotherhood, 67–68, 90

Mahir, Ahmad, 258

Mahmoud, Abd al-Mun'im, 125–26, 130, 140, 143, 145, 147; assessment of the Brotherhood by, 175–76; criticism of the Brotherhood's treatment of activist youth, 183; freezing of his membership in the Brotherhood, 142; opinion of the Guidance Bureau election process, 128, 129; opinion of reformers in the Brotherhood, 142

Mainwaring, Scott, 4, 8, 57

Malik, Hasan, 122

Mansour, Hamza, 208, 210–11, 319n71

March 20 Popular Campaign of Change, 108

Mashhour, Mustafa, 40, 67, 70, 294n15; on the Brotherhood's decision to enter the political process, 49–50; death of, 102; return of from exile, 66

McCoy, Jennifer L., 12

Mecham, Quinn, 4

Mekki, Ahmad, 267–68

Military Academy Group, 34

Mitchell, Richard P., 20–21, 22, 24, 25, 290n1

Moaddel, Mansour, 198

Mobilizing Islam (Wickham), 3, 63

"Moderation in Islam" conference, 217, 319n88

Morocco, 2, 3, 11, 15, 17, 196, 286, 287; and the "Arab Spring" protests, 245–46; bombings in Casablanca ("Morocco's 9/11"), 234; "February 20 Movement" in, 244; the Muslim Brotherhood in, 282, 285; Parti de Justice et Developpement (PJD) in, 230–31; secular nature of politics in, 238; the Shabiba movement and its successors in, 201–4

Mouvement Populaire Democratique and Constitutionnel (MPDC), 203; name change of, 203

Movement of Unity and Reform (MUR). *See* Harakat al-Tawhid wa al-Islah (Movement of Unity and Reform [MUR])

Mubarak, Hisham, 41

Mubarak, Hosni, 1, 50, 76, 77, 89, 145; blatant interference of in the 2010 parliamentary elections, 158; commitment of to gradual increase in public freedoms, 46, 136; inauguration of, 46; proposed amendment to Article 76 of the Egyptian Constitution, 111–12; resignation of, 154, 165–66; response to the Egyptian uprising protests, 163, 164; strategies of to rein in the Brotherhood, 121, 122; supervision of elections by, 97; trial of, 261; zero-tolerance approach of to the Brotherhood, 79–80, 120–24

Muhammad (the Prophet), 68

Muhammad V (king of Morocco), 244, 245

Muhammad VI (king of Morocco), 2, 233, 234–35

Muqbil, Nabil, 127

Mursi, Muhammad, 1, 126, 134, 151, 174, 175; advice of from the Brotherhood and from the FJP, 270; as the Brotherhood's "spare tire," 256; cancelling of SCAF's addendum to the Egyptian Constitution, 269; as candidate for the presidency of Egypt, 256–57, 259–60, 262–64; claim that child abuse and sexual violence did not exist in Egypt, 260; clash of with SCAF and the SCC, 266; disapproval of proposed youth conference, 182; as Egypt's first democratically elected president, 248, 264; as guardian of the people's will, 266–67; on an individual's right to question the precepts of Islam, 188; percentage of votes received by in the presidential election, 263–64, 325n55; policies toward the military, 270; reconvening of the dissolved parliament by, 266–68; as self-declared president of all citizens (both Muslim and Christian), 275–76; tourism campaign of, 272–73

Musa, Abdel Halim, 77, 298n11

Musa, ʿAmr, 257

Musbih, Muhammad, 262–63

Muslim Brotherhood, 1, 288; and Abu al-Futouh's proposal to break from the strategy of participation in politics, 146–48; accountability of to a global audience, 281; affiliates of in other countries, 20; aid of to victims of the Cairo earthquake, 77; ambitious social agenda of, 23–24; ambivalence toward formal political institutions, 25, 42; anti-government rallies of, 111, 305n68; anti-Semitism of, 33; as an "anti-system" group, 22; arrests of Brotherhood members, 27–28, 79, 122, 291n32; arrests of Brotherhood members after the assassination attempt on Nasser, 27, 291n31, 291n46; arrogance and snobbery of, 116; assertiveness of activist youth in the Brotherhood, 181–83; belief in a return to Islam as key to wresting Egypt from foreign control, 22–23; as a cadre organization, 268; calls of for the application of Shariʿa law, 187–90, 283–84; calls of for the democratic reform of the Brotherhood's internal practices, 71–73; charter (la'iha) of, 127, 130, 152, 181–82; commitment to democracy of, 280, 283–84; community projects of, 23; and the concept of jihad, 25–26; condemnation of Egypt's Emergency Laws, 55–56; conservative outlook on social and cultural issues, 44; conservative religious faction (daʿwa) of, 18, 23, 130, 131, 133, 144, 275, 280; contradictions in the political discourse of, 24–25, 44; daʿwa mission of, 48, 93–94, 95, 107, 147, 195, 280, 283; debate in over constitutional principles, 190–95; denunciation of Egypt's participation in the Madrid peace talks, 77; denunciation of Egyptian troops participating in the Gulf War, 76–77; denunciation of Israel, 33; dissolution of (1948), 26; during the Sadat era, 29–33, 43; effect of youthful bloggers on the Brotherhood's old guard, 141–42; effects of repression on, 80–81, 122, 124; efforts to promote Shariʿi law, 31; emphasis of on action (ʿamal) and organization (tandhiim) over ideology (fikra), 24; establishment of Brotherhood-affiliated NGOs, 185; expansion of, 22; expulsion of members for forming the Egyptian Current Party, 182–83; formation of the Rovers (jawwala) and the Battalions (kata'ib) by, 26; formation of a special section (al-nidham al-khass) in, 26; founding of, 3, 20; fragmentation of, 176–83; funding of weakened by arrests of Brotherhood leaders, 122; and the "Great Theft," 139; growing emphasis of on democracy, 151–53; hostility toward Israel, 277–78; and ideology, 136, 215; income of, 122, 307n12; infrastructure of, 123; internal elections of (2008–10), 127–32; internal elections of (2009–10), 144–46; Islamic upbringing (tarbiya) provided to members of, 23; and jihadist groups, 33–34; key aspects of the development of, 42–45; legislative assembly

Muslim Brotherhood (*cont.*)
(Majlis al-Shura) of, 68; marginalization of the reformist faction in, 177; membership requirements of, 183–84; moderation (gradualist approach) of, 6, 44–45; objectives of seen as illiberal, 44; origins of, 20–26; outreach to Islamist student associations by, 39–42; Palestinian members of, 215; participation in the People's Assembly, 134–35, 136; pragmatism of, 133–37, 145–46, 151, 275–78; proposed changes to the charter of, 181–82; questions concerning the Brotherhood's commitment to pluralism, 209–11, 284; Reform Initiative of, 104–7, 141–44, 303n46; and the regulation of public life, 135–36; reinstitution of (1951), 26; religious interpretation of the cause of Egypt's malaise, 22; repression of, 27–28, 42–43, 67, 79, 88, 102, 119, 120–24; in rural areas, 143–44; satellite television station of, 185; "secret apparatus" (*al-jihaz al-sirri*) of, 26, 27, 42, 67, 102, 121; as a "secret cell," 120; self-righteousness of, 25; sources of organizational discipline and coherence in, 183–86; student division (*qism al-tullab*) of, 156–57; and support for free political and artistic expression, 281; Supreme Guide(s) (*murshid*) of, 29, 30, 53, 66, 71–72, 89, 129, 131, 132, 145, 152, 177, 182, 276–77, 291n46; tensions between the middle generation and the old guard of, 66–68, 89–95, 184–85; under the Mubarak regime, 79–80, 87–89, 100, 116–17, 120–24, 134, 136, 138, 306–7n4; under the Nasser regime, 27–29, 42–43; views on women, 68–70. *See also* Guidance Bureau; Jordan, the Muslim Brotherhood in; Kuwait, the Muslim Brotherhood in; Muslim Brotherhood, during the transitional period in Egypt after the uprising; Muslim Brotherhood, and the Egyptian uprising; Muslim Brotherhood, and electoral politics; Muslim Brotherhood, internal leadership divisions of; Muslim Brotherhood, and professional associations ("syndicates" [*niqabat*]); Muslim Brotherhood, trajectory in the decade before the uprising

Muslim Brotherhood, during the transitional period in Egypt after the uprising, 169–74, 247, 272–75; appeal of because of its social work, 251; ascendancy of, 247–48; bid of for the presidency, 254–57; and the "double di-

lemma" (exercising the public mandate and advancing its own partisan agenda) facing the Brotherhood, 268–72; and the first round of presidential elections, 257–60, 323n30; and the improvement of Egypt's economy, 273–75; and the presidential run-off election, 262–66; role of in the new Egypt, 279–82; use of its experienced organizational machine in the voting process, 250–51

Muslim Brotherhood, and the Egyptian uprising, 154–55; and activist Brotherhood youth outreach to lower-income residents, 162–63; assessment of the Brotherhood's role in the uprising, 166–69; mobilization of all Brotherhood members into the uprising, 162; and the rise of a cross-partisan youth network, 155–57; role of the Brotherhood in the "Battle of the Camel," 167; role of Brotherhood youth in the uprising, 160–62; statement issued by the Brotherhood concerning the uprising, 167; united front of the Brotherhood during the uprising, 167–68

Muslim Brotherhood, and electoral politics, 46, 294n7; in the 2005 parliamentary elections, 117–19; alliance of with secular nationalists, 47; alliance of with the Socialist Labor Party and the Liberal Party (the Islamic Alliance), 47, 53; alliance of with the Wafd party, 48, 50; boycott of the 1990 elections by the Brotherhood, 56–57; choice of candidates by the Brotherhood, 97; controversies concerning the Brotherhood's entrance into politics, 50; draft party platform of (2007), 124–26, 307–8n28; and the "dual games" of electoral authoritarian regimes, 57–58; election of Brotherhood leaders to parliament, 31–32, 293–94n2, 294n9; female candidate of the Brotherhood, 98; and the gradual application of Shari'a law, 52–54, 55–56; and the last election of the Mubarak era, 148–50; and the legitimacy of political parties, 50–52; major achievement of the Brotherhood in parliament, 136; number of Brotherhood candidates registered for municipal elections, 122, 307n15; political participation during the Mubarak era, 150–53; political participation as an extension of the *da'wa* mission, 46–52; political participation as a strategic choice, 144–46; political skills of the Brotherhood, 55; and the possibility of forming a Muslim Brotherhood party, 51–52, 295n29; as a victim of its own political success, 120–24; and the voting process in Egypt, 98

Muslim Brotherhood, internal leadership divisions of, 132–33; the *da'wa* faction, 133; the pragmatic conservative faction, 133–37, 145–46, 151, 275–78; the reformist youth faction, 141–44; and the rise of a cross-partisan youth network, 155–57; waning of the reformist movement and resurgence of the old guard, 137–41

Muslim Brotherhood, and professional associations ("syndicates" [*niqabat*]), 58–59, 77–78, 79; and changes in middle generation behavior, 63, 139; dominant position of the Brotherhood in universities, 60; and the Engineers' Syndicate, 66, 67; growing influence of the Brotherhood's middle generation in the syndicates, 59, 65–66; and the Guidance Bureau, 66, 67; success of in the professional associations, 80; syndicate conferences, 61–62. *See also* Islamist Trend (al-tayyar al-islami); Islamist Voice (as-sawt al-islami); "reformist trend" (al-tayyar al-islami)

Muslim Brotherhood, trajectory in the decade before the uprising: and the 2005 parliamentary elections, 117–19; absence of the Brotherhood from pro-Palestinian and anti-American protests, 100–101; and the Brotherhood as a self-limiting (self-restraining) actor in Egypt's politics, 97–101, 145, 151; and the cross-party alliances of the Brotherhood, 114–15; leadership succession struggles of the Brotherhood (2002–4), 102–3; pattern of external pressure and internal group dynamics, 96; period of bold self-assertion, 96, 111–13; period of guardedness, 96; and the reform initiative of the Brotherhood, 104–7, 303n46; reversion to self-restraint, 96. *See also* "Kefaya" (Enough) network, and the Muslim Brotherhood

"Muslim Woman in Muslim Society and *Shura* and Party Pluralism, The" (position paper of the Muslim Brotherhood), 69

Mustafa, Hala, 31

Mustafa, Shukri, 34

Muti', 'Abdelkrim, 202

Nafi, Abd al-Hamid, 296n50

Naguib, Muhammad, 27

Nahda (Renaissance) Party, 177, 178, 287

Nahda (Renaissance) project, 255, 257

Nassar, Gamal, 145

Nasser, Gamal Abdel, 27–29, 42–43

Nasserist Club, 38

Nasserists, showing of in parliamentary elections, 302n9

Nasr, Hamid Abu, 53

Nasr, Osama, 128

National Action Plan for the Integration of Women in Development, 232–33

National Association for Change (NAC), 148–50, 155

National Charter, drafting committee of, 85–86

National Democratic Front, 149, 150

National Democratic Party (NDP), 48, 50, 54, 55, 78, 134–35, 150, 164, 258, 302n10, 324n33

"National Dialogue" conference, 85

National Islamic Coalition (NIC), 220

National Renewal Party. *See* Hizb al-Tajdid al-Watani (National Renewal Party)

Nazif, Ahmad, 120

New Civic Forum, 86

New Islamist Discourse (*al-khitab al-islami al-jadid*), 68

"new Islamist intellectuals," 68–69

"No Need to Be Afraid of Us" (al-Shatir), 134

Nubians, 265

Nuh, Mukhtar, 149

Nur, Ayman, 165

Nye, Joseph, 103

"On Behalf of an Egypt United against Torture" conference, 61, 296n66

Orange Movement, 224

Orange Revolution (Ukraine), 110

Order of the Hasafiyya, 21

Ottaway, Martina, 104, 231

Palestine, 15, 20

Parti de Justice et Developpement (PJD), 3, 15, 196, 203, 286; and the 2007 parliamentary elections, 242–43; and the appointment of 'Abdalla Benkirane as prime minister of Morocco, 244–46; break from the radical Shabibi organization and joining of the mainstream, 231–33; electoral self-restraint of, 233–34; Islamist character of its platform, 231; limits of its progressive shift,

Parti de Justice et Developpement (PJD) (*cont.*)
241–42; in Morocco, 230–31; pragmatism
of, 234–41; pragmatism of as a constraint of
democratic reform, 242–43; support of for
the Mudawwana reform, 235–36
"participation-moderation" thesis, 5–6; analysis of, 6–8; lessons of during the Murbarak
era, 150–53
Pasha, Nuqrashi, assassination of, 26
People's Assembly, 177
pluralism, 10, 68, 84, 275, 280, 284, 285; intellectual pluralism, 13; in Islamist society, 69;
questions concerning the Brotherhood's
commitment to, 209–11
political actors, and the emulation of prescribed norms of behavior, 11–12
"Political Forces and Their Positions on Freedom of Opinion and Thought and Belief"
(Egyptian Organization for Human Rights),
85
Political Parties Committee, 82
Political Parties Law (1977), 31, 82, 123
politics: as the "art of the possible," 278; reactions to Islamist actors as a leading force in
Arab politics, 2
Politics in Islam (Hudeibi), 94–95
Presidential Election Committee (PEC), 258,
262, 263; disqualification of presidential
candidates by, 255–56
Professional Syndicates' Coordinating Com-
mittee, 62
Przeworski, Adam, 4, 8

Qandil, Abd al-Halim, 304
Qandil, Amani, 77–78
Qasim, Hashim, 273; skepticism of concerning
the Brotherhood and democratic reform,
115–16
Qasim, Tal'at Fu'ad, 40, 293n90
Qasim, Muhammad Tawfiq, 58
Qassas, Muhammad, 156, 157, 179, 180, 184
Qurah, Abd al-Latif Abu, 197
Quran, the, 25, 28, 33, 68; on the authority of
men over women, 69–70; the "Quran inci-
dent," 113, 305n78
Qutb, Misbah, 297n82
Qutb, Sayyid, 33, 37, 45, 200, 202; arrest and
imprisonment of, 28, 291n33; debate con-
cerning the religious validity of his radical
thought, 28–29

Radi, Mushin, 150
Ragin, Charles, 16
Ramadan, 31
Ramadan, Abdel Azim, 30, 291n47; on the
jama'at leaders' view of the Brotherhood,
293n107
Ramid, Mustafa, 234, 236, 242
Ramih, Tal'at, 90, 296n66
"rational actors," 8; rational actor models, 9,
11. *See also* value-change in individual actors, implications of
Rbah, 'Aziz, 236, 237, 240
"reformist group" (*al-majmu' al-islahi*). *See*
"reformist trend" (al-tayyar al-islami)
"reformist trend" (*al-tayyar al-islami*), 67–69;
official position papers (*bayanat*) of, 69–70;
theoretical and methodological issues concerning, 73–75
"reformist" (*islahi*) trends: and reform of the
self (*al-islah al-dhati*), 13–14; scope and limits of Islamist self-reform, 15
repression-radicalization theory, 28, 87–89,
119, 123
Revkin, Mara, 255
Revolution of the Roses (Georgia), 110
Revolutionary Youth Union, 253–54
Rida, Rashid, 23
Riley, Meredith, 232
Rishwan, Diya', 38, 102, 109, 113, 125, 304n62;
on the Brotherhood and Shari'a, 115
Roberts, Kenneth M., 12
Rovers (*jawwala*), 26
Rudolph, Suzanne Hoeber, 12, 289n8
Ryan, Curtis, 4, 204

Saadi, Sa'd, 232
Sabahi, Hamdeen, 257
Sadat, Anwar, 29–33, 40, 43, 44; assassination
of, 34; as the "Believer-President," 30; confrontation with Abu al-Futouh 'Abd al-
Mun'im, 38–39; criticism of by the Muslim
Brotherhood, 32–33; executive privilege
granting greater rights to women ("Jehan's
law"), 32, 53; experiment of in political liberalization, 30–31; general amnesty given to
the Muslim Brotherhood by, 30; and Islamic
student associations, 34–36; and the Islamization of Egyptian law, 32; opening of the
Egyptian economy to market forces by (the
Infitah), 32; purge of Nasserist socialists by,

29–30; signing of the peace treaty with Israel, 32
Sadat, Jehan, 32
Sa'eed, Hammam, 199, 215
Sa'eed, Khaled, murder of, 159
Salafi Asala (Authenticity) Party, 194, 253
Salafi movement, 3–4, 144, 194–95
Salafi Nur Party, 265
Salem, Mahmoud, 160
Salih, Subhi, 170, 187, 253
Sallam, Hesham, 269–70
"Salsbil Affair," 71
Sami, Mahir, 267
Sartori, Giovanni, 88
Sawt al-Haqq (Voice of the Truth), 36
Schwedler, Jillian, 4, 207, 215
Sha'ban, Ahmad Baha', 108
Shabibi movement, 231. See also Morocco, the Shabiba movement and its successors in
Shadi, Salah, 53, 55–56
Shafiq, Ahmad, 257–60, 262–64, 324n33
Shahin, 'Isa, 224
Shahin, Mamdouh, 264–65
Sharaf, 'Esam, 170
Share, Donald, 4
Shari'a law, 2, 10, 11, 13, 24, 34, 84, 115, 236–37, 280, 287; application of, 52–54, 55–56, 137; authority of, 69; as a "chief source of legislation," 31; definitive rulings (ahkam qat'iyya) of, 188; disagreements concerning the application of, 126; general Shari'a principles (mabadi') of, 187–88, 189; higher objectives (maqasid) of, 237–238; specific rulings (ahkam) of, 189; tensions between democracy and Shari'a law, 186–90; traditional rulings (ahkam) of, 187
Sharqiyya, 133, 143, 158
Shehata, Samer, 4, 123, 134, 269
Shu'ayb, 'Alya, 222
Shukr, Abd al-Ghaffer, 304n51
Shukri, Ibrahim, 53
shura (consultation), 32, 58, 94, 138, 242, 284
Shura Council, 52, 102, 112, 127–28, 130, 138, 143, 175, 177, 181, 185, 254, 269, 282; choosing of Guidance Bureau members by, 127; elections of, 122, 129, 143, 250; women's participation in, 215–16, 218
Sidqi, 'Aziz, 305–6n86
Siman, Muhammad, 63
Sirriyya, Salih, 34

Social Reform Society, 199
Socialist Labor Party, 47, 53
Society of the Muslim Brothers (Jam'iyyat al-Ikhwan al-Muslimin). See Muslim Brotherhood
Society of Muslims, 34
Sprague, John, 4, 8
Springborg, Robert, 294n7
Stacher, Joshua, 4, 51, 123, 134, 307n15
"Statement to the People" (Bayan lil-Naas), 70
Stemman, Jean, 209
Sudan, 20
Suez Canal Company, 21
Suez Canal Zone, 21
Suleiman, Omar, 165, 169
Sultan, 'Esam, 64, 82, 109, 114, 252, 299n46, 300n51
Sultan, Farouq, 256, 259, 262
Sunna, the, 28
Sunni revivalist groups, 196
Supreme Constitutional Court (SCC), 248, 258, 264, 265–68; rulings of concerning the "deep state" institutions of Egypt, 260–62; as a "superconstitutional authority," 267
Supreme Council of the Armed Forces (SCAF), 154, 165, 166, 170, 190, 248, 249, 255; announcement of a "supplement" to the Constitutional Declaration, 264–65; cancelling by Mursi of SCAF's addendum to the Constitution, 269; declaration that it would assume legislative authority until a new parliament was elected, 261; mistrust of civilians and the political class in, 265; revised political party laws of, 172, 173; role of in defining the new Egyptian constitution, 250; talks of with the IMF, 274
"syndicates." See Muslim Brotherhood, and professional associations ("syndicates" [niqabat])
Syria, 20

Tagammu Party, 82, 148, 249, 300, 302n9, 311n113
Tahrir Square, demonstrations at, 100, 107, 162, 163, 164, 165, 167, 170, 193–95, 258, 279
takfir (act of designating nominal Muslims as kafir [non-believers]), 33

Tamman, Hossam, 51–52, 102, 138–39, 185; on the conservative faction of the Brotherhood, 145–46; on the shifting power base of the Brotherhood, 143–44

Tantawi, Hussein, 269

Taqrir 'an al-Hala al-Diniyya fii Misr (Report on Religious Conditions in Egypt), 71

tarbiya (bottom-up spiritual formation of society), 42

Tezcur, Gunes Murat, 4

thawabet al-umma (enduring values of the nation), 83, 84–85, 106–7

"third-wave" democratic transitions, 4, 12, 115

torture, 27, 66, 67, 105, 159

"[Toward a] Broad Psychological and Practical Opening" (al-Infitah al-Nafsi wa al-'Amali al-'Am), 90–92

Tozy, Muhammad, 202–3, 236, 244

Tunisia, 1, 243, 287; the "Jasmine Revolution" in, 158, 159

'Umar, Muhammed Abd al-Fattah, 121

'Umara, Abd al-Qadir, 202, 204, 235

umma (Muslim nation/community of believers), 69, 83–84, 88, 300n55; as the source of authority, 94–95

Union Socialiste des Union Nationale des Forces Populaires (USFP), 231

Upper Egypt Conference, 108

'Usman, Amal, 98

'Usman, Muhammad, 260

value-change in individual actors, implications of: commitment of Islamic movement reformers to a vision of Islam as both religion and state (*din wa dawla*), 14; differences in life histories of and subsequent differing personal reactions of individual actors, 14; and the problem of aggregation, 14–15; uneven ideological revision in mainstream Islamic groups, 14; value-change proceeds from ideology and is shaped by the social and cultural milieu of revivalist Islam, 14

Wafd Party, 47, 50, 148, 150, 191, 302n9; withdrawal from the Democratic Alliance, 249

Wardani, Lina, 194

Wasat (Center) Party, 76–81, 172, 178, 190, 191, 214, 217, 265, 301n78; backstory of the Wasat founders' split from the Brotherhood, 85–87; criticism of, 140–41; differences of with the IAF, 215–16; endorsement of women's rights by, 84; and the "enduring values of the nation" (*thawabet al-umma*), 83, 84–85; initiative to form the Wasat Party, 81–85; intellectual influences on, 84, 300n51; in Jordan, 217; number of Brotherhood members in the Wasat Party, 81; objections to the platform of, 84–85; platform of, 83–84, 92–93, 299n46; press coverage of in Egypt and the Arab world, 84; and the reformist critique of the Brotherhood's old guard, 89–95; and the repression-radicalization theory, 87–89; salient themes of, 83

Weaver, Mary Ann, 81

Wegner, Eva, 4, 240

Wiktorowicz, Quintan, 198

Willis, Michael, 4, 202, 203, 233, 234, 243

women's rights, 5, 232, 240, 252; citizenship rights of women, 68, 84, 92, 124, 126, 280–81; debate over women's political rights in Kuwait, 223–24, 225; endorsement of women's rights by the Wasat Party, 84; the IFA's stance on women's rights, 211; as an issue in the post-Mubarak presidential elections, 259, 260; and the *khul'* provision concerning divorce, 212–13, 319n71; support of women's rights among ICM leaders, 226–27

Yatim, Muhammad, 202, 242, 286; on the higher objectives (*maqasid*) of Shari'a law, 237–238

Yemen, 4

York, Jillian, 159

"Young Egypt" (Misr al-Fatah) movement, 53

Youssefi, Abdel Rahman, 231

Zagazig University Faculty Club, 60

Zamalek soccer team, 161–62

Zamzam, Muhammad, 293n90

Zant, Abd al-Mun'im Abu, 215

Zein el-Abidine, Ben Ali, 243

Zollner, Barbara, 28–29

Zuhdi, Karam, 41, 293n90

Zulfiqar, Mona, 173

Zürn, Michael, 12